Burt Franklin: Research & Source Works Series #343
(American Classics in History & Social Science #75)

THE WRITINGS

OF

THOMAS PAINE

THE WRITINGS

OF

THOMAS PAINE

COLLECTED AND EDITED BY

MONCURE DANIEL CONWAY

AUTHOR OF "THE LIFE OF THOMAS PAINE," "OMITTED CHAPTERS OF HISTORY
DISCLOSED IN THE LIFE AND PAPERS OF EDMUND RANDOLPH,"
"GEORGE WASHINGTON AND MOUNT VERNON," ETC.

VOLUME I.

1774-1779

Burt Franklin
New York

18199

Published by BURT FRANKLIN
235 East 44th St., New York, N. Y. 10017
Originally Published: (Vol. 1) New York, 1902
Reprinted: 1969
Printed in the U.S.A. on long-life paper

Library of Congress Catalog Card No.: 70-80227
Burt Franklin: Research & Source Works Series #343
American Classics in History & Social Science #75

CONTENTS.

THE WRITINGS

OF

THOMAS PAINE

COLLECTED AND EDITED BY

MONCURE DANIEL CONWAY

AUTHOR OF "THE LIFE OF THOMAS PAINE," "OMITTED CHAPTERS OF HISTORY
DISCLOSED IN THE LIFE AND PAPERS OF EDMUND RANDOLPH,"
"GEORGE WASHINGTON, AND MOUNT VERNON," ETC.

VOLUME II.

1779-1792

Burt Franklin
New York

Published by BURT FRANKLIN
235 East 44th St., New York, N. Y. 10017
Originally Published: (Vol. 2) New York, 1906
Reprinted: 1969
Printed in the U.S.A. on long-life paper

Library of Congress Catalog Card No.: 70-80227
Burt Franklin: Research & Source Works Series #343
American Classics in History & Social Science #75

CONTENTS.

I.

PEACE, AND THE NEWFOUNDLAND FISHERIES.[1]

(First Letter.)

MESSIEURS HALL AND SELLERS.

Gentlemen,

A piece of very extraordinary complexion made its appearance in your last paper, under the signature of *Americanus*, and what is equally as extraordinary, I have not yet met with one advocate in its favour. To write under the curse of universal reprobation is hard indeed, and proves that either the writer is too honest for the world he lives in, or the world, bad as it is, too honest for him to write in.

Some time last winter a worthy member of the Assembly of this State put into my hands, with some expressions of surprize, a motion which he had copied from an original shewn to him by another member, who intended to move it in the House. The purport of *that*, and the doctrine of Americanus, bear such strong resemblance to each other, that I make no hesitation in believing them both generated from the same parents. The intended motion, however, withered without being put, and Americanus, by venturing into being, has exposed himself to a less tranquil exit.

Whether Americanus sits in Congress or not, may be the subject of future enquiry ; at present I shall content myself with making some strictures on what he advances.

He takes it for granted that hints towards a negociation for peace have been made to Congress, and that a debate

---

[1] From the *Pennsylvania Gazette*, June 30, 1779.

has taken place in that House respecting the terms on which such a negociation shall be opened.

" It is reported," says he, " that Congress are still debating what the terms shall be, and that some men strenuously insist on such as others *fear* will not be agreed to, and as they *apprehend* may prevent any treaty at all, and such as our ally [France], by his treaties with us, is *by no* means bound to support us in demanding."

Americanus, after running through a variety of introductory matter, comes at last to the point, and intimates, or rather informs, that the particular subject of debate in Congress has been respecting the fisheries on the Banks of Newfoundland, some insisting thereon as a matter of right and urging it as a matter of absolute necessity, others doubting, or appearing to doubt whether we have any right at all, and indifferent whether the fisheries be claimed or not.   Among the latter of which Americanus appears to be one.

Either Americanus does not know how to make a bargain, or he has already made one, and his affectation of modesty is the dress of design.   How, I ask, can Americanus, or any other person, know what claims or proposals will be rejected or what agreed to, till they be made, offered or demanded. To suppose a rejection is to invite it, and to publish our " *apprehensions,*" as a reason for declining the claim, is encouraging the enemy to fulfil the prediction.   Americanus may think what he pleases, but for my own part, I hate a prophecier of ill-luck, because the pride of being thought wise often carries him to the wrong side.

That an inhabitant of America or a member of Congress should become an advocate for the exclusive right of Britain to the fisheries, and signify, as his opinion, that an American has not a right to fish in the American seas, is something very extraordinary.

" It is a question," says he, " whether the subjects of these states had any other right to fishing than what they *derived from their being subjects of Great Britain ; and as it cannot be pretended that they were in the possession and enjoyment of the right either at the*

*time of the declaration of independence or of signing the treaties of
Paris, nor that it was ever included in any one of the charters of the
United States*, it cannot be surprising that many, who judge a *peace*
necessary for the happiness of these states, should be *afraid* of
the consequences which may follow from making this an ultimatum in a negociation."

I should be glad to know what ideas Americanus affixes to
the words *peace* and *independence;* they frequently occur in
his publication, but he uses them in such a neutral manner,
that they have neither energy or signification.   Peace, it is
true, has a pleasant sound, but he has nibbled it round, like
Dr. Franklin's description of a gingerbread cake, till scarcely
enough is left to guess at the composition.   To be at peace
certainly implies something more than barely a cessation of
war.   It is supposed to be accompanied with advantages
adequate to the toils of obtaining it.   It is a state of prosperity as well as safety, and of honour as well as rest.   His
independence too is made up of the same letters which compose the independence of other nations, but it has something
so sickly and consumptive in its constitution, so limping and
lingering in its manner, that at best it is but in leading
strings, and fit rather for the cradle than the cabinet.   But
to return to his argument :
Americanus has placed all his reasons the wrong way, and
drawn the contrary conclusions to what he ought to have
done.   He doubts the right of the States to fish, because it
is not mentioned in any of the charters.   Whereas, had it
been mentioned, it might have been contended that the
right in America was only derivative ; and been given as an
argument that the original right lay in Britain.   Therefore
the silence of the charters, added to the undisturbed practice
of fishing, admit the right to exist in America *naturally*, and
not by *grant*, and in Britain only *consequentially ;* for Britain
did not possess the fisheries independent of America, but in
consequence of her dominions in America.   Her claiming
territory here was her title deed to the fisheries, in the same
manner that Spain claims Faulkland's Island, by possessing

the Spanish continent; and therefore her right to those fisheries was derived *through America*, and not the right of America through Britain. Wedded to the continent, she inherited its fortunes of islands and fisheries, but divorced therefrom, she ceases her pretentions.

What Americanus means by saying, *that it cannot be pretended we were in the possession and enjoyment of the right either at the time of the declaration of independence or of signing the treaty of Paris*, I am at a loss to conceive; for the right being natural in America, and not derivative, could never cease, and though by the events of war she was at that time dispossessed of the immediate enjoyment, she could not be dispossessed of the *right*, and needed no other proofs of her title than custom and situation.

Americanus has quoted the 2d and 11th articles of the treaty of Paris, by way of showing that the right to the fisheries is not one of those rights which France has undertaken to guarantee.

To which I answer, that he may say the same by any particular right, because those articles describe no particular rights, but are comprehensive of *every* right which appertains to sovereignty, of which fishing in the American seas must to us be one.

Will Americanus undertake to persuade, that it is not the interest of France to endeavour to secure to her ally a branch of trade which redounds to the mutual interest of both, and without which the alliance will lose half its worth? Were we to propose to surrender the right and practice of fishing to Britain, we might reasonably conclude that France would object to such a surrender on our part, because it would not only render us a less valuable ally in point of commerce as well as power, but furnish the enemy of both with a new acquisition of naval strength; the sure and natural consequence of possessing the fisheries.

Americanus admits the fisheries to be an "*object of great consequence to the United States, to two or three of them more especially.*"

Whatever is of consequence to any, is so to all; for wealth

like water soon spreads over the surface, let the place of entrance be ever so remote; and in like manner, any portion of strength which is lost or gained to any one or more States, is lost or gained to the whole; but this is more particularly true of the naval strength, because, when on the seas it acts immediately for the benefit of all, and the ease with which it transports itself takes in the whole coast of America, as expeditiously as the land forces of any particular State can be arranged for its own immediate defence. But of all the States of America, New York ought to be the most anxious to secure the fisheries as a nursery for a navy;—because the particular situation of that State, on account of its deep waters, is such, that it will ever be exposed to the approaches of an enemy, unless it be defended by a navy; and if any of the delegates of that State has acted a contrary part, he or they have either designedly or ignorantly betrayed the interest of their constituents, and deserve their severest censure.

Through the whole of this curious and equivocal piece, the premises and arguments have, in themselves, a suspicious appearance of being unfairly if not unjustly stated, in order to admit of, and countenance, wrong conclusions; for taking it for granted that Congress have been debating upwards of four months what the terms shall be on which they shall open a negociation, and that the House are divided respecting their opinion of those terms, it does not follow from thence that the "*public have been deceived*" with regard to the news said to have arrived last February; and if they are deceived, the question is who deceived them? Neither do several other conclusions follow which he has attempted to draw, of which the two I shall now quote are sufficient instances.

" If," says **Americanus**, " the *insisting* on terms which neither the *declaration of independence nor the treaties of Paris authorized us to challenge as our rights,* have caused the late, otherways unaccountable delays, and prevented a peace, or at least a negociation being opened for one, *those who have challenged and insisted on these claims are justly responsible for the consequences.*"

This I look on to be truly jesuitical; for the delay cannot be occasioned by those who *propose*, but by those who *oppose*, and therefore the construction should stand thus:

If the *objecting* to rights and claims, which are neither *inconsistent with the declaration of independence or the treaties of Paris, and naturally included and understood in both*, has caused the late, otherways unaccountable delays, and prevented a peace, or at least a negociation for one, *those who made such objections, and thereby caused such delays and prevented such negociations being gone into, are justly responsible for the consequences.*

His next position is of the same cast, and admits of the same reversion.

"Governor Johnstone," says he, "in the House of Commons freely declared he had made use, while in America, of other means to effect the purpose of his commission than those of reason and argument; *have we not*," continues Americanus, "*good right from present appearances to believe that in this instance he declared the truth.*"

To this wonderful supposition I shall apply another, viz. That if Governor Johnstone *did* declare the truth, *who have we most right to suspect, those who are for relinquishing the fisheries to Britain, or those who are for retaining them?*

Upon the whole, I consider the fisheries of the utmost importance to America, and her natural right thereto so clear and evident, that it does not admit of a debate, and to surrender them is a species of treason for which no punishment is too severe.

I have not stept out of my way to fetch in either an argument or a fact, but have confined my reply to the piece, without regard to who the author is, or whether any such debates have taken place or not, or how far it may or not have been carried on one side or the other.

COMMON SENSE.

PHILADELPHIA, June 26, 1779.

PEACE, AND THE NEWFOUNDLAND FISHERIES.[1]

(SECOND LETTER.)

AMERICANUS, in your last, has favoured the public with a description of himself as a preface to his piece. " I am," says he, " neither a Member of Congress or of the Assembly of this State, or of any other, but a private citizen, in moderate circumstances in point of fortune, *and whose political principles have never been questioned.*" All this may be very true, and yet nothing to the purpose ; neither can the declaration be admitted either as a positive or negative proof of *what his principles are.* They may be good, or they may not, and yet be so well known as not to be doubted by those who know the writer. Joseph Galloway formerly wrote under the signature of *Americanus*, and tho' every honest man condemns his principles, yet nobody pretends to question them. When a writer, and especially an anonymous one, readily means to declare his political principles as a reinforcement to his arguments, he ought to be full, clear, and decisive, but this declaration is so ambiguously constructed and so unmeaningly applied, that it may be used by any and every person either within or without the enemy's lines, for it does not declare what his principles are, but that, be they what they may, *they are not questioned.*

Before I proceed, I cannot help taking notice of another inconsistency in his publication of last week. " In my last," says he, " I said that it was very unhappy that this question has been touched on or agitated at all at this time, to which," continues he, " I will now add, it is particularly so, *that it is become a subject of discussion in the public papers.*" This is very extraordinary from the very man who first brought it into the public papers. A short piece or two, on the importance of fisheries in general, were anonymously published some time ago ; but as a matter of treaty debate in Congress, or as a matter of right in itself, with the arguments and grounds on which they proceeded, Americanus is originally

---

[1] From the *Pennsylvania Gazette*, July 14, 1779.

chargeable with the inconvenience he pretends to lament. I with some others had heard, or perhaps knew, that such a subject was in debate, and tho' I always laid myself out to give it a meeting in the papers when ever it should appear, I never hinted a thought that might tend to start it.

"To *permit* the public," says Americanus, "to be made acquainted with what are to be the *ultimate demands* in a proposed treaty is really something new and extraordinary, if not impolitic and absurd."—There is a compound of folly and arrogance in this declaration, which deserves to be severely censured. Had he said, that to publish all the arguments of Congress, on which any claim in a proposed treaty are founded or objected to, might be inconvenient and in some cases impolitic, he would have been nearly right; but the *ultimate demand itself ought* to be made known, together with the rights and reasons on which that demand is founded.

But who is this gentleman who undertakes to say, that to *permit* the public to be made acquainted is really impolitic and absurd? And to this question I will add, that if he distinguishes Congress into one body, and the public into another, I should be glad to know in what situation he places himself, so as not to be subject to his own charge of absurdity. If he belongs to the former, he has, according to his own position, a right to know but not to tell, and if to the latter, he has neither a right to know nor to tell, and yet in some character or other he has done both. If this gentleman's political principles were never questioned before, I think they ought to be questioned now; for a man must be a strange character indeed, whom no known character can suit.

I am the more inclined to suspect Americanus, because he most illiberally, and in contradiction to everything sensible and reasonable, endeavoured, in his former piece, to insinuate that Governor Johnstone had bribed a party in Congress to *insist on the right of the United States to fish on the Banks of Newfoundland.* An insinuation so impolitic and absurd, so wide and foreign to the purpose of Governor

Johnstone's commission, can only be understood the contrary way ; namely, that he had bribed somebody or other to *insist* that the right should *not be insisted on.*

The expression of Governor Johnstone, as printed in the English papers, is literally this. " I do not," says he, " mean to disavow I *have had* transactions, where *other means have been used* besides persuasion." Governor Johnstone was in no places in America but Philadelphia and New-York, and these *other* means must have been used in one or other, or both of these places. We have had evidence of one application of his, with an offer of ten thousand guineas, which was refused, and treated with the disdain it deserved ; for the offer of a bribe contains in it, to all men of spirit, the substance of an affront. But it is strange indeed, if the *one* that was refused was the *only one* that was offered. Let any person read Americanus in your paper of June 23, and if he can after that acquit him of all suspicion, he must be charitable indeed.

But why does not Americanus declare who he is? This is no time for concealment, neither are the presses, tho' free, to become the vehicles of disguised poison. I have had my eye on that signature these two months past, and to what lengths the gentleman meant to go himself can best decide.

In his first piece he loosely introduced his intended politics, and put himself in a situation to make further advances. His second was a rapid progress, and his last a retreat. The difference between the second and the last is visible. In the former of those two he endeavours to invalidate the right of the United States to fish on the Banks of Newfoundland, because, forsooth, it was not mentioned in any of the former charters. It is very extraordinary that these same charters, which marked out and were the instruments of our *dependence*, should now be introduced as describing the line of our *independence*. In the same piece Americanus likewise says, " it is a question whether the subjects of these states *had any other right* to that fishery, than what they derived from being the subjects of Great-Britain." If this be not advocating the cause of the enemy, I know not what is. It is news-paper advice to them to insist on an exclusive right to the fisheries, by insinuating ours to be only a derivative one from them; which, had it been the case, as it is not, would have been very improper doctrine to preach at the first instance of a negotiation. If they have any right, let them find those rights out themselves. We shall have enough to do to look to our own side of the question, and ought not to admit persons among us to join force with the enemy either in arms or argument.

Whether Americanus found himself approaching a stormy latitude, and fearing for the safety of his bark, thought proper to tack about in time, or whether he has changed his appetite, and become an epicure in fish, or his principles, and become an advocate for America, must be left for his own decision; but in his last week's publication he has surrendered the grounds of his former one, and changed the argument from a matter of right to a matter of supposed convenience only. He no more speaks of our right to the fisheries as a derivative right from Britain, in consequence of our formerly being subjects. Not a syllable of the charters, whose silence he had produced as invalidating or negativing our independent right. Neither has he endeavoured to support, or offered to renew, what he had before asserted—namely, that we were not in possession of the right of fishing at the time of the declaration of independence, or of the signing the treaties of Paris; but he has admitted a theorem which I had advanced in opposition to his suggestions, and which no man can contradict, viz. that our right to fish on the Banks of Newfoundland is a *natural right*. Now if our right is natural, it could not be derived from subjection, and as we never can but by our own voluntary consent be put out of the possession of a natural national right, tho' by the temporary events of war we may be put out of the enjoyment of such a right, and as the British fishery Act of Parliament in seventy-six to exclude us was no act of ours, and universally denied by us, therefore, from his own admission, he has contradicted himself, and allowed that we were as fully in *possession of the right* of fishing on those Banks, both at the time of the declaration of independence, and at the time of signing the treaties of Paris, as at any period preceding them.

That he has admitted the natural right in his last piece, in contradiction to his supposed derivative right in his former one, will appear from two or three quotations I shall make.

1st. He says, " The giving up of our *right to this object* (the fisheries) and the making an *express* demand to have it guarantied to us, or the passing it over in silence in negociation, are distinct things."

2d. " I am well assured," he says, " that there is not a member in Congress any ways disposed *to give up or relinquish our right to the Newfoundland fishery.*"

The "right" here admitted cannot be a right derived from subjection, because we are no longer British subjects; neither can it be a right conveyed by charters, because we not only know no charters now, but those charters we used to know are silent on the matter in question. It must therefore be a *natural right.* Neither does the situation of America and Britain admit of any other explanation, because they are, with respect to each other, in a state of nature, not being even within the law of nations; for the law of nations is the law of treaties, compounded with customary usage, and between America and Britain there is yet no treaty, nor any national custom established.

But the third quotation I shall make from his last piece will prove, from his own words, his assent to the *natural right* which I contended for in behalf of these states, and which he, in his former piece, impliedly disowned, by putting our whole right on a question, and making our former subjection the grounds on which that question stood.

" I drew no conclusion," he says, " to exclude these States, or bar them from the *right which by nature they are entitled to* with others, as well to the fishery on the *Banks of Newfoundland* as to those in the ocean at large."

As he now admits a *natural right*, and appears to contend for it, I ask, why then was his former piece published, and why was our right there put in the lowest terms possible? He does not in that piece even hint, or appear to think of, or suppose such a thing as a natural right, but stakes the issue on a question which does not apply to the case, and went as far as a man dared to go, in saying we had no right at all. From all this twisting and turning, this advancing and retreating, and appearing to own at last what he impliedly disowned at first, I think myself justified in drawing this conclusion, that either Americanus does not know how to conduct an argument, or he intended to be a traitor if he dared.

The natural right of the United States in those fisheries is either *whole* or in *part*. If to the whole, she can admit a participation to other nations. If to a part, she, in consequence of her natural right to partake, claims her share therein, which is for as much as she can catch and carry away. Nature, in her distribution of favors, seems to have appointed these fisheries as a property to the northern division of America, from Florida upwards, and therefore our claim of an exclusive right seems to be rationally and consistently founded ; but our natural right to what we can catch is clear, absolute and positive.

Had Americanus intended no more than to consider our claim, whether it should be made or not, as a matter of convenience only, which is the stage he has now brought it to, he ought by no means to have made even the slightest stroke at the right itself ; because to omit making the claim in the treaty, and to assign the doubtfulness of the right as a reason for the omission, is to surrender the fisheries upon the insufficiency of the pretension, and of consequence to exclude ourselves from the *practice* by the silence of the treaty, and from the *right* by the reasons upon record.

Had I time to laugh over my *fish*, I could in this place set Americanus up to a very agreeable ridicule. He has all this while been angling without a bait, and endeavouring to deceive with an empty hook, and yet this man says he under-

stands *fishing* as well as any man in America. " Very few,"
says he, " and *I speak it without vanity*, are better acquainted
with the fisheries than myself." If this be true, which I
hope it is not, it is the best reason that can be given for
relinquishing them, and if made known would, on the other
hand, be a great inducement to Britain to cede the whole
right, because by our being possessed of a right without
knowing how to use it, she would be under no apprehensions of our thinning the ocean, and we should only go out
with our vessels to buy, and not to catch.

If Americanus wished to persuade the Americans to say
nothing about the fisheries in a treaty with Britain, he
ought, as a politician of some kind or other, to have baited
his hook with a plausible something, and, instead of telling
them that their right was doubtful, he should have assured
them it was indisputable, that Britain never meant to question it, that it was needless to say anything about it, that all
nations knew our rights, and naturally meant to acknowledge them.   But he, like a wiseacre, has run against the post
instead of running past it, and has, by the arguments he has
used, produced a necessity for doing the very thing he was
writing to prevent ; and yet this man says he understands
fishing as well as any man in America—It must be a cod
indeed that should be catched by him !

COMMON SENSE.

PHILADELPHIA, July 12, 1779.

PEACE, AND THE NEWFOUNDLAND
FISHERIES.[1]

(THIRD LETTER.)

THE *importance* of the fisheries Americanus has kept
almost totally out of sight.   Why he has done so, his readers
will contrive to guess at, or himself may explain.   A bare
confession, loosely scattered here and there, and marked
with the countenance of reluctance, is all he gives on the
subject.   Surely, the public might have expected more from

[1] From the *Pennsylvania Gazette*, July 21, 1779.

a man, who declares " he can, without vanity say, that very few are better acquainted with the *nature* and *extent* of the American fisheries than himself." If he really possesses the knowledge he affirms, he ought to have been as prolific on the subject as the fish he was treating of: And as he has not, I am obliged to suspect either the reality of his knowledge, or the *sincerity* of his intentions. If the declaration be *not* true, there are enow to fix his *title*; and if true, it shews that a man may keep company all his life-time with cod, and be little the wiser. But to the point,——

There are but two natural sources of wealth and strength —the Earth and the Ocean—and to lose the right to either is, in our situation, to put up the other to sale. Without the fisheries, independence would be a bubble. It would not deserve the name; and however we might, in such a condition, please ourselves with the jingle of the word, the consequences that would follow would soon deprive us even of the title and the music.

I shall arrange the fisheries under the three following heads:

First. As an Employment.

Secondly. As producing National Supply and Commerce, and a means of National Wealth.

Thirdly. As a Nursery for Seamen.

As an employment, by which a living is procured, it more immediately concerns those who make it their business; and in this view, which is the least of the three, such of the States, or parts thereof, which do not follow fishing, are not so directly interested as those which do. I call it the least of the three, because as no man needs want employment in America, so the change from one employment to another, if that be all, is but little to him, and less to anybody else. And this is the narrow impolitic light in which some persons have understood the fisheries.

But when we view them as producing national supply and commerce, and a means of national wealth, we then consider the *fish*, not the fisherman, and regard the consequences of the employment more than the employment itself; in the same manner that I distinguish the coat that clothes me, from the man that made it. In this view, we neither enquire (unless for curiosity) who catch the fish, or whether they catched themselves—how they were catched, or where? The same supply would be produced, the same commerce occasioned, and the same wealth created, were they, by a natural impulse, to throw themselves annually on the shore, or be driven there by a periodical current or storm. And taking it in this point, it is no more to us, than it was to the Israelites whether the manna that fed them was brought there by an angel or an insect, an eastern or a western breeze, or whether it was congealed dew, or a concretion of vegetable juices. It is sufficient that they had manna, and we have fish.

I imagine myself within compass, when I suppose the fisheries to constitute a fourth part of the staple commerce of the United States, and that with this extraordinary advantage, it is a commerce which interferes with none, and promotes others. Take away a fourth from any part, and the whole United States suffers, in the same manner that the blood taken from the arm is drained from the whole man; and if, by the unskilfulness of the operation, the wounded arm should lose its use, the whole body would want its service. It is to no purpose for a man to say, I am not a fisherman, an indigo planter, a rice planter, a tobacco planter, or a corn planter, any more than for the leg to say, I am not an arm; for as, in the latter instance, the same blood invigorates both and all by circulation, so, in the former, each is enriched by the wealth which the other creates, and fed by the supply the other raises. Were it proposed that no town should have a market, are none concerned therein but butchers? And in like manner it may be asked, that if we lose the market for fish, are none affected thereby but those who catch them? He who digs the mine, or tills the earth, or fishes in the ocean, digs, tills and fishes for the world. The employment and the pittance it procures him are his; but the produce itself creates a traffic for thousands, a supply for millions.

The Eastern States by quitting agriculture for fishing become customers to the rest, partly by exchange and partly by the wealth they import. Of the Middle States, they purchase grain and flour; of Maryland and Virginia, tobacco, the food and pastime of the fisherman; of North and South-Carolina, and Georgia, rice and indigo. They may not happen to become the client of a lawyer in either of these states, but is it any reason that we are to be deprived of fish, one of the *instruments* of commerce, because it comes to him without a *case?*

The loss of the fisheries being at this time blended with other losses, which all nations at war are more or less subject to, is not particularly felt or distinguished in the general suspension: And the men who were employed therein being now called off into other departments, and supported by other means, feel not the want of the employment. War, in this view, contains a temporary relief for its own misfortunes, by creating a trade in lieu of the suspended one. But when, with the restoration of peace, trade shall open, the case will be very and widely different, and the fisherman like the farmer will expect to return to his occupation in quietude.

As my limits will not allow me to range, neither have I time if I had room, I shall close this second head, and proceed to the third, and finish with some remarks on the state the question is now said to stand in in Congress.

If as an *employment* one fourth of the United States are immediately affected, and if as a source of national supply and commerce and a means of national wealth all are deeply interested, what shall we say when we consider it as a *nursery for seamen.* Here the question seems to take almost a reversed turn, for the states which do *not fish* are herein *more concerned* than those which do. It happens, by some disposition of providence or ourselves, that those particular states whose employment is to fish are thickly settled, and secured by their internal strength from any extensive ravages of an enemy. The States, all the way from thence to the southward, beginning at New-York, are less populous, and have less of that ability in proportion to their extent. *Their* security, therefore, will hereafter be in a navy, and without a fishery there can be no navy worthy of the name.

Has nature given us timber and iron, pitch and tar, and cordage if we please, for nothing but to sell or burn? Has experience taught us the art of ship-building equal to any people on earth to become the workmen of other nations? Has she surrounded our coast with fisheries to create strength to our enemies, and make us the purchasers of our own property? Has she brought those fisheries almost to our own doors, to insult us with the prospect, and at the same time that she bar us from the enjoyment to threaten us with the constant approach of an enemy? Or has she given these things for our use, and instructed us to combine them for our own protection? Who, I ask, will undertake to answer me, Americanus or myself?

What would we now give for thirteen ships of the line to guard and protect the remote or weaker parts? How would Carolina feel deliverance from danger, and Georgia from despair, and assisted by such a fleet become the prison of their invaders? How would the whigs of New York look up and smile with inward satisfaction at the display of an Admiral's command, opening, like a " *key*," the door of their confinement? How would France solace herself at such a union of force, and reciprocally assisting and assisted traverse the ocean in safety? Yet all these, or their similar consequences, are staked upon the fisheries.

Americanus may understand the " nature of fisheries," as to season, catching and curing, or their " extent " as to latitude and longitude ; but as a great political question, involving with it the means and channels of commerce, and the probability of empire, he is wholly unequal to the subject, or he would not have, as he has done, limitted their effects to " *two or three states especially.*" By a judgment acquired from long acquaintance, he may be able to know a cod when he sees it, or describe the inconveniences or pleasures of a fishing voyage. Or, " *born and educated* " * among them, he

---

* *King of England's first speech to the British parliament.—Author.*

may entertain us with the growling memories of a New-foundland bear, or amuse us with the history of a foggy climate or a smoaky hut, with all the winter chit-chat of fatigue and hardship; and this, in his idea, may be to "*understand the fisheries.*"

I will venture to predict that America, even with the assistance of all the fisheries, will never be a *great*, much less a *dangerous* naval power, and without them she will be scarcely any. I am established in this opinion from the known cast and order of things. No country of a large extent ever yet, I believe, was powerful at sea, or ever will be. The natural reason of this appears to be that men do not, in any great numbers, turn their thoughts to the ocean, till either the country gets filled, or some peculiar advantage or necessity tempts them out. A maritime life is a kind of partial emigration, produced from a portion of the same causes with emigrations in general. The ocean becomes covered and the supply kept up from the constant swarm-ings of the landed hive; and as we shall never be able to fill the whole dominion of the Thirteen States, and there will ever be new land to cultivate, the necessity can never take place in America, and of course the consequences can never happen.

Paradoxical as it may appear, greatness at sea is the effect of littleness by land. Want of room and want of employ are the generating causes. Holland has the most powerful navy in the world, compared with the small extent of her crowded country. France and Spain have too much room, and the soil too luxuriant and tempting, to be quitted for the ocean. Were not this the case, and did the abilities for a navy like those for land service rise in proportion to the number of inhabitants only, France would rival more than any two powers in Europe, which is not the case.

Had not nature thrown the fisheries in our way and in-flicted a degree of natural sterility on such parts of the con-tinent as lie contiguous thereto, by way both of forcing and tempting their inhabitants to the ocean, America, consider-ing the present cast of the world, would have wanted the means of defence, for the far greater part of our seamen except those produced by the fisheries, are natives of other countries. And shall we unwisely trifle with what we ought to hug as a treasure, and nourish with the utmost care as a Protector? And must the W. H. D. forever mean that *We Have Dunces?* [1]

We seek not a fleet to insult the world, or range in foreign regions for conquests. We have more land than we can cultivate; more extent than we can fill. Our natural situation frees us from the distress of crowded countries, and from the thirst of ambitious ones. We covet not dominion, for we already possess a world; we want not to export our labouring poor, for where can they live better, or where can they be more useful? But we want just such a fleet as the fisheries will enable us to keep up, and without which we shall be for ever exposed, a burthen to our allies, and incapable of the necessary defence. The strength of America, on account of her vast extent, cannot be collected by land; but since experience has taught us to sail, and nature has put the means in our power, we ought in time to make provision for a navy, as the cheapest, safest, best, and most effectual security we can hereafter depend on.

Having in my first and second publications endeavoured to establish the right of America to the fisheries, and in this treated of their vast importance, I shall conclude with some remarks on the subject, as it is now said to stand in Congress, or rather the form in which it is thrown out to the public.

Americanus says (and I ask not how he came by his knowledge) that the question is, "Whether the insisting on an explicit acknowledgment of that right (meaning the right of fishing on the Banks of Newfoundland) is either *safe, prudent or politic.*"

Before I enter on the discussion of this point, it may not be improper to remark, that some intimations were made to Congress in February by the Minister of France, Mr. Gerard, respecting what the claims of America might be, in case any treaty of peace should be entered on with the enemy. And

---

[1] Probably W. H. D. were initials of some disputant on the subject.—*Editor.*

from this, with some account of the general disposition of the powers of Europe, the mighty buz of peace took its rise, and several who ought to have known better, were whispering wonderful secrets at almost every tea table.

It was a matter very *early* supposed by those who had any clear judgment, that Spain would not immediately join in the war, but would lie by as a mediatorial power. If she succeeded therein, the consequence would be a peace ; if she failed, she would then be perfectly at liberty to fulfil her engagements with France, etc.

Now in order to enable Spain to act this part, it was necessary that the claims of Congress in behalf of America should be made known *to their own Plenipotentiary at Paris,* Dr. *Franklin,* with such instructions, public or private, as might be proper to give thereon. But I observe several members, either so little acquainted with political arrangements, or supposing their constituents to be so, that they treat with Mr. Gerard as if that gentleman was *our* Minister, instead of the Minister of his Most Christian Majesty, and *his* name is brought in to a variety of business to which it has no proper reference. This remark may to some appear rather severe, but it is a necessary one. It is not every member of Congress who acts as if he felt the true importance of his character, or the dignity of the country he acts for. And we seem in some instances to forget, that as France is the great ally of America, so America is the great ally of France.

It may now be necessary to mention, that no instructions are yet gone to Dr. Franklin as a line for negotiation, and the reason is because none are agreed on. The reason why they are *not* agreed on is another point. But had the gentlemen who are for leaving the fisheries out agreed to have had them put in, instructions might have been sent more than four months ago ; and if not exactly convenient, might by this time have been returned and reconsidered. On whose side then does the fault lie?

I profess myself an advocate, out of doors, for clearly, absolutely, and unequivocally ascertaining the right of the

States to fish on the Banks of Newfoundland, as one of the first and most necessary articles. The right and title of the States thereto I have endeavoured to show. The importance of these fisheries I have endeavoured to prove. What reason then can be given why they should be omitted?

The seeds of almost every former war have been sown in the injudicious or defective terms of the preceding peace. Either the conqueror has insisted on too much, and thereby held the conquered, like an over-bent bow, in a continual struggle to snap the cord, or the latter has artfully introduced an equivocal article, to take such advantages under as the turn of future affairs might afford. We have only to consult our own feelings, and each man may from thence learn the spring of all national policy. And he, who does not this, may be fortunate enough to effect a temporary measure, but never will, unless by accident, accomplish a lasting one.

Perhaps the fittest condition any countries can be in to make a peace, calculated for duration, is when neither is conquered, and both are tired. The first of these suits England and America. I put England first in this case, because she began the war: And as she must be and *is* convinced of the impossibility of conquering America, and as America has no romantic ideas of extending her conquests to England, the object on the part of England is lost, and on the part of America is so far secure, that, unless she unwisely conquers herself, she is certain of not being conquered; and this being the case, there is no visible object to prevent the opening a negociation. But how far England is disposed thereto is a matter wholly unknown, and much to be doubted. A movement towards a negociation, and a disposition to enter into it, are very distinct things. The first is often made, as an army affects to retreat, in order to throw an enemy off his guard. To prevent which, the most vigorous preparations ought to be made for war at the very instant of negociating for a peace.

Let America make these preparations, and she may send her terms and claims whenever she pleases, without any ap-

prehension of appearing or acting out of character. Those
preparations relate now more to revenue than to force, and
that being wholly and immediately within the compass of
our own abilities, requires nothing but our consent to
accomplish.*

To leave the fisheries wholly out, on any pretence whatever,
is to sow the seeds of another war; and I will be content to
have the name of an ideot engraven for an epitaph, if it does
not produce that effect. The difficulties which are now given
will become a soil for those seeds to grow in, and future circumstances will quicken their vegetation. Nations are very
fond of appealing to treaties when it suits their purpose, and
tho' America might afterwards assign her *unquestioned* right
as a reason for her silence, yet all must know that treaties
are never to be explained by presumption, but wholly by
what is put in, and never by what is left out.

There has not yet been an argument given for omitting the
fisheries, but what might have been given as a stronger reason to the contrary. All which has been advanced rests only
on supposition, and that failing, leaves them no foundation.
They suppose Britain will not hereafter interrupt the right;
but the case is, they have no right to that supposition; and
it may likewise be parried by saying,—suppose she should?
Now the matter, as I conceive it, stands thus——

If the right of the States to fish on the Banks of Newfoundland be made and consented to as an article in a treaty
with Britain, it of consequence becomes expresly guarantied
by the eleventh article of the present treaty of alliance with

---

* *A plan has been proposed, and all who are judges have approved it, for stopping the emissions* [of paper money] *and raising a revenue, by subscription for
three years without interest, and in lieu thereof to take every subscriber's taxes out
of his subscription, and the balance at the expiration of that time to be returned.
If the States universally go into this measure, they will acquire a degree of strength
and ability fitted either for peace or war. It is, I am clearly convinced, the best
measure they can adopt, the best interest they can have, and the best security they
can hold. In short, it is carrying on or providing against war without expence,
because the remaining money in the country, after the subscriptions are made, will
be equal in value to the whole they now hold. Boston has proposed the same
measure.—Author.*

France; but if it be left out in a treaty with the former, it is not then guarantied in the present treaty with the latter, because the guaranteeing is limited to "the whole of their (our) possessions, as the same shall be fixed and assured to the said States at *the moment of the cessation of their present war with England."* Art II.

Were the States to claim, as a memorial to be recorded with themselves, an exclusive right to those fisheries, as a matter of right *only*, derived from natural situation, and to propose to their allies to guarantee to them expresly so much of that right as we may have occasion to use, and the States to guarantee to such allies such portion of the fisheries as they possessed by the last treaty of peace, there might be some pretence for not touching on the subject in a treaty with Britain; because, after the conclusion of the war, she would hardly venture to interrupt the States in a right, which, tho' not described in a treaty with her, should be powerfully guarrantied in a treaty with others. But to omit it wholly in one treaty, and to leave it unguarrantied in another, and to trust it entirely, as the phrase is, to the chapter of accidents, is too loose, too impolitic a mode of conducting national business.

" Had nothing," says Americanus, "been said on the subject of the fisheries, our fishermen, on the peace, might have returned to their old stations without interruption."

Is this talking like an American politician, or a seducing emissary ? Who authorised Americanus to intimate such an assurance ; or how came he to know what the British ministry would or would not hereafter do ; or how can he be certain they have told him truth ? If it be supposition only, he has, as I before remarked, no right to make it ; and if it be more than supposition, it must be the effect of secret correspondence. In the first of these cases he is foolish ; in the second worse. Does he not see that the fisheries are not expresly and only conditionally guarrantied, and that if in such a situation they be omitted in a treaty with Britain, and she should afterwards interrupt our right, that the

States stand single in the question, and have no right on the face of the present treaties to call on their Allies for assistance? And yet this man is persuading us to say nothing about them.

Americanus like some others is mightily fond of amusing his readers with "*the law of nations*," just as if there really was such a law, fixed and known like the law of the ten commandments. Whereas the law of nations is in theory the law of treaties compounded with customary usage, and in practice just what they can get and keep till it be taken from them. It is a term without any regular defined meaning, and as in some instances we have invented the thing first and given the name afterwards, so in this we have invented the name and the thing is yet to be made.

Some gentlemen say leave the fisheries to be settled afterwards in a treaty of commerce. This is really beginning business at the wrong end. For a treaty of peace cannot *precede* the settlement of disputes, but proceeds in consequence of all controverted points respecting right and dominion being adjusted and agreed on. There is one kind of treaty of commerce which may follow a treaty of peace, but that respects such articles only and the mode of traficking with them as are produced within, or imported into the known and described dominions of the parties; or to the rules of exchange, or paying or recovering debts, but never to the dominion itself; and comes more properly within the province of a Consul than the superior contracting powers.

With these remarks I shall, for the present, close the subject. It is a new one, and I have endeavoured to give it as systematical an investigation as the short time allowed and the other business I have on hand will admit of. How the affair stands in Congress, or how the cast of the House is on the question, I have, for several reasons, not enquired into; neither have I conversed with any gentleman of that Body on the subject. They have their opinion and I mine; and as I chuse to think my own reasons and write my own thoughts, I feel the more free the less I consult.

Who the writer of Americanus is I am not informed. I

never said or ever believed it to be Mr. Gouverneur Morris, or replied to it upon that supposition. The manner is not his, neither do I know that the principles are, and as that gentleman has disavowed it, the assurance is sufficient. I have likewise heard it supposed that Mr. Deane is the author, and that his friend Mr. Langworthy carried it to the press. But I know not who the author is. I have replied to the Piece rather than to the Man ; tho' for the sake of relief to the reader and amusement to myself, he now and then comes in for a stroke.[1]

COMMON SENSE.

PHILADELPHIA, July 17, 1779.

[1] Paine's contention in these letters was taken up by Dr. Franklin, while the Treaty of Peace was under discussion at Paris (autumn of 1782). After much disputation the third article was framed by which the Newfoundland Fisheries were held open, but the right to land and dry fish was limited to the parts of Nova Scotia then unsettled, and, on their settlement, to be subject to agreement with the inhabitants.—*Editor*.

II.

THE AMERICAN PHILOSOPHICAL SOCIETY.

AN ACT for incorporating the American Philosophical Society, held at Philadelphia for promoting useful knowledge.[1]

Whereas the cultivation of useful knowledge, and the advancement of the liberal Arts and Sciences in any country, have the most direct tendency towards the improvement of agriculture, the enlargement of trade, the ease and comfort of life, the ornament of society, and the ease and happiness of mankind. And whereas this country of North America, which the goodness of Providence hath given us to inherit, from the vastness of its extent, the variety of its climate, the fertility of its soil, the yet unexplored treasures of its bowels, the multitude of its rivers, lakes, bays, inlets, and other conveniences of navigation, offers to these United States one of the richest subjects of cultivation, ever presented to any people upon earth. And whereas the experience of ages shows that improvements of a public nature are best carried on by societies of liberal and ingenious men, uniting their labours without regard to nation, sect, or party, in one grand pursuit, alike interesting to all, whereby mutual prejudices are worn off, a humane and philosophical Spirit is cherished, and youth are stimulated to a laudable diligence and emulation in the pursuit of Wisdom : And whereas, upon these Principles, divers public-spirited gentlemen of Pennsylvania

---

[1] The second reading of this Bill, Monday, February 14, 1780, is entered by Thomas Paine, as Clerk of the General Assembly, and was subsequently published as his by his London friends as a " Broadside." A copy is in the British Museum.—*Editor*.

and other American States did heretofore Unite Themselves, under certain regulations into one voluntary Society, by the name of " The American Philosophical Society, held at Philadelphia for promoting useful knowledge," and by their successful labours and investigations, to the great credit of America, have extended their reputation so far, that men of the first eminence in the republic of letters in the most civilized nations of Europe have done honour to their publications, and desired to be enrolled among their Members: And whereas the said Society, after having been long interrupted in their laudable pursuits by the calamities of war, and the distresses of our country, have found means to revive their design, in hopes of being able to prosecute the same with their former success, and of being further encouraged therein by the public, for which purpose they have prayed us, " the Representatives of the Freemen of the Commonwealth of Pennsylvania, that they may be created One Body Politic and Corporate for ever, with such powers, and privileges, and immunities as may be necessary for answering the valuable purposes which the said Society had originally in view."

Wherefore, in order to encourage the said Society in the prosecution and advancement of all useful branches of knowledge, for the benefit of their Country and Mankind, Be it enacted, and it is hereby enacted by the Representatives of the Freemen of the Commonwealth of Pennsylvania, in General Assembly met, and by the authority of the same, That the members of the said Philosophical Society, heretofore voluntarily associated for promoting useful knowledge, and such other persons as have been duly elected Members and Officers of the same, agreeably to the fundamental laws and regulations of the said Society, comprised in twelve sections, prefixed to their first Volume of Transactions, published in Philadelphia, and such other laws and regulations as shall hereafter be duly made and enacted by the Society, according to the tenor hereof, be and for ever hereafter shall be, One Body Corporate and Politic in Deed, by the name and style of " The American Philosophical Society held at Philadelphia, for promoting useful knowledge."

And whereas—Nations truly civilized (however unhappily at variance on other accounts) will never wage war with the Arts and Sciences, and the Common Interests of Humanity; Be it further enacted by the authority aforesaid, That it shall and may be lawful for the said Society, by their proper officers, at all times, whether in peace or war, to correspond with learned societies, as well as individual learned men, of any nation or country; upon matters merely belonging to the business of the said Societies, such as the mutual communication of their discoveries and proceedings in philosophy and science; the procuring Books, Apparatus, Natural Curiosities, and such other articles and intelligence as are usually exchanged between learned bodies, for furthering their common pursuits: Provided always, That such correspondence of the said Society be at all times open to the inspection of the supreme Executive Council of this Commonwealth, etc.

III.

EMANCIPATION OF SLAVES.

PREAMBLE TO THE ACT PASSED BY THE PENNSYLVANIA
ASSEMBLY MARCH 1, 1780.

I. WHEN we contemplate our abhorrence of that condition, to which the arms and tyranny of Great Britain were exerted to reduce us, when we look back on the variety of dangers to which we have been exposed, and how miraculously our wants in many instances have been supplied, and our deliverances wrought, when even hope and human fortitude have become unequal to the conflict, we are unavoidably led to a serious and grateful sense of the manifold blessings, which we have undeservedly received from the hand of that Being, from whom every good and perfect gift cometh. Impressed with these ideas, we conceive that it is our duty, and we rejoice that it is in our power, to extend a portion of that freedom to others, which hath been extended to us, and release them from the state of thralldom, to which we ourselves were tyrannically doomed, and from which we have now every prospect of being delivered. It is not for us to enquire why, in the creation of mankind, the inhabitants of the several parts of the earth were distinguished by a difference in feature or complexion. It is sufficient to know that all are the work of the Almighty Hand. We find in the distribution of the human species, that the most fertile as well as the most barren parts of the earth are inhabited by men of complexions different from ours, and from each other ; from whence we may reasonably as well as religiously infer, that He, who placed them in their various situations, hath extended equally his care and protection to all, and that it becometh not us to counteract his mercies. We esteem it a peculiar blessing granted to us, that we are enabled this day to add one more step to universal civilization, by removing, as much as possible, the sorrows of those who have lived in undeserved bondage, and from which, by the assumed authority of the Kings of Great Britain, no effectual legal relief could be obtained. Weaned, by a long course of experience, from those narrow prejudices and partialities we had imbibed, we find our hearts enlarged with kindness and benevolence towards men of all conditions and nations ; and we conceive ourselves at this particular period particularly called upon by the blessings which we have received, to manifest the sincerity of our profession, and to give a substantial proof of our gratitude.

II. And whereas the condition of those persons, who have heretofore been denominated Negro and Mulatto slaves, has been attended with circumstances, which not only deprived them of the common blessings that they were by nature entitled to, but has cast them into the deepest afflictions, by an unnatural separation and sale of husband and wife from each other and from their children, an injury, the greatness of which can only be conceived by supposing that we were in the same unhappy case. In justice, therefore, to persons so unhappily circumstanced, and who, having no prospect before them whereon they may rest their sorrows and their hopes, have no reasonable inducement to render their service to society, which they otherwise might, and also in grateful commemoration of our own happy deliverance from that state of unconditional submission to which we were doomed by the tyranny of Britain,

III. *Be it enacted*, etc.[1]

---

[1] The provisions of this first Act of Emancipation in America were written by George Bryan. It was introduced on the day when Paine became Clerk of the Assembly (Nov. 2, 1779.) Although the authorship of this Preamble has been claimed for others, the steady tradition which has ascribed it to Paine can hardly be doubted by those who compare it with the plea for emancipation with which his career in America opened. See vol. i. of this work ; and my "Life of Paine," i., p. 154.—*Editor.*

IV.

PUBLIC GOOD.[1]

PREFACE.

THE following pages are on a subject hitherto little under-stood but highly interesting to the United States.

They contain an investigation of the claims of Virginia to the vacant Western territory, and of the right of the United States to the same ; with some outlines of a plan for laying out a new state, to be applied as a fund, for carrying on the war, or redeeming the national debt.

The reader, in the course of this publication, will find it studiously plain, and, as far as I can judge, perfectly candid. What materials I could get at I have endeavoured to place in a clear line, and deduce such arguments therefrom as the subject required. In the prosecution of it, I have considered myself as an advocate for the right of the states, and taken no other liberty with the subject than what a counsel would, and ought to do, in behalf of a client.

I freely confess that the respect I had conceived, and still preserve, for the character of Virginia, was a constant check upon those sallies of imagination, which are fairly and ad-vantageously indulged against an enemy, but ungenerous when against a friend.

If there is any thing I have omitted or mistaken, to the

---

[1] This pamphlet was published with the following title : "Public Good : Being an Examination into the Claim of Virginia to the Vacant Western Ter-ritory, and of the Right of the United States to the Same : to Which is Added Proposals for Laying off a New State, to be Applied as a Fund for Carrying on the War, or Redeeming the National Debt." [Published by Dunlap, Phila-delphia, December 30, 1780.]

31

injury of the intentions of Virginia or her claims, I shall gladly rectify it, or if there is any thing yet to add, should the subject require it, I shall as cheerfully undertake it ; being fully convinced, that to have matters fairly discussed, and properly understood, is a principal means of preserving harmony and perpetuating friendship.

THE AUTHOR.

PUBLIC GOOD.

WHEN we take into view the mutual happiness and united interests of the states of America, and consider the vast consequences to arise from a strict attention of each, and of all, to every thing which is just, reasonable, and honorable; or the evils that will follow from an inattention to those principles; there cannot, and ought not, to remain a doubt but the governing rule of right and of mutual good must in all public cases finally preside.

The hand of providence has cast us into one common lot, and accomplished the independence of America, by the unanimous consent of the several parts, concurring at once in time, manner and circumstances. No superiority of interest, at the expense of the rest, induced the one, more than the other, into the measure. Virginia and Maryland, it is true, might foresee that their staple commodity, tobacco, by being no longer monopolized by Britain, would bring them a better price abroad: for as the tax on it in England was treble its first purchase from the planter, and they being now no longer compelled to send it under that obligation, and in the restricted manner they formerly were, it is easy to see that the article, from the alteration of the circumstances of trade, will, and daily does, turn out to them with additional advantages.

But this being a natural consequence, produced by that common freedom and independence of which all are partakers, is therefore an advantage they are entitled to, and on which the rest of the states can congratulate them without feeling a wish to lessen, but rather to extend it. To contribute to the increased prosperity of another, by the same means which occasion our own, is an agreeable reflection;

and the more valuable any article of export becomes, the more riches will be introduced into and spread over the continent.

Yet this is an advantage which those two states derive from the independence of America, superior to the local circumstances of the rest; and of the two it more particularly belongs to Virginia than Maryland, because the staple commodity of a considerable part of Maryland is flour, which, as it is an article that is the growth of Europe as well as of America, cannot obtain a foreign market but by underselling, or at least by limiting it to the current price abroad. But tobacco commands its own price. It is not a plant of almost universal growth, like wheat. There are but few soils and climes that produce it to advantage, and before the cultivation of it in Virginia and Maryland, the price was from four to sixteen shillings sterling a pound in England.*

But the condition of the vacant western territory of America makes a very different case to that of the circumstances of trade in any of the states. Those very lands, formed, in contemplation, the fund by which the debt of America would in the course of years be redeemed. They were considered as the common right of all; and it is only till lately that any pretension of claim has been made to the contrary.

That difficulties and differences will arise in communities, ought always to be looked for. The opposition of interests, real or supposed, the variety of judgments, the contrariety of temper, and, in short, the whole composition of man, in his individual capacity, is tinctured with a disposition to contend; but in his social capacity there is either a right, which, being proved, terminates the dispute, or a reasonableness in the measure, where no direct right can be made out, which decides or compromises the matter.

As I shall have frequent occasion to mention the word *right*, I wish to be clearly understood in my definition of it. There are various senses in which this term is used, and custom has, in many of them, afforded it an introduction con-

---

* See Sir Dalby Thomas's Historical Account of the rise and growth of the West India Colonies.—*Author*.

trary to its true meaning. We are so naturally inclined to give the utmost degree of force to our own case, that we call every pretension, however founded, *a right*; and by this means the term frequently stands opposed to justice and reason.

After Theodore was elected king of Corsica, not many years ago, by the mere choice of the natives, for their own convenience in opposing the Genoese, he went over to England, run himself in debt, got himself into jail, and on his release therefrom, by the benefit of an act of insolvency, he surrendered up what he called *his* kingdom of Corsica, as a part of his personal property, for the use of his creditors; some of whom may hereafter call this a charter, or by any other name more fashionable, and ground thereon what they may term a right to the sovereignty and property of Corsica. But does not justice abhor such an action both in him and them, under the prostituted name of a *right*, and must not laughter be excited wherever it is told?

A right, to be truly so, must be right within itself: yet many things have obtained the name of rights, which are originally founded in wrong. Of this kind are all rights by mere conquest, power or violence. In the cool moments of reflection we are obliged to allow, that the mode by which such a right is obtained, is not the best suited to that spirit of universal justice which ought to preside equally over all mankind. There is something in the establishment of such a right, that we wish to slip over as easily as possible, and say as little about as can be. But in the case of a *right founded in right*, the mind is carried cheerfully into the subject, feels no compunction, suffers no distress, subjects its sensations to no violence, nor sees any thing in its way which requires an artificial smoothing.

From this introduction I proceed to examine into the claims of Virginia; first, as to the right, secondly as to the reasonableness, and lastly, as to the consequences.

The name, *Virginia*, originally bore a different meaning to what it does now. It stood in the place of the word North-America, and seems to have been a name comprehensive of all the English settlements or colonies on the continent, and not descriptive of any one as distinguished from the rest. All to the southward of the Chesapeake, as low as the gulf of Mexico, was called South-Virginia, and all to the northward, North-Virginia, in a similar line of distinction, as we now call the whole continent North and South America.*

The first charter, or patent, was to Sir Walter Raleigh by Queen Elizabeth, of England, in the year 1583, and had neither name nor bounds. Upon Sir Walter's return, the name *Virginia* was given to the whole country, including the now United States. Consequently the present Virginia, either as a province or state, can set up no exclusive claim to the Western territory under this patent, and that for two reasons: first, because the words of the patent run *to Sir Walter Raleigh, and such persons as he should nominate, themselves and their successors*; which is a line of succession Virginia does not pretend to stand in ; and secondly, because a prior question would arise, namely, who are to be understood by Virginians under this patent? and the answer would be, all the inhabitants of America, from New-England to Florida.

This patent, therefore, would destroy their exclusive claim, and invest the right collectively in the thirteen states.

But it unfortunately happened, that the settlers under this patent, partly from misconduct, the opposition of the Indians, and other calamities, discontinued the process, and the patent became extinct.

After this, James the first, who, in the year 1602, succeeded Elizabeth, issued a new patent, which I come next to describe.

This patent differed from the former in this essential point, that it had limits, whereas the other had none : the former was intended to promote discoveries wherever they could be made, which accounts why no limits were affixed, and this to settle discoveries already made, which likewise assigns a reason why limits should be described.

In this patent were incorporated two companies, called the South-Virginia company, and the North-Virginia company, and sometimes the London company, and the Plymouth company.

* Oldmixon's History of Virginia.—*Author.*

The South-Virginia or London company was composed
chiefly of London adventurers; the North-Virginia or Plymouth company was made up of adventurers from Plymouth
in Devonshire and other persons of the western part of
England.

Though they were not to fix together, yet they were
allowed to choose their places of settlement any where on
the coast of America, then called Virginia, between the lati-
tudes of 34 and 45 degrees, which was a range of 760 miles:
the south company was not to go below 34 degrees, nor the
north company above 45 degrees.   But the patent expressed,
that as soon as they had made their choice, each was to become limited to 50 miles each way on the coast, and 100 up
the country ; so that the grant to each company was a square
of 100 miles, and no more. The North-Virginia or Plymouth
company settled to the eastward, and in the year 1614,
changed the name, and called that part New-England. The
South-Virginia or London company settled near Cape Henry.

This then cannot be the patent of boundless extent, and
that for two reasons : first, because the limits are described,
namely, a square of 100 miles ; and secondly, because there
were two companies of equal rights included in the same
patent.

Three years after this, that is, in the year 1609, the South-
Virginia company applied for new powers from the crown of
England, which were granted them in a new patent, and the
boundaries of the grant enlarged ; and this is the charter, or
patent, on which some of the present Virginians ground
their pretension to boundless territory.

The first reflection that presents itself on this enlargement
of the grant is, that it must be supposed to bear some intended degree of reasonable comparison to that which it
superseded. The former could not be greater than a square
of one hundred miles ; and this new one being granted in
lieu of that, and that within the space of three years, and by
the same person, James the first, who was never famed either
for profusion or generosity, cannot, on a review of the time
and circumstances of the grant, be supposed a very extravagant or very extraordinary one.   If a square of one hundred

miles was not sufficiently large, twice that quantity was as much as could well be expected or solicited; but to suppose that he, who had caution enough to confine the first grant within moderate bounds, should, in so short a space as three years, supersede it by another grant of many million times greater extent, is, on the face of the affair, a circumstantial nullity.

Whether this patent, or charter, was in existence or not at the time the revolution commenced, is a matter I shall hereafter speak to, and confine myself in this place to the limits which the said patent or charter lays down. The words are as follow:

" Beginning at the cape or point of land called cape or point Comfort, thence all along the seacoast to the NORTHWARD 200 miles, and from the said point or cape Comfort, all along the seacoast to the *southward,* 200 miles; and all that space or circuit of land lying from the seacoast of the precinct aforesaid up into the land throughout, from sea to sea, WEST and *northwest."*

The first remark I shall offer on the words of this grant is, that they are uncertain, obscure, and unintelligible, and may be construed into such a variety of contradictory meanings as to leave at last no meaning at all.

Whether the two hundred miles each way from cape Comfort, were to be on a *straight* line, or ascertained by following the indented *line of the coast,* that is, " *all along the seacoast,"* in and out as the coast lay, cannot now be fully determined; because, as either will admit of supposition, and nothing but supposition can be produced, therefore neither can be taken as positive. Thus far may be said, that had it been intended to be a straight line, the word *straight* ought to have been inserted, which would have made the matter clear; but as no inference can be well drawn to the advantage of that which does *not appear,* against that which *does,* therefore the omission implies negatively in favor of the coast-indented line, or that the 400 miles were to be traced on the windings of the coast, that is " *all along the seacoast."*

But what is meant by the words "*west and northwest*" is still more unintelligible. Whether they mean a west line and a northwest line, or whether they apply to the general lying of the land from the Atlantic, without regard to lines, cannot again be determined. But if they are supposed to mean lines to be run, then a new difficulty of more magnitude than all the rest arises; namely, from which end of the extent on the coast is the west line and the northwest line to be set off? As the difference in the contents of the grant, occasioned by transposing them, is many hundred millions of acres; and either includes or excludes a far greater quantity of land than the whole thirteen United States contain.

In short, there is not a boundary in this grant that is clear, fixed and defined. The coast line is uncertain, and that being the base on which the others are to be formed, renders the whole uncertain. But even if this line was admitted, in either shape, the other boundaries would still be on supposition, till it might be said there is no boundary at all, and consequently no charter; for words which describe nothing can give nothing.

The advocates for the Virginia claim, laying hold of these ambiguities, have explained the grant thus:

Four hundred miles on the sea-coast, and from the south point a west line to the great South sea, and from the north point a northwest line to the said South sea. The figure which these lines produce will be thus:

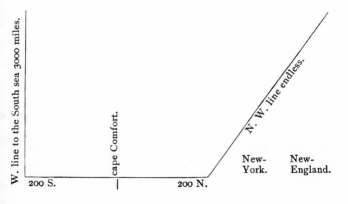

But why, I ask, must the west land line be set off from the south point, any more than the north point? The grant or patent does not say from which it shall be, neither is it clear that a line is the thing intended by the words: but admitting that it is, on what grounds do the claimants proceed in making this choice? The answer, I presume, is easily given, namely, because it is the most beneficial explanation to themselves they can possibly make; as it takes in many thousand times more extent of country than any other explanation would. But this, though it be a very good reason to them, is a very bad reason to us; and though it may do for the claimants to hope upon, will not answer to plead upon; especially to the very people, who, to confirm the partiality of the claimants' choice, must relinquish their own right and interest.

Why not set off the west land line from the north end of the coast line, and the northwest line from the south end of the same? There is some reason why this should be the construction, and none why the other should.

1st, Because if the line of two hundred miles each way from cape Comfort, be traced by following the indented line of the coast, which seems to be the implied intention of the words, and a west line set off from the north end, and a northwest line from the south end, these lines will all unite (which the other construction never can) and form a complete triangle, the contents of which will be about twenty-nine or thirty millions of acres, or something larger than Pennsylvania; and

2d, Because this construction is following the order of the lines as expressed in the grant; for the *first* mentioned *coast* line, which is to the *northward* of cape Comfort, and the *first* mentioned *land* line, which is the *west* line, have a numerical relation, being the first mentioned of each; and implies, that the west line was to be set off from the *north* point and *not* from the south point; and consequently the *two last* mentioned of each have the same numerical relation, and again implies that the *northwest* line was to be set off from the *south* point, and not from the *north* point. But why the claimants should break through the order of the lines, and contrary to implication, join the *first* mentioned of the *one*, to the last mentioned of the other, and thereby produce a shapeless monster, for which there is no name nor any parallel in the world, either as to extent of soil and sovereignty, is a construction that cannot be supported.

The figure produced by following the order of the lines is as follows * :

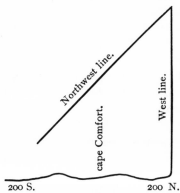

200 S.   200 N.

I presume that if 400 miles be traced by following the inflexes of any seashore, that the two extremes will not be more than 300 miles distant from each other, on a straight line. Therefore, to find the contents of a triangle, whose base is 300 miles, multiply the length of the base into half the perpendicular, which, in this case, is the west line, and the product will be the answer :

    300 miles, length of the base.
    150 half the perpendicular (supposing it a right-angled triangle).
    ————————
    15000
    300
    ————————
    45,000 contents of the grant in square miles.
       640 acres in a square mile.
    ————————
    1800000
    270000
    ————————
    28,800,000 contents in square acres.

* N. B. If the reader will cast his eye again over the words of the patent on p. 38, he will perceive the numerical relation alluded to, by observing, that the first mentioned coast line and the first mentioned land line are distinguished by CAPITALS. And the last mentioned of each by *italics*, which I have chosen to do to illustrate the explanation.—*Author*.

Now will any one undertake to say, that this explanation is not as fairly drawn (if not more so) from the words themselves, as any other that can be offered? Because it is not only justified by the exact words of the patent, grant, or charter, or any other name by which it may be called, but by their implied meaning; and is likewise of such contents as may be supposed to have been intended; whereas the claimants' explanation is without bounds, and beyond every thing that is reasonable. Yet, after all, who can say what was the precise meaning of terms and expressions so loosely formed, and capable of such a variety of contradictory interpretations?

Had the order of the lines been otherwise than they are in the patent, the reasonableness of the thing must have directed the manner in which they should be connected: but as the claim is founded in unreasonableness, and that unreasonableness endeavoured to be supported by a transposition of the lines, there remains no pretence for the claim to stand on.

Perhaps those who are interested in the claimants' explanation will say that as the South sea is spoken of, the lines must be as they explain them, in order to reach it.

To this I reply; first, that no man then knew how far it was from the Atlantic to the South sea, as I shall presently show, but believed it to be but a short distance: and,

Secondly, that the uncertain and ambiguous manner in which the South sea is alluded to (for it is not mentioned by name, but only "*from sea to sea*") serves to perplex the patent, and not to explain it; and as no right can be founded on an ambiguity, but on some proof cleared of ambiguity, therefore the allusive introduction of "from sea to sea" can yield no service to the claim.

There is likewise an ambiguous mention made of *two lands* in this patent, as well as of two *seas ; viz.* and all that "*space or circuit of land* lying from the sea-coast of the precinct aforesaid up into the *land throughout from sea to sea.*"

On which I remark, that the two lands here mentioned

have the appearance of a major and a minor, or the greater out of which the less is to be taken : and the term from " *sea to sea* " may be said to apply descriptively to the *land throughout* and not to the *space or circuit of land patented to the company ;* " in a similar manner that a former patent described a major of 706 miles in extent, out of which the minor, or square of one hundred miles, was to be chosen.

But to suppose that because the South sea is darkly alluded to, it must therefore (at whatever distance it might be, which then nobody knew, or for whatever purpose it might be introduced) be made a certain boundary, and that without regard to the reasonableness of the matter, or the order in which the lines are arranged, which is the only implication the patent gives for setting off the land lines, is a supposition that contradicts every thing which is reasonable.

The figure produced by following the order of the lines will be complete in itself, let the distance to the South sea be more or less ; because, if the *land throughout from sea to sea* had not been sufficiently extensive to admit the west land line and the northwest land line to close, the South sea, in that case, would have eventually become a boundary ; but if the extent of the *land throughout from sea to sea*, was so great that the lines closed without reaching the said South sea, the figure was complete without it.

Wherefore, as the order of the lines, when raised on the indented coast line, produces a regular figure of reasonable dimensions, and of about the same contents, though not of the same shape, which Virginia now holds within the Allegany mountains ; and by transposing them, another figure is produced, for which there is no name, and cannot be completed, as I shall presently explain, and of an extent greater than one half of Europe, it is needless to offer any other arguments to show that the order of the lines must be the rule, if any rule can be drawn from the words, for ascertaining from which point the west line and northwest line were to be set off. Neither is it possible to suppose any other rule could be followed ; because a northwest line set off two hundred miles above cape Comfort, would not only never touch the South sea, but would form a spiral line of infinite windings round the globe, and after passing over the northern parts of America and the frozen ocean, and then into the northern parts of Asia, would, when eternity should end, and not before, terminate in the north pole.

This is the only manner in which I can express the effect of a northwest line, set off as above ; because as its direction must always be between the north and the west, it consequently can never get into the pole nor yet come to a rest, and on the principle that matter or space is capable of being eternally divided, must proceed on for ever.

But it was a prevailing opinion, at the time this patent was obtained, that the South sea was at no great distance from the Atlantic, and therefore it was needless, under that supposition, to regard which way the lines should be run ; neither need we wonder at this error in the English government respecting America then, when we see so many and such glaring ones now, for which there is much less excuse.

Some circumstances favoured this mistake. Admiral Sir Francis Drake, not long before this, had, from the top of a mountain in the isthmus of Darien, which is the centre of North and South America, seen both the South sea and the Atlantic, the width of the part of the continent where he then was, not being above 70 miles ; whereas its width opposite Chesapeake bay is as great, if not greater, than in any other part, being from *sea to sea* about the distance it is from America to England. But this could not then be known, because only two voyages had been made across the South sea ; the one by the ship in which Magellan sailed, who died on his passage, and which was the first ship which sailed around the world, and the other by Sir Francis Drake ; but as neither of these sailed into a northern latitude in that ocean, high enough to fix the longitude of the western coast of America from the eastern, the distance across was entirely on supposition, and the errors they then ran into appear laughable to us who now know what the distance is.

That the company expected to come at the South sea without much trouble or travelling, and that the great body of land which intervened, so far from being their view in obtaining the charter, became their disappointment, may be collected from a circumstance mentioned in Stith's History of Virginia. He relates, that in the year 1608, which was at the time the company were soliciting this patent, they fitted up in England "a barge for captain Newport," (who was afterwards one of the joint deputy governors under the very charter we are now treating of,) "which, for convenience of carriage, might be taken into five pieces, and with which he and his company were instructed to go up James' river as far as the falls thereof, to discover the country of the Monakins, and from thence they were to proceed, *carrying their barge beyond the falls to convey them to the South sea;* being ordered not to return without a lump of gold, or a certainty of the said sea." And Hutchinson, in his history of New-England, which was called North Virginia at the time this patent was obtained, says "the geography of this part of America was less understood than at present. A line to the Spanish settlements was imagined to be much shorter than it really was. Some of Champlain's people in the beginning of the last century, who had been but a few days' march from Quebec, returned with great joy, supposing that from the top of a high mountain, they had discovered *the South sea.*"

From these matters, which are evidences on record, it appears that the adventurers had no knowledge of the distance it was to the South sea, but supposed it to be no great way from the Atlantic; and also that great extent of territory was not their object, but a short communication with the southern ocean, by which they might get into the neighborhood of the Gold coast, and likewise carry on a commerce with the East Indies.

Having thus shown the confused and various interpretations this charter is subject to, and that it may be made to mean any thing and nothing; I proceed to show, that, let the limits of it be more or less, the present state of Virginia does not, and cannot, as a matter of right, inherit under it.

I shall open this part of the subject by putting the following case:

Either Virginia stands in succession to the London company, to whom the charter was granted, or to the crown of England. If to the London company, then it becomes her, as an outset in the matter, to show who they were, and likewise that they were in possession to the commencement of the revolution.—If to the crown, then the charter is of consequence superseded; because the crown did not possess territories by charter, but by prerogative without charter. The notion of the crown chartering to itself is a nullity; and in this case, the unpossessed lands, be they little or much, are in the same condition as if they had never been chartered at all; and the sovereignty of them devolves to the sovereignty of the United States.

The charter or patent of 1609, as well as that of 1606, was to Sir Thomas Gates, Sir George Summers, the Rev. Richard Hacluit, prebend of Westminster, and others; and the government was then proprietary. These proprietors, by virtue of the charter of 1609, chose lord Delaware for their governor, and Sir Thomas Gates, Sir George Summers, and captain Newport, (the person who was to go with a boat to the South sea,) joint deputy governors. Was this the form of government either as to soil or constitution at the time the present revolution commenced? If not, the charter was not *in being ;* for it matters not to us how it came to be *out of being*, so long as the present Virginians, or their ancestors, neither are, nor were sufferers by the change then made.

But suppose it could not be proved to be in being, which it cannot, because *being*, in a charter, is power, it would only prove a right in behalf of the London company of adventurers; but how that right is to be disposed of is another question. We are not defending the right of the London company, deceased 150 years ago, but taking up the matter at the place where we found it, and so far as the authority of the crown of England was exercised when the revolution commenced. The charter was a contract between the crown of England and those adventurers for their own emolument, and not between the crown and the people of Virginia; and whatever was the occasion of the contract becoming void, or surrendered up, or superseded, makes no part of the question now.   It is sufficient that when the United States succeeded to sovereignty they found no such contract in existence, or even in litigation.   They found Virginia under the authority of the crown of England both as to soil and government, subject to quit-rents to the crown and not to the company, and had been so for upwards of 150 years: and that an in- strument or deed of writing, of a private nature, as all pro- prietary contracts are, so far as land is concerned, and which is now historically known, and in which Virginia was no party, and to which no succession in any line can be proved, and has ceased for 150 years, should now be raked from ob- livion and held up as a charter whereon to assume a right to boundless territory, and that by a pervertion of the order of it, is something very singular and extraordinary.

If there was any innovation on the part of the crown, the contest rested between the crown and the proprietors, the London company, and not between Virginia and the said crown.   It was not her charter; it was the company's charter, and the only parties in the case were the crown and the company.

But why, if Virginia contends for the immutability of char- ters, has she selected this in preference to the two former ones?   All her arguments, arising from this principle, must go to the first charter and not to the last; but by placing them to the last, instead of the first, she admits a fact against her principle; because, in order to establish the last, she proves the first to be vacated by the second in the space of 23 years, the second to be vacated by the third in the space of 3 years; and why the third should not be vacated by the fourth form of government, issuing from the same power with the former two, and which took place about 25 years after, and continued in being for 150 years since, and under which all her public and private business was transacted, her purchases made, her warrants for survey and patents for land obtained, is too mysterious to account for.

Either the re-assumption of the London company's charter into the hands of the crown was an usurpation, or it was not.

If it was, then, strictly speaking, is every thing which Virginia has done under that usurpation illegal, and she may be said to have lived in the most curious species of rebellion ever known; rebellion against the London company of adventurers. For if the charter to the company (for it was not to the Virginians) ought to be in being now, it ought to have been in being then; and why she should admit its vacation then and reject it now, is unaccountable; or why she should esteem her purchases of land good which were *then* made contrary to this charter, and now contend for the operation of the same charter to possess new territory by, are circumstances which cannot be reconciled.

But whether the charter, as it is called, ought to be extinct or not, cannot make a question with us. All the parties concerned in it are deceased, and no successors, in any regular line of succession, appear to claim. Neither the London company of adventurers, their heirs or assigns, were in possession of the exercise of this charter at the commencement of the revolution; and therefore the state of Virginia does not, in point of fact, succeed to and inherit from the company.

But, say they, we succeed to and inherit from the crown of England, which was the immediate possessor of the sovereignty at the time we entered, and had been so for 150 years.

To say this, is to say there is no charter at all. A charter is an assurance from one party to another, and cannot be from the same party to itself.

But before I enter further on this case, I shall concisely state how this charter came to be re-assumed by the power which granted it, the crown of England.

I have already stated that it was a proprietary charter, or grant, to Sir Thomas Gates and others, who were called the London company, and sometimes the South Virginia company, to distinguish them from those who settled to the eastward (now New-England) and were then called the North-Virginia or Plymouth company.

Oldmixon's History of Virginia (in his account of the British empire in America) published in the year 1708, gives a concise progress of the affair. He attributes it to the mis-conduct, contentions and mismanagements of the proprietors, and their innovations upon the Indians, which had so ex-asperated them, that they fell on the settlers, and destroyed at one time 334 men, women and children.

"Some time after this massacre," says he, "several gentlemen in England procured grants of land from the company, and others came over on their private accounts to make settlements ; among the former was one captain Martin, who was named to be of the council. This man raised so many differences among them, that new distractions followed, which the Indians observing, took heart, and once more fell upon the settlers on the borders, destroying, without pitying either age, sex, or condition.

"These and other calamities being chiefly imputed to the mis-management of the proprietors, whose losses had so discouraged most of their best members, that they sold their shares, and Charles I., on his accession to the throne, dissolved the company, and took the colony into his own immediate direction. He appointed the governor and council himself, ordered all patents and processes to issue in his own name, and reserved a quit-rent of two shillings sterling for every hundred acres."

Thus far our author. Now it is impossible for us at this distance of time to say what were all the exact causes of the change; neither have we any business with it. The company might surrender it, or they might not, or they might forfeit it by not fulfilling conditions, or they might sell it, or the crown might, as far as we know, take it from them. But what are either of these cases to Virginia, or any other which can be produced. She was not a party in the matter. It was not her charter, neither can she ingraft any right upon it, or suffer any injury under it.

If the charter was vacated, it must have been by the London company; if it was surrendered, it must be by the same ; and if it was sold, nobody else could sell it ; and if it was taken from them, nobody else could lose it ; and yet Virginia calls this her charter, which it was not within her power to hold, to sell, to vacate, or to lose.

But if she puts her right upon the ground that it never was sold, surrendered, lost, or vacated, by the London company, she admits that if they *had* sold, surrendered, lost, or vacated it, it would have become extinct, and to her no charter at all. And in this case, the only thing to prove is the fact, which is, has this charter been the rule of government, and of purchasing or procuring unappropriated lands in Virginia, from the time it was granted to the time of the revolution? Answer—the charter has not been the rule of government, nor of purchasing and procuring lands, neither have any lands been purchased or procured under its sanction or authority for upwards of 150 years.

But if she goes a step further, and says, that they could not vacate, surrender, sell, or lose it, by any act they could do, so neither could they vacate, surrender, sell, or lose that of 1606, which was three years prior to this; and this argument, so far from establishing the charter of 1609, would destroy it; and in its stead confirm the preceding one, which limited the company to a square of 100 miles. And if she still goes back to that of Sir Walter Raleigh, *that* only places her in the light of Americans in common with all.

The only fact that can be clearly proved is, that the crown of England exercised the power of dominion and government in Virginia, and of the disposal of the lands, and that the charter had neither been the rule of government or purchasing land for upwards of 150 years, and this places Virginia in succession to the crown, and not to the company. Consequently it proves a lapse of the charter into the hands of the crown by some means or other.

Now to suppose that the charter could return into the hands of the crown and yet remain in force, is to suppose that a man could be bound by a bond of obligation to himself.

Its very *being* in the hands of the crown, from which it issued, is a cessation of its existence; and an effectual unchartering all that part of the grant which was not before disposed of. And consequently the state of Virginia, standing thus in succession to the crown, can be entitled to no more extent of country as a state under the union, than what it possessed as a province under the crown. And all lands exterior to these bounds, as well of Virginia as the rest of the states, devolve, in the order of succession, to the sovereignty of the United States, for the benefit of all.

And this brings the case to what were the limits of Virginia as a province under the crown of England.

Charter it had none. Its limits then rested at the discretion of the authority to which it was subject. Maryland and Pennsylvania became its boundary to the eastward and northward, and North Carolina to the southward, therefore the boundary to the westward was the only principal line to be ascertained.

As Virginia from a proprietary soil and government was become what then bore the name of a royal one, the extent of the province, as the order of things then stood (for something must always be admitted whereon to form a beginning) was wholly at the disposal of the crown of England, who might enlarge or diminish, or erect new governments to the westward, by the same authoritative right that Virginia now can divide a county into two, if too large, or too inconvenient.

To say, as has been said, that Pennsylvania, Maryland, and North-Carolina, were taken out of Virginia, is no more than to say, they were taken out of America; because Virginia was the common name of all the country, north and south; and to say they were taken out of the chartered limits of Virginia, is likewise to say nothing; because, after the dissolution or extinction of the proprietary company, there was nobody to whom any provincial limits became chartered. The extinction of the company was the extinction of the chartered limits. The patent could not survive the company, because it was to them a right, which, when they expired, ceased to be any body's else in their stead.

But to return to the western boundary of Virginia at the commencement of the revolution.

Charters, like proclamations, were the sole act of the crown, and if the former were adequate to fix limits to the lands which it gave away, sold, or otherwise disposed of, the latter were equally adequate to fix limits or divisions to those which it retained ; and therefore, the western limits of Virginia, as the proprietary company was extinct and consequently the patent with it, must be looked for in the line of proclamations.

I am not fond of quoting these old remains of former arrogance, but as we must begin somewhere, and as the states have agreed to regulate the right of each state to territory, by the condition each stood in with the crown of England at the commencement of the revolution, we have no other rule to go by ; and any rule which can be agreed on is better than none.

From the proclamation then of 1763, the western limits of Virginia, as a province under the crown of England, are described so as not to extend beyond the heads of any of the rivers which empty themselves into the Atlantic, and consequently the limits did not pass over the Allegany mountains.

The following is an extract from the proclamation of 1763, so far as respects boundary :

"And whereas, it is *just* and *reasonable* and *essential to our interest*, and the security of our colonies, that the several nations or tribes of Indians, with whom we are connected, and who live under our protection, should not be molested or disturbed in the possession of such parts of our dominions and territories, *as, not having been ceded to, or purchased by us, are reserved to them or any of them as their hunting grounds ;* we do therefore, with the advice of our privy council, declare it to be our royal will and pleasure that no governor, or commander-in-chief, in any of our colonies of Quebec, East-Florida, or West-Florida, do presume upon any pretence whatever, to grant warrants of survey, or pass any patents for lands beyond the bounds of their respective governments, as described in their commissions : as ALSO that no governor or commander-in chief of our colonies or plantations in America, do presume, for the present, and until our further pleasure be known, to grant warrants of survey or pass patents for any lands *beyond the heads or sources of any of the rivers which fall into the Atlantic ocean, from the west or northwest*, or upon any lands whatever, *which not having been ceded to or purchased by us, as aforesaid, are reserved unto the said Indians, or any of them.*

"And we do further declare it to be our royal will and pleasure, for the present, as aforesaid, to reserve under our sovereignty, protection, and dominion, *for the use of the said Indians, all lands and territories*, not included within the limits of our said three new governments, or within the limits of the territory granted to the Hudson's bay company; as also, *all the lands and territories lying to the westward of the sources of the rivers, which fall into the sea from the west and northwest, as aforesaid ;* and we do hereby strictly forbid, on pain of our displeasure, all our loving subjects from making any purchases or settlements whatever, or taking possession of any of the lands above reserved, without our especial leave and license for that purpose first obtained.

"And we do further strictly enjoin and require all persons whatever, who have either willfully or inadvertently seated themselves upon any lands within the countries above described, or upon any other lands, *which, not having been ceded to, or purchased by us*, are still reserved to the said Indians, as aforesaid, forthwith to remove themselves from such settlements."

It is easy for us to understand, that the frequent and plausible mention of the Indians was only a pretext to create an idea of the humanity of government. The object and intention of the proclamation was the western boundary, which is here signified not to extend beyond the heads of the rivers: and these, then, are the western limits which Virginia had as a province under the crown of Britain.

And agreeable to the intention of this proclamation, and the limits described thereby, lord Hillsborough, then secretary of state in England, addressed an official letter, of the 31st of July, 1770, to lord Bottetourt, at that time governor of Virginia, which letter was laid before the council of Virginia by Mr. president Nelson, and by him answered on the 18th of October, in the same year, of which the following are extracts :

" On the evening of the day your lordship's letter to the governor was delivered to me (as it contains matters of great variety and importance) it was read in council, and, together with the several papers inclosed, it hath been maturely considered, and I now trouble your lordship with theirs as well as my own opinion upon the subject of them.

" We do not presume to say to whom our gracious sovereign shall grant the vacant lands," and " with regard to the establishment of a *new colony on the back of Virginia*, it is a subject of too great political importance for me to presume to give an opinion upon ; however, permit me, my lord, to observe, that when that part of the country shall become sufficiently populated it may be a wise and prudent measure."

On the death of lord Bottetourt, lord Dunmore was appointed to the government, and he, either from ignorance of the subject or other motives, made a grant of some lands on the Ohio to certain of his friends and favorites, which produced the following letter from lord Dartmouth, who succeeded lord Hillsborough as secretary of state :

" I think fit to inclose your lordship a copy of lord Hillsborough's letter to lord Bottetourt, of the 31st of July, 1770, the receipt of which was acknowledged by Mr. president Nelson, a few days before lord Bottetourt's death, and appears by his answer to it, to have been laid before the council. That board, therefore, could not be ignorant of what has passed here upon Mr. Walpole's application, nor of the king's express command, contained in lord Hillsborough's letter, that no lands should be granted beyond the limits of the royal proclamation of 1763, until the king's further pleasure was signified ; and I have only to observe, that it must have been a very extraordinary neglect in them not to have informed your lordship of that letter and those orders."

On these documents I shall make no remarks. They are their own evidence, and show what the limits of Virginia were while a British province ; and as there was then no other authority by which they could be fixed, and as the grant to the London company could not be a grant to any but themselves, and of consequence ceased to be when they ceased to exist, it remained a matter of choice in the crown, on its re-assumption of the lands, to limit or divide them into separate governments, as it judged best, and from which there was not, and could not, in the order of government, be any appeal. Neither was Virginia, as a province, affected by it, because the monies, in any case, arising from the sale of lands, did not go into her treasury ; and whether to the crown or to the proprietors was to her indifferent. And it is likewise evident, from the secretary's letter, and the president's answer, that it was in contemplation to lay out a new colony on the *back* of Virginia, between the Allegany mountains and the Ohio.

Having thus gone through the several charters, or grants, and their relation to each other, and shown that Virginia cannot stand in succession to a private grant, which has been extinct for upwards of 150 years—and that the western limits of Virginia, at the commencement of the revolution, were at the heads of the rivers emptying themselves into the Atlantic, none of which are beyond the Allegany mountains ; I now proceed to the second part, namely,

The reasonableness of her claims.

Virginia, as a British province, stood in a different situation with the crown of England to any of the other provinces, because she had no ascertained limits, but such as arose from laying off new provinces and the proclamation of 1763. For the same name, Virginia, as I have before mentioned, was the general name of all the country, and the dominion out of which the several governments were laid off : and, in strict propriety, conformable to the origin of names, the province of Virginia was taken out of the dominion of Virginia. For the term, *dominion*, could not appertain to the province, which retained the name of Virginia, but to the crown, and from thence was applied to the whole country, and signified its being an appendage to the crown of England, as they say now, " *our dominion of Wales.*"

It is not possible to suppose there could exist an idea that Virginia, as a British province, was to be extended to the

South sea, at the distance of three thousand miles. The dominion, as appertaining at that time to the crown, might be claimed to extend so far, but as a province the thought was not conceivable, nor the practice possible.

And it is more than probable, that the deception made use of to obtain the patent of 1609, by representing the South sea to be near where the Allegany mountains are, was one cause of its becoming extinct; and it is worthy of re-marking, that no history (at least that I have met with) mentions any dispute or litigation, between the crown and the company, in consequence of the extinction of the patent, and the re-assumption of the lands ; and, therefore, the nega-tive evidence corroborating with the positive, makes it as certain as such a case can possibly be, that either the com-pany received a compensation for the patent, or quitted it quietly, ashamed of the imposition they had practised, and their subsequent mal-administration. Men are not inclined to give up a claim where there is any ground to contend upon, and the silence in which the patent expired is a pre-sumptive proof that its fate, from whatever cause, was just.

There is one general policy which seems to have prevailed with the English in laying off new governments, which was, not to make them larger than their own country, that they might the easier hold them manageable : this was the case with every one except Canada, the extension of whose limits was for the politic purpose of recognizing new acquisitions of territory, not immediately convenient for colonization.

But, in order to give this matter a chance through all its cases, I will admit what no man can suppose, which is, that there is an English charter that fixes Virginia to extend from the Atlantic to the South sea, and contained within a due west line, set off two hundred miles below cape Comfort, and a northwest line, set off two hundred miles above it. Her side, then, on the Atlantic (according to an explanation given in Mr. Bradford's paper of Sept. 29, 1779, by an advo-cate for the Virginia claims) will be four hundred miles ; her side to the south three thousand ; her side to the west four thousand ; and her northwest line about five thousand ; and the quantity of land contained within these dimensions will be almost four thousand millions of acres, which is more than ten times the quantity contained within the present United States, and above an hundred times greater than the kingdom of England.

To reason on a case like this, is such a waste of time, and such an excess of folly, that it ought not to be reasoned upon. It is impossible to suppose that any patent to private persons could be so intentionally absurd, and the claim grounded thereon, is as wild as any thing the imagination of man ever conceived.

But if, as I before mentioned, there was a charter which bore such an explanation, and Virginia stood in succession to it, what would that be to us, any more than the will of Alexander, had he taken it into his head to have bequeathed away the world? Such a charter, or grant, must have been obtained by imposition and a false representation of the country, or granted in error, or both; and in any of, or all these cases, the United States must reject the matter as something they cannot know, for the merits will not bear an argument, and the pretension of right stands upon no better ground.

Our case is an original one; and many matters attending it must be determined on their own merits and reasonableness. The territory of the rest of the states is, in general, within known bounds of moderate extent, and the quota which each state is to furnish towards the expense and service of the war, must be ascertained upon some rule of comparison. The number of inhabitants of each state formed the first rule; and it was naturally supposed that those numbers bore nearly the same proportion to each other, which the territory of each state did. Virginia on this scale, would be about one fifth larger than Pennsylvania, which would be as much dominion as any state could manage with happiness and convenience.

When I first began this subject, my intention was to be extensive on the merits, and concise on the matter of the right; instead of which, I have been extensive on the matter

of right, and concise on the merits of reasonableness : and
this alteration in my design arose, consequentially, from the
nature of the subject ; for as a reasonable thing the claim
can be supported by no argument, and therefore, needs none
to refute it ; but as there is a strange propensity in mankind
to shelter themselves under the sanction of right, however
unreasonable that supposed right may be, I found it most
conducive to the interest of the case, to show, that the right
stands upon no better grounds than the reason. And shall
therefore proceed to make some observations on the consequences of the claim.

The claim being unreasonable in itself, and standing on no
ground of right, but such as, if true, must, from the quarter
it is drawn, be offensive, has a tendency to create disgust,
and sour the minds of the rest of the states. Those lands
are capable, under the management of the United States, of
repaying the charges of the war, and some of them, as I
shall hereafter show, may, I presume, be made an immediate advantage of.

I distinguish three different descriptions of land in America at the commencement of the revolution. Proprietary or
chartered lands, as was the case in Pennsylvania ; crown
lands, within the described limits of any of the crown governments ; and crown residuary lands, that were without or
beyond the limits of any province ; and those last were held
in reserve whereon to erect new governments, and lay out
new provinces ; as appears to have been the design by lord
Hillsborough's letter, and the president's answer, wherein he
says, " with respect to the establishment of a *new* colony on
the *back* of Virginia, it is a subject of too great political
importance for me to presume to give an opinion upon ;
however, permit me, my lord, to observe, that when that
part of the country shall become populated, it may be a wise
and prudent measure."

The expression is, a "*new colony* on the *back* of Virginia ;" and referred to lands between the heads of the
rivers and the Ohio. This is a proof that those lands
were not considered within, but beyond the limits of Vir-

ginia, as a colony; and the other expression in the letter is equally descriptive, namely, " *We do not presume to say, to whom our gracious sovereign shall grant his vacant lands.*" Certainly then, the same right, which, at that time rested in the crown, rests now in the more supreme authority of the United States; and therefore, addressing the president's letter to the circumstances of the revolution, it will run thus:

" We do not presume to say to whom the *sovereign United States* shall grant their vacant lands, and with respect to the settlement of a *new colony* on the *back* of Virginia, it is a matter of too much political importance for me to give an opinion upon; however, permit me to observe, that when that part of the country shall become populated it may be a wise and prudent measure."

It must occur to every person, on reflection, that those lands are too distant to be within the government of any of the present states; and, I may presume to suppose, that were a calculation justly made, Virginia has lost more by the decrease of taxables, than she has gained by what lands she has made sale of; therefore, she is not only doing the rest of the states wrong in point of equity, but herself and them an injury in point of strength, service, and revenue.

It is only the United States, and not any single state, that can lay off new states, and incorporate them in the union by representation; therefore, the situation which the settlers on those lands will be in, under the assumed right of Virginia, will be hazardous and distressing, and they will feel themselves at last like the aliens to the commonwealth of Israel, their habitations unsafe and their title precarious.

And when men reflect on that peace, harmony, quietude, and security, which are necessary to prosperity, especially in making new settlements, and think that when the war shall be ended, their happiness and safety will depend on a union with the states, and not a scattered people, unconnected with, and politically unknown to the rest, they will feel but little inclination to put themselves in a situation, which, however solitary and recluse it may appear at present, will then be uncertain and unsafe, and their troubles will have to begin where those of the United States shall end.

It is probable that some of the inhabitants of Virginia may be inclined to suppose that the writer of this, by taking up the subject in the manner he has done, is arguing unfriendly against their interest. To which he wishes to reply:

That the most extraordinary part of the whole is, that Virginia should countenance such a claim. For it is worthy of observing, that, from the beginning of the contest with Britain, and long after, there was not a people in America who discovered, through all the variety and multiplicity of public business, a greater fund of true wisdom, fortitude, and disinterestedness, than the then colony of Virginia. They were loved—They were reverenced. Their investigation of the assumed rights of Britain had a sagacity which was uncommon. Their reasonings were piercing, difficult to be equalled and impossible to be refuted, and their public spirit was exceeded by none. But since this unfortunate land scheme has taken place, their powers seem to be absorbed; a torpor has overshaded them, and every one asks, What is become of Virginia?

It seldom happens that the romantic schemes of extensive dominion are of any service to a government, and never to a people. They assuredly end at last in loss, trouble, division and disappointment. And was even the title of Virginia good, and the claim admissible, she would derive more lasting and real benefit by participating in it, than by attempting the management of an object so infinitely beyond her reach. Her share with the rest, under the supremacy of the United States, which is the only authority adequate to the purpose, would be worth more to her than what the whole would produce under the management of herself alone. And that for several reasons:

1st, Because her claim not being admissible nor yet manageable, she cannot make a good title to the purchasers, and consequently can get but little for the lands.

2d, Because the distance the settlers will be from her, will immediately put them out of all government and protection, so far, at least as relates to Virginia: and by this means she will render her frontiers a refuge to desperadoes, and a hiding place from justice; and the consequence will be perpetual unsafety to her own peace, and that of the neighbouring states.

3d, Because her quota of expense for carrying on the war, admitting her to engross such an immensity of territory, would be greater than she can either support or supply, and could not be less, upon a reasonable rule of proportion, than nine-tenths of the whole.   And,

4th, Because she must sooner or later relinquish them; therefore to see her own interest wisely at first, is preferable to the alternative of finding it out by misfortune at last.

I have now gone through my examination of the claim of Virginia, in every case which I proposed; and for several reasons, wish the lot had fallen to another person.   But as this is a most important matter, in which all are interested, and the substantial good of Virginia not injured but promoted, and as few men have leisure, and still fewer have inclination, to go into intricate investigation, I have at last ventured on the subject.

The succession of the United States to the vacant Western territory is a right they originally set out upon; and in the pamphlet " Common Sense," I frequently mentioned those lands as a national fund for the benefit of all; therefore, resuming the subject where I then left off, I shall conclude with concisely reducing to system what I then only hinted.

In my last piece, the " Crisis Extraordinary," I estimated the annual amount of the charge of war and the support of the several governments at two million pounds sterling, and the peace establishment at three quarters of a million, and, by a comparison of the taxes of this country with those of England, proved that the whole yearly expense to us, to defend the country, is but a third of what Britain would have drawn from us by taxes, had she succeeded in her attempt to conquer; and our peace establishment only an eighth part; and likewise showed, that it was within the ability of the states to carry on the whole of the war by taxation, without having recourse to any other modes or funds. To have a clear idea of taxation is necessary to every country, and the more funds we can discover and organize, the less will be the hope of the enemy, and the readier their disposition to peace, which it is now *their* interest more than *ours* to promote.

I have already remarked that only the United States, and not any particular state, can lay off new states and incorporate them into the union by representation; keeping, therefore, this idea in view, I ask, might not a substantial fund be quickly created by laying off a new state, so as to contain between twenty and thirty millions of acres, and opening a land office in all countries in Europe for hard money, and in this country for supplies in kind, at a certain price.

The tract of land that seems best adapted to answer this purpose is contained between the Allegany mountains and the river Ohio, as far north as the Pennsylvania line, thence extending down the said river to the falls thereof, thence due south into the latitude of the North-Carolina line, and thence east to the Allegany mountains aforesaid. I the more readily mention this tract, because it is fighting the enemy with their own weapons, as it includes the same ground on which a new colony would have been erected, for the emolument of the crown of England, as appears by the letters of lords Hillsborough and Dartmouth, had not the revolution prevented its being carried into effect.

It is probable that there may be some spots of private property within this tract, but to incorporate them into some government will render them more profitable to the owners, and the condition of the scattered settlers more eligible and happy than at present.

If twenty millions of acres of this new state be patented and sold at twenty pounds sterling per hundred acres, they will produce four million pounds sterling, which, if applied to continental expenses only, will support the war for three years, should Britain be so unwise as to prosecute it against her own direct interest and against the interest and policy of all Europe. The several states will then have to raise taxes for their internal government only, and the continental taxes, as soon as the fund begins to operate, will lessen, and if sufficiently productive, will cease.

Lands are the real riches of the habitable world, and the natural funds of America. The funds of other countries are, in general, artificially constructed; the creatures of necessity and contrivance; dependant upon credit, and always exposed to hazard and uncertainty. But lands can neither be annihilated nor lose their value; on the contrary, they universally rise with population, and rapidly so, when under the security of effectual government. But this it is impossible for Virginia to give, and therefore, that which is capable of defraying the expenses of the empire, will, under the management of any single state, produce only a fugitive support to wandering individuals.

I shall now inquire into the effects which the laying out a new state, under the authority of the United States, will have upon Virginia. It is the very circumstance she ought to, and must, wish for, when she examines the matter in all its bearings and consequences.

The present settlers beyond her reach, and her supposed authority over them remaining in herself, they will appear to her as revolters, and she to them as oppressors; and this will produce such a spirit of mutual dislike, that in a little time a total disagreement will take place, to the disadvantage of both. But under the authority of the United States the matter is manageable, and Virginia will be eased of a disagreeable consequence.

Besides this, a sale of the lands, continentally, for the purpose of supporting the expense of the war, will save her a greater share of taxes, than the small sale which she could make herself, and the small price she could get for them would produce.

She would likewise have two advantages which no other state in the union enjoys; first, a frontier state for her defence against the incursions of the Indians; and the second is, that the laying out and peopling a new state on the back of an old one, situated as she is, is doubling the quantity of its trade.

The new state which is here proposed to be laid out, may

send its exports down the Mississippi, but its imports must come through Chesapeake bay, and consequently Virginia will become the market for the new state; because, though there is a navigation from it, there is none into it, on account of the rapidity of the Mississippi.

There are certain circumstances that will produce certain events whether men think of them or not. The events do not depend upon thinking, but are the natural consequence of acting; and according to the system which Virginia has gone upon, the issue will be, that she will get involved with the back settlers in a contention about *rights*, till they dispute with their own claims; and, soured by the contention, will go to any other state for their commerce; both of which may be prevented, a perfect harmony established, the strength of the states increased, and the expenses of the war defrayed, by settling the matter now on the plan of a general right; and every day it is delayed, the difficulty will be increased and the advantages lessened.

But if it should happen, as it possibly may, that the war should end before the money, which the new state may produce, be expended, the remainder of the lands therein may be set apart to reimburse those whose houses have been burnt by the enemy, as this is a species of suffering which it was impossible to prevent, because houses are not moveable property; and it ought not to be that because we cannot do every thing, that we ought not to do what we can.

Having said this much on the subject, I think it necessary to remark, that the prospect of a new fund, so far from abating our endeavours in making every immediate provision for the army, ought to quicken us therein; for should the states see it expedient to go upon the measure, it will be at least a year before it can be productive. I the more freely mention this, because there is a dangerous species of popularity, which, I fear, some men are seeking from their constituents by giving them grounds to believe, that if they are elected they will lighten the taxes; a measure which, in the present state of things, cannot be done without exposing the country to the ravages of the enemy by disabling the army from defending it.

Where knowledge is a duty, ignorance is a crime ; and if any man whose duty it was to know better, has encouraged such an expectation, he has either deceived himself or them : besides, no country can be defended without expense, and let any man compare his portion of temporary inconveniences arising from taxation with the real distresses of the army for the want of supplies, and the difference is not only sufficient to strike him dumb, but make him thankful that worse consequences have not followed.

In advancing this doctrine, I speak with an honest freedom to the country ; for as it is their good to be defended, so it is their interest to provide that defence, at least till other funds can be organized.

As the laying out new states will some time or other be the business of the country, and as it is yet a new business to us, and as the influence of the war has scarcely afforded leisure for reflecting on distant circumstances, I shall throw together a few hints for facilitating that measure whenever it may be proper for adopting it.

The United States now standing on the line of sovereignty, the vacant territory is their property collectively, but the persons by whom it may hereafter be peopled will also have an equal right with ourselves ; and therefore, as new states shall be laid off and incorporated with the present, they will become partakers of the remaining territory with us who are already in possession. And this consideration ought to heighten the value of lands to new emigrants : because, in making the purchases, they not only gain an immediate property, but become initiated into the right and heirship of the states to a property in reserve, which is an additional advantage to what any purchasers under the late government of England enjoyed.

The setting off the boundary of any new state will naturally be the first step, and as it must be supposed not to be peopled at the time it is laid off, a constitution must be formed by the United States, as the rule of government in any new state, for a certain term of years (perhaps ten) or until the state becomes peopled to a certain number of inhabitants; after which, the whole and sole right of modelling their government to rest with themselves.

A question may arise, whether a new state should immediately possess an equal right with the present ones in all cases which may come before congress.

This, experience will best determine; but at a first view of the matter it appears thus: that it ought to be immediately incorporated into the union on the ground of a family right, such a state standing in the line of a younger child of the same stock; but as new emigrants will have something to learn when they first come to America, and a new state requiring aid rather than capable of giving it, it might be most convenient to admit its immediate representation into congress, there to sit, hear and debate on all questions and matters, but not to vote on any till after the expiration of seven years.

I shall in this place take the opportunity of renewing a hint which I formerly threw out in the pamphlet "Common Sense," and which the several states will, sooner or later, see the convenience if not the necessity of adopting; which is, that of electing a continental convention, for the purpose of forming a continental constitution, defining and describing the powers and authority of congress.

Those of entering into treaties, and making peace, they naturally possess, in behalf of the states, for their separate as well as their united good, but the internal control and dictatorial powers of congress are not sufficiently defined, and appear to be too much in some cases and too little in others; and therefore, to have them marked out legally will give additional energy to the whole, and a new confidence to the several parts.[1]

---

[1] When, at Washington's request, a bill to bestow on Paine an *honorarium* of £2000 for his services in the Revolution was introduced into the Virginia Legislature (June 30, 1784), it was lost by one vote, because (according to Richard Henry Lee) of his "having written a pamphlet injurious to our claim of Western Territory." Yet before this Virginia had conceded its claim, on certain conditions, to the United States. The concession was accepted by Congress (March 1, 1784), but the conditions neither admitted nor rejected; and this evasion seems to have left in Virginia a soreness which rendered Paine's pamphlet, which involved the formidable issue of State sovereignty, a costly effort of patriotism to himself. See my "Life of Paine," vol. i., pp. 163 *seq.*, 206.—*Editor.*

V.

LETTER TO THE ABBE RAYNAL.[1]

INTRODUCTION.

A LONDON translation of an original work in French, by the abbe Raynal, which treats of the revolution of North-America, having been re-printed in Philadelphia and other parts of the continent, and as the distance at which the abbe is placed from the American theatre of war and politics, has occasioned him to mistake several facts, or misconceive the causes or principles by which they were produced, the following tract, therefore, is published with a view to rectify them, and prevent even accidental errors from intermixing with history, under the sanction of time and silence.

The editor of the London edition has entitled it, " *The Revolution of America*, by the ABBE RAYNAL," and the American printers have followed the example. But I have understood, and I believe my information just, that the piece, which is more properly reflections on the revolution, was unfairly purloined from the printer whom the abbe employed, or from the manuscript copy, and is only part of a larger work then in the press, or preparing for it. The person who procured it, appears to have been an Englishman, and though, in an advertisement prefixed to the London edition, he has endeavoured to gloss over the embezzlement

---

with professions of patriotism, and to soften it with high
encomiums on the author, yet the action in any view in
which it can be placed, is illiberal and unpardonable.

" In the course of his travels," says he, " the translator happily
succeeded in obtaining a copy of this exquisite little piece which
has not made its appearance from any press. He publishes a
French edition, in favor of those who feel its eloquent reasoning
more forcibly in its native language, at the same time with the following translation of it : in which he has been desirous, perhaps
in vain, that all the warmth, the grace, the strength, the dignity of
the original, should not be lost. And he flatters himself, that the
indulgence of the illustrious historian will not be wanting to a man,
who, of his own motion, has taken the liberty to give this composition to the public, only from a strong pursuasion, that its momentous argument will be useful in a critical conjuncture, to that
country which he loves with an ardour that can be exceeded only
by the nobler flame, which burns in the bosom of the philanthropic
author, for the freedom and happiness of all the countries upon
earth."

This plausibility of setting off a dishonourable action, may
pass for patriotism and sound principles with those who do
not enter into its demerits, and whose interest is not injured
nor their happiness affected thereby. But it is more than
probable, notwithstanding the declarations it contains, that
the copy was obtained for the sake of profiting by the sale
of a new and popular work, and that the professions are but
a garb to the fraud.

It may with propriety be marked, that in all countries where
literature is protected, and it never can flourish where it is
not, the works of an author are his legal property; and to
treat letters in any other light than this, is to banish them
from the country, or strangle them in the birth.—The embezzlement from the abbe Raynal, was, it is true, committed
by one country upon another, and therefore shows no defect
in the laws of either. But it is nevertheless a breach of civil
manners and literary justice : neither can it be any apology,

that because the countries are at war, literature shall be entitled to depredation.*

But the forestalling the abbe's publication by London editions, both in French and English, and thereby not only defrauding him and throwing an expensive publication on his hands by anticipating the sale, are only the smaller injuries which such conduct may occasion. A man's opinions, whether written or in thought, are his own, until he pleases to publish them himself; and it is adding cruelty to injustice, to make him the author of what future reflection, or better information, might occasion him to suppress or amend. There are declarations and sentiments in the abbe's piece which, for my own part, I did not expect to find, and such as himself, on a revisal, might have seen occasion to change; but the anticipated piracy effectually prevented his having the opportunity, and precipitated him into difficulties, which, had it not been for such ungenerous fraud, might not have happened.

This mode of making an author appear before his time, will appear still more ungenerous, when we consider how very few men there are in any country, who can at once, and without the aid of reflection and revisal, combine warm passions with a cool temper, and the full expansion of the imagination with the natural and necessary gravity of judgment, so as to be rightly balanced within themselves, and to make a reader feel, fancy, and understand justly at the same time. To call three powers of the mind into action at once, in a manner that neither shall interrupt, and that each

---

* The state of literature in America must one day become a subject of legislative consideration. Hitherto it hath been a disinterested volunteer in the service of the revolution, and no man thought of profits: but when peace shall give time and opportunity for study, the country will deprive itself of the honour and service of letters and the improvement of science, unless sufficient laws are made to prevent depredations on literary property. It is well worth remarking, that Russia, who but a few years ago was scarcely known in Europe, owes a large share of her present greatness to the close attention she has paid, and the wise encouragement she has given, to every branch of science and learning: and we have almost the same instance in France, in the reign of Louis XIV.—*Author*.

shall aid and invigorate the other, is a talent very rarely possessed.

It often happens that the weight of an argument is lost by the wit of setting it off ; or the judgment disordered by an intemperate irritation of the passions : yet a certain degree of animation must be felt by the writer, and raised in the reader, in order to interest the attention ; and a sufficient scope given to the imagination, to enable it to create in the mind a sight of the persons, characters and circumstances of the subject : for without these, the judgment will feel little or no excitement to office, and its determinations will be cold, sluggish, and imperfect. But if either or both of the two former are raised too high, or heated too much, the judgment will be jostled from its seat, and the whole matter, however important in itself, will diminish into a pantomime of the mind, in which we create images that promote no other purpose than amusement.

The abbe's writings bear evident marks of that extension and rapidness of thinking and quickness of sensation, which of all others require revisal, and the more particularly so, when applied to the living characters of nations or individuals in a state of war. The least misinformation or misconception leads to some wrong conclusion, and an error believed, becomes the progenitor of others. And, as the abbe has suffered some inconveniences in France, by mistaking certain circumstances of the war, and the characters of the parties therein, it becomes some apology for him that those errors were precipitated into the world by the avarice of an ungenerous enemy.

LETTER TO THE ABBE RAYNAL.

To an author of such distinguished reputation as the abbe Raynal, it might very well become me to apologize for the present undertaking ; but, as *to be right* is the first wish of philosophy, and the first principle of history, he will, I presume, accept from me a declaration of my motives, which are those of doing justice, in preference to any complimental apology I might otherwise make. The abbe, in the course of his work, has, in some instances, extolled without a reason, and wounded without a cause. He has given fame where it was not deserved, and withheld it where it was justly due ; and appears to be so frequently in and out of temper with his subjects and parties, that few or none of them are decisively and uniformly marked.

It is yet too soon to write the history of the revolution, and whoever attempts it precipitately, will unavoidably mistake characters and circumstances, and involve himself in error and difficulty. Things, like men, are seldom understood rightly at first sight. But the abbe is wrong even in the foundation of his work ; that is, he has misconceived and mis-stated the causes which produced the rupture between England and her then colonies, and which led on, step by step, unstudied and uncontrived on the part of America, to a revolution, which has engaged the attention, and affected the interest of Europe.

To prove this, I shall bring forward a passage, which, though placed towards the latter part of the abbe's work, is more intimately connected with the beginning ; and in which, speaking of the original cause of the dispute, he declares himself in the following manner—

" None," says he, " of those energetic causes, which have produced so many revolutions upon the globe, existed in North-
America. Neither religion nor laws had there been outraged.
The blood of martyrs or patriots had not there streamed from
scaffolds. Morals had not there been insulted. Manners, customs, habits, no object dear to nations, had there been the sport
of ridicule. Arbitrary power had not there torn any inhabitant
from the arms of his family and friends, to drag him to a dreary
dungeon. Public order had not been there inverted. The principles of administration had not been changed there ; and the
maxims of government had there always remained the same. The
whole question was reduced to the knowing whether the mother
country had, or had not, a right to lay, directly or indirectly, a
slight tax upon the colonies."

On this extraordinary passage, it may not be improper, in
general terms, to remark, that none can feel like those who
suffer ; and that for a man to be a competent judge of the pro-
vocatives, or as the abbe styles them, the energetic causes of
the revolution, he must have resided at the time in America.

The abbe, in saying that the several particulars he has
enumerated, did not exist in America, and neglecting to
point out the particular period, in which he means they did
not exist, reduces thereby his declaration to a nullity, by
taking away all meaning from the passage.

They did not exist in 1763, and they all existed before
1776 ; consequently as there was a time when they did *not*,
and another, when they *did* exist, the *time when* constitutes
the essence of the fact, and not to give it is to withhold the
only evidence which proves the declaration right or wrong,
and on which it must stand or fall. But the declaration as
it now appears, unaccompanied by time, has an effect in
holding out to the world, that there was no real cause for
the revolution, because it denies the existence of all those
causes, which are supposed to be justifiable, and which the
abbe styles energetic.

I confess myself exceedingly at a loss to find out the time
to which the abbe alludes ; because, in another part of, the
work, in speaking of the stamp act, which was passed in

1764, he styles it "an *usurpation* of the Americans' *most precious and sacred rights*." Consequently he here admits the most energetic of all causes, that is, *an usurpation of their most precious and sacred rights*, to have existed in America twelve years before the declaration of independence, and ten years before the breaking out of hostilities. The time, therefore, in which the paragraph is true, must be antecedent to the stamp act, but as at that time there was no revolution, nor any idea of one, it consequently applies without a meaning; and as it cannot, on the abbe's own principle, be applied to any time *after* the stamp act, it is therefore a wandering solitary paragraph, connected with nothing and at variance with everything.

The stamp act, it is true, was repealed in two years after it was passed, but it was immediately followed by one of infinitely more mischievous magnitude; I mean the declaratory act, which asserted the right, as it was styled, of the British parliament, "*to bind America in all cases whatsoever.*"

If then the stamp act was an usurpation of the Americans' most precious and sacred rights, the declaratory act left them no rights at all; and contained the full grown seeds of the most despotic government ever exercised in the world. It placed America not only in the lowest, but in the basest state of vassalage; because it demanded an unconditional submission in every thing, or as the act expresses it, *in all cases whatsoever :* and what renders this act the more offensive, is, that it appears to have been passed as an act of mercy; truly then may it be said, that *the tender mercies of the wicked are cruel.*

All the original charters from the crown of England, under the faith of which the adventurers from the old world settled in the new, were by this act displaced from their foundations; because, contrary to the nature of them, which was that of a compact, they were now made subject to repeal or alteration at the mere will of one party only. The whole condition of America was thus put into the hands of the parliament or ministry, without leaving to her the least right in any case whatsoever.

There is no despotism to which this iniquitous law did not extend; and though it might have been convenient in the execution of it, to have consulted manners and habits, the principle of the act made all tyranny legal. It stopped no where. It went to every thing. It took in with it the whole life of a man, or if I may so express it, an eternity of circumstances. It is the nature of law to require obedience, but this demanded servitude; and the condition of an American, under the operation of it, was not that of a subject, but a vassal. Tyranny has often been established *without* law and sometimes *against* it, but the history of mankind does not produce another instance, in which it has been established *by* law. It is an audacious outrage upon civil government, and cannot be too much exposed, in order to be sufficiently detested.

Neither could it be said after this, that the legislature of that country any longer made laws for this, but that it gave out commands; for wherein differed an act of parliament constructed on this principle, and operating in this manner, over an unrepresented people, from the orders of a military establishment?

The parliament of England, with respect to America, was not septennial but *perpetual.* It appeared to the latter a body always in being. Its election or expiration were to her the same as if its members succeeded by inheritance, or went out by death, or lived for ever, or were appointed to it as a matter of office. Therefore, for the people of England to have any just conception of the mind of America, respecting this extraordinary act, they must suppose all election and expiration in that country to cease for ever, and the present parliament, its heirs, etc. to be perpetual; in this case, I ask, what would the most clamorous of them think, were an act to be passed, declaring the right of *such a parliament* to bind *them* in all cases whatsoever? For this word *whatsoever* would go as effectually to their *magna charta, bill of rights, trial by juries, etc.* as it went to the charters and forms of government in America.

I am persuaded, that the gentleman to whom I address

these remarks, will not, after the passing of this act, say, "that the *principles* of administration had not been *changed* in America, and that the maxims of government had there been *always the same.*" For here is, in principle, a total overthrow of the whole; and not a subversion only, but an annihilation of the foundation of liberty and absolute domination established in its stead.

The abbe likewise states the case exceedingly wrong and injuriously, when he says, that "*the whole* question was reduced to the knowing whether the mother country had, or had not, a right to lay, directly or indirectly, a *slight* tax upon the colonies." This was *not the whole* of the question; neither was the *quantity* of the tax the object either to the ministry or to the Americans. It was the principle, of which the tax made but a part, and the quantity still less, that formed the ground on which America resisted.

The tax on tea, which is the tax here alluded to, was neither more nor less than an experiment to establish the practice of the declaratory law upon; modelled into the more fashionable phrase *of the universal supremacy of parliament.* For until this time the declaratory law had lain dormant, and the framers of it had contented themselves with barely declaring an opinion.

Therefore the *whole* question with America, in the opening of the dispute, was, shall we be bound in all cases whatsoever by the British parliament, or shall we not? For submission to the tea or tax act implied an acknowledgment of the declaratory act, or, in other words, of the universal supremacy of parliament, which as they never intended to do, it was necessary they should oppose it, in its first stage of execution.

It is probable the abbe has been led into this mistake by perusing detached pieces in some of the American newspapers; for, in a case where all were interested, every one had a right to give his opinion; and there were many, who, with the best intentions, did not choose the best, nor indeed the true ground, to defend their cause upon. They felt themselves right by a general impulse, without being able to separate, analyze, and arrange the parts.

I am somewhat unwilling to examine too minutely into the whole of this extraordinary passage of the abbe, lest I should appear to treat it with severity ; otherwise I could show that not a single declaration is justly founded : for instance, the reviving an obsolete act of the reign of Henry VIII. and fitting it to the Americans, by authority of which they were to be seized and brought from America to England, and there imprisoned and tried for any supposed offences, was, in the worst sense of the words, *to tear them, by the arbitrary power of parliament, from the arms of their families and friends, and drag them not only to dreary but distant dungeons.* Yet this act was contrived some years before the breaking out of hostilities. And again, though the blood of martyrs and patriots had not streamed on the scaffolds, it streamed in the streets, in the massacre of the inhabitants of Boston, by the British soldiery in the year 1770.

Had the abbe said that the causes which produced the revolution in America were originally *different* from those which produced revolutions in other parts of the globe, he had been right. Here the value and quality of liberty, the nature of government, and the dignity of man, were known and understood, and the attachment of the Americans to these principles produced the revolution, as a natural and almost unavoidable consequence. They had no particular family to set up or pull down. Nothing of personality was incorporated with their cause. They started even-handed with each other, and went no faster into the several stages of it, than they were driven by the unrelenting and imperious conduct of Britain. Nay, in the last act, the declaration of independence, they had nearly been too late ; for had it not been declared at the exact time it was, I see no period in their affairs since, in which it could have been declared with the same effect, and probably not at all.

But the object being formed before the reverse of fortune took place, that is, before the operations of the gloomy campaign of 1776, their honour, their interest, their every thing, called loudly on them to maintain it ; and that glow of thought and energy of heart, which even a distant prospect of independence inspires, gave confidence to their hopes, and resolution to their conduct, which a state of dependance could never have reached. They looked forward to happier days and scenes of rest, and qualified the hardships of the campaign by contemplating the establishment of their new-born system.

If, on the other hand, we take a review of what part Britain has acted, we shall find everything which ought to make a nation blush,—the most vulgar abuse, accompanied by that species of haughtiness which distinguishes the hero of a mob from the character of a gentleman. It was equally as much from her manners as from her injustice that she lost the colonies. By the latter she provoked their principles, by the former she wore out their temper; and it ought to be held out as an example to the world, to show how necessary it is to conduct the business of government with civility. In short, other revolutions may have originated in caprice, or generated in ambition; but here, the most unoffending humility was tortured into rage, and the infancy of existence made to weep.

A union so extensive, continued and determined, suffering with patience and never in despair, could not have been produced by common causes. It must be something capable of reaching the whole soul of man and arming it with perpetual energy. It is in vain to look for precedents among the revolutions of former ages, to find out, by comparison, the causes of this. The spring, the progress, the object, the consequences, nay, the men, their habits of thinking, and all the circumstances of the country, are different. Those of other nations are, in general, little more than the history of their quarrels. They are marked by no important character in the annals of events; mixed in the mass of general matters, they occupy but a common page; and while the chief of the successful partisans stepped into power, the plundered multitude sat down and sorrowed. Few, very few of them are accompanied with reformation, either in government or manners; many of them with the most consummate profligacy. Triumph on the one side and misery on the other were the only events. Pains, punishments, torture, and death were made the business of mankind, until compassion, the fairest associate of the heart, was driven from its place, and the eye, accustomed to continual cruelty, could behold it without offence.

But as the principles of the present revolution differed from those which preceded it, so likewise did the conduct of America both in government and war. Neither the foul finger of disgrace nor the bloody hand of vengeance has hitherto put a blot upon her fame. Her victories have received lustre from a greatness of lenity ; and her laws have been permitted to slumber, where they might justly be awakened to punish. War, so much the trade of the world, has here been only the business of necessity ; and when the necessity shall cease, her very enemies must confess, that as she drew the sword in her just defence, she used it without cruelty, and sheathed it without revenge.

As it is not my design to extend these remarks to a history, I shall now take my leave of this passage of the abbe, with an observation, which, until something unfolds itself to convince me otherwise, I cannot avoid believing to be true ;— which is, that it was the fixed determination of the British cabinet to quarrel with America at all events.

They (the members who composed the cabinet) had no doubt of success, if they could once bring it to the issue of a battle, and they expected from a conquest, what they could neither propose with decency, nor hope for by negotiation. The charters and constitutions of the colonies were become to them matters of offence, and their rapid progress in property and population were disgustingly beheld as the growing and natural means of independence. They saw no way to retain them long but by reducing them in time. A conquest would at once have made them both lords and landlords ; and put them in the possession both of the revenue and the rental. The whole trouble of government would have ceased in a victory, and a final end put to remonstrance and debate. The experience of the stamp act had taught them how to quarrel with the advantages of cover and convenience, and they had nothing to do but to renew the scene, and put contention into motion. They hoped for a rebellion, and they made one. They expected a declaration of independence, and they were not disappointed. But after this, they looked for victory, and they obtained a defeat.

If this be taken as the generating cause of the contest, then is every part of the conduct of the British ministry consistent from the commencement of the dispute, until the signing the treaty of Paris, after which, conquest becoming doubtful, they retreated to negotiation, and were again defeated.

Though the abbe possesses and displays great powers of genius, and is a master of style and language, he seems not to pay equal attention to the office of an historian. His facts are coldly and carelessly stated. They neither inform the reader nor interest him. Many of them are erroneous, and most of them are defective and obscure. It is undoubtedly both an ornament and a useful addition to history, to accompany it with maxims and reflections. They afford likewise an agreeable change to the style, and a more diversified manner of expression; but it is absolutely necessary that the root from whence they spring, or the foundation on which they are raised, should be well attended to, which in this work is not. The abbe hastens through his narrations as if he was glad to get from them, that he may enter the more copious field of eloquence and imagination.

The actions of Trenton and Princeton, in New-Jersey, in December 1776, and January following, on which the fate of America stood for a while trembling on the point of suspense, and from which the most important consequences followed, are comprised within a single paragraph, faintly conceived, and barren of character, circumstance and description.

"On the 25th of December," says the abbe, "they (the Americans) crossed the Delaware, and fell *accidentally* upon Trenton, which was occupied by fifteen hundred of the twelve thousand

Hessians, sold in so base a manner by their avaricious master, to the king of Great-Britain. This corps was *massacred*, taken, or dispersed. Eight days after, three English regiments were, in like manner, driven from Princeton, but after having better supported their reputation than the foreign troops in their pay."

This is all the account which is given of these interesting events. The abbe has preceded them by two or three pages on the military operations of both armies, from the time of general Howe's arriving before New-York from Halifax, and the vast reinforcements of British and foreign troops with lord Howe from England. But in these, there is so much mistake, and so many omissions, that, to set them right, must be the business of a history and not of a letter. The action of Long-Island is but barely hinted at, and the operations at the White-plains wholly omitted; as are likewise the attack and loss of fort Washington, with a garrison of about two thousand five hundred men, and the precipitate evacuation of fort Lee, in consequence thereof: which losses were in a great measure the cause of the retreat through the Jerseys to the Delaware, a distance of about ninety miles. Neither is the manner of the retreat described; which, from the season of the year, the nature of the country, the nearness of the two armies (sometimes within sight and shot of each other, for such a length of way) the rear of the one employed in pulling down bridges, and the van of the other in building them up, must necessarily be accompanied with many interesting circumstances.

It was a period of distresses. A crisis rather of danger than of hope. There is no description can do it justice; and even the actors in it, looking back upon the scene, are surprised how they got through; and at a loss to account for those powers of the mind, and springs of animation, by which they withstood the force of accumulated misfortune.

It was expected, that the time for which the army was enlisted, would carry the campaign so far into the winter, that the severity of the season, and the consequent condition of the roads, would prevent any material operation of the enemy, until the new army could be raised for the next year. And I mention it, as a matter worthy of attention, by all future historians, that the movements of the American army, until the attack upon the Hessian post at Trenton, the 26th of December, are to be considered as operating to effect no other principal purpose than delay, and to wear away the campaign under all the disadvantages of an unequal force, with as little misfortune as possible.

But the loss of the garrison at fort Washington on the 16th of November, and the expiration of the time of a considerable part of the army, so early as the 30th of the same month, and which was to be followed by almost daily expirations afterwards, made retreat the only final expedient. To these circumstances may be added the forlorn and destitute condition of the few that remained; for the garrison of fort Lee, which composed almost the whole of the retreat, had been obliged to abandon it so instantaneously, that every article of stores and baggage was left behind, and in this destitute condition, without tent or blanket, and without any other utensils to dress their provision than what they procured by the way, they performed a march of about ninety miles, and had the address and management to prolong it to the space of nineteen days.

By this unexpected or rather unthought-of turn of affairs, the country was in an instant surprised into confusion, and found an enemy within its bowels, without an army to oppose him. There were no succours to be had, but from the free-will offering of the inhabitants. All was choice, and every man reasoned for himself.

It was in this situation of affairs, equally calculated to confound or to inspire, that the gentleman, the merchant, the farmer, the tradesman and the labourer mutually turned from all the conveniences of home, to perform the duties of private soldiers, and undergo the severities of a winter campaign. The delay so judiciously contrived on the retreat, afforded time for the volunteer reinforcements to join general Washington on the Delaware.

The abbe is likewise wrong in saying, that the American

army fell *accidentally* on Trenton. It was the very object for which general Washington crossed the Delaware in the dead of the night and in the midst of snow, storms, and ice; and which he immediately re-crossed with his prisoners, as soon as he had accomplished his purpose. Neither was the intended enterprise a secret to the enemy, information having been sent of it by letter, from a British officer at Princeton, to colonel Rolle, who commanded the Hessians at Trenton, which letter was afterwards found by the Americans. Nevertheless the post was completely surprised. A small circumstance, which had the appearance of mistake on the part of the Americans, led to a more capital and real mistake on the part of Rolle.

The case was this. A detachment of twenty or thirty Americans had been sent across the river, from a post a few miles above, by an officer unacquainted with the intended attack; these were met by a body of Hessians, on the night to which the information pointed, which was Christmas night, and repulsed. Nothing further appearing, and the Hessians mistaking this for the advanced party, supposed the enterprise disconcerted, which at that time was not begun, and under this idea returned to their quarters; so that, what might have raised an alarm, and brought the Americans into an ambuscade, served to take off the force of an information, and promote the success of the enterprise. Soon after daylight, general Washington entered the town, and after a little opposition, made himself master of it, with upwards of nine hundred prisoners.

This combination of equivocal circumstances, falling within what the abbe styles, "*the wide empire of chance*," would have afforded a fine field for thought, and I wish, for the sake of that elegance of reflection he is so capable of using, that he had known it.

But the action at Princeton was accompanied by a still greater embarrassment of matters, and followed by more extraordinary consequences. The Americans, by a happy stroke of generalship, in this instance, not only deranged and defeated all the plans of the British, in the intended moment of execution, but drew from their posts the enemy they were not able to drive, and obliged them to close the campaign. As the circumstance is a curiosity in war, and not well understood in Europe, I shall, as concisely as I can, relate the principal parts; they may serve to prevent future historians from error, and recover from forgetfulness a scene of magnificent fortitude.[1]

Immediately after the surprise of the Hessians at Trenton, general Washington re-crossed the Delaware, which at this place is about three quarters of a mile over, and reassumed his former post on the Pennsylvania side. Trenton remained unoccupied, and the enemy were posted at Princeton, twelve miles distant, on the road towards New-York. The weather was now growing very severe, and as there were very few houses near the shore where general Washington had taken his station, the greatest part of his army remained out in the woods and fields. These, with some other circumstances, induced the re-crossing the Delaware and taking possession of Trenton. It was undoubtedly a bold adventure, and carried with it the appearance of defiance, especially when we consider the panic-struck condition of the enemy on the loss of the Hessian post. But in order to give a just idea of the affair, it is necessary that I should describe the place.

Trenton is situated on a rising ground, about three quarters of a mile distant from the Delaware, on the eastern or Jersey side; and is cut into two divisions by a small creek or rivulet, sufficient to turn a mill which is on it, after which it empties itself at nearly right angles into the Delaware. The upper division, which is that to the northeast, contains about seventy or eighty houses, and the lower about forty or fifty. The ground on each side this creek, and on which the houses are, is likewise rising, and the two divisions present an agreeable prospect to each other, with the creek

---

[1] Paine, who had retreated with Washington, fought in the battles of Trenton and Princeton. It was in the camp near Princeton that Washington gave Paine an overcoat, his own having been stolen ("Life of Paine," ii., p. 469). A piece of this coat, erroneously labelled as "worn at Bunker Hill," in the Leicester (England) Museum is now undiscoverable.—*Editor*.

between, on which there is a small stone bridge of one arch.

Scarcely had general Washington taken post here, and before the several parties of militia, out on detachments, or on their way, could be collected, than the British, leaving behind them a strong garrison at Princeton, marched suddenly and entered Trenton at the upper or northeast quarter. A party of the Americans skirmished with the advanced party of the British, to afford time for removing the stores and baggage, and withdrawing over the bridge.

In a little time the British had possession of one half of the town, general Washington of the other; and the creek only separated the two armies. Nothing could be a more critical situation than this, and if ever the fate of America depended upon the event of a day, it was now. The Delaware was filling fast with large sheets of driving ice, and was impassable; of course no retreat into Pennsylvania could be effected, neither is it possible, in the face of an enemy, to pass a river of such extent. The roads were broken and rugged with the frost, and the main road was occupied by the enemy.

About four o'clock a party of the British approached the bridge, with a design to gain it, but were repulsed. They made no more attempts, though the creek itself is passable any where between the bridge and the Delaware. It runs in a rugged, natural made ditch, over which a person may pass with little difficulty, the stream being rapid and shallow. Evening was now coming on, and the British, believing they had all the advantages they could wish for, and that they could use them when they pleased, discontinued all further operations, and held themselves prepared to make the attack next morning.

But the next morning produced a scene as elegant as it was unexpected. The British were under arms and ready to march to action, when one of their light-horse from Princeton came furiously down the street, with an account that general Washington had that morning attacked and carried the British post at that place, and was proceeding on to seize the magazine at Brunswick; on which the British, who were then on the point of making an assault on the evacuated camp of the Americans, wheeled about, and in a fit of consternation marched for Princeton.

This retreat is one of those extraordinary circumstances, that in future ages may probably pass for fable. For it will with difficulty be believed, that two armies, on which such important consequences depended, should be crowded into so small a space as Trenton; and that the one, on the eve of an engagement, when every ear is supposed to be open, and every degree of watchfulness employed, should move completely from the ground, with all its stores, baggage and artillery, unknown and even unsuspected by the other. And so entirely were the British deceived, that when they heard the report of the cannon and small arms at Princeton, they supposed it to be thunder, though in the depth of winter.

General Washington, the better to cover and disguise his retreat from Trenton, had ordered a line of fires to be lighted up in front of his camp. These not only served to give an appearance of going to rest, and continuing that deception, but they effectually concealed from the British whatever was acting behind them, for flame can no more be seen through than a wall, and in this situation, it may with propriety be said, they became a pillar of fire to one army, and a pillar of cloud to the other. After this, by a circuitous march of about eighteen miles, the Americans reached Princeton early in the morning.

The number of prisoners taken were between two and three hundred, with which general Washington immediately set off. The van of the British army from Trenton entered Princeton about an hour after the Americans had left it, who, continuing their march for the remainder of the day, arrived in the evening at a convenient situation, wide of the main road to Brunswick, and about sixteen miles distant from Princeton. But so wearied and exhausted were they, with the continual and unabated service and fatigue of two days and a night, from action to action, without shelter, and almost without refreshment, that the bare and frozen ground, with no other covering than the sky, became to them a place of comfortable rest. By these two events, and with but a little comparative force to accomplish them, the Americans closed with advantage a campaign, which, but a few days before, threatened the country with destruction. The British army, apprehensive for the safety of their magazines at Brunswick, eighteen miles distant, marched immediately for that place, where they arrived late in the evening, and from which they made no attempts to move, for nearly five months.

Having thus stated the principal outlines of these two most interesting actions, I shall now quit them, to put the abbe right in his mis-stated account of the debt and paper money of America, wherein, speaking of these matters, he says:

" These ideal riches were rejected. The more the multiplication of them was urged by want, the greater did their depreciation grow. The congress was indignant at the affront given to its money, and declared all those to be traitors to their country, who should not receive it as they would have received gold itself.

" Did not this body know, that prepossessions are no more to be controlled than feelings are ? Did it not perceive that, in the present crisis, every rational man would be afraid of exposing his fortune ? Did it not see, that at the beginning of a republic, it permitted to itself the exercise of such acts of despotism as are unknown even in the countries which are moulded to, and become familiar with, servitude and oppression ? Could it pretend that it did not punish a want of confidence with the pains which would have been scarcely merited by revolt and treason ? Of all this was the congress well aware. But it had no choice of means. Its despised and despicable scraps of paper were actually thirty times below their original value, when more of them were ordered to be made. On the 13th of September, 1779, there was of this paper among the public, to the amount of 35,544,155*l.* The state owed moreover 8,385,356*l.* without reckoning the particular debts of single provinces."

In the above recited passages, the abbe speaks as if the United States had contracted a debt of upwards of forty million pounds sterling, besides the debts of the individual states.   After which, speaking of foreign trade with America, he says, that "those countries in Europe, which are truly commercial ones, knowing that North-America had been reduced to contract debts, at the epoch even of her greatest prosperity, wisely thought that, in her present distress, she would be able to pay but very little, for what might be carried to her."

I know it must be extremely difficult to make foreigners understand the nature and circumstances of our paper money, because there are natives, who do not understand it themselves.   But with us its fate is now determined.   Common consent has consigned it to rest with that kind of regard, which the long service of inanimate things insensibly obtains from mankind.   Every stone in the bridge, that has carried us over, seems to have a claim upon our esteem. But this was a corner stone, and its usefulness cannot be forgotten.   There is something in a grateful mind, which extends itself even to things that can neither be benefited by regard, nor suffer by neglect: but so it is; and almost every man is sensible of the effect.

But to return.   The paper money, though issued from congress under the name of dollars, did not come from that body always at that value.   Those which were issued the first year, were equal to gold and silver.   The second year less, the third still less, and so on, for nearly the space of five years: at the end of which, I imagine, that the whole value, at which congress might pay away the several emissions, taking them together, was about ten or twelve million pounds sterling.

Now as it would have taken ten or twelve millions sterling of taxes to carry on the war for five years, and, as while this money was issuing, and likewise depreciating down to nothing, there were none, or few valuable taxes paid; consequently the event to the public was the same, whether they sunk ten or twelve millions of expended money, by depreciation, or paid ten or twelve millions by taxation; for as they did not do both, and chose to do one, the matter which, in a general view, was indifferent.[1]   And therefore, what the abbe supposes to be a debt, has now no existence; it having been paid, by every body consenting to reduce, at his own expense, from the value of the bills continually passing among themselves, a sum, equal, nearly, to what the expense of the war was for five years.

Again.   The paper money having now ceased, and the depreciation with it, and gold and silver supplied its place, the war will now be carried on by taxation, which will draw from the public a considerable less sum than what the depreciation drew; but as while they pay the former, they do not suffer the latter, and as when they suffered the latter, they did not pay the former, the thing will be nearly equal, with this moral advantage, that taxation occasions frugality and thought, and depreciation produced dissipation and carelessness.

And again.   If a man's portion of taxes comes to less than what he lost by the depreciation, it proves that the alteration is in his favour.   If it comes to more, and he is justly assessed, it shows that he did not sustain his proper share of depreciation, because the one was as operatively his tax as the other.

It is true, that it never was intended, neither was it foreseen, that the debt contained in the paper currency should sink itself in this manner; but as, by the voluntary conduct of all and of every one, it has arrived at this fate, the debt is paid by those who owed it.   Perhaps nothing was ever so universally the act of a country as this.   Government had no hand in it.   Every man depreciated his own money by his own consent, for such was the effect, which the raising the nominal value of goods produced.   But as by such reduction he sustained a loss equal to what he must have paid to sink it by taxation, therefore the line of justice is to

---

[1] It was, however, remarked by a contemporary writer, that "if the currency is sunk by taxation it is done in equal proportion, but if by depreciation the burden is unequal."   That is, the "Tories," who distrusted the paper money, and possessed little of it, had an advantage over the patriots (Whigs) who had much.—*Editor*.

consider his loss by the depreciation as his tax for that time, and not to tax him when the war is over, to make that money good in any other person's hands, which became nothing in his own.

Again. The paper currency was issued for the express purpose of carrying on the war. It has performed that service, without any other material charge to the public, while it lasted. But to suppose, as some did, that, at the end of the war, it was to grow into gold or silver, or become equal thereto, was to suppose that we were to *get* two hundred millions of dollars by *going to war*, instead of *paying* the cost of carrying it on.

But if any thing in the situation of America, as to her currency or her circumstances, yet remains not understood, then let it be remembered, that this war is the public's war, —the country's war. It is *their* independence that is to be supported ; *their* property that is to be secured ; *their* country that is to be saved. Here, government, the army, and the people, are mutually and reciprocally one. In other wars, kings may lose their thrones, and their dominions; but here, the loss must fall on the majesty of the multitude, and the property they are contending to save. Every man being sensible of this, he goes to the field, or pays his portion of the charge, as the sovereign of his own possessions ; and when he is conquered a monarch falls.

The remark, which the abbe in the conclusion of the passage has made, respecting America's contracting debts in the time of her prosperity, (by which he means, before the breaking out of hostilities,) serves to show, though he has not made the application, the very great commercial difference between a dependant and an independent country. In a state of dependance, and with a fettered commerce, though with all the advantages of peace, her trade could not balance itself, and she annually run into debt. But now, in a state of independence, though involved in war, she requires no credit : her stores are full of merchandize, and gold and silver are become the currency of the country. How these things have established themselves is difficult to account for: but they are facts, and facts are more powerful than arguments.

As it is probable this letter will undergo a re-publication in Europe, the remarks here thrown together will serve to show the extreme folly of Britain in resting her hopes of success on the extinction of our paper currency. The expectation is at once so childish and forlorn, that it places her in the laughable condition of a famished lion watching for prey at a spider's web.

From this account of the currency, the abbe proceeds to state the condition of America in the winter of 1777, and the spring following; and closes his observations with mentioning the treaty of alliance, which was signed in France, and the propositions of the British ministry, which were rejected in America. But in the manner in which the abbe has arranged his facts, there is a very material error, that not only he, but other European historians have fallen into; none of them having assigned the true cause why the British proposals were rejected, and all of them have assigned a wrong one.

In the winter of 1778, and spring following, congress were assembled at York Town, in Pennsylvania, the British were in possession of Philadelphia, and general Washington with the army were encamped in huts at the Valley-Forge, twenty-five miles distant therefrom. To all, who can remember, it was a season of hardship, but not despair; and the abbe, speaking of this period and its inconveniences, says:

" A multitude of privations, added to so many other misfortunes, might make the Americans regret their former tranquillity, and incline them to an accommodation with England. In vain had the people been bound to the new government by the sacredness of oaths and the influence of religion. In vain had endeavours been used to convince them that it was impossible to treat safely with a country, in which one parliament might overturn what should have been established by another. In vain had they been threatened with the eternal resentment of an exasperated and vindictive enemy. It was possible that these distant troubles might not be balanced by the weight of present evils.

"So thought the British ministry, when they sent to the new world public agents, authorised to offer every thing except independence to these very Americans, from whom they had two years before exacted an unconditional submission. It is not improbable but, that by this plan of conciliation, a few months sooner, some effect might have been produced. But at the period, at which it was proposed by the court of London, it was rejected with disdain, because this measure appeared but as an argument of fear and weakness. The people were already reassured. The congress, the generals, the troops, the bold and skilful men, in each colony had possessed themselves of the authority ; every thing had recovered its first spirit. *This was the effect of a treaty of friendship and commerce between the United States and the court of Versailles, signed the 6th of February,* 1778."

On this passage of the abbe's I cannot help remarking, that, to unite time with circumstance, is a material nicety in history ; the want of which frequently throws it into endless confusion and mistake, occasions a total separation between causes and consequences and connects them with others they are not immediately, and sometimes not at all, related to.

The abbe, in saying that the offers of the British ministry "were rejected with disdain," is *right*, as to the *fact*, but *wrong* as to the *time ;* and this error in the time, has occasioned him to be mistaken in the cause.

The signing the treaty of Paris the 6th of February, 1778, could have no effect on the mind or politics of America, until it was *known in America :* and therefore, when the abbe says, that the rejection of the British offers was in consequence of the alliance, he must mean, that it was in consequence of the alliance *being known* in America ; which was not the case : and by this mistake he not only takes from her the reputation, which her unshaken fortitude in that trying situation deserves, but is likewise led very injuriously to suppose, that had she *not known* of the treaty, the offers would probably have been accepted ; whereas she knew nothing of the treaty at the time of the rejection, and consequently did not reject them on that ground.

The propositions or offers above mentioned, were contained

in two bills brought into the British parliament by lord North, on the 17th of February, 1778. Those bills were hurried through both houses with unusual haste, and before they had gone through all the customary forms of parliament, copies of them were sent over to lord Howe and general Howe, then in Philadelphia, who were likewise commissioners. General Howe ordered them to be printed in Philadelphia, and sent copies of them by a flag to general Washington, to be forwarded to congress at York Town, where they arrived the 21st of April, 1778. Thus much for the arrival of the bills in America.

Congress, as is their usual mode, appointed a committee from their own body, to examine them and report thereon. The report was brought in the next day, (the twenty-second,) was read, and unanimously agreed to, entered on their journals, and published for the information of the country. Now this report must be the rejection to which the abbe alludes, because congress gave no other formal opinion on those bills and propositions: and on a subsequent application from the British commissioners, dated the 27th of May, and received at York Town [Pa.] the 6th of June, congress immediately referred them for an answer, to their printed resolves of the 22d of April. Thus much for the rejection of the offers.

On the 2d of May, that is, eleven days after the above rejection was made, the treaty between the United States and France arrived at Yorktown; and until this moment congress had not the least notice or idea, that such a measure was in any train of execution. But lest this declaration of mine should pass only for assertion, I shall support it by proof, for it is material to the character and principle of the revolution to show, that no condition of America, since the declaration of independence, however trying and severe, ever operated to produce the most distant idea of yielding it up either by force, distress, artifice or persuasion. And this proof is the more necessary, because it was the system of the British ministry at this time, as well as before and since, to hold out to the European powers that America was unfixed in her resolutions and policy; hoping by this artifice to lessen her reputation in Europe, and weaken the confidence which those powers or any of them might be inclined to place in her.

At the time these matters were transacting, I was secretary in the foreign department of congress. All the *political* letters from the American commissioners rested in my hands, and all that were officially written went from my office; and so far from congress knowing any thing of the signing the treaty, at the time they rejected the British offers, they had not received a line of information from their commissioners at Paris, on any subject whatever, for upwards of a twelve-month. Probably the loss of the port of Philadelphia and the navigation of the Delaware, together with the danger of the seas, covered at this time with British cruisers, contributed to the disappointment.

One packet, it is true, arrived at Yorktown in January preceding, which was about three months before the arrival of the treaty; but, strange as it may appear, every letter had been taken out, before it was put on board the vessel which brought it from France, and blank white paper put in their stead.

Having thus stated the time when the proposals from the British commissioners were first received, and likewise the time when the treaty of alliance arrived, and shown that the rejection of the former was eleven days prior to the arrival of the latter, and without the least knowledge of such circumstance having taken place or being about to take place; the rejection, therefore, must, and ought to be attributed to the fixed, unvaried sentiments of America respecting the enemy she is at war with, and her determination to support her independence to the last public effort, and not to any new circumstance which had taken place in her favor, which at that time she did not and could not know of.

Besides, there is a vigor of determination and spirit of defiance in the language of the rejection, (which I here subjoin,) which derive their greatest glory by appearing before the treaty was known; for that, which is bravery in distress, becomes insult in prosperity: and the treaty placed America on such a strong foundation, that had she then known it, the answer which she gave, would have appeared rather as an air of triumph, than as the glowing serenity of fortitude.

Upon the whole, the abbe appears to have entirely mistaken the matter; for instead of attributing the rejection of the propositions to *our knowledge* of the treaty of alliance; he should have attributed the origin of them in the British cabinet, to *their knowledge* of that event. And then the reason why they were hurried over to America in the state of bills, that is, before they were passed into acts, is easily accounted for, which is that they might have the chance of reaching America before any knowledge of the treaty should arrive, which they were lucky enough to do, and there met the fate they so richly merited. That these bills were brought into the British parliament after the treaty with France was signed, is proved from the dates: the treaty being on the 6th, and the bills on the 17th of February. And that the signing the treaty was known in parliament, when the bills were brought in, is likewise proved by a speech of Mr. Fox, on the said 17th of February, who, in reply to lord North, informed the house of the treaty being signed, and challenged the minister's knowledge of the same fact.*

* In congress, April 22d, 1788.

"The committee to whom was referred the general's letter of the 18th, containing a certain printed paper sent from Philadelphia, purporting to be the draught of a bill for declaring the *intentions* of the parliament of Great Britain, as to the *exercise* of what they are pleased to term their *right* of imposing taxes within these United States: and also the draught of a bill to enable the king of Great Britain to appoint commissioners, with powers to treat, consult, and agree upon the means of quieting certain disorders within the said states, beg leave to observe,

"That the said paper being industriously circulated by emissaries of the enemy, in a partial and secret manner, the same ought to be forthwith printed for the public information.

"The committee cannot ascertain whether the contents of the said paper have been framed in Philadelphia, or in Great Britain, much less whether the same are really and truly intended to be brought into the parliament of that kingdom, or whether the said parliament will confer thereon the usual solemnities of their laws. But are inclined to believe this will happen, for the following reasons:

"1st, Because their general hath made divers feeble efforts to set on foot some kind of treaty during the last winter, though, either from a mistaken idea

Though I am not surprised to see the abbe mistaken in matters of history, acted at such a distance from his sphere of immediate observation, yet I am more than surprised to find him wrong (or at least what appears so to me) in the

of his own dignity and importance, the want of information, or some other cause, he hath not made application to those who are invested with a proper authority.

"2d, Because they suppose that the fallacious idea of a cessation of hostilities will render these states remiss in their preparations for war.

"3d, Because believing the Americans wearied with war, they suppose we will accede to their terms for the sake of peace.

"4th, Because they suppose our negotiations may be subject to a like corrupt influence with their debates.

"5th, Because they expect from this step the same effects they did from what one of their ministers thought proper to call his *conciliatory motion, viz.*, that it will prevent foreign powers from giving aid to these states ; that it will lead their own subjects to continue a little longer the present war : and that it will detach some weak men in America, from the cause of freedom and virtue.

"6th, Because their king, from his own showing, hath reason to apprehend that his fleets and armies, instead of being employed against the territories of these states, will be necessary for the defence of his own dominions. And,

"7th, Because the impracticability of subjugating this country being every day more and more manifest, it is their interest to extricate themselves from the war upon any terms.

"The committee beg leave further to observe, that upon a supposition the matters contained in the said paper will really go into the British statute books, they serve to show, in a clear point of view, the weakness and wickedness of the enemy.

"*Their weakness.*

"1st, Because they formerly declared, not only that they had a right to bind the inhabitants of these states in all cases whatsoever, but also that the said inhabitants should *absolutely* and *unconditionally* submit to the exercise of that right.   And this submission they have endeavored to exact by the sword.   Receding from this claim, therefore, under the present circumstances, shows their inability to enforce it.

"2d, Because their prince hath heretofore rejected the humblest petitions of the representatives of America, praying to be considered as subjects, and protected in the enjoyment of peace, liberty and safety : and hath waged a most cruel war against them, and employed the savages to butcher innocent women and children.   But now the same prince pretends to treat with those very representatives, and grant to the *arms* of America what he refused to her *prayers*.

"3d, Because they have uniformly labored to conquer this continent, rejecting every idea of accommodation proposed to them, from a confidence in their

well enlightened field of philosophical reflection. Here the materials are his own; created by himself; and the error, therefore, is an act of the mind.

Hitherto my remarks have been confined to circumstance;

own strength. Wherefore it is evident, from the change in their mode of attack, that they have lost this confidence. And,

"4th, Because the constant language, spoken, not only by their ministers, but by the most public and authentic acts of the nation, hath been, that it is incompatible with their dignity to treat with the Americans while they have arms in their hands. Notwithstanding which, an offer is now about to be made for treaty.

" *The wickedness and insincerity* of the enemy appear from the following considerations :

" 1st, Either the *bills* now to be passed contain a direct or indirect cession of a part of their former claims, or they do not. If they do, then it is acknowledged that they have sacrificed many brave men in an unjust quarrel. If they do not, then they are calculated to deceive America into terms, to which neither argument before the war, nor force since, could procure her assent.

" 2d, The first of these *bills* appears, from the title, to be a declaration of the *intentions* of the British parliament concerning the exercise of the *right of imposing taxes* within these states. Wherefore, should these states treat under the said bill, they would *indirectly* acknowledge that right, to obtain which acknowledgment the present war hath been avowedly undertaken and prosecuted on the part of Great Britain.

" 3d, Should such pretended right be so acquiesced in, then, of consequence the same right might be exercised whenever the British parliament should find themselves in a different *temper* and *disposition ;* since it must depend upon those, and such like contingencies, how far men will act according to their former *intentions.*

"4th, The said first bill, in the body thereof, containeth no new matter, but is precisely the same with the motion before-mentioned, and liable to all the objections which lay against the said motion, excepting the following particular, viz., that *by the motion* actual taxation was to be suspended, so long as America should give as much as the said parliament might think proper : whereas, *by the proposed bill*, it is to be suspended, as long as future parliaments continue of the same mind with the present.

" 5th, From the second bill it appears, that the British king may, if he pleases, appoint commissioners to *treat* and *agree* with those, whom they please, about a variety of things therein mentioned. But such treaties and agreements are to be of no validity without the concurrence of the said parliament, except so far as they relate to the *suspension* of hostilities, and of certain of their acts, the granting of pardons, and the appointing of governors to these sovereign, free and independent states. Wherefore, the said parliament have reserved to themselves, in *express words*, the power of setting aside any such treaty, and

the order in which they arose, and the events they produced. In these, my information being better than the abbe's, my task was easy. How I may succeed in controverting matters of sentiment and opinion, with one whom years, experience,

taking the advantage of any circumstances which may arise to subject this continent to their usurpations.

"6th, The said bill, by holding forth a tender of pardon, implies a criminality in our justifiable resistance, and consequently, to treat under it would be an implied acknowledgment, that the inhabitants of these states were what Britain has declared them to be, *Rebels*.

"7th, The inhabitants of these states being claimed by them as subjects, they may infer, from the nature of the negotiation now pretended to be set on foot, that the said inhabitants would of right be afterwards bound by such laws as they should make. Wherefore, any agreement entered into on such negotiation might at any future time be repealed. And,

"8th, Because the said bill purports, that the commissioners therein mentioned may treat with private individuals : a measure highly derogatory to the dignity of national character.

" From all which it appears evident to your committee, that the said bills are intended to operate upon the hopes and fears of the good people of these states, so as to create divisions among them, and a defection from the common cause, now by the blessing of divine providence drawing near to a favorable issue. That they are the sequel of that insidious plan, which from the days of the stamp act down to the present time, hath involved this country in contention and bloodshed. And that, as in other cases so in this, although circumstances may force them at times to recede from their unjustifiable claims, there can be no doubt but they will as heretofore, upon the first favorable occasion, again display that lust of domination, which hath rent in twain the mighty empire of Britain.

" Upon the whole matter, the committee beg leave to report it as their opinion, that as the Americans united in this arduous contest upon principles of common interest, for the defence of common rights and privileges, which union hath been cemented by common calamities and by mutual good offices and affection, so the great cause for which they contend, and in which all mankind are interested, must derive its success from the continuance of that union. Wherefore, any man, or body of men, who should presume to make any separate or partial convention or agreement with commissioners under the crown of Great Britain, or any of them, ought to be considered and treated as open and avowed enemies of the United States.

" And further your committee beg leave to report it as their opinion, that these United States cannot with propriety, hold any conference or treaty with *any* commissioners on the part of Great Britain, unless they shall, as a preliminary thereto, either withdraw their fleets and armies, or else, in positive and express terms, acknowledge the independence of the said states.

" And inasmuch as it appears to be the design of the enemies of these states

and long established reputation have placed in a superior line, I am less confident in; but as they fall within the scope of my observations it would be improper to pass them over.

From this part of the abbe's work to the latter end, I find several expressions, which appear to me to start, with cynical complexion, from the path of liberal thinking, or at least they are so involved as to lose many of the beauties which distinguish other parts of the performance.

The abbe having brought his work to the period when the

to lull them into a fatal security—to the end that they may act with becoming weight and importance, it is the opinion of your committee, that the several states be called upon to use the utmost strenuous exertions to have their respective quotas of continental troops in the field as soon as possible, and that all the militia of the said states be held in readiness, to act as occasion may require."

The following is the answer of congress to the second application of the commissioners :

"YORK-TOWN, June 6, 1778.

"SIR,

"I have had the honor of laying your letter of the 3d instant, with the acts of the British parliament which came inclosed, before congress: and I am instructed to acquaint you, sir, that they have already expressed their sentiments upon bills, not essentially different from those acts, in a publication of the 22d of April last.

"Be assured, sir, when the king of Great Britain shall be seriously disposed to put an end to the unprovoked and cruel war waged against these United States, congress will readily attend to such terms of peace, as may consist with the honour of independent nations, the interest of their constituents and the sacred regard they mean to pay to treaties. I have the honor to be, sir,

Your most obedient, and
most humble servant.
HENRY LAURENS,
President of Congress."[1]

His Excellency,
Sir Henry Clinton, K. B. Philadelphia.   —*Author.*

[1] These documents do not bear out, strictly, Paine's case. In the answer of Congress, April 22, willingness is expressed to treat if the fleets and armies are withdrawn; but in the answer of June 6 (after the treaty with France was known) Congress will attend only to such terms "as may consist with the honor of independent nations," and with their "treaties."—*Editor.*

treaty of alliance between France and the United States commenced, proceeds to make some remarks thereon.

"In short," says he, "philosophy, whose first sentiment is the desire to see all governments just and all people happy, in casting her eyes upon this alliance of a monarchy, with a people who are defending their liberty, *is curious to know its motive. She sees at once, too clearly, that the happiness of mankind has no part in it.*"

Whatever train of thinking or of temper the abbe might be in, when he penned this expression, matters not. They will neither qualify the sentiment, nor add to its defect. If right, it needs no apology; if wrong, it merits no excuse. It is sent into the world as an opinion of philosophy, and may be examined without regard to the author.

It seems to be a defect, connected with ingenuity, that it often employs itself more in matters of curiosity, than usefulness. Man must be the privy councillor of fate, or something is not right. He must know the springs, the whys and wherefores of everything, or he sits down unsatisfied. Whether this be a crime, or only a caprice of humanity, I am not inquiring into. I shall take the passage as I find it, and place my objections against it.

It is not so properly the *motives* which *produced* the alliance, as the *consequences* which are to be *produced from it*, that mark out the field of philosophical reflection. In the one we only penetrate into the barren cave of secrecy, where little can be known, and every thing may be misconceived; in the other, the mind is presented with a wide extended prospect of vegetative good, and sees a thousand blessings budding into existence.

But the expression, even within the compass of the abbe's meaning, sets out with an error, because it is made to declare that which no man has authority to declare. Who can say that the happiness of mankind made *no part of the motives* which produced the Alliance? To be able to declare this, a man must be possessed of the mind of all the parties concerned, and know that their motives were something else.

In proportion as the independence of America became contemplated and understood, the local advantages of it to the immediate actors, and the numerous benefits it promised mankind, appeared to be every day increasing ; and we saw not a temporary good for the present race only, but a continued good to all posterity ; these motives, therefore, added to those which preceded them, became the motives on the part of America, which led her to propose and agree to the treaty of alliance, as the best effectual method of extending and securing happiness ; and therefore, with respect to us, the abbe is wrong.

France, on the other hand, was situated very differently. She was not acted upon by necessity to seek a friend, and therefore her motive in becoming one, has the strongest evidence of being good, and that which is so, must have some happiness for its object. With regard to herself, she saw a train of conveniences worthy her attention. By lessening the power of an enemy, whom at the same time she sought neither to destroy nor distress, she gained an advantage without doing an evil, and created to herself a new friend by associating with a country in misfortune. The springs of thought that lead to actions of this kind, however political they may be, are nevertheless naturally beneficent ; for in all causes, good or bad, it is necessary there should be a fitness in the mind, to enable it to act in character with the object : therefore, as a bad cause cannot be prosecuted with a good motive, so neither can a good cause be long supported by a bad one ; and as no man acts without a motive, therefore in the present instance, as they cannot be bad, they must be admitted to be good. But the abbe sets out upon such an extended scale, that he overlooks the degrees by which it is measured, and rejects the beginning of good, because the end comes not out at once.

It is true that bad motives may in some degree be brought to support a good cause or prosecute a good object ; but it never continues long, which is not the case with France ; for either the object will reform the mind, or the mind corrupt the object, or else not being able, either way, to get into unison, they will separate in disgust : and this natural, though unperceived progress of association or contention between the mind and the object, is the secret cause of fidelity or defection. Every object a man pursues, is, for the time, a kind of mistress to his mind : if both are good or bad, the union is natural; but if they are in reverse, and neither can seduce nor yet reform the other, the opposition grows into dislike, and a separation follows.

When the cause of America first made its appearance on the stage of the universe, there were many, who, in the style of adventurers and fortune-hunters, were dangling in its train, and making their court to it with every profession of honour and attachment. They were loud in its praise and ostentatious in its service. Every place echoed with their ardour or their anger, and they seemed like men in love. But, alas ! they were fortune-hunters. Their expectations were excited, but their minds were unimpressed ; and finding it not to their purpose, nor themselves reformed by its influence, they ceased their suit, and in some instances deserted and betrayed it.

There were others, who at first beheld America with indifference, and unacquainted with her character were cautious of her company. They treated her as one who, under the fair name of liberty, might conceal the hideous figure of anarchy, or the gloomy monster of tyranny. They knew not what she was. If fair, she was fair indeed. But still she was suspected, and though born among us appeared to be a stranger.

Accident with some, and curiosity with others, brought on a distant acquaintance. They ventured to look at her. They felt an inclination to speak to her. One intimacy led to another, till the suspicion wore away, and a change of sentiment gradually stole upon the mind ; and having no self-interest to serve, no passion of dishonour to gratify, they became enamoured of her innocence, and, unaltered by misfortune or uninfluenced by success, shared with fidelity in the varieties of her fate.

This declaration of the abbe's, respecting motives, has led

me unintentionally into a train of metaphysical reasoning; but
there was no other avenue by which it could so properly be approached. To place presumption against presumption, assertion against assertion, is a mode of opposition that has no effect ; and therefore the more eligible method was to show that
the declaration does not correspond with the natural progress
of the mind, and the influence it has upon our conduct.   I
shall now quit this part and proceed to what I have before
stated, namely, that it is not so properly the motives
which produced the alliance, as the consequences to be
produced from it, that mark out the field of philosophical
reflection.

It is an observation I have already made in some former
publications, that the circle of civilization is yet incomplete.
Mutual wants have formed the individuals of each country
into a kind of national society, and here the progress of
civilization has stopped.   For it is easy to see, that nations
with regard to each other (notwithstanding the ideal civil
law, which every one explains as it suits him) are like individuals in a state of nature.   They are regulated by no fixed
principle, governed by no compulsive law, and each does independently what it pleases or what it can.

Were it possible we could have known the world when in
a state of barbarism, we might have concluded that it never
could be brought into the order we now see it.   The untamed
mind was then as hard, if not harder, to work upon in its individual state, than the national mind is in its present one.
Yet we have seen the accomplishment of the one, why then
should we doubt that of the other ?

There is a greater fitness in mankind to extend and complete the civilization of nations with each other at this day,
than there was to begin it with the unconnected individuals
at first ; in the same manner that it is somewhat easier to
put together the materials of a machine after they are formed,
than it was to form them from original matter.   The present
condition of the world, differing so exceedingly from
what it formerly was, has given a new cast to the mind of
man, more than what he appears to be sensible of.   The

wants of the individual, which first produced the idea of
society, are now augmented into the wants of the nation, and
he is obliged to seek from another country what before he
sought from the next person.

Letters, the tongue of the world, have in some measure
brought all mankind acquainted, and by an extension of
their uses are every day promoting some new friendship.
Through them distant nations become capable of conversation, and losing by degrees the awkwardness of strangers,
and the moroseness of suspicion, they learn to know and
understand each other. Science, the partisan of no country,
but the beneficent patroness of all, has liberally opened a
temple where all may meet. Her influence on the mind,
like the sun on the chilled earth, has long been preparing it
for higher cultivation and further improvement. The philosopher of one country sees not an enemy in the philosopher
of another: he takes his seat in the temple of science, and
asks not who sits beside him.

This was not the condition of the barbarian world. Then
the wants of men were few and the objects within his reach.
While he could acquire these, he lived in a state of individual
independence ; the consequence of which was, there were as
many nations as persons, each contending with the other,
to secure something which he had, or to obtain something
which he had not. The world had then no business to follow, no studies to exercise the mind. Their time was
divided between sloth and fatigue. Hunting and war were
their chief occupations ; sleep and food their principal
enjoyments.

Now it is otherwise. A change in the mode of life has
made it necessary to be busy ; and man finds a thousand
things to do now which before he did not. Instead of placing his ideas of greatness in the rude achievements of the
savage, he studies arts, sciences, agriculture and commerce,
the refinements of the gentleman, the principles of society,
and the knowledge of the philosopher.

There are many things which in themselves are neither
morally good nor bad, but they are productive of conse-

quences, which are strongly marked with one or other of these characters. Thus commerce, though in itself a moral nullity, has had a considerable influence in tempering the human mind. It was the want of objects in the ancient world, which occasioned in them such a rude and perpetual turn for war. Their time hung on their hands without the means of employment. The indolence they lived in afforded leisure for mischief, and being all idle at once, and equal in their circumstances, they were easily provoked or induced to action.

But the introduction of commerce furnished the world with objects, which, in their extent, reach every man, and give him something to think about and something to do ; by these his attention is mechanically drawn from the pursuits which a state of indolence and an unemployed mind occasioned, and he trades with the same countries, which in former ages, tempted by their productions, and too indolent to purchase them, he would have gone to war with.

Thus, as I have already observed, the condition of the world being materially changed by the influence of science and commerce, it is put into a fitness not only to admit of, but to desire, an extension of civilization. The principal and almost only remaining enemy, it now has to encounter, is *prejudice ;* for it is evidently the interest of mankind to agree and make the best of life. The world has undergone its divisions of empire, the several boundaries of which are known and settled. The idea of conquering countries, like the Greeks and Romans, does not now exist ; and experience has exploded the notion of going to war for the sake of profit. In short, the objects for war are exceedingly diminished, and there is now left scarcely any thing to quarrel about, but what arises from that demon of society, prejudice, and the consequent sullenness and untractableness of the temper.

There is something exceedingly curious in the constitution and operation of prejudice. It has the singular ability of accommodating itself to all the possible varieties of the human mind. Some passions and vices are but thinly scattered among mankind, and find only here and there a fitness of reception. But prejudice, like the spider, makes every place its home. It has neither taste nor choice of situation, and all that it requires is room. Every where, except in fire or water, a spider will live. So, let the mind be as naked as the walls of an empty and forsaken tenement, gloomy as a dungeon, or ornamented with the richest abilities of thinking, let it be hot, cold, dark or light, lonely or inhabited, still prejudice, if undisturbed, will fill it with cobwebs, and live, like the spider, where there seems nothing to live on. If the one prepares her food by poisoning it to her palate and her use, the other does the same; and as several of our passions are strongly characterized by the animal world, prejudice may be denominated the spider of the mind.

Perhaps no two events ever united so intimately and forcibly to combat and expel prejudice, as the revolution of America and the alliance with France. Their effects are felt, and their influence already extends as well to the old world as the new. Our style and manner of thinking have undergone a revolution, more extraordinary than the political revolution of the country. We see with other eyes; we hear with other ears; and think with other thoughts, than those we formerly used. We can look back on our own prejudices, as if they had been the prejudices of other people. We now see and know they were prejudices and nothing else; and, relieved from their shackles, enjoy a freedom of mind, we felt not before. It was not all the argument, however powerful, nor all the reasoning, however eloquent, that could have produced this change, so necessary to the extension of the mind, and the cordiality of the world, without the two circumstances of the revolution and the alliance.

Had America dropped quietly from Britain, no material change in sentiment had taken place. The same notions, prejudices, and conceits would have governed in both countries, as governed them before, and, still the slaves of error and education, they would have travelled on in the beaten track of vulgar and habitual thinking. But brought about by the means it has been, both with regard to ourselves, to

France and England, every corner of the mind is swept of its cobwebs, poison and dust, and made fit for the reception of generous happiness.

Perhaps there never was an alliance on a broader basis, than that between America and France, and the progress of it is worth attending to. The countries had been enemies, not properly of themselves, but through the medium of England. They originally had no quarrel with each other, nor any cause for one, but what arose from the interest of England, and her arming America against France. At the same time, the Americans at a distance from, and unacquainted with, the world, and tutored in all the prejudices which governed those who governed them, conceived it their duty to act as they were taught. In doing this, they expended their substance to make conquests, not for themselves but for their masters, who in return treated them as slaves.

A long succession of insolent severity, and the separation finally occasioned by the commencement of hostilities at Lexington, on the 19th of April, 1775, naturally produced a new disposition of thinking. As the mind closed itself towards England, it opened itself towards the world, and our prejudices like our oppressions, underwent, though less observed, a mental examination; until we found the former as inconsistent with reason and benevolence, as the latter were repugnant to our civil and political rights.

While we were thus advancing by degrees into the wide field of extended humanity, the alliance with France was concluded. An alliance not formed for the mere purpose of a day, but on just and generous grounds, and with equal and mutual advantages; and the easy, affectionate manner in which the parties have since communicated has made it an alliance not of courts only, but of countries. There is now an union of mind as well as of interest; and our hearts as well as our prosperity call on us to support it.

The people of England not having experienced this change, had likewise no idea of it. They were hugging to their bosoms the same prejudices we were trampling beneath our feet; and they expected to keep a hold upon America, by that narrowness of thinking which America disdained. What they were proud of, we despised ; and this is a principal cause why all their negotiations, constructed on this ground, have failed. We are now really another people, and cannot again go back to ignorance and prejudice. The mind once enlightened cannot again become dark. There is no possibility, neither is there any term to express the supposition by, of the mind *un*knowing any thing it already knows ; and therefore all attempts on the part of England, fitted to the former habit of America, and on the expectation of their applying now, will be like persuading a seeing man to become blind, and a sensible one to turn an idiot. The first of which is unnatural and the other impossible.

As to the remark which the abbe makes on the one country being a monarchy and the other a republic, it can have no essential meaning. Forms of government have nothing to do with treaties. The former are the internal police of the countries severally ; the latter their external police jointly : and so long as each performs its part, we have no more right or business to know how the one or the other conducts its domestic affairs, than we have to inquire into the private concerns of a family.

But had the abbe reflected for a moment, he would have seen, that courts, or the governing powers of all countries, be their forms what they may, are relatively republics with each other. It is the first and true principle of alliance. Antiquity may have given precedence, and power will naturally create importance, but their equal right is never disputed. It may likewise be worthy of remarking, that a monarchical country can suffer nothing in its popular happiness by an alliance with a republican one ; and republican governments have never been destroyed by their external connexions, but by some internal convulsion or contrivance. France has been in alliance with the republic of Switzerland for more than two hundred years, and still Switzerland retains her original form of government as entire as if she had been allied with a republic like herself ; therefore this remark of the abbe should go for nothing. Besides it is best mankind should mix.   There is ever something to learn, either of manners or principle; and it is by a free communication, without regard to domestic matters, that friendship is to be extended, and prejudice destroyed all over the world.

But notwithstanding the abbe's high professions in favor of liberty, he appears sometimes to forget himself, or that his theory is rather the child of his fancy than of his judgment: for in almost the same instant that he censures the alliance, as not originally or sufficiently calculated for the happiness of mankind, he, by a figure of implication, accuses France for having acted so generously and unreservedly in concluding it.   " Why did they (says he, meaning the court of France) tie themselves down by an inconsiderate treaty to conditions with the congress, which they might themselves have held in dependance by ample and regular supplies."

When an author undertakes to treat of public happiness he ought to be certain that he does not mistake passion for right, nor imagination for principle.   Principle, like truth, needs no contrivance.   It will ever tell its own tale, and tell it the same way.   But where this is not the case, every page must be watched, recollected, and compared like an invented story.

I am surprised at this passage of the abbe's.   It means nothing or it means ill; and in any case it shows the great difference between speculative and practical knowledge.   A treaty according to the abbe's language would have neither duration nor affection: it might have lasted to the end of the war, and then expired with it.   But France, by acting in a style superior to the little politics of narrow thinking, has established a generous fame and won the love of a country she was before a stranger to.   She had to treat with a people who thought as nature taught them; and, on her own part, she wisely saw there was no present advantage to be obtained by unequal terms, which could balance the more lasting ones that might flow from a kind and generous beginning.

From this part the abbe advances into the secret transac-

tions of the two cabinets of Versailles and Madrid respecting the independence of America ; through which I mean
not to follow him. It is a circumstance sufficiently striking
without being commented on, that the former union of
America with Britain produced a power which, in her hands,
was becoming dangerous to the world : and there is no improbability in supposing, that had the latter known as much
of the strength of the former, before she began the quarrel,,
as she has known since, that instead of attempting to reduce
her to unconditional submission, she would have proposed
to her the conquest of Mexico. But from the countries separately, Spain has nothing to apprehend, though from their
union she had more to fear than any other power in Europe.

The part which I shall more particularly confine myself
to, is that wherein the abbe takes an opportunity of compli-
menting the British ministry with high encomiums of admiration, on their rejecting the offered mediation of the
court of Madrid, in 1779.

It must be remembered that before Spain joined France
in the war, she undertook the office of a mediator, and made
proposals to the British king and ministry so exceedingly
favourable to their interest, that had they been accepted,
would have become inconvenient, if not inadmissible, to
America. These proposals were nevertheless rejected by the
British cabinet ; on which the abbe says,—

"It is in such a circumstance as this ; it is in the time when
noble pride elevates the soul superior to all terror ; when nothing
is seen more dreadful than the shame of receiving the law, and
when there is no doubt or hesitation which to choose, between
ruin and dishonour : it is then, that the greatness of a nation is
displayed. I acknowledge, however, that men, accustomed to
judge of things by the event, call great and perilous resolutions
heroism or madness, according to the good or bad success with
which they have been attended. If then, I should be asked,
what is the name which shall in years to come be given to the
firmness, which was in this moment exhibited by the English, I
shall answer that I do not know. But that which it deserves I
know. I know that the annals of the world hold out to us but

rarely, the august and majestic spectacle of a nation, which chooses rather to renounce its duration than its glory."

In this paragraph the conception is lofty and the expression elegant, but the colouring is too high for the original, and the likeness fails through an excess of graces. To fit the powers of thinking and the turn of language to the subject, so as to bring out a clear conclusion that shall hit the point in question and nothing else, is the true criterion of writing. But the greater part of the abbe's writings (if he will pardon me the remark) appear to me uncentral and burdened with variety. They represent a beautiful wilderness without paths; in which the eye is diverted by every thing without being particularly directed to any thing; and in which it is agreeable to be lost, and difficult to find the way out.

Before I offer any other remark on the spirit and composition of the above passage, I shall compare it with the circumstance it alludes to.

The circumstance then does not deserve the encomium. The rejection was not prompted by her fortitude but her vanity. She did not view it as a case of despair or even of extreme danger, and consequently the determination to renounce her duration rather than her glory, cannot apply to the condition of her mind. She had then high expectations of subjugating America, and had no other naval force against her than France; neither was she certain that rejecting the mediation of Spain would combine that power with France. New mediations might arise more favorable than those she had refused. But if they should not, and Spain should join, she still saw that it would only bring out her naval force against France and Spain, which was not wanted and could not be employed against America, and habits of thinking had taught her to believe herself superior to both.

But in any case to which the consequence might point, there was nothing to impress her with the idea of renouncing her duration. It is not the policy of Europe to suffer the extinction of any power, but only to lop off or prevent its dangerous increase. She was likewise freed by situation from the internal and immediate horrors of invasion; was rolling in dissipation and looking for conquests; and though she suffered nothing but the expense of war, she still had a greedy eye to magnificent reimbursement.

But if the abbe is delighted with high and striking singularities of character, he might, in America, have found ample field for encomium. Here was a people, who could not know what part the world would take for, or against them; and who were venturing on an untried scheme, in opposition to a power, against which more formidable nations had failed. They had every thing to learn but the principles which supported them, and every thing to procure that was necessary for their defence. They have at times seen themselves as low as distress could make them, without showing the least decrease of fortitude; and been raised again by the most unexpected events, without discovering an unmanly discomposure of joy. To hesitate or to despair are conditions equally unknown in America. Her mind was prepared for every thing; because her original and final resolution of succeeding or perishing included all possible circumstances.

The rejection of the British propositions in the year 1778, circumstanced as America was at that time, is a far greater instance of unshaken fortitude than the refusal of the Spanish mediation by the court of London: and other historians, besides the abbe, struck with the vastness of her conduct therein, have, like himself, attributed it to a circumstance, which was then unknown, the alliance with France. Their error shows their idea of its greatness; because in order to account for it, they have sought a cause suited to its magnitude, without knowing that the cause existed in the principles of the country.*

* Extract from "A short Review of the present Reign," in England, p. 45, in the new Annual Register, for the year 1780.

" The commissioners, who, in consequence of lord North's conciliatory bills, went over to America, to propose terms of peace to the colonies, were wholly

But this passionate encomium of the abbe is deservedly subject to moral and philosophical objections. It is the effusion of wild thinking, and has a tendency to prevent that humanity of reflection which the criminal conduct of Britain enjoins on her as a duty.—It is a laudanum to courtly iniquity.—It keeps in intoxicated sleep the conscience of a nation ; and more mischief is effected by wrapping up guilt in splendid excuse, than by directly patronizing it.

Britain is now the only country which holds the world in disturbance and war ; and instead of paying compliments to the excess of her crimes, the abbe would have appeared much more in character, had he put to her, or to her monarch, this serious question—

Are there not miseries enough in the world, too difficult to be encountered and too pointed to be borne, without studying to enlarge the list and arming it with new destruction ? Is life so very long that it is necessary, nay even a duty, to shake the sand and hasten out the period of duration ? Is the path so elegantly smooth, so decked on every side and carpeted with joys, that wretchedness is wanted to enrich it as a soil ? Go ask thine aching heart, when sorrow from a thousand causes wounds it, go ask thy sickened self, when every medicine fails, whether this be the case or not ?

Quitting my remarks on this head, I proceed to another, in which the abbe has let loose a vein of ill-nature, and, what is still worse, of injustice.

After cavilling at the treaty, he goes on to characterize the several parties combined in the war.

" Is it possible," says the abbe, " that a strict union should long subsist amongst confederates, of characters so opposite as the hasty, light, disdainful Frenchman, the jealous, haughty, sly, slow,

unsuccessful. The concessions which formerly would have been received with the utmost gratitude, were rejected with disdain. Now was the time of American pride and haughtiness. It is probable, however, that it was not pride and haughtiness alone that dictated the resolutions of congress, but a distrust of the sincerity of the offers of Britain, a determination not to give up their independence, and, *above all, the engagements into which they had entered by their late treaty with France.*"—*Author.*

circumspect Spaniard, and the American, who is secretly snatch-
ing a look at the mother country, and would rejoice, were they
compatible with his independence, at the disasters of his allies?"

To draw foolish portraits of each other, is a mode of attack
and reprisal, which the greater part of mankind are fond of
indulging.   The serious philosopher should be above it, more
especially in cases from which no good can arise, and mischief may, and where no received provocation can palliate
the offence.   The abbe might have invented a difference of
character for every country in the world, and they in return
might find others for him, till in the war of wit all real
character is lost.   The pleasantry of one nation or the gravity
of another may, by a little pencilling, be distorted into whimsical features, and the painter becomes as much laughed at
as the painting.

But why did not the abbe look a little deeper, and bring
forth the excellencies of the several parties?—Why did he
not dwell with pleasure on that greatness of character, that
superiority of heart, which has marked the conduct of France
in her conquests, and which has forced an acknowledgment
even from Britain?

There is one line, at least, (and many others might be discovered,) in which the confederates unite ; which is, that of
a rival eminence in their treatment of their enemies.   Spain
in her conquest of Minorca and the Bahama islands, confirms
this remark.   America has been invariable in her lenity from
the beginning of the war, notwithstanding the high provocations she has experienced.   It is England only who has been
insolent and cruel.

But why must America be charged with a crime undeserved
by her conduct, more so by her principles, and which, if a
fact, would be fatal to her honour.   I mean the want of
attachment to her allies, or rejoicing in their disasters.   She,
it is true, has been assiduous in showing to the world that
she was not the aggressor towards England, and that the
quarrel was not of her seeking, or, at that time, even of her
wishing.   But to draw inferences from her candour, and

even from her justification, to stab her character by, (and I see nothing else from which they can be supposed to be drawn,) is unkind and unjust.

Does her rejection of the British propositions in 1778, before she knew of any alliance with France, correspond with the abbe's description of her mind? Does a single instance of her conduct since that time justify it?—But there is a still better evidence to apply to, which is, that of all the mails which, at different times, have been waylaid on the road, in divers parts of America, and taken and carried into New-York, and from which the most secret and confidential private letters, as well as those from authority, have been published, not one of them, I repeat it, not a single one of them, gave countenance to such a charge.

This is not a country where men are under government restraint in speaking; and if there is any kind of restraint, it arises from a fear of popular resentment. Now if nothing in her private or public correspondence favors such a suggestion, and if the general disposition of the country is such as to make it unsafe for a man to show an appearance of joy at any disaster to her ally, on what grounds, I ask, can the accusation stand? What company the abbe may have kept in France, we cannot know; but this we know, that the account he gives does not apply to America.

Had the abbe been in America at the time the news arrived of the disaster of the fleet under count de Grasse, in the West Indies, he would have seen his vast mistake. Neither do I remember any instance, except the loss of Charleston, in which the public mind suffered more severe and pungent concern, or underwent more agitations of hope and apprehension as to the truth or falsehood of the report. Had the loss been all our own, it could not have had a deeper effect; yet it was not one of those cases which reached to the independence of America.

In the geographical account which the abbe gives of the thirteen states, he is so exceedingly erroneous, that to attempt a particular refutation, would exceed the limits I have prescribed to myself. And as it is a matter neither political,

historical, or sentimental, and which can always be contradicted by the extent and natural circumstances of the
country, I shall pass it over; with this additional remark,
that I never yet saw an European description of America
that was true, neither can any person gain a just idea of it,
but by coming to it.

Though I have already extended this letter beyond what
I at first proposed, I am, nevertheless, obliged to omit many
observations, I originally designed to have made. I wish
there had been no occasion for making any. But the wrong
ideas which the abbe's work had a tendency to excite, and
the prejudicial impressions they might make, must be an
apology for my remarks, and the freedom with which they
are made.

I observe the abbe has made a sort of epitome of a considerable part of the pamphlet "Common Sense," and introduced it in that form into his publication. But there are
other places where the abbe has borrowed freely from the
said pamphlet without acknowledging it. The difference
between society and government, with which the pamphlet
opens, is taken from it, and in some expressions almost
literally, into the abbe's work, as if originally his own; and
through the whole of the abbe's remarks on this head, the
idea in "Common Sense" is so closely copied and pursued,
that the difference is only in words, and in the arrangement
of the thoughts, and not in the thoughts themselves.*

---

* COMMON SENSE.

"Some writers have so confounded
society with government, as to leave
little or no distinction between them;
whereas they are not only different,
but have different origins."

"Society is produced by our wants
and governments by our wickedness;
the former promotes our happiness
positively, by uniting our affections—
the latter *negatively*, by restraining
our vices."

ABBE RAYNAL.

"Care must be taken not to confound together society with government. That they may be known distinctly, their origin should be considered."

"Society originates in the wants of
men, government in their vices. Society tends always to good—government ought always to tend to the
repression of evil."

In the following paragraphs there is less likeness in the language, but the ideas
in the one are evidently copied from the other.

But as it is time that I should come to the end of my letter, I shall forbear all future observations on the abbe's work, and take a concise view of the state of public affairs, since the time in which that performance was published.

A mind habituated to actions of meanness and injustice, commits them without reflection, or with a very partial one; for on what other ground than this, can we account for the declaration of war against the Dutch? To gain an idea of the politics which actuated the British ministry to this measure, we must enter into the opinion which they, and the English in general, had formed of the temper of the Dutch nation; and from thence infer what their expectation of the consequences would be.

Could they have imagined that Holland would have seriously made a common cause with France, Spain and America,

" In order to gain a clear and just idea of the design and end of the government, let us suppose a small number of persons, meeting in some sequestered part of the earth, unconnected with the rest; they will then represent the peopling of any country or of the world. In this state of natural liberty, society will be their first thought. A thousand motives will excite them thereto. The strength of one man is so unequal to his wants, and his mind so unfitted for perpetual solitude, that he is soon obliged to seek assistance of another, who, in his turn, requires the same. Four or five united would be able to raise a tolerable dwelling in the midst of a wilderness; but *one* man might labor out the common period of life, without accomplishing anything; after he had felled his timber, he could not remove it, nor erect it after it was removed—hunger, in the mean time would urge him from his work, and every different want call him a different way. Disease, nay, even misfortune would be death—for al-

" Man, thrown, as it were, by chance upon the globe, surrounded by all the evils of nature, obliged continually to defend and protect his life against the storms and tempests of the air, against the inundations of water, against the fire of volcanoes, against the intemperance of frigid and torrid zones, against the sterility of the earth which refuses him aliment, or its baneful fecundity, which makes poison spring up beneath his feet—in short against the teeth and claws of savage beasts, who dispute with him his habitation and his prey, and, attacking his person, seem resolved to render themselves rulers of this globe, of which he thinks himself to be the master : man, in this state, alone and abandoned to himself, could do nothing for his preservation. It was necessary, therefore, that he should unite himself, and associate with his like, in order to bring together their strength and intelligence in common stock. It is by this union that he has triumphed over so many evils, that he has fashioned

the British ministry would never have dared to provoke them. It would have been a madness in politics to have done so, unless their views were to hasten on a period of such emphatic distress, as should justify the concessions which they saw they must one day or other make to the world, and for which they wanted an apology to themselves. —There is a temper in some men which seeks a pretence for submission. Like a ship disabled in action, and unfitted to continue it, it waits the approach of a still larger one to strike to, and feels relief at the opportunity. Whither this is greatness or littleness of mind, I am not inquiring into. I should suppose it to be the latter, because it proceeds from the want of knowing how to bear misfortune in its original state.

But the subsequent conduct of the British cabinet has shown that this was not their plan of politics, and consequently their motives must be sought for in another line.

though neither might be immediately mortal, yet either of them would disable him from living, and reduce him to a state in which he might rather be said to perish than to die. Thus necessity, like a gravitating power, would form our newly arrived emigrants into society, the reciprocal benefits of which would supersede and render the obligations of law and government unnecessary, while they remained perfectly just to each other. But as nothing but heaven is impregnable to vice, it unavoidably happens, that in proportion as they surmount the first difficulties of emigration, which bound them together in a common cause, they will begin to relax in their duty and attachment to each other, and this remissness will point out the necessity of establishing some form of government to supply the defect of moral virtue."

this globe to his use, restrained the rivers, subjugated the seas, insured his subsistence, conquered a part of the animals in obliging them to serve him, and driven others far from his empire, to the depths of deserts or of woods, where their number diminishes from age to age.—What a man alone would not have been able to effect, men have executed in concert : and altogether they preserve their work. Such is the origin, such the advantages, and the end of society.— Government owes its birth to the necessity of preventing and repressing the injuries which the associated individuals had to fear from one another. It is the sentinel who watches, in order that the common laborers be not disturbed."

Author.

"Common Sense," on its publication, was at once forwarded by the French agent in America to his government. Part of it (the attack on royalism was omitted) was translated in vol. iv. of "Affaires de l'Angleterre et de l'Amerique." —*Editor.*

The truth is, that the British had formed a very humble opinion of the Dutch nation. They looked on them as a people who would submit to any thing; that they might insult them as they liked, plunder them as they pleased, and still the Dutch dared not to be provoked.

If this be taken as the opinion of the British cabinet, the measure is easily accounted for; because it goes on the supposition, that when, by a declaration of hostilities, they had robbed the Dutch of some millions sterling, (and to rob them was popular,) they could make peace with them again whenever they pleased, and on almost any terms the British ministry should propose. And no sooner was the plundering committed, than the accommodation was set on foot and failed.

When once the mind loses the sense of its own dignity, it loses, likewise, the ability of judging of it in another. And the American war has thrown Britain into such a variety of absurd situations, that, arguing from herself, she sees not in what conduct national dignity consists in other countries. From Holland she expected duplicity and submission, and this mistake arose from her having acted, in a number of instances during the present war, the same character herself.

To be allied to, or connected with, Britain seems to be an unsafe and impolitic situation. Holland and America are instances of the reality of this remark. Make those countries the allies of France or Spain, and Britain will court them with civility, and treat them with respect; make them her own allies, and she will insult and plunder them. In the first case, she feels some apprehensions at offending them because they have support at hand; in the latter, those apprehensions do not exist. Such, however, has hitherto been her conduct.

Another measure which has taken place since the publication of the abbe's work, and likewise since the time of my beginning this letter, is the change in the British ministry. What line the new cabinet will pursue respecting America, is, at this time, unknown; neither is it very material, unless they are seriously disposed to a general and honourable peace.

Repeated experience has shown, not only the impracticability of conquering America, but the still higher impossibility of conquering her mind, or recalling her back to her
former condition of thinking.   Since the commencement of
the war, which is now approaching to eight years, thousands
and tens of thousands have advanced, and are daily advancing into the first state of manhood, who know nothing of
Britain but as a barbarous enemy, and to whom the independence of America appears as much the natural and
established government of the country, as that of England
does to an Englishman.   And, on the other hand, thousands
of the aged, who had British ideas, have dropped, and are
daily dropping, from the stage of business and life.   The
natural progress of generation and decay operates every
hour to the disadvantage of Britain.   Time and death, hard
enemies to contend with, fight constantly against her interest ; and the bills of mortality, in every part of America,
are the thermometers of her decline.   The children in the
streets are from their cradle bred to consider her as their
only foe.   They hear of her cruelties ; of their fathers, uncles,
and kindred killed ; they see the remains of burnt and destroyed houses, and the common tradition of the school
they go to, tells them, *those things were done by the British.*

These are circumstances which the mere English state
politician, who considers man only in a state of manhood,
does not attend to.   He gets entangled with parties coeval
or equal with himself at home, and thinks not how fast the
rising generation in America is growing beyond knowledge
of them, or they of him.   In a few years all personal remembrance will be lost, and who is king or minister in
England, will be little known and scarcely inquired after.

The new British administration is composed of persons
who have ever been against the war, and who have constantly reprobated all the violent measures of the former
one.   They considered the American war as destructive to
themselves, and opposed it on that ground.   But what are
these things to America?   She has nothing to do with
English parties.   The ins and the outs are nothing to her.

It is the whole country she is at war with, or must be at peace with.

Were every minister in England a Chatham, it would now weigh little or nothing in the scale of American politics. Death has preserved to the memory of this statesman, *that fame*, which he, by living, would have lost. His plans and opinions, towards the latter part of his life, would have been attended with as many evil consequences, and as much reprobated here as those of lord North; and considering him a wise man, they abound with inconsistencies amounting to absurdities.

It has apparently been the fault of many in the late minority to suppose that America would agree to certain terms with them, were they in place, which she would not even listen to, from the then administration. This idea can answer no other purpose than to prolong the war; and Britain may, at the expense of many more millions, learn the fatality of such mistakes. If the new ministry wisely avoid this hopeless policy, they will prove themselves better pilots and wiser men than they are conceived to be; for it is every day expected to see their bark strike upon some hidden rock and go to pieces.

But there is a line in which they may be great. A more brilliant opening needs not to present itself; and it is such an one as true magnanimity would improve, and humanity rejoice in.

A total reformation is wanted in England. She wants an expanded mind,—a heart which embraces the universe. Instead of shutting herself up in an island, and quarrelling with the world, she would derive more lasting happiness, and acquire more real riches, by generously mixing with it, and bravely saying, I am the enemy of none. It is not now a time for little contrivances or artful politics. The European world is too experienced to be imposed upon, and America too wise to be duped. It must be something new and masterly that can succeed. The idea of seducing America from her independence, or corrupting her from her alliance, is a thought too little for a great mind, and impossible for any honest one, to attempt. Whenever politics are applied to debauch mankind from their integrity, and dissolve the virtue of human nature, they become detestable ; and to be a statesman on this plan, is to be a commissioned villain. He who aims at it, leaves a vacancy in his character, which may be filled up with the worst of epithets.

If the disposition of England should be such, as not to agree to a general and honorable peace, and the war must, at all events, continue longer, I cannot help wishing that the alliances which America has or may enter into, may become the only objects of the war. She wants an opportunity of showing to the world that she holds her honour as dear and sacred as her independence, and that she will in no situation forsake those whom no negotiations could induce to forsake her. Peace, to every reflecting mind, is a desirable object ; but *that peace* which is accompanied with a ruined character, becomes a crime to the seducer, and a curse upon the seduced.

But where is the impossibility or even the great difficulty of England's forming a friendship with France and Spain, and making it a national virtue to renounce for ever those prejudiced inveteracies it has been her custom to cherish ; and which, while they serve to sink her with an increasing enormity of debt, by involving her in fruitless wars, become likewise the bane of her repose, and the destruction of her manners. We had once the fetters that she has now, but experience has shown us the mistake, and thinking justly has set us right.

The true idea of a great nation, is that which extends and promotes the principles of universal society ; whose mind rises above the atmosphere of local thoughts, and considers mankind, of whatever nation or profession they may be, as the work of one Creator. The rage for conquest has had its fashion, and its day. Why may not the amiable virtues have the same? The Alexanders and Cæsars of antiquity have left behind them their monuments of destruction, and are remembered with hatred ; whilst those more exalted characters, who first taught society and sci-

ence, are blest with the gratitude of every age and country. Of more use was *one* philosopher, though a heathen
to the world, than all the heathen conquerors that ever
existed.

Should the present revolution be distinguished by opening a new system of extended civilization, it will receive
from heaven the highest evidence of approbation; and as
this is a subject to which the abbe's powers are so eminently suited, I recommend it to his attention with the
affection of a friend, and the ardour of a universal citizen.

Postscript.

Since closing the foregoing letter, some intimations respecting a general peace have made their way to America.
On what authority or foundation they stand, or how near
or remote such an event may be, are circumstances I am
not inquiring into. But as the subject must sooner or
later become a matter of serious attention, it may not be
improper, even at this early period, candidly to investigate
some points that are connected with it, or lead towards it.

The independence of America is at this moment as firmly
established as that of any other country in a state of war. It
is not length of time, but power that gives stability. Nations
at war, know nothing of each other on the score of antiquity.
It is their present and immediate strength, together with
their connexions, that must support them. To which we
may add, that a right which originated to-day, is as much a
right, as if it had the sanction of a thousand years; and
therefore the independence and present governments of
America are in no more danger of being subverted, because
they are modern, than that of England is secure, because it
is ancient.

The politics of Britain, so far as respects America, were
originally conceived in idiotism, and acted in madness. There
is not a step which bears the smallest trace of rationality.
In her management of the war, she has laboured to be

wretched, and studied to be hated ; and in all her former propositions for accommodation, she has discovered a total ignorance of mankind, and of those natural and unalterable sensations by which they are so generally governed. How she may conduct herself in the present or future business of negotiating a peace, is yet to be proved.

He is a weak politician who does not understand human nature, and penetrate into the effect which measures of government will have upon the mind. All the miscarriages of Britain have arisen from this defect. The former ministry acted as if they supposed mankind to be *without a mind ;* and the present ministry, as if America was *without a memory.* The one must have supposed we were incapable of feeling ; and the other, that we could not remember injuries.

There is likewise another line in which politicians mistake, which is, that of not rightly calculating, or rather of misjudging, the consequences which any given circumstance will produce. Nothing is more frequent, as well in common as in political life, than to hear people complain, that such or such means produced an event directly contrary to their intentions. But the fault lies in their not judging rightly what the event would be ; for the means produced only its proper and natural consequences.

It is very probable that, in a treaty of peace, Britain will contend for some post or other in North-America, perhaps Canada or Halifax, or both : and I infer this from the known deficiency of her politics, which have ever yet made use of means, whose natural event was against both her interest and her expectation. But the question with her ought to be, whether it is worth her while to hold them, and what will be the consequences.

Respecting Canada, one or other of the two following will take place, *viz.* if Canada should become populous, it will revolt ; and if it does not become so, it will not be worth the expense of holding. And the same may be said of Halifax, and the country round it. But Canada *never will* be populous ; neither is there any occasion for contrivances on one side or the other, for nature alone will do the whole.

Britain may put herself to great expenses in sending settlers to Canada; but the descendants of those settlers will be Americans, as others descendants have been before them. They will look round and see the neighboring states sovereign and free, respected abroad and trading at large with the world; and the natural love of liberty, the advantages of commerce, the blessings of independence, and of a happier climate, and a richer soil, will draw them southward; and the effect will be, that Britain will sustain the expense, and America reap the advantage.

One would think that the experience which Britain has had of America, would entirely sicken her of all thoughts of continental colonization, and any part she might retain will only become to her a field of jealousy and thorns, of debate and contention, for ever struggling for privileges, and meditating revolt. She may form new settlements, but they will be for us; they will become part of the United States of America; and that against all her contrivances to prevent it, or without any endeavours of ours to promote it. In the first place she cannot draw from them a revenue, until they are able to pay one, and when they are so they will be above subjection. Men soon become attached to the soil they live upon, and incorporated with the prosperity of the place: and it signifies but little what opinions they come over with, for time, interest, and new connexions will render them obsolete, and the next generation know nothing of them.

Were Britain truly wise, she would lay hold of the present opportunity to disentangle herself from all continental embarrassments in North-America, and that not only to avoid future broils and troubles, but to save expenses. To speak explicitly on the matter, I would not, were I an European power, have Canada, under the conditions that Britain must retain it, could it be given to me. It is one of those kind of dominions that is, and ever will be, a constant charge upon any foreign holder.

As to Halifax, it will become useless to England after the present war, and the loss of the United States. A harbour, when the dominion is gone, for the purpose of which only it was wanted, can be attended only with expense. There are, I doubt not, thousands of people in England, who suppose, that these places are a profit to the nation, whereas they are directly the contrary, and instead of producing any revenue, a considerable part of the revenue of England is annually drawn off, to support the expense of holding them.

Gibraltar is another instance of national ill-policy. A post which in time of peace is not wanted, and in time of war is of no use, must at all times be useless. Instead of affording protection to a navy, it requires the aid of one to maintain it. To suppose that Gibraltar commands the Mediterranean, or the pass into it, or the trade of it, is to suppose a detected falsehood; because though Britain holds the post she has lost the other three, and every benefit she expected from it. And to say that all this happens because it is besieged by land and water, is to say nothing, for this will always be the case in time of war, while France and Spain keep up superior fleets, and Britain holds the place. So that, though, as an impenetrable, inaccessible rock, it may be held by the one, it is always in the power of the other to render it useless and excessively chargeable.

I should suppose that one of the principal objects of Spain in besieging it, is to show to Britain, that though she may not take it, she can command it, that is she can shut it up, and prevent its being used as a harbour, though not as a garrison. But the short way to reduce Gibraltar is to attack the British fleet; for Gibraltar is as dependant on a fleet for support, as a bird is on its wing for food, and when wounded there it starves.

There is another circumstance which the people of England have not only not attended to, but seem to be utterly ignorant of, and that is, the difference between permanent power and accidental power, considered in a national sense.

By permanent power, I mean, a natural, inherent and perpetual ability in a nation, which though always in being, may not be always in action, or not advantageously directed; and by accidental power, I mean, a fortunate or accidental disposition or exercise of national strength, in whole or in part.

There undoubtedly was a time when any one European nation, with only eight or ten ships of war, equal to the present ships of the line, could have carried terror to all others, who had not began to build a navy, however great their natural ability might be for that purpose: but this can be considered only as accidental, and not as a standard to compare permanent power by, and could last no longer than until those powers built as many or more ships than the former. After this a larger fleet was necessary, in order to be superior; and a still larger would again supersede it. And thus mankind have gone on building fleet upon fleet, as occasion or situation dictated. And this reduces it to an original question, which is: Which power can build and man the largest number of ships? The natural answer to which is, that power which has the largest revenue and the greatest number of inhabitants, provided its situation of coast affords sufficient conveniences.

France being a nation on the continent of Europe, and Britain an island in its neighborhood, each of them derived different ideas from their different situations. The inhabitants of Britain could carry on no foreign trade, nor stir from the spot they dwelt upon, without the assistance of shipping; but this was not the case with France. The idea therefore of a navy did not arise to France from the same original and immediate necessity which produced it to England. But the question is, that when both of them turn their attention, and employ their revenues the same way, which can be superior?

The annual revenue of France is nearly double that of England, and her number of inhabitants more than twice as many. Each of them has the same length of coast on the channel, besides which, France has several hundred miles extent on the bay of Biscay, and an opening on the Mediterranean: and every day proves that practice and exercise make sailors, as well as soldiers, in one country as well as another.

If, then, Britain can maintain a hundred ships of the line, France can as well support a hundred and fifty, because her

revenues and her population are as equal to the one, as those
of England are to the other.   And the only reason why she
has not done it, is because she has not till very lately attended
to it.   But when she sees, as she now does, that a navy is the
first engine of power, she can easily accomplish it.

England, very falsely, and ruinously for herself, infers, that
because she had the advantage of France, while France had
the smaller navy, that for that reason it is always to be so.
Whereas it may be clearly seen, that the strength of France
has never yet been tried on a navy, and that she is able to be
as superior to England in the extent of a navy, as she is in the
extent of her revenues and her population.   And England
may lament the day, when, by her insolence and injustice,
she provoked in France a maritime disposition.

It is in the power of the combined fleets to conquer every
island in the West-Indies, and reduce all the British navy in
those places.   For were France and Spain to send their whole
naval force in Europe to those islands, it would not be in the
power of Britain to follow them with an equal force.   She
would still be twenty or thirty ships inferior, were she to send
every vessel she had, and in the meantime all the foreign
trade of England would lay exposed to the Dutch.

It is a maxim which, I am persuaded, will ever hold good,
and more especially in naval operations, that a great power
ought never to move in detachments, if it can possibly be
avoided ; but to go with its whole force to some important
object, the reduction of which shall have a decisive effect
upon the war.   Had the whole of the French and Spanish
fleets in Europe come last spring to the West-Indies, every
island had been their own, Rodney their prisoner, and his
fleet their prize.   From the United States the combined
fleets can be supplied with provisions, without the necessity
of drawing them from Europe, which is not the case with
England.

Accident has thrown some advantages in the way of England, which, from the inferiority of her navy, she had not a
right to expect.   For though she had been obliged to fly
before the combined fleets, yet Rodney has twice had the

fortune to fall in with detached squadrons, to which he was superior in numbers: the first off cape St. Vincent, where he had nearly two to one, and the other in the West-Indies, where he had a majority of six ships. Victories of this kind almost produce themselves. They are won without honour, and suffered without disgrace: and are ascribable to the chance of meeting, not to the superiority of fighting. For the same admiral, under whom they were obtained, was unable, in three former engagements, to make the least impression on a fleet consisting of an equal number of ships with his own, and compounded for the events by declining the actions.*

To conclude: if it may be said that Britain has numerous enemies, it likewise proves that she has given numerous offences. Insolence is sure to provoke hatred, whether in a nation or an individual. That want of manners in the British court may be seen even in its birth-days' and new-years' odes, which are calculated to infatuate the vulgar, and disgust the man of refinement: and her former overbearing rudeness, and insufferable injustice on the seas, have made every commercial nation her foe. Her fleets were employed as engines of prey, and acted on the surface of the deep the character which the shark does beneath it. On the other hand, the combined powers are taking a popular part, and will render their reputation immortal, by establishing the perfect freedom of the ocean, to which all countries have a right, and are interested in accomplishing. The sea is the world's highway; and he who arrogates a prerogative over it, transgresses the right, and justly bring on himself the chastisement of nations.[1]

Perhaps it might be of some service to the future tranquillity of mankind, were an article introduced into the next general peace, that no one nation should, in time of peace,

* See the accounts, either English or French, of three actions, in the West Indies, between count de Guichen and admiral Rodney, in 1780.—*Author*.

[1] Doctor Franklin made an effort to secure recognition of this principle of the freedom and immunity of commerce at sea, and gained the assent of the King of Prussia and of Vergennes. See "Diary of John Hall," in my "Life of Paine," vol. ii., p. 468.—*Editor*.

exceed a certain number of ships of war. Something of this kind seems necessary; for according to the present fashion, half the world will get upon the water, and there appears to be no end to the extent to which navies may be carried. Another reason is, that navies add nothing to the manners or morals of a people. The sequestered life which attends the service, prevents the opportunities of society, and is too apt to occasion a coarseness of ideas and of language, and that more in ships of war than in the commercial employ; because in the latter they mix more with the world, and are nearer related to it. I mention this remark as a general one: and not applied to any one country more than to another.

Britain has now had the trial of above seven years, with an expense of nearly an hundred million pounds sterling; and every month in which she delays to conclude a peace costs her another million sterling, over and above her ordinary expenses of government, which are a million more; so that her total *monthly* expense is two million pounds sterling, which is equal to the whole *yearly* expense of America, all charges included. Judge then who is best able to continue it.[1]

---

[1] The following correspondence took place at this time between Paine and Washington.

BORDENTOWN, Sept. 7, 1782.

SIR,

I have the honour of presenting you with fifty copies of my Letter to the Abbe Raynal, for the use of the army, and to repeat to you my acknowledgments for your friendship.

I fully believe we have seen our worst days over. The spirit of the war, on the part of the enemy, is certainly on the decline, full as much as we think for. I draw this opinion not only from the present promising appearance of things, and the difficulties we know the British cabinet is in; but I add to it the peculiar effect which certain periods of time have, more or less, upon all men.

The British have accustomed themselves to think of *seven years* in a manner different to other portions of time. They acquire this partly by habit, by reason, by religion, and by superstition. They serve seven years apprenticeship —they elect their parliament for seven years—they punish by seven years transportation, or the duplicate or triplicate of that term—they let their leases in the same manner, and they read that Jacob served seven years for one wife, and after that seven years for another; and this particular period of time, by a variety of concurrences, has obtained an influence in their minds.

They have now had seven years of war, and are no further on the Continent than when they began. The superstitious and populous part will therefore con-

She has likewise many atonements to make to an injured world, as well in one quarter as in another. And instead of pursuing that temper of arrogance, which serves only to sink her in the esteem, and entail on her the dislike of all nations,

clude that *it is not to be*, and the rational part of them will think they have tried an unsuccessful and expensive project long enough, and by these two joining issue in the same eventual opinion, the obstinate part among them will be beaten out ; unless, consistent with their former sagacity, they should get over the matter by an act of parliament, " *to bind* TIME *in all cases whatsoever*," *or declare him a rebel.*

I observe the affair of Captain Asgill seems to die away :—very probably it has been protracted on the part of Clinton and Carleton, to gain time, to state the case to the British ministry, where following close on that of Colonel Haynes, it will create new embarrassments to them.—For my own part, I am fully persuaded that a suspension of his fate, still holding it *in terrorem*, will operate on a greater quantity of their passions and vices, and restrain them more than his execution would do.—However, the change of measures which seems now to be taking place, gives somewhat of a new cast to former designs ; and if the case, without the execution, can be so managed as to answer all the purposes of the latter, it will look much better hereafter, when the sensations that now provoke, and the circumstances that would justify his exit, shall be forgotten.

I am your Excellency's obliged and obedient humble servant,

THOMAS PAINE.

His Excellency General WASHINGTON.

HEAD QUARTERS, VERPLANCK'S POINT,
Sept. 18, 1782.

SIR,

I have the pleasure to acknowledge your favour of the 7th inst., informing me of your proposal to present me with fifty copies of your last publication, for the amusement of the army.

For this intention you have my sincere thanks, not only on my own account, but for the pleasure, I doubt not, the gentlemen of the army will receive from the perusal of your pamphlets.

Your observations on the *period of seven years*, as it applies itself to, and affects British minds, are ingenious, and I wish it may not fail of its effects in the present instance. The measures, and the policy of the enemy, are at present in great perplexity and embarrassment—but I have my fears, whether their necessities (which are the only operative motive with them) are yet arrived to that point, which must drive them unavoidably into what they will esteem disagreeable and dishonourable terms of peace—such, for instance, as an absolute, unequivocal admission of American Independence, upon the terms on which she can alone accept it.

For this reason, added to the obstinacy of the king—and the probable consonant principles of some of his principal ministers, I have not so full a confi-

she would do well to reform her manners, retrench her expenses, live peaceably with her neighbours, and think of war no more.

PHILADELPHIA, August 21, 1782.

dence in the success of the present negociation for peace as some gentlemen entertain.

Should events prove my jealousies to be ill founded, I shall make myself happy under the mistake—consoling myself with the idea of having erred on the safest side, and enjoying with as much satisfaction as any of my countrymen, the pleasing issue of our severe contest.

The case of Captain Asgill has indeed been spun out to a great length—but, with you, I hope that its termination will not be unfavourable to this country.[1]

I am, sir, with great esteem and regard, Your most obedient servant,

G. WASHINGTON.

THOMAS PAINE, ESQ.

[1] Concerning Captain Asgill see *ante*, the "Supernumerary Crisis," vol. i., p. 355 and footnote to same, p. 359.—*Editor*.

VI.

DISSERTATIONS

ON GOVERNMENT; THE AFFAIRS OF THE BANK; AND
PAPER MONEY.

PREFACE.

I HERE present the public with a new performance. Some parts of it are more particularly adapted to the state of Pennsylvania, on the present state of its affairs: but there are others which are on a larger scale. The time bestowed on this work has not been long, the whole of it being written and printed during the short recess of the assembly.[1]

As to parties, merely considered as such, I am attached to no particular one. There are such things as right and wrong in the world, and so far as these are parties against each other, the signature of *Common Sense* is properly employed.

THOMAS PAINE.

PHILADELPHIA, Feb. 18, 1786.

[1] That is, between December 22, 1785, and February 18, 1786. Professor W. G. Sumner, in his work on Robert Morris, says that Paine was " hired " by Morris for this work ; but after re-examining his papers, writes me that his statement goes beyond any evidence in his possession. The pamphlet was disinterested and courageous ; it cost Paine valued friendships. See my " Life of Paine," ii., 466.—*Editor*.

DISSERTATIONS ON GOVERNMENT, ETC.

EVERY government, let its form be what it may, contains within itself a principle common to all, which is, that of a sovereign power, or a power over which there is no control, and which controls all others: and as it is impossible to construct a form of government in which this power does not exist, so there must of necessity be a place, if it may be so called, for it to exist in.

In despotic monarchies this power is lodged in a single person, or sovereign. His will is law; which he declares, alters or revokes as he pleases, without being accountable to any power for so doing. Therefore, the only modes of redress, in countries so governed, are by petition or insurrection. And this is the reason we so frequently hear of insurrections in despotic governments; for as there are but two modes of redress, this is one of them.

Perhaps it may be said that as the united ressistance of the people is able, by force, to control the will of the sovereign, that therefore, the controlling power lodges in them; but it must be understood that I am speaking of such powers only as are constituent parts of the government, not of those powers which are externally applied to resist and overturn it.

In republics, such as those established in America, the sovereign power, or the power over which there is no control, and which controls all others, remains where nature placed it—in the people; for the people in America are the fountain of power. It remains there as a matter of right, recognized in the constitutions of the country, and the exercise of it is constitutional and legal. This sovereignty is exercised in electing and deputing a certain number of persons to represent and act for the whole, and who, if they do not act right, may be displaced by the same power that placed them there, and others elected and deputed in their stead, and the wrong measures of former representatives corrected and brought right by this means. Therefore the republican form and principle leaves no room for insurrection, because it provides and establishes a rightful means in its stead.

In countries under a despotic form of government, the exercise of this power is an assumption of sovereignty ; a wresting it from the person in whose hand their form of government has placed it, and the exercise of it is there styled rebellion. Therefore the despotic form of government knows no intermediate space between being slaves and being rebels.

I shall in this place offer an observation which, though not immediately connected with my subject, is very naturally deduced from it, which is that the nature, if I may so call it, of a government over any people, may be ascertained from the modes which the people pursue to obtain redress of grievances ; for like causes will produce like effects. And therefore the government which Britain attempted to erect over America could be no other than a despotism, because it left to the Americans no other modes of redress than those which are left to people under despotic governments, petition and resistance : and the Americans, without ever attending to a comparison on the case, went into the same steps which such people go into, because no other could be pursued : and this similarity of effects leads up to, and ascertains the similarity of the causes or governments which produced them.

But to return. The repository where the sovereign power is placed is the first criterion of distinction between a country under a despotic form of government and a free country. In a country under a despotic government, the sovereign is the only free man in it. In a republic, the people, retaining the sovereignty themselves, naturally and necessarily retain their freedom with it : for wherever the sovereignty is, there must the freedom be.

As the repository where the sovereign power is lodged is the first criterion of distinction, so the second is the principles on which it is administered.

A despotic government knows no principle but *will.*—
Whatever the sovereign wills to do, the government admits
him the inherent right, and the uncontrolled power of doing.
He is restrained by no fixed rule of right and wrong, for he
makes the right and wrong himself, and as he pleases.   If
he happens (for a miracle may happen) to be a man of consummate wisdom, justice and moderation, of a mild affectionate disposition, disposed to business, and understanding and
promoting the general good, all the beneficial purposes of
government will be answered under his administration, and
the people so governed, may, while this is the case, be prosperous and easy.   But as there can be no security that this
disposition will last, and this administration continue, and
still less security that his successor shall have the same
qualities and pursue the same measures ; therefore no people
exercising their reason, and understanding their rights,
would, of their own choice, invest any one man with such
a power.

Neither is it consistent to suppose the knowledge of any
one man competent to the exercise of such a power.   A
sovereign of this sort, is brought up in such a distant line of
life ; lives so remote from the people, and from a knowledge
of everything which relates to their local situations and
interests, that he can know nothing from experience and
observation, and all which he does know he must be told.
Sovereign power without sovereign knowledge, that is, a full
knowledge of all the matters over which that power is to be
exercised, is a something which contradicts itself.

There is a species of sovereign power in a single person,
which is very proper when applied to a commander-in-chief
over an army, so far as relates to the military government
of an army, and the condition and purpose of an army constitute the reason why it is so.   In an army every man is of
the same profession, that is, he is a soldier, and the commander-in-chief is a soldier too : therefore the knowledge
necessary to the exercise of the power is within himself.   By
understanding what a soldier is, he comprehends the local
situation, interest and duty of every man within what may

be called the dominion of his command; and, therefore, the condition and circumstances of an army make a fitness for the exercise of the power.

The purpose, likewise, or object of an army, is another reason: for this power in a commander-in-chief, though exercised over the army, is not exercised against it; but is exercised through or over the army against the enemy. Therefore the enemy, and not the people, is the object it is directed to. Neither is it exercised over an army for the purpose of raising a revenue from it, but to promote its combined interest, condense its powers, and give it capacity for action.

But all these reasons cease when sovereign power is transferred from the commander of an army to the commander of a nation, and entirely loses its fitness when applied to govern subjects following occupations, as it governs soldiers following arms. A nation is quite another element, and every thing in it differs not only from each other, but all of them differ from those of an army. A nation is composed of distinct, unconnected individuals, following various trades, employments and pursuits: continually meeting, crossing, uniting, opposing and separating from each other, as accident, interest and circumstance shall direct. An army has but one occupation and but one interest.

Another very material matter in which an army and a nation differ, is that of temper. An army may be said to have but one temper; for however the *natural* temper of the persons composing the army may differ from each other, there is a second temper takes place of the first: a temper formed by discipline, mutuality of habits, union of objects and pursuits, and the style of military manners: but this can never be the case among all the individuals of a nation. Therefore the fitness, arising from those circumstances, which disposes an army to the command of a single person, and the fitness of a single person for that command, is not to be found either in one or the other, when we come to consider them as a sovereign and a nation.

Having already shown what a despotic government is, and

how it is administered, I now come to show what the administration of a republic is.

The administration of a republic is supposed to be directed by certain fundamental principles of right and justice, from which there cannot, because there ought not to be any deviation ; and whenever any deviation appears, there is a kind of stepping out of the republican principle, and an approach towards the despotic one. This administration is executed by a select number of persons, periodically chosen by the people, who act as representatives and in behalf of the whole, and who are supposed to enact the same laws, and pursue the same line of administration, as the people would do were they all assembled together.

The *public good* is to be their object. It is therefore necessary to understand what public good is.

Public good is not a term opposed to the good of individuals ; on the contrary, it is the good of every individual collected. It is the good of all, because it is the good of every one : for as the public body is every individual collected, so the public good is the collected good of those individuals.

The foundation-principle of public good is justice, and wherever justice is impartially administered the public good is promoted ; for as it is to the good of every man that no injustice be done to him, so likewise it is to his good that the principle which secures him should not be violated in the person of another, because such a violation weakens *his* security, and leaves to chance what ought to be to him a rock to stand on.

But in order to understand more minutely, how the public good is to be promoted, and the manner in which the representatives are to act to promote it, we must have recourse to the original or first principles, on which the people formed themselves into a republic.

When a people agree to form themselves into a republic (for the word *republic* means the *public good*, or the good of the whole, in contradistinction to the despotic form, which makes the good of the sovereign, or of one man, the only object of the government), when I say, they agree to do this, it is to be understood, that they mutually resolve and pledge themselves to each other, rich and poor alike, to support and maintain this rule of equal justice among them. They therefore renounce not only the despotic form, but the despotic principle, as well of governing as of being governed by mere will and power, and substitute in its place a government of justice.

By this mutual compact, the citizens of a republic put it out of their power, that is, they renounce, as detestable, the power of exercising, at any future time, any species of despotism over each other, or doing a thing not right in itself, because a majority of them may have strength of numbers sufficient to accomplish it.

In this pledge and compact * lies the foundation of the republic: and the security to the rich and the consolation to

---

* This pledge and compact is contained in the declaration of rights prefixed to the constitution [of Pennsylvania], and is as follows :

I. That all men are born equally free and independent, and have certain natural, inherent and unalienable rights, amongst which are, the enjoying and defending life and liberty, acquiring, possessing and protecting property, and pursuing and obtaining happiness and safety.

II. That all men have a natural and unalienable right to worship almighty God, according to the dictates of their own consciences and understanding : and that no man ought or of right can be compelled to attend any religious worship, or erect or support any place of worship, or maintain any ministry, contrary to, or against, his own free will and consent : nor can any man, who acknowledges the being of a God, be justly deprived or abridged of any civil right as a citizen, on account of his religious sentiments or peculiar mode of religious worship : and that no authority can or ought to be vested in, or assumed by, any power whatever, that shall in any case interfere with, or in any manner control, the right of conscience in the free exercise of religious worship.

III. That the people of this state have the sole, exclusive and inherent right of governing and regulating the internal police of the same.

IV. That all power being originally inherent in, and consequently derived from, the people ; therefore, all officers of government, whether legislative or executive, are their trustees and servants, and at all times accountable to them.

V. That government is, or ought to be, instituted for the common benefit, protection and security of the people, nation or community ; and not for the particular emolument or advantage of any single man, family, or set of men, who are a part only of that community : and that the community hath an indubitable, unalienable and indefeasible right to reform, alter or abolish govern-

the poor is, that what each man has is his own ; that no despotic sovereign can take it from him, and that the common cementing principle which holds all the parts of a republic together, secures him likewise from the despotism of numbers : for despotism may be more effectually acted by many over a few, than by one man over all.

Therefore, in order to know how far the power of an assembly, or a house of representatives can act in administering the affairs of a republic, we must examine how far the power of the people extends under the original compact they have made with each other; for the power of the representatives is in many cases less, but never can be greater than that of the people represented ; and whatever the people in their mutual original compact have renounced the power of doing

ment in such manner as shall be by that community judged most conducive to the public weal.

VI. That those who are employed in the legislative and executive business of the state may be restrained from oppression, the people have a right, at such periods as they may think proper, to reduce their public officers to a private station, and supply the vacancies by certain and regular elections.

VII. That all elections ought to be free ; and that all free men having a sufficient evident common interest with, and attachment to the community, have a right to elect officers, or to be elected into office.

VIII. That every member of society hath a right to be protected in the enjoyment of life, liberty and property, and therefore is bound to contribute his proportion towards the expense of that protection, and yield his personal service when necessary, or an equivalent thereto; but no part of a man's property can be justly taken from him, or applied to public uses, without his own consent, or that of his legal representatives : nor can any man who is conscientiously scrupulous of bearing arms, be justly compelled thereto, if he will pay such equivalent : nor are the people bound by any laws, but such as they have in like manner assented to, for their common good.

IX. That in all prosecutions for criminal offences, a man hath a right to be heard by himself and his counsel, to demand the cause and nature of his accusation, to be confronted with the witnesses, to call for evidence in his favour, and a speedy public trial, by an impartial jury of the country, without the unanimous consent of which jury he cannot be found guilty : nor can he be compelled to give evidence against himself ; nor can any man be justly deprived of his liberty, except by the laws of the land, or the judgment of his peers.

X. That the people have a right to hold themselves, their houses, papers, and possessions free from search or seizure ; and therefore warrants without oaths or affirmations, first made, affording a sufficient foundation for them,

towards, or acting over each other, the representatives cannot assume the power to do, because, as I have already said, the power of the representatives cannot be greater than that of the people they represent.

In this place it naturally presents itself that the people in their original compact of equal justice or first principles of a republic, renounced, as despotic, detestable and unjust, the assuming a right of breaking and violating their engagements, contracts and compacts with, or defrauding, imposing or tyrannizing over each other, and therefore the representatives cannot make an act to do it for them, and any such kind of act would be an attempt to depose not the personal sovereign, but the sovereign principle of the republic, and to introduce despotism in its stead.

and whereby any officer or messenger may be commanded or required to search suspected places, or to seize any person or persons, his or their property, not particularly described, are contrary to that right, and ought not to be granted.

XI. That in controversies respecting property, and in suits between man and man, the parties have a right to trial by jury, which ought to be held sacred.

XII. That the people have a right to freedom of speech, and of writing and publishing their sentiments : therefore the freedom of the press ought not to be restrained.

XIII. That the people have a right to bear arms for the defence of themselves and the state—and as standing armies, in the time of peace, are dangerous to liberty, they ought not to be kept up—and that the military should be kept under a strict subordination to, and governed by, the civil power.

XIV. That a frequent recurrence to fundamental principles, and a firm adherence to justice, moderation, temperance, industry and frugality are absolutely necessary to preserve the blessings of liberty and keep a government free—the people ought therefore to pay particular attention to these points in the choice of officers and representatives, and have a right to exact a due and constant regard to them, from their legislators and magistrates, in the making and executing such laws as are necessary for the good government of the state.

XV. That all men have a natural inherent right to emigrate from one state to another that will receive them, or to form a new state in vacant countries, or in such countries as they can purchase, whenever they think that thereby they may promote their own happiness.

XVI. That the people have a right to assemble together, to consult for their common good, to instruct their representatives, and to apply to the legislature for redress of grievances, by address, petition, or remonstrance.—*Author.*

It may in this place be proper to distinguish between that species of sovereignty which is claimed and exercised by despotic monarchs, and that sovereignty which the citizens of a republic inherit and retain. The sovereignty of a despotic monarch assumes the power of making wrong right, or right wrong, as he pleases or as it suits him. The sovereignty in a republic is exercised to keep right and wrong in their proper and distinct places, and never suffer the one to usurp the place of the other. A republic, properly understood, is a sovereignty of justice, in contradistinction to a sovereignty of will.

Our experience in republicanism is yet so slender, that it is much to be doubted, whether all our public laws and acts are consistent with, or can be justified on, the principles of a republican government.

We have been so much habited to act in committees at the commencement of the dispute, and during the interregnum of government, and in many cases since, and to adopt expedients warranted by necessity, and to permit to ourselves a discretionary use of power, suited to the spur and exigency of the moment, that a man transferred from a committee to a seat in the legislature, imperceptibly takes with him the ideas and habits he has been accustomed to, and continues to think like a committee-man instead of a legislator, and to govern by the spirit rather than by the rule of the constitution and the principles of the republic.

Having already stated that the power of the representatives can never exceed the power of the people whom they represent, I now proceed to examine more particularly, what the power of the representatives is.

It is, in the first place, the power of acting as legislators in making laws—and in the second place, the power of acting in certain cases, as agents or negotiators for the commonwealth, for such purposes as the circumstances of the commonwealth require.

A very strange confusion of ideas, dangerous to the credit, stability, and the good and honor of the commonwealth, has arisen, by confounding those two distinct powers and things together, and blending every act of the assembly, of whatever kind it may be, under one general name, of *Laws of the Commonwealth*, and thereby creating an opinion (which is truly of the despotic kind) that every succeeding assembly has an equal power over every transaction, as well as law, done by a former assembly.

All laws are acts, but all acts are not laws. Many of the acts of the assembly are acts of agency or negociation, that is they are acts of contract and agreement, on the part of the state, with certain persons therein mentioned, and for certain purposes therein recited. An act of this kind, after it has passed the house, is of the nature of a deed or contract, signed, sealed and delivered; and subject to the same general laws and principles of justice as all other deeds and contracts are: for in a transaction of this kind, the state stands as an individual, and can be known in no other character in a court of justice.

By "*laws*," as distinct from the agency transactions, or matters of negociation, are to be comprehended all those public acts of the assembly or commonwealth, which have a universal operation, or apply themselves to every individual of the commonwealth. Of this kind are the laws for the distribution and administration of justice, for the preservation of the peace, for the security of property, for raising the necessary revenue by just proportions, &c.

Acts of this kind are properly *laws*, and they may be altered, amended and repealed, or others substituted in their places, as experience shall direct, for the better effecting the purpose for which they were intended: and the right and power of the assembly to do this is derived from the right and power which the people, were they all assembled together, instead of being represented, would have to do the same thing: because, in acts or laws of this kind, there is no other party than the public. The law, or the alteration, or the repeal, is for themselves;—and whatever the effects may be, it falls on themselves;—if for the better, they have the benefit of it—if for the worse, they suffer the inconvenience. No violence to any one is here offered—no breach of faith is here committed. It is therefore one of those rights and powers which is within the sense, meaning and limits of the original compact of justice which they formed with each other as the foundation-principle of the republic, and being one of those rights and powers, it devolves on their representatives by delegation.

As it is not my intention (neither is it within the limits assigned to this work) to define every species of what may be called *laws* (but rather to distinguish that part in which the representatives act as agents or negotiators for the state from the legislative part,) I shall pass on to distinguish and describe those acts of the assembly which are acts of agency or negotiation, and to show that as they are different in their nature, construction and operation, from legislative acts, so likewise the power and authority of the assembly over them, after they are passed, is different.

It must occur to every person on the first reflection, that the affairs and circumstances of a commonwealth require other business to be done besides that of making laws, and, consequently, that the different kinds of business cannot all be classed under one name, or be subject to one and the same rule of treatment.—But to proceed—

By agency transactions, or matters of negociation, done by the assembly, are to be comprehended all that kind of public business, which the assembly, as representatives of the republic, transact in its behalf, with a certain person or persons, or part or parts of the republic, for purposes mentioned in the act, and which the assembly confirm and ratify on the part of the commonwealth, by affixing to it the seal of the state.

An act of this kind, differs from a law of the before-mentioned kind; because here are two parties and there but one, and the parties are bound to perform different and distinct parts: whereas, in the before-mentioned law, every man's part was the same.

These acts, therefore, though numbered among the laws, are evidently distinct therefrom, and are not of the legislative kind. The former are laws for the government of the commonwealth; these are transactions of business, such as, selling and conveying an estate belonging to the public, or buying one; acts for borrowing money, and fixing with the lender the terms and modes of payment; acts of agreement and contract, with a certain person or persons, for certain purposes: and, in short, every act in which two parties, the state being one, are particularly mentioned or described, and in which the form and nature of a bargain or contract is comprehended.—These, if for custom and uniformity sake we call them by the name of *laws*, are not laws for the government of the commonwealth, but for the government of the contracting parties, as all deeds and contracts are; and are not, properly speaking, acts of the assembly, but joint acts, or acts of the assembly in behalf of the commonwealth on one part, and certain persons therein mentioned on the other part.

Acts of this kind are distinguishable into two classes:—

1st, Those wherein the matters inserted in the act have already been settled and adjusted between the state on one part, and the persons therein mentioned on the other part. In this case the act is the completion and ratification of the contract or matters therein recited. It is in fact a deed signed, sealed and delivered.

2d, Those acts wherein the matters have not been already agreed upon, and wherein the act only holds forth certain propositions and terms to be accepted of and acceded to.

I shall give an instance of each of those acts. First, the state wants the loan of a sum of money—certain persons make an offer to government to lend that sum, and send in their proposals: the government accept these proposals, and all the matters of the loan and the payment are agreed on; and an act is passed according to the usual form of passing acts, ratifying and confirming this agreement. This act is final.

In the second case,—the state, as in the preceding one, wants a loan of money—the assembly passes an act holding forth the terms on which it will borrow and pay: this act has no force until the propositions and terms are accepted of and acceded to by some person or persons, and when those terms are accepted of and complied with, the act is binding on the state.—But if at the meeting of the next assembly, or any other, the whole sum intended to be borrowed, should not be borrowed, that assembly may stop where they are, and discontinue proceeding with the loan, or make new propositions and terms for the remainder; but so far as the subscriptions have been filled up, and the terms complied with, it is, as in the first case, a signed deed : and in the same manner are all acts, let the matters in them be what they may, wherein, as I have before mentioned, the state on one part, and certain individuals on the other part, are parties in the act.

If the state should become a bankrupt, the creditors, as in all cases of bankruptcy, will be sufferers; they will have but a dividend for the whole : but this is not a dissolution of the contract, but an accommodation of it, arising from necessity. And so in all cases of this kind, if an inability takes place on either side, the contract cannot be performed, and some accommodation must be gone into, or the matter falls through of itself.

It may likewise, though it ought not to, happen that in performing the matters, agreeably to the terms of the act, inconveniences, unforeseen at the time of making the act, may arise to either or both parties : in this case, those inconveniences may be removed by the mutual consent and agreement of the parties, and each finds its benefit in so doing : for in a republic it is the harmony of its parts that constitutes their several and mutual good.

But the acts themselves are legally binding, as much as if they had been made between two private individuals. The greatness of one party cannot give it a superiority or advantage over the other. The state, or its representatives, the assembly, has no more power over an act of this kind, after it has passed, than if the state was a private person. It is the glory of a republic to have it so, because it secures the individual from becoming the prey of power, and prevents *might* from overcoming *right*.

If any difference or dispute arise afterwards between the state and the individuals with whom the agreement is made respecting the contract, or the meaning, or extent of any of the matters contained in the act, which may affect the property or interest of either, such difference or dispute must be judged of, and decided upon, by the laws of the land, in a court of justice and trial by jury ; that is, by the laws of the land already in being at the time such act and contract was made.—No law made afterwards can apply to the case, either directly, or by construction or implication: for such a law would be a retrospective law, or a law made after the fact, and cannot even be produced in court as applying to the case before it for judgment.

That this is justice, that it is the true principle of republican government, no man will be so hardy as to deny.—If, therefore, a lawful contract or agreement, sealed and ratified, cannot be affected or altered by any act made afterwards, how much more inconsistent and irrational, despotic and unjust would it be, to think of making an act with the professed intention of breaking up a contract already signed and sealed.

That it is possible an assembly, in the heat and indiscretion of party, and meditating on power rather than on the principle by which all power in a republican government is governed, that of equal justice, may fall into the error of passing such an act, is admitted ;—but it would be an actless act, an act that goes for nothing, an act which the courts of justice, and the established laws of the land, could know nothing of.

Because such an act would be an act of one party only, not only without, but against the consent of the other ; and, therefore, cannot be produced to affect a contract made between the two.—That the violation of a contract should be set up as a justification to the violator, would be the same thing as to say, that a man by breaking his promise is freed from the obligation of it, or that by transgressing the laws, he exempts himself from the punishment of them.

Besides the constitutional and legal reasons why an

assembly cannot, of its own act and authority, undo or make void a contract made between the state (by a former assembly) and certain individuals, may be added what may be called the natural reasons, or those reasons which the plain rules of common sense point out to every man. Among which are the following:

The principals, or real parties in the contract, are the state and the persons contracted with. The assembly is not a party, but an agent in behalf of the state, authorised and empowered to transact its affairs.

Therefore it is the state that is bound on one part and certain individuals on the other part, and the performance of the contract, according to the conditions of it, devolves on succeeding assemblies, not as principals, but as agents.

Therefore, for the next or any other assembly to undertake to dissolve the state from its obligation is an assumption of power of a novel and extraordinary kind.—It is the servant attempting to free his master.

The election of new assemblies following each other makes no difference in the nature of the thing. The state is still the same state. The public is still the same body. These do not annually expire though the time of an assembly does. These are not new-created every year, nor can they be displaced from their original standing; but are a perpetual, permanent body, always in being and still the same.

But if we adopt the vague, inconsistent idea that every new assembly has a full and complete authority over every act done by the state in a former assembly, and confound together laws, contracts, and every species of public business, it will lead us into a wilderness of endless confusion and insurmountable difficulties. It would be declaring an assembly despotic for the time being.—Instead of a government of established principles administered by established rules, the authority of government by being strained so high, would, by the same rule, be reduced proportionably as low, and would be no other than that of a committee of the state, acting with discretionary powers for one year. Every new election would be a new revolution, or it would suppose the public of the former year dead and a new public in its place.

Having now endeavoured to fix a precise idea to, and distinguish between legislative acts and acts of negotiation and agency, I shall proceed to apply this distinction to the case now in dispute, respecting the charter of the bank.

The charter of the bank, or what is the same thing, the act for incorporating it, is to all intents and purposes an act of negotiation and contract, entered into, and confirmed between the state on one part, and certain persons mentioned therein on the other part. The purpose for which the act was done on the part of the state is therein recited, *viz.* the support which the finances of the country would derive therefrom. The incorporating clause.is the condition or obligation on the part of the state; and the obligation on the part of the bank, is "that nothing contained in that act shall be construed to authorise the said corporation to exercise any powers in this state repugnant to the laws or constitution thereof."

Here are all the marks and evidences of a contract. The parties—the purport—and the reciprocal obligations.

That this is a contract, or a joint act, is evident from its being in the power of either of the parties to have forbidden or prevented its being done. The state could not force the stockholders of the bank to be a corporation, and therefore as their consent was necessary to the making the act, their dissent would have prevented its being made; so on the other hand, as the bank could not force the state to incorporate them, the consent or dissent of the state would have had the same effect to do, or to prevent its being done; and as neither of the parties could make the act alone, for the same reason can neither of them dissolve it alone: but this is not the case with a law or act of legislation, and therefore the difference proves it to be an act of a different kind.

The bank may forfeit the charter by delinquency, but the delinquency must be proved and established by a legal process in a court of justice and trial by jury; for the state, or the assembly, is not to be a judge in its own case, but must come to the laws of the land for judgment ; for that which is law for the individual, is likewise law for the state.

Before I enter further into this affair, I shall go back to the circumstances of the country, and the condition the government was in, for some time before, as well as at the time it entered into this engagement with the bank, and this act of incorporation was passed : for the government of this state, and I suppose the same of the rest, were then in want of two of the most essential matters which governments could be destitute of—money and credit.

In looking back to those times, and bringing forward some of the circumstances attending them, I feel myself entering on unpleasant and disagreeable ground ; because some of the matters which the attacks on the bank now make it necessary to state, in order to bring the affair fully before the public, will not add honour to those who have promoted that measure and carried it through the late house of assembly ; and for whom, though my own judgment and opinion on the case oblige me to differ from, I retain my esteem, and the social remembrance of times past.   But, I trust, those gentlemen will do me the justice to recollect my exceeding earnestness with them, last spring, when the attack on the bank first broke out ; for it clearly appeared to me one of those overheated measures, which, neither the country at large, nor their own constituents, would justify them in, when it came to be fully understood ; for however high a party measure may be carried in an assembly, the people out of doors are all the while following their several occupations and employments, minding their farms and their business, and take their own time and leisure to judge of public measures; the consequence of which is, that they often judge in a cooler spirit than their representatives act in.

It may be easily recollected that the present bank was preceded by, and rose out of a former one, called the Pennsylvania bank which began a few months before ; the occasion of which I shall briefly state.

In the spring of 1780, the Pennsylvania assembly was composed of many of the same members, and nearly all of the same connexion, which composed the late house that began the attack on the bank. I served as clerk of the assembly of 1780, which station I resigned at the end of the year, and accompanied a much lamented friend, the late colonel John Laurens, on an embassy to France.

The spring of 1780 was marked with an accumulation of misfortunes. The reliance placed on the defence of Charleston failed, and exceedingly lowered or depressed the spirits of the country. The measures of government, from the want of money, means and credit, dragged on like a heavy loaded carriage without wheels, and were nearly got to what a countryman would understand by a dead pull.

The assembly of that year met, by adjournment, at an unusual time, the 10th of May, and what particularly added to the affliction, was, that so many of the members, instead of spiriting up their constituents to the most nervous exertions, came to the assembly furnished with petitions to be exempt from paying taxes. How the public measures were to be carried on, the country defended, and the army recruited, clothed, fed, and paid, when the only resource, and that not half sufficient, that of taxes, should be relaxed to almost nothing, was a matter too gloomy to look at. A language very different from that of petitions ought at this time to have been the language of every one. A declaration to have stood forth with their lives and fortunes, and a reprobation of every thought of partial indulgence would have sounded much better than petitions.

While the assembly was sitting, a letter from the commander-in-chief was received by the executive council and transmitted to the house. The doors were shut, and it fell officially to me to read.

In this letter the naked truth of things was unfolded. Among other informations, the general said, that notwithstanding his confidence in the attachment of the army to the cause of the country, the distress of it, from the want of every necessary which men could be destitute of, had arisen to such a pitch, that the appearances of mutiny and discontent were so strongly marked on the countenance of the army, that he dreaded the event of every hour.

When the letter was read, I observed a despairing silence in the house. Nobody spoke for a considerable time. At length a member, of whose fortitude to withstand misfortunes I had a high opinion, rose: "If," said he, "the account in that letter is a true state of things, and we are in the situation there represented, it appears to me in vain to contend the matter any longer. We may as well give up at first as at last."

The gentleman who spoke next, was (to the best of my recollection) a member of Bucks county, who, in a cheerful note, endeavored to dissipate the gloom of the house—"Well, well," said he, "don't let the house despair, if things are not so well as we wish, we must endeavour to make them better." And on a motion for adjournment, the conversation went no further.

There was now no time to lose, and something absolutely necessary to be done, which was not within the immediate power of the house to do; for what with the depreciation of the currency, and slow operation of taxes, and the petitions to be exempted therefrom, the treasury was moneyless, and the government creditless.

If the assembly could not give the assistance which the necessity of the case immediately required, it was very proper the matter should be known by those who either could or would endeavor to do it. To conceal the information within the house, and not provide the relief which that information required, was making no use of the knowledge, and endangering the public cause. The only thing that now remained, and was capable of reaching the case, was private credit, and the voluntary aid of individuals; and under this impression, on my return from the house, I drew out the salary due to me as clerk, enclosed five hundred dollars to a gentleman in this city, in part of the whole, and wrote fully to him on the subject of our affairs.

The gentleman to whom this letter was addressed is Mr. Blair M'Clenaghan. I mentioned to him, that notwithstanding the current opinion that the enemy were beaten from before Charleston, there were too many reasons to believe the place was then taken and in the hands of the enemy : the consequence of which would be, that a great part of the British force would return, and join at New-York. That our own army required to be augmented, ten thousand men, to be able to stand against the combined force of the enemy. I informed Mr. M'Clenaghan of general Washington's letter, the extreme distresses he was surrounded with, and the absolute occasion there was for the citizens to exert themselves at this time, which there was no doubt they would do, if the necessity was made known to them ; for that the ability of government was exhausted. I requested Mr. M'Clenaghan to propose a voluntary subscription among his friends, and added, that I had enclosed five hundred dollars as my mite thereto, and that I would increase it as far as the last ability would enable me to go.*

The next day Mr. M'Clenaghan informed me that he had communicated the contents of the letter at a meeting of gentlemen at the coffee-house, and that a subscription was immediately began ; that Mr. Robert Morris and himself had subscribed two hundred pounds each, in hard money, and that the subscription was going on very successfully. This subscription was intended as a donation, and to be given in bounties to promote the recruiting service. It is dated June 8th, 1780. The original subscription list is now in my possession—it amounts to four hundred pounds hard money, and one hundred and one thousand three hundred and sixty pounds continental.

While this subscription was going forward, information of the loss of Charleston arrived,† and on a communication from several members of congress to certain gentlemen of this city, of the increasing distresses and dangers then taking place, a meeting was held of the subscribers, and such other

---

* Mr. M'Clenaghan being now returned from Europe, has my consent to show this letter to any gentleman who may be inclined to see it.—*Author*.

† Colonel Tennant, aid to general Lincoln, arrived the 14th of June, with despatches of the capitulation of Charleston.—*Author*.

gentlemen who chose to attend, at the city tavern. This meeting was on the 17th of June, nine days after the subscriptions had begun.

At this meeting it was resolved to open a security-subscription, to the amount of three hundred thousand pounds, Pennsylvania currency, in real money ; the subscribers to execute bonds to the amount of their subscriptions, and to form a bank thereon for supplying the army. This being resolved on and carried into execution, the plan of the first subscriptions was discontinued, and this extended one established in its stead.

By means of this bank the army was supplied through the campaign, and being at the same time recruited, was enabled to maintain its ground ; and on the appointment of Mr. Morris to be superintendent of the finances the spring following, he arranged the system of the present bank, styled the bank of North America, and many of the subscribers of the former bank tranferred their subscriptions into this.

Towards the establishment of this bank, congress passed an ordinance of incorporation, December 21st, which the government of Pennsylvania recognized by sundry matters : and afterwards, on an application of the president and directors of the bank, through the mediation of the executive council, the assembly agreed to, and passed the state act of incorporation April 1st, 1782.

Thus arose the bank—produced by the distresses of the times and the enterprising spirit of patriotic individuals.— Those individuals furnished and risked the money, and the aid which the government contributed was that of incorporating them.—It would have been well if the State had made all its bargains and contracts with as much true policy as it made this : for a greater service for so small a consideration, that only of an act of incorporation, has not been obtained since the government existed.

Having now shown how the bank originated, I shall proceed with my remarks.

The sudden restoration of public and private credit, which took place on the establishment of the bank, is an event as extraordinary in itself as any domestic occurence during the progress of the revolution.

How far a spirit of envy might operate to produce the attack on the bank during the sitting of the late assembly, is best known and felt by those who began or promoted the attack. The bank had rendered services which the assembly of 1780 could not, and acquired an honour which many of its members might be unwilling to own, and wish to obscure.

But surely every government, acting on the principles of patriotism and public good, would cherish an institution capable of rendering such advantages to the community. The establishment of the bank in one of the most trying vicissitudes of the war, its zealous services in the public cause, its influence in restoring and supporting credit, and the punctuality with which all its business has been transacted, are matters, that so far from meriting the treatment it met with from the late assembly, are an honour to the state, and what the body of her citizens may be proud to own.

But the attack on the bank, as a chartered institution, under the protection of its violators, however criminal it may be as an error of government, or impolitic as a measure of party, is not to be charged on the constituents of those who made the attack. It appears from every circumstance that has come to light, to be a measure which that assembly contrived of itself. The members did not come charged with the affair from their constituents. There was no idea of such a thing when they were elected or when they met. The hasty and precipitate manner in which it was hurried through the house, and the refusal of the house to hear the directors of the bank in its defence, prior to the publication of the repealing bill for public consideration, operated to prevent their constituents comprehending the subject: therefore, whatever may be wrong in the proceedings lies not at the door of the public. The house took the affair on its own shoulders, and whatever blame there is, lies on them.

The matter must have been prejudged and predetermined

by a majority of the members out of the house, before it was brought into it.   The whole business appears to have been fixed at once, and all reasoning or debate on the case rendered useless.

Petitions from a very inconsiderable number of persons, suddenly procured, and so privately done, as to be a secret among the few that signed them, were presented to the house and read twice in one day, and referred to a committee of the house to *inquire* and report thereon.   I here subjoin the petition * and the report, and shall exercise the right

---

* Minutes of the assembly, March 21, 1785.   Petitions from a considerable number of the inhabitants of *Chester* county were read, representing that the bank established at *Philadelphia* has fatal effects upon the community ; that whilst men are enabled, by means of the bank, to receive near three times the rate of common interest, and at the same time receive their money at very short warning, whenever they have occasion for it, it will be impossible for the husbandman or mechanic to borrow on the former terms of legal interest and distant payments of the principal ; that the best security will not enable the person to borrow : that experience clearly demonstrates the mischievous consequences of this institution to the fair trader ; that imposters have been enabled to support themselves in a fictitious credit, by means of a temporary punctuality at the bank, until they have drawn in their honest neighbours to trust them with their property, or to pledge their credit as sureties, and have been finally involved in ruin and distress ; that they have repeatedly seen the stopping of discounts at the bank operate on the trading part of the community, with a degree of violence scarcely inferior to that of a stagnation of the blood in the human body, hurrying the wretched merchant who hath debts to pay into the hands of griping usurers : that the directors of the bank may give such preference in trade, by advances of money, to their particular favourites, as to destroy that equality which ought to prevail in a commercial country ; that paper money has often proved beneficial to the state, but the bank forbids it, and the people must acquiesce : therefore, and in order to restore public confidence and private security, they pray that a bill may be brought in and passed into a law for repealing the law for incorporating the bank.

March 28.   The report of the committee, read March 25, on the petitions from the counties of *Chester* and *Berks*, and the city of *Philadelphia* and its vicinity, praying the act of the assembly, whereby the bank was established at *Philadelphia*, may be repealed, was read the second time as follows—*viz.*

The committee to whom was referred the petitions concerning the bank established at *Philadelphia*, and who were instructed to inquire whether the said bank be compatible with the public safety, and that equality which ought ever to prevail between the individuals of a republic, beg leave to report, that it is the opinion of this committee that the said bank, as at present established,

and privilege of a citizen in examining their merits, not for the purpose of opposition, but with a design of making an intricate affair more generally and better understood.

So far as my private judgment is capable of comprehending the subject, it appears to me, that the committee were unacquainted with, and have totally mistaken, the nature and business of a bank, as well as the matter committed to them, considered as a proceeding of government.

They were instructed by the house to *inquire* whether the bank established at Philadelphia was compatible with the public safety. It is scarcely possible to suppose the instructions meant no more than that they were to inquire of one another. It is certain they made no inquiry at the bank, to inform themselves of the situation of its affairs, how they were conducted, what aids it had rendered the public cause, or whether any; nor do the committee produce in their report a single fact or circumstance to show that they made any inquiry at all, or whether the rumours then circulated were true or false; but content themselves with modelling the insinuations of the petitions into a report and giving an opinion thereon. It would appear from the report, that

is in every view incompatible with the public safety—that in the present state of our trade, the said bank has a direct tendency to banish a great part of the specie from the country, so as to produce a scarcity of money, and to collect into the hands of the stockholders of the said bank, almost the whole of the money which remains amongst us. That the accumulation of enormous wealth in the hands of a society, who claim perpetual duration, will necessarily produce a degree of influence and power, which cannot be intrusted in the hands of any set of men whatsoever, without endangering the public safety. That the said bank, in its corporate capacity, is empowered to hold estates to the amount of ten millions of dollars, and by the tenor of the present charter, is to exist forever, without being obliged to yield any emolument to the government, or to be at all dependent upon it. That the great profits of the bank which will daily increase as money grows scarcer, and which already far exceed the profits of European banks, have tempted foreigners to vest their money in this bank, and thus to draw from us large sums for interest.

That foreigners will doubtless be more and more induced to become stockholders, until the time may arrive when this enormous engine of power may become subject to foreign influence; this country may be agitated with the politics of European courts, and the good people of America reduced once more

the committee either conceived that the house had already
determined how it would act without regard to the case, and
that they were only a committee for form sake, and to give
a colour of inquiry without making any, or that the case was
referred to them, *as law-questions are sometimes referred to
law-officers for an opinion only.*

This method of doing public business serves exceedingly
to mislead a country.—When the constituents of an assembly
hear that an inquiry into any matter is directed to be made,
and a committee appointed for that purpose, they naturally
conclude that the inquiry *is made*, and that the future proceedings of the house are in consequence of the matters,
facts, and information obtained by means of that inquiry.—
But here is a committee of inquiry making no inquiry at all,
and giving an opinion on a case without inquiring into the
merits of it. This proceeding of the committee would justify
an opinion that it was not their wish to *get*, but to *get over*
information, and lest the inquiry should not suit their wishes,
omitted to make any. The subsequent conduct of the
house, in resolving not to hear the directors of the bank, on

into a state of subordination, and dependance upon some one or other of the
European powers. That at best, if it were even confined to the hands of Americans, it would be totally destructive of that equality which ought to prevail in
a republic. We have nothing in our free and equal government capable of
balancing the influence which this bank must create—and we see nothing,
which in the course of a few years, can prevent the directors of the bank from
governing Pennsylvania. Already we have felt its influence indirectly interfering in the measures of the legislature. Already the house of assembly, the
representatives of the people, have been threatened, that the credit of our paper
currency will be blasted by the bank ; and if this growing evil continues, we
fear the time is not very distant, when the bank will be able to dictate to the
legislature, what laws to pass and what to forbear.

Your committee therefore beg leave further to report the following resolution
to be adopted by the house—*viz.*

Resolved, that a committee be appointed to bring in a bill to repeal the act
of assembly passed the 1st day of April, 1782, entitled, " An act to incorporate
the subscribers to the bank of North-America : " and also to repeal one other
act of assembly, passed the 18th of March, 1782, entitled, " An act for preventing and punishing the counterfeiting of the common seal, bank bills and
bank notes of the president, directors and company, of the bank of North-
America, and for the other purposes therein mentioned."—*Author.*.

their application for that purpose, prior to the publication of
the bill for the consideration of the people, strongly cor-
roborates this opinion : for why should not the house hear
them, unless it was apprehensive that the bank, by such a
public opportunity, would produce proofs of its services
and usefulness, that would not suit the temper and views of
its oppressors?

But if the house did not wish or choose to hear the defence
of the bank, it was no reason that their constituents should
not. The constitution of this state, in lieu of having two
branches of legislature, has substituted, that, "to the end
that laws before they are enacted may be more *maturely
considered*, and the inconvenience of *hasty determinations* as
much as possible prevented, all bills of a public nature shall
be printed for the consideration of the people." * The people,
therefore, according to the constitution, stand in the place of
another house ; or, more properly speaking, are a house in
their own right. But in this instance, the assembly arrogates
the whole power to itself, and places itself as a bar to stop
the necessary information spreading among the people. The
application of the bank to be heard before the bill was published for public consideration had two objects. First, to the
house,—and secondly, through the house to the people, who
are as another house. It was as a defence in the first instance,
and as an appeal in the second. But the assembly absorbs
the right of the people to judge ; because, by refusing to hear
the defence, they barred the appeal. Were there no other
cause which the constituents of that assembly had for censuring its conduct, than the exceeding unfairness, partiality,
and arbitrariness with which its business was transacted, it
would be cause sufficient.

Let the constituents of assemblies differ, as they may, respecting certain peculiarities in the *form* of the constitution,
they will all agree in supporting its *principles*, and in repro-
bating unfair proceedings and despotic measures.—Every
constituent is a member of the republic, which is a station of
more consequence to him than being a member of a party,

* Constitution, sect. 15th.—*Author.*

and though they may differ from each other in their choice
of persons to transact the public business, it is of equal importance to all parties that the business be done on right
principles; otherwise our laws and acts, instead of being
founded in justice, will be founded in party, and be laws and
acts of retaliation; and instead of being a republic of free
citizens, we shall be alternately tyrants and slaves. But to
return to the report.

The report begins by stating that, "The committee to
whom was referred the petitions concerning the bank established at Philadelphia, and who were instructed to *inquire*
whether the said bank be compatible with the public safety,
and that equality which ought ever to prevail between the
individuals of a republic, beg leave to report " (not that they
have made any *inquiry*, but) "that it is the *opinion* of this
committee, that the said bank, as at present established, is,
in every view, incompatible with the public safety." But
why is it so? Here is an opinion unfounded and unwarranted. The committee have begun their report at the
wrong end; for an opinion, when given as a matter of judgment, is an action of the mind which follows a fact, but here
it is put in the room of one.

The report then says, "that in the present state of our
trade, the said bank has a direct tendency to banish a great
part of the specie from the country, and to collect into the
hands of the stockholders of the bank, almost the whole of
the money which remains among us."

Here is another mere assertion, just like the former, without a single fact or circumstance to show why it is made, or
whereon it is founded. Now the very reverse of what the
committee asserts is the natural consequence of a bank.
Specie may be called the stock in trade of the bank, it is
therefore its interest to prevent it from wandering out of the
country, and to keep a constant standing supply to be ready
for all domestic occasions and demands. Were it true that
the bank has a direct tendency to banish the specie from
the country, there would soon be an end to the bank;
and, therefore, the committee have so far mistaken the mat-

ter, as to put their fears in the place of their wishes : for if it is to happen as the committee states, let the bank alone and it will cease of itself, and the repealing act need not have been passed.

It is the interest of the bank that people should keep their cash there, and all commercial countries find the exceeding great convenience of having a general depository for their cash.   But so far from banishing it, there are no two classes of people in America who are so much interested in preserving hard money in the country as the bank and the merchant. Neither of them can carry on their business without it. Their opposition to the paper money of the late assembly was because it has a direct effect, as far as it is able, to banish the specie, and that without providing any means for bringing more in.

The committee must have been aware of this, and therefore chose to spread the first alarm, and, groundless as it was, to trust to the delusion.

As the keeping the specie in the country is the interest of the bank, so it has the best opportunities of preventing its being sent away, and the earliest knowledge of such a design. While the bank is the general depository of cash, no great sums can be obtained without getting it from thence, and as it is evidently prejudicial to its interest to advance money to be sent abroad, because in this case the money cannot by circulation return again, the bank, therefore, is interested in preventing what the committee would have it suspected of promoting.

It is to prevent the exportation of cash, and to retain it in the country, that the bank has, on several occasions, stopped the discounting notes till the danger has been passed.*   The

* The petitions say, " That they have frequently seen the stopping of discounts at the bank operate on the trading part of the community, with a degree of violence scarcely inferior to that of a stagnation of the blood in the human body, hurrying the wretched merchant who hath debts to pay into the hands of griping usurers."

As the persons who say or signed this live somewhere in Chester county, they are not, from situation, certain of what they say.   Those petitions have every appearance of being contrived for the purpose of bringing the matter on.   The first part, therefore, of the assertion, that of banishing the specie, contains an apprehension as needless as it is groundless, and which, had the committee understood, or been the least informed of the nature of a bank, they could not have made. It is very probable that some of the opposers of the bank are those persons who have been disappointed in their attempts to obtain specie for this purpose, and now disguise their opposition under other pretences.

I now come to the second part of the assertion, which is, that when the bank has banished a great part of the specie from the country, "it will collect into the hands of the stockholders almost the whole of the money which remains among us." But how, or by what means, the bank is to accomplish this wonderful feat, the committee have not informed us. Whether people are to give their money to the bank for nothing, or whether the bank is to charm it from them as a rattlesnake charms a squirrel from a tree, the committee have left us as much in the dark about as they were themselves.

Is it possible the committee should know so very little of the matter, as not to know that no part of the money which at any time may be in the bank belongs to the stockholders?

petitions and the report have strong evidence in them of being both drawn by the same person : for the report is as clearly the echo of the petitions as ever the address of the British parliament was the echo of the king's speech.

Besides the reason I have already given for occasionally stopping discounting notes at the bank, there are other necessary reasons. It is for the purpose of settling accounts : short reckonings make long friends. The bank lends its money for short periods, and by that means assists a great many different people : and if it did not sometimes stop discounting as a means of settling with the persons it has already lent its money to, those persons would find a way to keep what they had borrowed longer than they ought, and prevent others being assisted. It is a fact, and some of the committee know it to be so, that sundry of those persons who then opposed the bank acted this part.

The stopping the discounts do not, and cannot, operate to call in the loans sooner than the time for which they were lent, and therefore the charge is false that "it hurries men into the hands of griping usurers : " and the truth is, that it operates to keep them from them.

If petitions are to be contrived to cover the design of a house of assembly, and give a pretence for its conduct, or if a house is to be led by the nose by the idle tale of any fifty or sixty signers to a petition, it is time for the public to look a little closer into the conduct of its representatives.—*Author.*

Not even the original capital which they put in is any part of it their own, until every person who has a demand upon the bank is paid, and if there is not a sufficiency for this purpose, on the balance of loss and gain, the original money of the stockholders must make up the deficiency.

The money, which at any time may be in the bank, is the property of every man who holds a bank note, or deposits cash there, or who has a just demand upon it from the city of Philadelphia up to fort Pitt, or to any part of the United States; and he can draw the money from it when he pleases. Its being in the bank, does not in the least make it the property of the stockholders, any more than the money in the state treasury is the property of the state treasurer. They are only stewards over it for those who please to put it, or let it remain there: and, therefore, this second part of the assertion is somewhat ridiculous.

The next paragraph in the report is, " that the accumulation of *enormous wealth* in the hands of a *society* who claim perpetual duration, will necessarily produce a degree of influence and power which cannot be entrusted in the hands of any set of men whatsoever " (the committee I presume excepted) " without endangering public safety." There is an air of solemn fear in this paragraph which is something like introducing a ghost in a play to keep people from laughing at the players.

I have already shown that whatever wealth there may be, at any time, in the bank, is the property of those who have demands upon the bank, and not the property of the stockholders. As a society they hold no property, and most probably never will, unless it should be a house to transact their business in, instead of hiring one. Every half year the bank settles its accounts, and each individual stockholder takes his dividend of gain or loss to himself, and the bank begins the next half year in the same manner it began the first, and so on. This being the nature of a bank, there can be no accumulation of wealth among them as a society.

For what purpose the word "*society*" is introduced into the report I do not know, unless it be to make a false impression upon people's minds. It has no connexion with the subject, for the bank is not a society, but a company, and denominated so in the charter.   There are several religious societies incorporated in this state, which hold property as the right of those societies, and to which no person can belong that is not of the same religious profession.   But this is not the case with the bank.   The bank is a company for the promotion and convenience of commerce, which is a matter in which all the state is interested, and holds no property in the manner which those societies do.

But there is a direct contradiction in this paragraph to that which goes before it.   The committee, there, accuses the bank of banishing the specie, and here, of accumulating enormous sums of it.   So here are two enormous sums of specie; one enormous sum going out, and another enormous sum remaining.   To reconcile this contradiction, the committee should have added to their report, *that they suspected the bank had found out the philosopher's stone, and kept it a secret.*

The next paragraph is, "that the said bank, in its corporate capacity, is empowered to hold estates to the amount of ten millions of dollars, and by the tenor of the present charter is to exist for ever, without being obliged to yield any emolument to the government, or be in the least dependant on it."

The committee have gone so vehemently into this business, and so completely shown their want of knowledge in every point of it, as to make, in the first part of this paragraph, a fear of what, the greater fear is, will never happen.   Had the committee known any thing of banking, they must have known, that the objection against banks has been (not that they held great estates but) that they held none; that they had no real, fixed, and visible property, and that it is the maxim and practice of banks not to hold any.

The honourable chancellor Livingston, late secretary for foreign affairs, did me the honour of showing, and discoursing with me on, a plan of a bank he had drawn up for the state of New-York.   In this plan it was made a condition or obligation, that whatever the capital of the bank amounted to in specie, there should be added twice as much in real estates. But the mercantile interest rejected the proposition.

It was a very good piece of policy in the assembly which passed the charter act, to add the clause to empower the bank to purchase and hold real estates.   It was as an inducement to the bank to do it, because such estates being held as the property of the bank would be so many mortgages to the public in addition to the money capital of the bank.

But the doubt is that the bank will not be induced to accept the opportunity.   The bank has existed five years, and has not purchased a shilling of real property: and as such property or estates cannot be purchased by the bank but with the interest money which the stock produces, and as that is divided every half year among the stockholders, and each stockholder chooses to have the management of his own dividend, and if he lays it out in purchasing an estate to have that estate his own private property, and under his own immediate management, there is no expectation, so far from being any fear, that the clause will be accepted.

Where knowledge is a duty, ignorance is a crime; and the committee are criminal in not understanding this subject better.   Had this clause not been in the charter, the committee might have reported the want of it as a defect, in not empowering the bank to hold estates as a real security to its creditors: but as the complaint now stands, the accusation of it is, that the charter empowers the bank to *give real security* to its creditors.   A complaint never made, heard of, or thought of before.

The second article in this paragraph is, "that the bank, according to the tenor of the present charter, is to exist for ever."   Here I agree with the committee, and am glad to find that among such a list of errors and contradictions there is one idea which is not wrong, although the committee have made a wrong use of it.

As we are not to live for ever ourselves, and other generations are to follow us, we have neither the power nor the right to govern them, or to say how they shall govern themselves.   It is the summit of human vanity, and shows a covetousness of power beyond the grave, to be dictating to the world to come.   It is sufficient that we do that which is right in our own day, and leave them with the advantage of good examples.

As the generations of the world are every day both commencing and expiring, therefore, when any public act, of this sort, is done, it naturally supposes the age of that generation to be then beginning, and the time contained between coming of age, and the natural end of life, is the extent of time it has a right to go to, which may be about thirty years; for though many may die before, others will live beyond; and the mean time is equally fair for all generations.

If it was made an article in the constitution, that all laws and acts should cease of themselves in thirty years, and have no legal force beyond that time, it would prevent their becoming too numerous and voluminous, and serve to keep them within view in a compact compass. Such as were proper to be continued, would be enacted again, and those which were not, would go into oblivion. There is the same propriety that a nation should fix a time for a full settlement of its affairs, and begin again from a new date, as that an individual should; and to keep within the distance of thirty years would be a convenient period.

The British, from the want of some general regulation of this kind, have a great number of obsolete laws; which, though out of use and forgotten, are not out of force, and are occasionally brought up for particular purposes, and innocent, unwary persons trapanned thereby.

To extend this idea still further,—it would probably be a considerable improvement in the political system of nations, to make all treaties of peace for a limited time. It is the nature of the mind to feel uneasy under the idea of a condition perpetually existing over it, and to excite in itself apprehensions that would not take place were it not from that cause.

Were treaties of peace made for, and renewable every seven or ten years, the natural effect would be, to make peace continue longer than it does under the custom of making peace for ever. If the parties felt, or apprehended, any inconveniences under the terms already made, they would

look forward to the time when they should be eventually relieved therefrom, and might renew the treaty on improved
conditions.   This opportunity periodically occurring, and the
recollection of it always existing, would serve as a chimney
to the political fabric, to carry off the smoke and fume of
national fire.   It would naturally abate and honorably take
off the edge and occasion for fighting : and however the
parties might determine to do it, when the time of the treaty
should expire, it would then seem like fighting in cool blood :
the fighting temper would be dissipated before the fighting
time arrived, and negotiation supply its place.   To know
how probable this may be, a man need do no more than
observe the progress of his own mind on any private circumstance similar in its nature to a public one.   But to return to
my subject.

To give limitation is to give duration : and though it is
not a justifying reason, that because an act or contract is not
to last for ever, that it shall be broken or violated to-day, yet,
where no time is mentioned, the omission affords an opportunity for the abuse.   When we violate a contract on this
pretence, we assume a right that belongs to the next generation ; for though they, as a following generation, have the
right of altering or setting it aside, as not being concerned in
the making it, or not being done in their day, we, who made
it, have not that right ; and, therefore, the committee, in this
part of their report, have made a wrong use of a right principle ; and as this clause in the charter might have been
altered by the consent of the parties, it cannot be produced
to justify the violation.   And were it not altered there would
be no inconvenience from it.   The term " for ever " is an
absurdity that would have no effect.   The next age will
think for itself, by the same rule of right that we have done,
and not admit any assumed authority of ours to encroach
upon the system of their day.   Our *for ever* ends, where
their *for ever* begins.

The third article in this paragraph is, that the bank holds
its charter " without being obliged to yield any emolument
to the government."

Ingratitude has a short memory.   It was on the failure of
the government to support the public cause, that the bank
originated.   It stepped in as a support, when some of the
persons then in the government, and who now oppose the
bank, were apparently on the point of abandoning the cause,
not from disaffection, but from despair.   While the expenses
of the war were carried on by emissions of continental money,
any set of men, in government, might carry it on.   The means
being provided to their hands, required no great exertions of
fortitude or wisdom ; but when this means failed, they would
have failed with it, had not a public spirit awakened itself
with energy out of doors.   It was easy times to the governments while continental money lasted. The dream of wealth
supplied the reality of it ; but when the dream vanished, the
government did not awake.

But what right has the government to expect any emolument from the bank ?   Does the committee mean to set up
acts and charters for sale, or what do they mean ?   Because
it is the practice of the British ministry to grind a toll out
of every public institution they can get a power over, is the
same practice to be followed here ?

The war being now ended, and the bank having rendered
the service expected, or rather hoped for, from it, the principal public use of it, at this time, is for the promotion and
extension of commerce.   The whole community derives
benefit from the operation of the bank.   It facilitates the
commerce of the country.   It quickens the means of purchasing and paying for country produce, and hastens on the
exportation of it.   The emolument, therefore, being to the
community, it is the office and duty of government to give
protection to the bank.

Among many of the principal conveniences arising from
the bank, one of them is, that it gives a kind of life to, what
would otherwise be, dead money.   Every merchant and person in trade, has always in his hands some quantity of cash,
which constantly remains with him ; that is, he is never entirely without : this remnant money, as it may be called, is
of no use to him till more is collected to it.—He can neither

buy produce nor merchandize with it, and this being the case with every person in trade, there will be (though not all at the same time) as many of those sums lying uselessly by, and scattered throughout the city, as there are persons in trade, besides many that are not in trade.

I should not suppose the estimate overrated, in conjecturing, that half the money in the city, at any one time, lies in this manner. By collecting those scattered sums together, which is done by means of the bank, they become capable of being used, and the quantity of circulating cash is doubled, and by the depositors alternately lending them to each other, the commercial system is invigorated : and as it is the interest of the bank to preserve this money in the country for domestic uses only, and as it has the best opportunity of doing so, the bank serves as a sentinel over the specie.

If a farmer, or a miller, comes to the city with produce, there are but few merchants that can individually purchase it with ready money of their own ; and those few would command nearly the whole market for country produce ; but, by means of the bank, this monopoly is prevented, and the chance of the market enlarged. It is very extraordinary that the late assembly should promote monopolizing ; yet such would be the effect of suppressing the bank ; and it is much to the honour of those merchants, who are capable by their fortunes of becoming monopolizers, that they support the bank. In this case, honour operates over interest. They were the persons who first set up the bank, and their honour is now engaged to support what it is their interest to put down.

If merchants, by this means, or farmers, by similar means, among themselves, can mutually aid and support each other, what has the government to do with it? What right has it to expect emolument from associated industry, more than from individual industry? It would be a strange sort of government, that should make it illegal for people to assist each other, or pay a tribute for doing so.

But the truth is, that the government has already derived emoluments, and very extraordinary ones. It has already

received its full share, by the services of the bank during
the war ; and it is every day receiving benefits, because whatever promotes and facilitates commerce, serves likewise to
promote and facilitate the revenue.

The last article in this paragraph is, " that the bank is not
the least dependant on the government."

Have the committee so soon forgotten the principles of republican government, and the constitution, or are they so
little acquainted with them, as not to know, that this article
in their report partakes of the nature of treason ? Do they
not know, that freedom is destroyed by dependance, and the
safety of the state endangered thereby ? Do they not see,
that to hold any part of the citizens of the state, as yearly
pensioners on the favour of an assembly, is striking at the
root of free elections?

If other parts of their report discover a want of knowledge
on the subject of banks, this shows a want of principle in the
science of government.

Only let us suppose this dangerous idea carried into practice, and then see what it leads to. If corporate bodies are,
after their incorporation, to be annually dependant on an
assembly for the continuance of their charter, the citizens
which compose those corporations, are not free. The government holds an authority and influence over them, in a
manner different from what it does over other citizens, and
by this means destroys that equality of freedom, which is
the bulwark of the republic and the constitution.

By this scheme of government any party, which happens
to be uppermost in a state, will command all the corporations in it, and may create more for the purpose of extending that influence. The dependant borough towns in
England are the rotten parts of their government and this
idea of the committee has a very near relation to it.

" If you do not do so and so," expressing what was meant,
" take care of your charter," was a threat thrown out against
the bank. But as I do not wish to enlarge on a disagreeable circumstance, and hope that what is already said is
sufficient to show the anti-constitutional conduct and prin-

ciples of the committee, I shall pass on to the next paragraph
in the report.—Which is—

"That the great profits of the bank, which will daily increase as money grows scarcer, and which already far exceeds
the profits of European banks, have tempted foreigners to
vest their money in this bank, and thus to draw from us
large sums for interest."

Had the committee understood the subject, some dependance might be put on their opinion which now cannot.
Whether money will grow scarcer, and whether the profits
of the bank will increase, are more than the committee know,
or are judges sufficient to guess at. The committee are not
so capable of taking care of commerce, as commerce is
capable of taking care of itself. The farmer understands
farming, and the merchant understands commerce; and as
riches are equally the object of both, there is no occasion
that either should fear that the other will seek to be poor.
The more money the merchant has, so much the better for
the farmer who has produce to sell ; and the richer the
farmer is, so much the better for the merchant, when he
comes to his store.

As to the profits of the bank, the stockholders must take
their chance for it. It may some years be more and others
less, and upon the whole may mot be so productive as many
other ways that money may be employed. It is the convenience which the stockholders, as commercial men, derive
from the establishment of the bank, and not the mere interest they receive, that is the inducement to them. It is
the ready opportunity of borrowing alternately of each other
that forms the principal object : and as they pay as well
as receive a great part of the interest among themselves, it
is nearly the same thing, both cases considered at once,
whether it is more or less.

The stockholders are occasionally depositors and sometimes borrowers of the bank. They pay interest for what
they borrow, and receive none for what they deposit ; and
were a stockholder to keep a nice account of the interest he
pays for the one and loses on the other, he would find, at

the year's end, that ten per cent. on his stock would probably not be more than common interest on the whole, if so
much.

As to the committee complaining "that foreigners by
vesting their money in the bank will draw large sums from
us for interest," it is like a miller complaining, in a dry
season, that so much water runs into his dam some of it runs
over.

Could those foreigners draw this interest without putting
in any capital, the complaint would be well founded ; but as
they must first put money in before they can draw any out,
as they must draw many years before they can draw even the
numerical sum they put in at first, the effect for at least
twenty years to come, will be directly contrary to what the
committee states; because we draw *capital* from them and
they only *interest* from us, and as we shall have the use of
the money all the while it remains with us, the advantage will always be in our favour.—In framing this part of
the report, the committee must have forgotten which side
of the Atlantic they were on, for the case would be as they
state it if we put money into their bank instead of their putting it into ours.

I have now gone through, line by line, every objection
against the bank, contained in the first half of the report;
what follows may be called, *The lamentations of the committee*,
and a lamentable, pusillanimous, degrading thing it is.—It
is a public affront, a reflection upon the sense and spirit of
the whole country. I shall give the remainder together, as
it stands in the report, and then my remarks. The lamentations are :

"That foreigners will doubtless be more and more induced to
become stock holders, until the time may arrive when this *enormous* engine of power may become subject to foreign influence,
this country may be agitated by the politics of European courts,
and the good people of America reduced once more into a state
of subordination and dependance upon some one or other of the
European powers. That at best, if it were even confined to the
hands of Americans, it would be totally destructive of that equality

which ought to prevail in a republic. We have nothing in our free and equal government capable of balancing the influence which this bank must create ; and we see nothing which in the course of a few years can prevent the directors of the bank from governing Pennsylvania. Already we have felt its influence in-directly interfering in the measures of the legislature. Already the house of asembly, the representatives of the people, have been threatened, that the credit of our paper currency will be blasted by the bank ; and if this growing evil continues, we fear the time is not very distant when the bank will be able to dictate to the legislature, what laws to pass and what to forbear."

When the sky falls we shall all be killed. There is some-thing so ridiculously grave, so wide of probability, and so wild, confused and inconsistent in the whole composition of this long paragraph, that I am at a loss how to begin upon it.—It is like a drowning man crying fire ! fire !

This part of the report is made up of two dreadful pre-dictions. The first is, that if foreigners purchase bank stock, we shall be all ruined ;—the second is, that if the Americans keep the bank to themselves, we shall be also ruined.

A committee of fortune-tellers is a novelty in government, and the gentlemen, by giving this specimen of their art, have ingeniously saved their honour on one point, which is, that though the people may say they are not bankers, nobody can say they are not conjurors.—There is, however, one con-solation left, which is, that the committee do not know *exactly* how long it may be ; so there is some hope that we may all be in heaven when this dreadful calamity happens upon earth.

But to be serious, if any seriousness is necessary on so laughable a subject.—If the state should think there is any thing improper in foreigners purchasing bank stock, or any other kind of stock or funded property (for I see no reason why bank stock should be particularly pointed at) the legis-lature have authority to prohibit it. It is a mere political opinion that has nothing to do with the charter, or the charter with that ; and therefore the first dreadful prediction vanishes.

It has always been a maxim in politics, founded on, and

drawn from, natural causes and consequences, that the more foreign countries which any nation can interest in the prosperity of its own, so much the better. Where the treasure is, there will the heart be also; and therefore when foreigners vest their money with us, they naturally invest their good wishes with it; and it is we that obtain an influence over them, not they over us.—But the committee set out so very wrong at first, that the further they travelled, the more they were out of their way; and now they have got to the end of their report, they are at the utmost distance from their business.

As to the second dreadful part, that of the bank overturning the government, perhaps the committee meant that at the next general election themselves might be turned out of it, which has partly been the case; not by the influence of the bank, for it had none, not even enough to obtain the permission of a hearing from government, but by the influence of reason and the choice of the people, who most probably resent the undue and unconstitutional influence which that house and committee were assuming over the privileges of citizenship.

The committee might have been so modest as to have confined themselves to the bank, and not thrown a general odium on the whole country. Before the events can happen which the committee predict, the electors of Pennsylvania must become dupes, dunces, and cowards; and, therefore, when the committee predict the dominion of the bank they predict the disgrace of the people.

The committee having finished their report, proceed to give their advice, which is,

" That a committee be appointed to bring in a bill to repeal the act of assembly passed the first day of April, 1782, entitled, ' An act to incorporate the subscribers to the bank of North-America,' and also to repeal one other act of the assembly passed the 18th of March, 1782, entitled, ' An act for preventing and punishing the counterfeiting of the common seal, bank-bills and bank notes of the president, directors and company of the bank of North-America, and for other purposes therein mentioned.' "

There is something in this sequel to the report that is perplexed and obscure.

Here are two acts to be repealed.   One is, the incorporating act.   The other, the act for preventing and punishing the counterfeiting of the common seal, bank bills, and bank notes of the president, directors and company of the bank of North-America.

It would appear from the committee's manner of arranging them (were it not for the difference of their dates) that the act for punishing the counterfeiting the common seal, etc. of the bank, followed the act of incorporation, and that the common seal there referred to is a common seal which the bank held in consequence of the aforesaid incorporating act.—But the case is quite otherwise.   The act for punishing the counterfeiting the common seal, etc. of the bank, was passed prior to the incorporating act, and refers to the common seal which the bank held in consequence of the charter of congress, and the style which the act expresses, of president, directors and company of the bank of North-America, is the corporate style which the bank derives under the congress charter.

The punishing act, therefore, hath two distinct legal points. The one is, an authoritative public recognition of the charter of congress.   The second is, the punishment it inflicts on counterfeiting.

The legislature may repeal the punishing part, but it cannot undo the recognition, because no repealing act can say that the state has not recognized.   The recognition is a mere matter of fact, and no law or act can undo a fact, or put it, if I may so express it, in the condition it was before it existed. The repealing act therefore does not reach the full point the committee had in view; for even admitting it to be a repeal of the state charter, it still leaves another charter recognized in its stead.—The charter of congress, standing merely on itself, would have a doubtful authority, but recognition of it by the state gives it legal ability.   The repealing act, it is true sets aside the punishment, but does not bar the operation of the charter of congress as a charter recognized by the state, and therefore the committee did their business but by halves.

I have now gone entirely through the report of the committee, and a more irrational, inconsistent, contradictory report will scarcely be found on the journals of any legislature of America.

How the repealing act is to be applied, or in what manner it is to operate, is a matter yet to be determined. For admitting a question of law to arise, whether the charter, which that act attempts to repeal, is a law of the land in the manner which laws of universal operation are, or of the nature of a contract made between the public and the bank, (as I have already explained in this work,) the repealing act does not and cannot decide the question, because it is the repealing act that makes the question, and its own fate is involved in the decision. It is a question of law and not a question of legislation, and must be decided on in a court of justice and not by a house of assembly.

But the repealing act, by being passed prior to the decision of this point, assumes the power of deciding it, and the assembly in so doing erects itself unconstitutionally into a tribunal of judicature, and absorbs the authority and right of the courts of justice into itself.

Therefore the operation of the repealing act, in its very outset, requires injustice to be done. For it is impossible on the principles of a republican government and the constitution, to pass an act to forbid any of the citizens the right of appealing to the courts of justice on any matter in which his interest or property is affected; but the first operation of this act goes to shut up the courts of justice and holds them subservient to the assembly. It either commands or influences them not to hear the case, or to give judgment on it on the mere will of one party only.

I wish the citizens to awaken themselves on this subject. Not because the bank is concerned, but because their own constitutional rights and privileges are involved in the event. It is a question of exceeding great magnitude; for if an assembly is to have this power, the laws of the land and the courts of justice are but of little use.

Having now finished with the report, I proceed to the third and last subject—that of paper money.

I remember a German farmer expressing as much in a few words as the whole subject requires; "*money is money, and paper is paper.*"—All the invention of man cannot make them otherwise. The alchymist may cease his labours, and the hunter after the philosopher's stone go to rest, if paper can be metamorphosed into gold and silver, or made to answer the same purpose in all cases.

Gold and silver are the emissions of nature: paper is the emission of art. The value of gold and silver is ascertained by the quantity which nature has made in the earth. We cannot make that quantity more or less than it is, and therefore the value being dependant upon the quantity, depends not on man.—Man has no share in making gold or silver; all that his labours and ingenuity can accomplish is, to collect it from the mine, refine it for use and give it an impression, or stamp it into coin.

Its being stamped into coin adds considerably to its convenience but nothing to its value. It has then no more value than it had before. Its value is not in the impression but in itself. Take away the impression and still the same value remains. Alter it as you will, or expose it to any misfortune that can happen, still the value is not diminished. It has a capacity to resist the accidents that destroy other things. It has, therefore, all the requisite qualities that money can have, and is a fit material to make money of ; and nothing which has not all those properties, can be fit for the purpose of money.

Paper, considered as a material whereof to make money, has none of the requisite qualities in it. It is too plentiful, and too easily come at. It can be had any where, and for a trifle.

There are two ways in which I shall consider paper.

The only proper use for paper, in the room of money, is to write promissory notes and obligations of payment in specie upon. A piece of paper, thus written and signed, is worth the sum it is given for, if the person who gives it is

able to pay it ; because in this case, the law will oblige him.
But if he is worth nothing, the paper note is worth nothing.
The value, therefore, of such a note, is not in the note itself,
for that is but paper and promise, but in the man who is
obliged to redeem it with gold or silver.

Paper, circulating in this manner, and for this purpose, continually points to the place and person where, and of whom,
the money is to be had, and at last finds its home ; and, as
it were, unlocks its master's chest and pays the bearer.

But when an assembly undertake to issue paper *as* money,
the whole system of safety and certainty is overturned, and
property set afloat. Paper notes given and taken between
individuals as a promise of payment is one thing, but paper
issued by an assembly *as* money is another thing. It is like
putting an apparition in the place of a man ; it vanishes
with looking at it, and nothing remains but the air.

Money, when considered as the fruit of many years industry,
as the reward of labour, sweat and toil, as the widow's dowry
and children's portion, and as the means of procuring the
necessaries and alleviating the afflictions of life, and making
old age a scene of rest, has something in it sacred that is not
to be sported with, or trusted to the airy bubble of paper
currency.

By what power or authority an assembly undertakes to
make paper money, is difficult to say. It derives none from
the constitution, for that is silent on the subject. It is one
of those things which the people have not delegated, and
which, were they at any time assembled together, they would
not delegate. It is, therefore, an assumption of power which
an assembly is not warranted in, and which may, one day or
other, be the means of bringing some of them to punishment.

I shall enumerate some of the evils of paper money and
conclude with offering means for preventing them.

One of the evils of paper money is, that it turns the whole
country into stock jobbers. The precariousness of its value
and the uncertainty of its fate continually operate, night and
day, to produce this destructive effect. Having no real value
in itself it depends for support upon accident, caprice and

party, and as it is the interest of some to depreciate and of others to raise its value, there is a continual invention going on that destroys the morals of the country.

It was horrid to see, and hurtful to recollect, how loose the principles of justice were left, by means of the paper emissions during the war. The experience then had, should be a warning to any assembly how they venture to open such a dangerous door again.

As to the romantic, if not hypocritical, tale that a virtuous people need no gold and silver, and that paper will do as well, it requires no other contradiction than the experience we have seen. Though some well meaning people may be inclined to view it in this light, it is certain that the sharper always talks this language.

There are a set of men who go about making purchases upon credit, and buying estates they have not wherewithal to pay for; and having done this, their next step is to fill the newspapers with paragraphs of the scarcity of money and the necessity of a paper emission, then to have a legal tender under the pretence of supporting its credit, and when out, to depreciate it as fast as they can, get a deal of it for a little price, and cheat their creditors; and this is the concise history of paper money schemes.

But why, since the universal custom of the world has established money as the most convenient medium of traffic and commerce, should paper be set up in preference to gold and silver? The productions of nature are surely as innocent as those of art; and in the case of money, are abundantly, if not infinitely, more so. The love of gold and silver may produce covetousness, but covetousness, when not connected with dishonesty, is not properly a vice. It is frugality run to an extreme.

But the evils of paper money have no end. Its uncertain and fluctuating value is continually awakening or creating new sehemes of deceit. Every principle of justice is put to the rack, and the bond of society dissolved: the suppression, therefore, of paper money might very properly have been put into the act for preventing vice and immorality.

The pretence for paper money has been, that there was not a sufficiency of gold and silver. This, so far from being a reason for paper emissions, is a reason against them.

As gold and silver are not the productions of North America, they are, therefore, articles of importation ; and if we set up a paper manufactory of money, it amounts, as far as it is able, to prevent the importation of hard money, or to send it out again as fast as it comes in ; and by following this practice we shall continually banish the specie, till we have none left, and be continually complaining of the grievance instead of remedying the cause.

Considering gold and silver as articles of importation, there will in time, unless we prevent it by paper emissions, be as much in the country as the occasions of it require, for the same reasons there are as much of other imported articles. But as every yard of cloth manufactured in the country occasions a yard the less to be imported, so it is by money, with this difference, that in the one case we manufacture the thing itself and in the other we do not. We have cloth for cloth, but we have only paper dollars for silver ones.

As to the assumed authority of any assembly in making paper money, or paper of any kind, a legal tender, or in other language, a compulsive payment, it is a most presumptuous attempt at arbitrary power. There can be no such power in a republican government : the people have no freedom, and property no security where this practice can be acted : and the committee who shall bring in a report for this purpose, or the member who moves for it, and he who seconds it merit impeachment, and sooner or later may expect it.

Of all the various sorts of base coin, paper money is the basest. It has the least intrinsic value of any thing that can be put in the place of gold and silver. A hobnail or a piece of wampum far exceeds it. And there would be more propriety in making those articles a legal tender than to make paper so.

It was the issuing base coin, and establishing it as a tender, that was one of the principal means of finally overthrowing the power of the Stuart family in Ireland. The article is worth reciting as it bears such a resemblance to the process practised in paper money.

" Brass and copper of the basest kind, old cannon, broken bells, household utensils were assiduously collected ; and from every pound weight of such vile materials, valued at four-pence, pieces were coined and circulated to the amount of five pounds normal value. By the first proclamation they were made current in all payments to and from the king and the subjects of the realm, except in duties on the importation of foreign goods, money left in trust, or due by mortgage, bills or bonds ; and James promised that when the money should be decried, he would receive it in all payments, or make full satisfaction in gold and silver. The nominal value was afterwards raised by subsequent proclamations, the original restrictions removed, and this base money was ordered to be received in all kinds of payments. As brass and copper grew scarce, it was made of still viler materials, of tin and pewter, and old debts of one thousand pounds were discharged by pieces of vile metal amounting to thirty shillings in intrinsic value." *

Had king James thought of paper, he needed not to have been at the trouble or expense of collecting brass and copper, broken bells, and household utensils.

The laws of a country ought to be the standard of equity, and calculated to impress on the minds of the people the moral as well as the legal obligations of reciprocal justice. But tender laws, of any kind, operate to destroy morality, and to dissolve, by the pretence of law, what ought to be the principle of law to support, reciprocal justice between man and man : and the punishment of a member who should move for such a law ought to be *death*.[1]

When the recommendation of congress, in the year 1780, for repealing the tender laws was before the assembly of Pennsylvania, on casting up the votes, for and against bringing in a bill to repeal those laws, the numbers were equal,

* Leland's History of Ireland, vol. iv. p. 265.—*Author*.

[1] It is a curious indication of the tension caused by the bank controversy that a man of Quaker training could make such a statement as the above. A few years later Paine is found advocating abolition of the death-penalty, even for treason against the state, for which some would reserve it.—*Editor*.

and the casting vote rested on the speaker, colonel Bayard. " I give my vote," said he, " for the repeal, from a consciousness of justice ; the tender laws operate to establish iniquity by law." But when the bill was brought in, the house rejected it, and the tender laws continued to be the means of fraud.

If any thing had, or could have, a value equal to gold and silver, it would require no tender law : and if it had not that value it ought not to have such a law; and, therefore, all tender laws are tyrannical and unjust, and calculated to support fraud and oppression.

Most of the advocates for tender laws are those who have debts to discharge, and who take refuge in such a law, to violate their contracts and cheat their creditors. But as no law can warrant the doing an unlawful act, therefore the proper mode of proceeding, should any such laws be enacted in future, will be to impeach and execute the members who moved for and seconded such a bill, and put the debtor and the creditor in the same situation they were in, with respect to each other, before such a law was passed. Men ought to be made to tremble at the idea of such a barefaced act of injustice. It is in vain to talk of restoring credit, or complain that money cannot be borrowed at legal interest, until every idea of tender laws is totally and publicly reprobated and extirpated from among us.

As to paper money, in any light it can be viewed, it is at best a bubble. Considered as property, it is inconsistent to suppose that the breath of an assembly, whose authority expires with the year, can give to paper the value and duration of gold. They cannot even engage that the next assembly shall receive it in taxes. And by the precedent, (for authority there is none,) that one assembly makes paper money, another may do the same, until confidence and credit are totally expelled, and all the evils of depreciation acted over again. The amount, therefore, of paper money is this, that it is the illegitimate offspring of assemblies, and when their year expires, they leave a vagrant on the hands of the public.

Having now gone through the three subjects proposed in

the title to this work, I shall conclude with offering some thoughts on the present affairs of the state.

My idea of a single legislature was always founded on a hope, that whatever personal parties there might be in the state, they would all unite and agree in the general principles of good government—that these party differences would be dropped at the threshold of the statehouse, and that the public good, or the good of the whole, would be the governing principle of the legislature within it.

Party dispute, taken on this ground, would only be, who should have the honour of making the laws ; not what the laws should be.   But when party operates to produce party laws, a single house is a single person, and subject to the haste, rashness and passion of individual sovereignty.   At least, it is an aristocracy.

The form of the present constitution is now made to trample on its principles, and the constitutional members are anti-constitutional legislators.   They are fond of supporting the form for the sake of the power, and they dethrone the principle to display the sceptre.

The attack of the late assembly on the bank, discovers such a want of moderation and prudence, of impartiality and equity, of fair and candid inquiry and investigation, of deliberate and unbiassed judgment, and such a rashness of thinking and vengeance of power, as is inconsistent with the safety of the republic.   It was judging without hearing, and executing without trial.

By such rash, injudicious and violent proceedings, the interest of the state is weakened, its prosperity diminished, and its commerce and its specie banished to other places. Suppose the bank had not been in an immediate condition to have stood such a sudden attack, what a scene of instant distress would the rashness of that assembly have brought upon this city and state.   The holders of bank notes, whoever they might be, would have been thrown into the utmost confusion and difficulties.   It is no apology to say the house never thought of this, for it was their duty to have thought of every thing.

But by the prudent and provident management of the bank, (though unsuspicious of the attack,) it was enabled to stand the run upon it without stopping payment a moment, and to prevent the evils and mischiefs taking place which the rashness of the assembly had a direct tendency to bring on ; a trial that scarcely a bank in Europe, under a similar circumstance, could have withstood.

I cannot see reason sufficient to believe that the hope of the house to put down the bank was placed on the withdrawing the charter, so much as on the expectation of producing a bankruptcy of the bank, by starting a run upon it.   If this was any part of their project it was a very wicked one, because hundreds might have been ruined to gratify a party spleen.

But this not being the case, what has the attack amounted to, but to expose the weakness and rashness, the want of judgment as well as justice, of those who made it, and to confirm the credit of the bank more substantially than it was before ?

The attack, it is true, has had one effect, which is not in the power of the assembly to remedy ; it has banished many thousand hard dollars from the state.   By the means of the bank, Pennsylvania had the use of a great deal of hard money belonging to citizens of other states, and that without any interest, for it laid here in the nature of deposit, the depositors taking bank notes in its stead.   But the alarm called those notes in and the owners drew out their cash.

The banishing the specie served to make room for the paper money of the assembly, and we have now paper dollars where we might have had silver ones.   So that the effect of the paper money has been to make less money in the state than there was before.[1]   Paper money is like dram-drinking, it relieves for a moment by deceitful sensation, but gradually diminishes the natural heat, and leaves the body

---

[1] The reader may be reminded of the humorous scene in Goethe's " Faust," Part Second, where Mephistopheles fills the empty Treasury by simple expedient of a printing-press, and the Court fool shows his sagacity by hastening to spend all the paper money he possesses.—*Editor*

worse than it found it. Were not this the case, and could money be made of paper at pleasure, every sovereign in Europe would be as rich as he pleased. But the truth is, that it is a bubble and the attempt vanity. Nature has provided the proper materials for money, gold and silver, and any attempt of ours to rival her is ridiculous.

But to conclude. If the public will permit the opinion of a friend who is attached to no party, and under obligation to none, nor at variance with any, and who through a long habit of acquaintance with them has never deceived them, that opinion shall be freely given.

The bank is an institution capable of being made exceedingly beneficial to the state, not only as the means of extending and facilitating its commerce, but as a means of increasing the quantity of hard money in the state. The assembly's paper money serves directly to banish or crowd out the hard, because it is issued *as* money and put in the place of hard money. But bank notes are of a very different kind, and produce a contrary effect. They are promissory notes payable on demand, and may be taken to the bank and exchanged for gold or silver without the least ceremony or difficulty.

The bank, therefore, is obliged to keep a constant stock of hard money sufficient for this purpose ; which is what the assembly neither does, nor can do by their paper ; because the quantity of hard money collected by taxes into the treasury is trifling compared with the quantity that circulates in trade and through the bank.

The method, therefore, to increase the quantity of hard money would be to combine the security of the government and the bank into one. And instead of issuing paper money that serves to banish the specie, to borrow the sum wanted of the bank in bank notes, on the condition of the bank exchanging those notes at stated periods and quantities, with hard money.

Paper issued in this manner, and directed to this end, would, instead of banishing, work itself into gold and silver ; because it will then be both the advantage and duty of the bank, and of all the mercantile interests connected with it, to procure and import gold and silver from any part of the world, to give in exchange for the notes. The English bank is restricted to the dealing in no other articles of importation than gold and silver, and we may make the same use of our bank if we proceed properly with it.

Those notes will then have a double security, that of the government and that of the bank: and they will not be issued *as* money, but as hostages to be exchanged for hard money, and will, therefore, work the contrary way to what the paper of the assembly, uncombined with the security of the bank, produces: and the interest allowed the bank will be saved to government, by a saving of the expenses and charges attending paper emissions.

It is, as I have already observed in the course of this work, the harmony of all the parts of a republic, that constitutes their several and mutual good. A government that is constructed only to govern, is not a republican government. It is combining authority with usefulness, that in a great measure distinguishes the republican system from others.

Paper money appears, at first sight, to be a great saving, or rather that it costs nothing; but it is the dearest money there is. The ease with which it is emitted by an assembly at first, serves as a trap to catch people in at last. It operates as an anticipation of the next year's taxes. If the money depreciates, after it is out, it then, as I have already remarked, has the effect of fluctuating stock, and the people become stock-jobbers to throw the loss on each other. If it does not depreciate, it is then to be sunk by taxes at the price of *hard money;* because the same quantity of produce, or goods, that would procure a paper dollar to pay taxes with, would procure a silver one for the same purpose. Therefore, in any case of paper money, it is dearer to the country than hard money, by all the expense which the paper, printing, signing, and other attendant charges come to, and at last goes into the fire.

Suppose one hundred thousand dollars in paper money to be emitted every year by the assembly, and the same sum to be sunk every year by taxes, there will then be no more than one hundred thousand dollars out at any one time. If the expense of paper and printing, and of persons to attend the press while the sheets are striking off, signers, etc. be five per cent. it is evident that in the course of twenty years' emissions, the one hundred thousand dollars will cost the country two hundred thousand dollars. Because the papermaker's and printer's bills, and the expense of supervisors and signers, and other attendant charges, will in that time amount to as much as the money amounts to; for the successive emissions are but a re-coinage of the same sum.

But gold and silver require to be coined but once, and will last an hundred years, better than paper will one year, and at the end of that time be still gold and silver. Therefore, the saving to government, in combining its aid and security with that of the bank in procuring hard money, will be an advantage to both, and to the whole community.

The case to be provided against, after this, will be, that the government do not borrow too much of the bank, nor the bank lend more notes than it can redeem; and, therefore, should any thing of this kind be undertaken, the best way will be to begin with a moderate sum, and observe the effect of it. The interest given the bank operates as a bounty on the importation of hard money, and which may not be more than the money expended in making paper emissions.

But nothing of this kind, nor any other public undertaking, that requires security and duration beyond the year, can be gone upon under the present mode of conducting government. The late assembly, by assuming a sovereign power over every act and matter done by the state in former assemblies, and thereby setting up a precedent of overhauling, and overturning, as the accident of elections shall happen or party prevail, have rendered government incompetent to all the great objects of the state. They have eventually reduced the public to an annual body like themselves; whereas the public are a standing, permanent body, holding annual elections.

There are several great improvements and undertakings,

such as inland navigation, building bridges, opening roads of communication through the state, and other matters of a public benefit, that might be gone upon, but which now cannot, until this governmental error or defect is remedied. The faith of government, under the present mode of conducting it, cannot be relied on. Individuals will not venture their money in undertakings of this kind, on an act that may be made by one assembly and broken by another. When a man can say that he cannot trust the government, the importance and dignity of the public is diminished, sapped and undermined ; and, therefore, it becomes the public to restore their own honour by setting these matters to rights.

Perhaps this cannot be effectually done until the time of the next convention, when the principles, on which they are to be regulated and fixed, may be made a part of the constitution.

In the mean time the public may keep their affairs in sufficient good order, by substituting prudence in the place of authority, and electing men into the government, who will at once throw aside the narrow prejudices of party, and make the good of the whole the ruling object of their conduct. And with this hope, and a sincere wish for their prosperity, I close my book.[1]

[1] It was generally admitted that Paine's pamphlet was the means of defeating the Assembly's effort to repeal the charter of the Bank of North America, and the author suffered some martyrdom in consequence. Dr. Franklin believed that Paine could successfully deal with the subject and was not disappointed. See my "Life of Paine," vol i., pp. 213, 215, and ii., p. 466.—*Editor*.

VII.

THE SOCIETY FOR POLITICAL INQUIRIES.[1]

THE moral character and happiness of mankind are so interwoven with the operations of government, and the progress of the arts and sciences is so dependent on the nature of our political institutions, that it is essential to the advancement of civilized society to give ample discussion to these topics.

But important as these inquiries are to all, to the inhabitants of these republics they are objects of peculiar magnitude and necessity. Accustomed to look up to those nations, from whom we have derived our origin, for our laws, our opinions, and our manners, we have retained with undistinguishing reverence their errors with their improvements; have blended with our public institutions the policy of dissimilar countries; and have grafted on an infant commonwealth the manners of ancient and corrupted monarchies. In having effected a separate government, we have as yet effected but a partial independance. The revolution can only be said to be complete, when we shall have freed ourselves, no less from the influence of foreign prejudices than from the fetters of foreign power. When breaking through the bounds, in which a dependent people have been accustomed to think and act, we shall probably comprehend the character

[1] Unpublished "Rules and Regulations of the Society for Political Inquiries, established at Philadelphia, 9th Feb. 1787." This Society met at Dr. Franklin's house, where Paine read a paper, described by William Rawle as "a well-written dissertation on the inexpediency of incorporating towns." The paper was no doubt used in "Rights of Man," ii., ch. 5. Several passages in the same work suggest Paine's probable authorship of the above Preamble.—*Editor.*

we have assumed and adopt those maxims of policy, which are suited to our new situation. While objects of subordinate importance have employed the associated labours of learned and ingenious men, the arduous and complicated science of government has been generally left to the care of practical politicians, or the speculations of individual theorists. From a desire of supplying this deficiency, and of promoting the welfare of our country, it is now proposed to establish a society for mutual improvement in the knowledge of government, and for the advancement of political science.

With these views, the subscribers associate themselves under the title of THE SOCIETY FOR POLITICAL INQUIRIES, and under the following laws and regulations.

LAWS AND REGULATIONS.

I. This Society shall consist of fifty residing members, and shall meet every Friday fortnight, at half past six o'clock in the evening (the chair to be taken precisely at seven) except during the months of June, July, August and September, when their meetings shall be discontinued.

II. There shall be a president, two vice-presidents, a treasurer, and two secretaries, who shall be elected annually by ballot on the second Friday in February.

III. Persons residing at a distance shall be eligible into the Society as honorary members, but shall not be entitled to the privilege of electing.

IV. Every candidate for admission shall be proposed by at least two residing members, who shall give in his name in writing with their own subscribed to it. After which one of the acting secretaries shall read aloud the name of the candidate as well as of the nominating members, at two successive meetings previous to the election.

V. Every election shall be conducted by ballot, twelve members at least being present ; and the votes of three-fourths of the number present, shall be necessary to the admission of the candidate.

VI. Each residing member shall pay twenty shillings on his admission, as well as fifteen shillings annually, towards the expences of the Society.

VII. A committee of papers shall be appointed annually by

ballot, on the same evening that the officers of the Society are
elected. This committee shall consist of the president, vice-presidents, and six other members of the Society, and shall decide on
the propriety of reading or publishing any paper which shall be
presented to the Society. But they shall not proceed to any decision unless five of their number are present. Nor shall any essay,
or the name of its author be published, without previously obtaining his consent.

VIII. The attention of the Society shall be confined to subjects of *government and political œconomy.* And members having
any essays, facts, or observations on these subjects, that they wish
to have read in the Society, or any political queries that they may
be desirous of having discussed in conversation, shall give the
same into the hands of the president or vice-president who shall
communicate the same to the Committee of papers and take
order thereon.

IX. The president or vice-president shall announce to the
Society, what papers are to be read, and what subjects to be discussed at their next meeting.

X. A fair record shall be kept of the proceedings of the Society, which shall be open to the inspection of the members.

XI. Medals shall be adjudged at the discretion of the Society
to the authors (whether members or not) of the best essays upon
such subjects as the Society may propose for that purpose. The
votes in these cases shall be taken by ballot.

XII. If any person to whom a medal shall be adjudged, should
not be a member of the Society, he shall be included in the list of
honorary members.

XIII. The president or vice-president shall have power to call
at any time a special meeting of the Society.

XIV. The Society shall be subject to such laws and regulations
as shall be made from time to time. But no laws shall be enacted,
rescinded or altered without the presence of twelve members, and
without the consent of three-fourths of the number present : Nor
shall any such measures be proposed, without notice has been
previously given at two successive meetings of the alterations or
additions intended to be made.

XV. There shall be a penalty of one shilling paid by every
member not attending at any meeting, either stated or special,
provided he be not out of town or confined by sickness.

VIII.

PROSPECTS ON THE RUBICON:

OR AN INVESTIGATION INTO THE CAUSES AND CONSE-QUENCES OF THE POLITICS TO BE AGITATED AT THE NEXT MEETING OF PARLIAMENT.[1]

PREFACE.

AN expression in the British parliament respecting the American war, alluding to Julius Cæsar having passed the Rubicon, has on several occasions introduced that river as the figurative river of war.

Fortunately for England, she is yet on the peaceable side of the Rubicon; but as the flames once kindled are not always easily extinguished, the hopes of peace are not so clear as before the late mysterious dispute began.

But while the calm lasts, it may answer a very good purpose to take a view of the prospects, consistent with the maxim, that he that goeth to war should first sit down and count the cost.

The nation has a young and ambitious Minister at its head, fond of himself, and deficient in experience: and instances have often shown that judgment is a different thing from

---

[1] This pamphlet was written in Paris, where Paine arrived from America in May, 1787, and where he was in constant intercourse with Jefferson (United States Minister), Condorcet, Lafayette, Cardinal De Brienne, and other eminent men. The date, August 20, is no doubt that of the conclusion of the manuscript, for he arrived in London September 3; but much was probably added to the proofs, which were read at his mother's home in Thetford. The house is in Guildhall Street (then Heathenman), now (1894) occupied by Mr. Brett. Dr. Robinet and others have remarked in this pamphlet the prevision of an approaching revolution in France.—*Editor.*

genius, and that the affairs of a nation are but unsafely trusted where the benefit of experience is wanting.

Illustrations have been drawn from the circumstances of the war before last to decorate the character of the present Minister, and, perhaps, they may have been greatly overdrawn; for the management must have been bad to have done less than what was then done, when we impartially consider the means, the force, and the money employed.

It was then Great Britain and America against France singly, for Spain did not join till near the end of the war. The great number of troops which the American colonies then raised and paid themselves, were sufficient to turn the scale, if all other parts had been equal. France had not at that time attended to naval affairs so much as she has done since; and the capture of French sailors before any declaration of war was made, which, however it may be justified upon policy, will always be ranked among the clandestine arts of war, assured a certain, but unfair advantage against her, because it was like a man administering a disabling dose over night to the person whom he intends to challenge in the morning.

THE AUTHOR.

PUBLISHER'S NOTE TO THE ENGLISH EDITION OF 1793.

This pamphlet was written by Mr. Paine in the year 1787, on one of Mr. Pitt's armaments, namely, that against Holland. His object was to prevent the people of England from being seduced into a war, by stating clearly to them the consequences which would inevitably befall the credit of this country should such a calamity take place. The minister has at length, however, succeeded in his great project, after three expensive armaments in the space of seven years; and the event has proved how well founded were the predictions of Mr. Paine. The person who has the authority to bring forward this pamphlet in its present shape, thinks his doing so a duty which he owes both to Mr. P——— and the people of England, in order that the latter may judge what credit is due to (what a great judge calls) THE WILD THEORIES OF MR. PAINE.

PROSPECTS ON THE RUBICON.

RIGHT by chance and wrong by system are things so frequently seen in the political world, that it becomes a proof of prudence neither to censure nor applaud too soon.

"The Rubicon is passed," was once given as a reason for prosecuting the most expensive war that England ever knew. Sore with the event, and groaning beneath a galling yoke of taxes, she has again been led ministerially on to the shore of the same delusive and fatal river, without being permitted to know the object or the reason why.

Expensive preparations have been gone into; fears, alarms, dangers, apprehensions, have been mistically held forth, as if the existence of the nation was at stake, and at last the mountain has brought forth a Dutch mouse.

Whoever will candidly review the present national characters of England and France, cannot but be struck with surprize at the change that is taking place. The people of France are beginning to think for themselves, and the people of England are resigning up the privilege of thinking.

The affairs of Holland have been the bubble of the day; and a tax is to be laid on shoes and boots (so say the newspapers) for the service of the Stadtholder of Holland. This will undoubtedly do honour to the nation, by veryfying the old English proverb, " Over shoes, over boots."

But tho' Democritus could scarcely have forborne laughing at the folly, yet, as serious argument and sound reasoning are preferable to ridicule, it will be best to quit the vein of unprofitable humour, and give the cause a fair investigation. But before we do this, it may not be improper to take a general review of sundry political matters that will naturally lead to a better understanding of the subject.

What has been the event of all the wars of England, but
an amazing accumulation of debt, and an unparalleled burden of taxes? Sometimes the pretence has been to support
one outlandish cause, and sometimes another. At one time
Austria, at another time Prussia, another to oppose Russia,
and so on; but the consequence has always been TAXES. A
few men have enriched themselves by jobs and contracts,
and the groaning multitude bore the burthen. What has
England gained by war since the year 1738, only fifty years
ago, to recompence her for TWO HUNDRED MILLIONS sterling, incurred as a debt within that time, and under the
annual interest of which, besides what was incurred before,
she is now groaning? Nothing at all.

The glare of fancied glory has often been held up, and the
shadowy recompence imposed itself upon the senses. Wars
that might have been prevented have been madly gone into,
and the end has been debt and discontent. A sort of something which man cannot account for is mixed in his composition, and renders him the subject of deception by the very
means he takes not to be deceived.

That jealousy which individuals of every nation feel at
the supposed design of foreign powers, fits them to be the
prey of Ministers, and of those among themselves whose
trade is war, or whose livelihood is jobs and contracts.
" Confusion to the politics of Europe, and may every nation
be at war in six months," was a toast given in my hearing not
long since.—The man was in court to the Ministry for a job.
—Ye gentle Graces, if any such there be who preside over
human actions, how must ye weep at the viciousness
of man!

When we consider, for the feelings of Nature cannot be
dismissed, the calamities of war and the miseries it inflicts
upon the human species, the thousands and tens of thousands of every age and sex who are rendered wretched by
the event, surely there is something in the heart of man that
calls upon him to think! Surely there is some tender chord
tuned by the hand of its Creator, that struggles to emit in
the hearing of the soul a note of sorrowing sympathy. Let

it then be heard, and let man learn to feel, that the true greatness of a nation is founded on the principles of humanity ; and that to avoid a war when our own existence is not endangered, and wherein the happiness of man must be wantonly sacrificed, is a higher principle of true honour than madly to engage in it.

But independent of all civil and moral considerations, there is no possible event that a war could produce benefits to England or France, on the present occasion, that could in the most distant proportion recompence to either the expence she must be at. War involves in its progress such a train of unforeseen and unsupposed circumstances, such a combination of foreign matters, that no human wisdom can calculate the end. It has but one thing certain, and that is increase of TAXES. The policy of European courts is now so cast, and their interests so interwoven with each other, that however easy it may be to begin a war, the weight and influence of interfering nations compel even the conqueror to unprofitable conditions of peace.

Commerce and maritime strength are now becoming the fashion, or rather the rage of Europe, and this naturally excites in them a combined wish to prevent either England or France increasing its comparative strength by destroying, or even relatively weakening, the other, and therefore whatever views each may have at the commencement of a war, new enemies will arise as either gains the advantage, and continued obstacles ensue to embarrass success.

The greatness of Lewis the Fourteenth made Europe his enemy, and the same cause will produce the same consequence to any other European power. That nation, therefore, is only truly wise, who, contenting herself with the means of defence, creates to herself no unnecessary enemies by seeking to be greater than the system of Europe admits. The Monarch or the Minister who exceeds this line, knows but little of his business. It is what the poet on another occasion calls—

" The point where sense and nonsense join."

Perhaps there is not a greater instance of the folly of calculating upon events, than are to be found in the treaties of alliance. As soon as they have answered the immediate purpose of either of the parties they are but little regarded. Pretences afterwards are never wanting to explain them away, nor reasons to render them abortive. And if half the money which nations lavish on speculative alliances were reserved for their own immediate purpose, whenever the occasion shall arrive, it would be more productively and advantageously employed.

Monarchs and Ministers, from ambition or resentment, often contemplate to themselves schemes of future greatness, and set out with what appears to them the fairest prospect: In the meanwhile, the great wheel of time and fate revolves unobserved, and something never dreamed of turns up and blasts the whole. A few fancied or unprofitable laurels supply the absence of success, and the exhausted nation is HUZZA'D INTO NEW TAXES.

The politics and interests of European Courts are so frequently varying with regard to each other, that there is no fixing even the probability of their future conduct. But the great principle of alliancing seems to be but little understood, or little cultivated in Courts, perhaps the least of all, in that of England.—No alliance can be operative that does not embrace within itself, not only the attachment of the Sovereigns, but the real interest of the nations.

The alliance between France and Spain, however it may be spoken of as a mere family compact, derives its greatest strength from national interest. The mines of Peru and Mexico are the soul of this alliance. Were those mines extinct, the family compact would most probably dissolve.

There exists not a doubt in the mind of Spain, what part England would act, respecting those mines, could she demolish the maritime power of France; and therefore the interest of Spain feels itself continually united with France. Spain has high ideas of honour, but has not the same ideas of English honour. They consider England as wholly governed by principles of interest, and that whatever she thinks it her interest to do, and supposes she has the power of doing, she makes very little ceremony of attempting. But this is not all—There is not a nation in Europe but what is more satisfied that those mines should be in the possession of Spain, than in that of any other European nation ; because the wealth of those mines, sufficient to ruin Europe in the hands of some of its powers, is innocently employed with respect to Europe, and better and more peaceably distributed among them all, through the medium of Spain, than it would be through that of any other nation. This is one of the secret causes that combine so large a part of Europe in the interest of France, because they cannot but consider her as a standing barrier to secure to them the free and equal distribution of this wealth throughout all the dominions of Europe.

This alliance of interest is likewise one of the unseen cements that prevents Spain and Portugal, two nations not very friendly to each other, proceeding to hostilities. They are both in the same situation, and, whatever their dislikes may be, they cannot fail to consider that by giving way to resentment that would weaken and exhaust themselves, each would be exposed a prey to some stronger power.

In short, this alliance of national interest is the only one that can be trusted, and the only one that can be operative. All other alliances formed on the mere will and caprice of Sovereigns, of family connections, uncombined with national interests, are but the quagmire of politics, and never fail to become a loss to that nation who wastes its present substance on the expectancy of distant returns.

With regard to Holland, a man must know very little of the matter, not to know that there exists a stronger principle of rivalship between Holland and England in point of commerce, than prevails between England and France in point of power : and, therefore, whenever a Stadtholder of Holland shall see it his interest to unite with the principle of his country, and act in concert with the sentiments of the very people who pay him for his services, the means now taken by England to render him formidable, will operate contrary to the political expectations of the present day.

Circumstances will produce their own natural effects, and no other, let the hopes or expectations of man be what they may. It is not our doing a thing with a design that it shall answer such or such an end, that will cause it to produce that end; the means taken must have a natural ability and tendency within themselves to produce no other, for it is this, and not our wishes of policy, that governs the event.

The English Navigation Act was levelled against the interest of the Dutch as a whole nation, and therefore it is not to be supposed that the catching at the accidental circumstances of one man, as in the case of the present Stadtholder, can combine the interest of that country with this. A few years, perhaps a less time, may remove him to the place where all things are forgotten, and his successor, contemplating his father's troubles, will be naturally led to reprobate the means that produced them, and to repose himself on the interests of his country, in preference to the accidental and tumultuous assistance of exterior power.

England herself exhibits at this day a species of this kind of policy. The present reign, by embracing the Scotch, has tranquillized and conciliated the spirit that disturbed the two former reigns. Accusations were not wanting at that time to reprobate the policy as tinctured with ingratitude towards those who were the immediate means of the Hanover succession. The brilliant pen of Junius was drawn forth, but in vain. It enraptured without convincing; and tho' in the plenitude of its rage it might be said to give elegance to bitterness, yet the policy survived the blast.[1]

What then will be the natural consequence of this expence, on account of the Stadtholder, or of a war entered into from that cause? Search the various windings and caverns of the human heart, and draw from thence the most probable conclusion, for this is more to be depended upon than the projects or declarations of Ministers.

It may do very well for a paragraph in a miserable common news-paper, or the wild effusions of romantic politicians,

---

[1] It is strange that in the face of this allusion the notion should spring up that Paine was "Junius."—*Editor*.

or the mercenary views of those who wish for war on any
occasion, merely for the sake of jobs and contracts, to talk of
French finesse or French intrigue ; but the Dutch are not a
people to be impressed by the finesse or intrigue of France
or England, or any other nation. If there has been any
finesse in the case, it has been between the electorate of
Hanover, the king of Prussia, and the Stadtholder, in which
it is most probable the people of England will be finessed
out of a sum of money.

The Dutch, as is already observed, are not a people open
to the impression of finesse. It is lost upon them. They
are impressed by their commercial interest. It is the political soul of their country, the spring of their actions, and
when this principle coincides with their ideas of freedom, it
has all the impulse a Dutchman is capable of feeling.

The Opposition in Holland were the enemies of the Stadtholder, upon a conviction that he was not the friend of their
national interests. They wanted no other impulse but this.
Whether this defect in him proceeded from foreign attachment, from bribery or corruption, or from the well known
defects of his understanding is not the point of inquiry.
It was the effect rather than the cause that irritated the
Hollanders.

If the Stadtholder made use of the power he held in the
government to expose and endanger the interests and property of the very people who supported him, what other
incentive does any man in any country require ? If the
Hollanders conceived the conduct of the Stadtholder injurious to their national interest, they had the same right to
expel him which England had to expel the Stuarts ; and the
interference of England to re-establish him serves only to
confirm in the Hollanders the same hatred against England
which the attempt of Lewis XIV. to re-establish the Stuarts
caused in England against France ; therefore if the present
policy is intended to attach Holland to England, it goes on
a principle exceedingly erroneous.

Let us now consider the situation of the Stadtholder, as
making another part of the question.

He must place the cause of his troubles to some secret influence which governed his conduct during the late war, or, in other words, that he was suspected of being the tool of the then British Administration. Therefore, as every part of an argument ought to have its weight, instead of charging the French with intriguing with the Hollanders, the charge more consistently lies against the British Ministry for intriguing with the Stadtholder, and endangering the nation in a war without a sufficient object. That which the Ministry are now doing confirms the suspicion, and explains to the Hollanders that collusion of the Stadtholder, against their national interests, which he must wish to have concealed, and the explanation does him more hurt than the unnecessary parade of service has done him good.

Nothing but necessity should have operated with England to appear openly in a case that must put the Stadtholder on still worse terms with his countrymen. Had France made any disposition for war, had she armed, had she made any one hostile preparation, there might then have been some pretence for England taking a step that cannot fail to expose to the world that the suspicions of the Hollanders against the Stadtholder were well founded, and that their cause was just, however unsuccessful has been the event.

As to the consequence of Holland in the scale of Europe, (the great stake, says some of the news-papers, for which England is contending) that is naturally pointed out by her condition : As merchants for other nations her interest dictates to her to be a neutral power, and this she always will be unless she is made war upon, as was the case in the last war ; and any expectation beyond what is the line of her interest, that is, beyond neutrality, either in England or France, will prove abortive. It therefore cannot be policy to go to war to effect that at a great expence, which will naturally happen of itself, and beyond which there is nothing to expect.

Let Holland be allied with England or with France, or with neither, or with both, her national conduct, consequently arising out of her circumstances, will be nearly the same, that

is, she will be neutral. Alliances have such a natural tendency to sink into harmless unoperative things, that to make
them a cause for going to war, either to prevent their being
formed, or to break any already formed, is the silliest speculation that war can be made upon, or wealth wasted to accomplish. It would scarcely be worth the attempt, if war could
be carried on without expence, because almost the whole
that can be hoped at the risk and expence of a war, is effected
by their natural tendency to inactivity.

However pompous the declarations of an alliance may be,
the object of many of them is no other than good-will, and
reciprocally securing, as far as such security can go, that
neither shall join the enemies of the other in any war that
may happen. But the national circumstances of Holland,
operate to insure this tranquillity on her part as effectually
to the power she is not allied with, as the engagement itself
does to the power with whom she is allied ; therefore the
security from circumstances is as good as the security from
engagement.

As to a cordial union of interest between Holland and
England, it is as unnatural to happen as between two individual rivals in the same trade : And if there is any step that
England could take to put it at a still greater distance, it is
the part she is now acting. She has increased the animosity
of Holland on the speculative politics of interesting the
Stadtholder, whose future repose depends upon uniting with
the Opposition in Holland, as the present reign did with the
Scotch. How foolish then has been the policy, how needless the expence of engaging in a war on account of the
affairs of Holland.

A cordiality between England and France is less improbable than between England and Holland. It is not how
an Englishman feels but how a Dutchman feels, that decides
this question. Between England and France there is no
real rivalship of interest ; it is more the effect of temper,
disposition, and the jealousy of confiding in each other, than
any substantial cause, that keeps up the animosity. But on
the part of Holland towards England, there is over and

above the spirit of animosity, the more powerful motives of interested commercial rivalship, and the galling remembrance of past injuries. The making war upon them under Lord North's administration, when they were taking no part in the hostilities, but merely acting the business of merchants, is a circumstance that will not easily be forgotten by them. On these reasons, therefore, which are naturally deduced from the operative feelings of mankind, any expectation of attaching Holland to England, as a friendly power, is vague and futile. Nature has her own way of working in the heart, and all plans of politics not founded thereon will disappoint themselves.

Any one who will review the history of English politics for several years past, must perceive they have been directed without system. To establish this, it is only necessary to examine one circumstance, fresh in the mind of every man.

The American war was prosecuted at a very great expence, on the publicly declared opinion, that the retaining America was necessary to the existence of England; but America being now separated from England, the present politics are, that she is better without her than with her. Both these cannot be true, and their contradiction to each other shows want of system. If the latter is true, it amounts to an impeachment of the political judgment of government, because the discovery ought to have been made before the expence was gone into. This single circumstance, yet fresh in every man's mind, is sufficient to create a suspicion, whether the present measures are more wisely founded than the former ones; and whether experience may not prove, that going to war for the sake of the Stadtholder, or for the hope of retaining a partial interest in Holland, who under any connection, can from circumstances be no more than a neutral power, is not as weak policy as going to war to retain America.

If England is powerful enough to maintain her own ground and consequence in the world as an independent nation, she needs no foreign connection. If she is not, the fact contradicts the popular opinion that she is. Therefore, either her politics are wrong, or her true condition is not what she supposes it to be. Either she must give up her opinion to justify her politics, or renounce her politics to vindicate her opinion.

If some kind of connection with Holland is supposed to be an object worthy some expence to obtain, it may be asked why was that connection broken by making war upon her in the last war? If it was not then worth preserving without expence, is it now worth re-obtaining at a vast expence? If the Hollanders do not like the English, can they be made to like them against their wills? If it shall be said that under the former connection they were un-friendly, will they be more friendly under any other? They were then in as free a situation to chuse as any future circumstances can make them, and, therefore, the national governing sentiment of the country can be easily discovered; for it signifies not what or who a Stadtholder may be, that which governs Holland is, and always must be, a commercial principle, and it will follow this line in spite of politics. Interest is as predominant and as silent in its operations as love; it resists all the attempts of force, and countermines all the stratagem of controul.

The most able English Statesmen and Politicians have always held it as a principle, that foreign connections served only to embarrass and exhaust England. That, surrounded by the ocean, she could not be invaded, as countries are on the Continent of Europe, and that her insular situation dic-tated to her a different system of politics to what those countries required, and that to be enleagued with them was sacrificing the advantages of situation to a capricious system of politics. That tho' she might serve them they could not much serve her, and that as the service must at all times be paid for, it could always be procured when it was wanted; and that it would be better to take it up in this line than to embarrass herself with speculative alliances that served rather to draw her into a Continental war on their account, than extricate her from a war undertaken on her own account.

From this discussion of the affairs of Holland, and of the inadequacy of Holland as an object of war, we will proceed to show that neither England nor France are in a condition to go to war, and that there is no present object to the one or the other to recompence the expence that each must be at, or atone to the subjects of either for the additional burthens that must be brought upon them. I defend the cause of the poor, of the manufacturers, of the tradesmen, of the farmer, and of all those on whom the real burthen of taxes fall—but above all, I defend the cause of humanity.

It will always happen, that any rumour of war will be popular among a great number of people in London. There are thousands who live by it; it is their harvest; and the clamour which those people keep up in news-papers and conversations passes unsuspiciously for the voice of the people, and it is not till after the mischief is done, that the deception is discovered.

Such people are continually holding up, in very magnified terms, the wealth of the nation, and the depressed condition of France, as reasons for commencing a war, without knowing any thing of either of these subjects.

But admitting them to be as true as they are false, as will be hereafter shown, it certainly indicates a vileness in the national disposition of any country, that will make the accidental internal difficulties to which all nations are subject, and sometimes encumbered with, a reason for making war upon them. The amazing encrease and magnitude of the paper currency now floating in all parts of England, exposes her to a shock as much more tremendous than the shock occasioned by the bankruptcy of the South Sea funds, as the quantity of credit and paper currency is now greater than they were at that time. Whenever such a circumstance shall happen, and the wisest men in the nation are, and cannot avoid being, impressed with the danger, it would be looked upon as baseness in France to make the distress and misfortune of England a cause and opportunity for making war upon her, yet this hideous infidelity is publicly avowed in England. The bankruptcy of 1719 was precipitated by the great credit which the funds then had, and the confidence which people placed in them. Is not credit making infinitely greater strides now than it made then? Is not confidence equally as blind now as at that day? The people then supposed themselves as wise as they do now, yet they were miserably deceived, and the deception that has once happened will happen again from the same causes.

Credit is not money, and therefore it is not pay, neither can it be put in the place of money in the end. It is only the means of getting into debt, not the means of getting out, otherwise the national debt could not accumulate; and the delusion which nations are under respecting the extention of credit is exactly like that which every man feels respecting life, the end is always nearer than was expected; and we become bankrupts in time by the same delusion that nations become bankrupts in property.

The little which nations know, or are sometimes willing to know, of each other, serves to precipitate them into wars which neither would have undertaken, had they fully known the extent of the power and circumstances of each other; it may therefore be of some use to place the circumstances of England and France in a comparative point of view.

In order to do this the accidental circumstances of a nation must be thrown out of the account. By accidental circumstances is meant, those temporary disjointings and derangements of its internal system which every nation in the world is subject to, and which, like accidental fits of sickness in the human body, prevent in the interim the full exertion and exercise of its natural powers.

The substantial basis of the power of a nation arises out of its population, its wealth, and its revenues. To these may be added the disposition of the people. Each of these will be spoken of as we proceed.

Instances are not wanting to show that a nation confiding too much on its natural strength, is less inclined to be active in its operations than one of less natural powers who is obliged to supply that deficiency by encreasing its exertions.

This has often been the case between England and France. The activity of England, arising from its fears, has sometimes exceeded the exertions of France reposing on its confidence.

But as this depends on the accidental disposition of a people, it will not always be the same. It is a matter well known to every man who has lately been in France, that a very extraordinary change is working itself in the minds of the people of that nation. A spirit that will render France exceedingly formidable whenever its government shall embrace the fortunate opportunity of doubling its strength by allying, if it may be so expressed (for it is difficult to express a new idea by old terms), the majesty of the Sovereign with the majesty of the nation ; for of all alliances that is infinitely the strongest and the safest to be trusted to, because the interest so formed, and operating against external enemies, can never be divided.

It may be taken as a certain rule, that a subject of any country attached to the government on the principles above mentioned, is of twice the value he was before. Freedom in the subject is not a diminution, as was formerly believed, of the power of government, but an increase of it. Yet the progress by which changes of this kind are effected, requires to be nicely attended to.

Were governments to offer freedom to the people, or to show an anxiety for that purpose, the offer most probably would be rejected. The purpose for which it was offered might be mistrusted. Therefore the desire must originate with, and proceed from the mass of the people, and when the impression becomes universal, and not before, is the important moment for the most effectual consolidation of national strength and greatness that can take place.

While this change is working, there will appear a kind of chaos in the nation ; but the creation we enjoy arose out of chaos, and our greatest blessings appear to have a confused beginning.

Therefore we may take it for granted, that what has at this moment the appearance of disorder in France, is no more than one of the links in that great chain of circumstances by which nations acquire the summit of their greatness. The provincial assemblies already begun in France, are as full, or rather a fuller representation of the people than the parliaments of England are.

The French, or, as they were formerly called, the Franks, (from whence came the English word frank and free) were once the freest people in Europe ; and as nations appear to have their periodical revolutions, it is very probable they will be so again. The change is already begun. The people of France, as it was before observed, are beginning to think for themselves, and the people of England resigning up the prerogative of thinking.[1]

We shall now proceed to compare the present condition of England and France as to population, revenues and wealth, and show that neither is in a condition of going to war, and that war can end in nothing but loss, and, most probably, a temporary ruin to both nations.

To establish this point so necessary for both nations to be impressed with, a free investigation of all matters connected with it is indispensable : If, therefore, any thing herein advanced shall be disagreeable, it must be justified on the ground that it is better to be known in order to prevent ruin, than to be concealed, when such concealment serves only to hasten the ruin on.

Of POPULATION.—The population of France, being upwards of twenty-four millions, is more than double that of Great Britain and Ireland ; besides which France recruits more soldiers in Switzerland than England does in Scotland and Ireland. To this may likewise be added, that England and Ireland are not on the best terms. The suspicion that England governs Ireland for the purpose of keeping her low, to prevent her becoming her rival in trade and manufactures, will always operate to hold Ireland in a state of sentimental hostility with England.

[1] Dr. Robinet (*Danton Emigré*, p. 7) alludes to these "prophetic" paragraphs, written in the summer of 1787, as due to his personal intimacy with those who presently inaugurated the Revolution. It will be remarked that no overthrow of the French Monarchy is suggested.—*Editor*.

REVENUES.—The revenues of France are twenty-four millions sterling. The revenues of England fifteen millions and an half. The taxes per head in France are twenty shillings sterling; the taxes per head in England are two pounds four shillings and two pence. The national debt of France, including the life annuities (which are two fifths of the whole debt, and are annually expiring) at eleven years purchase, is one hundred and forty-two millions sterling. The national debt of England, the whole of which is on perpetual interest, is two hundred and forty-five millions. The national debt of France contains a power of annihilating itself without any new taxes for that purpose; because it needs no more than to apply the life annuities as they expire to the purchase of the other three-fifths, which are on perpetual interest: But the national debt of England has not this advantage, and therefore the million a year that is to be applied towards the reducing it is so much additional tax upon the people, over and above the current service.

WEALTH.—This is an important investigation: it ought therefore to be heard with patience, and judged of without prejudice.

Nothing is more common than for people to mistake one thing for another. Do not those who are crying up the wealth of the nation mistake a paper currency for riches? To ascertain this point may be one of the means of preventing that ruin which cannot fail to follow by persisting in the mistake.

The highest estimation that is made of the quantity of gold and silver in Britain at this present day is twenty millions: and those who are most conversant with money transactions, believe it to be considerably below that sum. Yet this is no more money than what the nation possessed twenty years ago, and therefore, whatever her trade may be, it has produced to her no profit. Certainly no man can be so unwise as to suppose that encreasing the quantity of bank notes, which is done with as little trouble as printing of newspapers, is national wealth.

The quantity of money in the nation was very well ascertained in the years 1773, '74, and '76, by calling in the light gold coin.

There were upwards of fifteen millions and a half of gold coin then called in, which, with upwards of two millions of heavy guineas that remained out, and the silver coin, made above twenty millions, which is more than there is at this day. There is an amazing increase in the circulation of Bank paper, which is no more national wealth than news-papers are; because an increase of promissary notes, the capital remaining unincreasing, or not increasing in the same proportion, is no increase of wealth. It serves to raise false ideas which the judicious soon discover, and the ignorant experience to their cost.

Out of twenty millions sterling, the present quantity of real money in the nation, it would be too great an allowance to say that one fourth of that sum, which is five millions, was in London. But even admitting this to be the case, it would require no very superior powers to ascertain pretty nearly what proportion of that sum of five millions could be in the Bank. It would be ridiculous to suppose it could be less than half a million, and extravagant to suppose it could be two millions.

It likewise requires no very extraordinary discernment to ascertain how immense the quantity of Bank Notes, compared to the capital in the Bank must be, when it is considered, that the national taxes are paid in Bank Notes, that all great transactions are done in Bank Notes, and that were a loan for twenty millions to be opened at the meeting of Parliament, it would most probably be subscribed in a few days: Yet all men must know the loan could not be paid in money, because it is at least four times greater than all the money in London, including the Bankers and the Bank amount too. In short, every thing shows, that the rage that overrun America, for paper money or paper currency, has reached to England under another name. There it was called Continental Money, and here it is called Bank Notes. But it signifies not what name it bears, if the capital is not equal to the redemption.

There is likewise another circumstance that cannot fail to
strike with some force when it is mentioned, because every
man that has any thing to do with money transactions will
feel the truth of it, tho' he may not before have reflected
upon it.   It is the embarrassed condition into which the gold
coin is thrown by the necessity of weighing it, and by refusing guineas that are even standing weight, and there
appears to be but few heavy ones.   Whether this is intended to force the Paper Currency into circulation, is not
here attempted to be asserted, but it certainly has that
effect to a very great degree, because people, rather than
submit to the trouble and hazard of weighing, will take
paper in preference to money.   This was once the case in
America.

The natural effect of encreasing and continuing to increase paper currencies is that of banishing the real money.
The shadow takes place of the substance till the country is
left with only shadows in its hands.

A trade that does not increase the quantity of real money
in a country, cannot be styled a profitable trade ; yet this is
certainly the case with England : and as to credit, of which
so much has been said, it may be founded on ignorance or a
false belief, as well as on real ability.

In Amsterdam, the money deposited in the Bank is never
taken out again.   The depositors, when they have debts
to pay, transfer their right to the persons to whom they are
indebted, and those again proceed by the same practice,
and the transfer of the right goes for payment ; now could
all the money deposited in the Bank of Amsterdam be
privately removed away, and the matter be kept a secret,
the ignorance, or the belief that the money was still there,
would give the same credit as if it had not been removed.
In short, credit is often no more than an opinion, and
the difference between credit and money is that money requires no opinion to support it.

All the countries in Europe annually increase in their
quantity of gold and silver except England. By the registers
kept at Lisbon and Cadiz, the two ports into which the gold

and silver from South America are imported, it appears that above eighty millions sterling have been imported within twenty years.* This has spread itself over Europe, and increased the quantity in all the countries on the Continent; yet twenty years ago there was as much gold and silver in England as there is at this time.

The value of the silver imported into Europe exceeds that of the gold, yet every one can see there is no increase of silver coin in England; very little silver coin appearing except what are called Birmingham shillings, which have a faint impression of King William on one side, and are smooth on the other.

In what is the profits of trade to show itself but by increasing the quantity of that which is the object of trade, money? An increase of paper is not an increase of national noney, and the confounding paper and money together, or not attending to the distinction, is a rock that the nation will one day split upon.

Whether the payment of interest to foreigners, or the trade to the East Indies, or the nation embroiling itself in foreign wars, or whether the amount of all the trade which England carries on with different parts of the world, collectively taken, balances itself without profit; whether one or all of these is the cause, why the quantity of money does not encrease in England, is not, in this place the object of enquiry. It is the fact and not the cause that is the matter here treated of.

Men immersed in trade and the concerns of a counting-house are not the most speculative in national affairs, or always the best judges of them. Accustomed to run risks in trade, they are habitually prepared to run risks with Government, and though they are the first to suffer, they are often the last to foresee an evil.

Let us now cast a look towards the manufactures. A great deal has been said of their flourishing condition, and

---

* From 1763 to 1777, a period of fifteen years of peace, the registered importations of gold and silver into Lisbon and Cadiz, was seventy millions sterling, besides what was privately landed.—*Author*.

perhaps a great deal too much, for it may again be asked, where is the profit if there is no encrease of money?

The woollen manufacture is the staple manufacture of England, and this is evidently on the decline, in some, if not in all its branches. The city of Norwich, one of the most populous cities in England, and wholly dependant on the woollen manufacture, is at this day, in a very impoverished condition, owing to the decline of its trade.

But not to rest the matter on a general assertion, or embarrass it with numerous statements, we will produce a circumstance by which the whole progress of the trade may be ascertained.

So long as thirty years ago, the price paid to the spinners of wool was one shilling for twenty-four skains, each skain containing five hundred and sixty yards. This, according to the term of the trade, was called giving a shilling for a shilling. A good hand would spin twelve skains, which was sixpence a day.

According to the increase of taxes, and the increased price of all the articles of life, they certainly ought now to get at least fifteen pence, for what thirty years ago they got a shilling for. But such is the decline of the trade, that the case is directly the contrary. They now get but nine pence for the shilling, that is, they get but nine pence for what thirty years ago they got a shilling for. Can these people cry out for war, when they are already half ruined by the decline of trade, and half devoured by the increase of taxes?

But this is not the whole of the misfortunes which that part of the country suffers, and which will extend to others. The Norfolk farmers were the first who went into the practice of manuring their land with marle; but time has shewn that though it gave a vigour to the land for some years, it operated in the end to exhaust its stamina; that the lands in many parts are worse than before they begun to marle, and that it will not answer to marle a second time.

The manufacturers of Manchester, Birmingham and Sheffield have had of late a considerable spring, but this appears

to be rather on speculation than certainty. The speculations on the American market have failed, and that on
Russia is becoming very precarious. Experience likewise
was wanting to ascertain the quantity which the treaty of
commerce with France would give sale to, and it is most
probable the estimations have been too high, more especially
as English goods will now become unpopular in France, which
was not the case before the present injudicious rupture.

But in the best state which manufactures can be in, they
are very unstable sources of national wealth. The reasons
are, that they seldom continue long in one state. The
market for them depends upon the caprice of fashions, and
sometimes of politics in foreign countries, and they are at
all times exposed to rivalship as well as to change. The
Americans have already several manufactures among them,
which they prefer to the English, such as axes, scythes,
sickles, ploughs, planes, nails, etc. Window glass, which was
once a considerable article of export from England to
America, the Americans now procure from other countries,
nearly as good as the English Crown Glass, and but little
dearer than the common green window glass.

It is somewhat remarkable that so many pens have been
displayed to shew what is called the increase of the commerce of England, and yet all of them have stopped short
of the grand point, that is, they have gone no further than
to shew that a larger proportion of shipping, and a greater
quantity of tonnage have been employed of late years than
formerly: But this is no more than what is happening in
other parts of Europe. The present fashion of the world is
commerce, and the quantity encreases in France as well as
in England.

But the object of all trade is profit, and profit shews itself,
not by an increase of paper currency, for that may be nationally had without the trouble of trade, but by an increase of
real money: therefore the estimation should have ended,
not in the comparative quantity of shipping and tonnage,
but in the comparative quantity of gold and silver.

Had the quantity of gold and silver increased in England,

the ministerial writers would not have stopt short at shipping and tonnage; but if they know any thing of the
matter, they must know that it does not increase, and that
the deception is occasioned by the increase of paper instead
of money, and that as paper continues to increase, gold
and silver will diminish.   Poorer in wealth, and richer in
delusion.

Something is radically wrong, and time will discover it to
be putting paper in the room of money.

Out of one hundred millions sterling of gold and silver,
which must have been imported into Europe from South
America since the commencement of the peace before last,
it does not appear that England has derived or retains any
portion of it.

M. Neckar states the annual increase of gold and silver in
France, that is, the proportion which France draws of the
annual importation into Europe, to be upwards of one
million sterling.   But England, in the space of twenty
years, does not appear to have encreased in any thing but
paper currency.

Credulity is wealth while credulity lasts, and credit is, in
a thousand instances, the child of credulity.   It requires no
more faith to believe paper to be money, than to believe a
man could go into a quart bottle; and the nation whose
credulity can be imposed upon by bottle conjuring, can, for
a time, be imposed upon by paper conjuring.

From these matters we pass on to make some observations on the national debt, which is another species of paper
currency.

In short, to whatever point the eye is directed, whether
to the money, the paper, the manufactures, the taxes, or the
debt, the inability of supporting a war is evident, unless it is
intended to carry it on by fleecing the skin over people's
ears by taxes; and therefore the endangering the nation in
a war for the sake of the Stadtholder of Holland, or the
king of Prussia, or any other foreign affairs, from which
England can derive no possible advantage, is an absurd and
ruinous system of politics.

France, perhaps, is not in a better situation, and therefore, a war where both must lose, and wherein they could only act the part of seconds, must historically have been denominated a boyish, foolish, unnecessary quarrel.

But before we enter on the subject of the national debt, it will be proper to make a general review of the different manner of carrying on war since the Revolution to what was the practice before.

Before the Revolution the intervals of peace and war always found means to pay off the expence, and leave the nation clear of incumbrance at the commencement of any succeeding war; and even for some years after the Revolution this practice was continued.

From the year 1688, (the æra of the Revolution) to the year 1702, a period of fourteen years, the sums borrowed by Government at different times, amounted to forty-four millions; yet this sum was paid off almost as fast as it was borrowed; thirty-four millions being paid off, at the commencement of the year 1702. This was a greater exertion than the nation has ever made since, for exertion is not in borrowing but in paying.

From that time wars have been carried on by borrowing and funding the capital on a perpetual interest, instead of paying it off, and thereby continually carrying forward and accumulating the weight and expence of every war into the next. By this means that which was light at first becomes immensely heavy at last. The nation has now on its shoulders the weight of all the wars from the time of Queen Anne. This practice is exactly like that of loading a horse with a feather at a time till you break his back.

The national debt exhibits at this day a striking novelty. It has travelled on in a circular progression till the amount of the annual interest has exactly overtaken, or become equal to, the first capital of the national debt, NINE MILLIONS. Here begins the evidence of the predictions so long foretold by the ablest calculators in the nation. The interest will in succession overtake all the succeeding capitals, and that with the proportioned rapidity with which those capitals accumulated ; because by continuing the practice, not only higher and higher premiums must be given for loans, but the money, or rather the paper, will not go so far as it formerly did, and therefore the debt will increase with a continually increasing velocity.

The expence of every war, since the national debt began, has, upon an average, been double the expence of the war preceding it ; the expence therefore of the next war will be at least two hundred millions, which will encrease the annual interest to at least seventeen millions, and consequently the taxes in the same proportion ; the following war will encrease the interest to thirty-three millions, and a third war will mount up the interest to sixty-five millions. This is not going on in the spirit of prediction, but taking what has already been as a rule for what will yet be, and therefore the nation has but a miserable prospect to look at. The weight of accumulating interest is not much felt till after many years have passed over ; but when it begins to be heavy, as it does now, the burthen encreases like that of purchasing a horse with a farthing for the first nail of the shoe and doubling it.

As to Mr. Pitt's scheme of reducing the national debt by a million a year, applied to the purchase of stock, it will turn out, to say the least of it, a ridiculous and frivolous project : For if a Minister has not experience enough to distinguish a feather in the air, and such there always will be, from the God of War, nor the clamours and interest of those who are seeking for jobs and contracts from the voice and interests of the people, he will soon precipitate the nation into some unnecessary war : and therefore any scheme of redemption of the debt, founded on the supposed continuance of peace, will, with such conduct, be no more than a balloon.

That the funding system contains within itself the seeds of its own destruction, is as certain as that the human body contains within itself the seeds of death. The event is as fixed as fate, unless it can be taken as a proof that because we are not dead we are not to die.

The consequence of the funding scheme, even if no other

event takes place, will be to create two violent parties in the nation. The one, goaded by taxes continually encreasing to pay the interest, the other reaping a benefit from the taxes by receiving the interest. This is very strongly shadowed forth, like the handwriting on the wall, by the ingenious author of the Commercial Atlas, in his observations on the national debt.

The slumber that for several years has over-shadowed the nation in all matters of public finance, cannot be supposed to last for ever. The people have not yet awakened to the subject, and it is taken for granted that they never will. But, if a supposed unnecessary expenditure of between five and six millions sterling in the finances of France (for the writer undertakes not to judge of the fact) has awakened that whole nation, a people supposed to be perfectly docile in all national matters, surely the people of England will not be less attentive to their rights and properties. If this should not be the case, the inference will be fairly drawn that England is losing the spirit that France is taking up, and that it is an ingenious device in the Ministry to compose the nation to unpopular and unnecessary taxes, by shamming a victory when there was no enemy at hand.

In short, every war serves to encrease every kind of paper currency in the nation, and to diminish the quantity of gold and silver, by sending it to Prussia and other foreign countries.

It will not be denied that credulity is a strong trait in the English character; and this has in no instance shewn itself more than in mistaking paper for money, except it be in the unaccountable ignorance of mistaking the debt of the nation for riches. But the suspicion is beginning to awake.

We will close this article with observing, that a new kind of paper currency has arisen within a few years, which is that of country Bank Notes; almost every town now has its Bank, its Paper Mint, and the coinage of paper is become universal. In the mean time the melting down the light guineas, and recoining them, passes with those who know no better for an encrease of money; because every new guinea they see, and which is but seldom, they naturally suppose to be a guinea more, when it is really nothing else than an old guinea new cast.

From this account of the money, paper, and national debt of England, we proceed to compare it with the money, paper, and national debt of France.

It is very well known that paper has not the same credit in France which it has in England, and that, consequently, there is much less of it. This has naturally operated to encrease the quantity of gold and silver in France, and prevent the encrease of paper.

The highest estimation of the quantity of gold and silver in England, as already stated, is twenty millions sterling, and the quantity of paper grafted thereon, immense.

The quantity of gold and silver in France is ninety millions sterling, and the quantity of paper grafted thereon trifling. France, therefore, has a long run of credit yet in reserve, which England has already expended ; and it will naturally follow, that when the Government of France and the nation shall adjust their differences by an amicable embrace of each other, that this reserved credit will be brought forth, and the power of France will be doubly encreased. The adjustment of these differences is but the business of a day, whenever its Government shall see the proper moment for doing it ; and nothing would precipitate this event more than a war. The cry of war, from the injudicious provocations given by the British Ministry, and the disadvantageous effect of the Commercial Treaty, is becoming popular in France.

The near situation of France to Spain and Portugal, the two countries which import gold and silver, and her manufactures being better adapted to the warm climate of those countries than the manufactures of England, give her superior opportunities of drawing money into the nation ; and as she has but little trade to the East Indies, the money so drawn in is not drawn out again, as in England. Another advantage is that, from the greatness of her dominions, she has no occasion to waste her wealth in hiring foreign troops, as is the practice with England ; and a third advantage is, that the money which England squanders in Prussia and other countries on the Continent serves to encrease the wealth of France, because a considerable part of it centres there through the medium of her commerce.

Admitting Great Britain and Ireland to contain ten millions of inhabitants, the quantity of money per head is forty shillings ; the money per head in France is three pounds fifteen shillings, which is nearly double.

The national debt of England, compared to the whole amount of money in the nation, is as twelve to one, that is, the debt is twelve times greater than all the money amounts to.

The national debt of France, compared to the whole amount of her money, is considerably less than as two is to one, that is, her debt is not so much as twice the amount of her money. France, therefore, as already stated, has an immense credit in reserve whenever the settlement of her present internal differences shall furnish her with the means of employing it ; and that period, so much to be dreaded by England, is hastening on.

The annual interest of the national debt of England and France are nearly equal, being NINE MILLIONS sterling ; but with this difference, that above three millions and a half of the annual interest of France are only life annuities. The interest, therefore, of her debt lessens every year, and she will have a surplus up to the amount of three millions and a half, to apply to the purchase of that part of the debt which is on perpetual interest ; therefore, without any new taxes for that purpose, she can discharge her whole debt in less than a third of the time in which it can be done in England, according to Mr. Pitt's plan, with his additional tax of a million a year.

But let the event of Mr. Pitt's plan be what it may, as to reducing the debt, there is one circumstance that cannot fail to accompany it, which is, that of making it the interest of Government, in executing this plan, to undermine the interest of its creditors, or the value of the funds, for the purpose of purchasing at a cheaper rate.

The plan is founded on the presumption of a long uninterrupted peace, and that future loans would not be wanted,
which cannot now be expected, for France in her turn is
getting into a temper for war.   The plan naturally strikes at
the credit of Government, in contracting further debts; for
were a loan to be opened to-morrow, the subscribers, naturally perceiving that it was the interest of Government to
undermine them as soon as they became creditors, would consequently seek to secure themselves by demanding higher
premiums at first.   It is a question whether a premium of
thirty per cent. is now as good as ten was before, and therefore the plan, in case of a war, instead of lessening the debt,
serves to push it more rapidly on.

The Minister certainly never understood the natural operation of his plan, or he would not have acted as he has done.
The plan has two edges, while he has supposed it to have only
one.   It strikes at the debt in peace, and at the credit in war.

The gentleman who originally furnished the Minister with
this plan, now gives it totally up.   He knew its operation
both in peace and war, but the Minister appears not to have
comprehended it : But if he has made a mistake, his youth
and inexperience must be his apology.

The plan, unless it should be altered, that is given out for
providing for the expence of the late armaments, is in reality
no other than the American plan of paper money, and it is
very probable that the Minister has received it from some
American refugee.

The plan given out is, that the Minister is to borrow the
MONEY of the Bank.   Here is the delusion.   The name of
MONEY covers the deception.   For the case is, that the Bank
does not lend the real money, but it issues out an emission
of Bank-paper, and the presumption is that there will be no
run upon the Bank in consequence of such an extraordinary
emission; but if there should, no man can be at a loss in
foreseeing the issue.

There are those who remember that on a former run the
Bank was obliged to prolong the time of paying shillings and
sixpences, and it is universally credited that a quantity of

silver is now preserved in the Bank for the same purpose; but the device, to every person of reflection, shows that the capital is not equal to the demands, and that the Chapter of Accidents is part of the Bible of Bank.

It may be asked why does not the Government issue the paper instead of the Bank? The answer is, that it is exactly the same thing in the end, only with this difference in the mode, that were the Government to do it, it would be too visible a system of paper currency, and that a disguise is necessary.

Having recourse to the Bank, is a kind of playing the Bank off against the Funds. Fighting one kind of paper against another, and in the combat both will be sufferers.

In short, the delusion of paper riches is working as rapidly in England as it did in America. A young and inexperienced Minister, like a young and inexperienced Congress, may suppose that he sees mines of wealth in a printing press, and that a nation cannot be exhausted while there is paper and ink enough to print paper money. Every new emission, until the delusion bursts, will appear to the nation an increase of wealth. Every merchant's coffers will appear a treasury, and he will swell with paper riches till he becomes a bankrupt.

When a Bank makes too free with its paper, it exposes itself in much the same manner which a Government does that makes too free with its power; too much credit is as bad as too little; and there is such a thing as governing too much, as well in a Bank, as in a Government. But nothing exposes a Bank more than being under the influence instead of the protection of Government, and whenever either the property or the credit of a Bank, can be commanded or influenced by a Government, or a Minister, its destruction is not far off.

We have now stated the comparative condition of England and France as to money matters. But there yet remain some things necessary to be touched upon.

It is an error very frequently committed in the world to mistake disposition for condition.

France, with a much better permanent condition for war than England, is in a less disposition to enter into one, and this want of disposition in her is mistaken in England for want of condition ; and on the other hand, the apparent disposition in England for war is mistaken by her for a condition to undertake and carry one on.

There appears a uniformity in all the works of Nature, from individual animals up to nations. The smaller animals are always the most fretful, passionate, and insulting. They mistake temper for strength, and often fall a sacrifice to vexatious impetuosity, while larger ones go calmly on, and require repeated provocations to incense them. France may yet be aggravated into war, and very probably will. Where the condition exists, the disposition may at any time take place. We may create temper, but we cannot create strength.

While the literature of England preserves an honourable rank among the nations of Europe, her national character is most miserably suffering in the world through her newspapers. The most barefaced perfidiousness, the most abandoned principles are daily propagated. A total disregard to all the obligations of national faith and honour are publicly professed. Instead of that true greatness of heart, that calm grandeur of sentiment, that generous disdain of vulgar littleness that ought always to accompany the disputes of nations, scarcely any thing is to be seen but mean abuse and low scurrility. This is not the case in any other country in the world but England.

We will now proceed to conclude with a few additional observations on the state of politics.

For several weeks the nation was amused with the daily rumours of some great Cabinet secret, and admiring how profoundly the secret was kept, when the only secret was, that there was no secret to divulge.

But this opinion of a secret very well shews that the opinion of the nation was opposed to the opinion of the Minister, or the supposition of some great secret would not have taken place, as the affairs of the Stadtholder were then

publicly known.   It shews that the nation did not think the
Stadtholder of Holland a sufficient reason for laying new
taxes on England, and running into the risk and expence of
a war, and great was the surprise when the declaration and
counter-declaration, like twin mice, peeped from the Cabinet.

But there is one secret that requires to be investigated,
which is, whether the Minister did not know that France
would not engage in a war, and whether the preparations
were not an idle parade, founded on that knowledge.

Whether it was not meanly putting England under the
banners of Prussia, and taking thereby a dishonourable
advantage of the internal perplexity which France was
then in, and which in its turn may happen to England, to
assume the air of a challenge, which it must be known
would not be accepted, because there was nothing to make
the acceptance necessary.

Whether this conduct in the Minister does not mischiev-
ously operate to destroy the harmony that appeared to be
growing up between the two nations; to lessen, if not totally
destroy, the advantages of the Commercial Treaty, and to
lay the seeds of future wars, when there was a prospect of
a long and uninterrupted peace.

When there are two ways of accomplishing the same
object, it almost always happens that the one is better
than the other; and whether the Minister has not chosen
the worst, a few observations will elucidate.

It signifies not what airy schemes, projects, or even
treaties may be formed, especially if done under the point
of the bayonet, for all that can be expected of Holland is
neutrality.   Her trade is with all nations, and it is from her
neutrality that this trade has arisen.   Destroy this neutrality
and Holland is destroyed.   Therefore it matters not what
sentiments party men may be of in Holland as to the Stadtholdership, because there is still a superior banner under
which all will unite.

Holland will not expose her trade to the devastations of
England by joining France in a war, neither will she expose it to France by joining England.   It may very well

be asked, what are England or France to Holland, that she should join with either in a war, unless she is compelled to it by one or the other making war upon her, as was the case in the last war?

Events may soon happen in Europe to make all the force that Prussia can raise necessary to her own defence, and Holland must be wise enough to see that, by joining England, she not only exposes her trade to France but likewise her dominions, because France can invade her in a quarter in which England cannot defend her, provided her Generals prove true, for Holland lies open to France by land. It is, therefore, more immediately the interest of Holland to keep on good terms with France; neither can England give her any equivalent to balance this circumstance. How foolish then are the politics which are directed to unnatural and impossible objects! Surely the experience of a century past is sufficient to shew to any man, except one of yesterday, what the conduct of Holland in all cases must be.

But there is another circumstance that does not fail to impress foreigners, and especially Holland; which is, that the immensity of the national debt of England, the prospect of its still encreasing, and the exorbitancy of her paper currencies, render her too insecure in herself to be much confided in by foreign nations for any length of time. Because that which must happen may soon happen.

Concerning the rescript delivered by the French Minister, there is one certain explanation to be put upon it, which is, that if France had been disposed for war, she would not have made that communication. The very making it goes to a full explanation of the parts; and as soon as Mr. Pitt obtained this knowledge, it appeared to him a safe moment to gird on his sword; and when he found that France was as well weaponed as himself, to propose to take it off again. This is in a few words the whole history of the campaign. A war Minister in peace, and a peace Minister in war. Brave where there is no danger, and prudent when there is.

The rescript could be nothing else than an explanation, on the part of France, of the situation she conceived herself to be subject to, and the probable consequences that might follow from it. This she was not obliged to make, and therefore her making it was a matter of civil communication towards a power she was at peace with, and which in return entitled her to a similar communication on the part of the British Cabinet. All this might have been done without either the expence, the tumult, the provocations, or the ill blood that has been created.

The alliance between France and the Dutch was formed while the Stadtholder was a part of the Government, therefore France could not, from that alliance, take a part either for or against him. She could only act when the whole interest of the Republic was exposed to a foreign enemy, and it was not certain that this might not be the case.

The rescript, therefore, instead of being taken as a ground for war, was in itself a ground for peace, because it tended to bring on a discussion of all the circumstances of France and England relative to Holland, which would not have failed to place Holland in a state of neutrality, and that only will be the final event now; because, independent of all parties, no other is consistent with the whole national interest of that Republic.

But this is not being done, it is now left to the Dutch to do it for themselves.

An alliance with England, at the same time there is one existing with France, will secure this neutrality, so necessary to the Dutch Republic. By this stroke of politics she will be free from all obligations to join with either in a war, and be guaranteed by both. Her alliance with England will debar England from molesting her trade by sea, and that with France will debar France from the same thing, and likewise from invading her by land in all future cases. There are so many probable circumstances to arise on the Continent of Europe, that the situation of Holland requires this safeguard, more especially from France, on account of her land connection.

The rising greatness of the Russian Empire, the probable union of this Empire with those of Germany and France, and consequently with Spain, whose interests cannot be separated, and the probability of a rupture between the Emperor and the King of Prussia, are matters that cannot fail to impress the Dutch with the necessity of securing themselves by land as well as by sea, and to prevent their being drawn into the quarrels either of England or France.

Upon the whole, as there was a civil as well as an uncivil line of politics to be pursued, every man of humane and generous sentiments must lament it was not chosen.

A disposition for peace was growing up in every part of France, and there appeared at the same time a mutual one rising in England. A silent wish on both sides was universally expanding itself, that wars, so fatal to the true interest and burthensome by taxes to the subjects of both countries, might exist no more, and that a long and lasting peace might take place.

But instead of cultivating this happy opportunity, the pettish vanity of a young and inexperienced Minister, who balanced himself between peace and war to take his choice of circumstances, instead of principles, and who went into an expensive armament when there was none to contend with, and not till after the affairs of Holland might be said to be terminated, has destroyed those seeds of harmony that might have been rendered of more value to both nations than their fleets and armies.

He has permitted the nation to run mad under the universal influence of a groundless belief of vast hostile armaments in the East and West Indies, and the supposition of a secret that never existed. By this means the sparks of ill will are afresh kindled up between the nations, the fair prospects of lasting peace are vanished, and a train of future evils fills up the scene, and that at a time when the internal affairs of France, however confused they at present appear, are naturally approaching to a great and harmonious encrease of its power.

THOMAS PAINE.

York Street, St. James's Square,
20th August, 1787.

IX.

SPECIFICATION OF THOMAS PAINE.

A.D. 1788 . . . . N° 1667.

CONSTRUCTING ARCHES, VAULTED ROOFS, AND CEILINGS.

To all to whom these presents shall come, I, Thomas Paine, send greeting.

Whereas His most Excellent Majesty King George the Third, by His Letters Patent under the Great Seal of Great Britain, bearing date the Twenty-sixth day of August, in the Twenty-eighth year of His reign, did give unto me, the said Thomas Paine, His special licence that I, the said Thomas Paine, during the term of fourteen years therein expressed, should and lawfully might make, use, exercise, and vend, within England, Wales, and Town of Berwick-upon-Tweed, my Invention of "A Method of Constructing of Arches, Vaulted Roofs, and Cielings, either in Iron or Wood, on Principles New and Different to anything hitherto practiced, by means of which Construction Arches, Vaulted Roofs, and Cielings may be Erected to the extent of several Hundred Feet beyond what can be performed in the present practice of Architecture;" in which said Letters Patent there is contained a proviso obliging me, the said Thomas Paine, to cause a particular description of the nature of my said Invention, and in what manner the same is to be performed, by an instrument in writing under my hand and seal, to be inrolled in His Majesty's High Court of Chancery

227

within one calendar month next and immediately after the date of the said recited Letters Patent, as in and by the same (relation being thereunto had) may more fully and at large appear.

NOW KNOW YE, that in compliance with the said proviso, I, the said Thomas Paine, do hereby declare that my said Invention of A Method of Constructing of Arches, Vaulted Roofs, and Cielings, either in Iron or Wood, on Principles New and Different to anything hitherto practiced, by means of which Construction, Arches, Vaulted Roofs, and Cielings may be Erected to the Extent of several Hundred Feet beyond what can be performed in the present practice of Architecture, is described in manner following (that is to say) :—

The idea and construction of this arch is taken from the figure of a spider's circular web, of which it resembles a section, and from a conviction that when nature empowered this insect to make a web she also instructed her in the strongest mechanical method of constructing it.

Another idea, taken from nature in the construction of this arch, is that of increasing the strength of matter by dividing and combining it, and thereby causing it to act over a larger space than it would occupy in a solid state, as is seen in the quills of birds, bones of animals, reeds, canes, etc. The curved bars of the arch are composed of pieces of any length joined together to the whole extent of the arch, and take curveture by bending. Those curves, to any number, height, or thickness, as the extent of the arch may require, are raised concentrically one above another, and separated, when the extent of the arch requires it, by the interposition of blocks, tubes, or pins, and the whole bolted close and fast together (the direction of the radius is the best) through the whole thickness of the arch, the bolts being made fast by a head pin or screw at each end of them. This connection forms one arched rib, and the number of ribs to be used is in proportion to the breadth and extent of the arch, and those separate ribs are also combined and braced together by bars passing 'cross all the ribs, and made

fast thereto above and below, and as often and wherever the
arch, from its extent, depth, and breadth, requires.   When
this arch is to be applied to the purpose of a bridge, which
requires more arches than one, they are to be connected in
the following manner (that is to say):—Wood piles are to
be driven into the earth ; over each of those piles are to be
let fall a hollow iron or metal case, with a broad foot let into
a bed ; the interspace between the case and the wood pile
to be filled up with a cement and pinned together.   The
whole number of those pillars are to be braced together, and
formed into a platform for receiving and connecting the
arches.   The interspaces of those pillars may be filled with
plates of iron or lattice work so as to resemble a pier, or left
open so as to resemble a colonade of any of the orders of
architecture.   Among the advantages of this construction is
that of rendering the construction of bridges into a portable
manufacture, as the bars and parts of which it is composed
need not be longer or larger than is convenient to be stowed
in a vessel, boat, or waggon, and that with as much compact-
ness as iron or timber is transported to or from Great Britain ;
and a bridge of any extent upon this construction may be
manufactured in Great Britain and sent to any part of the
world to be erected.   For the purpose of preserving the iron
from dust it is to be varnished over with a coat of melted
glass.   It ought to be observed, that extreme simplicity,
though striking to the view, is difficult to be conceived from
description, although such description exactly accords, upon
inspection, with the thing described.   A practicable method
of constructing arches to several hundred feet span, with a
small elevation, is the desideratum of bridge architecture,
and it is the principle and practicability of constructing and
connecting such arches so as totally to remove or effectually
lessen the danger and inconvenience of obstructing the chan-
nell of rivers, together with that of adding a new and important manufacture to the iron works of the nation, capable
of transportation and exportation, that is herein described.
When this arch is to be applied to the purpose of a roof and
cieling cords may be added to the arch to supply the want

of butments, which are to be braced to or connected with the arch by perpendiculars.

> In witness whereof, I, the said Thomas Paine, have hereunto set my hand and seal, the Twenty-fifth day of September, in the year of our Lord One thousand seven hundred and eighty-eight.
>
> THOMAS   (L.S.)   PAINE.

Sealed and delivered, being first duly
    stamped, in the presence of
        PETER WHITESIDE.

AND BE IT REMEMBERED, that on the Twenty-fifth day of September, in the twenty-eighth year of the reign of His Majesty King George the Third, the said Thomas Paine came before our said Lord the King in His Chancery, and acknowledged the Instrument aforesaid, and all and every thing therein contained and specified, in form above written. And also the Instrument aforesaid was stamped according to the tenor of the several Statutes made in the sixth year of the reign of the late King and Queen William and Mary of England, and so forth, and in the seventeenth and twenty-third years of the reign of His Majesty King George the Third.

> Inrolled the said Twenty-fifth day of September, in the year last above written.

LETTER TO JEFFERSON IN PARIS.

No. 13 Broad Street Buildings,
London, Feb. 16, 1789.

" DEAR SIR :—Your favour of the 23d Dec'r continued to
the — of Jan'y came safe to hand ; for which I thank you.
I begin this without knowing of any opportunity of conveyance, and shall follow the method of your letter by writing
on till an opportunity offers. I thank you for the many
and judicious observations about my bridge. I am exactly
in your Ideas, as you will perceive by the following account.
—I went to the Iron Works [Yorkshire] the latter end of
Oct'r. My intention at the time of writing to you was to
construct an experiment arch of 250 feet [an iron Bridge],
but in the first place the season was too far advanced to
work out of doors, and an arch of that extent could not be
worked within doors ; and *nextly*, there was a prospect of a
real Bridge being wanted on the spot, of 90 feet extent.
The person who appeared disposed to erect a Bridge was
Mr. Foljambe, nephew to the late Sir George Saville, and
Member in the last Parliament for Yorkshire. He lives
about three miles from the Works, and the river Don runs
in front of his house, over which there is an old ill-constructed
Bridge which he wants to remove. These circumstances
determined me to begin an arch of 90 feet, with an elevation
of five feet.—The foreman of the Works is a relative of the
Proprietors [Messrs. Walker], an excellent mechanic, who
fell in with all my Ideas with great ease and penetration. I
staid at the Works till one-half of the Rib, 45 feet, was compleated and framed horizontally together, and came up to

London at the meeting of Parliament on the 4th of December. The foreman, whom, as I told him, I should appoint 'President of the Board of Works' in my absence, wrote me word that he has got the other half together with much less trouble than the first. He is now preparing for erecting and I for returning.

"Feb. 26. A few days ago I received a letter from Mr. Foljambe in which he says, 'I saw the Rib of your Bridge. In point of elegance and beauty it far exceeded my expectations, and is certainly beyond anything I ever saw.'

"My Model and myself had many visitors while I was at the Works. A few days after I got there, Lord Fitz William, heir to the Marquis of Rockingham, came with Mr. [Edmund] Burke. The former gave the workmen five guineas and invited me to Wentworth House, a few miles distant from the Works, where I went, and staid a few days.

"This Bridge I expect will bring forth something greater, but in the meantime I feel like a bird from its nest [America], and wishing most anxiously to return; therefore as soon as I can bring anything to bear I shall dispose of the contract and bid adieu. I can very truly say that my mind is not at home.

"I am very much rejoiced at the account you give me of the state of affairs in France. I feel exceedingly interested in the affairs of that nation. They are now got or getting into the right way, and the present reign will be more immortalized in France than any that ever preceded it: they have all died away, forgotten in the common mass of things, but this will be to France like an Anno Mundi, or an Anno Domini.

"The happiness of doing good, and the pride of doing great things, unite themselves in this business. But as there are two kinds of Pride, the little and the great, the privileged orders will in some degree be governed by this division. Those of little pride (I mean little-minded pride) will be schismatical, and those of great pride will be orthodox, with respect to the States General. Interest will likewise have some share, and could this operate freely it would arrange itself on the orthodox side. To enrich a nation is to enrich the individuals which compose it. To enrich the farmer is to enrich the farm—and consequently the land-lord ;—for whatever the farmer is, the farm will be. The richer the subject, the richer the revenue, because the con-sumption from which taxes are raised are in proportion to the abilities of people to consume ; therefore the most effec-tual method to raise both the revenue and the rental of a country is to raise the condition of the people,—or that order known in France by the Tiers Etat. But I ought to ask pardon for entering into reasoning in a letter to you. I only do it because I like the subject.

" I observe in all the companies I go into the impression which the present circumstances of France have upon this country. *An internal Alliance* [of Throne and People] in France is an alliance which England never dreamed of, and which she most dreads. Whether she will be better or worse tempered afterwards I cannot judge of, but I believe she will be more cautious in giving offense. She is likewise impressed with an idea that a negotiation is on foot between the King [Louis XVI.] and the Emperor [of Germany] for adding Austrian Flanders to France. This appears to me such a probable thing, and may be rendered [so] conducive to the interest of all parties concerned, that I am inclined to give it credit and wish it success. I hope then to see the Scheld opened, for it is a sin to refuse the bounties of Nature. On these matters I shall be glad of your opinion. I think the States General of Holland could not be in earnest when they applied to France for the payment of the quota to the Emperor. All things considered, to request it was meanness and to expect it absurdity. I am more in-clined to think they made it an opportunity to find how they stood with France. Absalom (I think it was) set fire to his brother's field of corn to bring on a conversation.

" March 12. With respect to political matters here the truth is, the people are fools. They have no discernment into principles and consequences. Had Mr. Pitt proposed a National Convention at the time of the King's insanity, he had done right; but instead of this he has absorbed the right of the Nation into a right of Parliament,—one house of which (the Peers) is hereditary in its own right, and over which the people have no control (not as much as they have over their King); and the other elective by only a small part of the Nation. Therefore he has lessened instead of increased the rights of the people; but as they have not sense enough to see it, they have been huzzaing him. There can be no fixed principles of government, or anything like a Constitution, in a country where the government can alter itself, or one part of it supply the other.

"Whether a man that has been so compleatly mad as not to be managed but by force and the mad shirt can ever be confided in afterwards as a reasonable man, is a matter I have very little opinion of. Such a circumstance, in my estimation, if mentioned, ought to be a perpetual disqualification.

"Had the Regency gone on and the new Administration been formed I should have been able to communicate some matters of business to you, both with respect to America and France, as an interview for that purpose was agreed upon, and to take place as soon as the persons who were to fill the offices should succeed. I am the more confidential with those persons, as they are distinguished by the name of the Blue and Buff,—a dress taken up during the American war, and the undress uniform of General Washington with lapels, which they still wear. But at any rate, I do not think it worth while for Congress to appoint any Minister to this Court. The greater distance Congress observes on this point, the better. It will be all money thrown away to go to any expense about it,—at least during the present reign. I know the Nation well, and the line of acquaintance I am in enables me to judge better than any other American can judge, especially at a distance. If Congress should have any business to state to the Government here, it can be easily done thro' their Minister at Paris; but the seldomer the better.

" I believe I am not so much in the good graces of the Marquis of Lansdowne as I used to be. I do not answer his purpose. He was always talking of a sort of reconnection of England and America, and my coldness and reserve on this subject checked communication. I believe he would be a good Minister for England with respect to a better agreement with France.

" Remember me to the Marquis de la Fayette, Mr. Le Roy, Mr. De Corney. Please to inform me if anything further has been done about the Bridge; and likewise how the new Bridge in your neighbourhood goes on.

" I am, Dear Sir, with much respect,

    " Your sincere Friend,

      " and ob't H'ble servant,

        " THOMAS PAINE."

XI.

THOMAS PAINE'S ANSWER TO FOUR QUES-
TIONS ON THE LEGISLATIVE AND
EXECUTIVE POWERS.

Translated from the MS. by Condorcet.

I HAVE received from my friend M———— a note containing the four following propositions on which you are kind
enough to desire my opinion. I shall not take up your valuable time with compliments and apologies, but as a man who
looks upon himself as a member of the great human family.

On reading the four questions put to T. Paine, one perceives the intention of soliciting, and the hope of obtaining
for them, an affirmative answer. The inquirer took care to
let the stern Republican understand that should his opinion
perchance coincide with that hope, he might expect the

---

[1] This newly discovered document is given here though it was written after
Part I. of "Rights of Man"; and it is given entire, though it anticipates, and
nearly in the same language, one or two passages in Part II. of that work. The
slight differences, and the connection in which the passages were originally
written, are of historical interest. Although the exact date of the composition
is not given, the internal evidence proves it to have been begun in April or May,
1791, Paine being then in Paris, and finished in July of the same year. A
translation of Part I. of "Rights of Man" appeared in Paris in May, and it
will be seen that he was already well advanced on Part II. to which he alludes
as in preparation. This paper, plainly not written for publication, was elicited
by questions put to Paine, probably by Condorcet, perhaps by Lafayette, concerning the Constitution just submitted by the National Assembly. In the
following year it was translated by Condorcet, and printed in the *Chronique du
Mois*, May, June, July, 1792. The original manuscript has not been discovered, and I am indebted to my friend Miss Fritsch for a careful translation
of the work which has before never appeared in English, or in any collection
of Paine's Writings.—*Editor*.

gratitude that a work so conducive to the freedom of the human race would deserve.   But interested and eager as I am for its happiness wherever it is found on the face of the earth, and working as a brother and associate with you and all those who are contributing to its felicity, I will lay before you, as briefly as I can, the reflexions that your questions have suggested.   In the first place I must warn you that I shall not stop to consider whether our opinions agree in every particular; but in the assurance that our end is one and the same, I shall limit myself to discussing with you the means of attaining it.

First you agree that the basis of the French constitution is good ; then you ask whether it is not defective on several points, and

1.   Whether the legislative and executive powers are not so unequally balanced that there is cause to fear lest the former should encroach upon the latter?

2.   Whether the executive power is not too weak to insure obedience to the law and to secure the respect and confidence of the people ?

3.   Whether it is not to be feared that the legislative body consisting of one single chamber will be carried away by its own impetuosity and lack self-restraint ?

4.   Whether the organization of the system of administration is not too complicated and of a kind to make anarchy lasting ?

I shall first impart to you a few reflexions on these questions considered separately.   I shall next add some remarks that embrace them all.   Finally, without examining whether the French constitution is defective and could be improved by being added to, or curtailed, I will lay before you some easy means of modifying it without disturbing the order of government should experience show the necessity of such modifications.

With regard to your opening declaration *that the basis of the constitution is good*, this basis being no other than the rights of man, it rests on truths so well demonstrated that they can no longer be a subject of discussion—I will merely quote and apply to those who dispute them the well-known saying: The fool hath said in his heart there is no God.

FIRST QUESTION.

Are not the legislative and executive powers too unequally balanced, and is there not cause to fear that the former will encroach upon the latter?

If we consider the legislative and executive powers as emanating from a common source, the *nation*, and as a distribution of the national power aiming at the general good, it will be difficult to perceive any motive why the one should encroach upon the other, or to conceive any advantage to be derived by either from the success of such an undertaking. But if, on the contrary, we look upon these two powers as having a different origin and struggling against each other, the one for the rights of the nation, and the other for rights that are not those of the nation, your question is no longer the same, and the fear it formulates is no longer fear of evil, but fear for the public safety.

As your terms do not show under which of these two aspects it should be considered, and as it is difficult to discuss separately a question which is directly dependent on a preceding one, I will use to its full extent the liberty which the vagueness of the proposition allows me and put down a few remarks as they suggest themselves to my mind. I shall thus carry the problem to the point of solution rather than solve it myself.

Nations suffer so universally from the fatal custom of being ill governed, and the human soul "cribbed, cabined and confined" through so many centuries, is so unaccustomed to light, that it may be doubted whether the faculty of distinguishing prismatic hues is as yet fully developed within it.

If we rid our ideas of all superfluous words, and consider them in their natural bareness and simplicity, we perceive (as in the very forms of the proposition) only two main divisions of the powers that constitute government: the power of making laws, and that of causing them to be car-

ried out or administered. Thus all that pertains to government naturally falls under one or the other of these primary
divisions.

We have, I think, generally a more precise and fuller conception of the nature of the legislative power than of the
executive. By the first, we merely mean the delegated
power of making laws *in conformity with the basis and principles of the constitution.* For, without this conformity, the
legislative power would only be despotic power disguised
under another name.

But, when we examine the executive power in the vague
sense generally given to that term, we have not so precise
or so clear an idea of it as we have of the legislative power.
This idea seems to carry with it some admixture of arbitrary
power, with the inevitable result of creating suspicion rather
than confidence. Consequently, until these powers shall
have been defined with equal precision, it is difficult to
treat of the propositions that relate to them.

But, if any mutual invasion of these two powers be possible, it is as possible on the part of the one as of the other ;
and in this alternative, I should deem that nation safer
where an *elected* legislative body should possess itself of the
executive, than where a *non-elected* executive should assume
the power of making laws.

Independently of these considerations, I own that I do
not see how a government can with any exactness be compared to a pair of scales. What is there to balance? A
balance suggests the idea of opposition. This figure of
speech is, I think, borrowed from England, where circumstances had, at first, given it some appropriateness. The
English government being a tyranny founded on the Norman Conquest, the nation has constantly sought a counter-
poise to what it could not remove.

With the Norman Conquest, aristocracy came in, and the
nation had to struggle against a host of obstacles. *The
weight of the nation was then in the scale against the ruling
powers. It is what has since been called the national interest
to distinguish it from the interest of* THE COURT.

But the metaphor of a pair of scales is inconceivable in a country where all the powers of government have a common origin. In this case, the idea of two extremities in opposition to each other disappears, and we see only one edifice where union and harmony are the order of the day.

II.

I pass on to the second question, namely "Whether the executive power is not too weak to insure obedience to the law and to secure the respect and confidence of the people?" When there is a fundamental objection to the first proposition, this objection reappears necessarily in all the propositions that are derived from that first one, and here I ask again, What is the executive power? If, by this expression, is meant *the power of carrying out the laws*, these words refer naturally to every tribunal and court of justice whose business it is to enforce the law, since the last recourse is to them, wherever it is violated. The legislature is particularly interested in maintaining the power of the executive, considered from this point of view; for if the enforcement of the law is weakened, the laws themselves, and those who made them, will be weakened in proportion. But, if it should be admitted that the executive *is no longer able to enforce obedience to the laws and secure the respect and obedience of the people*, a great question presents itself, namely, what is the cause of this incapacity?

This question leads us to consider the term *executive power*, as referring, not to the immediate carrying out of the laws, but as designating a medium or centre through which they must pass to reach the point of execution. And this brings our thoughts to bear on that part of the constitution called the *monarchy*.

The original and direct meaning of the word "*monarch*" is *absolute power concentrated in one man*. This meaning is always the same and suffers no other interpretation. It must be admitted that the constitution, although sublime in its principles, offers here a contradiction between ideas and terms, and as such a contradiction ever brings suspicion in its train, let us examine to what extent suspicion leads, in its turn, to non-execution of the law.

If a remembrance of the nature and extent of monarchical power in old days, and the idea that is attached to those terms, continue to be identified with that of executive power, every scheme likely to strengthen the latter will only tend to increase suspicion and diminish confidence.

If there were a law of Nature, or a decree of the Almighty, made known to men, by which He had determined that all the successive holders of the same power should be endowed with the same heart, and that heart never deceived, suspicions, fears, and alarms would be appeased. But when we see Nature act as if she were determined to disown the monarchical system, producing monarchs as diverse in character as in person, making one wicked, the other stupid, a third mad, and another all these things at once, will it be possible, so long as reason remains a faculty of man, for him to give the least credence to this hereditary absurdity?

If the French should scorn reflexion as long as the English have done, their lethargic indifference might look like happiness, and their thoughtlessness like confidence; but confidence, to be lasting, must be an edifice raised by time on the foundation of reason.

III.

I pass on to the third question: *Is there not cause to fear that the legislative body, composed of a single chamber, may be carried away by its own impetuosity and lack self-restraint?*

This question may be considered under so many aspects, each of which is open to so many arguments, that it seems as yet hardly susceptible of a positive answer. I will nevertheless give you my ideas on this point.

A Constitution, in defining the limits of power, together with the principles which the legislature is bound to obey, has already provided a most powerful and trustworthy check upon any abuse of power.

If, for instance, a law were proposed in one of the legislatures of America, like that passed in the English Parliament (at the beginning of the reign of George I.), to prolong the duration of these Parliaments, such a law could never pass, because the constitution is opposed to it and says: "Thus far shall ye go and no farther."

But, although all the restrictions to power under its various forms should be provided for by the constitution itself, much will always have to be left to the prudence and discretion of the different legislative bodies.

However much skill is displayed in combining the various powers of a constitution, if you establish two chambers you cannot calculate beforehand, with any certainty, the degree of restraint they will exercise upon each other. They may have an understanding not to use that power of mutual restraint, either for good or for evil; but a check provided by the constitution will have a certain and beneficial effect.

As to my private opinion, I should prefer for the reasons I shall unfold, that the legislature should be divided in two sections at the beginning of a debate, to its being always one body, or to its forming two separate bodies.

It seems to me that in this matter of the division of the legislative body, reason is not so much to be taken into consideration, as the passions of men. For, whenever the object is to convince or to persuade, the influence of these passions should be turned to account.

Wherever the legislative body consists of one single chamber, it runs the risk of coming to rash decisions; whereas division offers one chance more for collected judgement. There is no doubt that discussion sheds light, and that a superior man may sometimes derive benefit from the ideas of a person less enlightened than himself. But, if he means to carry out these ideas, it is best he should himself take but little part in the debate. I suppose therefore that the legislative body consists of 100 persons: instead of opening the debate in one assembly, divide the chamber into two equal sections that shall deal with some question, not at the same time, but successively. By this means, one section would

listen to the arguments of the other, and when each separately
should have closed the debate, it might be renewed and the
vote put in the general assembly.   I think therefore it might
be possible to hit on some scheme preferable to one chamber, as at present established, and free from the drawbacks
that result from two chambers, some of which I shall proceed
to state.

In the first place, it is illogical that one division of the
legislature should have the power of coming to a final decision on any one question while this question is still under
discussion by another body and consequently still open to
new lights.

Secondly, it is possible and constantly happens that when
the votes of each chamber are taken separately, the minority
governs the majority in a way both shocking and ridiculous.

Let us suppose, for instance, that the two chambers are
composed of 50 members each.   If unanimity exists in the
one, and the other be divided in the proportion of 26 votes
against 24—then 26 shall carry it against 74, that is, one-
fourth of the votes and one over, shall govern the other
three-fourths.   If the chambers are in the proportion of 60
to 40, 70 to 30, or 80 to 20, the evil is greater still, for then
eleven votes can carry it against 89, if these eleven votes are
at the same time in opposition to the nine of their own, and
to the totality of the other chamber.

But if the legislative body be only divided in order to facilitate debate and not for the purpose of carrying resolutions, all the advantages of separate discussion result from
this division without the drawbacks of two chambers.

As to the two chambers which constitute the Parliament
of England, they seem absolutely fused into one, and as
legislative bodies to have no special character of their own.
In all respects they take that of the Premier of the day,
whatever it be, and whatever the epoch of his premiership.
He touches them with his soporific wand, and at once they
fall into the sleep of subserviency.

If we consider the individual merit of those who compose
these two chambers, we shall see that the one whose very

name (House of Lords *) is an outrage on nature, has been very justly deprived of talent and virtues by nature herself. Pitiable though the representation of England is, the Commons are in a virile state compared to the Lords. That wretched assembly is so little considered and appears so puerile, that the people never ask what it is about. It also comes most under ministerial influence. In the debate on war with Russia, the minister had a majority of over 90 in the Lords, whilst in the other chamber, which is twice as numerous, he had only a majority of 63. Chesterfield, a member of that assembly, and one of those who knew it best, had nicknamed it "*the Hospital for Incurables.*"

I am little inclined to admit the idea of two chambers with an arbitrary and reciprocal veto. Nothing in the principle of good representation shows that the one may be wiser than the other, and thus to intrust power where wisdom cannot be given to use it is as much to run a risk as to take a precaution.

All human institutions having been improved since their origin, we must believe that the representative system will be improved too and this hope is all the better established that this system is among our institutions one of those which have met with the greatest number of obstacles and have had the best chance of being perfected.

IV.

I pass on to the fourth question—Whether the organization of the administrative system is not too complicated and of such a nature as to perpetuate anarchy?

A great advance has been made in the science of government (especially where the state is of considerable extent) by the institution of a system which puts each part of a country in a position to govern all its private affairs. Not only is private and public business simplified thereby, but the waste of time and the expense consequent upon administration from a distance are avoided, as well as the mistakes that such a system of jurisdiction entails.

* Lord means Master.—*Author.*

Although the general utility of the institution referred to above is evident, a particular knowledge of local circumstances is necessary to judge of its details. I own I do not possess this particular knowledge, my purpose being rather to elucidate general principles of government; for, if these be good, the application of them to particular cases, will be good also. The science of government being still in its infancy I am satisfied with hoping that no system will be established likely to prevent us from profiting by the lessons of experience.

In spite of the study which has been made of the science of government, of its principles, its operations, and its manifold results, the following question has not yet been sufficiently examined, nor has enough light been thrown upon it: *How small a measure of government is necessary to civilized man?*

I cannot now go thoroughly into this question. To do so would be to exceed the limits I have prescribed to myself. Moreover, it is being considered in a work of mine now in course of composition.

But I am very decided in the opinion that the sum of necessary government is much less than is generally thought, and that we are not yet rid of the habit of excessive government.

If I ask any one to what extent he thinks himself in need of being governed, he gives me to understand that in his case "a little would be enough"; and I receive the same answer from every one. But if, reversing the question, I ask the same man what amount of government he deems necessary for another, he answers: "a great deal." As that other person decides the question in the same way for everybody else, the result of all these answers is excess of government. I conclude therefore that the amount really necessary is to be found between these two extremes. It is, namely, a little more than each wants for himself and a good deal less than he thinks necessary for others. Excess of government only tends to incite to and to create crimes which else had never existed.

The wretched traffic of former governments was in a great measure upheld by the care they took to throw everywhere seeds of division, and to encourage the growth of suspicion, not only from nation to nation, but also from man to man. Such a traffic can only perpetuate itself by destroying the very principles of society, and we are still suffering from the effects of that rotten system. We must therefore consider that the moral condition of man must needs change, and that under better principles of government, he will cease to be the suspicious creature he inevitably was under former systems. Already, as nations come nearer to adopting the principles of civilized government, the human mind acquires a new faculty. The people of England and those of France are no longer what they were two years ago with respect to each other, and the same principles that actuate the bulk of these nations will prevail in the private relations of each. But the moral changes which obtain between nations, or between individuals, although very rapid in their operation when they lead to evil, are very slow when they lead to good. It is easy enough to prompt suspicion, but difficult to eradicate it. Force cannot kill it : it must be undermined silently, and it will crumble away without noise.

If we consider the situation of France under the old régime, we see a government founded on suspicion, consequently on spies and eaves-droppers, whose business it was to report everything to the police. Every social circle was accustomed to suspect one or other of its members ; confidence, except as a word, did not exist. The master suspected his servants, neighbours suspected each other, government suspected them all, and all suspected government. Therefore, we should rather wonder at the new régime being able to obtain the degree of confidence it does enjoy, than lament its not obtaining more. So much must needs be forgotten in this respect, that I wish the nation had no memory for the past.

I now come to the last part of my letter—*to the consideration of the best means of perfecting the constitution* (should experience show the necessity of it) *without interrupting* the course of government. The best way to do so would be to insert in the constitution a clause by which the method of these improvements would be determined. As opinion is divided on this point, I shall make it the object of a special discussion. So far, France has been without a Constitution: not only is she now on the eve of establishing one, but of electing a legislative assembly. In this condition of things, it is more than ever necessary to distinguish between the situation of the nation, when delegating power to form a constitution, and its situation afterwards, when obliged to delegate its authority to a legislative body, organized in accordance with that constitution. The constitution itself, and the laws, are two things essentially distinct from the power of framing laws to meet special circumstances, in accordance with the principles of that constitution. If the primal authority to form a constitution were to come down as an inheritance to every legislative body in succession, it is clear there would no longer be such a thing as a constitution ; and legislation having become arbitrary, as in England, it would without difficulty set up any government it liked. The present National Assembly, or to speak more exactly and to distinguish it from ordinary legislatures, the *National Assembly of the Convention*, has been obliged by stress of circumstance to take the place of a legislature, at the same time that it was framing a constitution. It was called upon to destroy, to construct, and to provide for immediate needs, whilst completing the new edifice. The mass of business was enormous and its attention was called for on every side at the same time. Without mentioning the special business which occupied the Assembly, its labours, in order to frame a constitution, come under two heads : *what it has destroyed, what it has built up.* With respect to the first head, it could not err ; for the old edifice rested on an evil foundation, that is on usurped power.

After thus simplifying the question, it remains only to examine the second head, namely what has been set up in lieu of the old edifice.

The foundations, on which the new rests are undisputably good, and that alone is sufficient compensation for all the nation has suffered. But have the old materials been used too sparingly, or with too free a hand, in the new building? Do all the parts present an exact symmetry? Is this symmetry greater or less than experience shows to be necessary? These are points on which experience itself can alone pronounce. All the wisdom of the present moment must limit itself to putting no obstacles in the way of the improvement that time may bring.

Meanwhile the world is perfectly agreed on two points: the boldness of the undertaking, and the perseverance displayed in carrying it out. It is natural that zeal, together with the fear of a return of bad government, should have induced the men to whom the power of framing a constitution had been delegated, to establish permanently what is only relatively good, instead of risking a return of former evils. But since this final settlement prevents what is good from becoming better, the wisdom of such a measure is at least doubtful. The degree of enlightenment attained by a nation, or more generally by the world, is one of the points to be considered. Reason is beginning to throw such strong daylight upon all political questions that we should boldly and magnanimously repulse every sort of fear lest man should sink back in the black night of ignorance; and since, in all countries whatever, the interest of the greatest number makes for good rather than for evil, these different causes working together will bring the science of government to a degree of perfection of which we can, as yet, form no idea. We should not therefore hinder its progress. While it would not be wise in us to fetter ourselves, with respect to posterity it would be usurpation. Man has no authority over posterity —if he had, our rights would long since have been lost. Pride inclines us too much to cast our eyes toward the future, when considering this question; whereas, the best way of doing so, would be to reflect on the past, and see to what state we should be reduced, had our ancestors succeeded in putting upon us with any show of legitimacy, the yoke we are trying to impose upon our descendants. We should not have been able to do what we are doing at the present moment. It is not enough that man should have the enjoyment of his rights. The exercise of these rights must be secured to him by the principles of social order.

The best we can do for our children in the matter of government, is to bequeath to them freedom together with good examples. What is worthy of imitation will necessarily be imitated. The intrinsic merit of our institutions, and not the checks we might put upon posterity, will determine it to imitate these institutions. When a man bequeaths an inheritance, he does not impose upon his heirs the obligation to accept it; such a condition would be absolutely null and void. The inheritance will be accepted if it is worth anything, and refused if it be valueless. Can it be otherwise with respect to government? The rights of man are the rights of all generations. We should not let anxiety for their welfare carry us to the pitch of doubting their capacity. They might be wiser than we are. Let us not therefore be so blind as to usurp a power to which we have no right.

The means of amending itself is a very important part of the constitution. It is perhaps impossible to combine in one institution principles, opinions and practice, in such a way that time shall bring no alterations and show no drawbacks. The best way to obviate such an increase of these drawbacks as might discourage attempts at reform or provoke revolutions, is to provide means of correcting them as they arise. Such a constitution may be called a perpetual constitution, but no other deserves that name. The constitution of Pennsylvania, established 1776 by the convention of which Benjamin Franklin was president, contained a statute to the effect that at the end of seven years (a term of years supposed to extend beyond the duration of the war) a new convention should be elected to revise the constitution, to compare it with public opinion and to propose such additions or retrenchments as might be deemed useful or necessary. But the proposed amendments were to be the object of public attention for a considerable time before being either rejected or confirmed. This clause was altered in a subsequent convention, and *the right of the nation to alter or perfect the constitution whenever she should deem it necessary* was substituted for it.

For my part I think that a periodical exercise of that right is preferable to the above general declaration ; for, at the same time that the periodic exercise of their power does not destroy the everlasting right, it provides frequent opportunities of using it and thus helps to keep government within the principles of the constitution.

The federal government, or that which embraces the whole of the United States, framed by the convention of 1787, under the Presidency of General Washington, to-day President of Congress, also contains a clause which admits of every future improvement ; but to bring these about recourse must be had to the authority of the people, and to those very means by which the constitution itself was framed. Whilst establishing a good government, it is necessary to provide means to keep it so.

This precaution is in fact so necessary that a constitution would be incomplete without it. Experience having shown us how very difficult it is to carry out reforms, it is to the real advantage of posterity that we should devise beforehand means for their accomplishment.

A constitution which contains a clause giving facilities for its amendment, is protected against all opposition ; for the hopes that may desire improvements, or what they look upon as such, will operate to bring them the means which the constitution furnishes and by doing so, will carry on its authority. This measure has another advantage. It defines precisely wherein consists the crime of *high treason* against the constitution itself—*to seek to alter any part of it by other means than those it furnishes* (means equally within reach of all citizens) is a clear definition of those terms and serves to impress, not merely on individuals, but on the holders of power also, a wholesome fear lest they should prove guilty of high treason. The authority to frame a constitution does not necessarily imply the authority to establish it : it must first be proposed and then approved before the power to establish it can exist.   It is thus the matter has been settled in America.   But, in spite of different methods of action having been followed in that country and in France, results in both have shown a good deal of similarity.   The American Convention did not allow any part of its labours to appear until it was completed, when it published the whole and gave public opinion time to sanction it before putting it into execution.   The French National Assembly, on the contrary, has published its work as it proceeded with it, beginning with the declaration of rights.   Both methods therefore are alike in one particular, namely in appealing to the public approbation, and either system may be equally good.

It is not necessary, in order to add a precautionary clause, to examine whether the constitution is so perfect as to be under no need, or even susceptibility, of improvement. This clause extends to any alteration the constitution may require in the future, and to what we cannot even foresee. I do not believe that the men now living have produced every possible thought on government, and the Abbé Raynal has just proved to us that ancient errors have not yet died of old age.

When the general principles of a constitution are sound, the minor reforms which experience may demand are so easy to bring about that the nation will never be tempted to let abuses accumulate.   It seems to me good policy to fix the date for the first revision of the constitution to seven years hence ; for before those years are over, its advantages and defects will have had time to make themselves known.   We should remark also that some of the most important articles of the constitution have not been the result of reflexion, but of special circumstances ; such, for instance, is the decree on the right of peace and war. As, on the other hand, it is not to be supposed that the space of two years (the time which the Assembly took to frame the constitution) has been sufficient to produce every

possible circumstance, it is well, on the supposition of necessary additions or amendments, that the first period of
revision should not be deferred to a too distant date.   It is
not impossible—nay, it is even probable—that the whole
system of government in Europe will change, that the
ferocious use of war,—that truly barbarous cause of wretchedness, poverty and taxation,—will yield to pacific means
of putting an end to quarrels among nations.   Government
is now being revolutionized from West to East by a movement more rapid than the impulse it formerly received from
East to West.   I wish the National Assembly may be bold
enough to propose a Convention elected by the different
peoples of Europe for the general welfare of that portion
of the world.   Freedom for ourselves is merely happiness :
it becomes virtue when we seek to enable others to enjoy it.

A journey has prevented my finishing sooner this letter,
begun more than five weeks ago.   Since that time, circumstances have changed in France, owing to the flight and
arrestation of Louis XVI.   Every successive event incites
man to reason. He proceeds from idea to idea, from thought
to thought, without perceiving the immense progress he is
making.   Those who believe that France has reached the
end of its political knowledge, will soon find themselves, not
only mistaken, but left behind, unless they themselves advance at the same rate.   Every day brings forth something
new.   The mind, after having fought kings as individuals,
must look upon them as part of a system of government,
and conclude that what is called monarchy is only a superstition and a political fraud, unworthy of an enlightened
people.   It is with monarchy as with all those things which
depend on some slavish habit of mind.

Could we draw a circle round a man, and say to him : You
cannot get out of this, for beyond is an abyss ready to swallow you up—he will remain there as long as the terror of
the impression endures.   But if, by a happy chance, he sets
one foot outside the magic circle, the other will not be slow
to follow.

THOMAS PAINE.

XII.

ADDRESS AND DECLARATION.

At a select Meeting of the Friends of Universal Peace and Liberty, held at the Thatched House Tavern, St. James's Street, August 20, 1791, the following Address and Declaration to our Fellow Citizens was agreed on and ordered to be published.

FRIENDS AND FELLOW CITIZENS,

AT a moment like the present, when wilful misrepresentations are industriously spread by the partizans of arbitrary power, and the advocates of passive obedience and court government, we think it incumbent on us to declare to the world our principles, and the motives of our conduct.

We rejoice at the glorious event of the *French Revolution.*

If it be asked : What is the French Revolution to us?

We answer, (as it has been already answered in another place,*) *It is much* to us as men : much to us as Englishmen.

As men we rejoice in the freedom of twenty-five millions of our fellow men.   We rejoice in the prospect which such a magnificent example opens to the world.   We congratulate the French nation for having laid the axe to the root of tyranny, and for erecting government on the sacred *hereditary rights of man*—Rights which appertain to ALL, and not to any one more than to another.   We know of no human authority superior to that of a whole nation; and we pro-

---

* Declaration of the Volunteers of Belfast.—*Author.*

fess and proclaim it as our principle that every nation has at all times an inherent indefeasible right to constitute and establish such government for itself as best accords with its disposition, interest, and happiness.

As Englishmen we also rejoice, because we are *immediately* interested in the French Revolution.

Without enquiring into the justice on either side of the reproachful charges of intrigue and ambition, which the English and French Courts have constantly made on each other, we confine ourselves to this observation :—That if the Court of France only was in fault, and the numerous wars which have distressed both countries, are chargeable to her alone, that Court now exists no longer ; and the cause and the consequence must cease together. The French, therefore, by the revolution they have made, have conquered for us as well as for themselves ; if it be true that their Court only was in fault, and ours never.

On this state of the case, the French Revolution concerns us *immediately*. We are oppressed with a heavy national debt, a burthen of taxes, and an expensive administration of government, beyond those of any people in the world. We have also a very numerous poor ; and we hold that the moral obligation of providing for old age, helpless infancy, and poverty, is far superior to that of supplying the invented wants of courtly extravagance, ambition, and intrigue.

We believe there is no instance to be produced but in England, of *seven* millions of inhabitants, which make but little more than *one* million of families, paying yearly SEVEN-TEEN MILLIONS of taxes.

As it has always been held out by all administrations that the restless ambition of the Court of France rendered this expense necessary to us for our own defence, we consequently rejoice as men deeply interested in the French Revolution, for that Court, as we have already said, exists no longer ; and consequently the same enormous expenses need not continue to us.

Thus rejoicing, as we sincerely do, both as men and Englishmen, as lovers of universal peace and freedom, and as friends to our own national prosperity, and a reduction of our public expenses, we cannot but express our astonishment that any part, or any members of our own government, should reprobate the extinction of that very power in France, or wish to see it restored, to whose influence they formerly attributed (whilst they appeared to lament) the enormous increase of our own burthens and taxes. What, then, are they sorry that the pretence for new oppressive taxes, and the occasion for continuing many of the old taxes, will be at an end? If so, and if it is the policy of courts and of court governments, to prefer enemies to friends, and a system of war to that of peace, as affording more pretences for places, offices, pensions, revenue, and taxation, it is high time for the people of every nation to look with circumspection to their own interests.

Those who *pay* the expense, and *not* those who *participate* in the emoluments arising from it, are the persons immediately interested in inquiries of this kind. We are a part of that national body, on whom this annual expense of seventeen millions falls ; and we consider the present opportunity of the French Revolution as a most happy one for lessening the enormous load under which this nation groans. If this be not done, we shall then have reason to conclude, that the cry of intrigue and ambition against *other* courts, is no more than the common cant of *all* courts.

We think it also necessary to express our astonishment that a government, desirous of being called FREE, should prefer connection with the most despotic and arbitrary powers in Europe. We know of none more deserving this description than those of Turkey and Prussia, and the whole combination of German despots. Separated as we happily are by nature, from the tumults of the Continent, we reprobate all systems and intrigues which sacrifice (and that too at a great expense) the blessings of our natural situation. Such systems cannot have a national origin.

If we are asked, what government is?—We hold it to be nothing more than a NATIONAL ASSOCIATION, and we hold that to be the best which secures to every man his rights, and promotes the greatest quantity of happiness with the *least expence*.

We live to improve, or we live in vain ; and therefore we admit of no maxims of government or policy on the mere score of antiquity, or other men's authority, the *old* whigs or the *new*.

We will exercise the reason with which we are endued, or we possess it unworthily. As reason is given at all times, it is for the purpose of being used at all times.

Among the blessings which the French Revolution has produced to that nation, we enumerate the abolition of the feudal system of injustice and tyranny on the 4th of August, 1789. Beneath the feudal system all Europe has long groaned, and from it England is not yet free. Game laws, borough tenures, and tyrannical monopolies of numerous kinds, still remain amongst us ; but rejoicing as we sincerely do, in the freedom of others, till we shall happily accomplish our own, we intended to commemorate this prelude to the universal extirpation of the feudal system, by meeting on the anniversary of that day (the 4th of August) at the Crown and Anchor. From this meeting we were prevented by the interference of certain *unnamed* and *skulking* persons with the master of the Tavern, who informed us, that on *their* representations he could not receive us. Let those who live by, or countenance feudal oppressions, take the reproach of this ineffectual meanness and cowardice to themselves. They cannot stifle the public declaration of our honest, open, and avowed opinions.

These are our principles, and these our sentiments. They embrace the interest and happiness of the great body of the nation of which we are a part. As to riots and tumults, let those answer for them, who, by wilful misrepresentations, endeavor to excite and promote them ; or who seek to *stun* the sense of the nation, and to lose the great cause of public good in the outrages of a misinformed mob. We take our ground on principles that require no such riotous aid. We have nothing to apprehend from the poor ; for we are plead-ing their cause. And we fear not proud oppression, for we have truth on our side. We say, and we repeat it, that the French Revolution opens to the world an opportunity in which all good citizens must rejoice—that of promoting the general happiness of man. And that it moreover offers to this country in particular, an opportunity of reducing our enormous taxes.

These are our objects, and we will pursue them.

J. HORNE TOOKE,
Chairman.[1]

[1] Only signed by Tooke as Chairman, but written by Paine.—*Editor.*

XIII.

RIGHTS OF MAN.

WHEN Thomas Paine sailed from America for France, in April, 1787, he was perhaps as happy a man as any in the world. His most intimate friend, Jefferson, was Minister at Paris, and his friend Lafayette was the idol of France. His fame had preceded him, and he at once became, in Paris, the centre of the same circle of savants and philosophers that had surrounded Franklin. His main reason for proceeding at once to Paris was that he might submit to the Academy of Sciences his invention of an iron bridge, and with its favorable verdict he came to England, in September. He at once went to his aged mother at Thetford, leaving with a publisher (Ridgway), his "Prospects on the Rubicon." He next made arrangements to patent his bridge, and to construct at Rotherham the large model of it exhibited on Paddington Green, London. He was welcomed in England by leading statesmen, such as Lansdowne and Fox, and above all by Edmund Burke, who for some time had him as a guest at Beaconsfield, and drove him about in various parts of the country. He had not the slightest revolutionary purpose, either as regarded England or France. Towards Louis XVI. he felt only gratitude for the services he had rendered America, and towards George III. he felt no animosity whatever. His four months' sojourn in Paris had convinced him that there was approaching a reform of that country after the American model, except that the Crown would be preserved, a compromise he approved, provided the throne should not be hereditary. Events in France travelled more swiftly than he had anticipated, and Paine was summoned by Lafayette, Condorcet, and others, as an adviser in the formation of a new constitution.

Such was the situation immediately preceding the political and literary duel between Paine and Burke, which in the event turned out a tremendous war between Royalism and Republicanism in Europe. Paine was, both in France and in England, the inspirer of moderate counsels. Samuel Rogers relates that in early life he dined at a friend's house in London with Thomas Paine, when one of the toasts given was the " memory of Joshua,"—in allusion to the Hebrew leader's conquest of the kings of Canaan, and execution of them. Paine observed that he would not treat kings like Joshua. " I 'm of the Scotch parson's opinion," he said, "when he prayed against Louis XIV.—'Lord, shake him over the mouth of hell, but don't let him drop !' " Paine then gave as his toast, " The Republic of the World,"—which Samuel Rogers, aged twenty-nine, noted as a sublime idea. This was Paine's faith and hope, and with it he confronted the revolutionary storms which presently burst over France and England.

Until Burke's arraignment of France in his parliamentary speech (February 9, 1790), Paine had no doubt whatever that he would sympathize with the movement in France, and wrote to him from that country as if conveying glad tidings. Burke's " Reflections on the Revolution in France " appeared November 1, 1790, and Paine at once set himself to answer it. He was then staying at the Angel Inn, Islington. The inn has been twice rebuilt since that time, and from its contents there is preserved only a small image, which perhaps was meant to represent " Liberty,"—possibly brought from Paris by Paine as an ornament for his study. From the Angel he removed to a house in Harding Street, Fetter Lane. Rickman says Part First of " Rights of Man " was finished at Versailles, but probably this has reference to the preface only, as I cannot find Paine in France that year until April 8. The book had been printed by Johnson, in time

for the opening of Parliament, in February ; but this publisher became frightened after a few copies were out (there
is one in the British Museum), and the work was transferred
to J. S. Jordan, 166 Fleet Street, with a preface sent from
Paris (not contained in Johnson's edition, nor in the American editions). The pamphlet, though sold at the same price
as Burke's, three shillings, had a vast circulation, and Paine
gave the proceeds to the Constitutional Societies which
sprang up under his teachings in various parts of the
country.

Soon after appeared Burke's "Appeal from the New to
the Old Whigs." In this Burke quoted a good deal from
"Rights of Man," but replied to it only with exclamation
points, saying that the only answer such ideas merited was
"criminal justice." Paine's Part Second followed, published
February 17, 1792. In Part First Paine had mentioned a
rumor that Burke was a masked pensioner (a charge that
will be noticed in connection with its detailed statement in
a further publication); and as Burke had been formerly
arraigned in Parliament, while Paymaster, for a very ques-
tionable proceeding, this charge no doubt hurt a good deal.
Although the government did not follow Burke's suggestion
of a prosecution at that time, there is little doubt that it was
he who induced the prosecution of Part Second. Before the
trial came on, December 18, 1792, Paine was occupying his
seat in the French Convention, and could only be outlawed.

Burke humorously remarked to a friend of Paine and
himself, "We hunt in pairs." The severally representative
character aud influence of these two men in the revolutionary era, in France and England, deserve more adequate
study than they have received. While Paine maintained
freedom of discussion, Burke first proposed criminal prosecution for sentiments by no means libellous (such as Paine's
Part First). While Paine was endeavoring to make the
movement in France peaceful, Burke fomented the league
of monarchs against France which maddened its people,
and brought on the Reign of Terror. While Paine was
endeavoring to preserve the French throne ("phantom"

though he believed it), to prevent bloodshed, Burke was secretly writing to the Queen of France, entreating her not to compromise, and to "trust to the support of foreign armies" ("Histoire de France depuis 1789." Henri Martin, i., 151). While Burke thus helped to bring the King and Queen to the guillotine, Paine pleaded for their lives to the last moment. While Paine maintained the right of mankind to improve their condition, Burke held that "the awful Author of our being is the author of our place in the order of existence; and that, having disposed and marshalled us by a divine tactick, not according to our will, but according to his, he has, in and by that disposition, virtually subjected us to act the part which belongs to the place assigned us." Paine was a religious believer in eternal principles; Burke held that "political problems do not primarily concern truth or falsehood. They relate to good or evil. What in the result is likely to produce evil is politically false, that which is productive of good politically is true." Assuming thus the visionary's right to decide before the result what was "likely to produce evil," Burke vigorously sought to kindle war against the French Republic which might have developed itself peacefully, while Paine was striving for an international Congress in Europe in the interest of peace. Paine had faith in the people, and believed that, if allowed to choose representatives, they would select their best and wisest men; and that while reforming government the people would remain orderly, as they had generally remained in America during the transition from British rule to self-government. Burke maintained that if the existing political order were broken up there would be no longer a people, but "a number of vague, loose individuals, and nothing more." "Alas!" he exclaims, "they little know how many a weary step is to be taken before they can form themselves into a mass, which has a true personality." For the sake of peace Paine wished the revolution to be peaceful as the advance of summer; he used every endeavor to reconcile English radicals to some *modus vivendi* with the existing order, as he was willing to retain Louis XVI. as head of the executive in France : Burke resisted every tendency of English statesmanship to reform at home, or to negotiate with the French Republic, and was mainly responsible for the King's death and the war that followed between England and France in February, 1793. Burke became a royal favorite, Paine was outlawed by a prosecution originally proposed by Burke. While Paine was demanding religious liberty, Burke was opposing the removal of penal statutes from Unitarians, on the ground that but for those statutes Paine might some day set up a church in England. When Burke was retiring on a large royal pension, Paine was in prison, through the devices of Burke's confederate, the American Minister in Paris. So the two men, as Burke said, " hunted in pairs."

So far as Burke attempts to affirm any principle he is fairly quoted in Paine's work, and nowhere misrepresented. As for Paine's own ideas, the reader should remember that " Rights of Man " was the earliest complete statement of republican principles. They were pronounced to be the fundamental principles of the American Republic by Jefferson, Madison, and Jackson,—the three Presidents who above all others represented the republican idea which Paine first allied with American Independence. Those who suppose that Paine did but reproduce the principles of Rousseau and Locke will find by careful study of his well-weighed language that such is not the case. Paine's political principles were evolved out of his early Quakerism. He was potential in George Fox. The belief that every human soul was the child of God, and capable of direct inspiration from the Father of all, without mediator or priestly intervention, or sacramental instrumentality, was fatal to all privilege and rank. The universal Fatherhood implied universal Brotherhood, or human equality. But the fate of the Quakers proved the necessity of protecting the individual spirit from oppression by the majority as well as by privileged classes. For this purpose Paine insisted on surrounding the individual right with the security of the Declaration of Rights, not to be invaded by any government ; and would reduce

government to an association limited in its operations to the
defence of those rights which the individual is unable, alone,
to maintain.

From the preceding chapter it will be seen that Part Second of " Rights of Man " was begun by Paine in the spring
of 1791.   At the close of that year, or early in 1792, he took
up his abode with his friend Thomas " Clio " Rickman, at No.
7 Upper Marylebone Street.   Rickman was a radical publisher ; the house remains still a book-binding establishment,
and seems little changed since Paine therein revised the
proofs of Part Second on a table which Rickman marked
with a plate, and which is now in possession of Mr. Edward
Truelove.   As the plate states, Paine wrote on the same
table other works which appeared in England in 1792.

In 1795 D. I. Eaton published an edition of " Rights of
Man," with a preface purporting to have been written by
Paine while in Luxembourg prison.   It is manifestly spu-
rious.   The genuine English and French prefaces are given.

RIGHTS OF MAN

BEING AN ANSWER TO MR. BURKE'S ATTACK ON THE FRENCH REVOLUTION

THOMAS PAINE

SECRETARY FOR FOREIGN AFFAIRS TO CONGRESS IN THE
AMERICAN WAR, AND
AUTHOR OF THE WORKS ENTITLED "COMMON SENSE" AND "A LETTER TO THE ABBÉ RAYNAL"

GEORGE WASHINGTON,

PRESIDENT OF THE UNITED STATES OF AMERICA.

SIR,—

I present you a small treatise in defence of those principles of freedom which your exemplary virtue hath so eminently contributed to establish. That the Rights of Man may become as universal as your benevolence can wish, and that you may enjoy the happiness of seeing the New World regenerate the Old, is the prayer of

SIR,

Your much obliged, and

Obedient humble Servant,

THOMAS PAINE.

PREFACE TO THE ENGLISH EDITION.

FROM the part Mr. Burke took in the American Revolution, it was natural that I should consider him a friend to mankind; and as our acquaintance commenced on that ground, it would have been more agreeable to me to have had cause to continue in that opinion than to change it.

At the time Mr. Burke made his violent speech last winter in the English Parliament against the French Revolution and the National Assembly, I was in Paris, and had written to him but a short time before to inform him how prosperously matters were going on.[1] Soon after this I saw his advertisement of the Pamphlet he intended to publish: As the attack was to be made in a language but little studied, and less understood in France, and as everything suffers by translation, I promised some of the friends of the Revolution in that country that whenever Mr. Burke's Pamphlet came forth, I would answer it. This appeared to me the more

---

[1] My efforts to discover this letter have failed. The following is from Croly's "Life of Burke": "Among his [Paine's] earliest missives was a letter [from Paris] to Burke, whom he eagerly urged to introduce Revolution into England, by its established name of 'Reform.' Burke threw back the temptation, or the insult, at once. 'Do you *really* imagine, Mr. Paine,' was his reply, 'that the constitution of this kingdom requires such innovations, or *could exist with them*, or that any *reflecting man would seriously engage in them?* You are aware that I have, all my life, opposed such schemes of reform, because *I know them not to be Reform.*' Paine, however, continued his ill-received correspondence; and whether from the delight of molesting Burke, or the expectation of making him a convert to a side which had the grand charm for the conviction of his own profligate heart, plunder; he sent him narratives of the rapidly recurring triumphs of democracy. In one of those he stated that the Reformers had already determined on the total overthrow of the [French] monarchy, etc." This letter is said by the reverend biographer to have been written "exactly three days before the storming of the Bastille."—*Editor.*

necessary to be done, when I saw the flagrant misrepresentations which Mr. Burke's Pamphlet contains ; and that while it is an outrageous abuse on the French Revolution, and the principles of Liberty, it is an imposition on the rest of the world.

I am the more astonished and disappointed at this conduct in Mr. Burke, as (from the circumstances I am going to mention) I had formed other expectations.

I had seen enough of the miseries of war, to wish it might never more have existence in the world, and that some other mode might be found out to settle the differences that should occasionally arise in the neighbourhood of nations. This certainly might be done if Courts were disposed to set honestly about it, or if countries were enlightened enough not to be made the dupes of Courts. The people of America had been bred up in the same prejudices against France, which at that time characterised the people of England ; but experience and an acquaintance with the French Nation have most effectually shown to the Americans the falsehood of those prejudices ; and I do not believe that a more cordial and confidential intercourse exists between any two countries than between America and France.

When I came to France, in the spring of 1787, the Archbishop of Thoulouse was then Minister, and at that time highly esteemed. I became much acquainted with the private Secretary of that Minister, a man of an enlarged benevolent heart ; and found, that his sentiments and my own perfectly agreed with respect to the madness of war, and the wretched impolicy of two nations, like England and France, continually worrying each other, to no other end than that of a mutual increase of burdens and taxes. That I might be assured I had not misunderstood him, nor he me, I put the substance of our opinions into writing and sent it to him ; subjoining a request, that if I should see among the people of England, any disposition to cultivate a better understanding between the two nations than had hitherto prevailed, how far I might be authorised to say that the same disposition prevailed on the part of France? He answered me by letter in the most unreserved manner, and that not for himself only, but for the Minister, with whose knowledge the letter was declared to be written.

I put this letter into the hands of Mr. Burke almost three years ago, and left it with him, where it still remains; hoping, and at the same time naturally expecting, from the opinion I had conceived of him, that he would find some opportunity of making good use of it, for the purpose of removing those errors and prejudices which two neighbouring nations, from the want of knowing each other, had entertained, to the injury of both.

When the French Revolution broke out, it certainly afforded to Mr. Burke an opportunity of doing some good, had he been disposed to it; instead of which, no sooner did he see the old prejudices wearing away, than he immediately began sowing the seeds of a new inveteracy, as if he were afraid that England and France would cease to be enemies. That there are men in all countries who get their living by war, and by keeping up the quarrels of Nations, is as shocking as it is true; but when those who are concerned in the government of a country, make it their study to sow discord and cultivate prejudices between Nations, it becomes the more unpardonable.

With respect to a paragraph in this work alluding to Mr. Burke's having a pension, the report has been some time in circulation, at least two months; and as a person is often the last to hear what concerns him the most to know, I have mentioned it, that Mr. Burke may have an opportunity of contradicting the rumour, if he thinks proper.

THOMAS PAINE.

PAINE'S PREFACE TO THE FRENCH EDITION.[1]

THE astonishment which the French Revolution has caused throughout Europe should be considered from two different points of view : first as it affects foreign peoples, secondly as it affects their governments.

The cause of the French people is that of all Europe, or rather of the whole world ; but the governments of all those countries are by no means favorable to it. It is important that we should never lose sight of this distinction. We must not confuse the peoples with their governments; especially not the English people with its government.

The government of England is no friend to the revolution of France. Of this we have sufficient proofs in the thanks given by that weak and witless person, the Elector of Hanover, sometimes called the King of England, to Mr. Burke for the insults heaped on it in his book, and in the malevolent comments of the English Minister, Mr. Pitt, in his speeches in Parliament.

In spite of the professions of sincerest friendship found in the official correspondence of the English government with that of France, its conduct gives the lie to all its declarations, and shows us clearly that it is not a court to be trusted, but an insane court, plunging in all the quarrels and intrigues of Europe, in quest of a war to satisfy its folly and countenance its extravagance.

The English nation, on the contrary, is very favorably disposed towards the French Revolution, and to the progress

[1] Part I., translated by F. Soulès, was published in Paris in May, 1791. This Preface has not appeared in any American edition, but a translation was given in Carlile's edition, 1819. The present translation is from the original French. F. Lanthenas translated Parts I. and II. in 1792.—*Editor*.

of liberty in the whole world; and this feeling will become
more general in England as the intrigues and artifices of its
government are better known, and the principles of the revolution better understood.   The French should know that
most English newspapers are directly in the pay of government, or, if indirectly connected with it, always under its
orders; and that those papers constantly distort and attack
the revolution in France in order to deceive the nation.
But, as it is impossible long to prevent the prevalence of
truth, the daily falsehoods of those papers no longer have
the desired effect.

To be convinced that the voice of truth has been stifled
in England, the world needs only to be told that the government regards and prosecutes as a libel that which it
should protect.*   This outrage on morality is called *law*,
and judges are found wicked enough to inflict penalties on
truth.

The English government presents, just now, a curious
phenomenon.   Seeing that the French and English nations
are getting rid of the prejudices and false notions formerly
entertained against each other, and which have cost them
so much money, that government seems to be placarding its
need of a foe; for unless it finds one somewhere, no pretext
exists for the enormous revenue and taxation now deemed
necessary.

Therefore it seeks in Russia the enemy it has lost in
France, and appears to say to the universe, or to say to itself: " If nobody will be so kind as to become my foe, I
shall need no more fleets nor armies, and shall be forced to
reduce my taxes.   The American war enabled me to double
the taxes; the Dutch business to add more; the Nootka
humbug gave me a pretext for raising three millions sterling
more; but unless I can make an enemy of Russia the harvest
from wars will end.   I was the first to incite Turk against
Russian, and now I hope to reap a fresh crop of taxes."

If the miseries of war, and the flood of evils it spreads

---

* The main and uniform maxim of the judges is, the greater the truth the
greater the libel.—*Author*.

over a country, did not check all inclination to mirth, and turn laughter into grief, the frantic conduct of the government of England would only excite ridicule. But it is impossible to banish from one's mind the images of suffering which the contemplation of such vicious policy presents. To reason with governments, as they have existed for ages, is to argue with brutes. It is only from the nations themselves that reforms can be expected. There ought not now to exist any doubt that the peoples of France, England, and America, enlightened and enlightening each other, shall henceforth be able, not merely to give the world an example of good government, but by their united influence enforce its practice.

RIGHTS OF MAN.

AMONG the incivilities by which nations or individuals provoke and irritate each other, Mr. Burke's pamphlet on the French Revolution is an extraordinary instance. Neither the People of France, nor the National Assembly, were troubling themselves about the affairs of England, or the English Parliament; and that Mr. Burke should commence an unprovoked attack upon them, both in Parliament and in public, is a conduct that cannot be pardoned on the score of manners, nor justified on that of policy.

There is scarcely an epithet of abuse to be found in the English language, with which Mr. Burke has not loaded the French Nation and the National Assembly. Everything which rancour, prejudice, ignorance or knowledge could suggest, is poured forth in the copious fury of near four hundred pages. In the strain and on the plan Mr. Burke was writing, he might have written on to as many thousands. When the tongue or the pen is let loose in a phrenzy of passion, it is the man, and not the subject, that becomes exhausted.

Hitherto Mr. Burke has been mistaken and disappointed in the opinions he had formed of the affairs of France; but such is the ingenuity of his hope, or the malignancy of his despair, that it furnishes him with new pretences to go on. There was a time when it was impossible to make Mr. Burke believe there would be any Revolution in France. His opinion then was, that the French had neither spirit to undertake it nor fortitude to support it; and now that there is one, he seeks an escape by condemning it.

Not sufficiently content with abusing the National Assembly, a great part of his work is taken up with abusing

Dr. Price (one of the best-hearted men that lives) [1] and the two societies in England known by the name of the Revolution Society and the Society for Constitutional Information.

Dr. Price had preached a sermon on the 4th of November, 1789, being the anniversary of what is called in England the Revolution, which took place 1688.   Mr. Burke, speaking of this sermon, says: "The political Divine proceeds dogmatically to assert, that by the principles of the Revolution, the people of England have acquired three fundamental rights.

1. To choose our own governors.

2. To cashier them for misconduct.

3. To frame a government for ourselves."

Dr. Price does not say that the right to do these things exists in this or in that person, or in this or in that description of persons, but that it exists in the *whole ;* that it is a right resident in the nation.   Mr. Burke, on the contrary, denies that such a right exists in the nation, either in whole or in part, or that it exists anywhere ; and, what is still more strange and marvellous, he says : "that the people of England utterly disclaim such a right, and that they will resist the practical assertion of it with their lives and fortunes." That men should take up arms and spend their lives and fortunes, *not* to maintain their rights, but to maintain they have *not* rights, is an entirely new species of discovery, and suited to the paradoxical genius of Mr. Burke.

The method which Mr. Burke takes to prove that the people of England have no such rights, and that such rights do not now exist in the nation, either in whole or in part, or anywhere at all, is of the same marvellous and monstrous kind with what he has already said; for his arguments are that the persons, or the generation of persons, in whom they did exist, are dead, and with them the right is dead also.   To prove this, he quotes a declaration made by Parliament about a hundred years ago, to William and Mary, in these words: "The Lords Spiritual and Temporal, and Commons, do, in the name of the people aforesaid" (meaning the people of England then living) "most

[1] Richard Price, D.D., F.R.S., died April 19, 1791.

humbly and faithfully *submit* themselves, their *heirs* and *posterities*, for EVER." He quotes a clause of another Act of Parliament made in the same reign, the terms of which he says, " bind us "(meaning the people of their day), " our *heirs* and our *posterity*, to *them*, their *heirs* and *posterity*, to the end of time."

Mr. Burke conceives his point sufficiently established by producing those clauses, which he enforces by saying that they exclude the right of the nation for *ever*. And not yet content with making such declarations, repeated over and over again, he farther says, " that if the people of England possessed such a right before the Revolution " (which he acknowledges to have been the case, not only in England, but throughout Europe, at an early period), " yet that the *English Nation* did, at the time of the Revolution, most solemnly renounce and abdicate it, for themselves, and for *all their posterity, for ever.*"

As Mr. Burke occasionally applies the poison drawn from his horrid principles, not only to the English nation, but to the French Revolution and the National Assembly, and charges that august, illuminated and illuminating body of men with the epithet of *usurpers*, I shall, *sans cérémonie*, place another system of principles in opposition to his.

The English Parliament of 1688 did a certain thing, which, for themselves and their constituents, they had a right to do, and which it appeared right should be done. But, in addition to this right, which they possessed by delegation, *they set up another right by assumption*, that of binding and controlling posterity to the end of time. The case, therefore, divides itself into two parts ; the right which they possessed by delegation, and the right which they set up by assumption. The first is admitted ; but with respect to the second, I reply—

There never did, there never will, and there never can, exist a Parliament, or any description of men, or any generation of men, in any country, possessed of the right or the power of binding and controuling posterity to the " *end of time,*" or of commanding for ever how the world shall be governed, or who shall govern it; and therefore all such clauses, acts or declarations by which the makers of them attempt to do what they have neither the right nor the power to do, nor the power to execute, are in themselves null and void.   Every age and generation must be as free to act for itself *in all cases* as the age and generations which preceded it.   The vanity and presumption of governing beyond the grave is the most ridiculous and insolent of all tyrannies.   Man has no property in man; neither has any generation a property in the generations which are to follow. The Parliament or the people of 1688, or of any other period, had no more right to dispose of the people of the present day, or to bind or to control them *in any shape whatever*, than the parliament or the people of the present day have to dispose of, bind or control those who are to live a hundred or a thousand years hence.   Every generation is, and must be, competent to all the purposes which its occasions require.   It is the living, and not the dead, that are to be accommodated.   When man ceases to be, his power and his wants cease with him; and having no longer any participation in the concerns of this world, he has no longer any authority in directing who shall be its governors, or how its government shall be organised, or how administered.

I am not contending for nor against any form of government, nor for nor against any party, here or elsewhere. That which a whole nation chooses to do it has a right to do. Mr. Burke says, No.   Where, then, does the right exist? I am contending for the rights of the *living*, and against their being willed away and controuled and contracted for by the manuscript assumed authority of the dead, and Mr. Burke is contending for the authority of the dead over the rights and freedom of the living.   There was a time when kings disposed of their crowns by will upon their death-beds, and consigned the people, like beasts of the field, to whatever successor they appointed.   This is now so exploded as scarcely to be remembered, and so monstrous as hardly to be believed.   But the Parliamentary clauses upon which Mr. Burke builds his political church are of the same nature.

The laws of every country must be analogous to some common principle. In England no parent or master, nor all the authority of Parliament, omnipotent as it has called itself, can bind or control the personal freedom even of an individual beyond the age of twenty-one years. On what ground of right, then, could the Parliament of 1688, or any other Parliament, bind all posterity for ever?

Those who have quitted the world, and those who have not yet arrived at it, are as remote from each other as the utmost stretch of mortal imagination can conceive. What possible obligation, then, can exist between them—what rule or principle can be laid down that of two nonentities, the one out of existence and the other not in, and who never can meet in this world, the one should controul the other to the end of time?

In England it is said that money cannot be taken out of the pockets of the people without their consent. But who authorised, or who could authorise, the Parliament of 1688 to control and take away the freedom of posterity (who were not in existence to give or to withhold their consent), and limit and confine their right of acting in certain cases for ever?

A greater absurdity cannot present itself to the understanding of man than what Mr. Burke offers to his readers. He tells them, and he tells the world to come, that a certain body of men who existed a hundred years ago made a law, and that there does not now exist in the nation, nor ever will, nor ever can, a power to alter it. Under how many subtilties or absurdities has the divine right to govern been imposed on the credulity of mankind? Mr. Burke has discovered a new one, and he has shortened his journey to Rome by appealing to the power of this infallible Parliament of former days, and he produces what it has done as of divine authority, for that power must certainly be more than human which no human power to the end of time can alter.

But Mr. Burke has done some service—not to his cause, but to his country—by bringing those clauses into public

view. They serve to demonstrate how necessary it is at all
times to watch against the attempted encroachment of
power, and to prevent its running to excess. It is somewhat extraordinary that the offence for which James II.
was expelled, that of setting up power by *assumption*, should
be re-acted, under another shape and form, by the Parliament that expelled him. It shews that the Rights of Man
were but imperfectly understood at the Revolution, for
certain it is that the right which that Parliament set up by
assumption (for by delegation it had not, and could not
have it, because none could give it) over the persons and
freedom of posterity for ever was of the same tyrannical
unfounded kind which James attempted to set up over the
Parliament and the nation, and for which he was expelled.
The only difference is (for in principle they differ not) that
the one was an usurper over the living, and the other over
the unborn ; and as the one has no better authority to
stand upon than the other, both of them must be equally
null and void, and of no effect.

From what, or from whence, does Mr. Burke prove the
right of any human power to bind posterity for ever? He
has produced his clauses, but he must produce also his
proofs that such a right existed, and shew how it existed.
If it ever existed it must now exist, for whatever appertains
to the nature of man cannot be annihilated by man. It is
the nature of man to die, and he will continue to die as long
as he continues to be born. But Mr. Burke has set up a
sort of political Adam, in whom all posterity are bound
for ever. He must, therefore, prove that his Adam possessed such a power, or such a right.

The weaker any cord is, the less will it bear to be
stretched, and the worse is the policy to stretch it, unless
it is intended to break it. Had anyone proposed the overthrow of Mr. Burke's positions, he would have proceeded as
Mr. Burke has done. He would have magnified the authorities, on purpose to have called the *right* of them into
question ; and the instant the question of right was started,
the authorities must have been given up.

It requires but a very small glance of thought to perceive that altho' laws made in one generation often continue in force through succeeding generations, yet they continue to derive their force from the consent of the living.   A law not repealed continues in force, not because it *cannot* be repealed, but because it is *not* repealed ; and the non-repealing passes for consent.

But Mr. Burke's clauses have not even this qualification in their favor.   They become null, by attempting to become immortal.   The nature of them precludes consent.   They destroy the right which they *might* have, by grounding it on a right which they *cannot* have.   Immortal power is not a human right, and therefore cannot be a right of Parliament.   The Parliament of 1688 might as well have passed an act to have authorised themselves to live for ever, as to make their authority live for ever.   All, therefore, that can be said of those clauses is that they are a formality of words, of as much import as if those who used them had addressed a congratulation to themselves, and in the oriental style of antiquity had said : O Parliament, live for ever !

The circumstances of the world are continually changing, and the opinions of men change also ; and as government is for the living, and not for the dead, it is the living only that has any right in it.   That which may be thought right and found convenient in one age may be thought wrong and found inconvenient in another.   In such cases, who is to decide, the living or the dead ?

As almost one hundred pages of Mr. Burke's book are employed upon these clauses, it will consequently follow that if the clauses themselves, so far as they set up an *assumed usurped* dominion over posterity for ever, are unauthoritative, and in their nature null and void ; that all his voluminous inferences, and declamation drawn therefrom, or founded thereon, are null and void also ; and on this ground I rest the matter.

We now come more particularly to the affairs of France. Mr. Burke's book has the appearance of being written as instruction to the French nation ; but if I may permit myself

the use of an extravagant metaphor, suited to the extravagance of the case, it is darkness attempting to illuminate
light.

While I am writing this there are accidentally before me
some proposals for a declaration of rights by the Marquis
de la Fayette (I ask his pardon for using his former address,
and do it only for distinction's sake) to the National Assembly, on the 11th of July, 1789, three days before the taking
of the Bastille, and I cannot but remark with astonishment
how opposite the sources are from which that gentleman
and Mr. Burke draw their principles. Instead of referring
to musty records and mouldy parchments to prove that the
rights of the living are lost, " renounced and abdicated for
ever," by those who are now no more, as Mr. Burke has
done, M. de la Fayette applies to the living world, and
emphatically says: "Call to mind the sentiments which
nature has engraved on the heart of every citizen, and which
take a new force when they are solemnly recognised by all:
—For a nation to love liberty, it is sufficient that she knows
it; and to be free, it is sufficient that she wills it." How
dry, barren, and obscure is the source from which Mr. Burke
labors! and how ineffectual, though gay with flowers, are
all his declamation and his arguments compared with these
clear, concise, and soul-animating sentiments! Few and
short as they are, they lead on to a vast field of generous
and manly thinking, and do not finish, like Mr. Burke's
periods, with music in the ear, and nothing in the heart.

As I have introduced M. de la Fayette, I will take the
liberty of adding an anecdote respecting his farewel address
to the Congress of America in 1783, and which occurred
fresh to my mind, when I saw Mr. Burke's thundering
attack on the French Revolution. M. de la Fayette went
to America at the early period of the war, and continued
a volunteer in her service to the end. His conduct through
the whole of that enterprise is one of the most extraordinary that is to be found in the history of a young man,
scarcely then twenty years of age. Situated in a country that
was like the lap of sensual pleasure, and with the means of

enjoying it, how few are there to be found who would
exchange such a scene for the woods and wildernesses of
America, and pass the flowery years of youth in unprofitable
danger and hardship ! but such is the fact. When the war
ended, and he was on the point of taking his final departure, he presented himself to Congress, and contemplating
in his affectionate farewel the Revolution he had seen,
expressed himself in these words : " May this great monument raised to liberty serve as a lesson to the oppressor,
and an example to the oppressed ! " When this address
came to the hands of Dr. Franklin, who was then in France,
he applied to Count Vergennes to have it inserted in the
French Gazette, but never could obtain his consent. The
fact was that Count Vergennes was an aristocratical despot
at home, and dreaded the example of the American Revolution in France, as certain other persons now dread the
example of the French Revolution in England, and Mr.
Burke's tribute of fear (for in this light his book must be
considered) runs parallel with Count Vergennes' refusal.
But to return more particularly to his work.

   " We have seen," says Mr. Burke, " the French rebel against
a mild and lawful monarch, with more fury, outrage, and
insult, than any people has been known to rise against the
most illegal usurper, or the most sanguinary tyrant." This
is one among a thousand other instances, in which Mr.
Burke shows that he is ignorant of the springs and principles
of the French Revolution.

   It was not against Louis XVIth but against the despotic
principles of the Government, that the nation revolted. These
principles had not their origin in him, but in the original
establishment, many centuries back : and they were become
too deeply rooted to be removed, and the Augean stables of
parasites and plunderers too abominably filthy to be cleansed
by anything short of a complete and universal Revolution.
When it becomes necessary to do anything, the whole heart
and soul should go into the measure, or not attempt it.
That crisis was then arrived, and there remained no choice
but to act with determined vigor, or not to act at all.   The

king was known to be the friend of the nation, and this circumstance was favorable to the enterprise. Perhaps no man bred up in the style of an absolute king, ever possessed a heart so little disposed to the exercise of that species of power as the present King of France. But the principles of the Government itself still remained the same. The Monarch and the Monarchy were distinct and separate things ; and it was against the established despotism of the latter, and not against the person or principles of the former, that the revolt commenced, and the Revolution has been carried.

Mr. Burke does not attend to the distinction between men and principles , and, therefore, he does not see that a revolt may take place against the despotism of the latter, while there lies no charge of despotism against the former.

The natural moderation of Louis XVIth contributed nothing to alter the hereditary despotism of the monarchy. All the tyrannies of former reigns, acted under that hereditary despotism, were still liable to be revived in the hands of a successor. It was not the respite of a reign that would satisfy France, enlightened as she was then become. A casual discontinuance of the *practice* of despotism, is not a discontinuance of its *principles :* the former depends on the virtue of the individual who is in immediate possession of the power ; the latter, on the virtue and fortitude of the nation. In the case of Charles Ist and James IInd of England, the revolt was against the personal despotism of the men ; whereas in France, it was against the hereditary despotism of the established Government. But men who can consign over the rights of posterity for ever on the authority of a mouldy parchment, like Mr. Burke, are not qualified to judge of this Revolution. It takes in a field too vast for their views to explore, and proceeds with a mightiness of reason they cannot keep pace with.

But there are many points of view in which this Revolution may be considered. When despotism has established itself for ages in a country, as in France, it is not in the person of the king only that it resides. It has the appearance of being so in show, and in nominal authority ; but it is not so in practice and in fact. It has its standard everywhere. Every office and department has its despotism, founded upon custom and usage. Every place has its Bastille, and every Bastille its despot. The original hereditary despotism resident in the person of the king, divides and sub-divides itself into a thousand shapes and forms, till at last the whole of it is acted by deputation. This was the case in France ; and against this species of despotism, proceeding on through an endless labyrinth of office till the source of it is scarcely perceptible, there is no mode of redress. It strengthens itself by assuming the appearance of duty, and tyrannises under the pretence of obeying.

When a man reflects on the condition which France was in from the nature of her government, he will see other causes for revolt than those which immediately connect themselves with the person or character of Louis XVI. There were, if I may so express it, a thousand despotisms to be reformed in France, which had grown up under the hereditary despotism of the monarchy, and became so rooted as to be in a great measure independent of it. Between the Monarchy, the Parliament, and the Church there was a *rivalship* of despotism ; besides the feudal despotism operating locally, and the ministerial despotism operating everywhere. But Mr. Burke, by considering the king as the only possible object of a revolt, speaks as if France was a village, in which everything that passed must be known to its commanding officer, and no oppression could be acted but what he could immediately controul. Mr. Burke might have been in the Bastille his whole life, as well under Louis XVI as Louis XIV., and neither the one nor the other have known that such a man as Burke existed. The despotic principles of the government were the same in both reigns, though the dispositions of the men were as remote as tyranny and benevolence.

What Mr. Burke considers as a reproach to the French Revolution (that of bringing it forward under a reign more mild than the preceding ones) is one of its highest honors.

The Revolutions that have taken place in other European countries, have been excited by personal hatred. The rage was against the man, and he became the victim. But, in the instance of France we see a Revolution generated in the rational contemplation of the Rights of Man, and distinguishing from the beginning between persons and principles.

But Mr. Burke appears to have no idea of principles when he is contemplating Governments. " Ten years ago," says he, " I could have felicitated France on her having a Government, without inquiring what the nature of that Government was, or how it was administered." Is this the language of a rational man? Is it the language of a heart feeling as it ought to feel for the rights and happiness of the human race? On this ground, Mr. Burke must compliment all the Governments in the world, while the victims who suffer under them, whether sold into slavery, or tortured out of existence, are wholly forgotten. It is power, and not principles, that Mr. Burke venerates ; and under this abominable depravity he is disqualified to judge between them. Thus much for his opinion as to the occasions of the French Revolution. I now proceed to other considerations.

I know a place in America called Point-no-Point, because as you proceed along the shore, gay and flowery as Mr. Burke's language, it continually recedes and presents itself at a distance before you ; but when you have got as far as you can go, there is no point at all. Just thus it is with Mr. Burke's three hundred and sixty-six pages. It is therefore difficult to reply to him. But as the points he wishes to establish may be inferred from what he abuses, it is in his paradoxes that we must look for his arguments.

As to the tragic paintings by which Mr. Burke has outraged his own imagination, and seeks to work upon that of his readers, they are very well calculated for theatrical representation, where facts are manufactured for the sake of show, and accommodated to produce, through the weakness of sympathy, a weeping effect. But Mr. Burke should recollect that he is writing history, and not *plays*, and that

his readers will expect truth, and not the spouting rant of
high-toned exclamation.

When we see a man dramatically lamenting in a publication
intended to be believed that " *The age of chivalry is gone !*
that *The glory of Europe is extinguished for ever !* that *The*
unbought grace of life (if anyone knows what it is), *the*
cheap defence of nations, the nurse of manly sentiment and
heroic enterprise is gone !" and all this because the Quixot
age of chivalry nonsense is gone, what opinion can we
form of his judgment, or what regard can we pay to his
facts?   In the rhapsody of his imagination he has discovered
a world of wind mills, and his sorrows are that there are no
Quixots to attack them.   But if the age of aristocracy, like
that of chivalry, should fall (and they had originally some
connection) Mr. Burke, the trumpeter of the Order, may
continue his parody to the end, and finish with exclaiming:
" *Othello's occupation's gone !*"

Notwithstanding Mr. Burke's horrid paintings, when the
French Revolution is compared with the Revolutions of
other countries, the astonishment will be that it is marked
with so few sacrifices ; but this astonishment will cease
when we reflect that *principles*, and not *persons*, were the
meditated objects of destruction.   The mind of the nation
was acted upon by a higher stimulus than what the consideration of persons could inspire, and sought a higher conquest than could be produced by the downfal of an enemy.
Among the few who fell there do not appear to be any
that were intentionally singled out.   They all of them had
their fate in the circumstances of the moment, and were
not pursued with that long, cold-blooded unabated revenge
which pursued the unfortunate Scotch in the affair of
1745.

Through the whole of Mr. Burke's book I do not observe that the Bastille is mentioned more than once, and
that with a kind of implication as if he were sorry it was
pulled down, and wished it were built up again. " We have
rebuilt Newgate," says he, "and tenanted the mansion ;
and we have prisons almost as strong as the Bastille

for those who dare to libel the queens of France." *   As to
what a madman like the person called Lord G[eorge] G[or-
don] might say, and to whom Newgate is rather a bedlam
than a prison, it is unworthy a rational consideration.   It
was a madman that libelled, and that is sufficient apology;
and it afforded an opportunity for confining him, which
was the thing that was wished for.   But certain it is that
Mr. Burke, who does not call himself a madman (whatever
other people may do), has libelled in the most unprovoked
manner, and in the grossest style of the most vulgar abuse,
the whole representative authority of France, and yet Mr.
Burke takes his seat in the British House of Commons!
From his violence and his grief, his silence on some points
and his excess on others, it is difficult not to believe
that Mr. Burke is sorry, extremely sorry, that arbitrary
power, the power of the Pope and the Bastille, are pulled
down.

Not one glance of compassion, not one commiserating
reflexion that I can find throughout his book, has he bestowed on those who lingered out the most wretched of lives,
a life without hope in the most miserable of prisons.   It
is painful to behold a man employing his talents to corrupt
himself.   Nature has been kinder to Mr. Burke than he is to
her.   He is not affected by the reality of distress touching
his heart, but by the showy resemblance of it striking his
imagination.   He pities the plumage, but forgets the dying
bird.   Accustomed to kiss the aristocratical hand that hath
purloined him from himself, he degenerates into a composition of art, and the genuine soul of nature forsakes him.
His hero or his heroine must be a tragedy-victim expiring

---

* Since writing the above, two other places occur in Mr. Burke's pamphlet
in which the name of the Bastille is mentioned, but in the same manner.   In
the one he introduces it in a sort of obscure question, and asks : " Will any
ministers who now serve such a king, with but a decent appearance of respect,
cordially obey the orders of those whom but the other day, *in his name*, they
had committed to the Bastille ? "   In the other the taking it is mentioned
as implying criminality in the French guards, who assisted in demolishing it.
" They have not, "says he, " forgot the taking the king's castles at Paris."   This
is Mr. Burke, who pretends to write on constitutional freedom.—*Author*.

in show, and not the real prisoner of misery, sliding into
death in the silence of a dungeon.

As Mr. Burke has passed over the whole transaction of
the Bastille (and his silence is nothing in his favor), and has
entertained his readers with reflections on supposed facts
distorted into real falsehoods, I will give, since he has not,
some account of the circumstances which preceded that
transaction. They will serve to shew that less mischief
could scarcely have accompanied such an event when considered with the treacherous and hostile aggravations of the
enemies of the Revolution.

The mind can hardly picture to itself a more tremendous
scene than what the city of Paris exhibited at the time of
taking the Bastille, and for two days before and after, nor
perceive the possibility of its quieting so soon. At a distance this transaction has appeared only as an act of heroism
standing on itself, and the close political connection it had
with the Revolution is lost in the brilliancy of the achieve-
ment. But we are to consider it as the strength of the
parties brought man to man, and contending for the issue.
The Bastille was to be either the prize or the prison of the
assailants. The downfall of it included the idea of the
downfall of despotism, and this compounded image was
become as figuratively united as Bunyan's Doubting Castle
and Giant Despair.[1]

The National Assembly, before and at the time of taking
the Bastille, was sitting at Versailles, twelve miles distant
from Paris. About a week before the rising of the Parisians,
and their taking the Bastille, it was discovered that a plot
was forming, at the head of which was the Count d'Artois,
the king's youngest brother, for demolishing the National
Assembly, seizing its members, and thereby crushing, by a
coup de main, all hopes and prospects of forming a free government. For the sake of humanity, as well as freedom, it is well
this plan did not succeed. Examples are not wanting to show
how dreadfully vindictive and cruel are all old governments,
when they are successful against what they call a revolt.

[1] In the French edition this allusion is explained in a footnote.—*Editor.*

This plan must have been some time in contemplation; because, in order to carry it into execution, it was necessary to collect a large military force round Paris, and cut off the communication between that city and the National Assembly at Versailles. The troops destined for this service were chiefly the foreign troops in the pay of France, and who, for this particular purpose, were drawn from the distant provinces where they were then stationed. When they were collected to the amount of between twenty-five and thirty thousand, it was judged time to put the plan into execution. The ministry who were then in office, and who were friendly to the Revolution, were instantly dismissed and a new ministry formed of those who had concerted the project, among whom was Count de Broglio, and to his share was given the command of those troops. The character of this man as described to me in a letter which I communicated to Mr. Burke before he began to write his book, and from an authority which Mr. Burke well knows was good, was that of "a high-flying aristocrat, cool, and capable of every mischief."

While these matters were agitating the National Assembly stood in the most perilous and critical situation that a body of men can be supposed to act in. They were the devoted victims, and they knew it. They had the hearts and wishes of their country on their side, but military authority they had none. The guards of Broglio surrounded the hall where the Assembly sat, ready, at the word of command, to seize their persons, as had been done the year before to the Parliament of Paris. Had the National Assembly deserted their trust, or had they exhibited signs of weakness or fear, their enemies had been encouraged and their country depressed. When the situation they stood in, the cause they were engaged in, and the crisis then ready to burst, which should determine their personal and political fate and that of their country, and probably of Europe, are taken into one view, none but a heart callous with prejudice or corrupted by dependence can avoid interesting itself in their success.

The Archbishop of Vienne was at this time President of

the National Assembly—a person too old to undergo the
scene that a few days or a few hours might bring forth.   A
man of more activity and bolder fortitude was necessary,
and the National Assembly chose (under the form of a Vice-
President, for the Presidency still resided in the Archbishop)
M. de la Fayette ; and this is the only instance of a Vice-
President being chosen.   It was at the moment that this
storm was pending (July 11th) that a declaration of rights
was brought forward by M. de la Fayette, and is the same
which is alluded to in p. [282.] It was hastily drawn up, and
makes only a part of the more extensive declaration of
rights agreed upon and adopted afterwards by the National
Assembly.   The particular reason for bringing it forward at
this moment (M. de la Fayette has since informed me) was
that, if the National Assembly should fall in the threatened
destruction that then surrounded it, some trace of its principles might have the chance of surviving the wreck.

Everything now was drawing to a crisis.   The event was
freedom or slavery.   On one side, an army of nearly thirty
thousand men ; on the other, an unarmed body of citizens
—for the citizens of Paris, on whom the National Assembly
must then immediately depend, were as unarmed and as undisciplined as the citizens of London are now.   The French
guards had given strong symptoms of their being attached
to the national cause ; but their numbers were small, not a
tenth part of the force that Broglio commanded, and their
officers were in the interest of Broglio.

Matters being now ripe for execution, the new ministry
made their appearance in office.   The reader will carry in
his mind that the Bastille was taken the 14th July ; the
point of time I am now speaking of is the 12th.   Immediately on the news of the change of ministry reaching Paris,
in the afternoon, all the playhouses and places of entertainment, shops and houses, were shut up.   The change of
ministry was considered as the prelude of hostilities, and
the opinion was rightly founded.

The foreign troops began to advance towards the city.
The Prince de Lambesc, who commanded a body of German

cavalry, approached by the Place of Lewis XV., which connects itself with some of the streets. In his march, he insulted and struck an old man with a sword. The French are remarkable for their respect to old age ; and the insolence with which it appeared to be done, uniting with the general fermentation they were in, produced a powerful effect, and a cry of "To arms! to arms!" spread itself in a moment over the city.

Arms they had none, nor scarcely anyone who knew the use of them ; but desperate resolution, when every hope is at stake, supplies, for a while, the want of arms. Near where the Prince de Lambesc was drawn up, were large piles of stones collected for building the new bridge, and with these the people attacked the cavalry. A party of French guards upon hearing the firing, rushed from their quarters and joined the people ; and night coming on, the cavalry retreated.

The streets of Paris, being narrow, are favorable for defence, and the loftiness of the houses, consisting of many stories, from which great annoyance might be given, secured them against nocturnal enterprises ; and the night was spent in providing themselves with every sort of weapon they could make or procure : guns, swords, blacksmiths' hammers, carpenters' axes, iron crows, pikes, halberts, pitchforks, spits, clubs, etc., etc. The incredible numbers in which they assembled the next morning, and the still more incredible resolution they exhibited, embarrassed and astonished their enemies. Little did the new ministry expect such a salute. Accustomed to slavery themselves, they had no idea that liberty was capable of such inspiration, or that a body of unarmed citizens would dare to face the military force of thirty thousand men. Every moment of this day was employed in collecting arms, concerting plans, and arranging themselves into the best order which such an instantaneous movement could afford. Broglio continued lying round the city, but made no further advances this day, and the succeeding night passed with as much tranquility as such a scene could possibly produce.

But defence only was not the object of the citizens. They had a cause at stake, on which depended their freedom or their slavery. They every moment expected an attack, or to hear of one made on the National Assembly; and in such a situation, the most prompt measures are sometimes the best. The object that now presented itself was the Bastille; and the *éclat* of carrying such a fortress in the face of such an army, could not fail to strike terror into the new ministry, who had scarcely yet had time to meet. By some intercepted correspondence this morning, it was discovered that the Mayor of Paris, M. Deffleseslles, who appeared to be in the interest of the citizens, was betraying them; and from this discovery, there remained no doubt that Broglio would reinforce the Bastille the ensuing evening. It was therefore necessary to attack it that day; but before this could be done, it was first necessary to procure a better supply of arms than they were then possessed of.

There was, adjoining to the city a large magazine of arms deposited at the Hospital of the Invalids, which the citizens summoned to surrender; and as the place was neither defensible, nor attempted much defence, they soon succeeded. Thus supplied, they marched to attack the Bastille; a vast mixed multitude of all ages, and of all degrees, armed with all sorts of weapons. Imagination would fail in describing to itself the appearance of such a procession, and of the anxiety of the events which a few hours or a few minutes might produce. What plans the ministry were forming, were as unknown to the people within the city, as what the citizens were doing was unknown to the ministry; and what movements Broglio might make for the support or relief of the place, were to the citizens equally as unknown. All was mystery and hazard.

That the Bastille was attacked with an enthusiasm of heroism, such only as the highest animation of liberty could inspire, and carried in the space of a few hours, is an event which the world is fully possessed of. I am not undertaking the detail of the attack, but bringing into view the conspiracy against the nation which provoked it, and which fell with the Bastille. The prison to which the new ministry were dooming the National Assembly, in addition to its being the high altar and castle of despotism, became the proper object to begin with. This enterprise broke up the new ministry, who began now to fly from the ruin they had prepared for others. The troops of Broglio dispersed, and himself fled also.

Mr. Burke has spoken a great deal about plots, but he has never once spoken of this plot against the National Assembly, and the liberties of the nation ; and that he might not, he has passed over all the circumstances that might throw it in his way. The exiles who have fled from France, whose case he so much interests himself in, and from whom he has had his lesson, fled in consequence of the miscarriage of this plot. No plot was formed against them ; they were plotting against others ; and those who fell, met, not unjustly, the punishment they were preparing to execute. But will Mr. Burke say, that if this plot, contrived with the subtilty of an ambuscade, had succeeded, the successful party would have restrained their wrath so soon ? Let the history of all governments answer the question.

Whom has the National Assembly brought to the scaffold ? None. They were themselves the devoted victims of this plot, and they have not retaliated ; why, then, are they charged with revenge they have not acted ? In the tremendous breaking forth of a whole people, in which all degrees, tempers and characters are confounded, delivering themselves, by a miracle of exertion, from the destruction meditated against them, is it to be expected that nothing will happen ? When men are sore with the sense of oppressions, and menaced with the prospects of new ones, is the calmness of philosophy or the palsy of insensibility to be looked for? Mr. Burke exclaims against outrage ; yet the greatest is that which himself has committed. His book is a volume of outrage, not apologised for by the impulse of a moment, but cherished through a space of ten months ; yet Mr. Burke had no provocation—no life, no interest, at stake.

More of the citizens fell in this struggle than of their opponents : but four or five persons were seized by the populace,

and instantly put to death ; the Governor of the Bastille,
and the Mayor of Paris, who was detected in the act of betraying them ; and afterwards Foulon, one of the new
ministry, and Berthier, his son-in-law, who had accepted the
office of intendant of Paris.   Their heads were struck upon
spikes, and carried about the city ; and it is upon this mode
of punishment that Mr. Burke builds a great part of his
tragic scene.   Let us therefore examine how men came by
the idea of punishing in this manner.

They learn it from the governments they live under; and
retaliate the punishments they have been accustomed to
behold.   The heads stuck upon spikes, which remained for
years upon Temple Bar, differed nothing in the horror of
the scene from those carried about upon spikes at Paris ;
yet this was done by the English Government.   It may
perhaps be said that it signifies nothing to a man what is
done to him after he is dead ; but it signifies much to the
living ; it either tortures their feelings or hardens their
hearts, and in either case it instructs them how to punish
when power falls into their hands.

Lay then the axe to the root, and teach governments humanity.   It is their sanguinary punishments which corrupt
mankind.   In England the punishment in certain cases is
by *hanging, drawing* and *quartering ;* the heart of the sufferer is cut out and held up to the view of the populace.
In France, under the former Government, the punishments
were not less barbarous.   Who does not remember the execution of Damien, torn to pieces by horses ?   The effect of
those cruel spectacles exhibited to the populace is to destroy
tenderness or excite revenge ;   and by the base and false
idea of governing men by terror, instead of reason, they
become precedents.   It is over the lowest class of mankind
that government by terror is intended to operate, and it is
on them that it operates to the worst effect.   They have
sense enough to feel they are the objects aimed at ; and they
inflict in their turn the examples of terror they have been
instructed to practise.

There is in all European countries a large class of people

of that description, which in England is called the "*mob*."
Of this class were those who committed the burnings and
devastations in London in 1780, and of this class were those
who carried the heads upon spikes in Paris. Foulon and
Berthier were taken up in the country, and sent to Paris, to
undergo their examination at the Hotel de Ville; for the
National Assembly, immediately on the new ministry coming into office, passed a decree, which they communicated
to the King and Cabinet, that they (the National Assembly)
would hold the ministry, of which Foulon was one, responsible for the measures they were advising and pursuing;
but the mob, incensed at the appearance of Foulon and
Berthier, tore them from their conductors before they were
carried to the Hotel de Ville, and executed them on the
spot. Why then does Mr. Burke charge outrages of this
kind on a whole people? As well may he charge the riots
and outrages of 1780 on all the people of London, or those
in Ireland on all his countrymen.

But everything we see or hear offensive to our feelings
and derogatory to the human character should lead to other
reflections than those of reproach. Even the beings who
commit them have some claim to our consideration. How
then is it that such vast classes of mankind as are distinguished by the appellation of the vulgar, or the ignorant mob,
are so numerous in all old countries? The instant we ask
ourselves this question, reflection feels an answer. They
rise, as an unavoidable consequence, out of the ill construction of all old governments in Europe, England included
with the rest. It is by distortedly exalting some men, that
others are distortedly debased, till the whole is out of nature. A vast mass of mankind are degradedly thrown into
the back-ground of the human picture, to bring forward,
with greater glare, the puppet-show of state and aristocracy.
In the commencement of a revolution, those men are rather
the followers of the *camp* than of the *standard* of liberty,
and have yet to be instructed how to reverence it.

I give to Mr. Burke all his theatrical exaggerations for
facts, and I then ask him if they do not establish the cer-

tainty of what I here lay down ?   Admitting them to be
true, they show the necessity of the French Revolution, as
much as any one thing he could have asserted.   These outrages were not the effect of the principles of the Revolution, but of the degraded mind that existed before the
Revolution, and which the Revolution is calculated to reform.   Place them then to their proper cause, and take the
reproach of them to your own side.

It is the honour of the National Assembly and the city
of Paris that, during such a tremendous scene of arms and
confusion, beyond the controul of all authority, they have
been able, by the influence of example and exhortation, to
restrain so much.   Never were more pains taken to instruct
and enlighten mankind, and to make them see that their interest consisted in their virtue, and not in their revenge, than
have been displayed in the Revolution of France.   I now
proceed to make some remarks on Mr. Burke's account of
the expedition to Versailles, October the 5th and 6th.

I can consider Mr. Burke's book in scarcely any other
light than a dramatic performance ; and he must, I think,
have considered it in the same light himself, by the poetical
liberties he has taken of omitting some facts, distorting
others, and making the whole machinery bend to produce
a stage effect.   Of this kind is his acccunt of the expedition to Versailles.   He begins this account by omitting the
only facts which as causes are known to be true ; everything
beyond these is conjecture, even in Paris ; and he then works
up a tale accommodated to his own passions and prejudices.

It is to be observed throughout Mr. Burke's book that he
never speaks of plots *against* the Revolution ; and it is from
those plots that all the mischiefs have arisen.   It suits his
purpose to exhibit the consequences without their causes.
It is one of the arts of the drama to do so.   If the crimes
of men were exhibited with their sufferings, stage effect
would sometimes be lost, and the audience would be inclined to approve where it was intended they should com-
miserate.

After all the investigations that have been made into this

intricate affair (the expedition to Versailles), it still remains enveloped in all that kind of mystery which ever accompanies events produced more from a concurrence of awkward circumstances than from fixed design. While the characters of men are forming, as is always the case in revolutions, there is a reciprocal suspicion, and a disposition to misinterpret each other ; and even parties directly opposite in principle will sometimes concur in pushing forward the same movement with very different views, and with the hopes of its producing very different consequences. A great deal of this may be discovered in this embarrassed affair, and yet the issue of the whole was what nobody had in view.

The only things certainly known are that considerable uneasiness was at this time excited at Paris by the delay of the King in not sanctioning and forwarding the decrees of the National Assembly, particularly that of the *Declaration of the Rights of Man,* and the decrees of the *fourth of August,* which contained the foundation principles on which the constitution was to be erected. The kindest, and perhaps the fairest conjecture upon this matter is, that some of the ministers intended to make remarks and observations upon certain parts of them before they were finally sanctioned and sent to the provinces ; but be this as it may, the enemies of the Revolution derived hope from the delay, and the friends of the Revolution uneasiness.

During this state of suspense, the *Garde du Corps,* which was composed as such regiments generally are, of persons much connected with the Court, gave an entertainment at Versailles (October 1) to some foreign regiments then arrived ; and when the entertainment was at the height, on a signal given, the *Garde du Corps* tore the national cockade from their hats, trampled it under foot, and replaced it with a counter-cockade prepared for the purpose. An indignity of this kind amounted to defiance. It was like declaring war ; and if men will give challenges they must expect consequences. But all this Mr. Burke has carefully kept out of sight. He begins his account by saying : " History will record that on the morning of the 6th October, 1789, the

King and Queen of France, after a day of confusion, alarm,
dismay, and slaughter, lay down under the pledged security
of public faith to indulge nature in a few hours of respite,
and troubled melancholy repose." This is neither the sober
stile of history, nor the intention of it. It leaves everything to be guessed at and mistaken. One would at least
think there had been a battle; and a battle there probably
would have been had it not been for the moderating prudence of those whom Mr. Burke involves in his censures.
By his keeping the *Garde du Corps* out of sight Mr. Burke
has afforded himself the dramatic licence of putting the
King and Queen in their places, as if the object of the
expedition was against them. But to return to my account—

This conduct of the *Garde du Corps*, as might well be expected, alarmed and enraged the Parisians. The colors of
the cause, and the cause itself, were become too united to
mistake the intention of the insult, and the Parisians were
determined to call the *Garde du Corps* to an account. There
was certainly nothing of the cowardice of assassination in
marching in the face of the day to demand satisfaction, if
such a phrase may be used, of a body of armed men who
had voluntarily given defiance. But the circumstance which
serves to throw this affair into embarrassment is, that the
enemies of the Revolution appear to have encouraged it as
well as its friends. The one hoped to prevent a civil war by
checking it in time, and the other to make one. The hopes
of those opposed to the Revolution rested in making the
King of their party, and getting him from Versailles to
Metz, where they expected to collect a force and set up a
standard. We have, therefore, two different objects presenting themselves at the same time, and to be accomplished by the same means : the one to chastise the *Garde
du Corps*, which was the object of the Parisians ; the other
to render the confusion of such a scene an inducement to
the King to set off for Metz.

On the 5th of October a very numerous body of women,
and men in the disguise of women, collected round the Ho-

tel de Ville or town-hall at Paris, and set off for Versailles. Their professed object was the *Garde du Corps;* but prudent men readily recollect that mischief is more easily begun than ended ; and this impressed itself with the more force from the suspicions already stated, and the irregularity of such a cavalcade.   As soon, therefore, as a sufficient force could be collected, M. de la Fayette, by orders from the civil authority of Paris, set off after them at the head of twenty thousand of the Paris militia.   The Revolution could derive no benefit from confusion, and its opposers might.   By an amiable and spirited manner of address he had hitherto been fortunate in calming disquietudes, and in this he was extraordinarily successful; to frustrate, therefore, the hopes of those who might seek to improve this scene into a sort of justifiable necessity for the King's quitting Versailles and withdrawing to Metz, and to prevent at the same time the consequences that might ensue between the *Garde du Corps* and this phalanx of men and women, he forwarded expresses to the King, that he was on his march to Versailles, by the orders of the civil authority of Paris, for the purpose of peace and protection, expressing at the same time the necessity of restraining the *Garde du Corps* from firing upon the people.*

He arrived at Versailles between ten and eleven at night. The *Garde du Corps* was drawn up, and the people had arrived some time before, but everything had remained suspended.   Wisdom and policy now consisted in changing a scene of danger into a happy event.   M. de la Fayette became the mediator between the enraged parties; and the King, to remove the uneasiness which had arisen from the delay already stated, sent for the President of the National Assembly, and signed the *Declaration of the Rights of Man,* and such other parts of the constitution as were in readiness.

It was now about one in the morning.   Everything appeared to be composed, and a general congratulation took place.   By the beat of a drum a proclamation was made that

* I am warranted in asserting this, as I had it personally from M. de la Fayette, with whom I lived in habits of friendship for fourteen years.—*Author.*

the citizens of Versailles would give the hospitality of
their houses to their fellow-citizens of Paris. Those who
could not be accommodated in this manner remained in the
streets, or took up their quarters in the churches ; and at
two o'clock the King and Queen retired.

In this state matters passed till the break of day, when
a fresh disturbance arose from the censurable conduct of
some of both parties, for such characters there will be in
all such scenes. One of the *Garde du Corps* appeared at
one of the windows of the palace, and the people who had
remained during the night in the streets accosted him with
reviling and provocative language. Instead of retiring, as
in such a case prudence would have dictated, he presented
his musket, fired, and killed one of the Paris militia. The
peace being thus broken, the people rushed into the palace in
quest of the offender. They attacked the quarters of the
Garde de Corps within the palace, and pursued them throughout the avenues of it, and to the apartments of the King.
On this tumult, not the Queen only, as Mr. Burke has represented it, but every person in the palace, was awakened
and alarmed ; and M. de la Fayette had a second time to
interpose between the parties, the event of which was
that the *Garde du Corps* put on the national cockade, and
the matter ended as by oblivion, after the loss of two or
three lives.

During the latter part of the time in which this confusion
was acting, the King and Queen were in public at the
balcony, and neither of them concealed for safety's sake,
as Mr. Burke insinuates. Matters being thus appeased,
and tranquility restored, a general acclamation broke forth
of *Le Roi à Paris—Le Roi à Paris*—The King to Paris. It
was the shout of peace, and immediately accepted on the
part of the King. By this measure all future projects of
trapanning the King to Metz, and setting up the standard
opposition to the constitution, were prevented, and the
suspicions extinguished. The King and his family reached
Paris in the evening, and were congratulated on their arrival
by M. Bailly, the Mayor of Paris, in the name of the citi-

zens.   Mr. Burke, who throughout his book confounds things, persons, and principles, as in his remarks on M. Bailly's address, confounded time also.   He censures M. Bailly for calling it "*un bon jour*," a good day.   Mr. Burke should have informed himself that this scene took up the space of two days, the day on which it began with every appearance of danger and mischief, and the day on which it terminated without the mischiefs that threatened ; and that it is to this peaceful termination that M. Bailly alludes, and to the arrival of the King at Paris.   Not less than three hundred thousand persons arranged themselves in the procession from Versailles to Paris, and not an act of molestation was committed during the whole march.

Mr. Burke on the authority of M. Lally Tollendal, a deserter from the National Assembly, says, that on entering Paris, the people shouted " *Tous les évèques à la lanterne.*" All Bishops to be hanged at the lanthorn or lamp-posts. It is surprising that nobody could hear this but Lally Tollendal, and that nobody should believe it but Mr. Burke. It has not the least connexion with any part of the transaction, and is totally foreign to every circumstance of it.   The Bishops had never been introduced before into any scene of Mr. Burke's drama : why then are they, all at once, and altogether, *tout à coup, et tous ensemble*, introduced now ? Mr. Burke brings forward his Bishops and his lanthorn-like figures in a magic lanthorn, and raises his scenes by contrast instead of connection.   But it serves to show, with the rest of his book what little credit ought to be given where even probability is set at defiance, for the purpose of defaming ; and with this reflexion, instead of a soliloquy in praise of chivalry, as Mr. Burke has done, I close the account of the expedition to Versailles.*

I have now to follow Mr. Burke through a pathless wilderness of rhapsodies, and a sort of descant upon govern-

---

* An account of the expedition to Versailles may be seen in No. 13 of the *Revolution de Paris* containing the events from the 3rd to the 10th of October, 1789.—*Author*.

ments, in which he asserts whatever he pleases, on the presumption of its being believed, without offering either evidence or reasons for so doing.

Before anything can be reasoned upon to a conclusion, certain facts, principles, or data, to reason from, must be established, admitted, or denied. Mr. Burke with his usual outrage, abused the *Declaration of the Rights of Man*, published by the National Assembly of France, as the basis on which the constitution of France is built. This he calls "paltry and blurred sheets of paper about the rights of man." Does Mr. Burke mean to deny that *man* has any rights? If he does, then he must mean that there are no such things as rights anywhere, and that he has none himself; for who is there in the world but man? But if Mr. Burke means to admit that man has rights, the question then will be: What are those rights, and how man came by them originally?

The error of those who reason by precedents drawn from antiquity, respecting the rights of man, is that they do not go far enough into antiquity. They do not go the whole way. They stop in some of the intermediate stages of an hundred or a thousand years, and produce what was then done, as a rule for the present day. This is no authority at all. If we travel still farther into antiquity, we shall find a direct contrary opinion and practice prevailing; and if antiquity is to be authority, a thousand such authorities may be produced, successively contradicting each other; but if we proceed on, we shall at last come out right; we shall come to the time when man came from the hand of his Maker. What was he then? Man. Man was his high and only title, and a higher cannot be given him. But of titles I shall speak hereafter.

We are now got at the origin of man, and at the origin of his rights. As to the manner in which the world has been governed from that day to this, it is no farther any concern of ours than to make a proper use of the errors or the improvements which the history of it presents. Those who lived a hundred or a thousand years ago, were then moderns, as we are now. They had *their* ancients, and those ancients had others, and we also shall be ancients in our turn. If the mere name of antiquity is to govern in the affairs of life, the people who are to live an hundred or a thousand years hence, may as well take us for a precedent, as we make a precedent of those who lived an hundred or a thousand years ago. The fact is, that portions of antiquity, by proving everything, establish nothing. It is authority against authority all the way, till we come to the divine origin of the rights of man at the creation. Here our enquiries find a resting-place, and our reason finds a home. If a dispute about the rights of man had arisen at the distance of an hundred years from the creation, it is to this source of authority they must have referred, and it is to this same source of authority that we must now refer.

Though I mean not to touch upon any sectarian principle of religion, yet it may be worth observing, that the genealogy of Christ is traced to Adam. Why then not trace the rights of man to the creation of man? I will answer the question. Because there have been upstart governments, thrusting themselves between, and presumptuously working to *un-make* man.

If any generation of men ever possessed the right of dictating the mode by which the world should be governed for ever, it was the first generation that existed; and if that generation did it not, no succeeding generation can show any authority for doing it, nor can set any up. The illuminating and divine principle of the equal rights of man (for it has its origin from the Maker of man) relates, not only to the living individuals, but to generations of men succeeding each other. Every generation is equal in rights to generations which preceded it, by the same rule that every individual is born equal in rights with his contemporary.

Every history of the creation, and every traditionary account, whether from the lettered or unlettered world, however they may vary in their opinion or belief of certain particulars, all agree in establishing one point, *the unity of man;* by which I mean that men are all of *one degree*, and con-

sequently that all men are born equal, and with equal natural
right, in the same manner as if posterity had been continued
by *creation* instead of *generation*, the latter being the only
mode by which the former is carried forward ; and consequently every child born into the world must be considered as
deriving its existence from God.   The world is as new to him
as it was to the first man that existed, and his natural right
in it is of the same kind.

The Mosaic account of the creation, whether taken as
divine authority or merely historical, is full to this point,
the unity or equality of man.   The expression admits of no
controversy.   " And God said, Let us make man in our own
image.   In the image of God created he him ; male and
female created he them."   The distinction of sexes is pointed
out, but no other distinction is even implied.   If this be not
divine authority, it is at least historical authority, and shews
that the equality of man, so far from being a modern doctrine,
is the oldest upon record.

It is also to be observed that all the religions known in
the world are founded, so far as they relate to man, on the
unity of man, as being all of one degree.   Whether in heaven
or in hell, or in whatever state man may be supposed to exist hereafter, the good and the bad are the only distinctions.
Nay, even the laws of governments are obliged to slide into
this principle, by making degrees to consist in crimes and
not in persons.

It is one of the greatest of all truths, and of the highest
advantage to cultivate.   By considering man in this light,
and by instructing him to consider himself in this light, it
places him in a close connection with all his duties, whether
to his Creator or to the creation, of which he is a part ; and
it is only when he forgets his origin, or, to use a more fashionable phrase, his *birth and family*, that he becomes dissolute.   It is not among the least of the evils of the present
existing governments in all parts of Europe that man,
considered as man, is thrown back to a vast distance from
his Maker, and the artificial chasm filled up with a succession
of barriers, or sort of turnpike gates, through which he has

to pass. I will quote Mr. Burke's catalogue of barriers that he has set up between man and his Maker. Putting himself in the character of a herald, he says : " We fear God —we look with *awe* to kings—with affection to Parliaments—with duty to magistrates—with reverence to priests, and with respect to nobility." Mr. Burke has forgotten to put in "*chivalry*." He has also forgotten to put in Peter.

The duty of man is not a wilderness of turnpike gates, through which he is to pass by tickets from one to the other. It is plain and simple, and consists but of two points. His duty to God, which every man must feel ; and with respect to his neighbor, to do as he would be done by. If those to whom power is delegated do well, they will be respected : if not, they will be despised ; and with regard to those to whom no power is delegated, but who assume it, the rational world can know nothing of them.

Hitherto we have spoken only (and that but in part) of the natural rights of man. We have now to consider the civil rights of man, and to show how the one originates from the other. Man did not enter into society to become *worse* than he was before, nor to have fewer rights than he had before, but to have those rights better secured. His natural rights are the foundation of all his civil rights. But in order to pursue this distinction with more precision, it will be necessary to mark the different qualities of natural and civil rights.

A few words will explain this. Natural rights are those which appertain to man in right of his existence. Of this kind are all the intellectual rights, or rights of the mind, and also all those rights of acting as an individual for his own comfort and happiness, which are not injurious to the natural rights of others. Civil rights are those which appertain to man in right of his being a member of society. Every civil right has for its foundation some natural right pre-existing in the individual, but to the enjoyment of which his individual power is not, in all cases, sufficiently competent. Of this kind are all those which relate to security and protection.

From this short review it will be easy to distinguish between that class of natural rights which man retains after entering into society and those which he throws into the common stock as a member of society.

The natural rights which he retains are all those in which the *power* to execute is as perfect in the individual as the right itself. Among this class, as is before mentioned, are all the intellectual rights, or rights of the mind ; consequently religion is one of those rights. The natural rights which are not retained, are all those in which, though the right is perfect in the individual, the power to execute them is defective. They answer not his purpose. A man, by natural right, has a right to judge in his own cause; and so far as the right of the mind is concerned, he never surrenders it. But what availeth it him to judge, if he has not power to redress? He therefore deposits this right in the common stock of society, and takes the arm of society, of which he is a part, in preference and in addition to his own. Society *grants* him nothing. Every man is a proprietor in society, and draws on the capital as a matter of right.

From these premisses two or three certain conclusions will follow :

First, That every civil right grows out of a natural right ; or, in other words, is a natural right exchanged.

Secondly, That civil power properly considered as such is made up of the aggregate of that class of the natural rights of man, which becomes defective in the individual in point of power, and answers not his purpose, but when collected to a focus becomes competent to the purpose of every one.

Thirdly, That the power produced from the aggregate of natural rights, imperfect in power in the individual, cannot be applied to invade the natural rights which are retained in the individual, and in which the power to execute is as perfect as the right itself.

We have now, in a few words, traced man from a natural individual to a member of society, and shewn, or endeavoured to shew, the quality of the natural rights retained, and of those which are exchanged for civil rights. Let us now apply these principles to governments.

In casting our eyes over the world, it is extremely easy to distinguish the governments which have arisen out of society, or out of the social compact, from those which have not; but to place this in a clearer light than what a single glance may afford, it will be proper to take a review of the several sources from which governments have arisen and on which they have been founded.

They may be all comprehended under three heads. First, Superstition. Secondly, Power. Thirdly, the common interest of society and the common rights of man.

The first was a government of priestcraft, the second of conquerors, and the third of reason.

When a set of artful men pretended, through the medium of oracles, to hold intercourse with the Deity, as familiarly as they now march up the back-stairs in European courts, the world was completely under the government of superstition. The oracles were consulted, and whatever they were made to say became the law; and this sort of government lasted as long as this sort of superstition lasted.

After these a race of conquerors arose, whose government, like that of William the Conqueror, was founded in power, and the sword assumed the name of a sceptre. Governments thus established last as long as the power to support them lasts; but that they might avail themselves of every engine in their favor, they united fraud to force, and set up an idol which they called *Divine Right*, and which, in imitation of the Pope, who affects to be spiritual and temporal, and in contradiction to the Founder of the Christian religion, twisted itself afterwards into an idol of another shape, called *Church and State*. The key of St. Peter and the key of the Treasury became quartered on one another, and the wondering cheated multitude worshipped the invention.

When I contemplate the natural dignity of man, when I feel (for Nature has not been kind enough to me to blunt my feelings) for the honour and happiness of its character, I become irritated at the attempt to govern mankind by force and fraud, as if they were all knaves and fools, and can scarcely avoid disgust at those who are thus imposed upon.

We have now to review the governments which arise out of society, in contradistinction to those which arose out of superstition and conquest.

It has been thought a considerable advance towards establishing the principles of Freedom to say that Government is a compact between those who govern and those who are governed ; but this cannot be true, because it is putting the effect before the cause ; for as man must have existed before governments existed, there necessarily was a time when governments did not exist, and consequently there could originally exist no governors to form such a compact with.

The fact therefore must be that the *individuals themselves,* each in his own personal and sovereign right, *entered into a compact with each other* to produce a government : and this is the only mode in which governments have a right to arise, and the only principle on which they have a right to exist.

To possess ourselves of a clear idea of what government is, or ought to be, we must trace it to its origin. In doing this we shall easily discover that governments must have arisen either *out* of the people or *over* the people. Mr. Burke has made no distinction. He investigates nothing to its source, and therefore he confounds everything ; but he has signified his intention of undertaking, at some future opportunity, a comparison between the constitution of England and France. As he thus renders it a subject of controversy by throwing the gauntlet, I take him upon his own ground. It is in high challenges that high truths have the right of appearing ; and I accept it with the more readiness because it affords me, at the same time, an opportunity of pursuing the subject with respect to governments arising out of society.

But it will be first necessary to define what is meant by a *Constitution.* It is not sufficient that we adopt the word ; we must fix also a standard signification to it.

A constitution is not a thing in name only, but in fact. It has not an ideal, but a real existence ; and wherever it cannot be produced in a visible form, there is none. A constitution is a thing *antecedent* to a government, and a government is only the creature of a constitution. The constitution of a country is not the act of its government, but of the people constituting its government. It is the body of elements, to which you can refer, and quote article by article; and which contains the principles on which the government shall be established, the manner in which it shall be organised, the powers it shall have, the mode of elections, the duration of Parliaments, or by what other name such bodies may be called; the powers which the executive part of the government shall have; and in fine, everything that relates to the complete organization of a civil government, and the principles on which it shall act, and by which it shall be bound. A constitution, therefore, is to a government what the laws made afterwards by that government are to a court of judicature. The court of judicature does not make the laws, neither can it alter them; it only acts in conformity to the laws made: and the government is in like manner governed by the constitution.

Can, then, Mr. Burke produce the English Constitution? If he cannot, we may fairly conclude that though it has been so much talked about, no such thing as a constitution exists, or ever did exist, and consequently that the people have yet a constitution to form.

Mr. Burke will not, I presume, deny the position I have already advanced—namely, that governments arise either *out* of the people or *over* the people. The English Government is one of those which arose out of a conquest, and not out of society, and consequently it arose over the people; and though it has been much modified from the opportunity of circumstances since the time of William the Conqueror, the country has never yet regenerated itself, and is therefore without a constitution.

I readily perceive the reason why Mr. Burke declined going into the comparison between the English and French constitutions, because he could not but perceive, when he sat down to the task, that no such a thing as a constitution existed on his side the question. His book is certainly bulky enough to have contained all he could say on this subject, and it would have been the best manner in which people could have judged of their separate merits. Why then has he declined the only thing that was worth while to write upon? It was the strongest ground he could take, if the advantages were on his side, but the weakest if they were not ; and his declining to take it is either a sign that he could not possess it or could not maintain it.

Mr. Burke said, in a speech last winter in Parliament, "that when the National Assembly first met in three Orders (the Tiers Etats, the Clergy, and the Noblesse), France had then a good constitution." This shews, among numerous other instances, that Mr. Burke does not understand what a constitution is. The persons so met were not a *constitution*, but a *convention*, to make a constitution.

The present National Assembly of France is, strictly speaking, the personal social compact. The members of it are the delegates of the nation in its *original* character ; future assemblies will be the delegates of the nation in its *organised* character. The authority of the present Assembly is different from what the authority of future Assemblies will be. The authority of the present one is to form a constitution ; the authority of future assemblies will be to legislate according to the principles and forms prescribed in that constitution ; and if experience should hereafter shew that alterations, amendments, or additions are necessary, the constitution will point out the mode by which such things shall be done, and not leave it to the discretionary power of the future government.

A government on the principles on which constitutional governments arising out of society are established, cannot have the right of altering itself. If it had, it would be arbitrary. It might make itself what it pleased ; and wherever such a right is set up, it shows there is no constitution. The act by which the English Parliament empowered itself to sit seven years, shows there is no constitution in England. It might, by the same self-authority, have sat any great number of years, or for life. The bill which the present Mr.

Pitt brought into Parliament some years ago, to reform Parliament, was on the same erroneous principle. The right of reform is in the nation in its original character, and the constitutional method would be by a general convention elected for the purpose. There is, moreover, a paradox in the idea of vitiated bodies reforming themselves.

From these preliminaries I proceed to draw some comparisons. I have already spoken of the declaration of rights; and as I mean to be as concise as possible, I shall proceed to other parts of the French Constitution.

The constitution of France says, that every man who pays a tax of sixty sous *per annum* (2s. 6d. English) is an elector. What article will Mr. Burke place against this? Can anything be more limited, and at the same time more capricious, than the qualification of electors is in England? Limited—because not one man in an hundred (I speak much within compass) is admitted to vote. Capricious—because the lowest character that can be supposed to exist, and who has not so much as the visible means of an honest livelihood, is an elector in some places: while in other places, the man who pays very large taxes, and has a known fair character, and the farmer who rents to the amount of three or four hundred pounds a year, with a property on that farm to three or four times that amount, is not admitted to be an elector. Everything is out of nature, as Mr. Burke says on another occasion, in this strange chaos, and all sorts of follies are blended with all sorts of crimes. William the Conqueror and his descendants parcelled out the country in this manner, and bribed some parts of it by what they call charters to hold the other parts of it the better subjected to their will. This is the reason why so many of those charters abound in Cornwall; the people were averse to the Government established at the Conquest, and the towns were garrisoned and bribed to enslave the country. All the old charters are the badges of this conquest, and it is from this source that the capriciousness of election arises.

The French Constitution says, that the number of representatives for any place shall be in a ratio to the number of

taxable inhabitants or electors.   What article will Mr. Burke
place against this?   The county of York, which contains
nearly a million of souls, sends two county members; and
so does the county of Rutland, which contains not an
hundredth part of that number.   The town of Old Sarum,
which contains not three houses, sends two members;
and the town of Manchester, which contains upward of
sixty thousand souls, is not admitted to send any.   Is there
any principle in these things?[1]   Is there anything by
which you can trace the marks of freedom, or discover those
of wisdom?   No wonder then Mr. Burke has declined the
comparison, and endeavored to lead his readers from the
point by a wild, unsystematical display of paradoxical
rhapsodies.

The French Constitution says that the National Assembly
shall be elected every two years.   What article will Mr.
Burke place against this?   Why, that the nation has no
right at all in the case; that the government is perfectly arbitrary with respect to this point; and he can quote for his
authority the precedent of a former Parliament.

The French Constitution says there shall be no game laws,
that the farmer on whose lands wild game shall be found
(for it is by the produce of his lands they are fed) shall
have a right to what he can take; that there shall be no
monopolies of any kind—that all trades shall be free and
every man free to follow any occupation by which he can
procure an honest livelihood, and in any place, town, or city
throughout the nation.   What will Mr. Burke say to this?
In England, game is made the property of those at whose
expense it is not fed; and with respect to monopolies, the
country is cut up into monopolies.   Every chartered town

---

[1] The English rotten borough system was quoted in the United States Constitutional Convention, 1787, as precedent for the disproportionate representation
embodied in the Senate.   But the new Constitution in America had been little
studied in 1791 by Paine, and, fortunately for this argument, less by his opponents.   In a modern English edition Paine's text is invaded by the anachronism :
" It is admitted that all this is altered, but there is much to be done yet, before
we have a fair representation of the people."—*Editor*.

is an aristocratical monopoly in itself, and the qualification of
electors proceeds out of those chartered monopolies. Is
this freedom ? Is this what Mr. Burke means by a constitution ?

In these chartered monopolies, a man coming from another
part of the country is hunted from them as if he were a
foreign enemy. An Englishman is not free of his own
country ; every one of those places presents a barrier in his
way, and tells him he is not a freeman—that he has no rights.
Within these monopolies are other monopolies. In a city,
such for instance as Bath, which contains between twenty
and thirty thousand inhabitants, the right of electing representatives to Parliament is monopolised by about thirty-one
persons. And within these monopolies are still others. A
man even of the same town, whose parents were not in circumstances to give him an occupation, is debarred, in many
cases, from the natural right of acquiring one, be his genius
or industry what it may.

Are these things examples to hold out to a country regenerating itself from slavery, like France ? Certainly they
are not, and certain am I, that when the people of England
come to reflect upon them they will, like France, annihilate
those badges of ancient oppression, those traces of a conquered nation. Had Mr. Burke possessed talents similar to
the author of " On the Wealth of Nations," he would have
comprehended all the parts which enter into, and, by assemblage, form a constitution. He would have reasoned from
minutiæ to magnitude. It is not from his prejudices only,
but from the disorderly cast of his genius, that he is unfitted
for the subject he writes upon. Even his genius is without
a constitution. It is a genius at random, and not a genius
constituted. But he must say something. He has therefore mounted in the air like a balloon, to draw the eyes of
the multitude from the ground they stand upon.

Much is to be learned from the French Constitution.
Conquest and tyranny transplanted themselves with William the Conqueror from Normandy into England, and the
country is yet disfigured with the marks. May, then, the

example of all France contribute to regenerate the freedom which a province of it destroyed!

The French Constitution says that to preserve the national representation from being corrupt no member of the National Assembly shall be an officer of the government, a placeman or a pensioner. What will Mr. Burke place against this? I will whisper his answer; *Loaves and Fishes.* Ah! this government of loaves and fishes has more mischief in it than people have yet reflected on. The National Assembly has made the discovery, and it holds out the example to the world. Had governments agreed to quarrel on purpose to fleece their countries by taxes, they could not have succeeded better than they have done.

Everything in the English government appears to me the reverse of what it ought to be, and of what it is said to be.[1] The Parliament, imperfectly and capriciously elected as it is, is nevertheless *supposed* to hold the national purse in *trust* for the nation; but in the manner in which an English Parliament is constructed it is like a man being both mortgagor and mortgagee, and in the case of misapplication of trust it is the criminal sitting in judgment upon himself. If those who vote the supplies are the same persons who receive the supplies when voted, and are to account for the expenditure of those supplies to those who voted them, it is *themselves accountable to themselves*, and the Comedy of Errors concludes . with the pantomime of *Hush.* Neither the Ministerial party nor the Opposition will touch upon this case. The national purse is the common hack which each mounts upon. It is like what the country people call " Ride and tie—you ride a little way, and then I."* They order these things better in France.

---

[1] In Jordan's addition, which superseded Johnson's (of which only a few copies obtained circulation) this sentence begins, " Many things, etc." But Burke, in his " Appeal," was careful to quote the original sentence.—*Editor*.

* It is a practice in some parts of the country, when two travellers have but one horse, which, like the national purse, will not carry double, that the one mounts and rides two or three miles ahead, and then ties the horse to a gate and walks on. When the second traveller arrives he takes the horse, rides on, and passes his companion a mile or two, and ties again, and so on—*Ride and tie.—Author.*

The French Constitution says that the right of war and
peace is in the nation.   Where else should it reside but in
those who are to pay the expense?

In England this right is said to reside in a *metaphor* shown
at the Tower for sixpence or a shilling a piece : so are the
lions ; and it would be a step nearer to reason to say it resided in them, for any inanimate metaphor is no more than
a hat or a cap.   We can all see the absurdity of worshipping
Aaron's molten calf, or Nebuchadnezzar's golden image ;
but why do men continue to practise themselves the absurdities they despise in others?

It may with reason be said that in the manner the English nation is represented it signifies not where the right
resides, whether in the Crown or in the Parliament.   War
is the common harvest of all those who participate in the
division and expenditure of public money, in all countries.
It is the art of *conquering at home ;* the object of it is an
increase of revenue ; and as revenue cannot be increased
without taxes, a pretence must be made for expenditure.
In reviewing the history of the English Government, its
wars and its taxes, a bystander, not blinded by prejudice nor
warped by interest, would declare that taxes were not raised
to carry on wars, but that wars were raised to carry on taxes.

Mr. Burke, as a member of the House of Commons, is a
part of the English Government ; and though he professes
himself an enemy to war, he abuses the French Constitution, which seeks to explode it.   He holds up the English
Government as a model, in all its parts, to France ; but he
should first know the remarks which the French make upon
it.   They contend in favor of their own, that the portion
of liberty enjoyed in England is just enough to enslave a
country more productively than by despotism, and that as
the real object of all despotism is revenue, a government
so formed obtains more than it could do either by direct
despotism, or in a full state of freedom, and is, therefore on
the ground of interest, opposed to both.   They account
also for the readiness which always appears in such governments for engaging in wars by remarking on the different

motives which produced them. In despotic governments wars are the effect of pride ; but in those governments in which they become the means of taxation, they acquire thereby a more permanent promptitude.

The French Constitution, therefore, to provide against both these evils, has taken away the power of declaring war from kings and ministers, and placed the right where the expence must fall.

When the question of the right of war and peace was agitating in the National Assembly, the people of England appeared to be much interested in the event, and highly to applaud the decision. As a principle it applies as much to one country as another. William the Conqueror, *as a conqueror*, held this power of war and peace in himself, and his descendants have ever since claimed it under him as a right.

Although Mr. Burke has asserted the right of the Parliament at the Revolution to bind and controul the nation and posterity for *ever*, he denies at the same time that the Parliament or the nation had any right to alter what he calls the succession of the crown in anything but in part, or by a sort of modification. By his taking this ground he throws the case back to the *Norman Conquest*, and by thus running a line of succession springing from William the Conqueror to the present day, he makes it necessary to enquire who and what William the Conqueror was, and where he came from, and into the origin, history and nature of what are called prerogatives. Everything must have had a beginning, and the fog of time and antiquity should be penetrated to discover it. Let, then, Mr. Burke bring forward his William of Normandy, for it is to this origin that his argument goes. It also unfortunately happens, in running this line of succession, that another line parallel thereto presents itself, which is that if the succession runs in the line of the conquest, the nation runs in the line of being conquered, and it ought to rescue itself from this reproach.

But it will perhaps be said that tho' the power of declaring war descends in the heritage of the conquest, it is held in check by the right of Parliament to withhold the supplies.

It will always happen when a thing is originally wrong that amendments do not make it right, and it oftens happens that they do as much mischief one way as good the other, and such is the case here, for if the one rashly declares war as a matter of right, and the other peremptorily withholds the supplies as a matter of right, the remedy becomes as bad, or worse, than the disease. The one forces the nation to a combat, and the other ties its hands; but the more probable issue is that the contest will end in a collusion between the parties, and be made a screen to both.

On this question of war, three things are to be considered. First, the right of declaring it: secondly, the expense of supporting it: thirdly, the mode of conducting it after it is declared. The French constitution places the *right* where the *expense* must fall, and this union can only be in the nation. The mode of conducting it after it is declared, it consigns to the executive department. Were this the case in all countries, we should hear but little more of wars.

Before I proceed to consider other parts of the French Constitution, and by way of relieving the fatigue of argument, I will introduce an anecdote which I had from Dr. Franklin.

While the Doctor resided in France as Minister from America, during the war, he had numerous proposals made to him by projectors of every country and of every kind, who wished to go to the land that floweth with milk and honey, America; and among the rest, there was one who offered himself to be king. He introduced his proposal to the Doctor by letter, which is now in the hands of M. Beaumarchais, of Paris—stating, first, that as the Americans had dismissed or sent away * their King, that they would want another. Secondly, that himself was a Norman. Thirdly, that he was of a more ancient family than the Dukes of Normandy, and of a more honorable descent, his line having never been bastardised. Fourthly, that there was already a precedent in England of kings coming out of

* The word he used was renvoyé, dismissed or sent away.—*Author*.

Normandy, and on these grounds he rested his offer, *enjoining* that the Doctor would forward it to America. But as the Doctor neither did this, nor yet sent him an answer, the projector wrote a second letter, in which he did not, it is true, threaten to go over and conquer America, but only with great dignity proposed that if his offer was not accepted, an acknowledgment of about £30,000 might be made to him for his generosity! Now, as all arguments respecting succession must necessarily connect that succession with some beginning, Mr. Burke's arguments on this subject go to show that there is no English origin of kings, and that they are descendants of the Norman line in right of the Conquest. It may, therefore, be of service to his doctrine to make this story known, and to inform him, that in case of that natural extinction to which all mortality is subject, Kings may again be had from Normandy, on more reasonable terms than William the Conqueror ; and consequently, that the good people of England, at the revolution of 1688, *might have done much better*, had such a generous Norman as *this* known *their* wants, and they had known *his*. The chivalric character which Mr. Burke so much admires, is certainly much easier to make a bargain with than a *hard dealing Dutchman*. But to return to the matters of the constitution—

The French Constitution says, *There shall be no titles;* and, of consequence, all that class of equivocal generation which in some countries is called " *aristocracy* " and in others " *nobility*," is done away, and the *peer* is exalted into the MAN.

Titles are but nick-names, and every nickname is a title. The thing is perfectly harmless in itself, but it marks a sort of foppery in the human character, which degrades it. It reduces man into the diminutive of man in things which are great, and the counterfeit of women in things which are little. It talks about its fine *blue ribbon* like a girl, and shows its new *garter* like a child. A certain writer, of some antiquity, says : " When I was a child, I thought as a child ; but when I became a man, I put away childish things."

It is, properly, from the elevated mind of France that the folly of titles has fallen.   It has outgrown the baby clothes of *Count* and *Duke*, and breeched itself in manhood.   France has not levelled, it has exalted.   It has put down the dwarf, to set up the man.   The punyism of a senseless word like *Duke, Count* or *Earl* has ceased to please.   Even those who possessed them have disowned the gibberish, and as they outgrew the rickets, have despised the rattle.   The genuine mind of man, thirsting for its native home, society, contemns the gewgaws that separate him from it.   Titles are like circles drawn by the magician's wand, to contract the sphere of man's felicity.   He lives immured within the Bastille of a word, and surveys at a distance the envied life of man.

Is it, then, any wonder that titles should fall in France? Is it not a greater wonder that they should be kept up any-where?   What are they?   What is their worth, and " what is their amount?" When we think or speak of a *Judge* or a *General*, we associate with it the ideas of office and character; we think of gravity in one and bravery in the other ; but when we use the word *merely as a title*, no ideas associate with it.   Through all the vocabulary of Adam there is not such an animal as a Duke or a Count ; neither can we con-nect any certain ideas with the words.   Whether they mean strength or weakness, wisdom or folly, a child or a man, or the rider or the horse, is all equivocal.   What respect then can be paid to that which describes nothing, and which means nothing?   Imagination has given figure and character to centaurs, satyrs, and down to all the fairy tribe ; but titles baffle even the powers of fancy, and are a chimerical non-descript.

But this is not all.   If a whole country is disposed to hold them in contempt, all their value is gone, and none will own them.   It is common opinion only that makes them anything, or nothing, or worse than nothing. There is no occasion to take titles away, for they take themselves away when society con-curs to ridicule them.   This species of imaginary consequence has visibly declined in every part of Europe, and it hastens to its exit as the world of reason continues to rise.   There was a time when the lowest class of what are called nobility was more thought of than the highest is now, and when a man in armour riding throughout Christendom in quest of adventures was more stared at than a modern Duke. The world has seen this folly fall, and it has fallen by being laughed at, and the farce of titles will follow its fate. The patriots of France have discovered in good time that rank and dignity in society must take a new ground. The old one has fallen through. It must now take the substantial ground of character, instead of the chimerical ground of titles; and they have brought their titles to the altar, and made of them a burnt-offering to Reason.

If no mischief had annexed itself to the folly of titles they would not have been worth a serious and formal destruction, such as the National Assembly have decreed them ; and this makes it necessary to enquire farther into the nature and character of aristocracy.

That, then, which is called aristocracy in some countries and nobility in others arose out of the governments founded upon conquest. It was originally a military order for the purpose of supporting military government (for such were all governments founded in conquest); and to keep up a succession of this order for the purpose for which it was established, all the younger branches of those families were disinherited and the law of *primogenitureship* set up.

The nature and character of aristocracy shows itself to us in this law. It is the law against every other law of nature, and Nature herself calls for its destruction. Establish family justice, and aristocracy falls. By the aristocratical law of primogenitureship, in a family of six children five are exposed. Aristocracy has never more than one child. The rest are begotten to be devoured. They are thrown to the cannibal for prey, and the natural parent prepares the unnatural repast.

As everything which is out of nature in man affects, more or less, the interest of society, so does this. All the children which the aristocracy disowns (which are all except the eldest) are, in general, cast like orphans on a parish, to be provided for by the public, but at a greater charge. Unnecessary offices and places in governments and courts are created at the expense of the public to maintain them.

With what kind of parental reflexions can the father or mother contemplate their younger offspring? By nature they are children, and by marriage they are heirs; but by aristocracy they are bastards and orphans. They are the flesh and blood of their parents in the one line, and nothing akin to them in the other. To restore, therefore, parents to their children, and children to their parents—relations to each other, and man to society—and to exterminate the monster aristocracy, root and branch—the French Constitution has destroyed the law of PRIMOGENITURESHIP. Here then lies the monster; and Mr. Burke, if he pleases, may write its epitaph.

Hitherto we have considered aristocracy chiefly in one point of view. We have now to consider it in another. But whether we view it before or behind, or sideways, or any way else, domestically or publicly, it is still a monster.

In France aristocracy had one feature less in its countenance than what it has in some other countries. It did not compose a body of hereditary legislators. It was not "*a corporation of aristocracy,*" for such I have heard M. de la Fayette describe an English House of Peers. Let us then examine the grounds upon which the French Constitution has resolved against having such a House in France.

Because, in the first place, as is already mentioned, aristocracy is kept up by family tyranny and injustice.

Secondly. Because there is an unnatural unfitness in an aristocracy to be legislators for a nation. Their ideas of *distributive justice* are corrupted at the very source. They begin life by trampling on all their younger brothers and sisters, and relations of every kind, and are taught and educated so to do. With what ideas of justice or honor can that man enter a house of legislation, who absorbs in his own person the inheritance of a whole family of children or doles out to them some pitiful portion with the insolence of a gift?

Thirdly.   Because the idea of hereditary legislators is as inconsistent as that of hereditary judges, or hereditary juries; and as absurd as an hereditary mathematician, or an hereditary wise man; and as ridiculous as an hereditary poet laureate.

Fourthly.   Because a body of men, holding themselves accountable to nobody, ought not to be trusted by anybody.

Fifthly.   Because it is continuing the uncivilised principle of governments founded in conquest, and the base idea of man having property in man, and governing him by personal right.

Sixthly.   Because aristocracy has a tendency to deteriorate the human species.   By the universal economy of nature it is known, and by the instance of the Jews it is proved, that the human species has a tendency to degenerate, in any small number of persons, when separated from the general stock of society, and inter-marrying constantly with each other.   It defeats even its pretended end, and becomes in time the opposite of what is noble in man.   Mr. Burke talks of nobility; let him show what it is.   The greatest characters the world have known have arisen on the democratic floor.   Aristocracy has not been able to keep a proportionate pace with democracy.   The artificial NOBLE shrinks into a dwarf before the NOBLE of Nature; and in the few instances of those (for there are some in all countries) in whom nature, as by a miracle, has survived in aristocracy, THOSE MEN DESPISE IT.—But it is time to proceed to a new subject.

The French constitution has reformed the condition of the clergy.   It has raised the income of the lower and middle classes, and taken from the higher.   None are now less than twelve hundred livres, (fifty pounds sterling) nor any higher than two or three thousand pounds.   What will Mr. Burke place against this?   Hear what he says.

He says: "That the people of England can see without pain or grudging, an archbishop precede a duke; they can see a Bishop of Durham, or a Bishop of Winchester in possession of £ 10,000 a-year; and cannot see why it is in worse hands than estates to a like amount, in the hands of this

earl or that squire." And Mr. Burke offers this as an example
to France.

As to the first part, whether the archbishop precedes the
duke, or the duke the bishop, it is, I believe, to the people
in general, somewhat like *Sternhold* and *Hopkins*, or *Hopkins*
and *Sternhold;* you may put which you please first ; and as
I confess that I do not understand the merits of this case, I
will not contest it with Mr. Burke.

But with respect to the latter, I have something to say.
Mr. Burke has not put the case right. The comparison is
out of order, by being put between the bishop and the earl
or the squire. It ought to be put between the bishop and
the curate, and then it will stand thus :— " The people of
England can see without pain or grudging, a Bishop of Durham, or a Bishop of Winchester, in possession of ten thousand
pounds a-year, and a curate on thirty or forty pounds a-year,
or less." No, sir, they certainly do not see those things without great pain or grudging. It is a case that applies itself to
every man's sense of justice, and is one among many that
calls aloud for a constitution.

In France the cry of " *the church ! the church !* " was repeated as often as in Mr. Burke's book, and as loudly as
when the Dissenters' Bill was before the English Parliament ;
but the generality of the French clergy were not to be deceived by this cry any longer. They knew that whatever the
pretence might be, it was they who were one of the principal
objects of it. It was the cry of the high beneficed clergy, to
prevent any regulation of income taking place between those
of ten thousand pounds a-year and the parish priest. They
therefore joined their case to those of every other oppressed
class of men, and by this union obtained redress.

The French Constitution has abolished tythes, that source
of perpetual discontent between the tythe-holder and the
parishioner. When land is held on tythe, it is in the condition of an estate held between two parties ; the one receiving
one-tenth, and the other nine-tenths of the produce : and
consequently, on principles of equity, if the estate can be
improved, and made to produce by that improvement double

or treble what it did before, or in any other ratio, the expense of such improvement ought to be borne in like proportion between the parties who are to share the produce.   But this is not the case in tythes : the farmer bears the whole expense, and the tythe-holder takes a tenth of the improvement, in addition to the original tenth, and by this means gets the value of two-tenths instead of one.   This is another case that calls for a constitution.

The French Constitution hath abolished or renounced *Toleration* and *Intolerance* also, and hath established UNIVERSAL RIGHT OF CONSCIENCE.

Toleration is not the *opposite* of Intolerance, but is the *counterfeit* of it.   Both are despotisms.   The one assumes to itself the right of withholding Liberty of Conscience, and the other of granting it.   The one is the Pope armed with fire and faggot, and the other is the Pope selling or granting indulgences.   The former is church and state, and the latter is church and traffic.

But Toleration may be viewed in a much stronger light. Man worships not himself, but his Maker ; and the liberty of conscience which he claims is not for the service of himself, but of his God.   In this case, therefore, we must necessarily have the associated idea of two things ; the *mortal* who renders the worship, and the IMMORTAL BEING who is worshipped.   Toleration, therefore, places itself, not between man and man, nor between church and church, nor between one denomination of religion and another, but between God and man ; between the being who worships, and the BEING who is worshipped ; and by the same act of assumed authority which it tolerates man to pay his worship, it presumptuously and blasphemously sets itself up to tolerate the Almighty to receive it.

Were a bill brought into any Parliament, entitled, " An Act to tolerate or grant liberty to the Almighty to receive the worship of a Jew or a Turk," or " to prohibit the Almighty from receiving it," all men would startle and call it blasphemy.   There would be an uproar.   The presumption of toleration in religious matters would then present itself unmasked ; but the presumption is not the less because the name of " Man " only appears to those laws, for the associated idea of the *worshipper* and the *worshipped* cannot be separated.   Who then art thou, vain dust and ashes! by whatever name thou art called, whether a King, a Bishop, a Church, or a State, a Parliament, or anything else, that obtrudest thine insignificance between the soul of man and its Maker ?   Mind thine own concerns.   If he believes not as thou believest, it is a proof that thou believest not as he believes, and there is no earthly power can determine between you.

With respect to what are called denominations of religion, if every one is left to judge of its own religion, there is no such thing as a religion that is wrong ; but if they are to judge of each other's religion, there is no such thing as a religion that is right ; and therefore all the world is right, or all the world is wrong.   But with respect to religion itself, without regard to names, and as directing itself from the universal family of mankind to the Divine object of all adoration, *it is man bringing to his Maker the fruits of his heart ;* and though those fruits may differ from each other like the fruits of the earth, the grateful tribute of every one is accepted.

A Bishop of Durham, or a Bishop of Winchester, or the archbishop who heads the dukes, will not refuse a tythe-sheaf of wheat because it is not a cock of hay, nor a cock of hay because it is not a sheaf of wheat ; nor a pig, because it is neither one nor the other ; but these same persons, under the figure of an established church, will not permit their Maker to receive the varied tythes of man's devotion.

One of the continual choruses of Mr. Burke's book is " Church and State."   He does not mean some one particular church, or some one particular state, but any church and state ; and he uses the term as a general figure to hold forth the political doctrine of always uniting the church with the state in every country, and he censures the National Assembly for not having done this in France.   Let us bestow a few thoughts on this subject.

All religions are in their nature kind and benign, and united with principles of morality. They could not have made proselytes at first by professing anything that was vicious, cruel, persecuting, or immoral. Like everything else, they had their beginning ; and they proceeded by persuasion, exhortation, and example. How then is it that they lose their native mildness, and become morose and intolerant?

It proceeds from the connection which Mr. Burke recommends. By engendering the church with the state, a sort of mule-animal, capable only of destroying, and not of breeding up, is produced, called *the Church established by Law.* It is a stranger, even from its birth, to any parent mother, on whom it is begotten, and whom in time it kicks out and destroys.

The inquisition in Spain does not proceed from the religion originally professed, but from this mule-animal, engendered between the church and the state. The burnings in Smithfield proceeded from the same heterogeneous production ; and it was the regeneration of this strange animal in England afterwards, that renewed rancour and irreligion among the inhabitants, and that drove the people called Quakers and Dissenters to America. Persecution is not an original feature in *any* religion ; but it is alway the strongly-marked feature of all law-religions, or religions established by law. Take away the law-establishment, and every religion re-assumes its original benignity. In America, a catholic priest is a good citizen, a good character, and a good neighbour ; an episcopalian minister is of the same description : and this proceeds independently of the men, from there being no law-establishment in America.[1]

If also we view this matter in a temporal sense, we shall see the ill-effects it has had on the prosperity of nations. The union of church and state has impoverished Spain. The revoking the edict of Nantes drove the silk manufac-

---

[1] But on his return to America, after writing the " Age of Reason," Paine learned by sad experience that the disestablishment of a church does not imply the disestablishment of Dogmas or of Intolerance.—*Editor.*

ture from that country into England ; and church and state are now driving the cotton manufacture from England to America and France. Let then Mr. Burke continue to preach his antipolitical doctrine of Church and State. It will do some good. The National Assembly will not follow his advice, but will benefit by his folly. It was by observing the ill effects of it in England, that America has been warned against it ; and it is by experiencing them in France, that the National Assembly have abolished it, and, like America, have established UNIVERSAL RIGHT OF CONSCIENCE, AND UNIVERSAL RIGHT OF CITIZENSHIP.*

I will here cease the comparison with respect to the prin-

---

* When in any country we see extraordinary circumstances taking place, they naturally lead any man who has a talent for observation and investigation, to enquire into the causes. The manufacturers of Manchester, Birmingham, and Sheffield, are the principal manufacturers in England. From whence did this arise ? A little observation will explain the case. The principal, and the generality of the inhabitants of those places, are not of what is called in England, *the church established by law :* and they, or their fathers, (for it is within but a few years) withdrew from the persecution of the chartered towns, where test-laws more particularly operate, and established a sort of asylum for themselves in those places. It was the only asylum that then offered, for the rest of Europe was worse.—But the case is now changing. France and America bid all comers welcome, and initiate them into all the rights of citizenship. Policy and interest, therefore, will, but perhaps too late, dictate in England, what reason and justice could not. Those manufacturers are withdrawing, and arising in other places. There is now erecting in Passey, three miles from Paris, a large cotton manufactory, and several are already erected in America. Soon after the rejecting the Bill for repealing the test-law, one of the richest manufacturers in England said in my hearing, " England, Sir, is not a country for a dissenter to live in,—we must go to France." These are truths, and it is doing justice to both parties to tell them. It is chiefly the dissenters that have carried English manufactures to the height they are now at, and the same men have it in their power to carry them away ; and though those manufactures would afterwards continue in those places, the foreign market will be lost. There frequently appear in the London Gazette, extracts from certain acts to prevent machines and persons, as far as they can extend to persons, from going out of the country. It appears from these that the ill effects of the test-laws and church-establishment begin to be much suspected ; but the remedy of force can never supply the remedy of reason. In the progress of less than a century, all the unrepresented part of England, of all denominations, which is at least an hundred times the most numerous, may begin to feel the necessity of a constitution, and then all those matters will come regularly before them.—*Author.*

ciples of the French constitution, and conclude this part of
the subject with a few observations on the organization of
the formal parts of the French and English governments.

The executive power in each country is in the hands of a
person stiled the King ; but the French constitution distinguishes between the King and the Sovereign : It considers
the station of King as official, and places Sovereignty in the
nation.

The representatives of the nation, who compose the National Assembly, and who are the legislative power, originate
in and from the people by election, as an inherent right in
the people.—In England it is otherwise ; and this arises from
the original establishment of what is called its monarchy ;
for, as by the conquest all the rights of the people or the
nation were absorbed into the hands of the Conqueror, and
who added the title of King to that of Conqueror, those
same matters which in France are now held as rights in the
people, or in the nation, are held in England as grants from
what is called the crown.   The Parliament in England, in
both its branches, was erected by patents from the descendants of the conqueror.   The House of Commons did not
originate as a matter of right in the people to delegate or
elect, but as a grant or boon.

By the French Constitution the nation is always named
before the king.   The third article of the declaration of
rights says : " The nation is essentially the source (or fountain) of all sovereignty."   Mr. Burke argues that in England
a king is the fountain—that he is the fountain of all honor.
But as this idea is evidently descended from the conquest I
shall make no other remark upon it, than that it is the nature of conquest to turn everything upside down ; and as
Mr. Burke will not be refused the privilege of speaking
twice, and as there are but two parts in the figure, the *fountain* and the *spout*, he will be right the second time.

The French Constitution puts the legislative before the
executive, the law before the king ; *la loi, le roi.*   This also
is in the natural order of things, because laws must have
existence before they can have execution.

A king in France does not, in addressing himself to the National Assembly, say, " My Assembly," similar to the phrase used in England of *my* " Parliament"; neither can he use it consistently with the constitution, nor could it be admitted.   There may be propriety in the use of it in England, because as is before mentioned, both Houses of Parliament originated from what is called the crown by patent or boon—and not from the inherent rights of the people, as the National Assembly does in France, and whose name designates its origin.

The President of the National Assembly does not ask the King *to grant to the Assembly liberty of speech*, as is the case with the English House of Commons.   The constitutional dignity of the National Assembly cannot debase itself. Speech is, in the first place, one of the natural rights of man always retained ; and with respect to the National Assembly the use of it is their *duty*, and the nation is their *authority*. They were elected by the greatest body of men exercising the right of election the European world ever saw.   They sprung not from the filth of rotten boroughs, nor are they the vassal representatives of aristocratical ones.   Feeling the proper dignity of their character they support it.   Their Parliamentary language, whether for or against a question, is free, bold and manly, and extends to all the parts and cir-cumstances of the case.   If any matter or subject respecting the executive department or the person who presides in it (the king) comes before them it is debated on with the spirit of men, and in the language of gentlemen ; and their answer or their address is returned in the same style.   They stand not aloof with the gaping vacuity of vulgar ignorance, nor bend with the cringe of sycophantic insignificance.   The graceful pride of truth knows no extremes, and preserves, in every latitude of life, the right-angled character of man.

Let us now look to the other side of the question.   In the addresses of the English Parliaments to their kings we see neither the intrepid spirit of the old Parliaments of France, nor the serene dignity of the present National As-sembly ; neither do we see in them anything of the stile of

English manners, which border somewhat on bluntness.
Since then they are neither of foreign extraction, nor naturally
of English production, their origin must be sought for elsewhere, and that origin is the Norman Conquest. They are
evidently of the vassalage class of manners, and emphatically
mark the prostrate distance that exists in no other condition
of men than between the conqueror and the conquered.
That this vassalage idea and stile of speaking was not
got rid of even at the Revolution of 1688, is evident from
the declaration of Parliament to William and Mary in these
words: "We do most humbly and faithfully *submit* ourselves, our heirs and posterities, for ever." Submission
is wholly a vassalage term, repugnant to the dignity of
freedom, and an echo of the language used at the Conquest.

As the estimation of all things is by comparison, the
Revolution of 1688, however from circumstances it may
have been exalted beyond its value, will find its level. It
is already on the wane, eclipsed by the enlarging orb of
reason, and the luminous revolutions of America and
France. In less than another century it will go, as well as
Mr. Burke's labors, "to the family vault of all the Capu-
lets." Mankind will then scarcely believe that a country
calling itself free would send to Holland for a man, and
clothe him with power on purpose to put themselves in
fear of him, and give him almost a million sterling a year
for leave to *submit* themselves and their posterity, like
bondmen and bondwomen, for ever.

But there is a truth that ought to be made known; I have
had the opportunity of seeing it; which is, *that notwithstanding appearances, there is not any description of men that despise
monarchy so much as courtiers.* But they well know, that
if it were seen by others, as it is seen by them, the juggle
could not be kept up; they are in the condition of men who
get their living by a show, and to whom the folly of that
show is so familiar that they ridicule it; but were the audience to be made as wise in this respect as themselves,
there would be an end to the show and the profits with it.
The difference between a republican and a courtier with

respect to monarchy, is that the one opposes monarchy, believing it to be something; and the other laughs at it, knowing it to be nothing.

As I used sometimes to correspond with Mr. Burke believing him then to be a man of sounder principles than his book shows him to be, I wrote to him last winter from Paris, and gave him an account how prosperously matters were going on. Among other subjects in that letter, I referred to the happy situation the National Assembly were placed in; that they had taken ground on which their moral duty and their political interest were united. They have not to hold out a language which they do not themselves believe, for the fraudulent purpose of making others believe it. Their station requires no artifice to support it, and can only be maintained by enlightening mankind. It is not their interest to cherish ignorance, but to dispel it. They are not in the case of a ministerial or an opposition party in England, who, though they are opposed, are still united to keep up the common mystery. The National Assembly must throw open a magazine of light. It must show man the proper character of man; and the nearer it can bring him to that standard, the stronger the National Assembly becomes.

In contemplating the French Constitution, we see in it a rational order of things. The principles harmonise with the forms, and both with their origin. It may perhaps be said as an excuse for bad forms, that they are nothing more than forms; but this is a mistake. Forms grow out of principles, and operate to continue the principles they grow from. It is impossible to practise a bad form on anything but a bad principle. It cannot be ingrafted on a good one; and wherever the forms in any government are bad, it is a certain indication that the principles are bad also.

I will here finally close this subject. I began it by remarking that Mr. Burke had *voluntarily* declined going into a comparison of the English and French Constitutions. He apologises (in page 241) for not doing it, by saying that he had not time. Mr. Burke's book was upwards of eight

months in hand, and is extended to a volume of three
hundred and sixty-six pages. As his omission does injury
to his cause, his apology makes it worse ; and men on the
English side of the water will begin to consider, whether
there is not some radical defect in what is called the
English constitution, that made it necessary for Mr. Burke to
suppress the comparison, to avoid bringing it into view.

As Mr. Burke has not written on constitutions so neither
has he written on the French Revolution. He gives no
account of its commencement or its progress. He only
expresses his wonder. " It looks," says he, " to me, as if I
were in a great crisis, not of the affairs of France alone, but of
all Europe, perhaps of more than Europe. All circumstances taken together, the French Revolution is the
most astonishing that has hitherto happened in the world."

As wise men are astonished at foolish things, and other
people at wise ones, I know not on which ground to account
for Mr. Burke's astonishment ; but certain it is, that he does
not understand the French Revolution. It has apparently
burst forth like a creation from a chaos, but it is no more
than the consequence of a mental revolution priorily existing
in France. The mind of the nation had changed beforehand, and the new order of things has naturally followed
the new order of thoughts. I will here, as concisely as
I can, trace out the growth of the French Revolution, and
mark the circumstances that have contributed to produce it.

The despotism of Louis XIV., united with the gaiety of
his Court, and the gaudy ostentation of his character, had
so humbled, and at the same time so fascinated the mind of
France, that the people appeared to have lost all sense of
their own dignity, in contemplating that of their Grand
Monarch ; and the whole reign of Louis XV., remarkable
only for weakness and effeminacy, made no other alteration
than that of spreading a sort of lethargy over the nation,
from which it shewed no disposition to rise.

The only signs which appeared of the spirit of Liberty
during those periods, are to be found in the writings of the
French philosophers. Montesquieu, President of the Parlia-

ment of Bordeaux, went as far as a writer under a despotic government could well proceed; and being obliged to divide himself between principle and prudence, his mind often appears under a veil, and we ought to give him credit for more than he has expressed.

Voltaire, who was both the flatterer and the satirist of despotism, took another line. His forte lay in exposing and ridiculing the superstitions which priest-craft, united with state-craft, had interwoven with governments. It was not from the purity of his principles, or his love of mankind (for satire and philanthropy are not naturally concordant), but from his strong capacity of seeing folly in its true shape, and his irresistible propensity to expose it, that he made those attacks. They were, however, as formidable as if the motive had been virtuous; and he merits the thanks rather than the esteem of mankind.

On the contrary, we find in the writings of Rousseau, and the Abbé Raynal, a loveliness of sentiment in favor of liberty, that excites respect, and elevates the human faculties; but having raised this animation, they do not direct its operation, and leave the mind in love with an object, without describing the means of possessing it.

The writings of Quesnay, Turgot, and the friends of those authors, are of the serious kind; but they labored under the same disadvantage with Montesquieu; their writings abound with moral maxims of government, but are rather directed to œconomise and reform the administration of the government, than the government itself.

But all those writings and many others had their weight; and by the different manner in which they treated the subject of government, Montesquieu by his judgment and knowledge of laws, Voltaire by his wit, Rousseau and Raynal by their animation, and Quesnay and Turgot by their moral maxims and systems of œconomy, readers of every class met with something to their taste, and a spirit of political inquiry began to diffuse itself through the nation at the time the dispute between England and the then colonies of America broke out.

In the war which France afterwards engaged in, it is very well known that the nation appeared to be before-hand with the French ministry. Each of them had its view; but those views were directed to different objects; the one sought liberty, and the other retaliation on England. The French officers and soldiers who after this went to America, were eventually placed in the school of Freedom, and learned the practice as well as the principles of it by heart.

As it was impossible to separate the military events which took place in America from the principles of the American Revolution, the publication of those events in France necessarily connected themselves with the principles which produced them. Many of the facts were in themselves principles; such as the declaration of American Independence, and the treaty of alliance between France and America, which recognised the natural rights of man, and justified resistance to oppression.

The then Minister of France, Count Vergennes, was not the friend of America; and it is both justice and gratitude to say, that it was the Queen of France who gave the cause of America a fashion at the French Court. Count Vergennes was the personal and social friend of Dr. Franklin; and the Doctor had obtained, by his sensible gracefulness, a sort of influence over him; but with respect to principles Count Vergennes was a despot.

The situation of Dr. Franklin, as Minister from America to France, should be taken into the chain of circumstances. The diplomatic character is of itself the narrowest sphere of society that man can act in. It forbids intercourse by the reciprocity of suspicion; and a diplomatic is a sort of unconnected atom, continually repelling and repelled. But this was not the case with Dr. Franklin. He was not the diplomatic of a Court, but of MAN. His character as a philosopher had been long established, and his circle of society in France was universal.

Count Vergennes resisted for a considerable time the publication in France of American constitutions, translated into the French language: but even in this he was obliged to give way to public opinion, and a sort of propriety in admitting to appear what he had undertaken to defend. The American constitutions were to liberty what a grammar is to language: they define its parts of speech, and practically construct them into syntax.

The peculiar situation of the then Marquis de la Fayette is another link in the great chain. He served in America as an American officer under a commission of Congress, and by the universality of his acquaintance was in close friendship with the civil government of America, as well as with the military line. He spoke the language of the country, entered into the discussions on the principles of government, and was always a welcome friend at any election.

When the war closed, a vast reinforcement to the cause of Liberty spread itself over France, by the return of the French officers and soldiers. A knowledge of the practice was then joined to the theory; and all that was wanting to give it real existence was opportunity. Man cannot, properly speaking, make circumstances for his purpose, but he always has it in his power to improve them when they occur, and this was the case in France.

M. Neckar was displaced in May, 1781; and by the ill-management of the finances afterwards, and particularly during the extravagant administration of M. Calonne, the revenue of France, which was nearly twenty-four millions sterling per year, was become unequal to the expenditure, not because the revenue had decreased, but because the expenses had increased; and this was a circumstance which the nation laid hold of to bring forward a Revolution. The English Minister, Mr. Pitt, has frequently alluded to the state of the French finances in his budgets, without understanding the subject. Had the French Parliaments been as ready to register edicts for new taxes as an English Parliament is to grant them, there had been no derangement in the finances, nor yet any Revolution; but this will better explain itself as I proceed.

It will be necessary here to show how taxes were formerly raised in France. The King, or rather the Court or Ministry acting under the use of that name, framed the edicts for taxes at their own discretion, and sent them to the Parliaments to be registered; for until they were registered by the Parliaments they were not operative. Disputes had long existed between the Court and the Parliaments with respect to the extent of the Parliament's authority on this head. The Court insisted that the authority of Parliaments went no farther than to remonstrate or show reasons against the tax, reserving to itself the right of determining whether the reasons were well or ill-founded; and in consequence thereof, either to withdraw the edict as a matter of choice, or to *order* it to be enregistered as a matter of authority. The Parliaments on their part insisted that they had not only a right to remonstrate, but to reject; and on this ground they were always supported by the nation.

But to return to the order of my narrative. M. Calonne wanted money: and as he knew the sturdy disposition of the Parliaments with respect to new taxes, he ingeniously sought either to approach them by a more gentle means than that of direct authority, or to get over their heads by a manœuvre; and for this purpose he revived the project of assembling a body of men from the several provinces, under the style of an " Assembly of the Notables," or men of note, who met in 1787, and who were either to recommend taxes to the Parliaments, or to act as a Parliament themselves. An Assembly under this name had been called in 1617.

As we are to view this as the first practical step towards the Revolution, it will be proper to enter into some particulars respecting it. The Assembly of the Notables has in some places been mistaken for the States-General, but was wholly a different body, the States-General being always by election. The persons who composed the Assembly of the Notables were all nominated by the king, and consisted of one hundred and forty members. But as M. Calonne could not depend upon a majority of this Assembly in his favor, he very ingeniously arranged them in such a manner as to make forty-four a majority of one hundred and forty; to effect this he disposed of them into seven separate committees, of twenty members each.   Every general question was to be decided, not by a majority of persons, but by a majority of committees ; and as eleven votes would make a majority in a committee, and four committees a majority of seven, M. Calonne had good reason to conclude that as forty-four would determine any general question he could not be outvoted.   But all his plans deceived him, and in the event became his overthrow.

The then Marquis de la Fayette was placed in the second committee, of which the Count D'Artois was president, and as money matters were the object, it naturally brought into view every circumstance connected with it.   M. de la Fayette made a verbal charge against Calonne for selling crown lands to the amount of two millions of livres, in a manner that appeared to be unknown to the king.   The Count D'Artois (as if to intimidate, for the Bastille was then in being) asked the Marquis if he would render the charge in writing ?   He replied that he would.   The Count D'Artois did not demand it, but brought a message from the king to that purport.   M. de la Fayette then delivered in his charge in writing, to be given to the king, undertaking to support it.   No farther proceedings were had upon this affair, but M. Calonne was soon after dismissed by the king and set off to England.

As M. de la Fayette, from the experience of what he had seen in America, was better acquainted with the science of civil government than the generality of the members who composed the Assembly of the Notables could then be, the brunt of the business fell considerably to his share.   The plan of those who had a constitution in view was to contend with the Court on the ground of taxes, and some of them openly professed their object.   Disputes frequently arose between Count D'Artois and M. de la Fayette upon various subjects.   With respect to the arrears already incurred the latter proposed to remedy them by accommodating the expenses to the revenue instead of the revenue to the expenses ; and as objects of reform he proposed to abolish the Bastille and all the State prisons throughout the nation

(the keeping of which was attended with great expense),
and to suppress *Lettres de Cachet ;* but those matters were
not then much attended to, and with respect to *Lettres de
Cachet,* a *majority of the Nobles appeared to be in favour of
them.*

On the subject of supplying the Treasury by new taxes
the Assembly declined taking the matter on themselves,
concurring in the opinion that they had not authority.   In
a debate on this subject M. de la Fayette said that raising
money by taxes could only be done by a National Assembly,
freely elected by the people, and acting as their representatives.   Do you mean, said the Count D'Artois, the *States-
General?*   M. de la Fayette replied that he did.   Will you,
said the Count D'Artois, sign what you say to be given to
the king?   The other replied that he would not only do
this but that he would go farther, and say that the effectual
mode would be for the king to agree to the establishment
of a constitution.

As one of the plans had thus failed, that of getting the
Assembly to act as a Parliament, the other came into view,
that of recommending.   On this subject the Assembly
agreed to recommend two new taxes to be enregistered by
the Parliament : the one a stamp-tax and the other a territorial tax, or sort of land-tax.   The two have been estimated
at about five millions sterling per annum.   We have now to
turn our attention to the Parliaments, on whom the business
was again devolving.

The Archbishop of Thoulouse (since Archbishop of Sens,
and now a Cardinal), was appointed to the administration
of the finances soon after the dismission of Calonne.   He
was also made Prime Minister, an office that did not always
exist in France.   When this office did not exist, the chief
of each of the principal departments transacted business
immediately with the King, but when a Prime Minister was
appointed they did business only with him.   The Archbishop
arrived to more state-authority than any minister since the
Duke de Choiseul, and the nation was strongly disposed in
his favor ; but by a line of conduct scarcely to be ac-

counted for he perverted every opportunity, turned out a despot, and sunk into disgrace, and a Cardinal.

The Assembly of the Notables having broken up, the minister sent the edicts for the two new taxes recommended by the Assembly to the Parliaments to be enregistered. They of course came first before the Parliament of Paris, who returned for answer: "that with such a revenue as the nation then supported the name of taxes ought not to be mentioned but for the purpose of reducing them"; and threw both the edicts out.*

On this refusal the Parliament was ordered to Versailles, where, in the usual form, the King held what under the old government was called a Bed of Justice; and the two edicts were enregistered in presence of the Parliament by an order of State, in the manner mentioned, p. 337. On this the Parliament immediately returned to Paris, renewed their session in form, and ordered the enregistering to be struck out, declaring that everything done at Versailles was illegal. All the members of the Parliament were then served with Lettres de Cachet, and exiled to Trois; but as they continued as inflexible in exile as before, and as vengeance did not supply the place of taxes, they were after a short time recalled to Paris.

The edicts were again tendered to them, and the Count D'Artois undertook to act as representative of the King. For this purpose he came from Versailles to Paris, in a train of procession; and the Parliament were assembled to receive him. But show and parade had lost their influence in France; and whatever ideas of importance he might set off with, he had to return with those of mortification and disappointment. On alighting from his carriage to ascend the steps of the Parliament House, the crowd (which was numerously collected) threw out trite expressions, saying: " This is Monsieur D'Artois, who wants more of our money to spend." The marked disapprobation which he saw im-

---

* When the English Minister, Mr. Pitt, mentions the French finances again in the English Parliament, it would be well that he noticed this as an example. —*Author.*

pressed him with apprehensions, and the word *Aux armes!*
(*To arms!*) was given out by the officer of the guard who
attended him.   It was so loudly vociferated, that it echoed
through the avenues of the house, and produced a temporary confusion.   I was then standing in one of the
apartments through which he had to pass, and could not
avoid reflecting how wretched was the condition of a dis-
respected man.*

After this a new subject took place : In the various
debates and contests which arose between the Court and
the Parliaments on the subject of taxes, the Parliament of
Paris at last declared that although it had been customary
for Parliaments to enregister edicts for taxes as a matter
of convenience, the right belonged only to the *States-General;* and that, therefore, the Parliament could no longer
with propriety continue to debate on what it had not
authority to act.   The King after this came to Paris and
held a meeting with the Parliament, in which he continued
from ten in the morning till about six in the evening, and,
in a manner that appeared to proceed from him as if
unconsulted upon with the Cabinet or Ministry, gave his
word to the Parliament that the States-General should be
convened.

But after this another scene arose, on a ground different
from all the former.   The Minister and the Cabinet were
averse to calling the States-General.   They well knew that
if the States-General were assembled, themselves must fall ;
and as the King had not mentioned *any time*, they hit on a
project calculated to elude, without appearing to oppose.

For this purpose, the Court set about making a sort of
constitution itself.   It was principally the work of M.
Lamoignon, the Keeper of the Seals, who afterwards shot
himself.   This new arrangement consisted in establishing a
body under the name of a *Cour Plénière*, or Full Court, in
which were invested all the powers that the Government
might have occasion to make use of.   The persons composing this Court were to be nominated by the King ; the
contended right of taxation was given up on the part of the

* See Note, page 356.

King, and a new criminal code of laws and law proceedings
was substituted in the room of the former. The thing, in
many points, contained better principles than those upon
which the Government had hitherto been administered;
but with respect to the *Cour Plénière*, it was no other than
a medium through which despotism was to pass, without
appearing to act directly from itself.

The Cabinet had high expectations from their new contrivance. The persons who were to compose the *Cour Plénière*
were already nominated; and as it was necessary to carry a fair
appearance, many of the best characters in the nation
were appointed among the number. It was to commence
on May 8, 1788; but an opposition arose to it on two
grounds—the one as to principle, the other as to form.

On the ground of Principle it was contended that Government had not a right to alter itself, and that if the practice
was once admitted it would grow into a principle and be
made a precedent for any future alterations the Government
might wish to establish: that the right of altering the
Government was a national right, and not a right of
Government. And on the ground of form it was contended
that the *Cour Plénière* was nothing more than a larger
Cabinet.

The then Duke de la Rochefoucault, Luxembourg, De
Noailles, and many others, refused to accept the nomination, and strenuously opposed the whole plan. When the
edict for establishing this new court was sent to the Parliaments to be enregistered and put into execution, they
resisted also. The Parliament of Paris not only refused,
but denied the authority; and the contest renewed itself
between the Parliament and the Cabinet more strongly than
ever. While the Parliament were sitting in debate on this
subject, the Ministry ordered a regiment of soldiers to
surround the House and form a blockade. The members
sent out for beds and provisions, and lived as in a besieged
citadel: and as this had no effect, the commanding officer
was ordered to enter the Parliament House and seize them,
which he did, and some of the principal members were shut

up in different prisons. About the same time a deputation
of persons arrived from the province of Brittany to remonstrate against the establishment of the *Cour Plénière*, and
those the archbishop sent to the Bastille. But the spirit of
the nation was not to be overcome, and it was so fully
sensible of the strong ground it had taken—that of withholding taxes—that it contented itself with keeping up a
sort of quiet resistance, which effectually overthrew all the
plans at that time formed against it. The project of the
Cour Plénière was at last obliged to be given up, and the
Prime Minister not long afterwards followed its fate, and M.
Neckar was recalled into office.

The attempt to establish the *Cour Plénière* had an effect
upon the nation which itself did not perceive. It was a sort of
new form of government that insensibly served to put the
old one out of sight and to unhinge it from the superstitious
authority of antiquity. It was Government dethroning
Government; and the old one, by attempting to make a new
one, made a chasm.

The failure of this scheme renewed the subject of convening the States-General; and this gave rise to a new
series of politics. There was no settled form for convening
the States-General: all that it positively meant was a deputation from what was then called the Clergy, the Noblesse, and
the Commons; but their numbers or their proportions had
not been always the same. They had been convened only
on extraordinary occasions, the last of which was in 1614;
their numbers were then in equal proportions, and they voted
by orders.

It could not well escape the sagacity of M. Neckar, that
the mode of 1614 would answer neither the purpose of the
then government nor of the nation. As matters were at that
time circumstanced it would have been too contentious to
agree upon anything. The debates would have been endless
upon privileges and exemptions, in which neither the wants
of the Government nor the wishes of the nation for a Constitution would have been attended to. But as he did not
chuse to take the decision upon himself, he summoned again

the *Assembly of the Notables* and referred it to them. This body was in general interested in the decision, being chiefly of aristocracy and high-paid clergy, and they decided in favor of the mode of 1614. This decision was against the sense of the Nation, and also against the wishes of the Court ; for the aristocracy opposed itself to both and contended for privileges independent of either. The subject was then taken up by the Parliament, who recommended that the number of the Commons should be equal to the other two : and they should all sit in one house and vote in one body. The number finally determined on was 1,200 ; 600 to be chosen by the Commons (and this was less than their proportion ought to have been when their worth and consequence is considered on a national scale), 300 by the Clergy, and 300 by the Aristocracy ; but with respect to the mode of assembling themselves, whether together or apart, or the manner in which they should vote, those matters were referred.*

The election that followed, was not a contested election, but an animated one. The candidates were not men, but

---

* Mr. Burke, (and I must take the liberty of telling him that he is very unacquainted with French affairs,) speaking upon this subject, says, " The first thing that struck me in calling the States-General, was a great departure from the ancient course ; "—and he soon after says, " From the moment I read the list, I saw distinctly, and very nearly as it has happened, all that was to follow."—Mr. Burke certainly did not see all that was to follow. I endeavored to impress him, as well before as after the States-General met, that there would be a *revolution* ; but was not able to make him see it, neither would he believe it. How then he could distinctly see all the parts, when the whole was out of sight, is beyond my comprehension. And with respect to the " departure from the ancient course," besides the natural weakness of the remark, it shews that he is unacquainted with circumstances. The departure was necessary, from the experience had upon it, that the ancient course was a bad one. The States-General of 1614 were called at the commencement of the civil war in the minority of Louis XIII. ; but by the class of arranging them by orders, they increased the confusion they were called to compose. The author of *L'Intrigue du Cabinet*, (Intrigue of the Cabinet,) who wrote before any revolution was thought of in France, speaking of the States-General of 1614, says, " They held the public in suspense five months ; and by the questions agitated therein, and the heat with which they were put, it appears that the great (*les grands*) thought more to satisfy their *particular* passions, than to procure the goods of the nation ; and the whole time passed away in altercations, ceremonies and parade." L' Intrigue du Cabinet, vol. i. p. 329.—*Author.*

principles. Societies were formed in Paris, and committees of correspondence and communication established throughout the nation, for the purpose of enlightening the people, and explaining to them the principles of civil government ; and so orderly was the election conducted, that it did not give rise even to the rumor of tumult.

The States-General were to meet at Versailles in April 1789, but did not assemble till May. They situated themselves in three separate chambers, or rather the Clergy and Aristocracy withdrew each into a separate chamber. The majority of the Aristocracy claimed what they called the privilege of voting as a separate body, and of giving their consent or their negative in that manner ; and many of the bishops and the high-beneficed clergy claimed the same privilege on the part of their Order.

The *Tiers Etat* (as they were then called) disowned any knowledge of artificial orders and artificial privileges ; and they were not only resolute on this point, but somewhat disdainful. They began to consider the Aristocracy as a kind of fungus growing out of the corruption of society, that could not be admitted even as a branch of it ; and from the disposition the Aristocracy has shown by upholding Lettres de Cachet, and in sundry other instances, it was manifest that no constitution could be formed by admitting men in any other character than as National Men.

After various altercations on this head, the Tiers Etat or Commons (as they were then called) declared themselves (on a motion made for that purpose by the Abbé Sieyes) " THE REPRESENTATIVE OF THE NATION ; *and that the two Orders could be considered but as deputies of corporations, and could only have a deliberate voice when they assembled in a national character with the national representatives.*" *This* proceeding extinguished the style of *Etats Généraux*, or States-General, and erected it into the style it now bears, that of L'Assemblée Nationale, or National Assembly.

This motion was not made in a precipitate manner. It was the result of cool deliberation, and concerned between the national representatives and the patriotic members of

the two chambers, who saw into the folly, mischief, and injustice of artificial privileged distinctions.   It was become
evident, that no constitution, worthy of being called by that
name, could be established on anything less than a national
ground.   The Aristocracy had hitherto opposed the despotism of the Court, and affected the language of patriotism ;
but it opposed it as its rival (as the English Barons opposed
King John), and it now opposed the nation from the same
motives.

On carrying this motion, the national representatives, as
had been concerted, sent an invitation to the two chambers,
to unite with them in a national character, and proceed to
business.   A majority of the clergy, chiefly of the parish
priests, withdrew from the clerical chamber, and joined the
nation ; and forty-five from the other chamber joined in like
manner.   There is a sort of secret history belonging to this
last circumstance, which is necessary to its explanation ; it
was not judged prudent that all the patriotic members of
the chamber styling itself the Nobles, should quit it at
once; and in consequence of this arrangement, they drew
off by degrees, always leaving some, as well to reason the
case, as to watch the suspected.   In a little time the numbers
increased from forty-five to eighty, and soon after to a greater
number ; which, with the majority of the clergy, and the
whole of the national representatives, put the malcontents
in a very diminutive condition.

The King, who, very different from the general class called
by that name, is a man of a good heart, shewed himself disposed to recommend a union of the three chambers, on the
ground the National Assembly had taken ; but the malcontents exerted themselves to prevent it, and began now to
have another project in view.   Their numbers consisted of
a majority of the aristocratical chamber, and the minority
of the clerical chamber, chiefly of bishops and high-beneficed clergy ; and these men were determined to put everything to issue, as well by strength as by stratagem.   They
had no objection to a constitution ; but it must be such a one
as themselves should dictate, and suited to their own views

and particular situations.   On the other hand, the Nation disowned knowing anything of them but as citizens, and was determined to shut out all such up-start pretensions.   The more aristocracy appeared, the more it was despised ; there was a visible imbecility and want of intellects in the major- ity, a sort of *je ne sais quoi,* that while it affected to be more than citizen, was less than man.   It lost ground from con- tempt more than from hatred ; and was rather jeered at as an ass, than dreaded as a lion.   This is the general character of aristocracy, or what are called Nobles or Nobility, or rather No-ability, in all countries.

The plan of the mal-contents consisted now of two things ; either to deliberate and vote by chambers (or orders), more especially on all questions respecting a Constitution (by which the aristocratical chamber would have had a negative on any article of the Constitution) ; or, in case they could not accomplish this object, to overthrow the National As- sembly entirely.

To effect one or other of these objects they began to cul- tivate a friendship with the despotism they had hitherto at- tempted to rival, and the Count D'Artois became their chief. The king (who has since declared himself deceived into their measures) held, according to the old form, a *Bed of Justice,* in which he accorded to the deliberation and vote *par tête* (by head) upon several subjects ; but reserved the delibera- tion and vote upon all questions respecting a constitution to the three chambers separately.   This declaration of the king was made against the advice of M. Neckar, who now began to perceive that he was growing out of fashion at Court, and that another minister was in contemplation.

As the form of sitting in separate chambers was yet appar- ently kept up, though essentially destroyed, the national representatives immediately after this declaration of the King resorted to their own chambers to consult on a pro- test against it ; and the minority of the chamber (calling itself the Nobles), who had joined the national cause, re- tired to a private house to consult in like manner.   The mal-contents had by this time concerted their measures with

the court, which the Count D'Artois undertook to conduct;
and as they saw from the discontent which the declaration
excited, and the opposition making against it, that they
could not obtain a control over the intended constitution by
a separate vote, they prepared themselves for their final object—that of conspiring against the National Assembly, and
overthrowing it.

The next morning the door of the chamber of the National Assembly was shut against them, and guarded by
troops; and the members were refused admittance.   On
this they withdrew to a tennis-ground in the neighborhood
of Versailles, as the most convenient place they could find,
and, after renewing their session, took an oath never to separate from each other, under any circumstance whatever, death
excepted, until they had established a constitution.   As the
experiment of shutting up the house had no other effect than
that of producing a closer connection in the members, it was
opened again the next day, and the public business recom-
menced in the usual place.

We are now to have in view the forming of the new ministry, which was to accomplish the overthrow of the National
Assembly.   But as force would be necessary, orders were
issued to assemble thirty thousand troops, the command of
which was given to Broglio, one of the intended new ministry, who was recalled from the country for this purpose.
But as some management was necessary to keep this plan
concealed till the moment it should be ready for execution,
it is to this policy that a declaration made by Count D'Artois must be attributed, and which is here proper to be
introduced.

It could not but occur while the mal-contents continued
to resort to their chambers separate from the National Assembly, more jealousy would be excited than if they were
mixed with it, and that the plot might be suspected.   But
as they had taken their ground, and now wanted a pretence
for quitting it, it was necessary that one should be devised.
This was effectually accomplished by a declaration made by
the Count D'Artois: " *That if they took not a part in the*

National Assembly, the life of the king would be endangered" :
on which they quitted their chambers, and mixed with the
Assembly, in one body.

At the time this declaration was made, it was generally
treated as a piece of absurdity in Count D'Artois calculated
merely to relieve the outstanding members of the two
chambers from the diminutive situation they were put in;
and if nothing more had followed, this conclusion would
have been good.   But as things best explain themselves by
their events, this apparent union was only a cover to the
machinations which were secretly going on ; and the declaration accommodated itself to answer that purpose.   In
a little time the National Assembly found itself surrounded
by troops, and thousands more were daily arriving.   On this
a very strong declaration was made by the National Assembly to the King, remonstrating on the impropriety of the
measure, and demanding the reason.   The King, who was
not in the secret of this business, as himself afterwards declared, gave substantially for answer, that he had no other
object in view than to preserve the public tranquility, which
appeared to be much disturbed.

But in a few days from this time the plot unravelled itself.
M. Neckar and the ministry were displaced, and a new one
formed of the enemies of the Revolution ; and Broglio, with
between twenty-five and thirty thousand foreign troops, was
arrived to support them.   The mask was now thrown off,
and matters were come to a crisis.   The event was that in a
space of three days the new ministry and their abettors
found it prudent to fly the nation ; the Bastille was taken,
and Broglio and his foreign troops dispersed, as is already
related in the former part of this work.

There are some curious circumstances in the history of
this short-lived ministry, and this short-lived attempt at a
counter-revolution.   The Palace of Versailles, where the
court was sitting, was not more than four hundred yards
distant from the hall where the National Assembly was sitting.   The two places were at this moment like the separate
headquarters of two combatant armies; yet the Court was

as perfectly ignorant of the information which had arrived from Paris to the National Assembly, as if it had resided at an hundred miles distance.   The then Marquis de la Fayette, who (as has been already mentioned) was chosen to preside in the National Assembly on this particular occasion, named by order of the Assembly three successive deputations to the king, on the day and up to the evening on which the Bastille was taken, to inform and confer with him on the state of affairs ; but the ministry, who knew not so much as that it was attacked, precluded all communication, and were solacing themselves how dextrously they had succeeded ; but in a few hours the accounts arrived so thick and fast that they had to start from their desks and run.   Some set off in one disguise, and some in another, and none in their own character.   Their anxiety now was to outride the news, lest they should be stopt, which, though it flew fast, flew not so fast as themselves.

It is worth remarking that the National Assembly neither pursued those fugitive conspirators, nor took any notice of them, nor sought to retaliate in any shape whatever.   Occupied with establishing a constitution founded on the Rights of Man and the Authority of the People, the only authority on which Government has a right to exist in any country, the National Assembly felt none of those mean passions which mark the character of impertinent governments, founding themselves on their own authority, or on the absurdity of hereditary succession.   It is the faculty of the human mind to become what it contemplates, and to act in unison with its object.

The conspiracy being thus dispersed, one of the first works of the National Assembly, instead of vindictive proclamations, as has been the case with other governments, was to publish a declaration of the Rights of Man, as the basis on which the new constitution was to be built, and which is here subjoined :

DECLARATION

OF THE

RIGHTS OF MAN AND OF CITIZENS,

BY THE NATIONAL ASSEMBLY OF FRANCE.

" THE Representatives of the people of FRANCE, formed into a NATIONAL ASSEMBLY, considering that ignorance, neglect, or contempt of human rights, are the sole causes of public misfortunes and corruptions of Government, have resolved to set forth in a solemn declaration, these natural, imprescriptible, and inalienable rights : that this declaration being constantly present to the minds of the members of the body social, they may be forever kept attentive to their rights and their duties ; that the acts of the legislative and executive powers of Government, being capable of being every moment compared with the end of political institu-tions, may be more respected ; and also, that the future claims of the citizens, ·being directed by simple and incon-testible principles, may always tend to the maintenance of the Constitution, and the general happiness.

" For these reasons the NATIONAL ASSEMBLY doth recog-nise and declare, in the presence of the Supreme Being, and with the hope of his blessing and favor, the following *sacred* rights of men and of citizens:

" ' *I. Men are born, and always continue, free and equal in respect of their rights.   Civil distinctions, therefore, can be founded only on public utility.*

" ' *II. The end of all political associations is the preserva-tion of the natural and imprescriptible rights of man ; and these rights are liberty, property, security, and resistance of oppression.*

" ' *III. The nation is essentially the source of all sovereignty ; nor can any* INDIVIDUAL, *or* ANY BODY OF MEN, *be entitled to any authority which is not expressly derived from it.*

" ' IV. Political Liberty consists in the power of doing whatever does not injure another. The exercise of the natural rights of every man, has no other limits than those which are necessary to secure to every *other* man the free exercise of the same rights ; and these limits are determinable only by the law.

" ' V. The law ought to prohibit only actions hurtful to society. What is not prohibited by the law should not be hindered ; nor should anyone be compelled to that which the law does not require.

" ' VI. The law is an expression of the will of the community. All citizens have a right to concur, either personally or by their representatives, in its formation. It should be the same to all, whether it protects or punishes ; and all being equal in its sight, are equally eligible to all honors, places, and employments, according to their different abilities, without any other distinction than that created by their virtues and talents.

" ' VII. No man should be accused, arrested, or held in confinement, except in cases determined by the law, and according to the forms which it has prescribed. All who promote, solicit, execute, or cause to be executed, arbitrary orders, ought to be punished, and every citizen called upon, or apprehended by virtue of the law, ought immediately to obey, and renders himself culpable by resistance.

" ' VIII. The law ought to impose no other penalties but such as are absolutely and evidently necessary ; and no one ought to be punished, but in virtue of a law promulgated before the offence, and legally applied.

" ' IX. Every man being presumed innocent till he has been convicted, whenever his detention becomes indispensable, all rigor to him, more than is necessary to secure his person, ought to be provided against by the law.

" ' X. No man ought to be molested on account of his opinions, not even on account of his *religious* opinions, provided his avowal of them does not disturb the public order established by the law.

" ' XI. The unrestrained communication of thoughts and opinions being one of the most precious rights of man, every citizen may speak, write and publish freely, provided

he is responsible for the abuse of this liberty, in cases determined by the law.

" ' XII.   A public force being necessary to give security
to the rights of men and of citizens, that force is instituted
for the benefit of the community and not for the particular
benefit of the persons to whom it is intrusted.

" ' XIII.   A common contribution being necessary for the
support of the public force, and for defraying the other
expenses of government, it ought to be divided equally
among the members of the community, according to their
abilities.

" ' XIV.   Every citizen has a right, either by himself or
his representative, to a free voice in determining the necessity of public contributions, the appropriation of them,
and their amount, mode of assessment, and duration.

" ' XV.   Every community has a right to demand of all
its agents an account of their conduct.

" XVI.   Every community in which a separation of powers and a security of rights is not provided for, wants a constitution.

" ' XVII.   The right to property being inviolable and
sacred, no one ought to be deprived of it, except in cases of
evident public necessity, legally ascertained, and on condition of a previous just indemnity.' "

OBSERVATIONS

ON THE

DECLARATION OF RIGHTS.

THE first three articles comprehend in general terms the
whole of a Declaration of Rights, all the succeeding articles
either originate from them or follow as elucidations.   The
4th, 5th, and 6th define more particularly what is only
generally expressed in the 1st, 2nd, and 3rd.

The 7th, 8th, 9th, 10th, and 11th articles are declaratory of
principles upon which laws shall be constructed, conformable

to *rights* already declared. But it is questioned by some very good people in France, as well as in other countries, whether the 10th article sufficiently guarantees the right it is intended to accord with ; besides which it takes off from the divine dignity of religion, and weakens its operative force upon the mind, to make it a subject of human laws. It then presents itself to man like light intercepted by a cloudy medium, in which the source of it is obscured from his sight, and he sees nothing to reverence in the dusky ray.*

The remaining articles, beginning with the twelfth, are substantially contained in the principles of the preceding articles; but in the particular situation in which France then was, having to undo what was wrong, as well as to set up what was right, it was proper to be more particular than what in another condition of things would be necessary.

While the Declaration of Rights was before the National Assembly some of its members remarked that if a declaration of rights were published it should be accompanied by a Declaration of Duties. The observation discovered a mind that reflected, and it only erred by not reflecting far

---

* There is a single idea, which, if it strikes rightly upon the mind, either in a legal or a religious sense, will prevent any man or any body of men, or any government, from going wrong on the subject of religion ; which is, that before any human institutions of government were known in the world, there existed, if I may so express it, a compact between God and man, from the beginning of time : and that as the relation and condition which man in his *individual person* stands in towards his Maker cannot be changed by any human laws or human authority, that religious devotion, which is a part of this compact, cannot so much as be made a subject of human laws ; and that all laws must conform themselves to this prior existing compact, and not assume to make the compact conform to the laws, which, besides being human, are subsequent thereto. The first act of man, when he looked around and saw himself a creature which he did not make, and a world furnished for his reception, must have been devotion ; and devotion must ever continue sacred to every individual man, *as it appears right to him ;* and governments do mischief by interfering.—*Author.*

Edmund Randolph, first Attorney-General of the United States, writing to Madison (Feb. 29, 1788) remarks concerning the new constitution's Art. VI. Sect. 3 : " Does not this exception as to a religious test imply that the Congress, by the general words, had power over religion ?"—*Editor.*

enough. A Declaration of Rights is, by reciprocity, a Declaration of Duties also. Whatever is my right as a man is
also the right of another ; and it becomes my duty to guarantee as well as to possess.

The first three articles are the basis of Liberty, as well
individual as national ; nor can any country be called free
whose government does not take its beginning from the
principles they contain, and continue to preserve them
pure ; and the whole of the Declaration of Rights is of more
value to the world, and will do more good, than all the
laws and statutes that have yet been promulgated.

In the declaratory exordium which prefaces the Declaration of Rights we see the solemn and majestic spectacle of
a nation opening its commission, under the auspices of its
Creator, to establish a Government, a scene so new, and so
transcendantly unequalled by anything in the European
world, that the name of a Revolution is diminutive of its
character, and it rises into a Regeneration of man. What
are the present Governments of Europe but a scene of
iniquity and oppression ? What is that of England ? Do
not its own inhabitants say it is a market where every man
has his price, and where corruption is common traffic at the
expense of a deluded people ? No wonder, then, that the
French Revolution is traduced. Had it confined itself
merely to the destruction of flagrant despotism perhaps
Mr. Burke and some others had been silent. Their cry now
is, " It has gone too far "—that is, it has gone too far for
them. It stares corruption in the face, and the venal tribe
are all alarmed. Their fear discovers itself in their outrage,   .
and they are but publishing the groans of a wounded vice.
But from such opposition the French Revolution, instead of
suffering, receives an homage. The more it is struck the
more sparks it will emit ; and the fear is it will not be
struck enough. It has nothing to dread from attacks ;
truth has given it an establishment, and time will record it
with a name as lasting as his own.

Having now traced the progress of the French Revolution
through most of its principal stages, from its commencement

to the taking of the Bastille, and its establishment by the Declaration of Rights, I will close the subject with the energetic apostrophe of M. de la Fayette—"*May this great monument, raised to Liberty, serve as a lesson to the oppressor, and an example to the oppressed !* " *

* See page 18 of this work.—N. B. Since the taking of the Bastille, the occurrences have been published : but the matters recorded in this narrative, are prior to that period ; and some of them, as may be easily seen, can be but very little known.—*Author.*

NOTE : The Editor regrets that the following passage, which should have been inserted after the eighth line on page 341, was omitted :

He endeavoured to impress the Parliament by great words, and opened his authority by saying, "The King, our Lord and Master." The Parliament received him very coolly, and with their usual determination not to register the taxes : and in this manner the interview ended.

MISCELLANEOUS CHAPTER.

To prevent interrupting the argument in the preceding part of this work, or the narrative that follows it, I reserved some observations to be thrown together in a Miscellaneous Chapter; by which variety might not be censured for confusion. Mr. Burke's book is *all* Miscellany. His intention was to make an attack on the French Revolution; but instead of proceeding with an orderly arrangement, he has stormed it with a mob of ideas tumbling over and destroying one another.

But this confusion and contradiction in Mr. Burke's Book is easily accounted for.—When a man in a wrong cause attempts to steer his course by anything else than some polar truth or principle, he is sure to be lost. It is beyond the compass of his capacity to keep all the parts of an argument together, and make them unite in one issue, by any other means than having this guide always in view. Neither memory nor invention will supply the want of it. The former fails him, and the latter betrays him.

Notwithstanding the nonsense, for it deserves no better name, that Mr. Burke has asserted about hereditary rights, and hereditary succession, and that a Nation has not à right to form a Government of itself; it happened to fall in his way to give some account of what Government is. " *Government*," says he, " *is a contrivance of human wisdom.*"

Admitting that government is a contrivance of human *wisdom*, it must necessarily follow, that hereditary succession, and hereditary rights (as they are called), can make no part of it, because it is impossible to make wisdom hereditary; and on the other hand, *that* cannot be a wise contrivance, which in its operation may commit the government

of a nation to the wisdom of an idiot.   The ground which
Mr. Burke now takes is fatal to every part of his cause.
The argument changes from hereditary rights to hereditary
wisdom ; and the question is, Who is the wisest man ?   He
must now shew that every one in the line of hereditary succession was a Solomon, or his title is not good to be a king.
What a stroke has Mr. Burke now made !   To use a sailor's
phrase, he has *swabbed the deck*, and scarcely left a name
legible in the list of Kings ; and he has mowed down and
thinned the House of Peers, with a scythe as formidable as
Death and Time.

  But Mr. Burke appears to have been aware of this retort ;
and he has taken care to guard against it, by making government to be not only a *contrivance* of human wisdom, but
a *monopoly* of wisdom.   He puts the nation as fools on one
side, and places his government of wisdom, all wise men of
Gotham, on the other side ; and he then proclaims, and says
that " *Men have a* RIGHT *that their* WANTS *should be provided for by this wisdom.*"   Having thus made proclamation,
he next proceeds to explain to them what their *wants* are,
and also what their *rights* are.   In this he has succeeded
dextrously, for he makes their wants to be a *want* of wisdom ; but as this is cold comfort, he then informs them, that
they have a *right* (not to any of the wisdom) but to be governed by it ; and in order to impress them with a solemn
reverence for this monopoly-government of wisdom, and of
its vast capacity for all purposes, possible or impossible,
right or wrong, he proceeds with astrological mysterious importance, to tell to them its powers in these words : " The
rights of men in government are their advantages ; and
these are often in balance between differences of good ; and
in compromises sometimes between *good* and *evil*, and sometimes between *evil* and *evil*.   Political reason is a *computing
principle ;* adding—subtracting—multiplying—and dividing,
morally and not metaphysically or mathematically, true moral
denominations."

  As the wondering audience, whom Mr. Burke supposes
himself talking to, may not understand all this learned jar-

gon, I will undertake to be its interpreter.   The meaning,
then, good people, of all this, is : *That government is governed by no principle whatever ; that it can make evil good, or
good evil, just as it pleases.   In short, that government is arbitrary power.*

But there are some things which Mr. Burke has forgotten.
First, he has not shewn where the wisdom originally came
from : and *secondly*, he has not shewn by what authority it
first began to act.   In the manner he introduces the matter,
it is either government stealing wisdom, or wisdom stealing
government.   It is without an origin, and its powers without
authority.   In short, it is usurpation.

Whether it be from a sense of shame, or from a consciousness of some radical defect in a government necessary to be
kept out of sight, or from both, or from any other cause, I
undertake not to determine, but so it is, that a monarchical
reasoner never traces government to its source, or from its
source.   It is one of the *shibboleths* by which he may be
known.   A thousand years hence, those who shall live in
America or France, will look back with contemplative pride
on the origin of their government, and say, *This was the
work of our glorious ancestors !* But what can a monarchical
talker say ?   What has he to exult in?   Alas he has nothing.   A certain something forbids him to look back to a beginning, lest some robber, or some Robin Hood, should rise
from the long obscurity of time and say, *I am the origin.*
Hard as Mr. Burke labored at the Regency Bill and Hereditary Succession two years ago, and much as he dived for
precedents, he still had not boldness enough to bring up
William of Normandy, and say, *There is the head of the list !
there is the fountain of honor !* the son of a prostitute, and
the plunderer of the English nation.

The opinions of men with respect to government are
changing fast in all countries.   The Revolutions of America
and France have thrown a beam of light over the world,
which reaches into man.   The enormous expense of governments has provoked people to think, by making them feel ;
and when once the veil begins to rend, it admits not of re-

pair.   Ignorance is of a peculiar nature: once dispelled, it is impossible to re-establish it.   It is not originally a thing of itself, but is only the absence of knowledge; and though man may be *kept* ignorant, he cannot be *made* ignorant. The mind, in discovering truth, acts in the same manner as it acts through the eye in discovering objects; when once any object has been seen, it is impossible to put the mind back to the same condition it was in before it saw it.   Those who talk of a counter-revolution in France, show how little they understand of man.   There does not exist in the compass of language an arrangement of words to express so much as the means of effecting a counter-revolution.   The means must be an obliteration of knowledge; and it has never yet been discovered how to make man *unknow* his knowledge, or *unthink* his thoughts.

Mr. Burke is laboring in vain to stop the progress of knowledge; and it comes with the worse grace from him, as there is a certain transaction known in the city which renders him suspected of being a pensioner in a fictitious name. This may account for some strange doctrine he has advanced in his book, which though he points it at the Revolution Society, is effectually directed against the whole nation.

"The King of England," says he, "holds *his* crown (for it does not belong to the Nation, according to Mr. Burke) in *contempt* of the choice of the Revolution Society, who have not a single vote for a king among them either *individually* or *collectively;* and his Majesty's heirs each in their time and order, will come to the Crown *with the same contempt* of their choice, with which his Majesty has succeeded to that which he now wears."

As to who is King in England or elsewhere, or whether there is any King at all, or whether the people choose a Cherokee chief, or a Hessian hussar for a King, it is not a matter that I trouble myself about—be that to themselves; but with respect to the doctrine, so far as it relates to the Rights of Men and Nations, it is as abominable as anything ever uttered in the most enslaved country under heaven. Whether it sounds worse to my ear, by not being accustomed

to hear such despotism, than what it does to the ear of
another person, I am not so well a judge of; but of its
abominable principle I am at no loss to judge.

It is not the Revolution Society that Mr. Burke means;
it is the Nation, as well in its *original* as in its *representative*
character; and he has taken care to make himself understood,
by saying that they have not a vote either *collectively* or *individually.* The Revolution Society is composed of citizens
of all denominations, and of members of both the Houses
of Parliament; and consequently, if there is not a right to
a vote in any of the characters, there can be no right to
any either in the nation or in its Parliament. This ought
to be a caution to every country how it imports foreign
families to be kings. It is somewhat curious to observe,
that although the people of England had been in the habit
of talking about kings, it is always a Foreign House of
Kings; hating Foreigners yet governed by them.—It is now
the House of Brunswick, one of the petty tribes of Germany.

It has hitherto been the practice of the English Parliaments to regulate what was called the succession (taking it
for granted that the Nation then continued to accord to the
form of annexing a monarchical branch of its government;
for without this the Parliament could not have had authority
to have sent either to Holland or to Hanover, or to impose
a king upon the nation against its will.) And this must be the
utmost limit to which Parliament can go upon this case; but
the right of the Nation goes to the *whole* case, because it has
the right of changing its *whole* form of government. The
right of a Parliament is only a right in trust, a right by delegation, and that but from a very small part of the Nation;
and one of its Houses has not even this. But the right of
the Nation is an original right, as universal as taxation. The
nation is the paymaster of everything, and everything must
conform to its general will.

I remember taking notice of a speech in what is called the
English House of Peers, by the then Earl of Shelburne, and
I think it was at the time he was Minister, which is applic-

able to this case. I do not directly charge my memory with every particular; but the words and the purport, as nearly as I remember, were these: "*That the form of a Government was a matter wholly at the will of the Nation at all times, that if it chose a monarchical form, it had a right to have it so; and if it afterwards chose to be a Republic, it had a right to be a Republic, and to say to a King, 'We have no longer any occasion for you.'*"

When Mr. Burke says that "His Majesty's heirs and successors, each in their time and order, will come to the crown with the *same contempt* of their choice with which His Majesty had succeeded to that he wears," it is saying too much even to the humblest individual in the country; part of whose daily labor goes towards making up the million sterling a-year, which the country gives the person it styles a king. Government with insolence is despotism; but when contempt is added it becomes worse; and to pay for contempt is the excess of slavery. This species of government comes from Germany; and reminds me of what one of the Brunswick soldiers told me, who was taken prisoner by the Americans in the late war: "Ah!" said he, "America is a fine free country, it is worth the people's fighting for; I know the difference by knowing my own: in my country, if the prince says eat straw, we eat straw." God help that country, thought I, be it England or elsewhere, whose liberties are to be protected by German principles of government, and Princes of Brunswick!

As Mr. Burke sometimes speaks of England, sometimes of France, and sometimes of the world, and of government in general, it is difficult to answer his book without apparently meeting him on the same ground. Although principles of Government are general subjects, it is next to impossible, in many cases, to separate them from the idea of place and circumstance, and the more so when circumstances are put for arguments, which is frequently the case with Mr. Burke.

In the former part of his book, addressing himself to the people of France, he says: "No experience has taught us (meaning the English), that in any other course or method than that of a *hereditary crown*, can our liberties be regularly perpetuated and preserved sacred as our *hereditary right*." I ask Mr. Burke, who is to take them away? M. de la Fayette, in speaking to France, says: "*For a Nation to be free, it is sufficient that she wills it.*" But Mr. Burke represents England as wanting capacity to take care of itself, and that its liberties must be taken care of by a King holding it in "contempt." If England is sunk to this, it is preparing itself to eat straw, as in Hanover, or in Brunswick. But besides the folly of the declaration, it happens that the facts are all against Mr. Burke. It was by the government *being hereditary*, that the liberties of the people were endangered. Charles I. and James II. are instances of this truth; yet neither of them went so far as to hold the Nation in contempt.

As it is sometimes of advantage to the people of one country to hear what those of other countries have to say respecting it, it is possible that the people of France may learn something from Mr. Burke's book, and that the people of England may also learn something from the answers it will occasion. When Nations fall out about freedom, a wide field of debate is opened. The argument commences with the rights of war, without its evils, and as knowledge is the object contended for, the party that sustains the defeat obtains the prize.

Mr. Burke talks about what he calls an hereditary crown, as if it were some production of Nature; or as if, like Time, it had a power to operate, not only independently, but in spite of man; or as if it were a thing or a subject universally consented to. Alas! it has none of those properties, but is the reverse of them all. It is a thing in imagination, the propriety of which is more than doubted, and the legality of which in a few years will be denied.

But, to arrange this matter in a clearer view than what general expression can convey, it will be necessary to state the distinct heads under which (what is called) an hereditary crown, or more properly speaking, an hereditary succession to the Government of a Nation, can be considered; which are,

First,   The right of a particular Family to establish itself.

Secondly,   The right of a Nation to establish a particular Family.

With respect to the *first* of these heads, that of a Family establishing itself with hereditary powers on its own authority, and independent of the consent of a Nation, all men will concur in calling it despotism; and it would be trespassing on their understanding to attempt to prove it.

But the *second* head, that of a Nation establishing a particular Family with *hereditary powers*, does not present itself as despotism on the first reflexion; but if men will permit a second reflexion to take place, and carry that reflexion forward but one remove out of their own persons to that of their offspring, they will then see that hereditary succession becomes in its consequences the same despotism to others, which they reprobated for themselves. It operates to preclude the consent of the succeeding generations; and the preclusion of consent is despotism. When the person who at any time shall be in possession of a Government, or those who stand in succession to him, shall say to a Nation, I hold this power in "contempt" of you, it signifies not on what authority he pretends to say it. It is no relief, but an aggravation to a person in slavery, to reflect that he was sold by his parent; and as that which heightens the criminality of an act cannot be produced to prove the legality of it, hereditary succession cannot be established as a legal thing.

In order to arrive at a more perfect decision on this head, it will be proper to consider the generation which undertakes to establish a Family with *hereditary powers*, apart and separate from the generations which are to follow; and also to consider the character in which the *first* generation acts with respect to succeeding generations.

The generation which first selects a person, and puts him at the head of its Government, either with the title of King, or any other distinction, acts on its *own choice*, be it wise or foolish, as a free agent for itself. The person so set up is

not hereditary, but selected and appointed ; and the generation who sets him up, does not live under a hereditary
government, but under a government of its own choice
and establishment.   Were the generation who sets him
up, and the person so set up, to live for ever, it never
could become hereditary succession ; and of consequence
hereditary succession can only follow on the death of the
first parties.

As, therefore, hereditary succession is out of the question with respect to the *first* generation, we have now
to consider the character in which *that* generation acts with
respect to the commencing generation, and to all succeeding ones.

It assumes a character, to which it has neither right nor
title.   It changes itself from a *Legislator* to a *Testator*, and
effects to make its Will, which is to have operation after
the demise of the makers, to bequeath the Government ;
and it not only attempts to bequeath, but to establish
on the succeeding generation, a new and different form of
Government under which itself lived.   Itself, as already observed, lived not under a hereditary Government but under
a Government of its own choice and establishment ; and it
now attempts, by virtue of a will and testament (and which
it has not authority to make), to take from the commencing
generation, and all future ones, the rights and free agency
by which itself acted.

But, exclusive of the right which any generation has to
act collectively as a testator, the objects to which it applies
itself in this case, are not within the compass of any law, or
of any will or testament.

The rights of men in society, are neither devisable or
transferable, nor annihilable, but are descendable only, and
it is not in the power of any generation to intercept finally,
and cut off the descent.   If the present generation, or any
other, are disposed to be slaves, it does not lessen the
right of the succeeding generation to be free.   Wrongs cannot have a legal descent.   When Mr. Burke attempts to
maintain that the *English nation did at the Revolution of*

1688, most solemnly renounce and abdicate their rights for themselves, and for all their posterity forever, he speaks a language that merits not reply, and which can only excite contempt for his prostitute principles, or pity for his ignorance.

In whatever light hereditary succession, as growing out of the will and testament of some former generation, presents itself, it is an absurdity. A cannot make a will to take from B the property of B, and give it to C ; yet this is the manner in which (what is called) hereditary succession by law operates. A certain former generation made a will, to take away the rights of the commencing generation, and all future ones, and convey those rights to a third person, who afterwards comes forward, and tells them, in Mr. Burke's language, that they have *no rights*, that their rights are already bequeathed to him and that he will govern in *contempt* of them. From such principles, and such ignorance, good Lord deliver the world !

But, after all, what is this metaphor called a crown, or rather what is monarchy? Is it a thing, or is it a name, or is it a fraud ? Is it a "contrivance of human wisdom," or of human craft to obtain money from a nation under specious pretences? Is it a thing necessary to a nation? If it is, in what does that necessity consist, what service does it perform, what is its business, and what are its merits? Does the virtue consist in the metaphor, or in the man ? Doth the goldsmith that makes the crown, make the virtue also ? Doth it operate like Fortunatus's wishing-cap, or Harlequin's wooden sword ? Doth it make a man a conjurer ? In fine, what is it ? It appears to be something going much out of fashion, falling into ridicule, and rejected in some countries, both as unnecessary and expensive. In America it is considered as an absurdity ; and in France it has so far declined, that the goodness of the man, and the respect for his personal character, are the only things that preserve the appearance of its existence.

If government be what Mr. Burke describes it, "a contrivance of human wisdom," I might ask him, if wisdom was at such a low ebb in England, that it was become necessary to import it from Holland and from Hanover? But I will do the country the justice to say, that was not the case; and even if it was, it mistook the cargo. The wisdom of every country, when properly exerted, is sufficient for all its purposes; and there could exist no more real occasion in England to have sent for a Dutch Stadtholder, or a German Elector, than there was in America to have done a similar thing. If a country does not understand its own affairs, how is a foreigner to understand them, who knows neither its laws, its manners, nor its language? If there existed a man so transcendently wise above all others, that his wisdom was necessary to instruct a nation, some reason might be offered for monarchy; but when we cast our eyes about a country, and observe how every part understands its own affairs; and when we look around the world, and see that of all men in it, the race of kings are the most insignificant in capacity, our reason cannot fail to ask us— What are those men kept for?

If there is anything in monarchy which we people of America do not understand, I wish Mr. Burke would be so kind as to inform us. I see in America, a government extending over a country ten times as large as England, and conducted with regularity, for a fortieth part of the expense which Government costs in England. If I ask a man in America if he wants a King, he retorts, and asks me if I take him for an ideot? How is it that this difference happens? are we more or less wise than others? I see in America the generality of people living in a style of plenty unknown in monarchical countries; and I see that the principle of its government, which is that of the *equal Rights of Man*, is making a rapid progress in the world.

If monarchy is a useless thing, why is it kept up anywhere? and if a necessary thing, how can it be dispensed with? That *civil government* is necessary, all civilised nations will agree; but civil government is republican government. All that part of the government of England which begins with the office of constable, and proceeds through the department of magistrate, quarter-sessions, and general assize, including trial by jury, is republican government. Nothing of monarchy appears in any part of it, except in the name which William the Conqueror imposed upon the English, that of obliging them to call him " Their Sovereign Lord the King."

It is easy to conceive that a band of interested men, such as Placemen, Pensioners, Lords of the bed-chamber, Lords of the kitchen, Lords of the necessary-house, and the Lord knows what besides, can find as many reasons for monarchy as their salaries, paid at the expence of the country, amount to ; but if I ask the farmer, the manufacturer, the merchant, the tradesman, and down through all the occupations of life to the common laborer, what service monarchy is to him ? he can give me no answer. If I ask him what monarchy is, he believes it is something like a sinecure.

Notwithstanding the taxes of England amount to almost seventeen millions a year, said to be for the expences of Government, it is still evident that the sense of the Nation is left to govern itself, and does govern itself, by magistrates and juries, almost at its own charge, on republican principles, exclusive of the expence of taxes. The salaries of the judges are almost the only charge that is paid out of the revenue. Considering that all the internal government is executed by the people, the taxes of England ought to be the lightest of any nation in Europe ; instead of which, they are the contrary. As this cannot be accounted for on the score of civil government, the subject necessarily extends itself to the monarchical part.

When the people of England sent for George the First (and it would puzzle a wiser man than Mr. Burke to discover for what he could be wanted, or what service he could render), they ought at least to have conditioned for the abandonment of Hanover. Besides the endless German intrigues that must follow from a German Elector being King of England, there is a natural impossibility of uniting in the same person the principles of Freedom and the principles of Despotism, or as it is usually called in England

Arbitrary Power. A German Elector is in his electorate a despot; how then could it be expected that he should be attached to principles of liberty in one country, while his interest in another was to be supported by despotism? The union cannot exist; and it might easily have been foreseen that German Electors would make German Kings, or in Mr. Burke's words, would assume government with " contempt." The English have been in the habit of considering a King of England only in the character in which he appears to them; whereas the same person, while the connection lasts, has a home-seat in another country, the interest of which is different to their own, and the principles of the governments in opposition to each other. To such a person England will appear as a town-residence, and the Electorate as the estate. The English may wish, as I believe they do, success to the principles of liberty in France, or in Germany; but a German Elector trembles for the fate of despotism in his electorate; and the Duchy of Mecklenburgh, where the present Queen's family governs, is under the same wretched state of arbitrary power, and the people in slavish vassalage.

There never was a time when it became the English to watch continental intrigues more circumspectly than at the present moment, and to distinguish the politics of the Electorate from the politics of the Nation. The Revolution of France has entirely changed the ground with respect to England and France, as nations; but the German despots, with Prussia at their head, are combining against liberty; and the fondness of Mr. Pitt for office, and the interest which all his family connections have obtained, do not give sufficient security against this intrigue.

As everything which passes in the world becomes matter for history, I will now quit this subject, and take a concise review of the state of parties and politics in England, as Mr. Burke has done in France.

Whether the present reign commenced with contempt, I leave to Mr. Burke: certain, however, it is, that it had strongly that appearance. The animosity of the English nation, it is very well remembered, ran high ; and, had the true principles of Liberty been as well understood then as they now promise to be, it is probable the Nation would not have patiently submitted to so much.   George the First and Second were sensible of a rival in the remains of the Stu-arts ; and as they could not but consider themselves as standing on their good behaviour, they had prudence to keep their German principles of government to themselves ; but as the Stuart family wore away, the prudence became less necessary.

The contest between rights, and what were called preroga-tives, continued to heat the nation till some time after the conclusion of the American War, when all at once it fell a calm—Execration exchanged itself for applause, and Court popularity sprung up like a mushroom in a night.

To account for this sudden transition, it is proper to ob-serve that there are two distinct species of popularity ; the one excited by merit, and the other by resentment.   As the Nation had formed itself into two parties, and each was ex-tolling the merits of its parliamentary champions for and against prerogative, nothing could operate to give a more general shock than an immediate coalition of the champions themselves.[1]   The partisans of each being thus suddenly left in the lurch, and mutually heated with disgust at the measure, felt no other relief than uniting in a common exe-cration against both.   A higher stimulus of resentment being thus excited than what the contest on prerogatives occasioned, the nation quitted all former objects. of rights and wrongs, and sought only that of gratification.   The in-dignation at the Coalition so effectually superseded the in-dignation against the Court as to extinguish it ; and without any change of principles on the part of the Court, the same people who had reprobated its despotism united with it to revenge themselves on the Coalition Parliament.   The case was not, which they liked best, but which they hated most ; and the least hated passed for love.   The dissolution of the

---

[1] Fox and Lord North, with whom Burke also had united, though he and Fox had once proposed to impeach North.—*Editor.*

Coalition Parliament, as it afforded the means of gratifying
the resentment of the Nation, could not fail to be popular;
and from hence arose the popularity of the Court.

Transitions of this kind exhibit a Nation under the government of temper, instead of a fixed and steady principle;
and having once committed itself, however rashly, it feels itself urged along to justify by continuance its first proceeding. Measures which at other times it would censure it now
approves, and acts persuasion upon itself to suffocate its
judgment.

On the return of a new Parliament, the new Minister, Mr.
Pitt, found himself in a secure majority; and the Nation
gave him credit, not out of regard to himself, but because it
had resolved to do it out of resentment to another.   He
introduced himself to public notice by a proposed Reform of
Parliament, which in its operation would have amounted to
a public justification of corruption.   The Nation was to be
at the expence of buying up the rotten boroughs, whereas
it ought to punish the persons who deal in the traffic.

Passing over the two bubbles of the Dutch business and
the million a-year to sink the national debt, the matter which
most presents itself, is the affair of the Regency.   Never, in
the course of my observation, was delusion more successfully
acted, nor a nation more completely deceived.   But, to make
this appear, it will be necessary to go over the circumstances.

Mr. Fox had stated in the House of Commons, that the
Prince of Wales, as heir in succession, had a right in himself to assume the Government.   This was opposed by Mr.
Pitt; and, so far as the opposition was confined to the doctrine, it was just.   But the principles which Mr. Pitt maintained on the contrary side were as bad, or worse in their
extent, than those of Mr. Fox; because they went to establish an aristocracy over the nation, and over the small representation it has in the House of Commons.[1]

[1] George III. having become insane (1788), Pitt held, against Fox and Burke,
that the Prince of Wales had no more right than any private individual to reign
unless chosen by the two Houses of Parliament.   No doubt Paine regarded
this as virtually making over to the Peers a providential opportunity for a representative election.—*Editor.*

Whether the English form of Government be good or bad, is not in this case the question ; but, taking it as it stands, without regard to its merits or demerits, Mr. Pitt was farther from the point than Mr. Fox.

It is supposed to consist of three parts :—while therefore the Nation is disposed to continue this form, the parts have a *national standing*, independent of each other, and are not the creatures of each other.   Had Mr. Fox passed through Parliament, and said that the person alluded to claimed on the ground of the Nation, Mr. Pitt must then have contended what he called the right of the Parliament against the right of the Nation.

By the appearance which the contest made, Mr. Fox took the hereditary ground, and Mr. Pitt the Parliamentary ground ; but the fact is, they both took hereditary ground, and Mr. Pitt took the worst of the two.

What is called the Parliament is made up of two Houses, one of which is more hereditary, and more beyond the controul of the Nation than what the Crown (as it is called) is supposed to be.   It is an hereditary aristocracy, assuming and asserting indefeasible, irrevocable, rights and authority, wholly independent of the Nation.   Where, then, was the merited popularity of exalting this hereditary power over another hereditary power less independent of the Nation than what itself assumed to be, and of absorbing the rights of the Nation into a House over which it has neither election nor controul ?

The general impulse of the Nation was right ; but it acted without reflection.   It approved the opposition made to the right set up by Mr. Fox, without perceiving that Mr. Pitt was supporting another indefeasible right more remote from the Nation, in opposition to it.

With respect to the House of Commons, it is elected but by a small part of the Nation ; but were the election as universal as taxation, which it ought to be, it would still be only the organ of the Nation, and cannot possess inherent rights. —When the National Assembly of France resolves a matter, the resolve is made in right of the Nation ; but Mr. Pitt,

on all national questions, so far as they refer to the House
of Commons, absorbs the rights of the Nation into the organ, and makes the organ into a Nation, and the Nation
itself into a cypher.

In a few words, the question on the Regency was a question of a million a-year, which is appropriated to the executive department: and Mr. Pitt could not possess himself of
any management of this sum, without setting up the supremacy of Parliament; and when this was accomplished, it was
indifferent who should be Regent, as he must be Regent
at his own cost.   Among the curiosities which this contentious debate. afforded, was that of making the Great Seal
into a King, the affixing of which to an act was to be royal
authority.   If, therefore, Royal Authority is a Great Seal, it
consequently is in itself nothing; and a good Constitution
would be of infinitely more value to the Nation than what
the three Nominal Powers, as they now stand, are worth.

The continual use of the word *Constitution* in the English
Parliament shews there is none; and that the whole is merely a
form of government without a Constitution, and constituting
itself with what powers it pleases.   If there were a Constitution, it certainly could be referred to; and the debate on
any constitutional point would terminate by producing the
Constitution.   One member says this is Constitution, and
another says that is Constitution—To-day it is one thing;
and to-morrow something else—while the maintaining of
the debate proves there is none.   Constitution is now the
cant word of Parliament, tuning itself to the ear of the
Nation.   Formerly it was the *universal supremacy of Parliament*—the *omnipotence of Parliament :*   But since the progress of Liberty in France, those phrases have a despotic
harshness in their note; and the English Parliament have
catched the fashion from the National Assembly, but without the substance, of speaking of *Constitution.*

As the present generation of the people in England did
not make the Government, they are not accountable for any
of its defects; but, that sooner or later, it must come into
their hands to undergo a constitutional reformation, is as

certain as that the same thing has happened in France. If France, with a revenue of nearly twenty-four millions sterling, with an extent of rich and fertile country above four times larger than England, with a population of twenty-four millions of inhabitants to support taxation, with upwards of ninety millions sterling of gold and silver circulating in the nation, and with a debt less than the present debt of England—still found it necessary, from whatever cause, to come to a settlement of its affairs, it solves the problem of funding for both countries.

It is out of the question to say how long what is called the English constitution has lasted, and to argue from thence how long it is to last; the question is, how long can the funding system last? It is a thing but of modern invention, and has not yet continued beyond the life of a man; yet in that short space it has so far accumulated, that, together with the current expenses, it requires an amount of taxes at least equal to the whole landed rental of the nation in acres to defray the annual expenditure. That a government could not have always gone on by the same system which has been followed for the last seventy years, must be evident to every man ; and for the same reason it cannot always go on.

The funding system is not money; neither is it, properly speaking, credit. It, in effect, creates upon paper the sum which it appears to borrow, and lays on a tax to keep the imaginary capital alive by the payment of interest and sends the annuity to market, to be sold for paper already in circulation. If any credit is given, it is to the disposition of the people to pay the tax, and not to the government, which lays it on. When this disposition expires, what is supposed to be the credit of Government expires with it. The instance of France under the former Government shews that it is impossible to compel the payment of taxes by force, when a whole nation is determined to take its stand upon that ground,

Mr. Burke, in his review of the finances of France, states the quantity of gold and silver in France, at about eighty-eight millions sterling. In doing this, he has, I presume, divided by the difference of exchange, instead of the standard of twenty-four livres to a pound sterling; for M. Neckar's statement, from which Mr. Burke's is taken, is *two thousand two hundred millions of livres,* which is upwards of ninety-one millions and a half sterling.

M. Neckar in France, and Mr. George Chalmers at the Office of Trade and Plantation in England, of which Lord Hawkesbury is president, published nearly about the same time (1786) an account of the quantity of money in each nation, from the returns of the Mint of each Nation. Mr. Chalmers, from the returns of the English Mint at the Tower of London, states the quantity of money in England, including Scotland and Ireland, to be twenty millions sterling.*

M. Neckar † says that the amount of money in France, re-coined from the old coin which was called in, was two thousand five hundred millions of livres (upwards of one hundred and four millions sterling); and, after deducting for waste, and what may be in the West Indies and other possible circumstances, states the circulation quantity at home to be ninety-one millions and a half sterling; but, taking it as Mr. Burke has put it, it is sixty-eight millions more than the national quantity in England.

That the quantity of money in France cannot be under this sum, may at once be seen from the state of the French Revenue, without referring to the records of the French Mint for proofs. The revenue of France, prior to the Revolution, was nearly twenty-four millions sterling; and as paper had then no existence in France the whole revenue was collected upon gold and silver; and it would have been impossible to have collected such a quantity of revenue upon a less national quantity than M. Neckar has stated. Before the establishment of paper in England, the revenue was about a fourth part of the national amount of gold and

* See " Estimate of the Comparative Strength of Great Britain," by G. Chalmers.—*Author.*

† See " Administration of the Finances of France," vol. iii., by M. Neckar. —*Author.*

silver, as may be known by referring to the revenue prior to King William, and the quantity of money stated to be in the nation at that time, which was nearly as much as it is now.

It can be of no real service to a nation, to impose upon itself, or to permit itself to be imposed upon ; but the prejudices of some, and the imposition of others, have always represented France as a nation possessing but little money —whereas the quantity is not only more than four times what the quantity is in England, but is considerably greater on a proportion of numbers. To account for this deficiency on the part of England, some reference should be had to the English system of funding. It operates to multiply paper, and to substitute it in the room of money, in various shapes ; and the more paper is multiplied, the more opportunities are offered to export the specie ; and it admits of a possibility (by extending it to small notes) of increasing paper till there is no money left.

I know this is not a pleasant subject to English readers ; but the matters I am going to mention, are so important in themselves, as to require the attention of men interested in money transactions of a public nature. There is a circumstance stated by M. Neckar, in his treatise on the administration of the finances, which has never been attended to in England, but which forms the only basis whereon to estimate the quantity of money (gold and silver) which ought to be in every nation in Europe, to preserve a relative proportion with other nations.

Lisbon and Cadiz are the two ports into which (money) gold and silver from South America are imported, and which afterwards divide and spread themselves over Europe by means of commerce, and increase the quantity of money in all parts of Europe. If, therefore, the amount of the annual importation into Europe can be known, and the relative proportion of the foreign commerce of the several nations by which it can be distributed can be ascertained, they give a rule sufficiently true, to ascertain the quantity of money which ought to be found in any nation, at any given time.

M. Neckar shews from the registers of Lisbon and Cadiz, that the importation of gold and silver into Europe, is five millions sterling annually. He has not taken it on a single year, but on an average of fifteen succeeding years, from 1763 to 1777, both inclusive ; in which time, the amount was one thousand eight hundred million livres, which is seventy-five millions sterling.*

From the commencement of the Hanover succession in 1714 to the time Mr. Chalmers published, is seventy-two years ; and the quantity imported into Europe, in that time, would be three hundred and sixty millions sterling.

If the foreign commerce of Great Britain be stated at a sixth part of what the whole foreign commerce of Europe amounts to (which is probably an inferior estimation to what the gentlemen at the Exchange would allow) the proportion which Britain should draw by commerce of this sum, to keep herself on a proportion with the rest of Europe, would be also a sixth part which is sixty millions sterling ; and if the same allowance for waste and accident be made for England which M. Neckar makes for France, the quantity remaining after these deductions would be fifty-two millions ; and this sum ought to have been in the nation (at the time Mr. Chalmers published), in addition to the sum which was in the nation at the commencement of the Hanover succession, and to have made in the whole at least sixty-six millions sterling ; instead of which there were but twenty millions, which is forty-six millions below its proportionate quantity.

As the quantity of gold and silver imported into Lisbon and Cadiz is more exactly ascertained than that of any commodity imported into England, and as the quantity of money coined at the Tower of London is still more positively known, the leading facts do not admit of controversy. Either, therefore, the commerce of England is unproductive of profit, or the gold and silver which it brings in leak continually away by unseen means at the average rate of about three-quarters of a million a year, which, in the course of

* " Administration of the Finances of France," vol. iii.—*Author*.

seventy-two years, accounts for the deficiency; and its absence is supplied by paper.*

* Whether the English commerce does not bring in money, or whether the government sends it out after it is brought in, is a matter which the parties concerned can best explain ; but that the deficiency exists, is not in the power of either to disprove.   While Dr. Price, Mr. Eden, (now Auckland,) Mr. Chalmers, and others, were debating whether the quantity of money in England was greater or less than at the Revolution, the circumstance was not adverted to, that since the Revolution, there cannot have been less than four hundred millions sterling imported into Europe ; and therefore the quantity in England ought at least to have been four times greater than it was at the Revolution, to be on a proportion with Europe.   What England is now doing by paper, is what she would have been able to do by solid money, if gold and silver had come into the nation in the proportion it ought, or had not been sent out ; and she is endeavoring to restore by paper, the balance she has lost by money.   It is certain, that the gold and silver which arrive annually in the register-ships to Spain and Portugal, do not remain in those countries.   Taking the value half in gold and half in silver, it is about four hundred tons annually ; and from the number of ships and galloons employed in the trade of bringing those metals from South-America to Portugal and Spain, the quantity sufficiently proves itself, without referring to the registers.

In the situation England now is, it is impossible she can increase in money. High taxes not only lessen the property of the individuals, but they lessen also the money capital of the nation, by inducing smuggling, which can only be carried on by gold and silver.   By the politics which the British Government have carried on with the Inland Powers of Germany and the Continent, it has made an enemy of all the Maritime Powers, and is therefore obliged to keep up a large navy ; but though the navy is built in England, the naval stores must be purchased from abroad, and that from countries where the greatest part must be paid for in gold and silver.   Some fallacious rumours have been set afloat in England to induce a belief in money, and, among others, that of the French refugees bringing great quantities.   The idea is ridiculous.   The general part of the money in France is silver ; and it would take upwards of twenty of the largest broad wheel wagons, with ten horses each, to remove one million sterling of silver.   Is it then to be supposed, that a few people fleeing on horse-back or in post-chaises, in a secret manner, and having the French Custom-House to pass, and the sea to cross, could bring even a sufficiency for their own expences ?

When millions of money are spoken of, it should be recollected, that such sums can only accumulate in a country by slow degrees, and a long procession of time.   The most frugal system that England could now adopt, would not recover in a century the balance she has lost in money since the commencement of the Hanover succession.   She is seventy millions behind France, and she must be in some considerable proportion behind every country in Europe, because the returns of the English mint do not shew an increase of money, while the registers of Lisbon and Cadiz shew an European increase of between three and four hundred millions sterling.—*Author*.

The Revolution of France is attended with many novel circumstances, not only in the political sphere, but in the circle of money transactions. Among others, it shows that a government may be in a state of insolvency and a nation rich. So far as the fact is confined to the late Government of France, it was insolvent; because the nation would no longer support its extravagance, and therefore it could no longer support itself—but with respect to the nation all the means existed. A government may be said to be insolvent every time it applies to the nation to discharge its arrears. The insolvency of the late Government of France and the present Government of England differed in no other respect than as the dispositions of the people differ. The people of France refused their aid to the old Government; and the people of England submit to taxation without inquiry. What is called the Crown in England has been insolvent several times; the last of which, publicly known, was in May, 1777, when it applied to the nation to discharge upwards of £600,000 private debts, which otherwise it could not pay.

It was the error of Mr. Pitt, Mr. Burke, and all those who were unacquainted with the affairs of France to confound the French nation with the French Government. The French nation, in effect, endeavoured to render the late Government insolvent for the purpose of taking government into its own hands: and it reserved its means for the support of the new Government. In a country of such vast extent and population as France the natural means cannot be wanting, and the political means appear the instant the nation is disposed to permit them. When Mr. Burke, in a speech last winter in the British Parliament, " cast his eyes over the map of Europe, and saw a chasm that once was France," he talked like a dreamer of dreams. The same natural France existed as before, and all the natural means existed with it. The only chasm was that which the extinction of despotism had left, and which was to be filled up with a Constitution more formidable in resources than the power which had expired.

Although the French Nation rendered the late Government insolvent, it did not permit the insolvency to act towards the creditors; and the creditors, considering the Nation as the real pay-master, and the Government only as the agent, rested themselves on the nation, in preference to the Government. This appears greatly to disturb Mr. Burke, as the precedent is fatal to the policy by which governments have supposed themselves secure. They have contracted debts, with a view of attaching what is called the monied interest of a Nation to their support; but the example in France shews that the permanent security of the creditor is in the Nation, and not in the Government; and that in all possible revolutions that may happen in Governments, the means are always with the Nation, and the Nation always in existence. Mr. Burke argues that the creditors ought to have abided the fate of the Government which they trusted; but the National Assembly considered them as the creditors of the Nation, and not of the Government —of the master, and not of the steward.

Notwithstanding the late government could not discharge the current expenses, the present government has paid off a great part of the capital. This has been accomplished by two means; the one by lessening the expenses of government, and the other by the sale of the monastic and ecclesiastical landed estates. The devotees and penitent debauchees, extortioners and misers of former days, to ensure themselves a better world than that they were about to leave, had bequeathed immense property in trust to the priesthood for *pious uses;* and the priesthood kept it for themselves. The National Assembly has ordered it to be sold for the good of the whole nation, and the priesthood to be decently provided for.

In consequence of the revolution, the annual interest of the debt of France will be reduced at least six millions sterling, by paying off upwards of one hundred millions of the capital; which, with lessening the former expenses of government at least three millions, will place France in a situation worthy the imitation of Europe.

Upon a whole review of the subject, how vast is the contrast! While Mr. Burke has been talking of a general bankruptcy in France, the National Assembly has been paying off the capital of its debt; and while taxes have increased near a million a year in England, they have lowered several millions a year in France. Not a word has either Mr. Burke or Mr. Pitt said about the French affairs, or the state of the French finances, in the present Session of Parliament. The subject begins to be too well understood, and imposition serves no longer.

There is a general enigma running through the whole of Mr. Burke's book. He writes in a rage against the National Assembly; but what is he enraged about? If his assertions were as true as they are groundless, and that France by her Revolution, had annihilated her power, and become what he calls a *chasm*, it might excite the grief of a Frenchman (considering himself as a national man), and provoke his rage against the National Assembly; but why should it excite the rage of Mr. Burke? Alas! it is not the nation of France that Mr. Burke means, but the Court; and every Court in Europe, dreading the same fate, is in mourning. He writes neither in the character of a Frenchman nor an Englishman, but in the fawning character of that creature known in all countries, and a friend to none—a courtier. Whether it be the Court of Versailles, or the Court of St. James, or Carlton-House, or the Court in expectation, signifies not; for the caterpillar principle of all Courts and Courtiers are alike. They form a common policy throughout Europe, detached and separate from the interest of Nations: and while they appear to quarrel, they agree to plunder. Nothing can be more terrible to a Court or Courtier than the Revolution of France. That which is a blessing to Nations is bitterness to them: and as their existence depends on the duplicity of a country, they tremble at the approach of principles, and dread the precedent that threatens their overthrow.

CONCLUSION.

REASON and Ignorance, the opposites of each other, influence the great bulk of mankind. If either of these can be rendered sufficiently extensive in a country, the machinery of Government goes easily on. Reason obeys itself; and Ignorance submits to whatever is dictated to it.

The two modes of the Government which prevail in the world, are, *first*, Government by election and representation : *Secondly*, Government by hereditary succession. The former is generally known by the name of republic ; the latter by that of monarchy and aristocracy.

Those two distinct and opposite forms, erect themselves on the two distinct and opposite bases of Reason and Ignorance.—As the exercise of Government requires talents and abilities, and as talents and abilities cannot have hereditary descent, it is evident that hereditary succession requires a belief from man to which his reason cannot subscribe, and which can only be established upon his ignorance ; and the more ignorant any country is, the better it is fitted for this species of Government.

On the contrary, Government, in a well-constituted republic, requires no belief from man beyond what his reason can give. He sees the *rationale* of the whole system, its origin and its operation ; and as it is best supported when best understood, the human faculties act with boldness, and acquire, under this form of government, a gigantic manliness.

As, therefore, each of those forms acts on a different base, the one moving freely by the aid of reason, the other by ignorance ; we have next to consider, what it is that gives motion to that species of Government which is called mixed

Government, or, as it is sometimes ludicrously stiled, a Government of *this, that* and *t'other.*

The moving power in this species of Government, is of necessity, Corruption. However imperfect election and representation may be in mixed Governments, they still give exercise to a greater portion of reason than is convenient to the hereditary Part ; and therefore it becomes necessary to buy the reason up. A mixed Government is an imperfect everything, cementing and soldering the discordant parts together by corruption, to act as a whole. Mr. Burke appears highly disgusted that France, since she had resolved on a revolution, did not adopt what he calls " *A British Constitution*"*;* and the regretful manner in which he expresses himself on this occasion implies a suspicion that the British Constitution needed something to keep its defects in countenance.

In mixed Governments there is no responsibility : the parts cover each other till responsibility is lost ; and the corruption which moves the machine, contrives at the same time its own escape. When it is laid down as a maxim, that *a King can do no wrong,* it places him in a state of similar security with that of ideots and persons insane, and responsibility is out of the question with respect to himself. It then descends upon the Minister, who shelters himself under a majority in Parliament, which, by places, pensions, and corruption, he can always command ; and that majority justifies itself by the same authority with which it protects the Minister. In this rotatory motion, responsibility is thrown off from the parts, and from the whole.

When there is a Part in a Government which can do no wrong, it implies that it does nothing ; and is only the machine of another power, by whose advice and direction it acts. What is supposed to be the King in the mixed Governments, is the Cabinet ; and as the Cabinet is always a part of the Parliament, and the members justifying in one character what they advise and act in another, a mixed Government becomes a continual enigma ; entailing upon a country by the quantity of corruption necessary to solder the parts, the expence of supporting all the forms of government at once, and finally resolving itself into a Government by Committee; in which the advisers, the actors, the approvers, the justifiers, the persons responsible, and the persons not responsible, are the same persons.

By this pantomimical contrivance, and change of scene and character, the parts help each other out in matters which neither of them singly would assume to act. When money is to be obtained, the mass of variety apparently dissolves, and a profusion of parliamentary praises passes between the parts. Each admires with astonishment, the wisdom, the liberality, the disinterestedness of the other: and all of them breathe a pitying sigh at the burthens of the Nation.

But in a well-constituted republic, nothing of this soldering, praising, and pitying, can take place; the representation being equal throughout the country, and compleat in itself, however it may be arranged into legislative and executive, they have all one and the same natural source. The parts are not foreigners to each other, like democracy, aristocracy, and monarchy. As there are no discordant distinctions, there is nothing to corrupt by compromise, nor confound by contrivance. Public measures appeal of themselves to the understanding of the Nation, and, resting on their own merits, disown any flattering applications to vanity. The continual whine of lamenting the burden of taxes, however successfully it may be practised in mixed Governments, is inconsistent with the sense and spirit of a republic. If taxes are necessary, they are of course advantageous; but if they require an apology, the apology itself implies an impeachment. Why, then, is man thus imposed upon, or why does he impose upon himself?

When men are spoken of as kings and subjects, or when Government is mentioned under the distinct and combined heads of monarchy, aristocracy, and democracy, what is it that *reasoning* man is to understand by the terms? If there really existed in the world two or more distinct and separate *elements* of human power, we should then see the several origins to which those terms would descriptively apply ; but as there is but one species of man, there can be but one element of human power ; and that element is man himself. Monarchy, aristocracy, and democracy, are but creatures of imagination ; and a thousand such may be contrived as well as three.

————

From the Revolutions of America and France, and the symptoms that have appeared in other countries, it is evident that the opinion of the world is changing with respect to systems of Government, and that revolutions are not within the compass of political calculations. The progress of time and circumstances, which men assign to the accomplishment of great changes, is too mechanical to measure the force of the mind, and the rapidity of reflection, by which revolutions are generated : All the old governments have received a shock from those that already appear, and which were once more improbable, and are a greater subject of wonder, than a general revolution in Europe would be now.

When we survey the wretched condition of man, under the monarchical and hereditary systems of Government, dragged from his home by one power, or driven by another, and impoverished by taxes more than by enemies, it becomes evident that those systems are bad, and that a general revolution in the principle and construction of Governments is necessary.

What is government more than the management of the affairs of a Nation ?   It is not, and from its nature cannot be, the property of any particular man or family, but of the whole community, at whose expence it is supported ; and though by force and contrivance it has been usurped into an inheritance, the usurpation cannot alter the right of things. Sovereignty, as a matter of right, appertains to the Nation only, and not to any individual ; and a Nation has at all times an inherent indefeasible right to abolish any form of Government it finds inconvenient, and to establish such as accords with its interest, disposition and happiness.   The romantic and barbarous distinction of men into Kings and subjects, though it may suit the condition of courtiers, cannot that of citizens; and is exploded by the principle upon which Governments are now founded.   Every citizen is a member of the Sovereignty, and, as such, can acknowledge no personal subjection; and his obedience can be only to the laws.

When men think of what Government is, they must necessarily suppose it to possess a knowledge of all the objects and matters upon which its authority is to be exercised. In this view of Government, the republican system, as established by America and France, operates to embrace the whole of a Nation; and the knowledge necessary to the interest of all the parts, is to be found in the center, which the parts by representation form: But the old Governments are on a construction that excludes knowledge as well as happiness; Government by Monks, who knew nothing of the world beyond the walls of a Convent, is as consistent as government by Kings.

What were formerly called Revolutions, were little more than a change of persons, or an alteration of local circumstances. They rose and fell like things of course, and had nothing in their existence or their fate that could influence beyond the spot that produced them.   But what we now see in the world, from the Revolutions of America and France, are a renovation of the natural order of things, a system of principles as universal as truth and the existence of man, and combining moral with political happiness and national prosperity.

"I. *Men are born, and always continue, free and equal in respect of their rights. Civil distinctions, therefore, can be founded only on public utility.*

"II. *The end of all political associations is the preservation of the natural and imprescriptible rights of man; and these rights are liberty, property, security, and resistance of oppression.*

"III. *The nation is essentially the source of all sovereignty; nor can any* INDIVIDUAL, *or* ANY BODY OF MEN, *be entitled to any authority which is not expressly derived from it.*"

In these principles, there is nothing to throw a Nation into confusion by inflaming ambition. They are calculated to call forth wisdom and abilities, and to exercise them for the public good, and not for the emolument or aggrandisement of particular descriptions of men or families. Monarchical sovereignty, the enemy of mankind, and the source of misery, is abolished ; and the sovereignty itself is restored to its natural and original place, the Nation. Were this the case throughout Europe, the cause of wars would be taken away.

It is attributed to Henry the Fourth of France, a man of enlarged and benevolent heart, that he proposed, about the year 1610, a plan for abolishing war in Europe. The plan consisted in constituting an European Congress, or as the French authors stile it, a Pacific Republic; by appointing delegates from the several Nations who were to act as a Court of arbitration in any disputes that might arise between nation and nation.

Had such a plan been adopted at the time it was proposed, the taxes of England and France, as two of the parties, would have been at least ten millions sterling annually to each Nation less than they were at the commencement of the French Revolution.

To conceive a cause why such a plan has not been adopted (and that instead of a Congress for the purpose of *preventing* war, it has been called only to *terminate* a war, after a fruitless expence of several years) it will be necessary to consider the interest of Governments as a distinct interest to that of Nations.

Whatever is the cause of taxes to a Nation, becomes also the means of revenue to Government. Every war terminates with an addition of taxes, and consequently with an addition of revenue ; and in any event of war, in the manner they are now commenced and concluded, the power and interest of Governments are increased. War, therefore, from its productiveness, as it easily furnishes the pretence of necessity for taxes and appointments to places and offices, becomes a principal part of the system of old Governments ;

and to establish any mode to abolish war, however advantageous it might be to Nations, would be to take from such Government the most lucrative of its branches. The frivolous matters upon which war is made, shew the disposition and avidity of Governments to uphold the system of war, and betray the motives upon which they act.

Why are not Republics plunged into war, but because the nature of their Government does not admit of an interest distinct from that of the Nation? Even Holland, though an ill-constructed Republic, and with a commerce extending over the world, existed nearly a century without war: and the instant the form of Government was changed in France, the republican principles of peace and domestic prosperity and œconomy arose with the new Government ; and the same consequences would follow the cause in other Nations.

As war is the system of Government on the old construction, the animosity which Nations reciprocally entertain, is nothing more than what the policy of their Governments excites to keep up the spirit of the system. Each Government accuses the other of perfidy, intrigue, and ambition, as a means of heating the imagination of their respective Nations, and incensing them to hostilities. Man is not the enemy of man, but through the medium of a false system of Government. Instead, therefore, of exclaiming against the ambition of Kings, the exclamation should be directed against the principle of such Governments; and instead of seeking to reform the individual, the wisdom of a Nation should apply itself to reform the system.

Whether the forms and maxims of Governments which are still in practice, were adapted to the condition of the world at the period they were established, is not in this case the question. The older they are, the less correspondence can they have with the present state of things. Time, and change of circumstances and opinions, have the same progressive effect in rendering modes of Government obsolete as they have upon customs and manners.—Agriculture, commerce, manufactures, and the tranquil arts, by which the prosperity of Nations is best promoted, require a different system of Government, and a different species of knowledge to direct its operations, than what might have been required in the former condition of the world.

As it is not difficult to perceive, from the enlightened state of mankind, that hereditary Governments are verging to their decline, and that Revolutions on the broad basis of national sovereignty and Government by representation, are making their way in Europe, it would be an act of wisdom to anticipate their approach, and produce Revolutions by reason and accommodation, rather than commit them to the issue of convulsions.

From what we now see, nothing of reform in the political world ought to be held improbable. It is an age of Revolutions, in which everything may be looked for. The intrigue of Courts, by which the system of war is kept up, may provoke a confederation of Nations to abolish it: and an European Congress to patronise the progress of free Government, and promote the civilisation of Nations with each other, is an event nearer in probability, than once were the revolutions and alliance of France and America.

XIV.

RIGHTS OF MAN.

PART SECOND, COMBINING PRINCIPLE AND PRACTICE.
BY THOMAS PAINE.

FRENCH TRANSLATOR'S PREFACE.

(*1792.*)

THE work of which we offer a translation to the public has created the greatest sensation in England. Paine, that man of freedom, who seems born to preach "Common Sense" to the whole world with the same success as in America, explains in it to the people of England the theory of the practice of the Rights of Man.

Owing to the prejudices that still govern *that nation*, the author has been obliged to condescend to answer Mr. Burke. He has done so more especially in an extended preface which is nothing but a piece of very tedious controversy, in which he shows himself very sensitive to criticisms that do not really affect him. To translate it seemed an insult to the *free French people*, and similar reasons have led the editors to suppress also a dedicatory epistle addressed by Paine to Lafayette.

The French can no longer endure dedicatory epistles. A man should write privately to those he esteems: when he publishes a book his thoughts should be offered to the

public alone.   Paine, that uncorrupted friend of freedom,
believed too in the sincerity of Lafayette.   So easy is it to
deceive men of single-minded purpose!   Bred at a distance
from courts, that austere American does not seem any more
on his guard against the artful ways and speech of courtiers
than some Frenchmen who resemble him.

TO

M. DE LA FAYETTE.

AFTER an acquaintance of nearly fifteen years in difficult situations in America, and various consultations in Europe, I feel a pleasure in presenting to you this small treatise, in gratitude for your services to my beloved America, and as a testimony of my esteem for the virtues, public and private, which I know you too possess.

The only point upon which I could ever discover that we differed was not as to principles of government, but as to time. For my own part I think it equally as injurious to good principles to permit them to linger, as to push them on too fast. That which you suppose accomplishable in fourteen or fifteen years, I may believe practicable in a much shorter period. Mankind, as it appears to me, are always ripe enough to understand their true interest, provided it be presented clearly to their understanding, and that in a manner not to create suspicion by anything like self-design, nor offend by assuming too much. Where we would wish to reform we must not reproach.

When the American revolution was established I felt a disposition to sit serenely down and enjoy the calm. It did not appear to me that any object could afterwards arise great enough to make me quit tranquility and feel as I had felt before. But when principle, and not place, is the energetic cause of action, a man, I find, is everywhere the same.

I am now once more in the public world; and as I have not a right to contemplate on so many years of remaining life as you have, I have resolved to labour as fast as I can;

392

and as I am anxious for your aid and your company, I wish
you to hasten your principles and overtake me.

If you make a campaign the ensuing spring, which it is
most probable there will be no occasion for, I will come and
join you. Should the campaign commence, I hope it will
terminate in the extinction of German despotism, and in
establishing the freedom of all Germany. When France
shall be surrounded with revolutions she will be in peace and
safety, and her taxes, as well as those of Germany, will
consequently become less.

>   Your sincere,
>   Affectionate Friend,
>   THOMAS PAINE.

LONDON, Feb. 9, 1792.

PREFACE.

WHEN I began the chapter entitled the "*Conclusion*" in the former part of the RIGHTS OF MAN, published last year, it was my intention to have extended it to a greater length; but in casting the whole matter in my mind, which I wish to add, I found that it must either make the work too bulky, or contract my plan too much. I therefore brought it to a close as soon as the subject would admit, and reserved what I had further to say to another opportunity.

Several other reasons contributed to produce this determination. I wished to know the manner in which a work, written in a style of thinking and expression different to what had been customary in England, would be received before I proceeded farther. A great field was opening to the view of mankind by means of the French Revolution. Mr. Burke's outrageous opposition thereto brought the controversy into England. He attacked principles which he knew (from information) I would contest with him, because they are principles I believe to be good, and which I have contributed to establish, and conceive myself bound to defend. Had he not urged the controversy, I had most probably been a silent man.

Another reason for deferring the remainder of the work was, that Mr. Burke promised in his first publication to renew the subject at another opportunity, and to make a comparison of what he called the English and French Constitutions. I therefore held myself in reserve for him. He has published two works since, without doing this: which he certainly would not have omitted, had the comparison been in his favour.

In his last work, his "*Appeal from the New to the Old*

Whigs," he has quoted about ten pages from the RIGHTS OF MAN, and having given himself the trouble of doing this, says he "shall not attempt in the smallest degree to refute them," meaning the principles therein contained. I am enough acquainted with Mr. Burke to know that he would if he could. But instead of contesting them, he immediately after consoles himself with saying that "he has done his part."—He has not done his part. He has not performed his promise of a comparison of constitutions. He started the controversy, he gave the challenge, and has fled from it ; and he is now a *case in point* with his own opinion that "*the age of chivalry is gone !*"

The title, as well as the substance of his last work, his "*Appeal,*" is his condemnation. Principles must stand on their own merits, and if they are good they certainly will. To put them under the shelter of other men's authority, as Mr. Burke has done, serves to bring them into suspicion. Mr. Burke is not very fond of dividing his honours, but in this case he is artfully dividing the disgrace.

But who are those to whom Mr. Burke has made his appeal ? A set of childish thinkers, and half-way politicians born in the last century, men who went no farther with any principle than as it suited their purposes as a party ; the nation was always left out of the question ; and this has been the character of every party from that day to this. The nation sees nothing in such works, or such politics, worthy its attention. A little matter will move a party, but it must be something great that moves a nation.

Though I see nothing in Mr. Burke's "Appeal" worth taking much notice of, there is, however, one expression upon which I shall offer a few remarks. After quoting largely from the RIGHTS OF MAN, and declining to contest the principles contained in that work, he says : "This will most probably be done (*if such writings shall be thought to deserve any other refutation than that of criminal justice*) by others, who may think with Mr. Burke and with the same zeal." [1]

---

[1] In his "Appeal" Burke wrote of himself in the third person.—*Editor.*

In the first place, it has not yet been done by anybody. Not less, I believe than eight or ten pamphlets intended as answers to the former part of the RIGHTS OF MAN have been published by different persons, and not one of them to my knowledge, has extended to a second edition, nor are even the titles of them so much as generally remembered. As I am averse to unnecessarily multiplying publications, I have answered none of them. And as I believe that a man may write himself out of reputation when nobody else can do it, I am careful to avoid that rock.

But as I would decline unnecessary publications on the one hand, so would I avoid everything that might appear like sullen pride on the other. If Mr. Burke, or any person on his side the question, will produce an answer to the RIGHTS OF MAN that shall extend to a half, or even to a fourth part of the number of copies to which the RIGHTS OF MAN extended, I will reply to his work. But until this be done, I shall so far take the sense of the public for my guide (and the world knows I am not a flatterer) that what they do not think worth while to read, is not worth mine to answer. I suppose the number of copies to which the first part of the RIGHTS OF MAN extended, taking England, Scotland, and Ireland, is not less than between forty and fifty thousand.

I now come to remark on the remaining part of the quotation I have made from Mr. Burke.

" If," says he, " such writing shall be thought to deserve any other refutation than that of *criminal* justice."

Pardoning the pun, it must be *criminal* justice indeed that should condemn a work as a substitute for not being able to refute it. The greatest condemnation that could be passed upon it would be a refutation. But in proceeding by the method Mr. Burke alludes to, the condemnation would, in the final event, pass upon the criminality of the process and not upon the work, and in this case, I had rather be the author, than be either the judge or the jury that should condemn it.

But to come at once to the point. I have differed from some professional gentlemen on the subject of prosecutions, and I since find they are falling into my opinion, which I will here state as fully, but as concisely as I can.

I will first put a case with respect to any law, and then compare it with a government, or with what in England is, or has been, called a constitution.

It would be an act of despotism, or what in England is called arbitrary power, to make a law to prohibit investigating the principles, good or bad, on which such a law, or any other is founded.

If a law be bad it is one thing to oppose the practice of it, but it is quite a different thing to expose its errors, to reason on its defects, and to shew cause why it should be repealed, or why another ought to be substituted in its place. I have always held it an opinion (making it also my practice) that it is better to obey a bad law, making use at the same time of every argument to shew its errors and procure its repeal, than forcibly to violate it ; because the precedent of breaking a bad law might weaken the force, and lead to a discretionary violation, of those which are good.

The case is the same with respect to principles and forms of government, or to what are called constitutions and the parts of which they are composed.

It is for the good of nations and not for the emolument or aggrandisement of particular individuals, that government ought to be established, and that mankind are at the expence of supporting it. The defects of every government and constitution, both as to principle and form, must, on a parity of reasoning, be as open to discussion as the defects of a law, and it is a duty which every man owes to society to point them out. When those defects, and the means of remedying them, are generally seen by a nation, that nation will reform its government or its constitution in the one case, as the government repealed or reformed the law in the other. The operation of government is restricted to the making and the administering of laws ; but it is to a nation that the right of forming or reforming, generating or regenerating constitutions and governments belong ; and consequently those subjects, as subjects of investigation, are always before a country *as a matter of right*, and cannot, without invading the general rights of that country, be made subjects for prosecution.   On this ground I will meet Mr. Burke whenever he please.   It is better that the whole argument should come out than to seek to stifle it.   It was himself that opened the controversy, and he ought not to desert it.

I do not believe that monarchy and aristocracy will continue seven years longer in any of the enlightened countries in Europe.   If better reasons can be shewn for them than against them, they will stand ; if the contrary, they will not. Mankind are not now to be told they shall not think, or they shall not read ; and publications that go no farther than to investigate principles of government, to invite men to reason and to reflect, and to shew the errors and excellences of different systems, have a right to appear.   If they do not excite attention, they are not worth the trouble of a prosecution ; and if they do, the prosecution will amount to nothing, since it cannot amount to a prohibition of reading. This would be a sentence on the public, instead of the author, and would also be the most effectual mode of making or hastening revolutions.

On all cases that apply universally to a nation, with respect to systems of government, a jury of *twelve* men is not competent to decide.   Where there are no witnesses to be examined, no facts to be proved, and where the whole matter is before the whole public, and the merits or demerits of it resting on their opinion ; and where there is nothing to be known in a court, but what every body knows out of it, every twelve men is equally as good a jury as the other, and would most probably reverse each other's verdict ; or, from the variety of their opinions, not be able to form one.   It is one case, whether a nation approve a work, or a plan ; but it is quite another case, whether it will commit to any such jury the power of determining whether that nation have a right to, or shall reform its government or not. I mention those cases that Mr. Burke may see I have not written on Government without reflecting on what is Law,

as well as on what are Rights.—The only effectual jury in
such cases would be, a convention of the whole nation
fairly elected ; for in all such cases the whole nation
is the vicinage. If Mr. Burke will propose such a jury, I
will wave all privileges of being the citizen of another country,
and, defending its principles, abide the issue, provided he
will do the same ; for my opinion is, that his work and his
principles would be condemned instead of mine.

As to the prejudices which men have from education and
habit, in favour of any particular form or system of government, those prejudices have yet to stand the test of reason
and reflection. In fact, such prejudices are nothing. No
man is prejudiced in favour of a thing, knowing it to be
wrong. He is attached to it on the belief of its being right ;
and when he sees it is not so, the prejudice will be gone.
We have but a defective idea of what prejudice is. It
might be said, that until men think for themselves the whole
is prejudice, and *not opinion ;* for that only is opinion which is
the result of reason and reflection. I offer this remark,
that Mr. Burke may not confide too much in what have
been the customary prejudices of the country.

I do not believe that the people of England have ever
been fairly and candidly dealt by. They have been imposed upon by parties, and by men assuming the character
of leaders. It is time that the nation should rise above those
trifles. It is time to dismiss that inattention which has so
long been the encouraging cause of stretching taxation to
excess. It is time to dismiss all those songs and toasts
which are calculated to enslave, and operate to suffocate reflection. On all such subjects men have but to think, and
they will neither act wrong nor be misled. To say that any
people are not fit for freedom, is to make poverty their
choice, and to say they had rather be loaded with taxes
than not. If such a case could be proved, it would equally
prove, that those who govern are not fit to govern them, for
they are a part of the same national mass.

But admitting governments to be changed all over Europe ;
it certainly may be done without convulsion or revenge. It

is not worth making changes or revolutions, unless it be for some great national benefit : and when this shall appear to a nation, the danger will be, as in America and France, to those who oppose ; and with this reflection I close my Preface.

THOMAS PAINE.

LONDON, Feb. 9, 1792.

RIGHTS OF MAN.

PART II.

INTRODUCTION.

WHAT Archimedes said of the mechanical powers, may be applied to Reason and Liberty. " *Had we,*" said he, " *a place to stand upon, we might raise the world.*"

The revolution of America presented in politics what was only theory in mechanics. So deeply rooted were all the governments of the old world, and so effectually had the tyranny and the antiquity of habit established itself over the mind, that no beginning could be made in Asia, Africa, or Europe, to reform the political condition of man. Freedom had been hunted round the globe ; reason was considered as rebellion ; and the slavery of fear had made men afraid to think.

But such is the irresistible nature of truth, that all it asks, — and all it wants, — is the liberty of appearing. The sun needs no inscription to distinguish him from darkness ; and no sooner did the American governments display themselves to the world, than despotism felt a shock and man began to contemplate redress.

The independence of America, considered merely as a separation from England, would have been a matter but of little importance, had it not been accompanied by a revolution in the principles and practice of governments. She made a stand, not for herself only, but for the world, and looked beyond the advantages herself could receive. Even the Hessian, though hired to fight against her, may live to bless his defeat; and England, condemning the viciousness of its government, rejoice in its miscarriage.

As America was the only spot in the political world where the principle of universal reformation could begin, so also was it the best in the natural world. An assemblage of circumstances conspired, not only to give birth, but to add gigantic maturity to its principles. The scene which that country presents to the eye of a spectator, has something in it which generates and encourages great ideas. Nature appears to him in magnitude. The mighty objects he beholds, act upon his mind by enlarging it, and he partakes of the greatness he contemplates.—Its first settlers were emigrants from different European nations, and of diversified professions of religion, retiring from the governmental persecutions of the old world, and meeting in the new, not as enemies, but as brothers.[1] The wants which necessarily accompany the cultivation of a wilderness produced among them a state of society, which countries long harassed by the quarrels and intrigues of governments, had neglected to cherish. In such a situation man becomes what he ought. He sees his species, not with the inhuman idea of a natural enemy, but as kindred; and the example shews to the artificial world, that man must go back to Nature for information.

From the rapid progress which America makes in every species of improvement, it is rational to conclude that, if the governments of Asia, Africa, and Europe had begun on a principle similar to that of America, or had not been very early corrupted therefrom, those countries must by this time have been in a far superior condition to what they are. Age after age has passed away, for no other purpose than to behold their wretchedness. Could we suppose a spectator who knew nothing of the world, and who was put into it merely to make his observations, he would take a great part of the old world to be new, just struggling with the difficulties and hardships of an infant settlement. He could not suppose

[1] American colonial history, as explored since Paine's time, mars this rosy picture.—*Editor*.

that the hordes of miserable poor with which old countries
abound could be any other than those who had not yet had
time to provide for themselves. Little would he think they
were the consequence of what in such countries they call
government.

If, from the more wretched parts of the old world, we
look at those which are in an advanced stage of improvement we still find the greedy hand of government thrusting
itself into every corner and crevice of industry, and grasping
the spoil of the multitude. Invention is continually exercised to furnish new pretences for revenue and taxation. It
watches prosperity as its prey, and permits none to escape
without a tribute.

As revolutions have begun, (and as the probability is always greater against a thing beginning, than of proceeding
after it has begun) it is natural to expect that other revolutions will follow. The amazing and still increasing expences
with which old governments are conducted, the numerous
wars they engage in or provoke, the embarrassments they
throw in the way of universal civilization and commerce,
and the oppression and usurpation acted at home, have
wearied out the patience, and exhausted the property of the
world. In such a situation, and with such examples already
existing, revolutions are to be looked for. They are become
subjects of universal conversation, and may be considered
as the *Order of the day.*

If systems of government can be introduced less expensive and more productive of general happiness than those
which have existed, all attempts to oppose their progress
will in the end be fruitless. Reason, like time, will make its
own way, and prejudice will fall in a combat with interest.
If universal peace, civilisation, and commerce are ever to be
the happy lot of man, it cannot be accomplished but by a
revolution in the system of governments. All the monarchical governments are military. War is their trade, plunder
and revenue their objects. While such governments continue, peace has not the absolute security of a day. What is
the history of all monarchical governments but a disgustful

picture of human wretchedness, and the accidental respite of a few years' repose? Wearied with war, and tired with human butchery, they sat down to rest, and called it peace. This certainly is not the condition that heaven intended for man; and if *this be monarchy*, well might monarchy be reckoned among the sins of the Jews.

The revolutions which formerly took place in the world had nothing in them that interested the bulk of mankind. They extended only to a change of persons and measures, but not of principles, and rose or fell among the common transactions of the moment. What we now behold may not improperly be called a "*counter revolution.*" Conquest and tyranny, at some earlier period, dispossessed man of his rights, and he is now recovering them. And as the tide of all human affairs has its ebb and flow in directions contrary to each other, so also is it in this. Government founded on a *moral theory, on a system of universal peace, on the indefeasible hereditary Rights of Man,* is now revolving from west to east by a stronger impulse than the government of the sword revolved from east to west. It interests not particular individuals, but nations in its progress, and promises a new era to the human race.

The danger to which the success of revolutions is most exposed is that of attempting them before the principles on which they proceed, and the advantages to result from them, are sufficiently seen and understood. Almost everything appertaining to the circumstances of a nation, has been absorbed and confounded under the general and mysterious word *government*. Though it avoids taking to its account the errors it commits, and the mischiefs it occasions, it fails not to arrogate to itself whatever has the appearance of prosperity. It robs industry of its honours, by pedanticly making itself the cause of its effects; and purloins from the general character of man, the merits that appertain to him as a social being.

It may therefore be of use in this day of revolutions to discriminate between those things which are the effect of government, and those which are not. This will best be done by taking a review of society and civilisation, and the consequences resulting therefrom, as things distinct from what are called governments. By beginning with this investigation, we shall be able to assign effects to their proper causes and analize the mass of common errors.

CHAPTER I.

OF SOCIETY AND CIVILISATION.

GREAT part of that order which reigns among mankind is not the effect of government. It has its origin in the principles of society and the natural constitution of man. It existed prior to government, and would exist if the formality of government was abolished. The mutual dependence and reciprocal interest which man has upon man, and all the parts of civilised community upon each other, create that great chain of connection which holds it together. The landholder, the farmer, the manufacturer, the merchant, the tradesman, and every occupation, prospers by the aid which each receives from the other, and from the whole. Common interest regulates their concerns, and forms their law ; and the laws which common usage ordains, have a greater influence than the laws of government. In fine society performs for itself almost everything which is ascribed to government.

To understand the nature and quantity of government proper for man, it is necessary to attend to his character. As Nature created him for social life, she fitted him for the station she intended. In all cases she made his natural wants greater than his individual powers. No one man is capable, without the aid of society, of supplying his own wants ; and those wants, acting upon every individual, impel the whole of them into society, as naturally as gravitation acts to a centre.

But she has gone further. She has not only forced man into society by a diversity of wants which the reciprocal aid of each other can supply, but she has implanted in him a system of social affections, which, though not necessary to

his existence, are essential to his happiness. There is no
period in life when this love for society ceases to act. It
begins and ends with our being.

If we examine with attention into the composition and
constitution of man, the diversity of his wants, and the
diversity of talents in different men for reciprocally accommodating the wants of each other, his propensity to society,
and consequently to preserve the advantages resulting from
it, we shall easily discover, that a great part of what is called
government is mere imposition.

Government is no farther necessary than to supply the
few cases to which society and civilisation are not conveniently competent ; and instances are not wanting to
show, that everything which government can usefully add
thereto, has been performed by the common consent of
society, without government.

For upwards of two years from the commencement of the
American War, and to a longer period in several of the
American States, there were no established forms of
government. The old governments had been abolished,
and the country was too much occupied in defence to
employ its attention in establishing new governments; yet
during this interval order and harmony were preserved as
inviolate as in any country in Europe.[1] There is a natural
aptness in man, and more so in society, because it embraces
a greater variety of abilities and resource, to accommodate
itself to whatever situation it is in. The instant formal
government is abolished, society begins to act: a general
association takes place, and common interest produces common security.

So far is it from being true, as has been pretended, that
the abolition of any formal government is the dissolution
of society, that it acts by a contrary impulse, and brings the
latter the closer together. All that part of its organisation
which it had committed to its government, devolves again

---

[1] But a custom of "lynching" loyalists ("tories"), rebuked by Paine,
arose, and some parts of America have never recovered from that cowardly kind
of lawlessness.—*Editor.*

upon itself, and acts through its medium. When men, as well from natural instinct as from reciprocal benefits, have habituated themselves to social and civilised life, there is always enough of its principles in practice to carry them through any changes they may find necessary or convenient to make in their government. In short, man is so naturally a creature of society that it is almost impossible to put him out of it.

Formal government makes but a small part of civilised life ; and when even the best that human wisdom can devise is established, it is a thing more in name and idea than in fact. It is to the great and fundamental principles of society and civilisation—to the common usage universally consented to, and mutually and reciprocally maintained—to the unceasing circulation of interest, which, passing through its million channels, invigorates the whole mass of civilised man—it is to these things, infinitely more than to anything which even the best instituted government can perform, that the safety and prosperity of the individual and of the whole depends.

The more perfect civilisation is, the less occasion has it for government, because the more does it regulate its own affairs, and govern itself ; but so contrary is the practice of old governments to the reason of the case, that the expences of them increase in the proportion they ought to diminish. It is but few general laws that civilised life requires, and those of such common usefulness, that whether they are enforced by the forms of government or not, the effect will be nearly the same. If we consider what the principles are that first condense men into society, and what are the motives that regulate their mutual intercourse afterwards, we shall find, by the time we arrive at what is called government, that nearly the whole of the business is performed by the natural operation of the parts upon each other.

Man, with respect to all those matters, is more a creature of consistency than he is aware, or than governments would wish him to believe. All the great laws of society are laws of nature. Those of trade and commerce, whether with respect to the intercourse of individuals or of nations, are laws of mutual and reciprocal interest. They are followed and obeyed, because it is the interest of the parties so to do, and not on account of any formal laws their governments may impose or interpose.

But how often is the natural propensity to society disturbed or destroyed by the operations of government! When the latter, instead of being ingrafted on the principles of the former, assumes to exist for itself, and acts by partialities of favour and oppression, it becomes the cause of the mischiefs it ought to prevent.

If we look back to the riots and tumults which at various times have happened in England, we shall find that they did not proceed from the want of a government, but that government was itself the generating cause; instead of consolidating society it divided it; it deprived it of its natural cohesion, and engendered discontents and disorders which otherwise would not have existed. In those associations which men promiscuously form for the purpose of trade, or of any concern in which government is totally out of the question, and in which they act merely on the principles of society, we see how naturally the various parties unite; and this shews, by comparison, that governments, so far from being always the cause or means of order, are often the destruction of it. The riots of 1780 had no other source than the remains of those prejudices which the government itself had encouraged. But with respect to England there are also other causes.

Excess and inequality of taxation, however disguised in the means, never fail to appear in their effects. As a great mass of the community are thrown thereby into poverty and discontent, they are constantly on the brink of commotion; and deprived, as they unfortunately are, of the means of information, are easily heated to outrage. Whatever the apparent cause of any riots may be, the real one is always want of happiness. It shews that something is wrong in the system of government that injures the felicity by which society is to be preserved.

But as fact is superior to reasoning, the instance of America presents itself to confirm these observations. If there is a country in the world where concord, according to common calculation, would be least expected, it is America. Made up as it is of people from different nations,* accustomed to different forms and habits of government, speaking different languages, and more different in their modes of worship, it would appear that the union of such a people was impracticable; but by the simple operation of constructing government on the principles of society and the rights of man, every difficulty retires, and all the parts are brought into cordial unison. There the poor are not oppressed, the rich are not privileged. Industry is not mortified by the splendid extravagance of a court rioting at its expence. Their taxes are few, because their government is just: and as there is nothing to render them wretched, there is nothing to engender riots and tumults.

A metaphysical man, like Mr. Burke, would have tortured his invention to discover how such a people could be governed. He would have supposed that some must be managed by fraud, others by force, and all by some contrivance; that genius must be hired to impose upon ignorance, and shew and parade to fascinate the vulgar. Lost in the abundance of his researches, he would have resolved and re-resolved, and finally overlooked the plain and easy road that lay directly before him.

One of the great advantages of the American Revolution has been, that it led to a discovery of the principles, and

---

* That part of America which is generally called New-England, including New-Hampshire, Massachusetts, Rhode-Island, and Connecticut, is peopled chiefly by English descendants. In the state of New-York about half are Dutch, the rest English, Scotch, and Irish. In New-Jersey, a mixture of English and Dutch, with some Scotch and Irish. In Pennsylvania about one third are English, another Germans, and the remainder Scotch and Irish, with some Swedes. The States to the southward have a greater proportion of English than the middle States, but in all of them there is a mixture; and besides those enumerated, there are a considerable number of French, and some few of all the European nations, lying on the coast. The most numerous religious denomination are the Presbyterians; but no one sect is established above another, and all men are equally citizens.—*Author*.

laid open the imposition, of governments. All the revolutions till then had been worked within the atmosphere of a
court, and never on the great floor of a nation. The parties were always of the class of courtiers; and whatever was
their rage for reformation, they carefully preserved the fraud
of the profession.

In all cases they took care to represent government as a
thing made up of mysteries, which only themselves understood; and they hid from the understanding of the nation the
only thing that was beneficial to know, namely, *That government is nothing more than a national association acting on the
principles of society.*

Having thus endeavored to show that the social and civilised state of man is capable of performing within itself
almost everything necessary to its protection and government, it will be proper, on the other hand, to take a review
of the present old governments, and examine whether their
principles and practice are correspondent thereto.

CHAPTER II.

OF THE ORIGIN OF THE PRESENT OLD GOVERNMENTS.

It is impossible that such governments as have hitherto
existed in the world, could have commenced by any other
means than a total violation of every principle sacred and
moral. The obscurity in which the origin of all the present
old governments is buried, implies the iniquity and disgrace
with which they began. The origin of the present government of America and France will ever be remembered,
because it is honourable to record it; but with respect to the
rest, even Flattery has consigned them to the tomb of time,
without an inscription.

It could have been no difficult thing in the early and solitary ages of the world, while the chief employment of men
was that of attending flocks and herds, for a banditti of
ruffians to overrun a country, and lay it under contributions.
Their power being thus established, the chief of the band

contrived to lose the name of Robber in that of Monarch ; and hence the origin of Monarchy and Kings.

The origin of the Government of England, so far as relates to what is called its line of monarchy, being one of the latest, is perhaps the best recorded. The hatred which the Norman invasion and tyranny begat, must have been deeply rooted in the nation, to have outlived the contrivance to obliterate it. Though not a courtier will talk of the curfeubell, not a village in England has forgotten it.

Those bands of robbers having parcelled out the world, and divided it into dominions, began, as is naturally the case, to quarrel with each other. What at first was obtained by violence was considered by others as lawful to be taken, and a second plunderer succeeded the first. They alternately invaded the dominions which each had assigned to himself, and the brutality with which they treated each other explains the original character of monarchy. It was ruffian torturing ruffian. The conqueror considered the conquered, not as his prisoner, but his property. He led him in triumph rattling in chains, and doomed him, at pleasure, to slavery or death. As time obliterated the history of their beginning, their successors assumed new appearances, to cut off the entail of their disgrace, but their principles and objects remained the same. What at first was plunder, assumed the softer name of revenue ; and the power originally usurped, they affected to inherit.

From such beginning of governments, what could be expected but a continued system of war and extortion ? It has established itself into a trade. The vice is not peculiar to one more than to another, but is the common principle of all. There does not exist within such governments sufficient stamina whereon to engraft reformation ; and the shortest and most effectual remedy is to begin anew on the ground of the nation.

What scenes of horror, what perfection of iniquity, present themselves in contemplating the character and reviewing the history of such governments ! If we would delineate human nature with a baseness of heart and hypocrisy of

countenance that reflexion would shudder at and humanity
disown, it is kings, courts and cabinets that must sit for the
portrait. Man, naturally as he is, with all his faults about
him, is not up to the character.

Can we possibly suppose that if governments had originated in a right principle, and had not an interest in pursuing a wrong one, the world could have been in the wretched
and quarrelsome condition we have seen it? What inducement has the farmer, while following the plough, to lay aside
his peaceful pursuit, and go to war with the farmer of another country? or what inducement has the manufacturer?
What is dominion to them, or to any class of men in a nation? Does it add an acre to any man's estate, or raise its
value? Are not conquest and defeat each of the same price,
and taxes the never-failing consequence?—Though this reasoning may be good to a nation, it is not so to a government.
War is the Pharo-table of governments, and nations the dupes
of the game.

If there is anything to wonder at in this miserable scene of
governments more than might be expected, it is the progress
which the peaceful arts of agriculture, manufacture and commerce have made beneath such a long accumulating load of
discouragement and oppression. It serves to shew that instinct in animals does not act with stronger impulse than the
principles of society and civilisation operate in man. Under
all discouragements, he pursues his object, and yields to
nothing but impossibilities.

CHAPTER III.

OF THE OLD AND NEW SYSTEMS OF GOVERNMENT.

NOTHING can appear more contradictory than the principles on which the old governments began, and the condition
to which society, civilisation and commerce are capable of
carrying mankind. Government, on the old system, is an
assumption of power, for the aggrandisement of itself; on
the new, a delegation of power for the common benefit of

society.   The former supports itself by keeping up a system
of war; the latter promotes a system of peace, as the true
means of enriching a nation.   The one encourages national
prejudices; the other promotes universal society, as the
means of universal commerce.   The one measures its prosperity, by the quantity of revenue it extorts; the other
proves its excellence, by the small quantity of taxes it
requires.

Mr. Burke has talked of old and new whigs.   If he can
amuse himself with childish names and distinctions, I shall
not interrupt his pleasure.   It is not to him, but to the Abbé
Sieyès, that I address this chapter.   I am already engaged
to the latter gentleman to discuss the subject of monarchical
government; and as it naturally occurs in comparing the
old and new systems, I make this the opportunity of presenting to him my observations.[1]   I shall occasionally take
Mr. Burke in my way.

Though it might be proved that the system of government now called the NEW, is the most ancient in principle of
all that have existed, being founded on the original, inherent
Rights of Man: yet, as tyranny and the sword have suspended the exercise of those rights for many centuries past,
it serves better the purpose of distinction to call it the *new*,
than to claim the right of calling it the old.

The first general distinction between those two systems, is,
that the one now called the old is *hereditary*, either in whole
or in part; and the new is entirely *representative*.   It rejects
all hereditary government:

First, As being an imposition on mankind.

Secondly, As inadequate to the purposes for which government is necessary.

With respect to the first of these heads—It cannot be

[1] In *Le Républicain*, Paris, July, 1791, Paine wrote a letter in which he declared monarchy and hereditary succession incompatible with the Declaration
of Rights in the new French Constitution.   The Abbé Sieyès (*Moniteur*, July 8,)
announced his intention of maintaining the principle of monarchical executive
against the new party.   Paine accepted the challenge, but Sieyès wrote that he
had "no leisure to enter into controversy with republican *polycrats*."   See my
"Life of Paine," i. p. 312.—*Editor*.

proved by what right hereditary government could begin ; neither does there exist within the compass of mortal power a right to establish it. Man has no authority over posterity in matters of personal right ; and, therefore, no man, or body of men, had, or can have, a right to set up hereditary government. Were even ourselves to come again into existence, instead of being succeeded by posterity, we have not now the right of taking from ourselves the rights which would then be ours. On what ground, then, do we pretend to take them from others ?

All hereditary government is in its nature tyranny. An heritable crown, or an heritable throne, or by what other fanciful name such things may be called, have no other significant explanation than that mankind are heritable property. To inherit a government, is to inherit the people, as if they were flocks and herds.

With respect to the second head, that of being inadequate to the purposes for which government is necessary, we have only to consider what government essentially is, and compare it with the circumstances to which hereditary succession is subject.

Government ought to be a thing always in full maturity. It ought to be so constructed as to be superior to all the accidents to which individual man is subject ; and, therefore, hereditary succession, by being *subject to them all*, is the most irregular and imperfect of all the systems of government.

We have heard the *Rights of Man* called a *levelling* system ; but the only system to which the word *levelling* is truly applicable, is the hereditary monarchical system. It is a system of *mental levelling*. It indiscriminately admits every species of character to the same authority. Vice and virtue, ignorance and wisdom, in short, every quality, good or bad, is put on the same level. Kings succeed each other, not as rationals, but as animals. It signifies not what their mental or moral characters are. Can we then be surprised at the abject state of the human mind in monarchical countries, when the government itself is formed on such an abject levelling system?—It has no fixed character. To-day it is one thing; to-morrow it is something else. It changes with the temper of every succeeding individual, and is subject to all the varieties of each. It is government through the medium of passions and accidents. It appears under all the various characters of childhood, decrepitude, dotage, a thing at nurse, in leading-strings, or in crutches. It reverses the wholesome order of nature. It occasionally puts children over men, and the conceits of non-age over wisdom and experience. In short, we cannot conceive a more ridiculous figure of government, than hereditary succession, in all its cases, presents.

Could it be made a decree in nature, or an edict registered in heaven, and man could know it, that virtue and wisdom should invariably appertain to hereditary succession, the objection to it would be removed ; but when we see that nature acts as if she disowned and sported with the hereditary system ; that the mental character of successors, in all countries, is below the average of human understanding; that one is a tyrant, another an idiot, a third insane, and some all three together, it is impossible to attach confidence to it, when reason in man has power to act.

It is not to the Abbé Sieyès that I need apply this reasoning ; he has already saved me that trouble by giving his own opinion upon the case. "If it be asked," says he, "what is my opinion with respect to hereditary right, I answer without hesitation, That in good theory, an hereditary transmission of any power of office, can never accord with the laws of a true representation. Hereditaryship is, in this sense, as much an attaint upon principle, as an outrage upon society. But let us," continues he, "refer to the history of all elective monarchies and principalities : is there one in which the elective mode is not worse than the hereditary succession ?"

As to debating on which is the worst of the two, it is admitting both to be bad ; and herein we are agreed. The preference which the Abbé has given, is a condemnation of the thing that he prefers. Such a mode of reasoning on such a subject is inadmissible, because it finally amounts to

an accusation upon Providence, as if she had left to man no
other choice with respect to government than between two
evils, the best of which he admits to be " *an attaint upon principle, and an outrage upon society.*"

Passing over, for the present, all the evils and mischiefs
which monarchy has occasioned in the world, nothing can
more effectually prove its uselessness in a state of *civil government*, than making it hereditary. Would we make any
office hereditary that required wisdom and abilities to fill
it ? And where wisdom and abilities are not necessary,
such an office, whatever it may be, is superfluous or insignificant.

Hereditary succession is a burlesque upon monarchy.   It
puts it in the most ridiculous light, by presenting it as an
office which any child or ideot may fill.   It requires some
talents to be a common mechanic; but to be a king requires
only the animal figure of man—a sort of breathing automa-
ton.   This sort of superstition may last a few years more,
but it cannot long resist the awakened reason and interest
of man.

As to Mr. Burke, he is a stickler for monarchy, not altogether as a pensioner, if he is one, which I believe, but as a
political man.   He has taken up a contemptible opinion of
mankind, who, in their turn, are taking up the same of him.
He considers them as a herd of beings that must be governed
by fraud, effigy, and show ; and an idol would be as good a
figure of monarchy with him, as a man.   I will, however,
do him the justice to say that, with respect to America, he
has been very complimentary.   He always contended, at
least in my hearing, that the people of America were more
enlightened than those of England, or of any country in
Europe ; and that therefore the imposition of shew was not
necessary in their governments.

Though the comparison between hereditary and elective
monarchy, which the Abbé has made, is unnecessary to the
case, because the representative system rejects both : yet,
were I to make the comparison, I should decide contrary to
what he has done.

The civil wars which have originated from contested hereditary claims, are more numerous, and have been more dreadful, and of longer continuance, than those which have been
occasioned by election.   All the civil wars in France arose
from the hereditary system ; they were either produced by
hereditary claims, or by the imperfection of the hereditary
form, which admits of regencies or monarchy at nurse.   With
respect to England, its history is full of the same misfortunes.   The contests for succession between the houses of
York and Lancaster, lasted a whole century ; and others of a
similar nature, have renewed themselves since that period.
Those of 1715 and 1745, were of the same kind.   The succession war for the crown of Spain, embroiled almost half
Europe.   The disturbances in Holland are generated from
the hereditaryship of the Stadtholder.   A government calling itself free, with an hereditary office, is like a thorn in the
flesh, that produces a fermentation which endeavours to
discharge it.

But I might go further, and place also foreign wars, of whatever kind, to the same cause.   It is by adding the evil of
hereditary succession to that of monarchy, that a permanent
family interest is created, whose constant objects are dominion and revenue.   Poland, though an elective monarchy, has
had fewer wars than those which are hereditary ; and it
is the only government that has made a voluntary essay,
though but a small one, to reform the condition of the
country.

Having thus glanced at a few of the defects of the old,
or hereditary systems of government, let us compare it with
the new, or representative system.

The representative system takes society and civilisation
for its basis ; nature, reason, and experience, for its guide.

Experience, in all ages, and in all countries, has demonstrated that it is impossible to controul Nature in her distribution of mental powers.   She gives them as she pleases.
Whatever is the rule by which she, apparently to us, scatters
them among mankind, that rule remains a secret to man.   It
would be as ridiculous to attempt to fix the hereditaryship

of human beauty, as of wisdom. Whatever wisdom con-
stituently is, it is like a seedless plant; it may be reared
when it appears, but it cannot be voluntarily produced.
There is always a sufficiency somewhere in the general mass
of society for all purposes; but with respect to the parts of
society, it is continually changing its place. It rises in one
to-day, in another to-morrow, and has most probably visited
in rotation every family of the earth, and again withdrawn.

As this is in the order of nature, the order of government
must necessarily follow it, or government will, as we see it
does, degenerate into ignorance. The hereditary system,
therefore, is as repugnant to human wisdom as to human
rights; and is as absurd as it is unjust.

As the republic of letters brings forward the best literary
productions, by giving to genius a fair and universal chance;
so the representative system of government is calculated to
produce the wisest laws, by collecting wisdom from where it
can be found. I smile to myself when I contemplate the
ridiculous insignificance into which literature and all the sciences would sink, were they made hereditary; and I carry
the same idea into governments. An hereditary governor
is as inconsistent as an hereditary author. I know not
whether Homer or Euclid had sons; but I will venture an
opinion that if they had, and had left their works unfinished,
those sons could not have completed them.

Do we need a stronger evidence of the absurdity of hereditary government than is seen in the descendants of those
men, in any line of life, who once were famous? Is there
scarcely an instance in which there is not a total reverse of
the character? It appears as if the tide of mental faculties
flowed as far as it could in certain channels, and then for-
sook its course, and arose in others. How irrational then
is the hereditary system, which establishes channels of
power, in company with which wisdom refuses to flow! By
continuing this absurdity, man is perpetually in contradiction with himself; he accepts, for a king, or a chief magistrate, or a legislator, a person whom he would not elect
for a constable.

It appears to general observation, that revolutions create genius and talents; but those events do no more than bring them forward. There is existing in man, a mass of sense lying in a dormant state, and which, unless something excites it to action, will descend with him, in that condition, to the grave. As it is to the advantage of society that the whole of its faculties should be employed, the construction of government ought to be such as to bring forward, by a quiet and regular operation, all that extent of capacity which never fails to appear in revolutions.

This cannot take place in the insipid state of hereditary government, not only because it prevents, but because it operates to benumb. When the mind of a nation is bowed down by any political superstition in its government, such as hereditary succession is, it loses a considerable portion of its powers on all other subjects and objects. Hereditary succession requires the same obedience to ignorance, as to wisdom; and when once the mind can bring itself to pay this indiscriminate reverence, it descends below the stature of mental manhood. It is fit to be great only in little things. It acts a treachery upon itself, and suffocates the sensations that urge the detection.

Though the ancient governments present to us a miserable picture of the condition of man, there is one which above all others exempts itself from the general description. I mean the democracy of the Athenians. We see more to admire, and less to condemn, in that great, extraordinary people, than in anything which history affords.

Mr. Burke is so little acquainted with constituent principles of government, that he confounds democracy and representation together. Representation was a thing unknown in the ancient democracies. In those the mass of the people met and enacted laws (grammatically speaking) in the first person. Simple democracy was no other than the common hall of the ancients. It signifies the *form*, as well as the public principle of the government. As those democracies increased in population, and the territory extended, the simple democratical form became unwieldy and impracticable; and as the system of representation was not known,

the consequence was, they either degenerated convulsively
into monarchies, or became absorbed into such as then
existed. Had the system of representation been then understood, as it now is, there is no reason to believe that those
forms of government, now called monarchical or aristocratical, would ever have taken place. It was the want of some
method to consolidate the parts of society, after it became
too populous, and too extensive for the simple democratical
form, and also the lax and solitary condition of shepherds
and herdsmen in other parts of the world, that afforded opportunities to those unnatural modes of government to begin.

As it is necessary to clear away the rubbish of errors, into
which the subject of government has been thrown, I will
proceed to remark on some others.

It has always been the political craft of courtiers and
court-governments, to abuse something which they called
republicanism ; but what republicanism was, or is, they never
attempt to explain. Let us examine a little into this case.

The only forms of government are, the democratical, the
aristocratical, the monarchical, and what is now called the
representative.

What is called a *republic* is not any *particular form* of
government. It is wholly characteristical of the purport,
matter or object for which government ought to be instituted, and on which it is to be employed, RES-PUBLICA, the
public affairs, or the public good ; or, literally translated, the
public thing. It is a word of a good original, referring to
what ought to be the character and business of government ;
and in this sense it is naturally opposed to the word *monarchy*, which has a base original signification. It means
arbitrary power in an individual person ; in the exercise of
which, *himself*, and not the *res-publica*, is the object.

Every government that does not act on the principle of a
Republic, or in other words, that does not make the *res-
publica* its whole and sole object, is not a good government.
Republican government is no other than government established and conducted for the interest of the public, as well
individually as collectively. It is not necessarily connected
with any particular form, but it most naturally associates

with the representative form, as being best calculated to secure the end for which a nation is at the expense of supporting it.

Various forms of government have affected to style them-selves a republic. Poland calls itself a republic, which is an hereditary aristocracy, with what is called an elective mon-archy. Holland calls itself a republic, which is chiefly aristocratical, with an hereditary stadtholdership. But the government of America, which is wholly on the system of representation, is the only real Republic, in character and in practice, that now exists. Its government has no other object than the public business of the nation, and therefore it is properly a republic; and the Americans have taken care that THIS, and no other, shall always be the object of their government, by their rejecting everything hereditary, and establishing government on the system of representation only. Those who have said that a republic is not a *form* of government calculated for countries of great extent, mistook, in the first place, the *business* of a government, for a *form* of government; for the *res-publica* equally appertains to every extent of territory and population. And, in the second place, if they meant anything with respect to *form*, it was the simple democratical form, such as was the mode of government in the ancient democracies, in which there was no representation. The case, therefore, is not, that a repub-lic cannot be extensive, but that it cannot be extensive on the simple democratical form; and the question naturally presents itself, *What is the best form of government for con-ducting the* RES-PUBLICA, *or the* PUBLIC BUSINESS *of a nation, after it becomes too extensive and populous for the simple democratical form?* It cannot be monarchy, because mon-archy is subject to an objection of the same amount to which the simple democratical form was subject.

It is possible that an individual may lay down a system of principles, on which government shall be constitutionally established to any extent of territory. This is no more than an operation of the mind, acting by its own powers. But the practice upon those principles, as applying to the various and numerous circumstances of a nation, its agriculture,

manufacture, trade, commerce, etc., etc., requires a knowledge of a different kind, and which can be had only from
the various parts of society.   It is an assemblage of practical
knowledge, which no individual can possess; and therefore
the monarchical form is as much limited, in useful practice,
from the incompetency of knowledge, as was the democratical form, from the multiplicity of population.   The one
degenerates, by extension, into confusion; the other, into
ignorance and incapacity, of which all the great monarchies
are an evidence.   The monarchical form, therefore, could not
be a substitute for the democratical, because it has equal
inconveniences.

Much less could it when made hereditary.   This is the
most effectual of all forms to preclude knowledge.   Neither
could the high democratical mind have voluntarily yielded
itself to be governed by children and ideots, and all the
motley insignificance of character, which attends such a mere
animal system, the disgrace and the reproach of reason and
of man.

As to the aristocratical form, it has the same vices and
defects with the monarchical, except that the chance of
abilities is better from the proportion of numbers, but there
is still no security for the right use and application of
them.*

Referring them to the original simple democracy, it affords
the true data from which government on a large scale can
begin.   It is incapable of extension, not from its principle,
but from the inconvenience of its form ; and monarchy and
aristocracy, from their incapacity.   Retaining, then, democracy as the ground, and rejecting the corrupt systems of
monarchy and aristocracy, the representative system naturally
presents itself ; remedying at once the defects of the simple
democracy as to form, and the incapacity of the other two
with respect to knowledge.

Simple democracy was society governing itself without
the aid of secondary means.   By ingrafting representation

* For a character of aristocracy, the reader is referred to *Rights of Man*,
Part I., p. 319.—*Author*.

upon democracy, we arrive at a system of government capable of embracing and confederating all the various interests and every extent of territory and population; and that also with advantages as much superior to hereditary government, as the republic of letters is to hereditary literature.

It is on this system that the American government is founded. It is representation ingrafted upon democracy. It has fixed the form by a scale parallel in all cases to the extent of the principle. What Athens was in miniature America will be in magnitude. The one was the wonder of the ancient world; the other is becoming the admiration, the model of the present. It is the easiest of all the forms of government to be understood and the most eligible in practice; and excludes at once the ignorance and insecurity of the hereditary mode, and the inconvenience of the simple democracy.

It is impossible to conceive a system of government capable of acting over such an extent of territory, and such a circle of interests, as is immediately produced by the operation of representation. France, great and populous as it is, is but a spot in the capaciousness of the system. It is preferable to simple democracy even in small territories. Athens, by representation, would have outrivalled her own democracy.

That which is called government, or rather that which we ought to conceive government to be, is no more than some common center in which all the parts of society unite. This cannot be accomplished by any method so conducive to the various interests of the community, as by the representative system. It concentrates the knowledge necessary to the interest of the parts, and of the whole. It places government in a state of constant maturity. It is, as has already been observed, never young, never old. It is subject neither to nonage, nor dotage. It is never in the cradle, nor on crutches. It admits not of a separation between knowledge and power, and is superior, as government always ought to be, to all the accidents of individual man, and is therefore superior to what is called monarchy.

A nation is not a body, the figure of which is to be represented by the human body; but is like a body contained
within a circle, having a common center, in which every radius
meets; and that center is formed by representation. To
connect representation with what is called monarchy, is
eccentric government. Representation is of itself the delegated monarchy of a nation, and cannot debase itself by
dividing it with another.

Mr. Burke has two or three times, in his parliamentary
speeches, and in his publications, made use of a jingle of
words that convey no ideas. Speaking of government, he
says, " It is better to have monarchy for its basis, and
republicanism for its corrective, than republicanism for its
basis, and monarchy for its corrective."—If he means that
it is better to correct folly with wisdom, than wisdom with
folly, I will no otherwise contend with him, than that it
would be much better to reject the folly entirely.

But what is this thing which Mr. Burke calls monarchy?
Will he explain it? All men can understand what representation is; and that it must necessarily include a variety of
knowledge and talents. But what security is there for the
same qualities on the part of monarchy? or, when the monarchy is a child, where then is the wisdom? What does it
know about government? Who then is the monarch, or
where is the monarchy? If it is to be performed by
regency, it proves to be a farce. A regency is a mock
species of republic, and the whole of monarchy deserves no
better description. It is a thing as various as imagination
can paint. It has none of the stable character that government ought to possess. Every succession is a revolution,
and every regency a counter-revolution. The whole of it is
a scene of perpetual court cabal and intrigue, of which Mr.
Burke is himself an instance. To render monarchy consistent with government, the next in succession should not be
born a child, but a man at once, and that man a Solomon.
It is ridiculous that nations are to wait and government be
interrupted till boys grow to be men.

Whether I have too little sense to see, or too much to be

imposed upon; whether I have too much or too little pride, or of anything else, I leave out of the question; but certain it is, that what is called monarchy, always appears to me a silly, contemptible thing. I compare it to something kept behind a curtain, about which there is a great deal of bustle and fuss, and a wonderful air of seeming solemnity; but when, by any accident, the curtain happens to be open—and the company see what it is, they burst into laughter.

In the representative system of government, nothing of this can happen. Like the nation itself, it possesses a perpetual stamina, as well of body, as of mind, and presents itself on the open theatre of the world in a fair and manly manner. Whatever are its excellences or defects, they are visible to all. It exists not by fraud and mystery; it deals not in cant and sophistry; but inspires a language that, passing from heart to heart, is felt and understood.

We must shut our eyes against reason, we must basely degrade our understanding, not to see the folly of what is called monarchy. Nature is orderly in all her works; but this is a mode of government that counteracts nature. It turns the progress of the human faculties upside down. It subjects age to be governed by children, and wisdom by folly.

On the contrary, the representative system is always parallel with the order and immutable laws of nature, and meets the reason of man in every part. For example:

In the American Federal Government, more power is delegated to the President of the United States than to any other individual member of Congress.[1] He cannot, therefore, be elected to this office under the age of thirty-five years. By this time the judgment of man becomes more matured, and he has lived long enough to be acquainted with men and things, and the country with him.—But on the monarchial plan (exclusive of the numerous chances there are against every man born into the world, of drawing a prize in the lottery of human faculties), the next in succession, whatever he may be, is put at the head of a

---

[1] It was not uncommon in England, when the United States government began, to speak of the President as "the President of Congress."—Editor.

nation, and of a government, at the age of eighteen years.
Does this appear like an action of wisdom? Is it consistent
with the proper dignity and the manly character of a
nation? Where is the propriety of calling such a lad the
father of the people?—In all other cases, a person is a
minor until the age of twenty-one years. Before this period,
he is not trusted with the management of an acre of land,
or with the heritable property of a flock of sheep, or an herd
of swine; but, wonderful to tell! he may, at the age of
eighteen years, be trusted with a nation.

That monarchy is all a bubble, a mere court artifice to
procure money, is evident (at least to me,) in every character in which it can be viewed. It would be impossible, on
the rational system of representative government, to make
out a bill of expences to such an enormous amount as this
deception admits. Government is not of itself a very
chargeable institution. The whole expence of the federal
government of America, founded, as I have already said,
on the system of representation, and extending over a
country nearly ten times as large as England, is but six
hundred thousand dollars, or one hundred and thirty-five
thousand pounds sterling.

I presume, that no man in his sober senses, will compare
the character of any of the kings of Europe with that of
General Washington. Yet, in France, and also in England,
the expence of the civil list only, for the support of one
man, is eight times greater than the whole expence of the
federal government in America. To assign a reason for this,
appears almost impossible. The generality of people in
America, especially the poor, are more able to pay taxes,
than the generality of people either in France or England.

But the case is, that the representative system diffuses
such a body of knowledge throughout a nation, on the subject of government, as to explode ignorance and preclude
imposition. The craft of courts cannot be acted on that
ground. There is no place for mystery; nowhere for it to
begin. Those who are not in the representation, know as
much of the nature of business as those who are. An affec-

tation of mysterious importance would there be scouted. Nations can have no secrets; and the secrets of courts, like those of individuals, are always their defects.

In the representative system, the reason for everything must publicly appear. Every man is a proprietor in government, and considers it a necessary part of his business to understand. It concerns his interest, because it affects his property. He examines the cost, and compares it with the advantages; and above all, he does not adopt the slavish custom of following what in other governments are called LEADERS.

It can only be by blinding the understanding of man, and making him believe that government is some wonderful mysterious thing, that excessive revenues are obtained. Monarchy is well calculated to ensure this end. It is the popery of government; a thing kept up to amuse the ignorant, and quiet them into taxes.

The government of a free country, properly speaking, is not in the persons, but in the laws. The enacting of those requires no great expence; and when they are administered, the whole of civil government is performed—the rest is all court contrivance.

CHAPTER IV.

OF CONSTITUTIONS.

THAT men mean distinct and separate things when they speak of constitutions and of governments, is evident; or why are those terms distinctly and separately used? A constitution is not the act of a government, but of a people constituting a government; and government without a constitution, is power without a right.

All power exercised over a nation, must have some beginning. It must either be delegated or assumed. There are no other sources. All delegated power is trust, and all assumed power is usurpation. Time does not alter the nature and quality of either.

In viewing this subject, the case and circumstances of

America present themselves as in the beginning of a world; and our enquiry into the origin of government is shortened, by referring to the facts that have arisen in our own day. We have no occasion to roam for information into the obscure field of antiquity, nor hazard ourselves upon conjecture. We are brought at once to the point of seeing government begin, as if we had lived in the beginning of time. The real volume, not of history, but of facts, is directly before us, unmutilated by contrivance, or the errors of tradition.

I will here concisely state the commencement of the American constitutions; by which the difference between constitutions and governments will sufficiently appear.

It may not be improper to remind the reader that the United States of America consist of thirteen separate states, each of which established a government for itself, after the declaration of independence, done the 4th of July, 1776. Each state acted independently of the rest, in forming its governments; but the same general principle pervades the whole. When the several state governments were formed, they proceeded to form the federal government, that acts over the whole in all matters which concern the interest of the whole, or which relate to the intercourse of the several states with each other, or with foreign nations. I will begin with giving an instance from one of the state governments (that of Pennsylvania) and then proceed to the federal government.

The State of Pennsylvania, though nearly of the same extent of territory as England, was then divided into only twelve counties. Each of those counties had elected a committee at the commencement of the dispute with the English government; and as the city of Philadelphia, which also had its committee, was the most central for intelligence, it became the center of communication to the several county committees. When it became necessary to proceed to the formation of a government, the committee of Philadelphia proposed a conference of all the committees, to be held in that city, and which met the latter end of July, 1776.

Though these committees had been duly elected by the people, they were not elected expressly for the purpose, nor invested with the authority of forming a constitution ; and as they could not, consistently with the American idea of rights, assume such a power, they could only confer upon the matter, and put it into a train of operation. The conferees, therefore, did no more than state the case, and recommend to the several counties to elect six representatives for each county, to meet in convention at Philadelphia, with powers to form a constitution, and propose it for public consideration.

This convention, of which Benjamin Franklin was president, having met and deliberated, and agreed upon a constitution, they next ordered it to be published, not as a thing established, but for the consideration of the whole people, their approbation or rejection, and then adjourned to a stated time. When the time of adjournment was expired, the convention re-assembled ; and as the general opinion of the people in approbation of it was then known, the constitution was signed, sealed, and proclaimed on the *authority of the people* and the original instrument deposited as a public record. The convention then appointed a day for the general election of the representatives who were to compose the government, and the time it should commence ; and having done this they dissolved, and returned to their several homes and occupations.

In this constitution were laid down, first, a declaration of rights ; then followed the form which the government should have, and the powers it should possess—the authority of the courts of judicature, and of juries—the manner in which elections should be conducted, and the proportion of representatives to the number of electors—the time which each succeeding assembly should continue, which was one year— the mode of levying, and of accounting for the expenditure, of public money—of appointing public officers, etc., etc., etc.

No article of this constitution could be altered or infringed at the discretion of the government that was to ensue. It was to that government a law. But as it would have been unwise to preclude the benefit of experience, and in order also to prevent the accumulation of errors, if any should be found, and to preserve an unison of government with the circumstances of the State at all times, the constitution provided, that, at the expiration of every seven years, a convention should be elected, for the express purpose of revising the constitution, and making alterations, additions, or abolitions therein, if any such should be found necessary.

Here we see a regular process—a government issuing out of a constitution, formed by the people in their original character ; and that constitution serving, not only as an authority, but as an law of controul to the government. It was the political bible of the state. Scarcely a family was without it. Every member of the government had a copy ; and nothing was more common, when any debate arose on the principle of a bill, or on the extent of any species of authority, than for the members to take the printed constitution out of their pocket, and read the chapter with which such matter in debate was connected.

Having thus given an instance from one of the states, I will shew the proceedings by which the federal constitution of the United States arose and was formed.

Congress, at its two first meetings, in September 1774, and May 1775, was nothing more than a deputation from the legislatures of the several provinces, afterwards states ; and had no other authority than what arose from common consent, and the necessity of its acting as a public body. In everything which related to the internal affairs of America, congress went no further than to issue recommendations to the several provincial assemblies, who at discretion adopted them or not. Nothing on the part of congress was compulsive ; yet, in this situation, it was more faithfully and affectionately obeyed than was any government in Europe. This instance, like that of the national assembly in France, sufficiently shows, that the strength of government does not consist in any thing WITHIN itself, but in the attachment of a nation, and the interest which a people feel in supporting it. When this is lost, government is but a child in power ;

and though, like the old government in France, it may harrass individuals for a while, it but facilitates its own fall.

After the declaration of independence, it became consistent with the principle on which representative government is founded, that the authority of congress should be defined and established. Whether that authority should be more or less than congress then discretionarily exercised was not the question. It was merely the rectitude of the measure.

For this purpose, the act, called the act of confederation, (which was a sort of imperfect federal constitution), was proposed, and, after long deliberation, was concluded in the year 1781. It was not the act of congress, because it is repugnant to the principles of representative government that a body should give power to itself. Congress first informed the several states, of the powers which it conceived were necessary to be invested in the union, to enable it to perform the duties and services required from it; and the states severally agreed with each other, and concentrated in congress those powers.

It may not be improper to observe, that in both those instances, (the one of Pennsylvania, and the other of the United States), there is no such thing as the idea of a compact between the people on one side, and the government on the other. The compact was that of the people with each other, to produce and constitute a government. To suppose that any government can be a party in a compact with the whole people, is to suppose it to have existence before it can have a right to exist. The only instance in which a compact can take place between the people and those who exercise the government, is, that the people shall pay them, while they chuse to employ them.

Government is not a trade which any man, or any body of men, has a right to set up and exercise for his own emolument, but is altogether a trust, in right of those by whom that trust is delegated, and by whom it is always resumeable. It has of itself no rights; they are altogether duties.

Having thus given two instances of the original formation

of a constitution, I will shew the manner in which both
have been changed since their first establishment.

The powers vested in the governments of the several
states, by the state constitutions, were found, upon experience, to be too great; and those vested in the federal
government, by the act of confederation, too little. The
defect was not in the principle, but in the distribution of
power.

Numerous publications, in pamphlets and in the newspapers, appeared, on the propriety and necessity of new
modelling the federal government. After some time of
public discussion, carried on through the channel of the
press, and in conversations, the state of Virginia, experiencing some inconvenience with respect to commerce, proposed holding a continental conference; in consequence of
which, a deputation from five or six state assemblies met at
Annapolis, in Maryland, in 1786. This meeting, not conceiving itself sufficiently authorised to go into the business
of a reform, did no more than state their general opinions
of the propriety of the measure, and recommend that a convention of all the states should be held the year following.

The convention met at Philadelphia in May, 1787, of
which General Washington was elected president. He was
not at that time connected with any of the state governments, or with congress. He delivered up his commission
when the war ended, and since then had lived a private
citizen.

The Convention went deeply into all the subjects; and
having, after a variety of debate and investigation, agreed
among themselves upon the several parts of a federal constitution, the next question was, the manner of giving it
authority and practice.

For this purpose they did not, like a cabal of courtiers,
send for a Dutch Stadtholder, or a German Elector; but
they referred the whole matter to the sense and interest of
the country.

They first directed that the proposed constitution should be
published. Secondly, that each state should elect a conven-

tion, expressly for the purpose of taking it into consideration, and of ratifying or rejecting it ; and that as soon as the approbation and ratification of any nine states should be given, that those states shall proceed to the election of their proportion of members to the new federal government; and that the operation of it should then begin, and the former federal government cease.

The several States proceeded accordingly to elect their conventions. Some of those conventions ratified the constitution by very large majorities, and two or three unanimously. In others there were much debate and division of opinion. In the Massachussetts convention, which met at Boston, the majority was not above nineteen or twenty, in about three hundred members ; but such is the nature of representative government, that it quietly decides all matters by majority. After the debate in the Massachussetts convention was closed, and the vote taken, the objecting members rose and declared, "*That though they had argued and voted against it, because certain parts appeared to them in a different light to what they appeared to other members ; yet, as the vote had decided in favour of the constitution as proposed, they should give it the same practical support as if they had voted for it.*"

As soon as nine states had concurred (and the rest followed in the order their conventions were elected), the old fabric of the federal government was taken down, and the new one erected, of which General Washington is president. —In this place I cannot help remarking, that the character and services of this gentleman are sufficient to put all those men called kings to shame. While they are receiving from the sweat and labours of mankind, a prodigality of pay, to which neither their abilities nor their services can entitle them, he is rendering every service in his power, and refusing every pecuniary reward. He accepted no pay as commander-in-chief ; he accepts none as president of the United States.[1]

---

[1] It had not been made known to the world that Washington had receded from this determination, announced at his inauguration. He received payment like other Presidents.—*Editor*.

After the new federal constitution was established, the
state of Pennsylvania, conceiving that some parts of its own
constitution required to be altered, elected a convention for
that purpose. The proposed alterations were published,
and the people concurring therein, they were established.

In forming those constitutions, or in altering them, little
or no inconvenience took place. The ordinary course of
things was not interrupted, and the advantages have been
much. It is always the interest of a far greater number of
people in a nation to have things right, than to let them
remain wrong; and when public matters are open to debate,
and the public judgment free, it will not decide wrong,
unless it decides too hastily.

In the two instances of changing the constitutions, the
governments then in being were not actors either way.[1]
Government has no right to make itself a party in any
debate respecting the principles or modes of forming, or of
changing, constitutions. It is not for the benefit of those
who exercise the powers of government that constitutions,
and the governments issuing from them, are established.
In all those matters the right of judging and acting are in
those who pay, and not in those who receive.

A constitution is the property of a nation, and not of
those who exercise the government. All the constitutions
of America are declared to be established on the authority
of the people. In France, the word nation is used instead
of the people; but in both cases, a constitution is a thing
antecedent to the government, and always distinct therefrom.

In England it is not difficult to perceive that everything
has a constitution, except the nation. Every society and
association that is established, first agreed upon a number of
original articles, digested into form, which are its constitution. It then appointed its officers, whose powers and
authorities are described in that constitution, and the gov-

---

[1] Not quite correct as to the United States. The old Congress invited the
States to send delegates to the Constitutional Convention, appointed the day of
meeting, and submitted their work to the several States for ratification.—
Editor.

ernment of that society then commenced. Those officers, by whatever name they are called, have no authority to add to, alter, or abridge the original articles. It is only to the constituting power that this right belongs.

From the want of understanding the difference between a constitution and a government, Dr. Johnson, and all writers of his description, have always bewildered themselves. They could not but perceive, that there must necessarily be a *controuling* power existing somewhere, and they placed this power in the discretion of the persons exercising the government, instead of placing it in a constitution formed by the nation. When it is in a constitution, it has the nation for its support, and the natural and the political controuling powers are together. The laws which are enacted by governments, controul men only as individuals, but the nation, through its constitution, controuls the whole government, and has a natural ability to do so. The final controuling power, therefore, and the original constituting power, are one and the same power.

Dr. Johnson could not have advanced such a position in any country where there was a constitution ; and he is himself an evidence that no such thing as a constitution exists in England. But it may be put as a question, not improper to be investigated, that if a constitution does not exist, how came the idea of its existence so generally established ?

In order to decide this question, it is necessary to consider a constitution in both its cases :—First, as creating a government and giving it powers. Secondly, as regulating and restraining the powers so given.

If we begin with William of Normandy, we find that the government of England was originally a tyranny, founded on an invasion and conquest of the country. This being admitted, it will then appear, that the exertion of the nation, at different periods, to abate that tyranny, and render it less intolerable, has been credited for a constitution.

Magna Charta, as it was called (it is now like an almanack of the same date), was no more than compelling the govern-

ment to renounce a part of its assumptions. It did not
create and give powers to government in a manner a constitution does; but was, as far as it went, of the nature of a
re-conquest, and not a constitution; for could the nation
have totally expelled the usurpation, as France has done its
despotism, it would then have had a constitution to form.

The history of the Edwards and the Henries, and up to
the commencement of the Stuarts, exhibits as many instances of tyranny as could be acted within the limits to
which the nation had restricted it. The Stuarts endeavoured
to pass those limits, and their fate is well known. In all
those instances we see nothing of a constitution, but only
of restrictions on assumed power.

After this, another William, descended from the same
stock, and claiming from the same origin, gained possession;
and of the two evils, *James* and *William*, the nation pre-
ferred what it thought the least; since, from circumstances,
it must take one. The act, called the Bill of Rights, comes
here into view. What is it, but a bargain, which the parts of
the government made with each other to divide powers,
profits, and privileges? You shall have so much, and I will
have the rest; and with respect to the nation, it said, for
your share, YOU *shall have the right of petitioning.* This
being the case, the bill of rights is more properly a bill of
wrongs, and of insult. As to what is called the convention
parliament, it was a thing that made itself, and then made
the authority by which it acted. A few persons got together, and called themselves by that name. Several of them
had never been elected, and none of them for the purpose.

From the time of William a species of government arose,
issuing out of this coalition bill of rights; and more so,
since the corruption introduced at the Hanover succession
by the agency of Walpole; that can be described by no
other name than a despotic legislation. Though the parts
may embarrass each other, the whole has no bounds; and
the only right it acknowledges out of itself, is the right of
petitioning. Where then is the constitution either that
gives or restrains power?

It is not because a part of the government is elective, that makes it less a despotism, if the persons so elected possess afterwards, as a parliament, unlimited powers. Election, in this case, becomes separated from representation, and the candidates are candidates for despotism.[1]

I cannot believe that any nation, reasoning on its own rights, would have thought of calling these things *a constitution*, if the cry of constitution had not been set up by the government. It has got into circulation like the words *bore* and *quoz* [*quiz*], by being chalked up in the speeches of parliament, as those words were on window shutters and doorposts; but whatever the constitution may be in other respects, it has undoubtedly been *the most productive machine of taxation that was ever invented.* The taxes in France, under the new constitution, are not quite thirteen shillings per head,* and the taxes in England, under what is called its present constitution, are forty-eight shillings and sixpence per head—men, women, and children—amounting to nearly seventeen millions sterling, besides the expence of collecting, which is upwards of a million more.

---

[1] This and the three preceding paragraphs were omitted by Paine in his cheap edition (Symonds, 1792) with the following statement : "Here follow, on page 52 of the original edition, four paragraphs. As those paragraphs are put into the information, and will publicly appear with the pleadings thereon, when the prosecution shall be brought to an issue, they are not verbally recited here, except the first of them, which is added in the annexed note, for the purpose of shewing the spirit of the prosecuting party, and the sort of matter which has been selected from the work for prosecution." After the note he adds : "Query. Does the prosecuting party mean to deny that instances of tyranny were acted by the Edwards and Henries ? Does he mean to deny that the Stuarts endeavoured to pass the limits which the nation had prescribed ? Does he mean to prove it libellous in any person to say that they did ? "— *Editor.*

* The whole amount of the assessed taxes of France, for the present year, is three hundred millions of francs, which is twelve millions and a half sterling ; and the incidental taxes are estimated at three millions, making in the whole fifteen millions and a half ; which among twenty-four millions of people, is not quite thirteen shillings per head. France has lessened her taxes since the revolution, nearly nine millions sterling annually. Before the revolution, the city of Paris paid a duty of upwards of thirty per cent. on all articles brought into the city. This tax was collected at the city gates. It was taken off on the first of last May, and the gates taken down.—*Author.*

In a country like England, where the whole of the civil
Government is executed by the people of every town and
county, by means of parish officers, magistrates, quarterly
sessions, juries, and assize; without any trouble to what is
called the government or any other expence to the revenue
than the salary of the judges, it is astonishing how such a
mass of taxes can be employed. Not even the internal
defence of the country is paid out of the revenue. On all
occasions, whether real or contrived, recourse is continually
had to new loans and new taxes. No wonder, then, that a
machine of government so advantageous to the advocates
of a court, should be so triumphantly extolled! No wonder, that St. James's or St. Stephen's should echo with the
continual cry of constitution; no wonder, that the French
revolution should be reprobated, and the *res-publica* treated
with reproach! The *red book* of England, like the red
book of France, will explain the reason.*

I will now, by way of relaxation, turn a thought or two
to Mr. Burke. I ask his pardon for neglecting him so long.

" America," says he (in his speech on the Canada Constitution bill), " never dreamed of such absurd doctrine as the
Rights of Man."

Mr. Burke is such a bold presumer, and advances his assertions and his premises with such a deficiency of judgment,
that, without troubling ourselves about principles of philosophy or politics, the mere logical conclusions they produce,
are ridiculous. For instance,

If governments, as Mr. Burke asserts, are not founded on
the Rights of MAN, and are founded on *any rights* at all,
they consequently must be founded on the right of *something* that is *not man.* What then is that something?

Generally speaking, we know of no other creatures that
inhabit the earth than man and beast; and in all cases,
where only two things offer themselves, and one must be
admitted, a negation proved on any one, amounts to an

---

* What was called the *livre rouge*, or the red book, in France, was not
exactly similar to the court calender in England; but it sufficiently showed
how a great part of the taxes was lavished.—*Author.*

affirmative on the other; and therefore, Mr. Burke, by proving against the Rights of *Man*, proves in behalf of the *beast;*
and consequently, proves that government is a beast; and
as difficult things sometimes explain each other, we now
see the origin of keeping wild beasts in the Tower; for
they certainly can be of no other use than to shew the origin
of the government. They are in the place of a constitution.
O John Bull, what honours thou hast lost by not being a
wild beast. Thou mightest, on Mr. Burke's system, have
been in the Tower for life.

If Mr. Burke's arguments have not weight enough to keep
one serious, the fault is less mine than his; and as I am
willing to make an apology to the reader for the liberty I
have taken, I hope Mr. Burke will also make his for giving
the cause.

Having thus paid Mr. Burke the compliment of remembering him, I return to the subject.

From the want of a constitution in England to restrain
and regulate the wild impulse of power, many of the laws
are irrational and tyrannical, and the administration of them
vague and problematical.

The attention of the government of England (for I rather
chuse to call it by this name than the English government) appears, since its political connection with Germany,
to have been so completely engrossed and absorbed by foreign
affairs, and the means of raising taxes, that it seems to exit
for no other purposes. Domestic concerns are neglected;
and with respect to regular law, there is scarcely such a thing.

Almost every case must now be determined by some
precedent, be that precedent good or bad, or whether it
properly applies or not; and the practice is become so general as to suggest a suspicion, that it proceeds from a deeper
policy than at first sight appears.

Since the revolution of America, and more so since that
of France, this preaching up the doctrines of precedents,
drawn from times and circumstances antecedent to those
events, has been the studied practice of the English government. The generality of those precedents are founded on

principles and opinions, the reverse of what they ought ; and
the greater distance of time they are drawn from, the more
they are to be suspected.   But by associating those precedents with a superstitious reverence for ancient things, as
monks shew relics and call them holy, the generality of
mankind are deceived into the design.   Governments now
act as if they were afraid to awaken a single reflection in man.
They are softly leading him to the sepulchre of precedents,
to deaden his faculties and call attention from the scene of
revolutions.   They feel that he is arriving at knowledge
faster than they wish, and their policy of precedents is the
barometer of their fears.   This political popery, like the
ecclesiastical popery of old, has had its day, and is hastening to its exit.   The ragged relic and the antiquated precedent, the monk and the monarch, will moulder together.

Government by precedent, without any regard to the
principle of the precedent, is one of the vilest systems that
can be set up.   In numerous instances, the precedent ought
to operate as a warning, and not as an example, and requires
to be shunned instead of imitated ; but instead of this, precedents are taken in the lump, and put at once for constitution and for law.

Either the doctrine of precedents is policy to keep a man
in a state of ignorance, or it is a practical confession that wisdom degenerates in governments as governments increase
in age, and can only hobble along by the stilts and crutches
of precedents.   How is it that the same persons who would
proudly be thought wiser than their predecessors, appear at
the same time only as the ghosts of departed wisdom?
How strangely is antiquity treated !   To some purposes it
is spoken of as the times of darkness and ignorance, and to
answer others, it is put for the light of the world.

If the doctrine of precedents is to be followed, the expences of government need not continue the same.   Why
pay men extravagantly, who have but little to do ?   If
everything that can happen is already in precedent, legislation is at an end, and precedent, like a dictionary, determines every case.   Either, therefore, government has arrived

at its dotage, and requires to be renovated, or all the occasions for exercising its wisdom have occurred.

We now see all over Europe, and particularly in England, the curious phenomenon of a nation looking one way, and the government the other—the one forward and the other backward. If governments are to go on by precedent, while nations go on by improvement, they must at last come to a final separation; and the sooner, and the more civilly they determine this point, the better.*

Having thus spoken of constitutions generally, as things distinct from actual governments, let us proceed to consider the parts of which a constitution is composed.

Opinions differ more on this subject than with respect to the whole. That a nation ought to have a constitution, as a rule for the conduct of its government, is a simple question in which all men, not directly courtiers, will agree. It is only on the component parts that questions and opinions multiply.

But this difficulty, like every other, will diminish when put into a train of being rightly understood.

The first thing is, that a nation has a right to establish a constitution.

Whether it exercises this right in the most judicious manner at first is quite another case. It exercises it agreeably to the judgment it possesses; and by continuing to do so, all errors will at last be exploded.

When this right is established in a nation, there is no fear that it will be employed to its own injury. A nation can have no interest in being wrong.

Though all the constitutions of America are on one gen-

---

* In England the improvements in agriculture, useful arts, manufactures, and commerce, have been made in opposition to the genius of its government, which is that of following precedents. It is from the enterprise and industry of the individuals, and their numerous associations, in which, tritely speaking, government is neither pillow nor bolster, that these improvements have proceeded. No man thought about government, or who was *in*, or who was *out*, when he was planning or executing those things; and all he had to hope, with respect to government, was, *that it would let him alone*. Three or four very silly ministerial newspapers are continually offending against the spirit of national improvement, by ascribing it to a minister. They may with as much truth ascribe this book to a minister.—*Author*.

eral principle, yet no two of them are exactly alike in their
component parts, or in the distribution of the powers which
they give to the actual governments.   Some are more, and
others less complex.

In forming a constitution, it is first necessary to consider
what are the ends for which government is necessary?
Secondly, what are the best means, and the least expensive,
for accomplishing those ends?

Government is nothing more than a national association;
and the object of this association is the good of all, as well
individually as collectively.   Every man wishes to pursue
his occupation, and to enjoy the fruits of his labours and the
produce of his property in peace and safety, and with the
least possible expence.   When these things are accomplished, all the objects for which government ought to be
established are answered.

It has been customary to consider government under
three distinct general heads.   The legislative, the executive,
and the judicial.

But if we permit our judgment to act unincumbered by
the habit of multiplied terms, we can perceive no more than
two divisions of power, of which civil government is composed, namely, that of legislating or enacting laws, and that
of executing or administering them.   Everything, therefore,
appertaining to civil government, classes itself under one or
other of these two divisions.

So far as regards the execution of the laws, that which is
called the judicial power, is strictly and properly the executive power of every country.   It is that power to which
every individual has appeal, and which causes the laws to be
executed; neither have we any other clear idea with respect
to the official execution of the laws.   In England, and also
in America and France, this power begins with the magistrate,
and proceeds up through all the courts of judicature.

I leave to courtiers to explain what is meant by calling
monarchy the executive power.   It is merely a name in
which acts of government are done; and any other, or none
at all, would answer the same purpose.   Laws have neither

more nor less authority on this account.   It must be from the justness of their principles, and the interest which a nation feels therein, that they derive support ; if they require any other than this, it is a sign that something in the system of government is imperfect.   Laws difficult to be executed cannot be generally good.

With respect to the organization of the *legislative power,* different modes have been adopted in different countries. In America it is generally composed of two houses.   In France it consists but of one, but in both countries, it is wholly by representation.

The case is, that mankind (from the long tyranny of assumed power) have had so few opportunities of making the necessary trials on modes and principles of government, in order to discover the best, *that government is but now beginning to be known,* and experience is yet wanting to determine many particulars.

The objections against two houses are, first, that there is an inconsistency in any part of a whole legislature, coming to a final determination by vote on any matter, whilst *that matter,* with respect to *that whole,* is yet only in a train of deliberation, and consequently open to new illustrations.

Secondly, That by taking the vote on each, as a separate body, it always admits of the possibility, and is often the case in practice, that the minority governs the majority, and that, in some instances, to a degree of great inconsistency.

Thirdly, That two houses arbitrarily checking or controuling each other is inconsistent ; because it cannot be proved on the principles of just representation, that either should be wiser or better than the other.   They may check in the wrong as well as in the right—and therefore to give the power where we cannot give the wisdom to use it, nor be assured of its being rightly used, renders the hazard at least equal to the precaution.*

* With respect to the two houses, of which the English parliament is composed, they appear to be effectually influenced into one, and, as a legislature, to have no temper of its own.   The minister, whoever he at any time may be, touches it as with an opium wand, and it sleeps obedience.

But if we look at the distinct abilities of the two houses, the difference will

The objection against a single house is, that it is always in a condition of committing itself too soon.—But it should at the same time be remembered, that when there is a constitution which defines the power, and establishes the principles within which a legislature shall act, there is already a more effectual check provided, and more powerfully operating, than any other check can be.   For example,

Were a Bill to be brought into any of the American legislatures similar to that which was passed into an act by the English parliament, at the commencement of George the First, to extend the duration of the assemblies to a longer period than they now sit, the check is in the constitution, which in effect says, Thus far shalt thou go and no further.

But in order to remove the objection against a single house, (that of acting with too quick an impulse,) and at the same time to avoid the inconsistencies, in some cases absurdities, arising from two houses, the following method has been proposed as an improvement upon both.

First, To have but one representation.

Secondly, To divide that representation, by lot, into two or three parts.

Thirdly, That every proposed bill, shall be first debated in those parts by succession, that they may become the hearers of each other, but without taking any vote.   After

appear so great, as to show the inconsistency of placing power where there can be no certainty of the judgment to use it.   Wretched as the state of representation is in England, it is manhood compared with what is called the house of Lords ; and so little is this nick-named house regarded, that the people scarcely inquire at any time what it is doing.   It appears also to be most under influence, and the furthest removed from the general interest of the nation.   In the debate on engaging in the Russian and Turkish war, the majority in the house of peers in favor of it was upwards of ninety, when in the other house ; which was more than double its numbers, the majority was sixty-three.

The proceedings on Mr. Fox's bill, respecting the rights of juries, merits also to be noticed.   The persons called the peers were not the objects of that bill.   They are already in possession of more privileges than that bill gave to others.   They are their own jury, and if any one of that house were prosecuted for a libel, he would not suffer, even upon conviction, for the first offence.   Such inequality in laws ought not to exist in any country.   The French constitution says, that *the law is the same to every individual, whether to protect or to punish.   All are equal in its sight.—Author.*

which the whole representation to assemble for a general debate and determination by vote.

To this proposed improvement has been added another, for the purpose of keeping the representation in the state of constant renovation; which is, that one-third of the representation of each county, shall go out at the expiration of one year, and the number be replaced by new elections. Another third at the expiration of the second year replaced in like manner, and every third year to be a general election.*

But in whatever manner the separate parts of a constitution may be arranged, there is *one* general principle that distinguishes freedom from slavery, which is, that all *hereditary government over a people is to them a species of slavery, and representative government is freedom.*

Considering government in the only light in which it should be considered, that of a NATIONAL ASSOCIATION, it ought to be so constructed as not to be disordered by any accident happening among the parts; and, therefore, no extraordinary power, capable of producing such an effect, should be lodged in the hands of any individual. The death, sickness, absence or defection, of any one individual in a government, ought to be a matter of no more consequence, with respect to the nation, than if the same circumstance had taken place in a member of the English Parliament, or the French National Assembly.

Scarcely anything presents a more degrading character of national greatness, than its being thrown into confusion, by anything happening to or acted by any individual; and the ridiculousness of the scene is often increased by the natural insignificance of the person by whom it is occasioned. Were a government so constructed, that it could not go on unless a goose or a gander were present in the senate, the difficulties would be just as great and as real, on the flight or sickness of the goose, or the gander, as if it were called a King. We laugh at individuals for the silly difficulties they

---

*As to the state of representation in England, it is too absurd to be reasoned upon. Almost all the represented parts are decreasing in population, and the unrepresented parts are increasing. A general convention of the nation is necessary to take the whole form of government into consideration.—*Author.*

make to themselves, without perceiving that the greatest of all ridiculous things are acted in governments.*

All the constitutions of America are on a plan that excludes the childish embarrassments which occur in monarchical countries. No suspension of government can there take place for a moment, from any circumstances whatever. The system of representation provides for everything, and is the only system in which nations and governments can always appear in their proper character.

As extraordinary power ought not to be lodged in the hands of any individual, so ought there to be no appropriations of public money to any person, beyond what his services in a state may be worth. It signifies not whether a man be called a president, a king, an emperor, a senator, or by any other name which propriety or folly may devise or arrogance assume; it is only a certain service he can perform in the state; and the service of any such individual in the routine of office, whether such office be called monarchical, presidential, senatorial, or by any other name or title, can never exceed the value of ten thousand pounds a year. All the great services that are done in the world are performed by volunteer characters, who accept nothing for them; but the routine of office is always regulated to such a general standard of abilities as to be within the compass of numbers in every country to perform, and therefore cannot merit very extraordinary recompense. *Government,* says Swift, *is a plain thing, and fitted to the capacity of many heads.*

* It is related that in the canton of Berne, in Switzerland, it has been customary, from time immemorial, to keep a bear at the public expense, and the people had been taught to believe, that if they had not a bear they should all be undone. It happened some years ago that the bear, then in being, was taken sick, and died too suddenly to have his place immediately supplied with another. During this interregnum the people discovered that the corn grew, and the vintage flourished, and the sun and moon continued to rise and set, and everything went on the same as before, and taking courage from these circumstances, they resolved not to keep any more bears; for, said they, "a bear is a very voracious expensive animal, and we were obliged to pull out his claws, lest he should hurt the citizens." The story of the bear of Berne was related in some of the French newspapers, at the time of the flight of Louis XVI., and the application of it to monarchy could not be mistaken in France; but it seems that the aristocracy of Berne applied it to themselves, and have since prohibited the reading of French newspapers.—*Author.*

It is inhuman to talk of a million sterling a year, paid out of the public taxes of any country, for the support of any individual, whilst thousands who are forced to contribute thereto, are pining with want, and struggling with misery. Government does not consist in a contrast between prisons and palaces, between poverty and pomp ; it is not instituted to rob the needy of his mite, and increase the wretchedness of the wretched.—But on this part of the subject I shall speak hereafter, and confine myself at present to political observations.

When extraordinary power and extraordinary pay are allotted to any individual in a government, he becomes the center, round which every kind of corruption generates and forms. Give to any man a million a-year, and add thereto the power of creating and disposing of places, at the expence of a country, and the liberties of that country are no longer secure. What is called the splendor of a throne is no other than the corruption of the state. It is made up of a band of parasites, living in luxurious indolence, out of the public taxes.

When once such a vicious system is established it becomes the guard and protection of all inferior abuses. The man who is in the receipt of a million a year is the last person to promote a spirit of reform, lest, in the event, it should reach to himself. It is always his interest to defend inferior abuses, as so many outworks to protect the citadel ; and on this species of political fortification, all the parts have such a common dependence that it is never to be expected they will attack each other.*

Monarchy would not have continued so many ages in the world, had it not been for the abuses it protects. It is the

---

* It is scarcely possible to touch on any subject, that will not suggest an allusion to some corruption in governments. The simile of "*fortifications*," unfortunately involves with it a circumstance, which is directly in point with the matter above alluded to.

Among the numerous instances of abuse which have been acted or protected by governments, ancient or modern, there is not a greater than that of quartering a man and his heirs upon the public, to be maintained at his expence.

Humanity dictates a provision for the poor ; but by what right, moral or political, does any government assume to say, that the person called the Duke of Richmond, shall be maintained by the public ? Yet, if common report is true,

master-fraud, which shelters all others.   By admitting a participation of the spoil, it makes itself friends ; and when it ceases to do this it will cease to be the idol of courtiers.

As the principle on which constitutions are now formed rejects all hereditary pretensions to government, it also rejects all that catalogue of assumptions known by the name of prerogatives.

If there is any government where prerogatives might with apparent safety be entrusted to any individual, it is in the fœderal government af America.   The president of the United States of America is elected only for four years. He is not only responsible in the general sense of the word, but a particular mode is laid down in the constitution for trying him.   He cannot be elected under thirty-five years of age ; and he must be a native of the country.

In a comparison of these cases with the Government of England, the difference when applied to the latter amounts to an absurdity.   In England the person who exercises prerogative is often a foreigner ; always half a foreigner, and always married to a foreigner.   He is never in full natural or political connexion with the country, is not responsible for anything, and becomes of age at eighteen years ; yet such a person is permitted to form foreign alliances, without even the knowledge of the nation, and to make war and peace without its consent.

But this is not all.   Though such a person cannot dispose of the government in the manner of a testator, he dictates the marriage connexions, which, in effect, accomplish a great part of the same end.   He cannot directly bequeath half the

not a beggar in London can purchase his wretched pittance of coal, without paying towards the civil list of the Duke of Richmond.   Were the whole produce of this imposition but a shilling a year, the iniquitous principle would be still the same ; but when it amounts, as it is said to do, to no less than twenty thousand pounds per annum, the enormity is too serious to be permitted to remain.   This is one of the effects of monarchy and aristocracy.

In stating this case I am led by no personal dislike.   Though I think it mean in any man to live upon the public, the vice originates in the government ; and so general is it become, that whether the parties are in the ministry or in the opposition, it makes no difference : they are sure of the guarantee of each other.—*Author*.

government to Prussia, but he can form a marriage partnership that will produce almost the same thing. Under such circumstances, it is happy for England that she is not situated on the Continent, or she might, like Holland, fall under the dictatorship of Prussia. Holland, by marriage, is as effectually governed by Prussia, as if the old tyranny of bequeathing the government had been the means.

The presidency in America (or, as it is sometimes called, the executive) is the only office from which a foreigner is excluded, and in England it is the only one to which he is admitted. A foreigner cannot be a member of Parliament, but he may be what is called a king. If there is any reason for excluding foreigners, it ought to be from those offices where mischief can most be acted, and where, by uniting every bias of interest and attachment, the trust is best secured. But as nations proceed in the great business of forming constitutions, they will examine with more precision into the nature and business of that department which is called the executive. What the legislative and judicial departments are every one can see ; but with respect to what, in Europe, is called the executive, as distinct from those two, it is either a political superfluity or a chaos of unknown things.

Some kind of official department, to which reports shall be made from the different parts of a nation, or from abroad, to be laid before the national representatives, is all that is necessary ; but there is no consistency in calling this the executive ; neither can it be considered in any other light than as inferior to the legislative. The sovereign authority in any country is the power of making laws, and everything else is an official department.

Next to the arrangement of the principles and the organization of the several parts of a constitution, is the provision to be made for the support of the persons to whom the nation shall confide the administration of the constitutional powers.

A nation can have no right to the time and services of any person at his own expence, whom it may choose to employ or intrust in any department whatever; neither can any reason be given for making provision for the support of any one part of a government and not for the other.

But admitting that the honour of being entrusted with
any part of a government is to be considered a sufficient
reward, it ought to be so to every person alike. If the
members of the legislature of any country are to serve at
their own expence that which is called the executive,
whether monarchical or by any other name, ought to serve
in like manner. It is inconsistent to pay the one, and accept
the service of the other gratis.

In America, every department in the government is decently provided for ; but no one is extravagantly paid.
Every member of Congress, and of the Assemblies, is allowed
a sufficiency for his expences. Whereas in England, a most
prodigal provision is made for the support of one part of the
Government, and none for the other, the consequence of
which is that the one is furnished with the means of corruption and the other is put into the condition of being corrupted. Less than a fourth part of such expence, applied as
it is in America, would remedy a great part of the corruption.

Another reform in the American constitution is the explod-
ing all oaths of personality. The oath of allegiance in America is to the nation only. The putting any individual as a
figure for a nation is improper. The happiness of a nation
is the superior object, and therefore the intention of an oath
of allegiance ought not to be obscured by being figuratively
taken, to, or in the name of, any person. The oath, called
the civic oath, in France, viz., " *the nation, the law, and the
king,*" is improper. If taken at all, it ought to be as in
America, to the nation only. The law may or may not be
good ; but, in this place, it can have no other meaning, than
as being conducive to the happiness of a nation, and therefore is included in it. The remainder of the oath is improper,
on the ground, that all personal oaths ought to be abolished.
They are the remains of tyranny on one part and slavery on
the other ; and the name of the CREATOR ought not to be
introduced to witness the degradation of his creation ; or if
taken, as is already mentioned, as figurative of the nation, it
is in this place redundant. But whatever apology may be
made for oaths at the first establishment of a government,
they ought not to be permitted afterwards. If a government

requires the support of oaths, it is a sign that it is not worth supporting, and ought not to be supported. Make government what it ought to be, and it will support itself.

To conclude this part of the subject :—One of the greatest improvements that have been made for the perpetual security and progress of constitutional liberty, is the provision which the new constitutions make for occasionally revising, altering, and amending them.

The principle upon which Mr. Burke formed his political creed, that of "*binding and controuling posterity to the end of time*, and of *renouncing and abdicating the rights of all posterity, for ever*," is now become too detestable to be made a subject of debate ; and therefore, I pass it over with no other notice than exposing it.

Government is but now beginning to be known. Hitherto it has been the mere exercise of power, which forbad all effectual enquiry into rights, and grounded itself wholly on possession. While the enemy of liberty was its judge, the progress of its principles must have been small indeed.

The constitutions of America, and also that of France, have either affixed a period for their revision, or laid down the mode by which improvement shall be made. It is perhaps impossible to establish anything that combines principles with opinions and practice, which the progress of circumstances, through a length of years, will not in some measure derange, or render inconsistent ; and, therefore, to prevent inconveniencies accumulating, till they discourage reformations or provoke revolutions, it is best to provide the means of regulating them as they occur. The Rights of Man are the rights of all generations of men, and cannot be monopolised by any. That which is worth following, will be followed for the sake of its worth, and it is in this that its security lies, and not in any conditions with which it may be encumbered. When a man leaves property to his heirs, he does not connect it with an obligation that they shall accept it. Why, then, should we do otherwise with respect to constitutions ? The best constitution that could now be devised, consistent with the condition of the present moment, may be far short of that excellence which a few

years may afford.   There is a morning of reason rising upon
man on the subject of government, that has not appeared
before.   As the barbarism of the present old governments
expires, the moral conditions of nations with respect to each
other will be changed.   Man will not be brought up with
the savage idea of considering his species as his enemy,
because the accident of birth gave the individuals existence
in countries distinguished by different names ; and as constitutions have always some relation to external as well as
to domestic circumstances, the means of benefitting by every
change, foreign or domestic, should be a part of every constitution.   We already see an alteration in the national
disposition of England and France towards each other,
which, when we look back to only a few years, is itself a
Revolution.   Who could have foreseen, or who could have
believed, that a French National Assembly would ever
have been a popular toast in England, or that a friendly
alliance of the two nations should become the wish of either?
It shews, that man, were he not corrupted by governments,
is naturally the friend of man, and that human nature is not
of itself vicious.   That spirit of jealousy and ferocity, which
the governments of the two countries inspired, and which
they rendered subservient to the purpose of taxation, is now
yielding to the dictates of reason, interest, and humanity.
The trade of courts is beginning to be understood, and the
affectation of mystery, with all the artificial sorcery by which
they imposed upon mankind, is on the decline.   It has received its death-wound ; and though it may linger, it will
expire.   Government ought to be as much open to improvement as anything which appertains to man, instead of which
it has been monopolised from age to age, by the most ignorant
and vicious of the human race.   Need we any other proof of
their wretched management, than the excess of debts and
taxes with which every nation groans, and the quarrels into
which they have precipitated the world?   Just emerging
from such a barbarous condition, it is too soon to determine to what extent of improvement government may yet
be carried.   For what we can foresee, all Europe may form
but one great Republic, and man be free of the whole.

CHAPTER V.

WAYS AND MEANS OF IMPROVING THE CONDITION OF EUROPE,
INTERSPERSED WITH MISCELLANEOUS OBSERVATIONS.

IN contemplating a subject that embraces with equatorial magnitude the whole region of humanity it is impossible to confine the pursuit in one single direction. It takes ground on every character and condition that appertains to man, and blends the individual, the nation, and the world. From a small spark, kindled in America, a flame has arisen not to be extinguished. Without consuming, like the *Ultima Ratio Regum*, it winds its progress from nation to nation, and conquers by a silent operation. Man finds himself changed, he scarcely perceives how. He acquires a knowledge of his rights by attending justly to his interest, and discovers in the event that the strength and powers of despotism consist wholly in the fear of resisting it, and that, in order " *to be free, it is sufficient that he wills it.*"

Having in all the preceding parts of this work endeavoured to establish a system of principles as a basis on which governments ought to be erected, I shall proceed in this, to the ways and means of rendering them into practice. But in order to introduce this part of the subject with more propriety, and stronger effect, some preliminary observations, deducible from, or connected with, those principles, are necessary.

Whatever the form or constitution of government may be, it ought to have no other object than the *general* happiness. When, instead of this, it operates to create and encrease wretchedness in any of the parts of society, it is on a wrong system, and reformation is necessity. Customary language has classed the condition of man under the two descriptions of civilised and uncivilised life. To the one it has ascribed felicity and affluence ; to the other hardship and want. But, however our imagination may be impressed by painting and comparison, it is nevertheless true, that a great portion of mankind, in what are called civilised countries, are in a state of poverty and wretchedness, far below the condition of an Indian. I speak not of one country, but of all. It is so in England, it is so all over Europe. Let us enquire into the cause.

It lies not in any natural defect in the principles of civilisation, but in preventing those principles having a universal
operation ; the consequence of which is, a perpetual system
of war and expence, that drains the country, and defeats
the general felicity of which civilisation is capable.   All the
European governments (France now excepted) are constructed not on the principle of universal civilisation, but on
the reverse of it.   So far as those governments relate to each
other, they are in the same condition as we conceive of
savage uncivilised life ; they put themselves beyond the law
as well of GOD as of man, and are, with respect to principle
and reciprocal conduct, like so many individuals in a state
of nature.   The inhabitants of every country, under the
civilisation of laws, easily civilise together, but governments
being yet in an uncivilised state, and almost continually at
war, they pervert the abundance which civilised life produces to carry on the uncivilised part to a greater extent.
By thus engrafting the barbarism of government upon the
internal civilisation of a country, it draws from the latter,
and more especially from the poor, a great portion of those
earnings, which should be applied to their own subsistence
and comfort.   Apart from all reflections of morality and
philosophy, it is a melancholy fact that more than one-
fourth of the labour of mankind is annually consumed
by this barbarous system.   What has served to continue
this evil, is the pecuniary advantage which all the governments of Europe have found in keeping up this state of un-
civilisation.   It affords to them pretences for power, and
revenue, for which there would be neither occasion nor
apology, if the circle of civilisation were rendered complete.
Civil government alone, or the government of laws, is not
productive of pretences for many taxes ; it operates at home,
directly under the eye of the country, and precludes the possibility of much imposition.   But when the scene is laid in
the uncivilised contention of governments, the field of pretences is enlarged, and the country, being no longer a judge,
is open to every imposition, which governments please to
act.   Not a thirtieth, scarcely a fortieth, part of the taxes
which are raised in England are either occasioned by, or ap-

plied to, the purpose of civil government. It is not difficult
to see, that the whole which the actual government does in
this respect, is to enact laws, and that the country adminis-
ters and executes them, at its own expence, by means of
magistrates, juries, sessions, and assize, over and above the
taxes which it pays. In this view of the case, we have two
distinct characters of government ; the one the civil government, or the government of laws, which operates at home,
the other the court or cabinet government, which operates
abroad, on the rude plan of uncivilised life ; the one attended
with little charge, the other with boundless extravagance ;
and so distinct are the two, that if the latter were to sink, as
it were, by a sudden opening of the earth, and totally dis-
appear, the former would not be deranged. It would still
proceed, because it is the common interest of the nation that
it should, and all the means are in practice. Revolutions,
then, have for their object a change in the moral condition
of governments, and with this change the burthen of public
taxes will lessen, and civilisation will be left to the enjoyment of that abundance, of which it is now deprived. In
contemplating the whole of this subject, I extend my views
into the department of commerce. In all my publications,
where the matter would admit, I have been an advocate for
commerce, because I am a friend to its effects. It is a pacific
system, operating to cordialise mankind, by rendering
nations, as well as individuals, useful to each other. As to
the mere theoretical reformation, I have never preached it
up. The most effectual process is that of improving the
condition of man by means of his interest ; and it is on this
ground that I take my stand. If commerce were permitted
to act to the universal extent it is capable, it would extirpate the system of war, and produce a revolution in the uncivilised state of governments. The invention of commerce
has arisen since those governments began, and is the greatest
approach towards universal civilisation that has yet been
made by any means not immediately flowing from moral
principles. Whatever has a tendency to promote the
civil intercourse of nations by an exchange of benefits,
is a subject as worthy of philosophy as of politics.

Commerce is no other than the traffic of two individuals, multiplied on a scale of numbers ; and by the same rule that nature intended for the intercourse of two, she intended that of all. For this purpose she has distributed the materials of manufactures and commerce, in various and distant parts of a nation and of the world ; and as they cannot be procured by war so cheaply or so commodiously as by commerce, she has rendered the latter the means of extirpating the former. As the two are nearly the opposite of each other, consequently, the uncivilised state of the European governments is injurious to commerce. Every kind of destruction or embarrassment serves to lessen the quantity, and it matters but little in what part of the commercial world the reduction begins. Like blood, it cannot be taken from any of the parts, without being taken from the whole mass in circulation, and all partake of the loss. When the ability in any nation to buy is destroyed, it equally involves the seller. Could the government of England destroy the commerce of all other nations, she would most effectually ruin her own. It is possible that a nation may be the carrier for the world, but she cannot be the merchant. She cannot be the seller and buyer of her own merchandise. The ability to buy must reside out of herself ; and, therefore, the prosperity of any commercial nation is regulated by the prosperity of the rest. If they are poor she cannot be rich, and her condition, be what it may, is an index of the height of the commercial tide in other nations. That the principles of commerce, and its universal operation may be understood, without understanding the practice, is a position that reason will not deny ; and it is on this ground only that I argue the subject. It is one thing in the counting-house, in the world it is another. With respect to its operation it must necessarily be contemplated as a reciprocal thing ; that only one-half its powers resides within the nation, and that the whole is as effectually destroyed by the destroying the half that resides without, as if the destruction had been committed on that which is within ; for neither can act without the other. When in the last, as well as in former wars, the commerce of England sunk, it

was because the quantity was lessened everywhere; and it
now rises, because commerce is in a rising state in every
nation. If England, at this day, imports and exports more
than at any former period, the nations with which she trades
must necessarily do the same; her imports are their exports, and *vice versa.* There can be no such thing as a
nation flourishing alone in commerce: she can only participate; and the destruction of it in any part must necessarily
affect all. When, therefore, governments are at war, the attack is made upon a common stock of commerce, and the
consequence is the same as if each had attacked his own.
The present increase of commerce is not to be attributed to
ministers, or to any political contrivances, but to its own
natural operation in consequence of peace. The regular
markets had been destroyed, the channels of trade broken
up, the high road of the seas infested with robbers of every
nation, and the attention of the world called to other objects. Those interruptions have ceased, and peace has restored the deranged condition of things to their proper
order. * It is worth remarking that every nation reckons
the balance of trade in its own favour; and therefore something must be irregular in the common ideas upon this subject. The fact, however, is true, according to what is called
a balance; and it is from this cause that commerce is universally supported. Every nation feels the advantage, or it
would abandon the practice: but the deception lies in the
mode of making up the accounts, and in attributing what
are called profits to a wrong cause. Mr. Pitt has sometimes
amused himself, by showing what he called a balance of
trade from the custom-house books. This mode of calculating, not only affords no rule that is true, but one that is
false. In the first place, Every cargo that departs from the
custom-house, appears on the books as an export; and, ac-

---

* In America the increase of commerce is greater in proportion than in England. It is, at this time, at least one half more than at any period prior to the
revolution. The greatest number of vessels cleared out of the port of Philadelphia, before the commencement of the war, was between eight and nine
hundred. In the year 1788, the number was upwards of twelve hundred. As
the State of Pennsylvania is estimated at an eighth part of the United States
in population, the whole number of vessels must now be nearly ten thousand.
—*Author.*

cording to the custom-house balance, the losses at sea, and
by foreign failures, are all reckoned on the side of profit because they appear as exports.

Secondly, Because the importation by the smuggling trade
does not appear on the custom-house, books, to arrange
against the exports.

No balance, therefore, as applying to superior advantages,
can be drawn from these documents ; and if we examine the
natural operation of commerce, the idea is fallacious ; and if
true, would soon be injurious.   The great support of commerce consists in the balance being a level of benefits among
all nations.

Two merchants of different nations trading together, will
both become rich, and each makes the balance in his own
favour ; consequently, they do not get rich of each other;
and it is the same with respect to the nations in which they
reside.   The case must be, that each nation must get rich
out of its own means, and increases that riches by something
which it procures from another in exchange.

If a merchant in England sends an article of English
manufacture abroad which costs him a shilling at home, and
imports something which sells for two, he makes a balance
of one shilling in his favour; but this is not gained out of
the foreign nation or the foreign merchant, for he also does
the same by the articles he receives, and neither has the advantage upon the other.   The original value of the two
articles in their proper countries were but two shillings ; but
by changing their places, they acquire a new idea of value,
equal to double what they had first, and that increased value
is equally divided.

There is no otherwise a balance on foreign than on domestic commerce.   The merchants of London and Newcastle trade on the same principles, as if they resided in
different nations, and make their balances in the same
manner : yet London does not get rich out of Newcastle,
any more than Newcastle out of London : but coals, the
merchandize of Newcastle, have an additional value at London, and London merchandize has the same at Newcastle.

Though the principal of all commerce is the same, the

domestic, in a national view, is the part the most beneficial; because the whole of the advantages, on both sides, rests within the nation; whereas, in foreign commerce, it is only a participation of one-half.

The most unprofitable of all commerce is that connected with foreign dominion. To a few individuals it may be beneficial, merely because it is commerce; but to the nation it is a loss. The expence of maintaining dominion more than absorbs the profits of any trade. It does not increase the general quantity in the world, but operates to lessen it; and as a greater mass would be afloat by relinquishing dominion, the participation without the expence would be more valuable than a greater quantity with it.

But it is impossible to engross commerce by dominion; and therefore it is still more fallacious. It cannot exist in confined channels, and necessarily breaks out by regular or irregular means, that defeat the attempt: and to succeed would be still worse. France, since the Revolution, has been more indifferent as to foreign possessions, and other nations will become the same when they investigate the subject with respect to commerce.

To the expence of dominion is to be added that of navies, and when the amounts of the two are subtracted from the profits of commerce, it will appear, that what is called the balance of trade, even admitting it to exist, is not enjoyed by the nation, but absorbed by the Government.

The idea of having navies for the protection of commerce is delusive. It is putting means of destruction for the means of protection. Commerce needs no other protection than the reciprocal interest which every nation feels in supporting it—it is common stock—it exists by a balance of advantages to all; and the only interruption it meets, is from the present uncivilised state of governments, and which it is its common interest to reform.*

---

* When I saw Mr. Pitt's mode of estimating the balance of trade, in one of his parliamentary speeches, he appeared to me to know nothing of the nature and interest of commerce; and no man has more wantonly tortured it than himself. During a period of peace it has been havocked with the calamities of war. Three times has it been thrown into stagnation, and the vessels unmanned by impressing, within less than four years of peace.—*Author.*

Quitting this subject, I now proceed to other matters.—
As it is necessary to include England in the prospect of a
general reformation, it is proper to inquire into the defects
of its government. It is only by each nation reforming its
own, that the whole can be improved, and the full benefit of
reformation enjoyed. Only partial advantages can flow
from partial reforms.

France and England are the only two countries in Europe
where a reformation in government could have successfully
begun. The one secure by the ocean, and the other by the
immensity of its internal strength, could defy the malignancy of foreign despotism. But it is with revolutions as
with commerce, the advantages increase by their becoming
general, and double to either what each would receive alone.

As a new system is now opening to the view of the world,
the European courts are plotting to counteract it. Alliances,
contrary to all former systems, are agitating, and a common
interest of courts is forming against the common interest of
man. This combination draws a line that runs throughout
Europe, and presents a cause so entirely new as to exclude
all calculations from former circumstances. While despotism
warred with despotism, man had no interest in the contest ;
but in a cause that unites the soldier with the citizen, and
nation with nation, the despotism of courts, though it feels
the danger and meditates revenge, is afraid to strike.

No question has arisen within the records of history that
pressed with the importance of the present. It is not
whether this or that party shall be in or not, or Whig or Tory,
high or low shall prevail; but whether man shall inherit his
rights, and universal civilisation take place? Whether the
fruits of his labours shall be enjoyed by himself or consumed
by the profligacy of governments? Whether robbery shall
be banished from courts, and wretchedness from countries?

When, in countries that are called civilised, we see age
going to the workhouse and youth to the gallows, something
must be wrong in the system of government. It would
seem, by the exterior appearance of such countries, that all
was happiness; but there lies hidden from the eye of common observation, a mass of wretchedness, that has scarcely

any other chance, than to expire in poverty or infamy. Its entrance into life is marked with the presage of its fate ; and until this is remedied, it is in vain to punish.

Civil government does not exist in executions ; but in making such provision for the instruction of youth and the support of age, as to exclude, as much as possible, profligacy from the one and despair from the other. Instead of this, the resources of a country are lavished upon kings, upon courts, upon hirelings, impostors and prostitutes ; and even the poor themselves, with all their wants upon them, are compelled to support the fraud that oppresses them.

Why is it that scarcely any are executed but the poor? The fact is a proof, among other things, of a wretchedness in their condition. Bred up without morals, and cast upon the world without a prospect, they are the exposed sacrifice of vice and legal barbarity. The millions that are superfluously wasted upon governments are more than sufficient to reform those evils, and to benefit the condition of every man in a nation, not included within the purlieus of a court. This I hope to make appear in the progress of this work.

It is the nature of compassion to associate with misfortune. In taking up this subject I seek no recompense—I fear no consequence. Fortified with that proud integrity, that disdains to triumph or to yield, I will advocate the Rights of Man.

It is to my advantage that I have served an apprenticeship to life. I know the value of moral instruction, and I have seen the danger of the contrary.

At an early period—little more than sixteen years of age, raw and adventurous, and heated with the false heroism of a master * who had served in a man-of-war—I began the carver of my own fortune, and entered on board the Terrible Privateer, Captain Death. From this adventure I was happily prevented by the affectionate and moral remonstrance of a good father, who, from his own habits of life, being of the Quaker profession, must begin to look upon

* Rev. William Knowle, master of the grammar school of Thetford, in Norfolk.—*Author.*

me as lost. But the impression, much as it effected at the time, began to wear away, and I entered afterwards in the King of Prussia Privateer, Captain Mendez, and went with her to sea. Yet, from such a beginning, and with all the inconvenience of early life against me, I am proud to say, that with a perseverence undismayed by difficulties, a disinterestedness that compelled respect, I have not only contributed to raise a new empire in the world, founded on a new system of government, but I have arrived at an eminence in political literature, the most difficult of all lines to succeed and excel in, which aristocracy with all its aids has not been able to reach or to rival.*

* Politics and self-interest have been so uniformly connected that the world, from being so often deceived, has a right to be suspicious of public characters, but with regard to myself I am perfectly easy on this head. I did not, at my first setting out in public life, nearly seventeen years ago, turn my thoughts to subjects of government from motives of interest, and my conduct from that moment to this proves the fact. I saw an opportunity in which I thought I could do some good, and I followed exactly what my heart dictated. I neither read books, nor studied other people's opinion. I thought for myself. The case was this : —

During the suspension of the old governments in America, both prior to and at the breaking out of hostilities, I was struck with the order and decorum with which everything was conducted, and impressed with the idea that a little more than what society naturally performed was all the government that was necessary, and that monarchy and aristocracy were frauds and impositions upon mankind. On these principles I published the pamphlet *Common Sense*. The success it met with was beyond anything since the invention of printing. I gave the copyright to every state in the Union, and the demand ran to not less than one hundred thousand copies. I continued the subject in the same manner, under the title of *The Crisis*, till the complete establishment of the Revolution.

After the declaration of independence Congress unanimously, and unknown to me, appointed me Secretary in the Foreign Department. This was agreeable to me, because it gave me the opportunity of seeing into the abilities of foreign courts, and their manner of doing business. But a misunderstanding arising between congress and me, respecting one of their commissioners then in Europe, Mr. Silas Deane, I resigned the office, and declined at the same time the pecuniary offers made by the Ministers of France and Spain, M. Gerald and Don Juan Mirralles.

I had by this time so completely gained the ear and confidence of America, and my own independence was become so visible, as to give me a range in political writing beyond, perhaps, what any man ever possessed in any country, and, what is more extraordinary, I held it undiminished to the end of the war,

Knowing my own heart and feeling myself as I now do, superior to all the skirmish of party, the inveteracy of interested or mistaken opponents, I answer not to falsehood or abuse, but proceed to the defects of the Engltsh Government.

and enjoy it in the same manner to the present moment. As my object was not myself, I set out with the determination, and happily with the disposition, of not being moved by praise or censure, friendship or calumny, nor of being drawn from my purpose by any personal altercation, and the man who cannot do this is not fit for a public character.

When the war ended I went from Philadelphia to Borden-Town, on the east bank of the Delaware, where I have a small place. Congress was at this time at Prince-Town, fifteen miles distant, and General Washington had taken his headquarters at Rocky Hill, within the neighborhood of Congress, for the purpose of resigning up his commission (the object for which he accepted it being accomplished), and of retiring to private life. While he was on this business he wrote me the letter which I here subjoin : —

"Rocky-Hill, Sept. 10, 1783.

"I have learned since I have been at this place that you are at Borden-Town. Whether for the sake of retirement or economy I know not. Be it for either, for both, or whatever it may, if you will come to this place, and partake with me, I shall be exceedingly happy to see you at it.

"Your presence may remind Congress of your past services to this country, and if it is in my power to impress them, command my best exertions with freedom, as they will be rendered cheerfully by one who entertains a lively sense of the importance of your works, and who, with much pleasure, subscribes himself, Your sincere friend,   G. WASHINGTON."

During the war, in the latter end of the year 1780, I formed to myself a design of coming over to England, and communicated it to General Greene, who was then in Philadelphia on his route to the southward, General Washington being then at too great a distance to communicate with immediately. I was strongly impressed with the idea that if I could get over to England without being known, and only remain in safety till I could get out a publication, that I could open the eyes of the country with respect to the madness and stupidity of its Government. I saw that the parties in Parliament had pitted themselves as far as they could go, and could make no new impressions on each other. General Greene entered fully into my views, but the affair of Arnold and André happening just after, he changed his mind, under strong apprehensions for my safety, wrote very pressingly to me from Annapolis, in Maryland, to give up the design, which, with some reluctance, I did. Soon after this I accompanied Colonel Lawrens, son of Mr. Lawrens, who was then in the Tower, to France on business from Congress. We landed at L'Orient, and while I remained there, he being gone forward, a circumstance occurred that renewed my former design. An English packet from Falmouth to New York,

I begin with charters and corporations. [1]

It is a perversion of terms to say that a charter gives rights. It operates by a contrary effect—that of taking rights away. Rights are inherently in all the inhabitants; but charters, by annulling those rights, in the majority, leave the right, by exclusion, in the hands of a few. If charters were constructed so as to express in direct terms, " *that every inhabitant, who is not a member of a corporation, shall not exercise the right of voting,*" such charters would, in the face, be charters not of rights, but of exclusion. The effect is the same under the form they now stand ; and the only persons on whom they operate are the persons whom they exclude. Those whose rights are guaranteed, by not being taken away, exercise no other rights than as members of the community they are entitled to without a charter; and, therefore, all charters have no other than an indirect negative operation. They do not give rights to A, but they

with the Government dispatches on board, was brought into L'Orient. That a packet should be taken is no extraordinary thing, but that the dispatches should be taken with it will scarcely be credited, as they are always slung at the cabin window in a bag loaded with cannon-ball, and ready to be sunk at a moment. The fact, however, is as I have stated it, for the dispatches came into my hands, and I read them. The capture, as I was informed, succeeded by the following stratagem :—The captain of the " Madame " privateer, who spoke English, on coming up with the packet, passed himself for the captain of an English frigate, and invited the captain of the packet on board, which, when done, he sent some of his own hands back, and secured the mail. But be the circumstance of the capture what it may, I speak with certainty as to the Government dispatches. They were sent up to Paris to Count Vergennes, and when Colonel Lawrens and myself returned to America we took the originals to Congress.

By these dispatches I saw into the stupidity of the English Cabinet far more than I otherwise could have done, and I renewed my former design. But Colonel Lawrens was so unwilling to return alone, more especially as, among other matters, we had a charge of upwards of two hundred thousand pounds sterling in money, that I gave in to his wishes, and finally gave up my plan. But I am now certain that if I could have executed it that it would not have been altogether unsuccessful.—*Author.*

[1] At a Society for Political Inquiries which met at Dr. Franklin's house, 1787. (Philadelphia), Paine read a paper " On the inexpediency of incorporating, towns." (" Penn. Hist. Soc. Memoirs," 1840.) The essay has not been discovered.—*Editor.*

make a difference in favour of A by taking away the right of B, and consequently are instruments of injustice.

But charters and corporations have a more extensive evil effect than what relates merely to elections. They are sources of endless contentions in the places where they exist, and they lessen the common rights of national society. A native of England, under the operation of these charters and corporations, cannot be said to be an Englishman in the full sense of the word. He is not free of the nation, in the same manner that a Frenchman is free of France, and an American of America. His rights are circumscribed to the town, and, in some cases, to the parish of his birth; and all other parts, though in his native land, are to him as a foreign country. To acquire a residence in these, he must undergo a local naturalisation by purchase, or he is forbidden or expelled the place. This species of feudality is kept up to aggrandise the corporations at the ruin of towns; and the effect is visible.

The generality of corporation towns are in a state of solitary decay, and prevented from further ruin only by some circumstance in their situation, such as a navigable river, or a plentiful surrounding country. As population is one of the chief sources of wealth (for without it land itself has no value), everything which operates to prevent it must lessen the value of property; and as corporations have not only this tendency, but directly this effect, they cannot but be injurious. If any policy were to be followed, instead of that of general freedom, to every person to settle where he chose (as in France or America) it would be more consistent to give encouragement to new comers than to preclude their admission by exacting premiums from them.*

The persons most immediately interested in the abolition of corporations are the inhabitants of the towns where cor-

* It is difficult to account for the origin of charter and corporation towns, unless we suppose them to have arisen out of, or been connected with, some species of garrison service. The times in which they began justify this idea. The generality of those towns have been garrisons, and the corporations were charged with the care of the gates of the towns, when no military garrison was present. Their refusing or granting admission to strangers, which has produced

porations are established. The instances of Manchester,
Birmingham, and Sheffield shew, by contrast, the injuries
which those Gothic institutions are to property and commerce. A few examples may be found, such as that of London, whose natural and commercial advantage, owing to its
situation on the Thames, is capable of bearing up against the
political evils of a corporation ; but in almost all other cases
the fatality is too visible to be doubted or denied.

Though the whole nation is not so directly affected by the
depression of property in corporation towns as the inhabitants themselves, it partakes of the consequence. By lessening the value of property, the quantity of national commerce
is curtailed. Every man is a customer in proportion to his
ability ; and as all parts of a nation trade with each other,
whatever affects any of the parts must necessarily communicate to the whole.

As one of the Houses of the English Parliament is, in a
great measure, made up of elections from these corporations ;
and as it is unnatural that a pure stream should flow from a
foul fountain, its vices are but a continuation of the vices of
its origin. A man of moral honour and good political principles cannot submit to the mean drudgery and disgraceful
arts, by which such elections are carried. To be a successful
candidate, he must be destitute of the qualities that constitute a just legislator : and being thus disciplined to corruption
by the mode of entering into Parliament, it is not to be expected that the representative should be better than the man.

Mr. Burke, in speaking of the English representation, has
advanced as bold a challenge as ever was given in the days
of chivalry. " Our representation," says he, " has been found
perfectly adequate to all the purposes for which a representation of the people can be desired or devised." " I defy,"
continues he, " the enemies of our constitution to shew the

the custom of giving, selling, and buying freedom, has more of the nature of
garrison authority than civil government. Soldiers are free of all corporations
throughout the nation, by the same propriety that every soldier is free of every
garrison, and no other persons are. He can follow any employment, with the
permission of his officers, in any corporation towns throughout the nation.—
Author.

contrary."—This declaration from a man who has been in constant opposition to all the measures of parliament the whole of his political life, a year or two excepted, is most extraordinary ; and, comparing him with himself, admits of no other alternative, than that he acted against his judgment as a member, or has declared contrary to it as an author.

But it is not in the representation only that the defects lie, and therefore I proceed in the next place to the aristocracy.

What is called the House of Peers, is constituted on a ground very similar to that, against which there is a law in other cases. It amounts to a combination of persons in one common interest. No better reason can be given, why a house of legislation should be composed entirely of men whose occupation consists in letting landed property, than why it should be composed of those who hire, or of brewers, or bakers, or any other separate class of men.

Mr. Burke calls this house " *the great ground and pillar of security to the landed interest.*" Let us examine this idea.

What pillar of security does the landed interest require more than any other interest in the state, or what right has it to a distinct and separate representation from the general interest of a nation ? The only use to be made of this power (and which it has always made,) is to ward off taxes from itself, and throw the burthen upon such articles of consumption by which itself would be least affected.

That this has been the consequence, (and will always be the consequence) of constructing governments on combinations, is evident with respect to England, from the history of its taxes.

Notwithstanding taxes have encreased and multiplied upon every article of common consumption, the land-tax, which more particularly affects this " pillar," has diminished. In 1778 the amount of the land-tax was £1,950,000, which is half-a-million less than it produced almost a hundred years ago,* notwithstanding the rentals are in many instances doubled since that period.

* See Sir John Sinclair's *History of the Revenue.* The land tax in 1646 was £2,473,499.—*Author.*

Before the coming of the Hanoverians, the taxes were divided in nearly equal proportions between the land and articles of consumption, the land bearing rather the largest share : but since that æra nearly thirteen millions annually of new taxes have been thrown upon consumption. The consequence of which has been a constant encrease in the number and wretchedness of the poor, and in the amount of the poor-rates. Yet here again the burthen does not fall in equal proportions on the aristocracy with the rest of the community. Their residences, whether in town or country, are not mixed with the habitations of the poor. They live apart from distress, and the expence of relieving it. It is in manufacturing towns and labouring villages that those burthens press the heaviest ; in many of which it is one class of poor supporting another.

Several of the most heavy and productive taxes are so contrived, as to give an exemption to this pillar, thus standing in its own defence. The tax upon beer brewed for sale does not affect the aristocracy, who brew their own beer free from this duty. It falls only on those who have not conveniency or ability to brew, and who must purchase it in small quantities. But what will mankind think of the justice of taxation, when they know, that this tax alone, from which the aristocracy are from circumstances exempt, is nearly equal to the whole of the land-tax, being in the year 1788, and it is not less now, £1,666,152, and with its proportion of the taxes on malt and hops, it exceeds it.—That a single article, thus partially consumed, and that chiefly by the working part, should be subject to a tax, equal to that on the whole rental of a nation, is, perhaps, a fact not to be paralleled in the histories of revenues.

This is one of the consequences resulting from a house of legislation, composed on the ground of a combination of common interest ; for whatever their separate politics as to parties may be, in this they are united. Whether a combination acts to raise the price of any article for sale, or the rate of wages ; or whether it acts to throw taxes from itself upon another class of the community, the principle and the

effect are the same; and if the one be illegal, it will be difficult to shew that the other ought to exist.

It is no use to say, that taxes are first proposed in the
house of commons; for as the other house has always a
negative, it can always defend itself; and it would be ridiculous to suppose that its acquiescence in the measures to be
proposed were not understood before hand. Besides which,
it has obtained so much influence by borough-traffic, and so
many of its relations and connexions are distributed on both
sides the commons, as to give it, besides an absolute negative in one house, a preponderancy in the other, in all matters of common concern.

It is difficult to discover what is meant by the *landed
interest*, if it does not mean a combination of aristocratical
landholders, opposing their own pecuniary interest to that
of the farmer, and every branch of trade, commerce, and
manufacture. In all other respects it is the only interest
that needs no partial protection. It enjoys the general protection of the world. Every individual, high or low, is
interested in the fruits of the earth; men, women, and
children, of all ages and degrees, will turn out to assist the
farmer, rather than a harvest should not be got in; and they
will not act thus by any other property. It is the only one
for which the common prayer of mankind is put up, and the
only one that can never fail from the want of means. It is
the interest, not of the policy, but of the existence of man,
and when it ceases, he must cease to be.

No other interest in a nation stands on the same united
support. Commerce, manufactures, arts, sciences, and
everything else, compared with this, are supported but in
parts. Their prosperity or their decay has not the same
universal influence. When the valleys laugh and sing, it is
not the farmer only, but all creation that rejoice. It is a
prosperity that excludes all envy; and this cannot be said
of anything else.

Why then, does Mr. Burke talk of his house of peers as
the pillar of the landed interest? Were that pillar to sink
into the earth, the same landed property would continue,

and the same ploughing, sowing, and reaping would go on.
The aristocracy are not the farmers who work the land, and
raise the produce, but are the mere consumers of the rent;
and when compared with the active world are the drones, a
seraglio of males, who neither collect the honey nor form
the hive, but exist only for lazy enjoyment.

Mr. Burke, in his first essay, called aristocracy "*the Co-
rinthian capital of polished society.*" Towards compleating
the figure, he has now added the pillar; but still the base is
wanting; and whenever a nation chuse to act a Samson, not
blind, but bold, down will go the temple of Dagon, the
Lords and the Philistines.

If a house of legislation is to be composed of men of one
class, for the purpose of protecting a distinct interest, all the
other interests should have the same. The inequality, as
well as the burthen of taxation, arises from admitting it in
one case, and not in all. Had there been a house of farmers, there had been no game laws; or a house of merchants
and manufacturers, the taxes had neither been so unequal
nor so excessive. It is from the power of taxation being in
the hands of those who can throw so great a part of it from
their own shoulders, that it has raged without a check.

Men of small or moderate estates are more injured by the
taxes being thrown on articles of consumption, than they
are eased by warding it from landed property, for the following reasons:

First, They consume more of the productive taxable articles, in proportion to their property, than those of large
estates.

Secondly, Their residence is chiefly in towns, and their
property in houses; and the encrease of the poor-rates,
occasioned by taxes on consumption, is in much greater
proportion than the land-tax has been favoured. In Birmingham, the poor-rates are not less than seven shillings in
the pound. From this, as is already observed, the aristocracy are in a great measure exempt.

These are but a part of the mischiefs flowing from the
wretched scheme of an house of peers.

As a combination, it can always throw a considerable portion of taxes from itself; and as an hereditary house, accountable to nobody, it resembles a rotten borough, whose consent is to be courted by interest. There are but few of its members, who are not in some mode or other participators, or disposers of the public money. One turns a candle-holder, or a lord in waiting; another a lord of the bed-chamber, a groom of the stole, or any insignificant nominal office to which a salary is annexed, paid out of the public taxes, and which avoids the direct appearance of corruption. Such situations are derogatory to the character of man; and where they can be submitted to, honour cannot reside.

To all these are to be added the numerous dependants, the long list of younger branches and distant relations, who are to be provided for at the public expence: in short, were an estimation to be made of the charge of aristocracy to a nation, it will be found nearly equal to that of supporting the poor. The Duke of Richmond alone (and there are cases similar to his) takes away as much for himself as would maintain two thousand poor and aged persons. Is it, then, any wonder, that under such a system of government, taxes and rates have multiplied to their present extent?

In stating these matters, I speak an open and disinterested language, dictated by no passion but that of humanity. To me, who have not only refused offers, because I thought them improper, but have declined rewards I might with reputation have accepted, it is no wonder that meanness and imposition appear disgustful. Independence is my happiness, and I view things as they are, without regard to place or person; my country is the world, and my religion is to do good.[1]

---

[1] The motto of the *Liberator* (Boston, U. S., Jan. 1, 1831) was : " Our country is the world, our countrymen are all mankind." In adopting this motto Garrison was not aware of Paine's sentence above, nor that Paine had been a pioneer in the cause of emancipation in America. The facts were pointed out to me by one of Mr. Garrison's sons. See my " Life of Paine," vol. i., p. 52—*Editor*.

Mr. Burke, in speaking of the aristocratical law of primogeniture, says, "it is the standing law of our landed inheritance; and which, without question, has a tendency, and I
think," continues he, " a happy tendency, to preserve a character of weight and consequence."

Mr. Burke may call this law what he pleases, but humanity and impartial reflection will denounce it as a law of brutal
injustice.   Were we not accustomed to the daily practice,
and did we only hear of it as the law of some distant part of
the world, we should conclude that the legislators of such
countries had not arrived at a state of civilisation.

As to its preserving a character of *weight and consequence,*
the case appears to me directly the reverse.   It is an attaint
upon character; a sort of privateering on family property.
It may have weight among dependent tenants, but it gives
none on a scale of national, and much less of universal character.   Speaking for myself, my parents were not able to
give me a shilling, beyond what they gave me in education;
and to do this they distressed themselves: yet, I possess
more of what is called consequence, in the world, than any
one in Mr. Burke's catalogue of aristocrats.

Having thus glanced at some of the defects of the two
houses of parliament, I proceed to what is called the crown,
upon which I shall be very concise.

It signifies a nominal office of a million sterling a year,
the business of which consists in receiving the money.
Whether the person be wise or foolish, sane or insane, a
native or a foreigner, matters not.   Every ministry acts
upon the same idea that Mr. Burke writes, namely, that the
people must be hood-winked, and held in superstitious ignorance by some bugbear or other; and what is called the
crown answers this purpose, and therefore it answers all the
purposes to be expected from it.   This is more than can be
said of the other two branches.

The hazard to which this office is exposed in all countries,
is not from anything that can happen to the man, but from
what may happen to the nation—the danger of its coming
to its senses.

It has been customary to call the crown the executive power, and the custom is continued, though the reason has ceased.[1]

It was called the *executive*, because the person whom it signified used, formerly, to act in the character of a judge, in administering or executing the laws. The tribunals were then a part of the court. The power, therefore, which is now called the judicial, is what was called the executive and, consequently, one or other of the terms is redundant, and one of the offices useless. When we speak of the crown now, it means nothing; it signifies neither a judge nor a general: besides which it is the laws that govern, and not the man. The old terms are kept up, to give an appearance of consequence to empty forms; and the only effect they have is that of increasing expences.

Before I proceed to the means of rendering governments more conducive to the general happiness of mankind, than they are at present, it will not be improper to take a review of the progress of taxation in England.

It is a general idea, that when taxes are once laid on, they are never taken off. However true this may have been of late, it was not always so. Either, therefore, the people of former times were more watchful over government than

---

[1] The two paragraphs preceding this were omitted by Paine in the cheap edition (Symonds, 1792) with the following in parenthesis : " Those two short paragraphs are taken into the information as prosecutable matter ; but on what ground such a prosecution can be supported I am at a loss to discover. Every part of which a government is composed must be alike open to examination and investigation ; and where this is not the case the country is not in a state of freedom ; for it is only by the free and rational exercise of this right, that errors, impositions, and absurdities can be detected and remedied either in the parts severally, or in the whole.—If there be any part in a government on which the exercise of this right ought to be more fully insisted upon by a nation than on another part, it is on that part for which a nation pays the most money, and which, in England, is called the crown."

It may be noted that the two prosecuted paragraphs might now be quoted by conservatism in favour of the English monarchy, since Paine agrees that it is the laws that govern, and not the man. Practically, he regards retention of the throne as merely a question of expense.—*Editor*.

those of the present, or government was administered with
less extravagance.

It is now seven hundred years since the Norman conquest,
and the establishment of what is called the crown. Taking
this portion of time in seven separate periods of one hundred
years each, the amount of annual taxes, at each period, will
be as follows—

Annual taxes by William the Conqueror, beginning in the year 1066. .£400,000
Annual taxes at 100 years from the conquest (1166)...... 200,000
Annual taxes at 200 years from the conquest (1266)................. 150,000
Annual taxes at 300 years from the conquest (1366)................. 130,000
Annual taxes at 400 years from the conquest (1466)................. 100,000

These statements and those which follow, are taken from
Sir John Sinclair's History of the Revenue; by which it appears, that taxes continued decreasing for four hundred years,
at the expiration of which time they were reduced three-
fourths, viz., from four hundred thousand pounds to one
hundred thousand. The people of England of the present
day, have a traditionary and historical idea of the bravery
of their ancestors ; but whatever their virtues or their vices
might have been, they certainly were a people who would
not be imposed upon, and who kept governments in awe as
to taxation, if not as to principle. Though they were not
able to expel the monarchical usurpation, they restricted it to
a republican economy of taxes.

Let us now review the remaining three hundred years.

Annual amount of taxes at 500 years from the conquest (1566)..... £500,000
Annual amount of taxes at 600 years from the conquest (1666)..... 1,800,000
Annual amount of taxes at the present time (1791).............. 17,000,000

The difference between the first four hundred years and
the last three, is so astonishing, as to warrant an opinion,
that the national character of the English has changed. It
would have been impossible to have dragooned the former
English, into the excess of taxation that now exists; and
when it is considered that the pay of the army, the navy, and
of all the revenue officers, is the same now as it was about a
hundred years ago, when the taxes were not above a tenth
part of what they are at present, it appears impossible to ac-

count for the enormous increase and expenditure on any other ground, than extravagance, corruption, and intrigue.*

With the Revolution of 1688, and more so since the Hanover succession, came the destructive system of continental intrigues, and the rage for foreign wars and foreign dominion; systems of such secure mystery that the expences admit of no accounts; a single line stands for millions. To what excess taxation might have extended, had not the

---

* Several of the court newspapers have of late made frequent mention of Wat Tyler. That his memory should be traduced by court sycophants and all those who live on the spoil of a public is not to be wondered at. He was, however, the means of checking the rage and injustice of taxation in his time, and the nation owed much to his valour. The history is concisely this :—In the time of Richard II. a poll tax was levied of one shilling per head upon every person in the nation of whatever estate or condition, on poor as well as, rich, above the age of fifteen years. If any favour was shewn in the law it was to the rich rather than to the poor, as no person could be charged more than twenty shillings for himself, family and servants, though ever so numerous ; while all other families, under the number of twenty were charged per head. Poll taxes had always been odious, but this being also oppressive and unjust, it excited as it naturally must, universal detestation among the poor and middle classes. The person known by the name of Wat Tyler, whose proper name was Walter, and a tiler by trade, lived at Deptford. The gatherer of the poll tax, on coming to his house, demanded tax for one of his daughters, whom Tyler declared was under the age of fifteen. The tax-gatherer insisted on satisfying himself, and began an indecent examination of the girl, which, enraging the father, he struck him with a hammer that brought him to the ground, and was the cause of his death. This circumstance served to bring the discontent to an issue. The inhabitants of the neighborhood espoused the cause of Tyler, who in a few days was joined, according to some histories, by upwards of fifty thousand men, and chosen their chief. With this force he marched to London, to demand an abolition of the tax and a redress of other grievances. The Court, finding itself in a forlorn condition, and, unable to make resistance, agreed, with Richard at its head, to hold a conference with Tyler in Smithfield, making many fair professions, courtier-like, of its dispositions to redress the oppressions. While Richard and Tyler were in conversation on these matters, each being on horseback, Walworth, then Mayor of London, and one of the creatures of the Court, watched an opportunity, and like a cowardly assassin, stabbed Tyler with a dagger, and two or three others falling upon him, he was instantly sacrificed. Tyler appears to have been an intrepid disinterested man with respect to himself. All his proposals made to Richard were on a more just and public ground than those which had been made to John by the Barons, and notwithstanding the sycophancy of historians and men like Mr. Burke, who seek to gloss over a base action of the Court by traducing Tyler, his fame will outlive their falsehood. If the Barons merited a monument to be erected at Runnymede, Tyler merited one in Smithfield.—*Author.*

French revolution contributed to break up the system, and put an end to pretences, is impossible to say. Viewed, as that revolution ought to be, as the fortunate means of lessening the load of taxes of both countries, it is of as much importance to England as to France; and, if properly improved to all the advantages of which it is capable, and to which it leads, deserves as much celebration in one country as the other.

In pursuing this subject, I shall begin with the matter that first presents itself, that of lessening the burthen of taxes; and shall then add such matter and propositions, respecting the three countries of England, France, and America, as the present prospect of things appears to justify: I mean, an alliance of the three, for the purposes that will be mentioned in their proper place.

What has happened may happen again. By the statement before shown of the progress of taxation, it is seen that taxes have been lessened to a fourth part of what they had formerly been. Though the present circumstances do not admit of the same reduction, yet they admit of such a beginning, as may accomplish that end in less time than in the former case.

The amount of taxes for the year ending at Michaelmas 1788, was as follows: Land-tax, £1,950,000; Customs, 3,789,274; Excise (including old and new malt), 6,751,727; Stamps, 1,278,214; Miscellaneous taxes and incidents, 1,803,755: total, 15,572,970.

Since the year 1788, upwards of one million new taxes have been laid on, besides the produce of the lotteries; and as the taxes have in general been more productive since than before, the amount may be taken, in round numbers, at £17,000,000. (The expence of collection and the drawbacks, which together amount to nearly two millions, are paid out of the gross amount; and the above is the nett sum paid into the exchequer). This sum of seventeen millions is applied to two different purposes; the one to pay the interest of the National Debt, the other to the current expences of each year. About nine millions are appropriated to the former; and the remainder, being nearly eight millions, to the latter. As to the million, said to be applied to the reduction of the debt, it is so much like paying with one hand and taking out with the other, as not to merit much notice. It happened, fortunately for France, that she possessed national domains for paying off her debt, and thereby lessening her taxes; but as this is not the case with England, her reduction of taxes can only take place by reducing the current expences, which may now be done to the amount of four or five millions annually, as will hereafter appear. When this is accomplished it will more than counter-balance the enormous charge of the American war; and the saving will be from the same source from whence the evil arose. As to the national debt, however heavy the interest may be in taxes, yet, as it serves to keep alive a capital useful to commerce, it balances by its effects a considerable part of its own weight; and as the quantity of gold and silver is, by some means or other, short of its proper proportion, being not more than twenty millions, whereas it should be sixty, (foreign intrigue, foreign wars, foreign dominions, will in a great measure account for the deficiency), it would, besides the injustice, be bad policy to extinguish a capital that serves to supply that defect. But with respect to the current expense, whatever is saved therefrom is gain. The excess may serve to keep corruption alive, but it has no re-action on credit and commerce, like the interest of the debt.

It is now very probable that the English Government (I do not mean the nation) is unfriendly to the French Revolution. Whatever serves to expose the intrigue and lessen the influence of courts, by lessening taxation, will be unwelcome to those who feed upon the spoil. Whilst the clamour of French intrigue, arbitrary power, popery, and wooden shoes could be kept up, the nation was easily allured and alarmed into taxes. Those days are now past: deception, it is to be hoped, has reaped its last harvest, and better times are in prospect for both countries, and for the world.

Taking it for granted that an alliance may be formed between England, France, and America for the purposes hereafter to be mentioned, the national expences of France and England may consequently be lessened. The same fleets and armies will no longer be necessary to either, and the reduction can be made ship for ship on each side. But to accomplish these objects the governments must necessarily be fitted to a common and correspondent principle. Confidence can never take place while an hostile disposition remains in either, or where mystery and secrecy on one side is opposed to candour and openness on the other.

These matters admitted, the national expences might be put back, *for the sake of a precedent,* to what they were at some period when France and England were not enemies. This, consequently, must be prior to the Hanover succession, and also to the Revolution of 1688.* The first instance that presents itself, antecedent to those dates, is in

---

* I happened to be in England at the celebration of the centenary of the Revolution of 1688. The characters of William and Mary have always appeared to be detestable ; the one seeking to destroy his uncle, and the other her father, to get possession of power themselves ; yet, as the nation was disposed to think something of that event, I felt hurt at seeing it ascribe the whole reputation of it to a man who had undertaken it as a jobb, and who, besides what he otherwise got, charged six hundred thousand pounds for the expence of the fleet that brought him from Holland. George the First acted the same close-fisted part as William had done, and bought the Duchy of Bremen with the money he got from England, two hundred and fifty thousand pounds over and above his pay as king, and having thus purchased it at the expence of England, added it to his Hanoverian dominions for his own private profit. In fact, every nation that does not govern itself is governed as a jobb. England has been the prey of jobbs ever since the Revolution.—*Author.*

For the above footnote was substituted by Paine in the cheap edition (Symonds, 1792.):

" On page 116 of the original edition of this work is a note in which similar remarks are made on the characters of William and Mary, the one fighting against his uncle, and the other against her own father, as have been made by other writers. Dr. Johnson, I believe, even while he was a pensioner of the present court, expressed himself in stronger terms of disapprobation than I have done. Why a change of policy has now taken place, of prosecuting at this time, what was permitted and apparently encouraged at another time, the persons concerned can best explain. In the same note it is stated that William charged six hundred thousand pounds for the expences of the Dutch fleet that brought him from Holland ; and that George the First purchased the Duchies of Bremen and Verden with two hundred and fifty thousand pounds, which he got from England, and added them to his Hanoverian dominions for his own use. The note in which these matters are contained are put into the prosecution ; but for what purpose I do not discover.

" The bill of costs delivered in for the Dutch fleet, as stated in Sir John Sin-the very wasteful and profligate times of Charles the Second; at which time England and France acted as allies. If I have chosen a period of great extravagance, it will serve to shew modern extravagance in a still worse light; especially as the pay of the navy, the army, and the revenue officers has not encreased since that time.

The peace establishment was then as follows (see Sir John Sinclair's History of the Revenue):—

Navy	£300,000
Army	212,000
Ordnance	40,000
Civil List	462,115
	£1,014,115

The parliament, however, settled the whole annual peace establishment at $1,200,000.* If we go back to the time of Elizabeth the amount of all the taxes was but half a million, yet the nation sees nothing during that period that reproaches it with want of consequence.

All circumstances, then, taken together, arising from the French revolution, from the approaching harmony and reciprocal interest of the two nations, the abolition of the court intrigue on both sides, and the progress of knowledge in the science of government, the annual expenditure might be put back to one million and a half, viz:—

clair's History of the Revenue (Part the third, p. 40) was 686,500*l*, and was reduced to 600,000 by parliament. And in 1701 the House of Commons came to a resolution, by which it appears that William was not very scrupulous or very careful in his expenditure of English money. The resolution is as follows:—' That it is notorious that many millions of money had been given to his majesty [meaning the said William] for the service of the public, which remain yet unaccounted for.' See the Journal.

"As to the purchase of Bremen and Verden, with the money obtained from England, by George the First, the Journals of Parliament will prove the fact, and the opposition it met with in parliament will shew the manner in which it was very generally considered by the faction."

* Charles, like his predecessors and successors, finding that war was the harvest of governments, engaged in a war with the Dutch, the expence of which encreased the annual expenditure to £1,800,000, as stated under the date of 1666; but the peace establishment was but £1,200,000.—*Author.*

Navy..............................	£500,000
Army..............................	500,000
Expences of Government.............	500,000
	£1,500,000

Even this sum is six times greater than the expences of government are in America, yet the civil internal government in England (I mean that administered by means of quarter sessions, juries and assize, and which, in fact, is nearly the whole, and performed by the nation), is less expence upon the revenue, than the same species and portion of government is in America.

It is time that nations should be rational, and not be governed like animals, for the pleasure of their riders. To read the history of kings, a man would be almost inclined to suppose that government consisted in stag-hunting, and that every nation paid a million a-year to a huntsman. Man ought to have pride, or shame enough to blush at being thus imposed upon, and when he feels his proper character he will. Upon all subjects of this nature, there is often passing in the mind, a train of ideas he has not yet accustomed himself to encourage and communicate. Restrained by something that puts on the character of prudence, he acts the hypocrite upon himself as well as to others. It is, however, curious to observe how soon this spell can be dissolved. A single expression, boldly conceived and uttered, will sometimes put a whole company into their proper feelings: and whole nations are acted on in the same manner.

As to the offices of which any civil government may be composed, it matters but little by what names they are described. In the rotine of business, as before observed, whether a man be styled a president, a king, an emperor, a senator, or anything else, it is impossible that any service he can perform, can merit from a nation more than ten thousand pounds a year; and as no man should be paid beyond his services, so every man of a proper heart will not accept more. Public money ought to be touched with the most scrupulous consciousness of honour.   It is not the produce of riches only, but of the hard earnings of labour and poverty.   It is drawn even from the bitterness of want and misery.   Not a beggar passes, or perishes in the streets, whose mite is not in that mass.

Were it possible that the Congress of America, could be so lost to their duty, and to the interest of their constituents, as to offer General Washington, as president of America, a million a year, he would not, and he could not, accept it.   His sense of honour is of another kind.   It has cost England almost seventy millions sterling, to maintain a family imported from abroad, of very inferior capacity to thousands in the nation ; and scarcely a year has passed that has not produced some new mercenary application.   Even the physicians' bills have been sent to the public to be paid.   No wonder that jails are crowded, and taxes and poor rates encreased.   Under such systems, nothing is to be looked for but what has already happened ; and as to reformation, whenever it come, it must be from the nation, and not from the government.

To shew that the sum of five hundred thousand pounds is more than sufficient to defray all the expences of the government, exclusive of navies and armies, the following estimate is added, for any country, of the same extent as England.

In the first place, three hundred representatives fairly elected, are sufficient for all the purposes to which legislation can apply, and preferable to a larger number.   They may be divided into two or three houses, or meet in one, as in France, or in any manner a constitution shall direct.

As representation is always considered, in free countries, as the most honourable of all stations, the allowance made to it is merely to defray the expence which the representatives incur by that service, and not to it as an office.

If an allowance, at the rate of five hundred pounds per annum, be made to every representative, deducting for non-attendance, the expence, if the whole number attended for six months, each year, would be.. £75,000

The official departments cannot reasonably exceed the following
number, with the salaries annexed :—

Three offices at ten thousand pounds each...................	£30,000
Ten ditto, at five thousand pounds each....................	50,000
Twenty ditto, at two thousand pounds each.................	40,000
Forty ditto, at one thousand pounds each..................	40,000
Two hundred ditto, at five hundred pounds each............	100,000
Three hundred ditto, at two hundred pounds each..........	60,000
Five hundred ditto, at one hundred pounds each............	50,000
Seven hundred ditto, at seventy five pounds each............	52,500
	£497,500

If a nation chuse, it can deduct four *per cent.* from all
offices, and make one of twenty thousand *per annum.*

All revenue officers are paid out of the monies they collect, and therefore, are not in this estimation.

The foregoing is not offered as an exact detail of offices.
but to shew the number of rate of salaries which five hundred thousand pounds will support ; and it will, on experience, be found impracticable to find business sufficient to
justify even this expence. As to the manner in which office
business is now performed, the Chiefs, in several offices, such
as the post-office, and certain offices in the exchequer, etc.,
do little more than sign their names three or four times a
year ; and the whole duty is performed by under-clerks.

Taking, therefore, one million and a half as a sufficient
peace establishment for all the honest purposes of government, which is three hundred thousand pounds more than
the peace establishment in the profligate and prodigal times
of Charles the Second (notwithstanding, as has been already
observed, the pay and salaries of the army, navy, and revenue officers, continue the same as at that period), there will
remain a surplus of upwards of six millions out of the present current expences. The question then will be, how to
dispose of this surplus.

Whoever has observed the manner in which trade and
taxes twist themselves together, must be sensible of the impossibility of separating them suddenly.

First. Because the articles now on hand are already

charged with the duty, and the reduction cannot take place on the present stock.

Secondly. Because, on all those articles on which the duty is charged in the gross, such as *per* barrel, hogshead, hundred weight, or ton, the abolition of the duty does not admit of being divided down so as fully to relieve the consumer, who purchases by the pint, or the pound. The last duty laid on strong beer and ale, was three shillings *per* barrel, which, if taken off, would lessen the purchase only half a farthing *per* pint, and consequently, would not reach to practical relief.

This being the condition of a great part of the taxes, it will be necessary to look for such others as are free from this embarrassment and where the relief will be direct and visible, and capable of immediate operation.

In the first place, then, the poor-rates are a direct tax which every housekeeper feels, and who knows also, to a farthing, the sum which he pays. The national amount of the whole of the poor-rates is not positively known, but can be procured. Sir John Sinclair, in his History of the Revenue has stated it at £2,100,587. A considerable part of which is expended in litigations, in which the poor, instead of being relieved, are tormented. The expence, however, is the same to the parish from whatever cause it arises.

In Birmingham, the amount of poor-rates is fourteen thousand pounds a year. This, though a large sum, is moderate, compared with the population. Birmingham is said to contain seventy thousand souls, and on a proportion of seventy thousand to fourteen thousand pounds poor-rates, the national amount of poor-rates, taking the population of England as seven millions, would be but one million four hundred thousand pounds. It is, therefore, most probable, that the population of Birmingham is over-rated. Fourteen thousand pounds is the proportion upon fifty thousand souls, taking two millions of poor-rates, as the national amount.

Be it, however, what it may, it is no other than the consequence of excessive burthen of taxes, for, at the time when the taxes were very low, the poor were able to maintain themselves ; and there were no poor-rates.* In the present state of things a laboring man, with a wife or two or three children, does not pay less than between seven and eight pounds a year in taxes. He is not sensible of this, because it is disguised to him in the articles which he buys, and he thinks only of their dearness ; but as the taxes take from him, at least, a fourth part of his yearly earnings, he is consequently disabled from providing for a family, especially, if himself, or any of them, are afflicted with sickness.

The first step, therefore, of practical relief, would be to abolish the poor-rates entirely, and in lieu thereof, to make a remission of taxes to the poor of double the amount of the present poor-rates, viz., four millions annually out of the surplus taxes. By this measure, the poor would be benefited two millions, and the house-keepers two millions. This alone would be equal to a reduction of one hundred and twenty millions of the National Debt, and consequently equal to the whole expence of the American War.

It will then remain to be considered, which is the most effectual mode of distributing this remission of four millions.

It is easily seen, that the poor are generally composed of large families of children, and old people past their labour. If these two classes are provided for, the remedy will so far reach to the full extent of the case, that what remains will be incidental, and, in a great measure, fall within the compass of benefit clubs, which, though of humble invention, merit to be ranked among the best of modern institutions.

Admitting England to contain seven millions of souls ; if one-fifth thereof are of that class of poor which need support, the number will be one million four hundred thousand. Of this number, one hundred and forty thousand will be aged poor, as will be hereafter shewn, and for which a distinct provision will be proposed.

There will then remain one million two hundred and sixty thousand which, at five souls to each family, amount to two

---

* Poor rates began about the time of Henry VIII., when the taxes began to encrease, and they have encreased as the taxes encreased ever since.— *Author.*

hundred and fifty-two thousand families, rendered poor from the expence of children and the weight of taxes.

The number of children under fourteen years of age, in each of those families, will be found to be about five to every two families ; some having two, and others three ; some one, and others four : some none, and others five ; but it rarely happens that more than five are under fourteen years of age, and after this age they are capable of service or of being apprenticed.

Allowing five children (under fourteen years) to every two families,

The number of children will be...................... 630,000

The number of parents, were they all living, would be.... 504,000

It is certain, that if the children are provided for, the parents are relieved of consequence, because it is from the expence of bringing up children that their poverty arises.

Having thus ascertained the greatest number that can be supposed to need support on account of young families, I proceed to the mode of relief or distribution, which is,

To pay as a remission of taxes to every poor family, out of the surplus taxes, and in room of poor-rates, four pounds a year for every child under fourteen years of age ; enjoining the parents of such children to send them to school, to learn reading, writing, and common arithmetic ; the ministers of every parish, of every denomination to certify jointly to an office, for that purpose, that this duty is performed. The amount of this expence will be,

For six hundred and thirty thousand children at £4 *per annum* each....... .... £2,520,000

By adopting this method, not only the poverty of the parents will be relieved, but ignorance will be banished from the rising generation, and the number of poor will hereafter become less, because their abilities, by the aid of education, will be greater.   Many a youth, with good natural genius, who is apprenticed to a mechanical trade, such as a carpenter, joiner, millwright, shipwright, blacksmith, etc., is pre-

vented getting forward the whole of his life from the want
of a little common education when a boy.

I now proceed to the case of the aged.

I divide age into two classes. First, the approach of age,
beginning at fifty. Secondly, old age commencing at sixty.

At fifty, though the mental faculties of man are in full
vigor, and his judgment better than at any preceding date,
the bodily powers for laborious life are on the decline. He
cannot bear the same quantity of fatigue as at an earlier
period. He begins to earn less, and is less capable of
enduring wind and weather ; and in those more retired
employments where much sight is required, he fails apace,
and sees himself, like an old horse, beginning to be turned
adrift.

At sixty his labour ought to be over, at least from direct
necessity. It is painful to see old age working itself to
death, in what are called civilised countries, for daily bread.

To form some judgment of the number of those above
fifty years of age, I have several times counted the persons
I met in the streets of London, men, women, and children,
and have generally found that the average is about one in
sixteen or seventeen. If it be said that aged persons do not
come much into the streets, so neither do infants ; and a
great proportion of grown children are in schools and in
work-shops as apprentices. Taking, then, sixteen for a
divisor, the whole number of persons in England of fifty
years and upwards, of both sexes, rich and poor, will be four
hundred and twenty thousand.

The persons to be provided for out of this gross number
will be husbandmen, common labourers, journeymen of
every trade and their wives, sailors, and disbanded soldiers,
worn out servants of both sexes, and poor widows.

There will be also a considerable number of middling
tradesmen, who having lived decently in the former part of
life, begin, as age approaches, to lose their business, and at
last fall to decay.

Besides these there will be constantly thrown off from the
revolutions of that wheel which no man can stop nor regu-

late, a number from every class of life connected with commerce and adventure.

To provide for all those accidents, and whatever else may
befal, I take the number of persons who, at one time or
other of their lives, after fifty years of age, may feel it
necessary or comfortable to be better supported, than they
can support themselves, and that not as a matter of grace
and favour, but of right, at one-third of the whole number,
which is one hundred and forty thousand, as stated in a
previous page, and for whom a distinct provision was proposed to be made.   If there be more, society, notwithstanding the shew and pomposity of government, is in a deplorable
condition in England.

Of this one hundred and forty thousand, I take one half,
seventy thousand, to be of the age of fifty and under sixty,
and the other half to be sixty years and upwards.   Having
thus ascertained the probable proportion of the number of
aged persons, I proceed to the mode of rendering their
condition comfortable, which is :

To pay to every such person of the age of fifty years, and
until he shall arrive at the age of sixty, the sum of six
pounds *per annum* out of the surplus taxes, and ten pounds
per annum during life after the age of sixty.   The expence
of which will be,

> Seventy thousand persons, at £6 *per annum*........ £420,000
> Seventy thousand ditto, at £10 *per annum*.......... 700,000
>
> £1,120,000

This support, as already remarked, is not of the nature of
a charity but of a right.   Every person in England, male
and female, pays on an average in taxes two pounds eight
shillings and six pence *per annum* from the day of his (or
her) birth; and, if the expence of collection be added, he
pays two pounds eleven shillings and sixpence; consequently, at the end of fifty years he has paid one hundred
and twenty-eight pounds fifteen shillings; and at sixty one
hundred and fifty-four pounds ten shillings.   Converting,
therefore, his (or her) individual tax in a tontine, the money

he shall receive after fifty years is but little more than the legal interest of the nett money he has paid ; the rest is made up from those whose circumstances do not require them to draw such support, and the capital in both cases defrays the expences of government. It is on this ground that I have extended the probable claims to one-third of the number of aged persons in the nation.—Is it, then, better that the lives of one hundred and forty thousand aged persons be rendered comfortable, or that a million a year of public money be expended on any one individual, and him often of the most worthless or insignificant character? Let reason and justice, let honor and humanity, let even hypocrisy, sycophancy and Mr. Burke, let George, let Louis, Leopold, Frederic, Catherine, Cornwallis, or Tippoo Saib, answer the question.*

The sum thus remitted to the poor will be,

To two hundred and fifty-two thousand poor families, containing six hundred and thirty thousand children....	£2,520,000
To one hundred and forty thousand aged persons........	1,120,000
	£3,640,000

There will then remain three hundred and sixty thousand

* Reckoning the taxes by families, five to a family, each family pays on an average £12 17s. 6d. *per annum*. To this sum are to be added the poor rates. Though all pay taxes in the articles they consume, all do not pay poor rates. About two millions are exempted—some as not being housekeepers, others as not being able, and the poor themselves who receive the relief. The average, therefore, of poor rates on the remaining number, is forty shillings for every family of five persons, which make the whole average amount of taxes and rates £14 17s. 6d. For six persons £17 17s. For seven persons £20 16s. 6d.

The average of taxes in America, under the new or representative system of government, including the interest of the debt contracted in the war, and taking the population at four millions of souls, which it now amounts to, and it is daily encreasing, is five shillings per head, men, women, and children. The difference, therefore, between the two governments is as under :—

	England			America		
	£	s.	d.	£	s.	d.
For a family of five persons	14	17	6	1	5	0
For a family of six persons.........	17	17	0	1	10	0
For a family of seven persons.......	20	16	6	1	15	0

—Author.

pounds out of the four millions, part of which may be applied as follows :—

After all the above cases are provided for there will still be a number of families who, though not properly of the class of poor, yet find it difficult to give education to their children ; and such children, under such a case, would be in a worse condition than if their parents were actually poor. A nation under a well-regulated government should permit none to remain uninstructed. It is monarchical and aristocratical government only that requires ignorance for its support.

Suppose, then, four hundred thousand children to be in this condition, which is a greater number than ought to be supposed after the provisions already made, the method will be :

To allow for each of those children ten shillings a year for the expense of schooling for six years each, which will give them six months schooling each year, and half a crown a year for paper and spelling books.

The expense of this will be annually £250,000.*

There will then remain one hundred and ten thousand pounds.

Notwithstanding the great modes of relief which the best instituted and best principled government may devise, there will be a number of smaller cases, which it is good policy as well as beneficence in a nation to consider.

Were twenty shillings to be given immediately on the birth

---

* Public schools do not answer the general purpose of the poor. They are chiefly in corporation towns from which the country towns and villages are excluded, or, if admitted, the distance occasions a great loss of time. Education, to be useful to the poor, should be on the spot, and the best method, I believe, to accomplish this is to enable the parents to pay the expenses themselves. There are always persons of both sexes to be found in every village, especially when growing into years, capable of such an undertaking. Twenty children at ten shillings each (and that not more than six months each year) would be as much as some livings amount to in the remotest parts of England, and there are often distressed clergymen's widows to whom such an income would be acceptable. Whatever is given on this account to children answers two purposes. To them it is education—to those who educate them it is a livelihood.—*Author*.

of a child, to every woman who should make the demand,
and none will make it whose circumstances do not require it,
it might relieve a great deal of instant distress.

There are about two hundred thousand births yearly in
England ; and if claimed by one fourth,

> The amount would be........................£50,000

And twenty shillings to every new-married couple who
should claim in like manner.   This would not exceed the sum
of £20,000.

Also twenty thousand pounds to be appropriated to defray
the funeral expences of persons, who, travelling for work, may
die at a distance from their friends.   By relieving parishes
from this charge, the sick stranger will be better treated.

I shall finish this part of the subject with a plan adapted
to the particular condition of a metropolis, such as London.

Cases are continually occurring in a metropolis, different
from those which occur in the country, and for which a different, or rather an additional, mode of relief is necessary.   In
the country, even in large towns, people have a knowledge
of each other, and distress never rises to that extreme height
it sometimes does in a metropolis.   There is no such thing
in the country as persons, in the literal sense of the word,
starved to death, or dying with cold from the want of a lodging.   Yet such cases, and others equally as miserable, happen
in London.

Many a youth comes up to London full of expectations,
and with little or no money, and unless he get immediate
employment he is already half undone ; and boys bred up in
London without any means of a livelihood, and as it often
happens of dissolute parents, are in a still worse condition ;
and servants long out of place are not much better off.   In
short, a world of little cases is continually arising, which busy
or affluent life knows not of, to open the first door to distress.
Hunger is not among the postponable wants, and a day,
even a few hours, in such a condition is often the crisis of a
life of ruin.

These circumstances which are the general cause of the

little thefts and pilferings that lead to greater, may be prevented. There yet remain twenty thousand pounds out of the four millions of surplus taxes, which with another fund hereafter to be mentioned, amounting to about twenty thousand pounds more, cannot be better applied than to this purpose. The plan will then be :

First,—To erect two or more buildings, or take some already erected, capable of containing at least six thousand persons, and to have in each of these places as many kinds of employment as can be contrived, so that every person who shall come may find something which he or she can do.

Secondly,—To receive all who shall come, without enquiring who or what they are. The only condition to be, that for so much, or so many hours' work, each person shall receive so many meals of wholesome food, and a warm lodging, at least as good as a barrack. That a certain portion of what each person's work shall be worth shall be reserved, and given to him or her, on their going away ; and that each person shall stay as long or as short a time, or come as often as he chuse, on these conditions.

If each person staid three months, it would assist by rotation twenty-four thousand persons annually, though the real number, at all times, would be but six thousand. By establishing an asylum of this kind, such persons to whom temporary distresses occur, would have an opportunity to recruit themselves, and be enabled to look out for better employment.

Allowing that their labor paid but one half the expence of supporting them, after reserving a portion of their earnings for themselves, the sum of forty thousand pounds additional would defray all other charges for even a greater number than six thousand.

The fund very properly convertible to this purpose, in addition to the twenty thousand pounds, remaining of the former fund, will be the produce of the tax upon coals, so iniquitously and wantonly applied to the support of the Duke of Richmond. It is horrid that any man, more especially at the price coals now are, should live on the distresses of a community ; and any government permitting such an abuse, deserves to be dismissed. This fund is said to be about twenty thousand pounds *per annum.*

I shall now conclude this plan with enumerating the several particulars, and then proceed to other matters.

The enumeration is as follows :—

First—Abolition of two millions poor-rates.

Secondly—Provision for two hundred and fifty thousand poor families.

Thirdly—Education for one million and thirty thousand children.

Fourthly—Comfortable provision for one hundred and forty thousand aged persons.

Fifthly—Donation of twenty shillings each for fifty thousand births.

Sixthly—Donation of twenty shillings each for twenty thousand marriages.

Seventhly—Allowance of twenty thousand pounds for the funeral expences of persons travelling for work, and dying at a distance from their friends.

Eighthly—Employment, at all times, for the casual poor in the cities of London and Westminster.

By the operation of this plan, the poor laws, those instruments of civil torture, will be superseded, and the wasteful expence of litigation prevented. The hearts of the humane will not be shocked by ragged and hungry children, and persons of seventy and eighty years of age, begging for bread. The dying poor will not be dragged from place to place to breathe their last, as a reprisal of parish upon parish. Widows will have a maintenance for their children, and not be carted away, on the death of their husbands, like culprits and criminals ; and children will no longer be considered as encreasing the distresses of their parents. The haunts of the wretched will be known, because it will be to their advantage ; and the number of petty crimes, the offspring of distress and poverty, will be lessened. The poor, as well as the rich, will then be interested in the support of government, and the cause and apprehension of riots and tumults will cease.—Ye who sit in ease, and solace yourselves in plenty, and such there are in Turkey and Russia, as well as in England, and who say to yourselves, "Are we not well off?" have ye thought of these things? When ye do, ye will cease to speak and feel for yourselves alone.

The plan is easy in practice. It does not embarrass trade by a sudden interruption in the order of taxes, but effects the relief by changing the application of them; and the money necessary for the purpose can be drawn from the excise collections, which are made eight times a year in every market town in England.

Having now arranged and concluded this subject, I proceed to the next.

Taking the present current expences at seven millions and an half, which is the least amount they are now at, there will remain (after the sum of one million and an half be taken for the new current expenses and four millions for the before-mentioned service) the sum of two millions; part of which to be applied as follows:

Though fleets and armies, by an alliance with France, will, in a great measure, become useless, yet the persons who have devoted themselves to those services, and have thereby unfitted themselves for other lines of life, are not to be sufferers by the means that make others happy. They are a different description of men from those who form or hang about a court.

A part of the army will remain, at least for some years, and also of the navy, for which a provision is already made in the former part of this plan of one million, which is almost half a million more than the peace establishment of the army and navy in the prodigal times of Charles the Second.

Suppose, then, fifteen thousand soldiers to be disbanded, and that an allowance be made to each of three shillings a week during life, clear of all deductions, to be paid in the same manner as the Chelsea College pensioners are paid, and for them to return to their trades and their friends; and also that an addition of fifteen thousand sixpences per week be made to the pay of the soldiers who shall remain; the annual expences will be, to the pay of—

Fifteen thousand disbanded soldiers at 3s. per week................	£117,000
Additional pay to the remaining soldiers..........................	19,000
Suppose that the pay to the officers of the disbanded corps be the same amount as to the men	117,000
To prevent bulky estimations, admit the same sum to the disbanded navy as to the army, and the same increase of pay.............	253,500
Total....................	£507,000

Every year some part of this sum of half a million (I omit the odd seven thousand pounds for the purpose of keeping the account unembarrassed) will fall in, and the whole of it in time, as it is on the ground of life annuities, except the encreased pay of twenty-nine thousand pounds. As it falls in, part of the taxes may be taken off; and as, for instance, when thirty thousand pounds fall in, the duty on hops may be wholly taken off; and as other parts fall in, the duties on candles and soap may be lessened, till at last they will totally cease. There now remains at least one million and a half of surplus taxes.

The tax on houses and windows is one of those direct taxes, which, like the poor rates, is not confounded with trade; and, when taken off, the relief will be instantly felt. This tax falls heavy on the middle class of people. The amount of this tax, by the returns of 1788, was: by the act of 1766, £385,459 11 7; by the act of 1779, £130,739 14 5½; total, £516,199 6 0½.

If this tax be struck off, there will then remain about one million of surplus taxes; and as it is always proper to keep a sum in reserve, for incidental matters, it may be best not to extend reductions further in the first instance, but to consider what may be accomplished by other modes of reform.

Among the taxes most heavily felt is the commutation-tax. I shall therefore offer a plan for its abolition, by substituting another in its place, which will effect three objects at once: 1, that of removing the burthen to where it can best be borne; 2, restoring justice among families by a distribution of property; 3, extirpating the overgrown influence arising from the unnatural law of primogeniture, which is one of the principal sources of corruption at elections. The amount of commutation-tax by the returns of 1788, was £771,657.

When taxes are proposed, the country is amused by the plausible language of taxing luxuries. One thing is called a luxury at one time, and something else at another; but the real luxury does not consist in the article, but in the means of procuring it, and this is always kept out of sight.

I know not why any plant or herb of the field should be a greater luxury in one country than another; but an overgrown estate in either is a luxury at all times, and, as such, is the proper object of taxation. It is, therefore, right to take those kind tax-making gentlemen up on their own word, and argue on the principle themselves have laid down, that of *taxing luxuries*. If they or their champion, Mr. Burke, who, I fear, is growing out of date, like the man in armor, can prove that an estate of twenty, thirty, or forty thousand pounds a year is not a luxury, I will give up the argument.

Admitting that any annual sum, say, for instance, one thousand pounds, is necessary or sufficient for the support of a family, consequently the second thousand is of the nature of a luxury, the third still more so, and by proceeding on, we shall at last arrive at a sum that may not improperly be called a prohibitable luxury. It would be impolitic to set bounds to property acquired by industry, and therefore it is right to place the prohibition beyond the probable acquisition to which industry can extend; but there ought to be a limit to property or the accumulation of it by bequest. It should pass in some other line. The richest in every nation have poor relations, and those often very near in consanguinity.

The following table of progressive taxation is constructed on the above principles, and as a substitute for the commutation tax. It will reach the point of prohibition by a regular operation, and thereby supercede the aristocratical law of primogeniture.

TABLE I.

A tax on all estates of the clear yearly value of £50, after deducting the land tax, and up

		per			per
	s. d.	pound		s. d.	pound
To £500	.. 0 3	"	On the twelfth thousand	9 0	"
From £500 to £1,000..	0 6	"	On the thirteenth "	10 0	"
On the second thousand.	0 9	"	On the fourteenth "	11 0	"
On the third "	1 0	"	On the fifteenth "	12 0	"
On the fourth "	1 6	"	On the sixteenth "	13 0	"
On the fifth "	2 0	"	On the seventeenth "	14 0	"
On the sixth "	3 0	"	On the eighteenth "	15 0	"
On the seventh "	4 0	"	On the nineteenth "	16 0	"
On the eighth "	5 0	"	On the twentieth "	17 0	"
On the ninth "	6 0	"	On the twenty-first "	18 0	"
On the tenth "	7 0	"	On the twenty-second "	19 0	"
On the eleventh "	8 0	"	On the twenty-third "	20 0	"

The foregoing table shows the progression per pound on every progressive thousand. The following table shows the amount of the tax on every thousand separately, and in the last column the total amount of all the separate sums collected.

TABLE II.

An estate of			
£50 *per annum*, at 3d., pays, £0 12 6	£300 *per annum*, at 3d., pays, £3 15 0
100 " " " 1 5 0	400 " " " 5 0 0
200 " " " 2 10 0	500 " " " 7 5 0

After £500, the tax of 6d. per pound takes place on the second £500; consequently an estate of £1,000 *per annum* pays £21, 15s, and so on.

For the	£	s.	d.	£ s.	£ s.			£	s.	d.	£ s.	£ s.
1st £500 at	0	3—		7 5 }	21 15		12th 1000 at	9	0—	450	0	2380 5
2nd "	0	6—		14 10 }			13th "	10	0—	500	0	2880 5
2nd 1000 at	0	9—		37 11	59 5		14th "	11	0—	550	0	3430 5
3rd "	1	0—		50 0	109 5		15th "	12	0—	600	0	4030 5
4th "	1	6—		75 0	184 5		16th "	13	0—	650	0	4680 5
5th "	2	0—		100 0	284 5		17th "	14	0—	700	0	5380 5
6th "	3	0—		150 0	434 5		18th "	15	0—	750	0	6130 5
7th "	4	0—		200 0	634 5		19th "	16	0—	800	0	6930 5
8th "	5	0—		250 0	880 5		20th "	17	0—	850	0	7780 5
9th "	6	0—		300 0	1100 5		21st "	18	0—	900	0	8680 5
10th "	7	0—		350 0	1530 5		22nd "	19	0—	950	0	9630 5
11th "	8	0—		400 0	1930 5		23rd "	20	0—1000		0	10630 5-

At the twenty-third thousand the tax becomes 20s. in the pound, and consequently every thousand beyond that sum can produce no profit but by dividing the estate. Yet formidable as this tax appears, it will not, I believe, produce so much as the commutation tax; should it produce more, it ought to be lowered to that amount upon estates under two or three thousand a year.

On small and middling estates it is lighter (as it is intended to be) than the commutation tax. It is not till after seven or eight thousand a-year, that it begins to be heavy. The object is not so much the produce of the tax as the justice of the measure. The aristocracy has screened itself too much, and this serves to restore a part of the lost equilibrium.

As an instance of its screening itself, it is only necessary to look back to the first establishment of the excise laws, at what is called the Restoration, or the coming of Charles the Second. The aristocratical interest then in power, commuted the feudal services itself was under, by laying a tax on beer brewed for sale; that is, they compounded with Charles for an exemption from those services for themselves and their heirs, by a tax to be paid by other people. The aristocracy do not purchase beer brewed for sale, but brew their own beer free of the duty, and if any commutation at that time were necessary, it ought to have been at the expence of those for whom the exemptions from those services were intended*; instead of which, it was thrown on an entirely different class of men.

But the chief object of this progressive tax (besides the justice of rendering taxes more equal than they are) is, as already stated, to extirpate the overgrown influence arising from the unnatural law of primogeniture, and which is one of the principal sources of corruption at elections.

It would be attended with no good consequences to enquire how such vast estates as thirty, forty, or fifty thou-

---

* The tax on beer brewed for sale, from which the aristocracy are exempt, is almost one million more than the present commutation tax, being by the returns of 1788, 1,666,152*l.*—and, consequently, they ought to take on themselves the amount of the commutation tax, as they are already exempted from one which is almost a million greater.

sand a-year could commence, and that at a time when commerce and manufactures were not in a state to admit of such
acquisitions.   Let it be sufficient to remedy the evil by putting them in a condition of descending again to the community by the quiet means of apportioning them among all
the heirs and heiresses of those families.   This will be the
more necessary, because hitherto the aristocracy have
quartered their younger children and connexions upon the
public in useless posts, places and offices, which when abolished
will leave them destitute, unless the law of primogeniture be
also abolished or superceded.

A progressive tax will, in a great measure, effect this object,
and that as a matter of interest to the parties most immediately concerned, as will be seen by the following table ;
which shews the nett produce upon every estate, after subtracting the tax.   By this it will appear, that after an estate
exceeds thirteen or fourteen thousand a-year, the remainder
produces but little profit to the holder, and consequently,
will pass either to the younger children, or to other kindred.

TABLE III.

Shewing the nett produce of every estate from one thousand to twenty-three
thousand pounds a year.

No. of thousands per ann.	Total tax subtracted.	Nett produce.
1000*l*.	21*l*.	979*l*.
2000	59	1941
3000	109	2891
4000	184	3861
5000	284	4716
6000	434	5566
7000	634	6366
8000	880	7120
9000	1100	7820
10,000	1530	8470
11,000	1930	9070
12,000	2380	9620
13,000	2880	10,120
14,000	3430	10,570
15,000	4030	10,970
16,000	4680	11,320
17,000	5380	11,620
18,000	6130	11,870
19,000	6930	12,170
20,000	7780	12,220
21,000	8680	12,320
22,000	9630	12,370
23,000	10,630	12,370

N. B.   The odd shillings are dropped in this table.

According to this table, an estate cannot produce more than 12,370*l.* clear of the land tax and the progressive tax, and therefore the dividing such estates will follow as a matter of family interest.   An estate of 23,000*l.* a year, divided into five estates of four thousand each and one of three, will be charged only 1129*l.* which is but five *per cent.*, but if held by one possessor, will be charged 10,630*l.*

Although an enquiry into the origin of those estates be unnecessary, the continuation of them in their present state is another subject.   It is a matter of national concern.   As hereditary estates, the law has created the evil, and it ought also to provide the remedy.   Primogeniture ought to be abolished, not only because it is unnatural and unjust, but because the country suffers by its operation.   By cutting off (as before observed) the younger children from their proper portion of inheritance, the public is loaded with the expence of maintaining them ; and the freedom of elections violated by the overbearing influence which this unjust monoply of family property produces.   Nor is this all.   It occasions a waste of national property.   A considerable part of the land of the country is rendered unproductive, by the great extent of parks and chases which this law serves to keep up, and this at a time when the annual production of grain is not equal to the national consumption.*—In short, the evils of the aristocratical system are so great and numerous, so inconsistent with every thing that is just, wise, natural, and beneficent, that when they are considered, there ought not to be a doubt that many, who are now classed under that description, will wish to see such a system abolished.

What pleasure can they derive from contemplating the exposed condition, and almost certain beggary of their younger offspring?   Every aristocratical family has an appendage of family beggars hanging round it, which in a few ages, or a few generations, are shook off, and console themselves with telling their tale in almshouses, workhouses, and prisons.   This is the natural consequence of aristocracy.   The peer and the beggar are often of the same family.   One extreme produces the other : to make one

* See the Reports on the Corn Trade.—*Author.*

rich many must be made poor; neither can the system be supported by other means.

There are two classes of people to whom the laws of England are particularly hostile, and those the most helpless; younger children, and the poor. Of the former I have just spoken; of the latter I shall mention one instance out of the many that might be produced, and with which I shall close this subject.

Several laws are in existence for regulating and limiting work-men's wages. Why not leave them as free to make their own bargains, as the law-makers are to let their farms and houses? Personal labour is all the property they have. Why is that little, and the little freedom they enjoy, to be infringed? But the injustice will appear stronger, if we consider the operation and effect of such laws. When wages are fixed by what is called a law, the legal wages remain stationary, while every thing else is in progression; and as those who make that law, still continue to lay on new taxes by other laws, they encrease the expence of living by one law, and take away the means by another.

But if these gentlemen law-makers and tax-makers thought it right to limit the poor pittance which personal labour can produce, and on which a whole family is to be supported, they certainly must feel themselves happily indulged in a limitation on their own part, of not less than twelve thousand a-year, and that of property they never acquired, (nor probably any of their ancestors) and of which they have made so ill a use.

Having now finished this subject, I shall bring the several particulars into one view, and then proceed to other matters.

The first eight articles are brought forward from p. 493:

1. Abolition of two millions poor-rates.

2. Provision for two hundred and fifty-two thousand poor families, at the rate of four pounds per head for each child under fourteen years of age; which, with the addition of two hundred and fifty thousand pounds, provides also education for one million and thirty thousand children.

3. Annuity of six pounds (per annum) each for all poor persons, decayed tradesmen, and others (supposed seventy thousand) of the age of fifty years, and until sixty.

4. Annuity of ten pounds each for life for all poor persons, decayed tradesmen, and others (supposed seventy thousand) of the age of sixty years.

5. Donation of twenty shillings each for fifty thousand births.

6. Donation of twenty shillings each for twenty thousand marriages.

7. Allowance of twenty thousand pounds for the funeral expenses of persons travelling for work, and dying at a distance from their friends.

8. Employment at all times for the casual poor in the cities of London and Westminster.

Second enumeration:

9. Abolition of the tax on houses and windows.

10. Allowance of three shillings per week for life to fifteen thousand disbanded soldiers, and a proportionate allowance to the officers of the disbanded corps.

11. Encrease of pay to the remaining soldiers of 19,500*l.* annually.

12. The same allowance to the disbanded navy, and the same encrease of pay, as to the army.

13. Abolition of the commutation tax.

14. Plan of a progressive tax, operating to extirpate the unjust and unnatural law of primogeniture, and the vicious influence of the aristocratical system *

* When inquiries are made into the condition of the poor, various degrees of distress will most probably be found, to render a different arrangement preferable to that which is already proposed. Widows with families will be in greater want than where there are husbands living. There is also a difference in the expence of living in different counties: and more so in fuel.

Suppose then fifty thousand extraordinary cases, at the rate of ten
      pounds per family per ann................................... 500,000*l.*
100,000 families, at 8*l.* per family per ann..................... 800,000
100,000 families, at 7*l.* per   "   "   700,000
104,000 families, at 5*l.* per   "   "   520,000
And instead of ten shillings per head for the education of other
      children, to allow fifty shillings per family for that purpose to
      fifty thousand families................................... 250,000

                                                                 2,770,000
140,000 aged persons as before,   1,120,000

                                                                 3,890,000*l.*

This arrangement amounts to the same sum as stated in p. 489, including the 250,000*l.* for education; but it provides (including the aged people) for four hundred and four thousand families, which is almost one third of all the families in England.—*Author.*

There yet remains, as already stated, one million of surplus taxes. Some part of this will be required for circumstances that do not immediately present themselves, and such part as shall not be wanted, will admit of a further reduction of taxes equal to that amount.

Among the claims that justice requires to be made, the condition of the inferior revenue-officers will merit attention. It is a reproach to any government to waste such an immensity of revenue in sinecures and nominal and unnecessary places and officers, and not allow even a decent livelihood to those on whom the labour falls. The salary of the inferior officers of the revenue has stood at the petty pittance of less than fifty pounds a year for upwards of one hundred years. It ought to be seventy. About one hundred and twenty thousand pounds applied to this purpose, will put all those salaries in a decent condition.

This was proposed to be done almost twenty years ago, but the treasury-board then in being, startled at it, as it might lead to similar expectations from the army and navy ; and the event was, that the King, or somebody for him, applied to parliament to have his own salary raised an hundred thousand pounds a year, which being done, every thing else was laid aside.[1]

With respect to another class of men, the inferior clergy, I forbear to enlarge on their condition ; but all partialities and prejudices for, or against, different modes and forms of religion aside, common justice will determine, whether there ought to be an income of twenty or thirty pounds a year to one man, and of ten thousand to another: I speak on this subject with the more freedom, because I am known not to be a Presbyterian ; and therefore the cant cry of court sycophants, about church and meeting, kept up to amuse and bewilder the nation, cannot be raised against me.

Ye simple men on both sides the question, do you not see

---

[1] In 1772, Paine, then Exciseman at Lewes, wrote *The Case of the officers of Excise ; with remarks on the qualifications of officers ; and of the numerous evils arising to the Revenue from the insufficiency of the present salary. Humbly addressed to the Hon. and Right Hon. Members of both Houses of Parliament.* Though printed it was not published until 1793. It will appear in the Appendix of our final volume.—*Editor.*

through this courtly craft? If ye can be kept disputing and wrangling about church and meeting, ye just answer the purpose of every courtier, who lives the while on the spoils of the taxes, and laughs at your credulity. Every religion is good that teaches man to be good; and I know of none that instructs him to be bad.

All the before-mentioned calculations suppose only sixteen millions and an half of taxes paid into the exchequer, after the expence of collection and drawbacks at the customhouse and excise-office are deducted; whereas the sum paid into the exchequer is very nearly, if not quite, seventeen millions. The taxes raised in Scotland and Ireland are expended in those countries, and therefore their savings will come out of their own taxes; but if any part be paid into the English exchequer, it might be remitted. This will not make one hundred thousand pounds a year difference.

There now remains only the national debt to be considered. In the year 1789, the interest, exclusive of the tontine, was 9,150,138*l.* How much the capital has been reduced since that time the minister best knows. But after paying the interest, abolishing the tax on houses and windows, the commutation tax, and the poor-rates; and making all the provisions for the poor, for the education of children, the support of the aged, the disbanded part of the army and navy, and encreasing the pay of the remainder, there will be a surplus of one million.

The present scheme of paying off the national debt appears to me, speaking as an indifferent person, to be an ill-concerted, if not a fallacious job. The burthen of the national debt consists not in its being so many millions, or so many hundred millions, but in the quantity of taxes collected every year to pay the interest. If this quantity continues the same, the burthen of the national debt is the same to all intents and purposes, be the capital more or less. The only knowledge which the public can have of the reduction of the debt, must be through the reduction of taxes for paying the interest. The debt, therefore, is not reduced one farthing to the public by all the millions that have been paid; and it would require more money now to purchase up the capital, than when the scheme began.

Digressing for a moment at this point, to which I shall return again, I look back to the appointment of Mr. Pitt, as minister.

I was then in America. The war was over; and though resentment had ceased, memory was still alive.

When the news of the coalition arrived, though it was a matter of no concern to me as a citizen of America, I felt it as a man. It had something in it which shocked, by publicly sporting with decency, if not with principle. It was impudence in Lord North; it was a want of firmness in Mr. Fox.

Mr. Pitt was, at that time, what may be called a maiden character in politics. So far from being hackneyed, he appeared not to be initiated into the first mysteries of court intrigue. Every thing was in his favour. Resentment against the coalition served as friendship to him, and his ignorance of vice was credited for virtue. With the return of peace, commerce and prosperity would rise of itself; yet even this encrease was thrown to his account.

When he came to the helm, the storm was over, and he had nothing to interrupt his course. It required even ingenuity to be wrong, and he succeeded. A little time shewed him the same sort of man as his predecessors had been. Instead of profiting by those errors which had accumulated a burthen of taxes unparalleled in the world, he sought, I might almost say, he advertised for enemies, and provoked means to encrease taxation. Aiming at something, he knew not what, he ransacked Europe and India for adventures, and abandoning the fair pretensions he began with, he became the knight-errant of modern times.

It is unpleasant to see character throw itself away. It is more so to see one's-self deceived. Mr. Pitt had merited nothing, but he promised much. He gave symptoms of a mind superior to the meanness and corruption of courts. His apparent candour encouraged expectations; and the public confidence, stunned, wearied, and confounded by a chaos of parties, revived and attached itself to him. But mistaking, as he has done, the disgust of the nation against the coalition, for merit in himself, he has rushed into measures, which a man less supported would not have presumed to act.

All this seems to show that change of ministers amounts to nothing. One goes out, another comes in, and still the same measures, vices, and extravagance are pursued. It signifies not who is minister. The defect lies in the system. The foundation and the superstructure of the government is bad. Prop it as you please, it continually sinks into court government, and ever will.

I return, as I promised, to the subject of the national debt, that offspring of the Dutch-Anglo-revolution, and its handmaid the Hanover succession.

But it is now too late to enquire how it began. Those to whom it is due have advanced the money; and whether it was well or ill spent, or pocketed, is not their crime. It is, however, easy to see, that as the nation proceeds in contemplating the nature and principles of government, and to understand taxes, and make comparisons between those of America, France, and England, it will be next to impossible to keep it in the same torpid state it has hitherto been. Some reform must, from the necessity of the case, soon begin. It is not whether these principles press with little or much force in the present moment. They are out. They are abroad in the world, and no force can stop them. Like a secret told, they are beyond recall; and he must be blind indeed that does not see that a change is already beginning.

Nine millions of dead taxes is a serious thing; and this not only for bad, but in a great measure for foreign government. By putting the power of making war into the hands of the foreigners who came for what they could get, little else was to be expected than what has happened.

Reasons are already advanced in this work, shewing that whatever the reforms in the taxes may be, they ought to be made in the current expences of government, and not in the part applied to the interest of the national debt. By remitting the taxes of the poor, *they* will be totally relieved, and all discontent will be taken away; and by striking off such of the taxes as are already mentioned, the nation will more than recover the whole expence of the mad American war.

There will then remain only the national debt as a subject of discontent; and in order to remove, or rather to prevent this, it would be good policy in the stock-holders themselves to consider it as property, subject like all other property, to bear some portion of the taxes. It would give to it both popularity and security, and as a great part of its present inconvenience is balanced by the capital which it keeps alive, a measure of this kind would so far add to that balance as to silence objections.

This may be done by such gradual means as to accomplish all that is necessary with the greatest ease and convenience.

Instead of taxing the capital, the best method would be to tax the interest by some progressive ratio, and to lessen the public taxes in the same proportion as the interest diminished.

Suppose the interest was taxed one halfpenny in the pound the first year, a penny more the second, and to proceed by a certain ratio to be determined upon, always less than any other tax upon property. Such a tax would be subtracted from the interest at the time of payment, without any expence of collection.

One halfpenny in the pound would lessen the interest and consequently the taxes, twenty thousand pounds. The tax on waggons amounts to this sum, and this tax might be taken off the first year. The second year the tax on female servants, or some other of the like amount might also be taken off, and by proceeding in this manner, always applying the tax raised from the property of the debt toward its extinction, and not carry it to the current services, it would liberate itself.

The stockholders, notwithstanding this tax, would pay less taxes than they do now. What they would save by the extinction of the poor-rates, and the tax on houses and windows, and the commutation tax, would be considerably greater than what this tax, slow, but certain in its operation, amounts to.

It appears to me to be prudence to look out for measures that may apply under any circumstance that may approach. There is, at this moment, a crisis in the affairs of Europe that requires it. Preparation now is wisdom. If taxation be once let loose, it will be difficult to re-instate it; neither would the relief be so effectual, as if it proceeded by some certain and gradual reduction.

The fraud, hypocrisy, and imposition of governments, are now beginning to be too well understood to promise them any long career. The farce of monarchy and aristocracy, in all countries, is following that of chivalry, and Mr. Burke is dressing for the funeral. Let it then pass quietly to the tomb of all other follies, and the mourners be comforted.

The time is not very distant when England will laugh at itself for sending to Holland, Hanover, Zell, or Burnswick for men, at the expence of a million a year, who understood neither her laws, her language, nor her interest, and whose capacities would scarcely have fitted them for the office of a parish constable. If government could be trusted to such hands, it must be some easy and simple thing indeed, and materials fit for all the purposes may be found in every town and village in England.

When it shall be said in any country in the world, my poor are happy; neither ignorance nor distress is to be found among them; my jails are empty of prisoners, my streets of beggars; the aged are not in want, the taxes are not oppressive; the rational world is my friend, because I am the friend of its happiness: when these things can be said, then may that country boast its constitution and its government.

Within the space of a few years we have seen two revolutions, those of America and France. In the former, the contest was long, and the conflict severe; in the latter, the nation acted with such a consolidated impulse, that having no foreign enemy to contend with, the revolution was complete in power the moment it appeared. From both those instances it is evident, that the greatest forces that can be brought into the field of revolutions, are reason and common interest. Where these can have the opportunity of acting, opposition dies with fear, or crumbles away by conviction. It is a great standing which they have now universally obtained; and we may hereafter hope to see revolutions, or changes in governments, produced with the same quiet operation by which any measure, determinable by reason and discussion, is accomplished.

When a nation changes its opinion and habits of thinking, it is no longer to be governed as before; but it would not only be wrong, but bad policy, to attempt by force what ought to be accomplished by reason. Rebellion consists in forcibly opposing the general will of a nation, whether by a party or by a government. There ought, therefore, to be in every nation a method of occasionally ascertaining the state of public opinion with respect to government. On this point the old government of France was superior to the present government of England, because, on extraordinary occasions, recourse could be had to what was then called the States General. But in England there are no such occasional bodies; and as to those who are now called Representatives, a great part of them are mere machines of the court, placemen, and dependants.

I presume, that though all the people of England pay taxes, not an hundredth part of them are electors, and the members of one of the houses of parliament represent nobody but themselves. There is, therefore, no power but the voluntary will of the people that has a right to act in any matter respecting a general reform; and by the same right that two persons can confer on such a subject, a thousand may. The object, in all such preliminary proceedings, is to find out what the general sense of a nation is, and to be governed by it. If it prefer a bad or defective government to a reform or chuse to pay ten times more taxes than there is any occasion for, it has a right so to do; and so long as the majority do not impose conditions on the minority, different from what they impose upon themselves, though there may be much error, there is no injustice. Neither will the error continue long. Reason and discussion will soon bring things right, however wrong they may begin. By such a process no tumult is to be apprehended. The poor, in all countries, are naturally both peaceable and grateful in all reforms in which their interest and happiness is included. It is only by neglecting and rejecting them that they become tumultuous.

The objects that now press on the public attention are, the French revolution, and the prospect of a general revolution in governments. Of all nations in Europe there is none so much interested in the French revolution as England, Enemies for ages, and that at a vast expence, and without any national object, the opportunity now presents itself of amicably closing the scene, and joining their efforts to reform the rest of Europe. By doing this they will not only prevent the further effusion of blood, and encrease of taxes, but be in a condition of getting rid of a considerable part of their present burthens, as has been already stated. Long experience however has shewn, that reforms of this kind are not those which old governments wish to promote, and therefore it is to nations, and not to such governments, that these matters present themselves.

In the preceding part of this work, I have spoken of an alliance between England, France, and America, for purposes that were to be afterwards mentioned. Though I have no direct authority on the part of America, I have good reason to conclude, that she is disposed to enter into a consideration of such a measure, provided, that the governments with which she might ally, acted as national governments, and not as courts enveloped in intrigue and mystery. That France as a nation, and a national government, would prefer an alliance with England, is a matter of certainty. Nations, like individuals, who have long been enemies, without knowing each other, or knowing why, become the better friends when they discover the errors and impositions under which they had acted.

Admitting, therefore, the probability of such a connection, I will state some matters by which such an alliance, together with that of Holland, might render service, not only to the parties immediately concerned, but to all Europe.

It is, I think, certain, that if the fleets of England, France, and Holland were confederated, they could propose, with effect, a limitation to, and a general dismantling of, all the navies in Europe, to a certain proportion to be agreed upon.

First, That no new ship of war shall be built by any power in Europe, themselves included.

Second, That all the navies now in existence shall be put back, suppose to one-tenth of their present force. This will save to France and England, at least two millions sterling annually to each, and their relative force be in the same proportion as it is now. If men will permit themselves to think, as rational beings ought to think, nothing can appear more ridiculous and absurd, exclusive of all moral reflections, than to be at the expence of building navies, filling them with men, and then hauling them into the ocean, to try which can sink each other fastest. Peace, which costs nothing, is attended with infinitely more advantage, than any victory with all its expence. But this, though it best answers the purpose of nations, does not that of court governments, whose habited policy is pretence for taxation, places, and offices.

It is, I think, also certain, that the above confederated powers, together with that of the United States of America, can propose with effect, to Spain, the independence of South America, and the opening those countries of immense extent and wealth to the general commerce of the world, as North America now is.

With how much more glory, and advantage to itself, does a nation act, when it exerts its powers to rescue the world from bondage, and to create itself friends, than when it employs those powers to increase ruin, desolation, and misery. The horrid scene that is now acting by the English government in the East-Indies, is fit only to be told of Goths and Vandals, who, destitute of principle, robbed and tortured the world they were incapable of enjoying.

The opening of South America would produce an immense field of commerce, and a ready money market for manufactures, which the eastern world does not. The East is already a country full of manufactures, the importation of which is not only an injury to the manufactures of England, but a drain upon its specie. The balance against England by this trade is regularly upwards of half a million annually sent out in the East-India ships in silver; and this is the reason, together with German intrigue, and German subsidies, that there is so little silver in England.

But any war is harvest to such governments, however ruinous it may be to a nation. It serves to keep up deceitful expectations which prevent people from looking into the defects and abuses of government. It is the *lo here!* and the *lo there!* that amuses and cheats the multitude.

Never did so great an opportunity offer itself to England, and to all Europe, as is produced by the two Revolutions of America and France. By the former, freedom has a national champion in the western world; and by the latter, in Europe. When another nation shall join France, despotism and bad government will scarcely dare to appear. To use a trite expression, the iron is becoming hot all over Europe. The insulted German and the enslaved Spaniard, the Russ and the Pole, are beginning to think. The present age will hereafter merit to be called the Age of reason,[1] and the present generation will appear to the future as the Adam of a new world.

When all the governments of Europe shall be established on the representative system, nations will become acquainted, and the animosities and prejudices fomented by the intrigue and artifice of courts, will cease. The oppressed soldier will become a freeman; and the tortured sailor, no longer dragged through the streets like a felon, will pursue his mercantile voyage in safety. It would be better that nations should continue the pay of their soldiers during their lives, and give them their discharge and restore them to freedom and their friends, and cease recruiting, than retain such multitudes at the same expence, in a condition useless to society and to themselves. As soldiers have

---

[1] It was about a year later that Paine used this phrase as the title of his work on religion, which, however, did not appear until 1794.—*Editor.*

hitherto been treated in most countries, they might be said to be without a friend. Shunned by the citizen on an apprehension of their being enemies to liberty, and too often insulted by those who commanded them, their condition was a double oppression. But where genuine principles of liberty pervade a people, every thing is restored to order; and the soldier civilly treated, returns the civility.

In contemplating revolutions, it is easy to perceive that they may arise from two distinct causes; the one, to avoid or get rid of some great calamity; the other, to obtain some great and positive good; and the two may be distinguished by the names of active and passive revolutions. In those which proceed from the former cause, the temper becomes incensed and sowered; and the redress, obtained by danger, is too often sullied by revenge. But in those which proceed from the latter, the heart, rather animated than agitated, enters serenely upon the subject. Reason and discussion, persuasion and conviction, become the weapons in the contest, and it is only when those are attempted to be suppressed that recourse is had to violence. When men unite in agreeing that a *thing is good*, could it be obtained, such for instance as relief from a burden of taxes and the extinction of corruption, the object is more than half accomplished. What they approve as the end, they will promote in the means.

Will any man say, in the present excess of taxation, falling so heavily on the poor, that a remission of five pounds annually of taxes to one hundred and four thousand poor families is not a *good thing?* Will he say, that a remission of seven pounds annually to one hundred thousand other poor families—of eight pounds annually to another hundred thousand poor families, and of ten pounds annually to fifty thousand poor and widowed families, are not *good things?* And, to proceed a step further in this climax, will he say, that to provide against the misfortunes to which all human life is subject, by securing six pounds annually for all poor, distressed, and reduced persons of the age of fifty and until sixty, and of ten pounds annually after sixty, is not a *good thing?*

Will he say, that an abolition of two millions of poor-rates
to the house-keepers, and of the whole of the house and
window-light tax and of the commutation tax is not a *good
thing?* Or will he say, that to abolish corruption is a *bad
thing?*

If, therefore, the good to be obtained be worthy of a passive, rational, and costless revolution, it would be bad policy
to prefer waiting for a calamity that should force a violent
one. I have no idea, considering the reforms which are now
passing and spreading throughout Europe, that England
will permit herself to be the last; and where the occasion
and the opportunity quietly offer, it is better than to wait
for a turbulent necessity. It may be considered as an honour to the animal faculties of man to obtain redress by
courage and danger, but it is far greater honour to the
rational faculties to accomplish the same object by reason,
accommodation, and general consent.*

As reforms, or revolutions, call them which you please,
extend themselves among nations, those nations will form
connections and conventions, and when a few are thus confederated, the progress will be rapid, till despotism and corrupt government be totally expelled, at least out of two
quarters of the world, Europe and America. The Algerine

* I know it is the opinion of many of the most enlightened characters in
France (there always will be those who see further into events than others,)
not only among the general mass of citizens, but of many of the principal
members of the former National Assembly, that the monarchical plan will not
continue many years in that country. They have found out, that as wisdom
cannot be made hereditary, power ought not; and that, for a man to merit a
million sterling a year from a nation, he ought to have a mind capable of comprehending from an atom to a universe, which, if he had, he would be above
receiving the pay. But they wished not to appear to lead the nation faster
than its own reason and interest dictated. In all the conversations where I
have been present upon this subject, the idea always was, that when such a
time, from the general opinion of the nation, shall arrive, that the honourable
and liberal method would be, to make a handsome present in fee simple to the
person, whoever he may be, that shall then be in the monarchical office, and
for him to retire to the enjoyment of private life, possessing his share of general rights and privileges, and to be no more accountable to the public for his
time and his conduct than any other citizen.—*Author.*

Monarchy was formally abolished in France Sept. 21, 1792.—*Editor.*

piracy may then be commanded to cease, for it is only by the malicious policy of old governments, against each other that it exists.[1]

Throughout this work, various and numerous as the subjects are, which I have taken up and investigated, there is only a single paragraph upon religion, *viz. "that every religion is good that teaches man to be good."*

I have carefully avoided to enlarge upon the subject, because I am inclined to believe, that what is called the present ministry, wish to see contentions about religion kept up, to prevent the nation turning its attention to subjects of government. It is, as if they were to say, *"Look that way, or any way, but this."*

But as religion is very improperly made a political machine, and the reality of it is thereby destroyed, I will conclude this work with stating in what light religion appears to me.

If we suppose a large family of children, who, on any particular day, or particular circumstance, made it a custom to present to their parents some token of their affection and gratitude, each of them would make a different offering, and most probably in a different manner. Some would pay their congratulations in themes of verse and prose, by some little devices, as their genius dictated, or according to what they thought would please; and, perhaps, the least of all, not able to do any of those things, would ramble into the garden, or the field, and gather what it thought the prettiest flower it could find, though, perhaps, it might be but a simple weed. The parent would be more gratified by such a variety, than if the whole of them had acted on a concerted plan, and each had made exactly the same offering. This would have the cold appearance of contrivance, or the harsh one of controul. But of all unwelcome things, noth-

---

[1] In a MS. Note-Book of Thomas ' Clio' Rickman, an anecdote, entered about 1818, is told as follows : " The Duke of Kent, when at Gibraltar, some years since, visited in great state The Dey of Algiers. The Dey, wishing to ingratiate himself, said, *Your father is the greatest Pirate in the world, and I am the next !*" —*Editor.*

ing could more afflict the parent than to know, that the whole of them had afterwards gotten together by the ears, boys and girls, fighting, scratching, reviling, and abusing each other about which was the best or the worst present.

Why may we not suppose, that the great Father of all is pleased with variety of devotion; and that the greatest offence we can act, is that by which we seek to torment and render each other miserable? For my own part, I am fully satisfied that what I am now doing, with an endeavour to conciliate mankind, to render their condition happy, to unite nations that have hitherto been enemies, and to extirpate the horrid practice of war, and break the chains of slavery and oppression is acceptable in his sight, and being the best service I can perform, I act it chearfully.

I do not believe that any two men, on what are called doctrinal points, think alike who think at all. It is only those who have not thought that appear to agree. It is in this case as with what is called the British constitution. It has been taken for granted to be good, and encomiums have supplied the place of proof. But when the nation comes to examine into its principles and the abuses it admits, it will be found to have more defects than I have pointed out in this work and the former.

As to what are called national religions, we may, with as much propriety, talk of national Gods. It is either political craft or the remains of the Pagan system, when every nation had its separate and particular deity. Among all the writers of the English church clergy, who have treated on the general subject of religion, the present Bishop of Landaff has not been excelled, and it is with much pleasure that I take this opportunity of expressing this token of respect.[1]

I have now gone through the whole of the subject, at least, as far as it appears to me at present. It has been my intention for the five years I have been in Europe, to offer an address to the people of England on the subject of

[1] Richard Watson (1737-1816). This homage in 1792 to the writer whose fame rests chiefly on his answer to Paine's *Age of Reason* ("Apology for the Bible," 1796) is worthy of note.—*Editor*.

overnment, if the opportunity presented itself before I
eturned to America.   Mr. Burke has thrown it in my way,
nd I thank him.   On a certain occasion, three years ago, I
ressed him to propose a national convention, to be fairly
lected, for the purpose of taking the state of the nation
nto consideration ; but I found, that however strongly the
arliamentary current was then setting against the party he
cted with, their policy was to keep every thing within that
ield of corruption, and trust to accidents.   Long experience
ad shewn that parliaments would follow any change of
ninisters, and on this they rested their hopes and their ex-
ectations.

Formerly, when divisions arose respecting governments,
ecourse was had to the sword, and a civil war ensued.
That savage custom is exploded by the new system, and
eference is had to national conventions.   Discussion and
he general will arbitrates the question, and to this, private
pinion yields with a good grace, and order is preserved
ininterrupted.

Some gentlemen have affected to call the principles upon
which this work and the former part of *Rights of Man* are
ounded, " a new-fangled doctrine."   The question is not
whether those principles are new or old, but whether they
re right or wrong.   Suppose the former, I will shew their
ffect by a figure easily understood.

It is now towards the middle of February.   Were I to
ake a turn into the country, the trees would present a leaf-
ess, wintery appearance.   As people are apt to pluck twigs
s they walk along, I perhaps might do the same, and by
hance might observe, that a *single bud* on that twig had
egun to swell.   I should reason very unnaturally, or rather
ot reason at all, to suppose this was the *only* bud in Eng-
and which had this appearance.   Instead of deciding thus, I
hould instantly conclude, that the same appearance was
eginning, or about to begin, every where ; and though the
vegetable sleep will continue longer on some trees and plants
han on others, and though some of them may not *blossom*
or two or three years, all will be in leaf in the summer, ex-

cept those which are *rotten.* What pace the political summer may keep with the natural, no human foresight ca determine. It is, however, not difficult to perceive that th spring is begun.—Thus wishing, as I sincerely do, freedom and happiness to all nations, I close the SECOND PART.

APPENDIX.

As the publication of this work has been delayed beyond the time intended, I think it not improper, all circumstances considered, to state the causes that have occasioned that delay.

The reader will probably observe, that some parts in the plan contained in this work for reducing the taxes, and certain parts in Mr. Pitt's speech at the opening of the present session, Tuesday, January 31, are so much alike, as to induce a belief, that either the author had taken the hint from Mr. Pitt, or Mr. Pitt from the author.—I will first point out the parts that are similar, and then state such circumstances as I am acquainted with, leaving the reader to make his own conclusion.

Considering it as almost an unprecedented case, that taxes should be proposed to be taken off, it is equally extraordinary that such a measure should occur to two persons at the same time; and still more so (considering the vast variety and multiplicity of taxes) that they should hit on the same specific taxes. Mr. Pitt has mentioned, in *his* speech, the tax on *Carts* and *Wagons*—that on *Female Servants*—the lowering the tax on *Candles* and the taking off the tax of three shillings on *Houses* having under seven windows.

Every one of those specific taxes are a part of the plan contained in this work, and proposed also to be taken off. Mr. Pitt's plan, it is true, goes no further than to a reduction of three hundred and twenty thousand pounds; and the reduction proposed in this work, to nearly six millions. I have made my calculations on only sixteen millions and an half of revenue, still asserting that it was " very nearly, if not quite, seventeen millions." Mr. Pitt states it at 16,690,-

ooo.   I know enough of the matter to say, that he has no
*over*stated it.   Having thus given the particulars, whic
correspond in this work and his speech, I will state a chai
of circumstances that may lead to some explanation.

The first hint for lessening the taxes, and that as a cons
quence flowing from the French revolution, is to be found i
the ADDRESS and DECLARATION of the Gentlemen wh
met at the Thatched-House Tavern, August 20, 179
Among many other particulars stated in that Address, is th
following, put as an interrogation to the government op
posers of the French Revolution.   *" Are they sorry that th
pretence for new oppressive taxes, and the occasion for continu
ing many old taxes will be at an end ? "*

It is well known, that the persons who chiefly frequen
the Thatched-House Tavern, are men of court connection
and so much did they take this Address and Declaratio
respecting the French Revolution, and the reduction of taxe
in disgust, that the Landlord was under the necessity o
informing the Gentlemen, who composed the meeting of th
20th of August, and who proposed holding another meeting
that he could not receive them.*

What was only hinted in the Address and Declaratio
respecting taxes and principles of government, will be foun

* The gentleman who signed the address and declaration as chairman of th
meeting, Mr. Horne Tooke, being generally supposed to be the person wh
drew it up, and having spoken much in commendation of it, has been joculari
accused of praising his own work.   To free him from this embarrassment, an
to save him the repeated trouble of mentioning the author, aş he has not faile
to do, I make no hesitation in saying, that as the opportunity of benefiting b
the French Revolution easily occurred to me, I drew up the publication in ques
tion, and shewed it to him and some other gentlemen, who, fully approving i
held a meeting for the purpose of making it public, and subscribed to th
amount of fifty guineas to defray the expence of advertising.   I believe the
are at this time, in England, a greater number of men acting on disintereste
principles, and determined to look into the nature and practices of governmen
themselves, and not blindly trust, as has hitherto been the case, either to go
ernment generally, or to parliaments, or to parliamentary opposition, than a
any former period.   Had this been done a century ago, corruption and taxatio
had not arrived to the height they are now at.—*Author*.

The Address and Declaration alluded to above is No. XII. in the presen
volume.—*Editor*.

reduced to a regular system in this work.   But as Mr Pitt's
speech contains some of the same things respecting taxes, I
now come to give the circumstances before alluded to.

The case is : This work was intended to be published just
before the meeting of Parliament, and for that purpose a
considerable part of the copy was put into the printer's
hands in September, and all the remaining copy, as far as
page 160, which contains the part to which Mr. Pitt's speech
is similar, was given to him full six weeks before the meeting of parliament, and he was informed of the time at which
it was to appear.   He had composed nearly the whole about
a fortnight before the time of Parliament meeting, and had
printed as far as page 112, and had given me a proof of the
next sheet, up to page 128.   It was then in sufficient for-
wardness to be out at the time proposed, as two other sheets
were ready for striking off.   I had before told him, that if
he thought he should be straitened for time, I could get
part of the work done at another press, which he desired me
not to do.   In this manner the work stood on the Tuesday
fortnight preceding the meeting of Parliament, when all at
once, without any previous intimation, though I had been
with him the evening before, he sent me, by one of his work-
men, all the remaining copy, from page 112, declining to go
on with the work *on any consideration.*

To account for this extraordinary conduct I was totally at
a loss, as he stopped at the part where the arguments on
systems and principles of government closed, and where the
plan for the reduction of taxes, the education of children,
and the support of the poor and the aged begins ; and still
more especially, as he had, at the time of his beginning to
print, and before he had seen the whole copy, offered a
thousand pounds for the copy-right, together with the future
copy-right of the former part of the Rights of Man.   I told
the person who brought me this offer that I should not accept it, and wished it not to be renewed, giving him as my
reason, that though I believed the printer to be an honest
man, I would never put it in the power of any printer or publisher to suppress or alter a work of mine, by making him

master of the copy, or give to him the right of selling it to any minister, or to any other person, or to treat as a mere matter of traffic, that which I intended should operate as a principle.

His refusal to complete the work (which he could not purchase) obliged me to seek for another printer, and this of consequence would throw the publication back till after the meeting of Parliament, otherways it would have appeared that Mr. Pitt had only taken up a part of the plan which I had more fully stated.

Whether that gentleman, or any other, had seen the work, or any part of it, is more than I have authority to say. But the manner in which the work was returned, and the particular time at which this was done, and that after the offers he had made, are suspicious circumstances. I know what the opinion of booksellers and publishers is upon such a case, but as to my own opinion, I chuse to make no declaration. There are many ways by which proof sheets may be procured by other persons before a work publicly appears; to which I shall add a certain circumstance, which is,

A ministerial bookseller in Piccadilly who has been employed, as common report says, by a clerk of one of the boards closely connected with the ministry (the board of trade and plantation, of which Hawkesbury is president) to publish what he calls my Life,[1] (I wish his own life and those of the cabinet were as good,) used to have his books printed at the same printing-office that I employed; but when the former part of *Rights of Man* came out, he took his work away in dudgeon; and about a week or ten days before the printer returned my copy, he came to make him an offer of his work again, which was accepted. This would consequently give him admission into the printing-office where the

---

[1] " The Life of Thomas Pain, Author of the ' Rights of Men,' with a Defence of his Writings. By Francis Oldys, A.M. of the University of Pennsylvania." George Chalmers, the clerk alluded to, by this purely fictitious claim to American connection, and pretence to " Defence," proved himself quite equal to the surreptitious action suspected by Paine. His libellous " Life" proves him well acquainted with Paine's transactions with the first printer. See my " Life of Paine," i., 330.—*Editor*.

sheets of this work were then lying ; and as booksellers and printers are free with each other, he would have the opportunity of seeing what was going on.—Be the case, however, as it may, Mr. Pitt's plan, little and diminutive as it is, would have made a very awkward appearance, had this work appeared at the time the printer had engaged to finish it.

I have now stated the particulars which occasioned the delay, from the proposal to purchase, to the refusal to print. If all the Gentlemen are innocent, it is very unfortunate for them that such a variety of suspicious circumstances should, without any design, arrange themselves together.

Having now finished this part, I will conclude with stating another circumstance.

About a fortnight or three weeks before the meeting of Parliament, a small addition, amounting to about twelve shillings and sixpence a year, was made to the pay of the soldiers, or rather their pay was docked so much less.   Some Gentlemen who knew, in part, that this work would contain a plan of reforms respecting the oppressed condition of soldiers, wished me to add a note to the work, signifying that the part upon that subject had been in the printer's hands some weeks before that addition of pay was proposed.   I declined doing this, lest it should be interpreted into an air of vanity, or an endeavour to excite suspicion (for which perhaps there might be no grounds) that some of the government gentlemen had, by some means or other, made out what this work would contain: and had not the printing been interrupted so as to occasion a delay beyond the time fixed for publication, nothing contained in this appendix would have appeared.

THOMAS PAINE.

END OF VOLUME II.

INTRODUCTION.

No apology is needed for an edition of Thomas Paine's writings, but rather for the tardiness of its appearance. For although there have been laborious and useful collections of his more famous works, none of them can be fairly described as adequate. The compilers have failed to discover many characteristic essays, they printed from imperfect texts, and were unable to find competent publishers courageous enough to issue in suitable form the Works of Paine. It is not creditable that the world has had to wait so long for a complete edition of writings which excited the gratitude and admiration of the founders of republican liberty in America and Europe; nevertheless those writings, so far as accessible, have been read and pondered by multitudes, and are to-day in large and increasing demand.

This indeed is not wonderful. Time, which destroys much literature, more slowly overtakes that which was inspired by any great human cause. "It was the cause of America that made me an author," wrote Paine at the close of the American Revolution; and in the preface to his first pamphlet he had said: "The cause of America is in a great measure the cause of all mankind." In the presence of such great argument he made no account of the poems and magazine essays published before the appearance of his first pamphlet, "Common Sense,"—the earliest plea for an independent American Republic. The magazine essays, which are printed in this volume, and the poems, reserved for the last, while they prove Paine's literary ability, also reveal in him an overpowering moral sentiment and human sympathy which must necessarily make his literary art their organ. Paine knew the secret of good writing.   In criticising a passage from the Abbé Raynal's " Revolution of America " he writes :

" In this paragraph the conception is lofty, and the expression elegant ; but the colouring is too high for the original, and the likeness fails through an excess of graces.   To fit the powers of thinking and the turn of language to the subject, so as to bring out a clear conclusion that shall hit the point in question, and nothing else, is the true criterion of writing.   But the greater part of the Abbé's writings (if he will pardon me the remark) appear to me uncentral, and burthened with variety.   They represent a beautiful wilderness without paths ; in which the eye is diverted by every thing, without being particularly directed to any thing ; and in which it is agreeable to be lost, and difficult to find the way out."

One cannot but wonder how Paine acquired his literary equipment, almost as complete in his first work as in his last. In his thirty-second year, when exciseman at Lewes, he made on the intelligent gentlemen of the White Hart Club an impression which led one of them, Mr. Lee, to apostrophize him in such lines as these :

> " Thy logic vanquish'd error, and thy mind
> No bounds but those of right and truth confined.
> Thy soul of fire must sure ascend the sky,
> Immortal Paine, thy fame can never die."

This was written of a man who had never published a word, and who, outside his club, was one of the poorest and most obscure men in England.   He must in some way have presently gained reputation for superior intelligence among his fellow-excisemen, who appointed him to write their plea to Parliament for an increase of salary.   This document, printed but not published in 1772 (reserved for an appendix to our last volume), is written in the lucid and simple style characteristic of all Paine's works,—" hitting the point in question and nothing else."   But with all of this power he would appear to have been without literary ambition, and writes to Goldsmith: " It is my first and only attempt, and even now I should not have undertaken it had I not been particularly applied to by some of my superiors in office." Such, when nearly thirty-six, was the man who three years later published in America the book which made as much history as any ever written.

These facts suggest some explanation of the effectiveness of Paine's work. Possessed of a style which, as Edmund Randolph said, insinuated itself into the hearts of learned and unlearned, he wrote not for the sake of writing, penned no word for personal fame, cared not for the morrow of his own reputation. His Quaker forerunner, George Fox, was never more surrendered to the moving spirit of the moment. Absorbed in the point to be carried, discarding all rhetoric that did not feather his arrow, dealing with every detail as well as largest events and principles, his works are now invaluable to the student of American history. In them the course of political events from 1774 to 1787 may be followed almost from hour to hour, and even his military narratives are of great importance. Previous editors of Paine's works, concerned mainly with his theories, have overlooked many of these occasional writings ; but the historian, for whom such occasions are never past, will find in these recovered writings testimony all the more valuable because not meant for any day beyond that which elicited it. Chief-Justice Jay confided to a friend his belief that the history of the American Revolution would never be written, on account of the reputations that would be affected were the truth fully told. That the history has not been really written is known to those who have critically examined the Stevens " Facsimiles," the Letters of George III. and of George Washington. To these actual materials, awaiting the competent and courageous historian, are now added the writings of Thomas Paine, second to none in importance. Certainly there was no witness with better opportunities of information, one more sleeplessly vigilant, or more thoroughly representative of public sentiment during the twelve momentous years in which the American government was founded.

While Paine's American writings are historical documents, their value as such is not limited to the mere record or interpretation of events. They possess very great value for the student of political institutions and constitutional development. Although there are no indications in Paine's writings of direct indebtedness to other writers, such as Rousseau and Locke, he breathes their philosophical atmosphere; but his genius is from the first that of an inventor. His utilitarian schemes, following statements of great principles, are sometimes even somewhat droll, as if a woodcutter should describe gravitation as a law for bringing down his axe upon its log. It was, however, this union in Paine of the theocratic-democratic Quaker visionary with the practical ironworker and engineer which had made him so representative of the theoretical and the concrete, the religious and the political, forces at work in the American Revolution. He utters the pertinent word, whether of sentiment or finance, ethics or gunpowder, local government or national organization, at every stage up to the formation of the federal Union which he was the first to devise. The United States Constitution departed, indeed, from several of the principles maintained by Paine,—as in its bicameral legislature, its disproportionate representation in the Senate, and the degree of non-amenability accorded to the States; but Paine's ideas on these subjects harmonize more nearly with much of the advanced political philosophy of the present day, and his arguments are often used by writers and statesmen who seem unacquainted with his works. The writings of Thomas Paine are therefore of living interest, not only for the light they shed on important events, but as studies and illustrations of political and constitutional evolution.

The present editor has followed the earliest editions, and has preserved Paine's own spelling. Nothing is suppressed, and nothing altered except manifest misprints, and, in a very few cases, punctuations which might impair the sense.

PREFATORY NOTE

TO PAINE'S FIRST ESSAY.

THIS essay is here for the first time printed since its original appearance in the *Postscript to the Pennsylvania Journal and the Weekly Advertiser*, Philadelphia, March 8, 1775. Dr. Benjamin Rush, who was much impressed by the essay, says, " He [Paine] told me the essay to which I alluded was the first thing he had ever published in his life."   Dr. Rush, writing thirty-four years after the interview, and in extreme age, must have reported Paine's remark inexactly, for several articles by Paine were published a little earlier in 1775. But there are indications that this antislavery essay was written at the close of 1774, immediately after Paine's arrival in America (November 30).   It was therefore the first essay he wrote for publication, though its appearance was delayed by the editor.   Probably there was hesitation about publishing it at all.   It was given a place in the *Postscript*. In the same issue " a stout healthy young negro man " is offered for sale, for whom those interested may " enquire of the Printers."   Slavery existed in all of the colonies,—there were nearly 6,000 slaves in Pennsylvania—nor had any one proposed immediate abolition of the system in America.

Attention was called to the Slave Trade by an anonymous pamphlet, small and cheap, entitled " A Short Account of that Part of Africa inhabited by the Negroes, etc."   This was published in Philadelphia, the second edition (probably the first also) dated 1762.   In 1767 the Quaker Anthony Benezet wrote " A Caution and Warning to Great Britain and Her Colonies, etc." (Philadelphia), in which the English denunciations of the Slave Trade were quoted. In 1772 the eminent Dr. Benjamin Rush published two brief pamphlets inveighing against the Slave Trade, and the cruelties of some masters. Although Dr. Rush recognized the injustice of Slavery he made no suggestion for its abolition. In the preface to his "Essays, literary, moral, and philosophical" (Philadelphia, 1798), Dr. Rush says: "The author has omitted in this Collection two pamphlets which he published in the year 1772 upon the Slavery of the Negroes, because he conceived the object of them had been in part accomplished, and because the Citizens of the United States have since that time been furnished from Great Britain and other countries with numerous tracts upon that subject more calculated to complete the effect intended by the author, than his early publications." When this was written Slavery was more powerful than in 1772, and the only object "in part accomplished" was the approaching end of the Slave Trade (1808). It will be seen therefore that the few antislavery protests in America preceding Paine's essay by no means anticipated it. Their aim was to excite horror of the traffic in Africans abroad, but they did not propose to restrict the home traffic, much less to emancipate the slaves. So far as I can discover, to Thomas Paine belongs the honor of being the first American abolitionist. Unnoted as this fact has been from that period to the present, the blow seems to have had far-reaching effects. "This," says Dr. Rush, "excited my desire to be better acquainted with him. We met soon afterwards in Mr. Aitkin's bookstore, where I did homage to his principles and pen upon the subject of the enslaved Africans." Those who know anything of the high position and influence of Dr. Rush can hardly doubt that the "essay with which [he] was much pleased" must have produced some agitation in the small circle of persons interested in the subject, among whom Rush was supreme. Soon after the appearance of Paine's antislavery essay the first American Anti-slavery Society was organized. It was founded at Philadelphia, in the Sun Tavern, Second

Street, April 14, 1775, under title of " The Society for the Relief of Free Negroes, unlawfully held in bondage." There can be little doubt that Paine was among these founders, and it will be seen on a farther page that he partly drafted, and signed, the Act of Pennsylvania abolishing Slavery, March 1, 1780,—the first legislative measure of negro-emancipation in Christendom.

I.

AFRICAN SLAVERY IN AMERICA.

Messrs. BRADFORD,

Please to insert the following, and oblige yours

A. B.

TO AMERICANS.

THAT some desperate wretches should be willing to steal and enslave men by violence and murder for gain, is rather lamentable than strange. But that many civilized, nay, christianized people should approve, and be concerned in the savage practice, is surprising; and still persist, though it has been so often proved contrary to the light of nature, to every principle of Justice and Humanity, and even good policy, by a succession of eminent men,* and several late publications.

Our Traders in MEN (*an unnatural commodity !*) must know the wickedness of that SLAVE-TRADE, if they attend to reasoning, or the dictates of their own hearts; and such as shun and stiffle all these, wilfully sacrifice Conscience, and the character of integrity to that golden Idol.

The Managers of that Trade themselves, and others, testify, that many of these African nations inhabit fertile

* Dr. Ames, Baxter, Durham, Locke, Carmichael, Hutcheson, Montesquieu, and Blackstone, Wallace, etc., etc. Bishop of Gloucester.—*Author.*

[What work of Dr. (? William) Ames is referred to I have not found. The others are Baxter's "Christian Directory"; James Durham's "Law Unsealed"; John Locke's "Of Government"; Gerschomus Carmichael's "Puffendorf"; Francis Hutcheson's "System of Moral Philosophy"; Montesquieu's "Spirit of the Laws"; Blackstone's "Commentaries"; Dr. George Wallace on the ancient peerages of Scotland; "Sermon before the Society for the Propagation of the Gospel, 21 February 1766," by the Bishop of Gloucester (Warburton). —*Editor.*]

countries, are industrious farmers, enjoy plenty, and lived quietly, averse to war, before the Europeans debauched them with liquors, and bribing them against one another; and that these inoffensive people are brought into slavery, by stealing them, tempting Kings to sell subjects, which they can have no right to do, and hiring one tribe to war against another, in order to catch prisoners. By such wicked and inhuman ways the English are said to enslave towards one hundred thousand yearly; of which thirty thousand are supposed to die by barbarous treatment in the first year; besides all that are slain in the unnatural wars excited to take them. So much innocent blood have the Managers and Supporters of this inhuman Trade to answer for to the common Lord of all!

Many of these were not prisoners of war, and redeemed from savage conquerors, as some plead; and they who were such prisoners, the English, who promote the war for that very end, are the guilty authors of their being so; and if they were redeemed, as is alleged, they would owe nothing to the redeemer but what he paid for them.

They show as little Reason as Conscience who put the matter by with saying—" Men, in some cases, are lawfully made Slaves, and why may not these?" So men, in some cases, are lawfully put to death, deprived of their goods, without their consent; may any man, therefore, be treated so, without any conviction of desert? Nor is this plea mended by adding—" They are set forth to us as slaves, and we buy them without farther inquiry, let the sellers see to it." Such men may as well join with a known band of robbers, buy their ill-got goods, and help on the trade; ignorance is no more pleadable in one case than the other; the sellers plainly own how they obtain them. But none can lawfully buy without evidence that they are not concurring with Men-Stealers; and as the true owner has a right to reclaim his goods that were stolen, and sold; so the slave, who is proper owner of his freedom, has a right to reclaim it, however often sold.

Most shocking of all is alledging the Sacred Scriptures to

favour this wicked practice.   One would have thought none
but infidel cavillers would endeavour to make them appear
contrary to the plain dictates of natural light, and Conscience, in a matter of common Justice and Humanity;
which they cannot be.   Such worthy men, as referred to
before, judged otherways; Mr. BAXTER declared, *the Slave-
Traders should be called Devils, rather than Christians; and
that it is a heinous crime to buy them.*   But some say, " the
practice was permitted to the Jews."   To which may be
replied,

  1. The example of the Jews, in many things, may not be
imitated by us; they had not only orders to cut off several
nations altogether, but if they were obliged to war with
others, and conquered them, to cut off every male; they
were suffered to use polygamy and divorces, and other
things utterly unlawful to us under clearer light.

  2. The plea is, in a great measure, false; they had no permission to catch and enslave people who never injured them.

  3. Such arguments ill become us, *since the time of reformation came,* under Gospel light.   All distinctions of nations,
and privileges of one above others, are ceased; Christians
are taught to *account all men their neighbours; and love
their neighbours as themselves; and do to all men as they
would be done by; to do good to all men; and Man-stealing is
ranked with enormous crimes.*   Is the barbarous enslaving
our inoffensive neighbours, and treating them like wild beasts
subdued by force, reconcilable with all these *Divine precepts?*
Is this doing to them as we would desire they should do to
us?   If they could carry off and enslave some thousands of
us, would we think it just?—One would almost wish they
could for once; it might convince more than Reason, or the
Bible.

  As much in vain, perhaps, will they search ancient history
for examples of the modern Slave-Trade.   Too many nations
enslaved the prisoners they took in war.   But to go to
nations with whom there is no war, who have no way provoked, without farther design of conquest, purely to catch
inoffensive people, like wild beasts, for slaves, is an hight of

outrage against Humanity and Justice, that seems left by Heathen nations to be practised by pretended Christians. How shameful are all attempts to colour and excuse it!

As these people are not convicted of forfeiting freedom, they have still a natural, perfect right to it; and the Governments whenever they come should, in justice set them free, and punish those who hold them in slavery.

So monstrous is the making and keeping them slaves at all, abstracted from the barbarous usage they suffer, and the many evils attending the practice; as selling husbands away from wives, children from parents, and from each other, in violation of sacred and natural ties; and opening the way for adulteries, incests, and many shocking consequences, for all of which the guilty Masters must answer to the final Judge.

If the slavery of the parents be unjust, much more is their children's; if the parents were justly slaves, yet the children are born free; this is the natural, perfect right of all mankind; they are nothing but a just recompense to those who bring them up: And as much less is commonly spent on them than others, they have a right, in justice, to be proportionably sooner free.

Certainly one may, with as much reason and decency, plead for murder, robbery, lewdness, and barbarity, as for this practice : They are not more contrary to the natural dictates of Conscience, and feelings of Humanity; nay, they are all comprehended in it.

But the chief design of this paper is not to disprove it, which many have sufficiently done; but to entreat Americans to consider.

1. With what consistency, or decency they complain so loudly of attempts to enslave them, while they hold so many hundred thousands in slavery; and annually enslave many thousands more, without any pretence of authority, or claim upon them?

2. How just, how suitable to our crime is the punishment with which Providence threatens us? We have enslaved multitudes, and shed much innocent blood in doing it; and

now are threatened with the same. And while other evils are confessed, and bewailed, why not this especially, and publicly; than which no other vice, if all others, has brought so much guilt on the land?

3. Whether, then, all ought not immediately to discontinue and renounce it, with grief and abhorrence? Should not every society bear testimony against it, and account obstinate persisters in it bad men, enemies to their country, and exclude them from fellowship; as they often do for much lesser faults?

4. The great Question may be—What should be done with those who are enslaved already? To turn the old and infirm free, would be injustice and cruelty; they who enjoyed the labours of their better days should keep, and treat them humanely. As to the rest, let prudent men, with the assistance of legislatures, determine what is practicable for masters, and best for them. Perhaps some could give them lands upon reasonable rent, some, employing them in their labour still, might give them some reasonable allowances for it; so as all may have some property, and fruits of their labours at their own disposal, and be encouraged to industry; the family may live together, and enjoy the natural satisfaction of exercising relative affections and duties, with civil protection, and other advantages, like fellow men. Perhaps they might sometime form useful barrier settlements on the frontiers. Thus they may become interested in the public welfare, and assist in promoting it; instead of being dangerous, as now they are, should any enemy promise them a better condition.

5. The past treatment of Africans must naturally fill them with abhorrence of Christians; lead them to think our religion would make them more inhuman savages, if they embraced it; thus the gain of that trade has been pursued in opposition to the Redeemer's cause, and the happiness of men: Are we not, therefore, bound in duty to him and to them to repair these injuries, as far as possible, by taking some proper measures to instruct, not only the slaves here, but the Africans in their own countries? Primitive Chris-

tians laboured always to spread their *Divine Religion ;* and this is equally our duty while there is an Heathen nation : But what singular obligations are we under to these injured people !

These are the sentiments of

JUSTICE AND HUMANITY.

II.

A DIALOGUE BETWEEN GENERAL WOLFE AND GENERAL GAGE IN A WOOD NEAR BOSTON.[1]

Gen. WOLFE.   Welcome my old friend to this retreat.

Gen. GAGE.   I am glad to see you my dear Mr. Wolfe, but what has brought you back again to this world?

Gen. WOLFE.   I am sent by a group of British heroes to remonstrate with you upon your errand to this place. You are come upon a business unworthy a British soldier, and a freeman. You have come here to deprive your fellow subjects of their liberty.

Gen. GAGE.   God forbid! I am come here to execute the orders of my Sovereign,—a Prince of unbounded wisdom and goodness, and who aims at no higher honor than that of being the King of a free people.

Gen. WOLFE.   Strange language from a British soldier! I honour the crown of Great-Britain as an essential part of her excellent constitution. I served a Sovereign to whom the impartial voice of posterity has ascribed the justice of the man as well as the magnanimity of a King, and yet such was the free spirit of the troops under my command, that I could never animate them with a proper martial spirit without setting before them the glorious objects, of their King and their COUNTRY.

Gen. GAGE.   The orders of my Sovereign have been sanctified by the Parliament of Great-Britain. All the wisdom and liberty of the whole empire are collected in that august Assembly. My troops therefore cannot want the same glorious motives which animated yours, in the present ex-

---

[1] From the *Pennsylvania Journal*, January 4, 1775.

pedition.   They will fight for their country as well as their King.

Gen. WOLFE.   The wisest assemblies of men are as liable as individuals, to corruption and error.   The greatest ravages which have ever been committed upon the liberty and happiness of mankind have been by weak and corrupted republics.   The American colonies are entitled to all the privileges of British subjects.   Equality of liberty is the glory of every Briton.   He does not forfeit it by crossing the Ocean.   He carries it with him into the most distant parts of the world, because he carries with him the immutable laws of nature.   A Briton or an American ceases to be a British subject when he ceases to be governed by rulers chosen or approved of by himself.   This is the essence of liberty and of the British constitution.

Gen. GAGE.   The inhabitants of the province of Massachusetts Bay, have not only thrown off the jurisdiction of the British Parliament, but they are disaffected to the British crown.   They cannot even bear with that small share of regal power and grandeur which have been delegated to the Governors of this province.   They traduced Sir Francis Bernard, and petitioned the King to remove Mr. Hutchinson from the seat of government.   But their opposition to my administration has arisen to open rebellion.   They have refused to obey my proclamations.   They have assembled and entered into associations to eat no mutton and to wear clothes manufactured in this country,—they have even provided themselves with arms and ammunition, and have acquired a complete knowledge of the military exercises, in direct opposition to my proclamations.

Gen. WOLFE.   The inhabitants of Massachusetts Bay were once a brave and *loyal* people.   If they are disaffected to his present Majesty, it is because his Ministers have sent counterfeit impressions of his royal virtues to govern them. Bernard and Hutchinson must have been a composition of all the base and wicked qualities in human nature to have diminished the loyalty of those illustrious subjects, or weakened their devotion to every part of the British constitution.

—I must add here that the late proceedings of the British
Parliament towards the American colonists have reached the
British heroes in Elysium, and have produced a suspension of their happiness.   The Quebec Bill in a particular
manner has roused their resentment.   It was once the glory
of Englishmen to draw the sword only in defence of liberty
and the protestant religion, or to extend the blessings of
both to their unhappy neighbours.   These godlike motives
reconciled me to all the hardships of that campaign which
ended in the reduction of Canada.   These godlike motives
likewise reconciled me to the horror I felt in being obliged
to shed the blood of those brave Frenchmen, who opposed
me on the plains of Abraham.   I rejoiced less in the hour
of my death, in the honor of my victory, than in the glory
of having communicated to an inslaved people the glorious
privileges of an English constitution.   While my fellow
soldiers hailed me as their conqueror, I exulted only in being
their DELIVERER.   But popery and French laws in Canada
are but a part of that system of despotism, which has been
prepared for the colonies.   The edicts of the British Parliament (for they want the sanction of British laws) which
relate to the province of Massachusetts Bay are big with
destruction to the whole British empire.   I come therefore
in the name of Blakeney—Cumberland—Granby—and an
illustrious band of English heroes to whom the glory of Old
England is still dear, to beg you to have no hand in the
execution of them.   Remember Sir you are a man as well
as a soldier.   You did not give up your privileges as a citizen
when you put on your sword.   British soldiers are not
machines, to be animated only with the voice of a Minister
of State.   They disdain those ideas of submission which
preclude them from the liberty of thinking for themselves,
and degrade them to an equality with a war horse, or an
elephant.   If you value the sweets of peace and liberty,—
if you have any regard to the glory of the British name, and
if you prefer the society of Grecian, Roman, and British
heroes in the world of spirits, to the company of Jeffries,
Kirk, and other royal executioners, I conjure you imme-

diately to resign your commission. Assign the above reasons to your Sovereign for your conduct, and you will have
the *sole* glory of performing an action which would do honour
to an angel. You will restore perpetual harmony between
Britain and her colonies.

III.

THE MAGAZINE IN AMERICA.[1]

IN a country whose reigning character is the love of
science, it is somewhat strange that the channels of communication should continue so narrow and limited. The
weekly papers are at present the only vehicles of public
information. Convenience and necessity prove that the
opportunities of acquiring and communicating knowledge
ought always to inlarge with the circle of population.
America has now outgrown the state of infancy: her
strength and commerce make large advances to manhood;
and science in all its branches has not only blossomed, but
even ripened on the soil. The cottages as it were of yesterday have grown to villages, and the villages to cities; and
while proud antiquity, like a skeleton in rags, parades the
streets of other nations, their genius, as if sickened and disgusted with the phantom, comes hither for recovery.

The present enlarged and improved state of things gives

[1] Introductory of the *Pennsylvania Magazine, or American Museum,*
Philadelphia, published by Robert Aitkin. Paine was its first editor, and Dr.
Rush says that some of his writings in it "gave it a sudden currency which few
works of the kind have since had in our country." His salary was fifty pounds.
I conclude to omit several brief articles in it by Paine, giving descriptions of
scientific machines, as they require reproduction of the plates, and are technical.
Several of Paine's poems were first published in this magazine, including the
Song on "The Death of General Wolfe" (with music), which, though written
in England, was not published in the *Gentleman's Magazine* (as some have
stated), or elsewhere in that country. Paine wrote under various signatures in
his magazine, but I feel certain, after careful investigation, that the articles
reproduced from the magazine in this volume are from his pen. It may be
remarked that in the September number (1775) a picture of the battle of Bunker
Hill appears, displaying for the first time, I believe, the stripes of the American
flag.—*Editor*.

every encouragement which the editor of a New Magazine can reasonably hope for. The failure of former ones cannot be drawn as a parallel now. Change of times adds propriety to new measures. In the early days of colonization, when a whisper was almost sufficient to have negotiated all our internal concerns, the publishing even of a newspaper would have been premature. Those times are past ; and population has established both their use and their credit. But their plan being almost wholly devoted to news and commerce, affords but a scanty residence to the Muses. Their path lies wide of the field of science, and has left a rich and unexplored region for new adventurers.

It has always been the opinion of the learned and curious, that a magazine, when properly conducted, is the nursery of genius ; and by constantly accumulating new matter, becomes a kind of market for wit and utility. The opportunities which it affords to men of abilities to communicate their studies, kindle up a spirit of invention and emulation. An unexercised genius soon contracts a kind of mossiness, which not only checks its growth, but abates its natural vigour. Like an untenanted house it falls into decay, and frequently ruins the possessor.

The British magazines, at their commencement, were the repositories of ingenuity : They are now the retailers of tale and nonsense. From elegance they sunk to simplicity, from simplicity to folly, and from folly to voluptuousness. The Gentleman's, the London, and the Universal, Magazines, bear yet some marks of their originality; but the Town and Country, the Covent-Garden, and the Westminster, are no better than incentives to profligacy and dissipation. They have added to the dissolution of manners, and supported Venus against the Muses.

America yet inherits a large portion of her first-imported virtue. Degeneracy is here almost a useless word. Those who are conversant with Europe would be tempted to believe that even the air of the Atlantic disagrees with the constitution of foreign vices; if they survive the voyage, they either expire on their arrival, or linger away in an in-curable consumption. There is a happy something in the climate of America, which disarms them of all their power both of infection and attraction.

But while we give no encouragement to the importation of foreign vices, we ought to be equally as careful not to create any. A vice begotten might be worse than a vice imported. The latter, depending on favour, would be a sycophant ; the other, by pride of birth, would be a tyrant : To the one we should be dupes, to the other slaves.

There is nothing which obtains so general an influence over the manners and morals of a people as the Press ; from *that*, as from a fountain, the streams of vice or virtue are poured forth over a country : And of all publications, none are more calculated to improve or infect than a periodical one. All others have their rise and their exit ; but *this* renews the pursuit. If it has an evil tendency, it debauches by the power of repetition ; if a good one, it obtains favor by the gracefulness of soliciting it. Like a lover, it woos its mistress with unabated ardor, nor gives up the pursuit without a conquest.

The two capital supports of a magazine are Utility **and** Entertainment : The first is a boundless path, the other an endless spring. To suppose that arts and sciences are exhausted subjects, is doing them a kind of dishonour. The divine mechanism of creation reproves such folly, and shews us by comparison, the imperfection of our most refined inventions. I cannot believe that this species of vanity is peculiar to the present age only. I have no doubt but that it existed before the flood, and even in the wildest ages of antiquity. 'Tis folly we have inherited, not created ; and the discoveries which every day produces, have greatly contributed to dispossess us of it. Improvement and the world will expire together : And till that period arrives, we may plunder the mine, but can never exhaust it ! That " *We have found out every thing*," has been the motto of every age. Let our ideas travel a little into antiquity, and we shall find larger portions of it than now ; and so unwilling were our ancestors to descend from this mountain of perfection,

that when any new discovery exceeded the common standard, the discoverer was believed to be in alliance with the
devil. It was not the ignorance of the age only, but the
vanity of it, which rendered it dangerous to be ingenious.
The man who first planned and erected a tenable hut, with
a hole for the smoke to pass, and the light to enter, was
perhaps called an able architect, but he who first improved
it with a chimney, could be no less than a prodigy ; yet had
the same man been so unfortunate as to have embellished it
with glass windows, he might probably have been burnt for
a magician. Our fancies would be highly diverted could we
look back, and behold a circle of original Indians harranguing
on the sublime perfection of the age : Yet 'tis not impossible but future times may exceed us almost as much as we
have exceeded them.

I would wish to extirpate the least remains of this impolitic vanity. It has a direct tendency to unbrace the
nerves of invention, and is peculiarly hurtful to young
colonies. A magazine can never want matter in America,
if the inhabitants will do justice to their own abilities. Agriculture and manufactures owe much of their improvement
in England, to hints first thrown out in some of their magazines. Gentlemen whose abilities enabled them to make
experiments, frequently chose that method of communication, on account of its convenience. And why should not
the same spirit operate in America? I have no doubt of
seeing, in a little time, an American magazine full of more
useful matter than I ever saw an English one : Because we
are not exceeded in abilities, have a more extensive field for
enquiry ; and, whatever may be our political state, *Our happiness will always depend upon ourselves.*

Something useful will always arise from exercising the
invention, though perhaps, like the witch of Endor, we shall
raise up a being we did not expect. We owe many of our
noblest discoveries more to accident than wisdom. In quest
of a pebble we have found a diamond, and returned enriched
with the treasure. Such happy accidents give additional
encouragement to the making experiments ; and the con-

venience which a magazine affords of collecting and conveying them to the public, enhances their utility.   Where
this opportunity is wanting, many little inventions, the fore-
runners of improvement, are suffered to expire on the spot
that produced them ; and, as an elegant writer beautifully
expresses on another occasion,

"They waste their sweetness on the desert air."—*Gray*.

In matters of humour and entertainment there can be no
reason to apprehend a deficiency.   Wit is naturally a volunteer, delights in action, and under proper discipline is capable of great execution.   'Tis a perfect master in the art of
bush-fighting ; and though it attacks with more subtility
than science, has often defeated a whole regiment of heavy
artillery.—Though I have rather exceeded the line of gravity
in this description of wit, I am unwilling to dismiss it without being a little more serious.—'Tis a qualification which,
like the passions, has a natural wildness that requires governing.   Left to itself, it soon overflows its banks, mixes with
common filth, and brings disrepute on the fountain.   We
have many valuable springs of it in America, which at present
run purer streams, than the generality of it in other countries.
In France and Italy, 'tis froth highly fomented : In England
it has much of the same spirit, but rather a browner complexion.   European wit is one of the worst articles we can
import.   It has an intoxicating power with it, which
debauches the very vitals of chastity, and gives a false colouring to every thing it censures or defends.   We soon grow
fatigued with the excess, and withdraw like gluttons sickened
with intemperance.   On the contrary, how happily are the
sallies of innocent humour calculated to amuse and sweeten
the vacancy of business !   We enjoy the harmless luxury
without surfeiting, and strengthen the spirits by relaxing
them.

The Press has not only a great influence over our manners
and morals, but contributes largely to our pleasures ; and a
magazine when properly enriched, is very conveniently calculated for this purpose.   Voluminous works weary the

patience, but here we are invited by conciseness and variety. As I have formerly received much pleasure from perusing these kind of publications, I wish the *present* success; and have no doubt of seeing a proper diversity blended so agreeably together, as to furnish out an *Olio* worthy of the company for whom it is designed.

I consider a magazine as a kind of bee-hive, which both allures the swarm, and provides room to store their sweets. Its division into cells, gives every bee a province of its own ; and though they all produce honey, yet perhaps they differ in their taste for flowers, and extract with greater dexterity from one than from another. Thus, we are not all PHI-LOSOPHERS, all ARTISTS, nor all POETS.

IV.

USEFUL AND ENTERTAINING HINTS.[1]

" The real value of a thing,
Is as much money as 'twill bring."

IN the possession of the Philadelphia Library Company
is a cabinet of fossils,* with several specimens of earth, clay,
sand, etc., with some account of each, and where brought
from.

I have always considered these kinds of researches as productive of many advantages, and in a new country they are
particularly so. As subjects for speculation, they afford
entertainment to the curious; but as objects of utility they
merit a closer attention. The same materials which delight
the Fossilist, enrich the manufacturer and the merchant.
While the one is scientifically examining their structure and
composition, the others, by industry and commerce, are
transmuting them to gold. Possessed of the power of pleasing, they gratify on both sides; the one contemplates their
natural beauties in the cabinet, the others, their *re-created*
ones in the coffer.

'Tis by the researches of the virtuoso that the hidden
parts of the earth are brought to light, and from his discoveries of its qualities, the potter, the glassmaker, and
numerous other artists, are enabled to furnish us with their

[1] From the *Pennsylvania Magazine*, Feb., 1775.—*Editor.*

* In the catalogue it is called a collection of American fossils, etc., but a
considerable part of them are foreign ones. I presume that the collector, in
order to judge the better of such as he might discover here, made first a collection of such foreign ones whose value were known, in order to compare by : as
his design seems rather bent towards discovering the treasures of America than
merely to make a collection.—*Author.*

productions. Artists considered *merely* as such, would have made but a slender progress, had they not been led on by the enterprising spirit of the curious. I am unwilling to dismiss this remark without entering my protest against that unkind, ungrateful, and impolitic custom of ridiculing unsuccessful experiments. And of informing those unwise or overwise pasquinaders, that half the felicities they enjoy sprung originally from generous curiosity.

Were a man to propose or set out to bore his lands as a carpenter does a board, he might probably bring on himself a shower of witticisms ; and tho' he could not be jested at for *building castles in the air,* yet many *magnanimous* laughs might break forth at his expence, and vociferously predict the explosion of a mine in his subterraneous pursuits. I am led to this reflection by the present domestic state of America, because it will unavoidably happen, that before we can arrive at that perfection of things which other nations have acquired, many hopes will fail, many whimsical attempts will become fortunate, and many reasonable ones end in air and expence. *The degree of improvement which America has already arrived at is unparalleled and astonishing,* but 'tis miniature to what she will one day boast of, if heaven continue her happiness. We have nearly one whole region yet unexplored : I mean the internal region of the earth. By industry and tillage we have acquired a considerable knowledge of what America will *produce,* but very little of what it *contains.* The bowels of the earth have been only slightly inquired into : We seem to content ourselves with such parts of it as are absolutely necessary, and cannot well be imported ; as brick, stone, etc., but have gone very little further, except in the article of iron. The glass and the pottery manufactures are yet very imperfect, and will continue so, till some curious researcher finds out the proper material.

COPPER, LEAD, [1] and TIN articles valuable both in their simple state, and as being the component parts of other metals (viz. brass and pewter) are at present but little known

[1] A footnote explaining the preparation of white lead, and correcting an error in the Philadelphia catalogue, is omitted.—*Editor.*

throughout the continent in their mineral form: yet I doubt not, but very valuable mines of them, are daily travelled over in the western parts of America. Perhaps a few feet of surface conceal a treasure sufficient to enrich a kingdom.

The value of the interior part of the earth (like ourselves) cannot be judged certainly of by the surface, neither do the corresponding strata lie with the unvariable order of the colours of the rainbow, and if they ever did (which I do not believe) age and misfortune have now broken in upon their union; earthquakes, deluges, and volcanoes have so dis-united and re-united them, that in their present state they appear like a world in ruins.—Yet the ruins are beautiful. —The caverns, museums of antiquities.

Tho' nature is gay, polite, and generous abroad, she is sullen, rude, and niggardly at home: Return the visit, and she admits you with all the suspicion of a miser, and all the reluctance of an antiquated beauty retired to replenish her charms. Bred up in antediluvian notions, she has not yet acquired the European taste of receiving visitants in her dressing-room: she locks and bolts up her private recesses with extraordinary care, as if not only resolved to preserve her hoards, but to conceal her age, and hide the remains of a face that was young and lovely in the days of Adam. He that would view nature in her undress, and partake of her internal treasures, must proceed with the resolution of a robber, if not a ravisher. She gives no invitation to follow her to the cavern.—The external earth makes no proclama-tion of the interior stores, but leaves to chance and industry, the discovery of the whole. In such gifts as nature can annually re-create, she is noble and profuse, and entertains the whole world with the interest of her fortunes; but watches over the capital with the care of a miser. Her gold and jewels lie concealed in the earth, in caves of utter dark-ness; and hoards of wealth, heaps upon heaps, mould in the chests, like the riches of a Necromancer's cell. It must be very pleasant to an adventurous speculist to make excursions into these Gothic regions; and in his travels he may possi-bly come to a cabinet locked up in some rocky vault, whose treasures shall reward his toil, and enable him to shine on his return, as splendidly as nature herself.

By a small degree of attention to the order and origin of things, we shall perceive, that though the *surface* of the earth produce us the *necessaries* of life, yet 'tis from the mine we extract the *conveniences* thereof. Our houses would diminish to wigwams, furnished in the Indian style, and ourselves resemble the building, were it not for the ores of the earth. Agriculture and manufactures would wither away for want of tools and implements, and commerce stand still for want of materials. The beasts of the field would elude our power, and the birds of the air get beyond our reach. Our dominion would shrink to a narrow circle, and the mind itself, partaking of the change, would contract its prospects, and lessen into almost animal instinct. Take away but the single article of iron, and half the felicities of life fall with it. Little as we may prize this common ore, the loss of it would *cut* deeper than the use of it: And by the way of laughing off misfortunes 'tis easy to prove, by this method of investigation, that *an iron age is better than a golden one.*

Since so great a portion of our enjoyments is drawn from the mine, it is certainly an evidence of our prudence to inquire and know what our possessions are. Every man's landed property extends to the [centre] [1] of the earth. Why then should he sit down contented with a part, and practise upon his estate those fashionable follies in life, which prefer the superfice to the solid? Curiosity alone, should the thought occur conveniently, would move an active mind to examine (tho' not to the bottom) at least to a considerable depth.

The propriety and reasonableness of these internal enquiries are continually pointed out to us by numberless occurrences. Accident is almost every day turning out some new secret from the earth. How often has the plow-share or the spade broken open a treasure, which for ages, perhaps for ever, had lain just beneath the surface? And tho' every estate have not mines of gold or silver, yet they may contain

[1] " Surface " in the original, but surely a clerical error.—*Editor.*

some strata of valuable earth, proper for manufactures; and if they have not those, there is a great probability of their having chalk, marl, or some rich soil proper for manure, which only requires to be removed to the surface.

I have been informed of some land in England being raised to four times its former value by the discovery of a chalk or marl pit, in digging a hole to fix a post in; and in embanking a meadow in the Jerseys, the laborers threw out with the soil, a fine blue powderly earth, resembling indigo, which, when mixed with oil, was used for paint. I imagine the vein is now exhausted. [1]

Many valuable ores, clays, etc. appear in such rude forms in their natural state, as not even to excite *curiosity*, much less *attention*. A true knowledge of their different value can only be obtained by experiment: As soil proper for manure, they may be judged of by the planter; but as matter, they come under the enquiry of the philosopher. This leads me to reflect with inexpressible pleasure, on the numberless benefits arising to a community, by the institution of societies for promoting useful knowledge.

The American Philosophical Society, like the Royal Society in England, by having public spirit for its support, and public good for its object, is a treasure we ought to glory in. Here the defective knowledge of the individual is supplied by the common stock. Societies without endangering private fortunes, are enabled to proceed in their enquiries by analysis and experiment: But individuals are seldom furnished with conveniences for so doing, and generally rest their opinion on reasonable conjecture.

I presume that were samples of different soils from different parts of America, presented to the society for their inspection and examination, it would greatly facilitate our knowledge of the internal earth, and give a new spring both to agriculture and manufactures.

These hints are not intended to lament any loss of time, or remissness in the pursuit of useful knowledge, but to

---

[1] A description of the boring apparatus, inserted here by Paine, is omitted.— *Editor.*

furnish matter for future studies; that while we glory in what we are, we may not neglect what we *are to be*.

Of the present state we may justly say, that no nation under heaven ever struck out in so short a time, and with so much spirit and reputation, into the labyrinth of art and science; and that, not in the *acquisition* of knowledge only, but in the happy advantages flowing *from* it. The world does not at this day exhibit a parallel, neither can history produce its equal.

ATLANTICUS.

PHILADELPHIA, Feb. 10.

V.

NEW ANECDOTES OF ALEXANDER THE GREAT.[1]

IN one of those calm and gloomy days,which have a strange effect in disposing the mind to pensiveness, I quitted the busy town and withdrew into the country. As I passed towards the Schuylkill, my ideas enlarged with the prospect, and sprung from place to place with an agility for which nature had not a simile. Even the eye is a loiterer, when compared with the rapidity of the thoughts. Before I could reach the ferry, I had made the tour of the creation, and paid a regular visit to almost every country under the sun ; and while I was crossing the river, I passed the Styx, and made large excursions into the shadowy regions ; but my ideas relanded with my person, and taking a new flight inspected the state of things unborn. This happy wildness of imagination makes a man a lord of the world, and discovers to him the value and the vanity of all it possesses.

Having discharged the two terrestrial Charons, who ferried me over the Schuylkill, I took up my staff and walked into the woods. Every thing conspired to hush me into a pleasing kind of melancholy—the trees seemed to sleep—and the air hung round me with such unbreathing silence, as if listening to my very thoughts. Perfectly at rest from care or business, I suffered my ideas to pursue their own unfettered fancies ; and in less time than what is required to express it in, they had again passed the Styx and toured many miles into the new country.

[1] From the *Pennsylvania Magazine*, February, 1775.

As the servants of great men always imitate their masters abroad, so my ideas, habiting themselves in my likeness, figured away with all the consequence of the person they belonged to; and calling themselves when united, I and *Me*, wherever they went, brought me on their return the following anecdotes of Alexander, viz.

Having a mind to see in what manner Alexander lived in the Plutonian world, I crossed the Styx, (without the help of Charon, for the dead only are his fare,) and enquired of a melancholy looking shade, who was sitting on the banks of the river, if he could give me any account of him, *Yonder he comes*, replied the shade, *get out of the way or you 'll be run over.* Turning myself round I saw a grand equipage rolling towards me, which filled the whole avenue.   Bless me! thought I, the gods still continue this man in his insolence and pomp! The chariot was drawn by eight horses in golden harness, and the whole represented his triumphal return, after he had conquered the world.   It passed me with a splendour I had never seen before, and shined so luminously up into the country, that I discovered innumerable shades sitting under the trees, which before were invisible.   As there were two persons in the chariot equally splendid, I could not distinguish which was Alexander, and on requiring that information of the shade, who still stood by, he replied, *Alexander is not there.*   Did you not, continued I, tell me that Alexander was coming, and bid me get out of the way?   *Yes*, answered the shade, *because he was the forehorse on the side next to us.*   Horse! I mean Alexander the Emperor.   *I mean the same*, replied the shade, *for whatever he was on the other side of the water is nothing now, he is a* HORSE *here; and not always that, for when he is apprehensive that a good licking is intended for him, he watches his opportunity to roll out of the stable in the shape of a piece of dung, or in any other disguise he can escape by.*   On this information I turned instantly away, not being able to bear the thought of such astonishing degradation, notwithstanding the aversion I have to his character.   But curiosity got the better of my compassion, and having a mind to see what sort of a figure the con-

queror of the world cut in the stable, I directed my flight
thither ; he was just returned with the rest of the horses from
the journey, and the groom was rubbing him down with a
large furz bush, but turning himself round to get a still larger
and more prickly one that was newly brought in, Alexander
catched the opportunity, and instantly disappeared, on which
I quitted the place, lest I should be suspected of stealing
him : when I had reached the bands of the river, and was
preparing to take my flight over, I perceived that I had
picked up a *bug* among the Plutonian gentry, and thinking
it was needless to increase the breed on this side the water,
was going to dispatch it, when the little wretch screamed out,
Spare Alexander the GREAT.   On which I withdrew the violence I was offering to his person, and holding up the emperor between my finger and thumb, he exhibited a most
contemptible figure of the downfall of tyrant greatness. Affected with a mixture of concern and compassion (*which he
was always a stranger to*) I suffered him to nibble on a pim-
ple that was newly risen on my hand, in order to refresh
him ; after which I placed him on a tree to hide him, but a
Tom Tit coming by, chopped him up with as little ceremony
as he put whole kingdoms to the sword.   On which I took
my flight, reflecting with pleasure,—That I was not ALEX-
ANDER THE GREAT.

ESOP.

VI.

REFLECTIONS ON THE LIFE AND DEATH OF
LORD CLIVE.[1]

AH! The tale is told—The scene is ended—and the curtain falls. As an emblem of the vanity of all earthly pomp, let his Monument be a globe, but be that globe a bubble ; let his Effigy be a man walking round it in his sleep ; and let Fame, in the character of a shadow, inscribe his honours on the air.

I view him but as yesterday on the burning plains of Plassey,* doubtful of life, health, or victory. I see him in the instant when " *To be or not to be*," were equal chances to a human eye. To be a lord or a slave, to return loaded with the spoils, or remain mingled with the dust of India.—Did necessity always justify the severity of a conqueror, the rude tongue of censure would be silent, and however painfully he might look back on scenes of horror, the pensive reflection would not alarm him. Though his feelings suffered, his conscience would be acquitted. The sad remembrance would move serenely, and leave the mind without a wound.—But Oh India! thou loud proclaimer of European cruelties, thou bloody monument of unnecessary deaths, be tender in the day of enquiry, and show a Christian world thou canst suffer and forgive.

Departed from India, and loaded with plunder, I see him doubling the Cape and looking wistfully to Europe. I see him

[1] From the *Pennsylvania Magazine*, March, 1775.

* Battle of Plassey, in the East Indies, where Lord Clive, at that time Colonel Clive, acquired an immense fortune, and from which place his title is taken.— *Author*.

contemplating on years of pleasure, and gratifying his ambition with expected honours. I see his arrival pompously announced in every newspaper, his eager eye rambling thro' the crowd in quest of homage, and his ear listening lest an applause should escape him. Happily for him he arrived before his *fame*, and the short interval was a time of rest. From the crowd I follow him to the court, I see him enveloped in the sunshine of sovereign favour, rivalling the great in honours, the proud in splendour, and the rich in wealth. From the court I trace him to the country, his equipage moves like a camp ; every village bell proclaims his coming ; the wondering peasants admire his pomp, and his heart runs over with joy.

But, alas! not satisfied with uncountable thousands, I accompany him *again* to India. I mark the variety of countenances which appear at his landing. Confusion spreads the news. Every passion seems alarmed. The wailing widow, the crying orphan, and the childless parent remember and lament ; the rival Nabobs court his favour ; the rich dread his power, and the poor his severity. Fear and terror march like pioneers before his camp, murder and rapine accompany it, famine and wretchedness follow in the rear.

Resolved on accumulating an unbounded fortune, he enters into all the schemes of war, treaty, and intrigue. The British sword is set up for sale ; the heads of contending Nabobs are offered at a price, and the bribe taken from both sides. Thousands of men or money are trifles in an India bargain. The field is an empire, and the treasure almost without end. The wretched inhabitants are glad to compound for offences never committed, and to purchase at any rate the privilege to breathe ; while he, the sole lord of their lives and fortunes, disposes of either as he pleases, and prepares for Europe.*

---

* In April, 1773, a Committee of the House of Commons, under the name of the Select Committee, were appointed by the House to enquire into the state of the East India affairs, and the conduct of the several Governors of Bengal. The Committee having gone through the examinations, General Burgoyne, the chairman, prefaced their report to the House, informing them, "that the reports

Uncommon fortunes require an uncommon date of life to enjoy them in. The usual period is spent in preparing to live: And unless nature prolongs the time, fortune bestows her excess of favours in vain.

The conqueror of the east having nothing more to expect from the one, has all his court to make to the other. Anxiety for wealth gives place to anxiety for life ; and wisely recollecting that the sea is no respecter of persons, resolves on taking his route to Europe by land. Little beings move unseen, or unobserved, but he engrosses whole kingdoms in his march, and is gazed at like a comet. The burning desert, the pathless mountains, and the fertile valleys, are in their turns explored and passed over. No material accident distresses his progress, and England once more receives the spoiler.

How sweet is rest to the weary traveller ; the retrospect heightens the enjoyment ; and if the future prospect be serene, the days of ease and happiness are arrived. An uninquiring observer might have been inclined to consider Lord

contained accounts shocking to human nature, that the most infamous designs had been carried into execution by perfidy and murder." He recapitulated the wretched situation of the East-Indian princes, who held their dignities on the precarious condition of being the highest bribers. No claim, however just on their part, he said, could be admitted without being introduced with enormous sums of rupees, nor any prince suffered to reign long, who did not quadrate with this idea ; and that Lord Clive, over and above the enormous sums he might with some appearance of justice lay claim to, had obtained others to which he could have no title. He (General Burgoyne) therefore moved, " That it appears to this house, that Robert Lord Clive, baron of Plassey, about the time of deposing Surajah Dowla, Nabob of Bengal, and establishing Meer Jaffier in his room, did, through the influence of the power with which he was intrusted, as member of the Select Committee in India, and Commander in Chief of the British forces there, obtain and possess himself of two lacks of rupees, as member of the Select Committee ; a further sum of two lacks and 80,000 rupees, as member of the Select Committee ; a further sum of two lacks of rupees, as Commander in Chief ; a further sum of 16 lacks of rupees, or more, under the denomination of *private donations ;* which sums, amounting together to 20 lacks and 80,000 rupees, were of the value, in English money, of £234,000,* and that in so doing, the said Robert Lord Clive abused the powers with which he was intrusted, to the evil example of the servants of the public."—*Author.*

* Equal to £340,000 Pennsylvania currency.—*Author.*

Clive, under all these agreeable circumstances, one whose every care was over, and who had nothing to do but sit down and say, *Soul, take thine ease, thou hast goods laid up in store for many years.*

The reception which he met with on his second arrival, was in every instance equal to, and in many exceeded, the honours of the first. 'Tis the peculiar temper of the English to applaud before they think. Generous of their praise, they frequently bestow it unworthily: but when once the truth arrives, the torrent stops, and rushes back again with the same violence.* Scarcely had the echo of applause ceased upon the ear, than the rude tongue of censure took up the

---

* Lord Clive, in the defence which he made in the House of Commons, against the charges mentioned in the preceding note, very positively insists on his innocence, and very pathetically laments his situation ; and after informing the House of the thanks which he had some years before received, for the same actions which they are now endeavouring to censure him for, he says,

" After such certificates as these, Sir, am I to be brought here like a criminal, and the very best part of my conduct construed into crimes against the state? Is this the reward that is now held out to persons who have performed such important services to their country? If it is, Sir, the future consequences that will attend the execution of any important trust, committed to the persons who have the care of it, will be fatal indeed ; and I am sure the noble Lord upon the treasury bench, whose great humanity and abilities I revere, would never have consented to the resolutions that passed the other night, if he had thought on the dreadful consequences that would attend them. Sir, I cannot say that I either sit or rest easy, when I find that all I have in the world is likely to be confiscated, and that no one will take my security for a shilling. These, Sir, are dreadful apprehensions to remain under, and I cannot but look upon myself as a bankrupt. I have not anything left which I can call my own, except my paternal fortune of £500 per annum, and which has been in the family for ages past. But upon this I am contented to live, and perhaps I shall find more real content of mind and happiness than in the trembling affluence of an unsettled fortune. But, Sir, I must make one more observation, that, if the definition of the Hon. Gentleman, [General Burgoyne,] and of this House, is that the *State*, as expressed in these resolutions is, *quoad hoc*, the Company, then, Sir, every farthing that I enjoy is granted to me. But to be called, after sixteen years have elapsed, to account for my conduct in this manner, and after an uninterrupted enjoyment of my property, to be questioned and considered as obtaining it unwarrantably, is hard indeed ! and a treatment I should not think the British Senate capable of. But if it should be the case, I have a conscious innocence within me, that tells me my conduct is irreproachable. *Frangas, non flectes.* They may take from me what I have ; they may, as they think, make

tale.   The newspapers, fatal enemies to ill-gotten wealth!
began to buz a general suspicion of his conduct, and the in-
quisitive public soon refined it into particulars.   Every post
gave a stab to his fame—a wound to his peace—and a nail
to his coffin.   Like spectres from the grave they haunted
him in every company, and whispered murder in his ear.
A life chequered with uncommon varieties is seldom a
long one.   Action and care will in time wear down the
strongest frame, but guilt and melancholy are poisons of
quick despatch.

Say, cool deliberate reflection was the prize, though abstracted from the guilt, worthy of the pains?   Ah no!
Fatigued with victory he sat down to rest, and while he
was recovering breath he lost it.   A conqueror more fatal
than himself beset him, and revenged the injuries done
to India.

As a cure for avarice and ambition let us take a view of
him in his latter years.   Hah! what gloomy being wanders
yonder?   How visibly is the melancholy heart delineated
on his countenance.   He mourns no common care—His
very steps are timed to sorrow—He trembles with a kind of
mental palsy.   Perhaps 'tis some broken hearted parent,
some David mourning for his Absalom, or some Heraclitus
weeping for the world.—I hear him mutter something
about wealth.—Perhaps he is poor, and hath not wherewithal to hide his head.   Some debtor started from his
sleepless pillow, to ruminate on poverty, and ponder on the
horrors of a jail.   Poor man!   I'll to him and relieve him.
Hah! 'tis Lord Clive himself!   Bless me, what a change!
He makes, I see, for yonder cypress shade—fit scene for
melancholy hearts!—I'll watch him there and listen to
his story.

LORD CLIVE.   "Can I but suffer when a beggar pities
me.   Erewhile I heard a ragged wretch, who every mark of

me poor, *but I will be happy!*   I mean not this as my defence.   My defence
will be made at the bar ; and before I sit down, I have one request to make to
the House, *that when they come to decide upon my honour, they will not forget
their own.*"—*Author*.

poverty had on, say to a sooty sweep, Ah, poor Lord Clive! while he the negro-coloured vagrant, more mercifully cruel, curst me in my hearing.

"There was a time when fortune, like a yielding mistress, courted me with smiles—She never waited to be told my wishes, but studied to discover them, and seemed not happy to herself, but when she had some favour to bestow. Ah! little did I think the fair enchantress would desert me thus; and after lavishing her smiles upon me, turn my reproacher, and publish me in folio to the world. Volumes of morality are dull and spiritless compared to me. Lord Clive is himself a treatise upon vanity, printed in a golden type. The most unlettered clown writes explanatory notes thereon, and reads them to his children. Yet I could bear these insults could I but bear myself.—A strange unwelcome something hangs about me. In company I seem no company at all.—The festive board appears to me a stage, the crimson coloured port resembles blood—Each glass is strangely metamorphosed to a man in armour, and every bowl appears a Nabob. The joyous toast is like the sound of murder, and the loud laughs are groans of dying men. The scenes of India are all rehearsed, and no one sees the tragedy but myself.—Ah! I discover things which are not, and hear unuttered sounds——

"O peace, thou sweet companion of the calm and innocent! Whither art thou fled? Here take my gold, and all the world calls mine, and come thou in exchange. Or thou, thou noisy sweep, who mix thy food with soot and relish it, who canst descend from lofty heights and walk the humble earth again, without repining at the change, come teach that *mystery* to me. Or thou, thou ragged wandering beggar, who, when thou canst not beg successfully, will pilfer from the hound, and eat the dirty morsel sweetly; be thou Lord Clive, and I will beg, so I may laugh like thee.

"Could I unlearn what I've already learned—unact what I've already acted—or would some sacred power convey me back to youth and innocence, I'd act another part—I'd keep within the vale of humble life, nor wish for what the world calls pomp.

> " But since this cannot be,
> And only a few days and sad remain for me,
> I'll haste to quit the scene ; for what is life
> When every passion of the soul 's at strife ? " *

ATLANTICUS.

* Some time before his death he became very melancholy—subject to strange imaginations—and was found dead at last.—*Author.*

VII.

CUPID AND HYMEN.[1]

An Original.

As the little amorous deity was one day winging his way over a village in Arcadia, he was drawn by the sweet sound of the pipe and tabor, to descend and see what was the matter. The gods themselves are sometimes ravished with the simplicity of mortals. The groves of Arcadia were once the country seats of the celestials, where they relaxed from the business of the skies, and partook of the diversions of the villagers. Cupid being descended, was charmed with the lovely appearance of the place. Every thing he saw had an air of pleasantness. Every shepherd was in his holyday dress, and every shepherdess was decorated with a profusion of flowers. The sound of labour was not heard among them. The little cottages had a peaceable look, and were almost hidden with arbours of jessamine and myrtle. The way to the temple was strewed with flowers, and enclosed with a number of garlands and green arches. Surely, quoth Cupid, here is a festival today. I'll hasten and enquire the matter.

So saying, he concealed his bow and quiver, and took a turn thro' the village: As he approached a building distinguished from all the rest by the elegance of its appearance, he heard a sweet confusion of voices mingled with instrumental music. What is the matter, said Cupid to a swain who was sitting under a sycamore by the way-side, and humming a very melancholy tune, why are you not at the

[1] From the *Pennsylvania Magazine*, April, 1775.

feast, and why are you so sad? I sit here, answered the swain, to see a sight, and a sad sight 'twill be. What is it, said Cupid, come tell me, for perhaps I can help you. I was once happier than a king, replied the swain, and was envied by all the shepherds of the place, but now everything is dark and gloomy, because—Because what? said Cupid—Because I am robbed of my Ruralinda; Gothic, the Lord of the manor, hath stolen her from me, and this is to be the nuptial day. A wedding, quoth Cupid, and I know nothing of it, you must be mistaken, shepherd, I keep a record of marriages, and no such thing has come to my knowledge. 'Tis no wedding, I assure you, if I am not consulted about it. The Lord of the manor, continued the shepherd, consulted nobody but Ruralinda's mother, and she longed to see her fair daughter the Lady of the manor: He hath spent a deal of money to make all this appearance, for money will do anything; I only wait here to see her come by, and then farewell to the hills and dales. Cupid bade him not be rash, and left him. This is another of Hymen's tricks, quoth Cupid to himself, he hath frequently served me thus, but I'll hasten to him, and have it out with him. So saying, he repaired to the mansion. Everything there had an air of grandeur rather than of joy, sumptuous but not serene. The company were preparing to walk in procession to the temple. The Lord of the manor looked like the father of the village, and the business he was upon gave a foolish awkwardness to his age and dignity. Ruralinda smiled, because she *would* smile, but in that smile was sorrow. Hymen with a torch faintly burning on one side only stood ready to accompany them. The gods when they please can converse in silence, and in that language Cupid began on Hymen.

Know, Hymen, said he, that I am your master. Indulgent Jove gave you to me as a clerk, not as a rival, much less a superior. 'Tis my province to form the union, and yours to witness it. But of late you have treacherously assumed to set up for yourself. 'Tis true you may chain couples together like criminals, but you cannot yoke them like lovers;

besides you are such a dull fellow when I am not with you, that you poison the felicities of life. You have not a grace but what is borrowed from me. As well may the moon attempt to enlighten the earth without the sun, as you to bestow happiness when I am absent. At best you are but a temporal and a temporary god, whom Jove has appointed not to bestow, but to secure happiness, and restrain the infidelity of mankind. But assure yourself that I'll complain of you to the Synod.

This is very high indeed, replied Hymen, to be called to an account by such a boy of a god as you are. You are not of such importance in the world as your vanity thinks; for my own part I have enlisted myself with another master, and can very well do without you. Plutus * and I are greater than Cupid; you may complain and welcome, for Jove himself descended in a silver shower and conquered: and by the same power the Lord of the manor hath won a damsel, in spite of all the arrows in your quiver.

Cupid, incensed at this reply, resolved to support his authority, and expose the folly of Hymen's pretentions to independance. As the quarrel was carried on in silence, the company were not interrupted by it. The procession began to set forward to the temple, where the ceremony was to be performed. The Lord of the manor led the beautiful Ruralinda like a lamb devoted to sacrifice. Cupid immediately despatched a petition for assistance to his mother on one of the sun-beams, and the same messenger returning in an instant, informed him that whatever he wished should be done. He immediately cast the old Lord and Ruralinda into one of the most extraordinary sleeps ever known. They continued walking in the procession, talking to each other, and observing every ceremony with as much order as if they had been awake; their souls had in a manner crept from their bodies, as snakes creep from their skin, and leave the perfect appearance of themselves behind: And so rapidly does imagination change the landscape of life, that in the same space of time which passed over while they were walking to

* God of riches.—*Author*.

the temple, they both ran through, in a strange variety of dreams, seven years of wretched matrimony. In which imaginary time, Gothic experienced all the mortification which age wedded to youth must expect; and she all the infelicity which such a sale and sacrifice of her person justly deserved.

In this state of reciprocal discontent they arrived at the temple: Cupid still continued them in their slumber, and in order to expose the consequences of such marriages, he wrought so magically on the imaginations of them both, that he drove Gothic distracted at the supposed infidelity of his wife, and she mad with joy at the supposed death of her husband; and just as the ceremony was about to be performed, each of them broke out into such passionate soliloquies, as threw the whole company into confusion. He exclaiming, she rejoicing; he imploring death to relieve him, and she preparing to bury him; gold, quoth Ruralinda, may be bought too dear, but the grave has befriended me.—The company believing them mad, conveyed them away, Gothic to his mansion, and Ruralinda to her cottage. The next day they awoke, and being grown wise without loss of time, or the pain of real experience, they mutually declined proceeding any farther.—The old Lord continued as he was, and generously bestowed a handsome dowry on Ruralinda, who was soon after wedded to the young shepherd, that had piteously bewailed the loss of her.—The authority of Cupid was re-established, and Hymen ordered never more to appear in the village, unless Cupid introduced him.

ESOP.

VIII.

DUELLING.[1]

"Cursory Reflections on the Single Combat or Modern Duel. Addressed to Gentlemen in every Class of Life."

GOTHIC and absurd as the custom of duelling is generally allowed to be, there are advocates for it on principle; reasoners, who coolly argue for the necessity and even convenience, of this mode of accommodating certain kinds of personal differences, and of redressing certain species of injuries, for which the laws have not provided proper or adequate remedies : they conclude, therefore, that an appeal to the sword is a requisite supplement to the law, and that this sort of satisfaction for extra judicial offences, must take place, till some other mode shall be devised and established. The learned Dr. Robertson has observed, in favour of this practice—even while he condemns it—that its influence on modern manners, has been found, in some respects, beneficial to mankind.

" To this absurd custom," says he, " we must ascribe, in some degree, the extraordinary gentleness and complaisance of modern manners, and that respectful attention of one man to another, which, at present, render the social intercourses of life far more agreeable and decent than amongst the most civilized nations of antiquity." [2]

[1] From the *Pennsylvania Magazine*, May, 1775. I have not discovered the author of the pamphlet reviewed, " Cursory Reflections," etc.—*Editor*.

[2] " Reign of Emperor Charles V.," Book V. (Dr. William Robertson).—*Editor*.

The author of these considerations ["Cursory Reflections"] reduces the arguments which have been offered in behalf of the private combat to these two.

I. That the duel is the only expedient to obtain satisfaction for those injuries of which the laws take no cognizance.

II. That a man of honour is bound on pain of infamy to resent every indignity that may be offered to him with the point of his sword or with a pistol.

These positions our sensible author undertakes to refute; and we shall give a specimen of his reasoning: but, first, it will not be improper to lay before our readers part of what he has said on the origin of the single combat, or duel.

"The ancient states," says he, "of Greece and Rome, from whence we derive the noblest models of heroism, supported private honour, without delivering down to us any evidences of this baneful custom of demanding so severe a decision of private affronts; which, considering the military spirit of these nations, must, if it obtained at all, have proved more destructive to them at home, than the united swords of their enemies abroad. The practice is in fact of later and more ignoble birth; the judicial combat, the parent of modern duels, springing from monkish superstition, grafted on feudal barbarism. Whoever reads Hurd's entertaining and ingenious "Letters on Chivalry and Romance," with Robertson's elaborate "History of the Emperor Charles V.," will no longer hesitate concerning the clear fact.

"The judicial combat obtained in ignorant ages, on a conclusion that in this appeal to Providence, innocence and right would be pointed out by victory, and guilt stigmatised and punished by defeat. But alas! experience at length taught us not to expect a miraculous interposition, whenever superior strength, superior skill, and superior bravery or ferocity, either or all of them, happened to appear on the side of injustice."

Dr. Robertson, above quoted, denies the *fashion* (as the writer of these reflections has observed) of terminating private differences by the sword, or pistol, by the illustrious example of the challenge sent by Francis I. of France to the Emperor Charles V. This was not, indeed, the first instance of such challenges, among princes; but, as our author remarks, the dignity of the parties, in the present case, afforded a sufficient sanction for extending this mode of deciding differences; to which we may add, that the spirit of chivalry and romantic knighthood still prevailing in those fighting times, was continually exciting the heroes of the age to this mode of proving their personal prowess and valour.

We now return to our author's manner of reasoning upon the postulata before stated:

" With respect to the first argument," says he, " if we annex any determined ideas to our words, by satisfaction we are to understand redress, compensation, amends or atonement. Now, Gentlemen ! for the sake of all that is valuable in life, condescend for a minute to bring down your refined notions to the sure standard of common sense, and then weigh the satisfaction to be obtained in a duel.

" Is satisfaction to be enforced from an adversary by putting a weapon into his hand, and standing a contention with him, life for life, upon an equal chance ?

" Is an offender against the rules of gentility, or against the obligations of morality, a man presumptively destitute of honour himself, fairly entitled to this equal chance of extending an injury already committed, to the irreparable degree of taking the life also from an innocent man ?

" If a gentleman is infatuated enough to meet a person who has degraded himself from the character of a gentleman, upon these equal terms, and loses a limb, or his life, what species of satisfaction can that be called ?—But it is better to suffer death than indignity. What, from the injurious hand ? Correct your ideas, and you will esteem life too valuable to be complimented away for a mistaken notion.

" If the aggressor falls, the full purpose of the injured person is thus answered, but what is the satisfaction ? The survivor becomes a refugee, like a felon ; or if he should be cleared by the equivocal tenderness of a court of justice, must he not be a barbarian instead of a gentleman, who can feed upon this inhuman bloody satisfaction, without experiencing the pangs of self-reproach, for having sacrificed the life of a fellow creature to a mere punctilio ; and perhaps involved the ruin of an innocent family by the brutal deed ? If, on the other hand, he is really a mistaken man of humanity, what has he obtained ? The satisfaction of imbittering all the remainder of his life with the keenest sorrow ; of having forfeited all his future peace of mind by a consciousness of guilt, from which his notions of honour can never release him, till the load drags him down to the grave !

" If a man of strict honour is reduced to beg his life of a mere pretender to honour, a scoundrel ; what satisfaction can this be esteemed ? Is not this a mortifying, a painful aggravation of a wrong already sustained ? What consolation can honour afford for such a disgrace ? "

Our author has some other very sensible animadversions on this first branch of the argument in defence of duelling ; after which, he proceeds to the second plea, viz. " The obligation of resenting affronts in this manner, founded on the infamy of suspected courage" ; and, in our opinion, he satisfactorily proves that this argument is by no means irrefragable : but for his reasoning on this delicate point, we must refer to his pamphlet, and proceed to take notice of his plan for putting a stop to the practice of duelling.

In the first place, he recommends that a law be passed, " declaring the act of sending a challenge, or the reducing a person to defend his life with sword or pistol, to be felony ; and the killing a person in a duel, to be punished as murder, without benefit of clergy, unless sufficient proof is made that the party killed, really urged the combat."

As this first part of his proposal relates rather to the mode of punishing, than the means of preventing duels, he proceeds :

" In every quarrel between two gentlemen where satisfaction is thought necessary, let the parties be empowered to summon a jury of honour from among their friends, six to be appointed by one gentleman, and six by the other, or in case of a refusal of either party, let the six chosen by the other complete the number by their own appointment, each nominating one ; and finally, let all this be done, if possible, free from the embarrassing intervention of lawyers.

"Let this jury of honour, when duly assembled, discuss the merits of the dispute in question, and form their opinion by a majority of votes ; but to guard against generating fresh quarrels by the discovery of the votes on either side, let the whole twelve be bound to secrecy upon their honour, and the whole twelve sign the verdict of the majority.   Let a copy of this verdict be delivered to the gentleman whose conduct is condemned ; and if he refuses to make the required concession or due satisfaction, let this opinion be published in such a manner as may be thought proper, and be understood to divest him of his character as a gentleman so long as he remains contumacious.

" By this single expedient, conveyed in few words, it is hoped the necessity of duels may be effectually superseded, the practice suppressed, and ample satisfaction enforced for all injuries of honour.   In the examination of subjects of importance we are often tempted to overlook the thing we want, on a supposition that it cannot be near at hand.   This plan may perhaps admit of amendment, but it is feared the more complicated it is rendered, the more difficult it may prove to carry into execution : and it is hoped, as it is, it will not be the worse thought of, for coming from an unknown pen."

With respect to the practicability of this scheme, we apprehend that the great difficulty would lie in obliging the quarrelling parties, or either of them (who by the author's plan are merely empowered), to refer the matter to a court of honour.   But the writer does not give this as a finished plan : he barely suggests the hint ; leaving others to improve upon it, if thought worthy of farther consideration.

As to the proposed act for punishing the survivor, where one of the parties has fallen in the conflict, it is, indeed, a melancholy truth, that our laws in being have been found inadequate to the purpose of preventing duels by the dread of legal consequences.   The King of Sweden's method was virtually the same which is here recommended ; and it is said to have been effectual in that Kingdom.

The great Gustavus Adolphus, finding that the custom of duelling was becoming alarmingly prevalent among the officers in his army, was determined to suppress, if possible,

those false notions of honour. Soon after the King had
formed this resolution, and issued some very rigorous
edicts against the practice, a quarrel arose between two of
his generals; who agreed to crave His Majesty's pardon to
decide the quarrel by the laws of honour. The King consented, and said he would be a spectator of the combat; he
went, accordingly, to the place appointed, attended by a
body of guards, and the public executioner. He then told
the combatants that "they must fight till one of them
died"; and turning to the executioner, he added, "Do you
immediately strike off the head of the survivor." The monarch's inflexibility had the desired effect: the difference between the two officers was adjusted; and no more challenges
were heard of in the army of Gustavus Adolphus.

From the peculiar prevalence of this custom in countries
where the religious system is established, which, of all others,
most expressly prohibits the gratification of revenge, with
every species of outrage and violence, we too plainly see,
how little mankind are, in reality, influenced by the principles of the religion by which they profess to be guided, and
in defence of which they will occasionally risk even their
lives.

IX.

REFLECTIONS ON TITLES.[1]

Ask me what's honour? I'll the truth impart:
Know, honour then, is *Honesty of Heart.*

WHITEHEAD.

WHEN I reflect on the pompous titles bestowed on unworthy men, I feel an indignity that instructs me to despise
the absurdity. The *Honourable* plunderer of his country, or
the *Right Honourable* murderer of mankind, create such a
contrast of ideas as exhibit a monster rather than a man.
Virtue is inflamed at the violation, and sober reason calls it
nonsense.

Dignities and high sounding names have different effects
on different beholders. The lustre of the *Star* and the title
of *My Lord*, over-awe the superstitious vulgar, and forbid
them to inquire into the character of the possessor: Nay
more, they are, as it were, bewitched to admire in the great,
the vices they would honestly condemn in themselves. This
sacrifice of common sense is the certain badge which distinguishes slavery from freedom; for when men yield up the
privilege of thinking, the last shadow of liberty quits the
horizon.

But the reasonable freeman sees through the magic of a
title, and examines the man before he approves him. To
him the honours of the worthless serve to write their
masters' vices in capitals, and their stars shine to no other
end than to read them by. The possessors of undue honours
are themselves sensible of this; for when their repeated
guilt renders their persons unsafe, they disown their rank,

[1] From the *Pennsylvania Magazine*, May, 1775.—*Editor.*

and, like glow-worms, extinguish themselves into common reptiles, to avoid discovery. Thus Jeffries sunk into a fisherman, and his master escaped in the habit of a peasant.

Modesty forbids men, separately or collectively, to assume titles. But as all honours, even that of Kings, originated from the public, the public may justly be called the fountain of true honour. And it is with much pleasure I have heard the title of *Honourable* applied to a body of men, who nobly disregarding private ease and interest for public welfare, have justly merited the address of The Honourable Continental Congress.

Vox Populi.

X.

THE DREAM INTERPRETED.[1]

PARCHED with thirst and wearied with a fatiguing journey to Virginia, I turned out of the road to shelter myself among the shades; in a little time I had the good fortune to light on a spring, and the refreshing draught went sweetly down. How little of luxury does nature want! This cooling stream administered more relief than all the wines of Oporto; I drank and was satisfied; my fatigue abated, my wasted spirits were reinforced, and 'tis no wonder after such a delicious repast that I sunk insensibly into slumber. The wildest fancies in that state of forgetfulness always appear regular and connected; nothing is wrong in a dream, be it ever so unnatural. I am apt to think that the wisest men dream the most inconsistently: for as the judgment has nothing or very little to do in regulating the circumstances of a dream, it necessarily follows that the more powerful and creative the imagination is, the wilder it runs in that state of unrestrained invention: While those who are unable to wander out of the track of common thinking when awake, never exceed the boundaries of common nature when asleep.

But to return from my digression, which in this place is nothing more than that wandering of fancy which every dreamer is entitled to, and which cannot in either case be applied to myself, as in the dream I am about to relate I was only a spectator, and had no other business to do than to remember.

To what scene or country my ideas had conveyed themselves, or whether they had created a region on purpose to

[1] From the *Pennsylvania Magazine*, June, 1775.—*Editor*.

explore, I know not, but I saw before me one of the most
pleasing landscapes I have ever beheld. I gazed at it, till my
mind partaking of the prospect became incorporated therewith, and felt all the tranquillity of the place.   In this state
of ideal happiness I sat down on the side of a mountain,
totally forgetful of the world I had left behind me.   The
most delicious fruits presented themselves to my hands, and
one of the clearest rivers that ever watered the earth rolled
along at the foot of the mountain, and invited me to drink.
The distant hills were blue with the tincture of the skies,
and seemed as if they were the threshold of the celestial
region. But while I gazed the whole scene began to change,
by an almost insensible gradation.   The sun, instead of
administering life and health, consumed everything with an
intolerable heat. The verdure withered. The hills appeared
burnt and black. The fountains dried away ; and the atmosphere became a motionless lake of air, loaded with
pestilence and death. After several days of wretched suf-
focation, the sky grew darkened with clouds from every
quarter, till one extended storm excluded the face of heaven.
A dismal silence took place, as if the earth, struck with a
general panic, was listening like a criminal to the sentence
of death. The glimmering light with which the sun feebly
penetrated the clouds began to fail, till Egyptian darkness
added to the horror. The beginning of the tempest was
announced by a confusion of distant thunders, till at length
a general discharge of the whole artillery of heaven was
poured down upon the earth.   Trembling I shrunk into
the side of a cave, and dreaded the event. The mountain
shook, and threatened me with instant destruction. The
rapid lightning at every blaze exhibited the landscape of a
world on fire, while the accumulating torrent, not in rain,
but floods of water, resembled another deluge.

At length the fury of the storm abated, and nature, fatigued
with fear and watching, sank into rest. But when the morning rose, and the universal lamp of heaven emerged from
the deep, how was I struck with astonishment ! I expected
to have seen a world in ruins, which nothing but a new

creation could have restored. Instead of which, the prospect was lovely and inviting, and had all the promising appearance of exceeding its former glory. The air, purged of
its poisonous vapours, was fresh and healthy. The dried
fountains were replenished, the waters sweet and wholesome.
The sickly earth, recovered to new life, abounded with vegetation. The groves were musical with innumerable song-
sters, and the long-deserted fields echoed with the joyous
sound of the husbandman. All, all was felicity ; and what
I had dreaded as an evil, became a blessing. At this happy
reflection I awoke; and having refreshed myself with
another draught from the friendly spring, pursued my
journey.

After travelling a few miles I fell in with a companion,
and as we rode through a wood but little frequented by
travellers, I began, for the sake of chatting away the tedious-
ness of the journey, to relate my dream. I think, replied
my friend, that I can interpret it : That beautiful country
which you saw is America. The sickly state you beheld her
in, has been coming on her for these ten years past. Her
commerce has been drying up by repeated restrictions, till
by one merciless edict the ruin of it is compleated. The
pestilential atmosphere represents that ministerial corruption which surrounds and exercises its dominion over her,
and which nothing but a storm can purify. The tempest is
the present contest, and the event will be the same. She
will rise with new glories from the conflict, and her fame be
established in every corner of the globe; while it will be
remembered to her eternal honour, that she has not sought
the quarrel, but has been driven into it. He who guides the
natural tempest will regulate the political one, and bring
good out of evil. In our petition to Britain we asked but
for peace; but the prayer was rejected. The cause is now
before a higher court, the court of providence, before whom
the arrogance of kings, the infidelity of ministers, the general
corruption of government, and all the cobweb artifice of
courts, will fall confounded and ashamed.

Bucks County.

XI.

REFLECTIONS ON UNHAPPY MARRIAGES.[1]

THOUGH 't is confessed on all hands that the weal or woe of life depends on no one circumstance so critical as matrimony, yet how few seem to be influenced by this universal acknowledgement, or act with a caution becoming the danger.

Those that are undone this way, are the young, the rash and amorous, whose hearts are ever glowing with desire, whose eyes are ever roaming after beauty; these doat on the first amiable image that chance throws in their way, and when the flame is once kindled, would risk eternity itself to appease it.—But, still like their first parents, they no sooner taste the tempting fruit, but their eyes are opened: the folly of their intemperance becomes visible; shame succeeds first, and then repentance; but sorrow for themselves soon returns to anger with the innocent cause of their unhappiness. Hence flow bitter reproaches, and keen invectives, which end in mutual hatred and contempt: Love abhors clamour and soon flies away, and happiness finds no entrance when love is gone; Thus for a few hours of dalliance, I will not call it affection, the repose of all their future days are sacrificed; and those who but just before seem'd to live only for each other, now would almost cease to live, that the separation might be eternal.

But hold, says the man of phlegm and economy, all are not of this hasty turn—I allow it—there are persons in the

---

[1] From the *Pennsylvania Magazine*, June, 1775, where it is appended to a series of papers ("The Old Bachelor") which Paine did not write. The writer says he has "transcribed" it.—*Editor*.

world who are young without passions, and in health without appetite : these hunt out a wife as they go to *Smithfield* for a horse ; and inter-marry fortunes, not minds, or even bodies :   In this case the Bridegroom has no joy but in taking possession of the portion, and the bride dreams of little beside new clothes, visits and congratulations.   Thus, as their expectations of pleasure are not very great, neither is the disappointment very grievous ; they just keep each other in countenance, live decently, and are exactly as fond the twentieth year of matrimony, as the first.   But I would not advise any one to call this state of insipidity happiness, because it would argue him both ignorant of its nature, and incapable of enjoying it.   Mere absence of pain will undoubtedly constitute ease ; and, without ease, there can be no happiness :   Ease, however, is but the medium, through which happiness is tasted, and but passively receives what the last actually bestows ; if therefore the rash who marry inconsiderately, perish in the storms raised by their own passions, these slumber away their days in a sluggish calm, and rather dream they live, than experience it by a series of actual sensible enjoyments.

As matrimonial happiness is neither the result of insipidity, or ill-grounded passion, surely those, who make their court to age, ugliness, and all that's detestable both in mind and body, cannot hope to find it, tho' qualified with all the riches that avarice covets, or *Plutus* could bestow.   Matches of this kind are downright prostitution, however softened by the letter of the law ; and he or she who receives the golden equivalent of youth and beauty, so wretchedly bestowed, can never enjoy what they so dearly purchased : The shocking incumbrance would render the sumptuous banquet tasteless, and the magnificent bed loathsome ; rest would disdain the one, and appetite sicken at the other ; uneasiness wait upon both ; even gratitude itself would almost cease to be obliging, and good-manners grow such a burden, that the best bred or best-natured people breathing, would be often tempted to throw it down.

But say we should not wonder that those who either

marry gold without love, or love without gold, should be
miserable : I can't forbear being astonished, if such whose
fortunes are affluent, whose desires were mutual, who equally
languished for the happy moment before it came, and
seemed for a while to be equally transported when it had
taken place :   If even these should, in the end, prove as unhappy as either of the others !   And yet how often is this
the melancholy circumstance !   As extasy abates, coolness
succeeds, which often makes way for indifference, and that
for neglect: Sure of each other by the nuptial band, they
no longer take any pains to be mutually agreeable ; careless
if they displease ; and yet angry if reproached ; with so little relish for each other's company, that anybody's else is
welcome, and more entertaining.   Their union thus broke,
they pursue separate pleasures ; never meet but to wrangle,
or part but to find comfort in other society.   After this the
descent is easy to utter aversion, which having wearied itself
out with heart-burnings, clamours, and affronts, subsides
into a perfect insensibility ; when fresh objects of love step
in to their relief on either side, and mutual infidelity makes
way for mutual complaisance, that each may be the better
able to deceive the other.

I shall conclude with the sentiments of an American savage on this subject, who being advised by one of our countrymen to marry according to the ceremonies of the church,
as being the ordinance of an infinitely wise and good God,
briskly replied, "That either the Christians' God was not
so good and wise as he was represented, or he never med-
dled with the marriages of his people ; since not one in a
hundred of them had anything to do either with happiness
or common sense.   Hence," continued he, " as soon as ever
you meet you long to part ; and, not having this relief in
your power, by way of revenge, double each other's misery :
Whereas in ours, which have no other ceremony than mutual
affection, and last no longer than they bestow mutual pleasures, we make it our business to oblige the heart we are
afraid to lose ; and being at liberty to separate, seldom or
never feel the inclination.   But if any should be found so

wretched among us, as to hate where the only commerce ought to be love, we instantly dissolve the band : God made us all in pairs ; each has his mate somewhere or other ; and 't is our duty to find each other out, since no creature was ever intended to be miserable."

XII.

THOUGHTS ON DEFENSIVE WAR.[1]

COULD the peaceable principle of the Quakers be universally established, arms and the art of war would be wholly
extirpated : But we live not in a world of angels. The
reign of Satan is not ended ; neither are we to expect to be
defended by miracles. The pillar of the cloud existed only
in the wilderness. In the nonage of the Israelites. It protected them in their retreat from Pharaoh, while they were
destitute of the natural means of defence, for they brought
no arms from Egypt ; but it neither fought their battles nor
shielded them from dangers afterwards.

I am thus far a Quaker, that I would gladly agree with all
the world to lay aside the use of arms, and settle matters by
negotiation ; but unless the whole will, the matter ends, and
I take up my musket and thank heaven he has put it in my
power.

Whoever considers the unprincipled enemy we have to
cope with, will not hesitate to declare that nothing but arms
or miracles can reduce them to reason and moderation.
They have lost sight of the limits of humanity. The portrait
of a parent red with the blood of her children is a picture fit
only for the galleries of the infernals. From the House of
Commons the troops of Britain have been exhorted to fight,
not for the defence of their natural rights, not to repel the
invasion or the insult of enemies; but on the vilest of all
pretences, gold. " Ye fight for solid revenue " was vociferated in the House. Thus America *must suffer* because she

[1] From the *Pennsylvania Magazine*, July, 1775. Probably by Paine—*Editor*.

has something to lose. Her crime is property. That which allures the Highwayman has allured the ministry under a gentler name. But the position laid down by Lord Sandwich, is a clear demonstration of the justice of defensive arms. The Americans, quoth this Quixote of modern days, *will not fight;* therefore we will. His Lordship's plan when analized amounts to this. These people are either too superstitiously religious, or too cowardly for arms; they either *cannot* or *dare not* defend; their property is open to any one who has the courage to attack them. Send but your troops and the prize is ours. Kill a few and take the whole. Thus the peaceable part of mankind will be continually overrun by the vile and abandoned, while they neglect the means of self defence. The supposed quietude of a good man allures the ruffian; while on the other hand, arms like laws discourage and keep the invader and the plunderer in awe, and preserve order in the world as well as property. The balance of power is the scale of peace. The same balance would be preserved were all the world destitute of arms, for all would be alike; but since some *will not*, others *dare not* lay them aside. And while a single nation refuses to lay them down, it is proper that all should keep them up. Horrid mischief would ensue were one half the world deprived of the use of them; for while avarice and ambition have a place in the heart of man, the weak will become a prey to the strong. The history of every age and nation establishes these truths, and facts need but little arguments when they prove themselves.

But there is a point to view this matter in of superior consequence to the defence of property; and that point is *Liberty* in all its meanings. In the barbarous ages of the world, men in general had no liberty. The strong governed the weak at will; 'till the coming of Christ there was no such thing as political freedom in any known part of the earth. The Jewish kings were in point of government as absolute as the Pharaohs. Men were frequently put to death without trial at the will of the Sovereign. The

Romans held the world in slavery, and were themselves the slaves of their emperors. The madman of Macedon governed by caprice and passion, and strided as arrogantly over the world as if he had made and peopled it; and it is needless to imagine that other nations at that time were more refined. Wherefore political as well as spiritual freedom is the gift of God through Christ. The second in the catalogue of blessings; and so intimately related, so sympathetically united with the first, that the one cannot be wounded without communicating an injury to the other. Political liberty is the visible .pass which guards the religions. It is the outwork by which the church militant is defended, and the attacks of the enemy are frequently made through this fortress. The same power which has established a restraining Port Bill in the Colonies, has established a restraining Protestant Church Bill in Canada.

I had the pleasure and advantage of hearing this matter wisely investigated, by a gentleman, in a sermon to one of the battalions of this city; and am fully convinced, that spiritual freedom is the root of political liberty.

First. Because till spiritual freedom was made manifest, political liberty did not exist.

Secondly. because in proportion that *spiritual freedom* has been manifested, *political liberty* has encreased.

Thirdly. Whenever the visible church has been oppressed, political freedom has suffered with it. Read the history of Mary and the Stuarts. The popish world at this day by not knowing the full manifestation of spiritual freedom, enjoy but a shadow of political liberty.—Though I am unwilling to accuse the present government of popish principles, they cannot, I think, be clearly acquitted of popish practices : the facility with which they perceive the dark and ignorant are governed, in popish nations, will always be a temptation to the lovers of arbitrary power to adopt the same methods.

As the union between spiritual freedom and political liberty seems nearly inseparable, it is our duty to defend both. And defence in the first instance is best. The lives of hundreds of both countries had been preserved had America been in arms a year ago. Our enemies have mistaken our peace for cowardice, and supposing us unarmed have begun the attack.

A Lover of Peace.

XIII.

AN OCCASIONAL LETTER ON THE FEMALE SEX.[1]

O Woman ! lovely Woman !
Nature made thee to temper man,
We had been Brutes without you.

OTWAY.

IF we take a survey of ages and of countries, we shall find the women, almost—without exception—at all times and in all places, adored and oppressed. Man, who has never neglected an opportunity of exerting his power, in paying homage to their beauty, has always availed himself of their weakness. He has been at once their tyrant and their slave.

Nature herself, in forming beings so susceptible and tender, appears to have been more attentive to their charms than to their happiness. Continually surrounded with griefs and fears, the women more than share all our miseries, and are besides subjected to ills which are peculiarly their own. They cannot be the means of life without exposing themselves to the loss of it ; every revolution which they undergo, alters their health, and threatens their existence. Cruel distempers attack their beauty—and the hour, which confirms their release from those, is perhaps the most melancholy of their lives. It robs them of the most essential characteristic of their sex. They can then only hope for protection from the humiliating claims of pity, or the feeble voice of gratitude.

Society, instead of alleviating their condition, is to them the source of new miseries. More than one half of the globe

[1] From the *Pennsylvania Magazine*, August, 1775.—*Editor*.

is covered with savages; and among all these people women are completely wretched.   Man, in a state of barbarity, equally cruel and indolent, active by necessity, but naturally inclined to repose, is acquainted with little more than the physical effects of love ; and, having none of those moral ideas which only can soften the empire of force, he is led to consider it as his supreme law, subjecting to his despotism those whom reason had made his equal, but whose imbecility betrayed them to his strength.   " Nothing " (says Professor Miller, speaking of the women of barbarous nations) " can exceed the dependence and subjection in which they are kept, or the toil and drudgery which they are obliged to undergo.   The husband, when he is not engaged in some warlike exercise, indulges himself in idleness, and devolves upon his wife the whole burden of his domestic affairs.   He disdains to assist her in any of those servile employments. She sleeps in a different bed, and is seldom permitted to have any conversation or correspondence with him."

The women among the Indians of America are what the Helots were among the Spartans, a vanquished people, obliged to toil for their conquerors.   Hence on the banks of the Oroonoko, we have seen mothers slaying their daughters out of compassion, and smothering them in the hour of their birth.   They consider this barbarous pity as a virtue.

" The men (says Commodore Byron, in his account of the in-habitants of South-America) exercise a most despotic authority over their wives, whom they consider in the same view they do any other part of their property, and dispose of them accord-ingly : Even their common treatment of them is cruel ; for though the toil and hazard of procuring food lies entirely on the women, yet they are not suffered to touch any part of it till the husband is satisfied ; and then he assigns them their portion, which is generally very scanty, and such as he has not a stomach for himself."

Among the nations of the East we find another kind of despotism and dominion prevail—the Seraglio, and the domestic servitude of woman, authorised by the manners and established by the laws. In Turkey, in Persia, in India, in Japan, and over the vast empire of China, one half of the human species is oppressed by the other.

The excess of oppression in those countries springs from the excess of love.

All Asia is covered with prisons, where beauty in bondage waits the caprices of a master. The multitude of women there assembled have no will, no inclinations but his : Their triumphs are only for a moment ; and their rivalry, their hate, and their animosities, continue till death. There the lovely sex are obliged to repay even their servitude with the most tender affections; or, what is still more mortifying, with the counterfeit of an affection, which they do not feel : There the most gloomy tyranny has subjected them to creatures, who, being of neither sex, are a dishonour to both : There, in short, their education tends only to debase them ; their virtues are forced ; their very pleasures are involuntary and joyless; and after an existence of a few years —till the bloom of youth is over—their period of neglect commences, which is long and dreadful. In the temperate latitude where the climates, giving less ardour to passion, leave more confidence in virtue, the women have not been deprived of their liberty, but a severe legislation has, at all times, kept them in a state of dependence. One while, they were confined to their own apartments, and debarred at once from business and amusement ; at other times, a tedious guardianship defrauded their hearts, and insulted their understandings. Affronted in one country by polygamy, which gives them their rivals for their inseparable companions; inslaved in another by indissoluble ties, which often join the gentle to the rude, and sensibility to brutality : Even in countries where they may be esteemed most happy, constrained in their desires in the disposal of their goods, robbed of freedom of will by the laws, the slaves of opinion, which rules them with absolute sway, and construes the slightest appearances into guilt ; surrounded on all sides by judges, who are at once tyrants and their seducers, and who, after having prepared their faults, punish every lapse with

dishonour—nay, usurp the right of degrading them on suspicion! Who does not feel for the tender sex? Yet such,
I am sorry to say, is the lot of woman over the whole earth.
Man with regard to them, in all climates, and in all ages,
has been either an insensible husband or an oppressor; but
they have sometimes experienced the cold and deliberate
oppression of pride, and sometimes the violent and terrible
tyranny of jealousy. When they are not beloved they are
nothing; and, when they are, they are tormented. They
have almost equal cause to be afraid of indifference and of
love. Over three quarters of the globe nature has placed
them between contempt and misery.

"The melting desires, or the fiery passions," says Professor
Ferguson, "which in one climate take place between the sexes,
are, in another, changed into a sober consideration, or a patience
of mutual disgust. This change is remarked in crossing the
Mediterranean, in following the course of the Mississippi, in
ascending the mountains of Caucasus, and in passing from the
Alps and the Pyrenees to the shores of the Baltic.

"The burning ardours and torturing jealousies of the Seraglio
and Harem, which have reigned so long in Asia and Africa, and
which, in the southern parts of Europe, have scarcely given way
to the differences of religion and civil establishments, are found,
however, with an abatement of heat in the climate, to be more
easily changed, in one latitude, into a temporary passion, which
engrosses the mind without infeebling it, and which excites to
romantic atchievments. By a farther progress to the north it is
changed into a spirit of gallantry, which employs the wit and
fancy more than the heart, which prefers intrigue to enjoyment,
and substitutes affection and vanity where sentiment and desire
have failed. As it departs from the sun, the same passion is farther composed into a habit of domestic connection, or frozen into
a state of insensibility, under which the sexes at freedom scarcely
choose to unite their society."

Even among people where beauty received the highest
homage, we find men who would deprive the sex of every
kind of reputation: "The most virtuous woman," says a
celebrated Greek, "is she who is least talked of." That

morose man, while he imposes duties upon women, would deprive them of the sweets of public esteem, and in exacting virtues from them, would make it a crime to aspire at honour.

If a woman were to defend the cause of her sex, she might address him in the following manner:

"How great is your injustice? If we have an equal right with you to virtue, why should we not have an equal right to praise? The public esteem ought to wait upon merit. Our duties are different from yours, but they are not therefore less difficult to fulfil, or of less consequence to society: They are the fountains of your felicity, and the sweetness of life. We are wives and mothers. 'T is we who form the union and the cordiality of families: 'T is we who soften that savage rudeness which considers everything as due to force, and which would involve man with man in eternal war. We cultivate in you that humanity which makes you feel for the misfortunes of others, and our tears forewarn you of your own danger. Nay, you cannot be ignorant that we have need of courage not less than you: More feeble in ourselves, we have perhaps more trials to encounter. Nature assails us with sorrow, law and custom press us with constraint, and sensibility and virtue alarm us with their continual conflict. Sometimes also the name of citizen demands from us the tribute of fortitude. When you offer your blood to the State think that it is ours. In giving it our sons and our husbands we give more than ourselves. You can only die on the field of battle, but we have the misfortune to survive those whom we love most. Alas! while your ambitious vanity is unceasingly labouring to cover the earth with statues, with monuments, and with inscriptions to eternize, if possible, your names, and give yourselves an existence, when this body is no more, why must we be condemned to live and to die unknown? Would that the grave and eternal forgetfulness should be our lot. Be not our tyrants in all: Permit our names to be sometimes pronounced beyond the narrow circle in which we live: Permit friendship, or at least love, to inscribe its emblems on the tomb where our ashes repose; and deny us not that public esteem which, after the esteem of one's self, is the sweetest reward of well doing."

All men, however, it must be owned, have not been equally unjust to their fair companions. In some countries public honours have been paid to women. Art has erected them monuments. Eloquence has celebrated their virtues, and History has collected whatever could adorn their character.

XIV.

A SERIOUS THOUGHT.[1]

WHEN I reflect on the horrid cruelties exercised by Britain in the East Indies—How thousands perished by artificial famine—How religion and every manly principle of honour and honesty were sacrificed to luxury and pride—When I read of the wretched natives being blown away, for no other crime than because, sickened with the miserable scene, they refused to fight—When I reflect on these and a thousand instances of similar barbarity, I firmly believe that the Almighty, in compassion to mankind, will curtail the power of Britain.

And when I reflect on the use she hath made of the discovery of this new world—that the little paltry dignity of earthly kings hath been set up in preference to the great cause of the King of kings—That instead of Christian examples to the Indians, she hath basely tampered with their passions, imposed on their ignorance, and made them tools of treachery and murder—And when to these and many other melancholy reflections I add this sad remark, that ever since the discovery of America she hath employed herself in the most horrid of all traffics, that of human flesh, unknown to the most savage nations, hath yearly (without provocation and in cold blood) ravaged the hapless shores of Africa, robbing it of its unoffending inhabitants to cultivate her stolen dominions in the West—When I reflect on these, I hesitate not for a moment to believe that the Almighty

---

[1] *Pennsylvania Journal*, October 18, 1775. This was probably the earliest anticipation of the Declaration of Independence written and published in America.—*Editor*.

will finally separate America from Britain. Call it Independence or what you will, if it is the cause of God and humanity it will go on.

And when the Almighty shall have blest us, and made us a people *dependent only upon Him*, then may our first gratitude be shown by an act of continental legislation, which shall put a stop to the importation of Negroes for sale, soften the hard fate of those already here, and in time procure their freedom.

HUMANUS.

COMMON SENSE.[1]

INTRODUCTION.

PERHAPS the sentiments contained in the following pages, are not *yet* sufficiently fashionable to procure them general Favor ; a long Habit of not thinking a Thing *wrong*, gives it a superficial appearance of being *right*, and raises at first a formidable outcry in defence of Custom. But the Tumult soon subsides. Time makes more Converts than Reason.

As a long and violent abuse of power is generally the means of calling the right of it in question, (and in matters too which might never have been thought of, had not the sufferers been aggravated into the inquiry,) and as the King of England hath undertaken in his *own right*, to support the Parliament in what he calls *Theirs*, and as the good People of this Country are grievously oppressed by the Combination, they have an undoubted privilege to enquire into the

---

[1] This pamphlet, whose effect has never been paralleled in literary history, was published January 10, 1776, with the following title :

COMMON SENSE : Addressed to the Inhabitants of America, on the following Interesting Subjects, viz.: I. Of the Origin and Design of Government in General ; with Concise Remarks on the English Constitution. II. Of Monarchy and Hereditary Succession. III. Thoughts on the Present State of American Affairs. IV. Of the Present Ability of America ; with some Miscellaneous Reflections.

Man knows no master save creating HEAVEN,
Or those whom choice and common good ordain.

THOMSON.

Philadelphia : Printed, and Sold, by R. BELL, in Third Street. MDCCLXXVI.

a...
Comp...
thereof.
a Pamphlet ; ...
unfriendly will cease ...
bestowed upon their conversions.

The cause of America is in a great measure the cause of all mankind. Many circumstances have, and will arise, which are not local, but universal, and through which the principles of all lovers of mankind are affected, and in the event of which their affections are interested. The laying a country desolate with fire and sword, declaring war against the natural rights of all mankind, and extirpating the defenders thereof from the face of the earth, is the concern of every man to whom nature hath given the power of feeling ; of which class, regardless of party censure, is

THE AUTHOR.

Postscript to Preface in the third edition.

P. S. The Publication of this new Edition hath been delayed, with a view of taking notice (had it been necessary) of any attempt to refute the Doctrine of Independence : As no answer hath yet appeared, it is now presumed that none will, the time needful for getting such a Performance ready for the Public being considerably past.

Who the Author of this Production is, is wholly unnecessary to the Public, as the Object for Attention is the *Doctrine itself*, not the *Man*. Yet it may not be unnecessary to say, That he is unconnected with any party, and under no sort of Influence, public or private, but the influence of reason and principle.

PHILADELPHIA, February 14, 1776.

COMMON SENSE.

ON THE ORIGIN AND DESIGN OF GOVERNMENT IN GENERAL, WITH CONCISE REMARKS ON THE ENGLISH CONSTITUTION.

SOME writers have so confounded society with government, as to leave little or no distinction between them ; whereas they are not only different, but have different origins. Society is produced by our wants, and government by our wickedness ; the former promotes our happiness *possitively* by uniting our affections, the latter *negatively* by restraining our vices. The one encourages intercourse, the other creates distinctions. The first is a patron, the last a punisher.

Society in every state is a blessing, but Government, even in its best state, is but a necessary evil; in its worst state an intolerable one : for when we suffer, or are exposed to the same miseries *by a Government*, which we might expect in a country *without Government*, our calamity is heightened by reflecting that we furnish the means by which we suffer. Government, like dress, is the badge of lost innocence ; the palaces of kings are built upon the ruins of the bowers of paradise. For were the impulses of conscience clear, uniform and irresistibly obeyed, man would need no other lawgiver ; but that not being the case, he finds it necessary to surrender up a part of his property to furnish means for the protection of the rest ; and this he is induced to do by the same prudence which in every other case advises him, out of two evils to choose the least. Wherefore, security being the true design and end of government, it unanswerably follows that whatever form thereof appears most likely to ensure it to us, with the least expence and greatest benefit, is preferable to all others.

In order to gain a clear and just idea of the design and end of government, let us suppose a small number of persons settled in some sequestered part of the earth, unconnected with the rest; they will then represent the first peopling of any country, or of the world. In this state of natural liberty, society will be their first thought. A thousand motives will excite them thereto; the strength of one man is so unequal to his wants, and his mind so unfitted for perpetual solitude, that he is soon obliged to seek assistance and relief of another, who in his turn requires the same. Four or five united would be able to raise a tolerable dwelling in the midst of a wilderness, but one man might labour out the common period of life without accomplishing any thing; when he had felled his timber he could not remove it, nor erect it after it was removed; hunger in the mean time would urge him to quit his work, and every different want would call him a different way. Disease, nay even misfortune, would be death; for though neither might be mortal, yet either would disable him from living, and reduce him to a state in which he might rather be said to perish than to die.

Thus necessity, like a gravitating power, would soon form our newly arrived emigrants into society, the reciprocal blessings of which would supercede, and render the obligations of law and government unnecessary while they remained perfectly just to each other; but as nothing but Heaven is impregnable to vice, it will unavoidably happen that in proportion as they surmount the first difficulties of emigration, which bound them together in a common cause, they will begin to relax in their duty and attachment to each other: and this remissness will point out the necessity of establishing some form of government to supply the defect of moral virtue.

Some convenient tree will afford them a State House, under the branches of which the whole Colony may assemble to deliberate on public matters. It is more than probable that their first laws will have the title only of Regulations and be enforced by no other penalty than public disesteem. In this first parliament every man by natural right will have a seat.

But as the Colony encreases, the public concerns will encrease likewise, and the distance at which the members may
be separated, will render it too inconvenient for all of them
to meet on every occasion as at first, when their number was
small, their habitations near, and the public concerns few and
trifling. This will point out the convenience of their consenting to leave the legislative part to be managed by a select number chosen from the whole body, who are supposed
to have the same concerns at stake which those have who
appointed them, and who will act in the same manner as the
whole body would act were they present. If the colony
continue encreasing, it will become necessary to augment the
number of representatives, and that the interest of every
part of the colony may be attended to, it will be found best
to divide the whole into convenient parts, each part sending
its proper number : and that the *elected* might never form to
themselves an interest separate from the *elector*s, prudence
will point out the propriety of having elections often : because as the *elected* might by that means return and mix
again with the general body of the *electors* in a few months,
their fidelity to the public will be secured by the prudent
reflection of not making a rod for themselves. And as this
frequent interchange will establish a common interest with
every part of the community, they will mutually and naturally support each other, and on this, (not on the unmeaning
name of king,) depends the *strength of government, and the
happiness of the governed.*

Here then is the origin and rise of government ; namely,
a mode rendered necessary by the inability of moral virtue
to govern the world ; here too is the design and end of
government, viz. Freedom and security. And however our
eyes may be dazzled with show, or our ears deceived by sound ;
however prejudice may warp our wills, or interest darken our
understanding, the simple voice of nature and reason will
say, 'tis right.

I draw my idea of the form of government from a principle in nature which no art can overturn, viz. that the more
simple any thing is, the less liable it is to be disordered, and

the easier repaired when disordered; and with this maxim in view I offer a few remarks on the so much boasted constitution of England. That it was noble for the dark and slavish times in which it was erected, is granted. When the world was overrun with tyranny the least remove therefrom was a glorious rescue. But that it is imperfect, subject to convulsions, and incapable of producing what it seems to promise, is easily demonstrated.

Absolute governments, (tho' the disgrace of human nature) have this advantage with them, they are simple; if the people suffer, they know the head from which their suffering springs; know likewise the remedy; and are not bewildered by a variety of causes and cures. But the constitution of England is so exceedingly complex, that the nation may suffer for years together without being able to discover in which part the fault lies; some will say in one and some in another, and every political physician will advise a different medicine.

I know it is difficult to get over local or long standing prejudices, yet if we will suffer ourselves to examine the component parts of the English constitution, we shall find them to be the base remains of two ancient tyrannies, compounded with some new Republican materials.

First.—The remains of Monarchical tyranny in the person of the King.

Secondly.—The remains of Aristocratical tyranny in the persons of the Peers.

Thirdly.—The new Republican materials, in the persons of the Commons, on whose virtue depends the freedom of England.

The two first, by being hereditary, are independant of the People; wherefore in a *constitutional sense* they contribute nothing towards the freedom of the State.

To say that the constitution of England is an *union* of three powers, reciprocally *checking* each other, is farcical; either the words have no meaning, or they are flat contradictions.

To say that the Commons is a check upon the King, presupposes two things.

First.—That the King is not to be trusted without being looked after; or in other words, that a thirst for absolute power is the natural disease of monarchy.

Secondly.—That the Commons, by being appointed for that purpose, are either wiser or more worthy of confidence than the Crown.

But as the same constitution which gives the Commons a power to check the King by withholding the supplies, gives afterwards the King a power to check the Commons, by empowering him to reject their other bills; it again supposes that the King is wiser than those whom it has already supposed to be wiser than him. A mere absurdity!

There is something exceedingly ridiculous in the composition of Monarchy; it first excludes a man from the means of information, yet empowers him to act in cases where the highest judgment is required. The state of a king shuts him from the World, yet the business of a king requires him to know it thoroughly; wherefore the different parts, by unnaturally opposing and destroying each other, prove the whole character to be absurd and useless.

Some writers have explained the English constitution thus: the King, say they, is one, the people another; the Peers are a house in behalf of the King, the commons in behalf of the people; but this hath all the distinctions of a house divided against itself; and though the expressions be pleasantly arranged, yet when examined they appear idle and ambiguous; and it will always happen, that the nicest construction that words are capable of, when applied to the description of something which either cannot exist, or is too incomprehensible to be within the compass of description, will be words of sound only, and though they may amuse the ear, they cannot inform the mind: for this explanation includes a previous question, viz. *how came the king by a power which the people are afraid to trust, and always obliged to check?* Such a power could not be the gift of a wise people, neither can any power, *which needs checking*, be from God; yet the provision which the constitution makes supposes such a power to exist.

But the provision is unequal to the task ; the means either cannot or will not accomplish the end, and the whole affair is a *Felo de se :* for as the greater weight will always carry up the less, and as all the wheels of a machine are put in motion by one, it only remains to know which power in the constitution has the most weight, for that will govern : and tho' the others, or a part of them, may clog, or, as the phrase is, check the rapidity of its motion, yet so long as they cannot stop it, their endeavours will be ineffectual :   The first moving power will at last have its way, and what it wants in speed is supplied by time.

That the crown is this overbearing part in the English constitution needs not be mentioned, and that it derives its whole consequence merely from being the giver of places and pensions is self-evident ; wherefore, though we have been wise enough to shut and lock a door against absolute Monarchy, we at the same time have been foolish enough to put the Crown in possession of the key.

The prejudice of Englishmen, in favour of their own government, by King, Lords and Commons, arises as much or more from national pride than reason.   Individuals are undoubtedly safer in England than in some other countries : but the will of the king is as much the law of the land in Britain as in France, with this difference, that instead of proceeding directly from his mouth, it is handed to the people under the formidable shape of an act of parliament.   For the fate of Charles the First hath only made kings more subtle —not more just.

Wherefore, laying aside all national pride and prejudice in favour of modes and forms, the plain truth is that *it is wholly owing to the constitution of the people, and not to the constitution of the government* that the crown is not as oppressive in England as in Turkey.

An inquiry into the *constitutional errors* in the English form of government, is at this time highly necessary ; for as we are never in a proper condition of doing justice to others, while we continue under the influence of some leading partiality, so neither are we capable of doing it to our-

selves while we remain fettered by any obstinate prejudice.
And as a man who is attached to a prostitute is unfitted
to choose or judge of a wife, so any prepossession in
favour of a rotten constitution of government will disable us
from discerning a good one.

OF MONARCHY AND HEREDITARY SUCCESSION.

MANKIND being originally equals in the order of creation,
the equality could only be destroyed by some subsequent
circumstance: the distinctions of rich and poor may in a
great measure be accounted for, and that without having
recourse to the harsh ill-sounding names of oppression and
avarice. Oppression is often the *consequence*, but seldom or
never the *means* of riches; and tho' avarice will preserve a
man from being necessitously poor, it generally makes him
too timorous to be wealthy.

But there is another and greater distinction for which no
truly natural or religious reason can be assigned, and that
is the distinction of men into KINGS and SUBJECTS. Male
and female are the distinctions of nature, good and bad the
distinctions of Heaven; but how a race of men came into the
world so exalted above the rest, and distinguished like some
new species, is worth inquiring into, and whether they are the
means of happiness or of misery to mankind.

In the early ages of the world, according to the scripture
chronology there were no kings; the consequence of which
was, there were no wars; it is the pride of kings which
throws mankind into confusion. Holland, without a king
hath enjoyed more peace for this last century than any of ·
the monarchical governments in Europe. Antiquity favours
the same remark; for the quiet and rural lives of the first
Patriarchs have a happy something in them, which vanishes
when we come to the history of Jewish royalty.

Government by kings was first introduced into the world
by the Heathens, from whom the children of Israel copied
the custom. It was the most prosperous invention the
Devil ever set on foot for the promotion of idolatry. The

Heathens paid divine honours to their deceased kings, and the Christian World hath improved on the plan by doing the same to their living ones. How impious is the title of sacred Majesty applied to a worm, who in the midst of his splendor is crumbling into dust!

As the exalting one man so greatly above the rest cannot be justified on the equal rights of nature, so neither can it be defended on the authority of scripture; for the will of the Almighty as declared by Gideon, and the prophet Samuel, expressly disapproves of government by Kings. All anti-monarchical parts of scripture, have been very smoothly glossed over in monarchical governments, but they undoubtedly merit the attention of countries which have their governments yet to form. *Render unto Cesar the things which are Cesar's,* is the scripture doctrine of courts, yet it is no support of monarchical government, for the Jews at that time were without a king, and in a state of vassalage to the Romans.

Near three thousand years passed away, from the Mosaic account of the creation, till the Jews under a national delusion requested a king. Till then their form of government (except in extraordinary cases where the Almighty interposed) was a kind of Republic, administered by a judge and the elders of the tribes. Kings they had none, and it was held sinful to acknowledge any being under that title but the Lord of Hosts. And when a man seriously reflects on the idolatrous homage which is paid to the persons of kings, he need not wonder that the Almighty, ever jealous of his honour, should disapprove a form of government which so impiously invades the prerogative of Heaven.

Monarchy is ranked in scripture as one of the sins of the Jews, for which a curse in reserve is denounced against them. The history of that transaction is worth attending to.

The children of Israel being oppressed by the Midianites, Gideon marched against them with a small army, and victory thro' the divine interposition decided in his favour. The Jews, elate with success, and attributing it to the generalship of Gideon, proposed making him a king, saying, *Rule thou over us, thou and thy son, and thy son's son.* Here was temptation in its fullest extent; not a kingdom only, but an hereditary one; but Gideon in the piety of his soul replied, *I will not rule over you, neither shall my son rule over you.* THE LORD SHALL RULE OVER YOU. Words need not be more explicit; Gideon doth not decline the honour, but denieth their right to give it; neither doth he compliment them with invented declarations of his thanks, but in the positive stile of a prophet charges them with disaffection to their proper Sovereign, the King of Heaven.

About one hundred and thirty years after this, they fell again into the same error. The hankering which the Jews had for the Idolatrous customs of the Heathens, is something exceedingly unaccountable; but so it was, that laying hold of the misconduct of Samuel's two sons, who were intrusted with some secular concerns, they came in an abrupt and clamorous manner to Samuel, saying, *Behold thou art old, and thy sons walk not in thy ways, now make us a king to judge us like all the other nations.* And here we cannot but observe that their motives were bad, viz. that they might be *like* unto other nations, i. e. the Heathens, whereas their true glory lay in being as much *unlike* them as possible. *But the thing displeased Samuel when they said, give us a King to judge us; and Samuel prayed unto the Lord, and the Lord said unto Samuel, hearken unto the voice of the people in all that they say unto thee, for they have not rejected thee, but they have rejected me,* THAT I SHOULD NOT REIGN OVER THEM. *According to all the works which they have done since the day that I brought them up out of Egypt even unto this day, wherewith they have forsaken me, and served other Gods: so do they also unto thee. Now therefore hearken unto their voice, howbeit, protest solemnly unto them and show them the manner of the King that shall reign over them,* i. e. not of any particular King, but the general manner of the Kings of the earth whom Israel was so eagerly copying after. And notwithstanding the great distance of time and difference of manners, the character is still in fashion. *And Samuel told all the words of the Lord unto the people, that asked of him a King. And he said, This shall be the manner of the King that shall reign over you. He will take your sons and appoint them for himself for his chariots and to be his horsemen, and some shall run before his chariots* (this description agrees with the present mode of impressing men) *and he will appoint him captains over thousands and captains over fifties, will set them to ear his ground and to reap his harvest, and to make his instruments of war, and instruments of his chariots. And he will take your daughters to be confectionaries, and to be cooks, and to be bakers* (this describes the expense and luxury as well as the oppression of Kings) *and he will take your fields and your vineyards, and your olive yards, even the best of them, and give them to his servants. And he will take the tenth of your seed, and of your vineyards, and give them to his officers and to his servants* (by which we see that bribery, corruption, and favouritism, are the standing vices of Kings) *and he will take the tenth of your men servants, and your maid servants, and your goodliest young men, and your asses, and put them to his work: and he will take the tenth of your sheep, and ye shall be his servants, and ye shall cry out in that day because of your king which ye shall have chosen,* AND THE LORD WILL NOT HEAR YOU IN THAT DAY. This accounts for the continuation of Monarchy ; neither do the characters of the few good kings which have lived since, either sanctify the title, or blot out the sinfulness of the origin ; the high encomium given of David takes no notice of him *officially as a King,* but only as a *Man* after God's own heart. *Nevertheless the people refused to obey the voice of Samuel, and they said, Nay but we will have a king over us, that we may be like all the nations, and that our king may judge us, and go out before us and fight our battles.* Samuel continued to reason with them but to no purpose ; he set before them their ingratitude, but all would not avail ; and seeing them fully bent on their folly, he cried out, *I will call unto the Lord, and he shall send thunder and rain* (which was then a punishment, being in the time of wheat harvest) *that ye may perceive and see that your wickedness is great which ye have done in the sight of the Lord,* IN ASKING YOU A KING. *So Samuel called unto the Lord, and the Lord sent thunder and rain that day, and all the people greatly feared the Lord and Samuel. And all the people said unto Samuel, Pray for thy servants unto the Lord thy God that we die not, for* WE HAVE ADDED UNTO OUR SINS THIS EVIL, TO ASK A KING. These portions of scripture are direct and positive. They admit of no equivocal construction. That the Almighty hath here entered his protest against monarchical government is true, or the scripture is false. And a man hath good reason to believe that there is as much of kingcraft as priestcraft in withholding the scripture from the public in popish countries. For monarchy in every instance is the popery of government.

To the evil of monarchy we have added that of hereditary succession; and as the first is a degradation and lessening of ourselves, so the second, claimed as a matter of right, is an insult and imposition on posterity. For all men being originally equals, no one by birth could have a right to set up his own family in perpetual preference to all others for ever, and tho' himself might deserve some decent degree of honours of his cotemporaries, yet his descendants might be far too unworthy to inherit them. One of the strongest natural proofs of the folly of hereditary right in Kings, is that nature disapproves it, otherwise she would not so frequently turn it into ridicule, by giving mankind an *Ass for a Lion.*

Secondly, as no man at first could possess any other public honors than were bestowed upon him, so the givers of those honors could have no power to give away the right of posterity, and though they might say "We choose you for our head," they could not without manifest injustice to their children say "that your children and your children's children shall reign over ours forever." Because such an unwise, unjust, unnatural compact might (perhaps) in the next succession put them under the government of a rogue or a fool. Most wise men in their private sentiments have ever treated hereditary right with contempt; yet it is one of those evils which when once established is not easily removed; many submit from fear, others from superstition, and the more powerful part shares with the king the plunder of the rest.

This is supposing the present race of kings in the world to have had an honorable origin: whereas it is more than probable, that, could we take off the dark covering of antiquity and trace them to their first rise, we should find the first of them nothing better than the principal ruffian of some restless gang, whose savage manners or pre-eminence in subtilty obtained him the title of chief among plunderers: and who by increasing in power and extending his depredations, overawed the quiet and defenceless to purchase their safety by frequent contributions. Yet his electors could have no idea of giving hereditary right to his descendants, because such a perpetual exclusion of themselves was incompatible with the free and unrestrained principles they professed to live by. Wherefore, hereditary succession in the early ages of monarchy could not take place as a matter of claim, but as something casual or complemental; but as few or no records were extant in those days, and traditionary history stuff'd with fables, it was very easy, after the lapse of a few generations, to trump up some superstitious tale conveniently timed, Mahomet-like, to cram hereditary right down the throats of the vulgar. Perhaps the disorders which threatened, or seemed to threaten, on the decease of a leader and the choice of a new one (for elections among ruffians could not be very orderly) induced many at first to favour hereditary pretensions; by which means it happened, as it hath happened since, that what at first was submitted to as a convenience was afterwards claimed as a right.

England since the conquest hath known some few good monarchs, but groaned beneath a much larger number of bad ones: yet no man in his senses can say that their claim under William the Conqueror is a very honourable one. A French bastard landing with an armed Banditti and establishing himself king of England against the consent of the natives, is in plain terms a very paltry rascally original. It certainly hath no divinity in it. However it is needless to spend much time in exposing the folly of hereditary right ; if there are any so weak as to believe it, let them promiscuously worship the Ass and the Lion, and welcome. I shall neither copy their humility, nor disturb their devotion.

Yet I should be glad to ask how they suppose kings came at first? The question admits but of three answers, viz. either by lot, by election, or by usurpation. If the first king was taken by lot, it establishes a precedent for the next, which excludes hereditary succession. Saul was by lot, yet the succession was not hereditary, neither does it appear from that transaction that there was any intention it ever should. If the first king of any country was by election, that likewise establishes a precedent for the next ; for to say, that the right of all future generations is taken away, by the act of the first electors, in their choice not only of a king but of a family of kings for ever, hath no parallel in or out of scripture but the doctrine of original sin, which supposes the free will of all men lost in Adam ; and from such comparison, and it will admit of no other, hereditary succession can derive no glory. For as in Adam all sinned, and as in the first electors all men obeyed ; as in the one all mankind were subjected to Satan, and in the other to sovereignty ; as our innocence was lost in the first, and our authority in the last ; and as both disable us from re-assuming some former state and privilege, it unanswerably follows that original sin and hereditary succession are parallels. Dishonourable rank ! inglorious connection ! yet the most subtle sophist cannot produce a juster simile.

As to usurpation, no man will be so hardy as to defend it ; and that William the Conqueror was an usurper is a fact not to be contradicted. The plain truth is, that the antiquity of English monarchy will not bear looking into.

But it is not so much the absurdity as the evil of hereditary succession which concerns mankind. Did it ensure a race of good and wise men it would have the seal of divine authority, but as it opens a door to the *foolish*, the *wicked*, and the *improper*, it hath in it the nature of oppression. Men who look upon themselves born to reign, and others to obey, soon grow insolent. Selected from the rest of mankind, their minds are early poisoned by importance ; and the world they act in differs so materially from the world at large, that they have but little opportunity of knowing its true interests, and when they succeed to the government are frequently the most ignorant and unfit of any throughout the dominions.

Another evil which attends hereditary succession is, that the throne is subject to be possessed by a minor at any age ; all which time the regency acting under the cover of a king have every opportunity and inducement to betray their trust. The same national misfortune happens when a king worn out with age and infirmity enters the last stage of human weakness. In both these cases the public becomes a prey to every miscreant who can tamper successfully with the follies either of age or infancy.

The most plausible plea which hath ever been offered in favor of hereditary succession is, that it preserves a nation from civil wars ; and were this true, it would be weighty ; whereas it is the most bare-faced falsity ever imposed upon mankind. The whole history of England disowns the fact. Thirty kings and two minors have reigned in that distracted kingdom since the conquest, in which time there has been (including the revolution) no less than eight civil wars and nineteen Rebellions. Wherefore instead of making for peace, it makes against it, and destroys the very foundation it seems to stand upon.

The contest for monarchy and succession, between the houses of York and Lancaster, laid England in a scene of blood for many years. Twelve pitched battles besides skirmishes and sieges were fought between Henry and Edward. Twice was Henry prisoner to Edward, who in his turn was prisoner to Henry. And so uncertain is the fate of war and the temper of a nation, when nothing but personal matters are the ground of a quarrel, that Henry was taken in triumph from a prison to a palace, and Edward obliged to fly from a palace to a foreign land ; yet, as sudden transitions of temper are seldom lasting, Henry in his turn was driven from the throne, and Edward re-called to succeed him. The parliament always following the strongest side.

This contest began in the reign of Henry the Sixth, and was not entirely extinguished till Henry the Seventh, in whom the families were united. Including a period of 67 years, viz. from 1422 to 1489.

In short, monarchy and succession have laid (not this or that kingdom only) but the world in blood and ashes. 'Tis a form of government which the word of God bears testimony against, and blood will attend it.

If we enquire into the business of a King, we shall find that in some countries they may have none ; and after sauntering away their lives without pleasure to themselves or advantage to the nation, withdraw from the scene, and leave their successors to tread the same idle round. In absolute monarchies the whole weight of business civil and military lies on the King ; the children of Israel in their request for a king urged this plea, " that he may judge us, and go out before us and fight our battles." But in countries where he is neither a Judge nor a General, as in England, a man would be puzzled to know what *is* his business.

The nearer any government approaches to a Republic, the less business there is for a King. It is somewhat difficult to find a proper name for the government of England. Sir William Meredith calls it a Republic ; but in its present state it is unworthy of the name, because the corrupt influence of the Crown, by having all the places in its disposal, hath so effectually swallowed up the power, and eaten out the virtue of the House of Commons (the Republican part in the constitution) that the government of England is nearly as monarchical as that of France or Spain. Men fall out with names without understanding them. For 'tis the Republican and not the Monarchical part of the constitution of England which Englishmen glory in, viz. the liberty of choosing an House of Commons from out of their own body—and it is easy to see that when Republican virtues fails, slavery ensues. Why is the constitution of England sickly, but because monarchy hath poisoned the Republic ; the Crown hath engrossed the Commons.

In England a King hath little more to do than to make

war and give away places; which, in plain terms, is to empoverish the nation and set it together by the ears. A pretty business indeed for a man to be allowed eight hundred thousand sterling a year for, and worshipped into the bargain! Of more worth is one honest man to society, and in the sight of God, than all the crowned ruffians that ever lived.

THOUGHTS ON THE PRESENT STATE OF AMERICAN AFFAIRS.

IN the following pages I offer nothing more than simple facts, plain arguments, and common sense: and have no other preliminaries to settle with the reader, than that he will divest himself of prejudice and prepossession, and suffer his reason and his feelings to determine for themselves : that he will put on, or rather that he will not put off, the true character of a man, and generously enlarge his views beyond the present day.

Volumes have been written on the subject of the struggle between England and America. Men of all ranks have embarked in the controversy, from different motives, and with various designs; but all have been ineffectual, and the period of debate is closed. Arms as the last resource decide the contest; the appeal was the choice of the King, and the Continent has accepted the challenge.

It hath been reported of the late Mr. Pelham (who tho' an able minister was not without his faults) that on his being attacked in the House of Commons on the score that his measures were only of a temporary kind, replied, " *they will last my time*." Should a thought so fatal and unmanly possess the Colonies in the present contest, the name of ancestors will be remembered by future generations with detestation.

The Sun never shined on a cause of greater worth. 'Tis not the affair of a City, a County, a Province, or a Kingdom; but of a Continent—of at least one eighth part of the habitable Globe. 'Tis not the concern of a day, a year, or an age ; posterity are virtually involved in the contest, and will

be more or less affected even to the end of time, by the proceedings now.   Now is the seed-time of Continental union,
faith and honour.   The least fracture now will be like a name
engraved with the point of a pin on the tender rind of a
young oak ; the wound would enlarge with the tree, and
posterity read it in full grown characters.

By referring the matter from argument to arms, a new
æra for politics is struck—a new method of thinking hath
arisen.   All plans, proposals, &c. prior to the nineteenth of
April, *i. e.* to the commencement of hostilities,[1] are like the
almanacks of the last year ;   which tho' proper then, are
superceded and useless now.   Whatever was advanced by
the advocates on either side of the question then, terminated
in one and the same point, viz. a union with Great Britain ;
the only difference between the parties was the method of
effecting it ; the one proposing force, the other friendship ;
but it hath so far happened that the first hath failed, and the
second hath withdrawn her influence.

As much hath been said of the advantages of reconciliation, which, like an agreeable dream, hath passed away and
left us as we were, it is but right that we should examine
the contrary side of the argument, and enquire into some
of the many material injuries which these Colonies sustain,
and always will sustain, by being connected with and dependant on Great-Britain.   To examine that connection and
dependance, on the principles of nature and common sense,
to see what we have to trust to, if separated, and what we
are to expect, if dependant.

I have heard it asserted by some, that as America has
flourished under her former connection with Great-Britain,
the same connection is necessary towards her future happiness, and will always have the same effect.   Nothing can be
more fallacious than this kind of argument.   We may as
well assert that because a child has thrived upon milk, that
it is never to have meat, or that the first twenty years of
our lives is to become a precedent for the next twenty. But
even this is admitting more than is true ; for I answer

[1] At Lexington, Massachusetts, 1775.—*Editor.*

roundly, that America would have flourished as much, and probably much more, had no European power taken any notice of her. The commerce by which she hath enriched herself are the necessaries of life, and will always have a market while eating is the custom of Europe.

But she has protected us, say some. That she hath engrossed us is true, and defended the Continent at our expense as well as her own, is admitted ; and she would have defended Turkey from the same motive, *viz.* for the sake of trade and dominion.

Alas ! we have been long led away by ancient prejudices and made large sacrifices to superstition. We have boasted the protection of Great Britain, without considering, that her motive was *interest* not *attachment ;* and that she did not protect us from *our enemies* on *our account ;* but from *her enemies* on *her own account,* from those who had no quarrel with us on any *other account,* and who will always be our enemies on the *same account.* Let Britain waive her pretensions to the Continent, or the Continent throw off the dependance, and we should be at peace with France and Spain, were they at war with Britain. The miseries of Hanover last war ought to warn us against connections.

It hath lately been asserted in parliament, that the Colonies have no relation to each other but through the Parent Country, *i. e.* that Pennsylvania and the Jerseys, and so on for the rest, are sister Colonies by the way of England ; this is certainly a very roundabout way of proving relationship, but it is the nearest and only true way of proving enmity (or enemyship, if I may so call it.) France and Spain never were, nor perhaps ever will be, our enemies as *Americans,* but as our being the *subjects of Great Britain.*

But Britain is the parent country, say some. Then the more shame upon her conduct. Even brutes do not devour their young, nor savages make war upon their families ; Wherefore, the assertion, if true, turns to her reproach ; but it happens not to be true, or only partly so, and the phrase *parent* or *mother country* hath been jesuitically adopted by the King and his parasites, with a low papistical design of gaining an unfair bias on the credulous weakness of our minds. Europe, and not England, is the parent country of America. This new World hath been the asylum for the persecuted lovers of civil and religious liberty from *every part* of Europe. Hither have they fled, not from the tender embraces of the mother, but from the cruelty of the monster ; and it is so far true of England, that the same tyranny which drove the first emigrants from home, pursues their descendants still.

In this extensive quarter of the globe, we forget the narrow limits of three hundred and sixty miles (the extent of England) and carry our friendship on a larger scale ; we claim brotherhood with every European Christian, and triumph in the generosity of the sentiment.

It is pleasant to observe by what regular gradations we surmount the force of local prejudices, as we enlarge our acquaintance with the World. A man born in any town in England divided into parishes, will naturally associate most with his fellow parishioners (because their interests in many cases will be common) and distinguish him by the name of *neighbour ;* if he meet him but a few miles from home, he drops the narrow idea of a street, and salutes him by the name of *townsman ;* if he travel out of the county and meet him in any other, he forgets the minor divisions of street and town, and calls him *countryman, i. e. countyman* : but if in their foreign excursions they should associate in France, or any other part of *Europe*, their local remembrance would be enlarged into that of *Englishmen*. And by a just parity of reasoning, all Europeans meeting in America, or any other quarter of the globe, are *countrymen ;* for England, Holland, Germany, or Sweden, when compared with the whole, stand in the same places on the larger scale, which the divisions of street, town, and county do on the smaller ones ; Distinctions too limited for Continental minds. Not one third of the inhabitants, even of this province, [Pennsylvania], are of English descent. Wherefore, I reprobate the phrase of Parent or Mother Country applied to England only, as being false, selfish, narrow and ungenerous.

But, admitting that we were all of English descent, what does it amount to? Nothing. Britain, being now an open enemy, extinguishes every other name and title: and to say that reconciliation is our duty, is truly farcical. The first king of England, of the present line (William the Conqueror) was a Frenchman, and half the peers of England are descendants from the same country; wherefore, by the same method of reasoning, England ought to be governed by France.

Much hath been said of the united strength of Britain and the Colonies, that in conjunction they might bid defiance to the world: But this is mere presumption; the fate of war is uncertain, neither do the expressions mean any thing; for this continent would never suffer itself to be drained of inhabitants, to support the British arms in either Asia, Africa, or Europe.

Besides, what have we to do with setting the world at defiance? Our plan is commerce, and that, well attended to, will secure us the peace and friendship of all Europe; because it is the interest of all Europe to have America a free port. Her trade will always be a protection, and her barrenness of gold and silver secure her from invaders.

I challenge the warmest advocate for reconciliation to show a single advantage that this continent can reap by being connected with Great Britain. I repeat the challenge; not a single advantage is derived. Our corn will fetch its price in any market in Europe, and our imported goods must be paid for buy them where we will.

But the injuries and disadvantages which we sustain by that connection, are without number; and our duty to mankind at large, as well as to ourselves, instruct us to renounce the alliance: because, any submission to, or dependance on, Great Britain, tends directly to involve this Continent in European wars and quarrels, and set us at variance with nations who would otherwise seek our friendship, and against whom we have neither anger nor complaint. As Europe is our market for trade, we ought to form no partial connection with any part of it. It is the true interest of America to steer clear of European contentions, which she never can do, while, by her dependance on Britain, she is made the make-weight in the scale of British politics.

Europe is too thickly planted with Kingdoms to be long at peace, and whenever a war breaks out between England and any foreign power, the trade of America goes to ruin, *because of her connection with Britain.* The next war may not turn out like the last, and should it not, the advocates for reconciliation now will be wishing for separation then, because neutrality in that case would be a safer convoy than a man of war. Every thing that is right or reasonable pleads for separation. The blood of the slain, the weeping voice of nature cries, 'TIS TIME TO PART. Even the distance at which the Almighty hath placed England and America is a strong and natural proof that the authority of the one over the other, was never the design of Heaven. The time like-wise at which the Continent was discovered, adds weight to the argument, and the manner in which it was peopled, en-creases the force of it. The Reformation was preceded by the discovery of America: As if the Almighty graciously meant to open a sanctuary to the persecuted in future years, when home should afford neither friendship nor safety.

The authority of Great Britain over this continent, is a form of government, which sooner or later must have an end : And a serious mind can draw no true pleasure by looking forward, under the painful and positive conviction that what he calls "the present constitution" is merely temporary. As parents, we can have no joy, knowing that this government is not sufficiently lasting to ensure any thing which we may bequeath to posterity : And by a plain method of argument, as we are running the next generation into debt, we ought to do the work of it, otherwise we use them meanly and piti-fully. In order to discover the line of our duty rightly, we should take our children in our hand, and fix our station a few years farther into life ; that eminence will present a prospect which a few present fears and prejudices conceal from our sight.

Though I would carefully avoid giving unnecessary offence, yet I am inclined to believe, that all those who espouse the doctrine of reconciliation, may be included within the following descriptions.

Interested men, who are not to be trusted, weak men who *cannot* see, prejudiced men who will not see, and a certain set of moderate men who think better of the European world than it deserves; and this last class, by an ill-judged deliberation, will be the cause of more calamities to this Continent than all the other three.

It is the good fortune of many to live distant from the scene of present sorrow; the evil is not sufficiently brought to their doors to make them feel the precariousness with which all American property is possessed. But let our imaginations transport us a few moments to Boston; that seat of wretchedness will teach us wisdom, and instruct us for ever to renounce a power in whom we can have no trust. The inhabitants of that unfortunate city who but a few months ago were in ease and affluence, have now no other alternative than to stay and starve, or turn out to beg. Endangered by the fire of their friends if they continue within the city, and plundered by the soldiery if they leave it, in their present situation they are prisoners without the hope of redemption, and in a general attack for their relief they would be exposed to the fury of both armies.

Men of passive tempers look somewhat lightly over the offences of Great Britain, and, still hoping for the best, are apt to call out, *Come, come, we shall be friends again for all this.* But examine the passions and feelings of mankind: bring the doctrine of reconciliation to the touchstone of nature, and then tell me whether you can hereafter love, honour, and faithfully serve the power that hath carried fire and sword into your land? If you cannot do all these, then are you only deceiving yourselves, and by your delay bringing ruin upon posterity. Your future connection with Britain, whom you can neither love nor honour, will be forced and unnatural, and being formed only on the plan of present convenience, will in a little time fall into a relapse more wretched than the first. But if you say, you can still pass the violations over, then I ask, hath your house been burnt? Hath your property been destroyed before your face? Are your wife and children destitute of a bed to lie on, or bread to live on? Have you lost a parent or a child by their hands, and yourself the ruined and wretched survivor? If you have not, then are you not a judge of those who have. But if you have, and can still shake hands with the murderers, then are you unworthy the name of husband, father, friend, or lover, and whatever may be your rank or title in life, you have the heart of a coward, and the spirit of a sycophant.

This is not inflaming or exaggerating matters, but trying them by those feelings and affections which nature justifies, and without which we should be incapable of discharging the social duties of life, or enjoying the felicities of it. I mean not to exhibit horror for the purpose of provoking revenge, but to awaken us from fatal and unmanly slumbers, that we may pursue determinately some fixed object. 'Tis not in the power of Britain or of Europe to conquer America, if she doth not conquer herself by delay and timidity. The present winter is worth an age if rightly employed, but if lost or neglected the whole Continent will partake of the misfortune; and there is no punishment which that man doth not deserve, be he who, or what, or where he will, that may be the means of sacrificing a season so precious and useful.

'Tis repugnant to reason, to the universal order of things, to all examples from former ages, to suppose that this Continent can long remain subject to any external power. The most sanguine in Britain doth not think so. The utmost stretch of human wisdom cannot, at this time, compass a plan, short of separation, which can promise the continent even a year's security. Reconciliation is *now* a fallacious dream. Nature hath deserted the connection, and art cannot supply her place. For, as Milton wisely expresses, "never can true reconcilement grow where wounds of deadly hate have pierced so deep."

Every quiet method for peace hath been ineffectual. Our prayers have been rejected with disdain; and hath tended to

convince us that nothing flatters vanity or confirms obstinacy
in Kings more than repeated petitioning—and nothing hath
contributed more than that very measure to make the
Kings of Europe absolute.   Witness Denmark and Sweden.
Wherefore, since nothing but blows will do, for God's sake
let us come to a final separation, and not leave the next generation to be cutting throats under the violated unmeaning
names of parent and child.

To say they will never attempt it again is idle and visionary ; we thought so at the repeal of the stamp act, yet a
year or two undeceived us ; as well may we suppose that
nations which have been once defeated will never renew the
quarrel.   ·

As to government matters, 'tis not in the power of
Britain to do this continent justice : the business of it will
soon be too weighty and intricate to be managed with any
tolerable degree of convenience, by a power so distant from
us, and so very ignorant of us ; for if they cannot conquer
us, they cannot govern us.   To be always running three or
four thousand miles with a tale or a petition, waiting four or
five months for an answer, which, when obtained, requires
five or six more to explain it in, will in a few years be looked
upon as folly and childishness.   There was a time when it
was proper, and there is a proper time for it to cease.

Small islands not capable of protecting themselves are
the proper objects for government [1] to take under their care ;
but there is something absurd, in supposing a Continent to
be perpetually governed by an island.   In no instance hath
nature made the satellite larger than its primary planet ;
and as England and America, with respect to each other,
reverse the common order of nature, it is evident that they
belong to different systems.   England to Europe : America
to itself.

I am not induced by motives of pride, party, or resentment to espouse the doctrine of separation and independence ; I am clearly, positively, and conscientiously persuaded
that it is the true interest of this Continent to be so ; that

---

[1] In some later editions " kingdoms."—*Editor.*

every thing short of *that* is mere patchwork, that it can afford
no lasting felicity,—that it is leaving the sword to our children,
and shrinking back at a time when a little more, a little
further, would have rendered this Continent the glory of
the earth.

As Britain hath not manifested the least inclination
towards a compromise, we may be assured that no terms can
be obtained worthy the acceptance of the Continent, or any
ways equal to the expence of blood and treasure we have
been already put to.

The object contended for, ought always to bear some just
proportion to the expense. The removal of North, or the
whole detestable junto, is a matter unworthy the millions
we have expended.   A temporary stoppage of trade was an
inconvenience, which would have sufficiently ballanced the
repeal of all the acts complained of, had such repeals been
obtained ; but if the whole Continent must take up arms, if
every man must be a soldier, 'tis scarcely worth our while to
fight against a contemptible ministry only.   Dearly, dearly
do we pay for the repeal of the acts, if that is all we fight
for ; for, in a just estimation 'tis as great a folly to pay a
Bunker-hill price for law as for land.   As I have always considered the independancy of this continent, as an event
which sooner or later must arrive, so from the late rapid
progress of the Continent to maturity, the event cannot be
far off.   Wherefore, on the breaking out of hostilities, it was
not worth the while to have disputed a matter which time
would have finally redressed, unless we meant to be in
earnest : otherwise it is like wasting an estate on a suit at
law, to regulate the trespasses of a tenant whose lease is just
expiring.   No man was a warmer wisher for a reconciliation
than myself, before the fatal nineteenth of April, 1775, but
the moment the event of that day was made known, I rejected the hardened, sullen-tempered Pharaoh of England
for ever ; and disdain the wretch, that with the pretended
title of FATHER OF HIS PEOPLE can unfeelingly hear of
their slaughter, and composedly sleep with their blood upon
his soul.

But admitting that matters were now made up, what would be the event? I answer, the ruin of the Continent. And that for several reasons.

First. The powers of governing still remaining in the hands of the King, he will have a negative over the whole legislation of this Continent. And as he hath shown himself such an inveterate enemy to liberty, and discovered such a thirst for arbitrary power, is he, or is he not, a proper person to say to these colonies, *You shall make no laws but what I please! ?* And is there any inhabitant of America so ignorant as not to know, that according to what is called the *present constitution,* this Continent can make no laws but what the king gives leave to; and is there any man so unwise as not to see, that (considering what has happened) he will suffer no law to be made here but such as suits *his* purpose? We may be as effectually enslaved by the want of laws in America, as by submitting to laws made for us in England. After matters are made up (as it is called) can there be any doubt, but the whole power of the crown will be exerted to keep this continent as low and humble as possible? Instead of going forward we shall go backward, or be perpetually quarrelling, or ridiculously petitioning. We are already greater than the King wishes us to be, and will he not hereafter endeavor to make us less? To bring the matter to one point, Is the power who is jealous of our prosperity, a proper power to govern us? Whoever says *No,* to this question, is an Independant for independency means no more than this, whether we shall make our own laws, or, whether the King, the greatest enemy this continent hath, or can have, shall tell us *there shall be no laws but such as I like.*

But the King, you will say, has a negative in England; the people there can make no laws without his consent. In point of right and good order, it is something very ridiculous that a youth of twenty-one (which hath often happened) shall say to several millions of people older and wiser than himself, "I forbid this or that act of yours to be law." But in this place I decline this sort of reply, though I will never cease to expose the absurdity of it, and only answer that England being the King's residence, and America not so, makes quite another case. The King's negative here is ten times more dangerous and fatal than it can be in England ; for there he will scarcely refuse his consent to a bill for putting England into as strong a state of defense as possible, and in America he would never suffer such a bill to be passed.

America is only a secondary object in the system of British politics. England consults the good of this country no further than it answers her own purpose. Wherefore, her own interest leads her to suppress the growth of ours in every case which doth not promote her advantage, or in the least interferes with it. A pretty state we should soon be in under such a second hand government, considering what has happened ! Men do not change from enemies to friends by the alteration of a name : And in order to show that reconciliation now is a dangerous doctrine, I affirm, *that it would be policy in the King at this time to repeal the acts, for the sake of reinstating himself in the government of the provinces ;* In order that HE MAY ACCOMPLISH BY CRAFT AND SUBTLETY, IN THE LONG RUN, WHAT HE CANNOT DO BY FORCE AND VIOLENCE IN THE SHORT ONE. Reconciliation and ruin are nearly related.

Secondly. That as even the best terms which we can expect to obtain can amount to no more than a temporary expedient, or a kind of government by guardianship, which can last no longer than till the Colonies come of age, so the general face and state of things in the interim will be unsettled and unpromising. Emigrants of property will not choose to come to a country whose form of government hangs but by a thread, and who is every day tottering on the brink of commotion and disturbance ; and numbers of the present inhabitants would lay hold of the interval to dispose of their effects, and quit the Continent.

But the most powerful of all arguments is, that nothing but independance, *i. e.* a Continental form of government, can keep the peace of the Continent and preserve it inviolate from civil wars. I dread the event of a reconciliation with Britain now, as it is more than probable that it will be followed by a revolt some where or other, the consequences of which may be far more fatal than all the malice of Britain.

Thousands are already ruined by British barbarity; (thousands more will probably suffer the same fate.) Those men have other feelings than us who have nothing suffered. All they now possess is liberty; what they before enjoyed is sacrificed to its service, and having nothing more to lose they disdain submission. Besides, the general temper of the Colonies, towards a British government will be like that of a youth who is nearly out of his time; they will care very little about her: And a government which cannot preserve the peace is no government at all, and in that case we pay our money for nothing; and pray what is it that Britain can do, whose power will be wholly on paper, should a civil tumult break out the very day after reconciliation? I have heard some men say, many of whom I believe spoke without thinking, that they dreaded an independance, fearing that it would produce civil wars: It is but seldom that our first thoughts are truly correct, and that is the case here; for there is ten times more to dread from a patched up connection than from independance. I make the sufferer's case my own, and I protest, that were I driven from house and home, my property destroyed, and my circumstances ruined, that as a man, sensible of injuries, I could never relish the doctrine of reconciliation, or consider myself bound thereby.

The Colonies have manifested such a spirit of good order and obedience to Continental government, as is sufficient to make every reasonable person easy and happy on that head. No man can assign the least pretence for his fears, on any other grounds, than such as are truly childish and ridiculous, viz., that one colony will be striving for superiority over another.

Where there are no distinctions there can be no superiority; perfect equality affords no temptation. The Republics of Europe are all (and we may say always) in peace. Holland and Switzerland are without wars, foreign or domestic:

Monarchical governments, it is true, are never long at rest: the crown itself is a temptation to enterprising ruffians at home ; and that degree of pride and insolence ever attendant on regal authority, swells into a rupture with foreign powers in instances where a republican government, by being formed on more natural principles, would negociate the mistake.

If there is any true cause of fear respecting independance, it is because no plan is yet laid down. Men do not see their way out. Wherefore, as an opening into that business I offer the following hints ; at the same time modestly affirming, that I have no other opinion of them myself, than that they may be the means of giving rise to something better. Could the straggling thoughts of individuals be collected, they would frequently form materials for wise and able men to improve into useful matter.

Let the assemblies be annual, with a president only. The representation more equal, their business wholly domestic, and subject to the authority of a Continental Congress.

Let each Colony be divided into six, eight, or ten, convenient districts, each district to send a proper number of Delegates to Congress, so that each Colony send at least thirty. The whole number in Congress will be at least 390. Each congress to sit   and to choose a President by the following method. When the Delegates are met, let a Colony be taken from the whole thirteen Colonies by lot, after which let the Congress choose (by ballot) a president from out of the Delegates of that Province. In the next Congress, let a Colony be taken by lot from twelve only, omitting that Colony from which the president was taken in the former Congress, and so proceeding on till the whole thirteen shall have had their proper rotation. And in order that nothing may pass into a law but what is satisfactorily just, not less than three fifths of the Congress to be called a majority. He that will promote discord, under a government so equally formed as this, would have joined Lucifer in his revolt.

But as there is a peculiar delicacy from whom, or in what manner, this business must first arise, and as it seems most agreeable and consistent that it should come from some intermediate body between the governed and the governors, that is, between the Congress and the People, let a Continental Conference be held in the following manner, and for the following purpose,

A Committee of twenty six members of congress, *viz.* Two for each Colony. Two Members from each House of Assembly, or Provincial Convention; and five Representatives of the people at large, to be chosen in the capital city or town of each Province, for, and in behalf of the whole Province, by as many qualified voters as shall think proper to attend from all parts of the Province for that purpose; or, if more convenient, the Representatives may be chosen in two or three of the most populous parts thereof. In this conference, thus assembled, will be united the two grand principles of business, *knowledge* and *power*. The Members of Congress, Assemblies, or Conventions, by having had experience in national concerns, will be able and useful counsellors, and the whole, being impowered by the people, will have a truly legal authority.

The conferring members being met, let their business be to frame a Continental Charter, or Charter of the United Colonies; (answering to what is called the Magna Charta of England) fixing the number and manner of choosing Members of Congress, Members of Assembly, with their date of sitting; and drawing the line of business and jurisdiction between them: Always remembering, that our strength is Continental, not Provincial. Securing freedom and property to all men, and above all things, the free exercise of religion, according to the dictates of conscience; with such other matter as it is necessary for a charter to contain. Immediately after which, the said conference to dissolve, and the bodies which shall be chosen conformable to the said charter, to be the Legislators and Governors of this Continent for the time being: Whose peace and happiness, may GOD preserve. AMEN.

Should any body of men be hereafter delegated for this or some similar purpose, I offer them the following extracts from that wise observer on Governments, Dragonetti. " The

science," says he, " of the Politician consists in fixing the
true point of happiness and freedom. Those men would
deserve the gratitude of ages, who should discover a mode
of government that contained the greatest sum of individual
happiness, with the least national expense." (Dragonetti
on " Virtues and Reward.")

But where, say some, is the King of America? I'll tell
you, friend, he reigns above, and doth not make havoc of
mankind like the Royal Brute of Great Britain. Yet that
we may not appear to be defective even in earthly honours,
let a day be solemnly set apart for proclaiming the Charter ;
let it be brought forth placed on the Divine Law, the Word
of God ; let a crown be placed thereon, by which the world
may know, that so far as we approve of monarchy, that in
America the law is king. For as in absolute governments
the King is law, so in free countries the law ought to be
king ; and there ought to be no other. But lest any ill use
should afterwards arise, let the Crown at the conclusion of
the ceremony be demolished, and scattered among the
people whose right it is.

A government of our own is our natural right : and when
a man seriously reflects on the precariousness of human
affairs, he will become convinced, that it is infinitely wiser
and safer, to form a constitution of our own in a cool deliberate manner, while we have it in our power, than to trust
such an interesting event to time and chance. If we omit
it now, some Massanello* may hereafter arise, who, laying
hold of popular disquietudes, may collect together the
desperate and the discontented, and by assuming to themselves the powers of government, finally sweep away the
liberties of the Continent like a deluge. Should the government of America return again into the hands of Britain, the
tottering situation of things will be a temptation for some
desperate adventurer to try his fortune ; and in such a case,

---

* Thomas Anello, otherwise Massanello, a fisherman of Naples, who after
spiriting up his countrymen in the public market place, against the oppression
of the Spaniards, to whom the place was then subject, prompted them to revolt,
and in the space of a day became King.—*Author*.

what relief can Britain give? Ere she could hear the news, the fatal business might be done; and ourselves suffering like the wretched Britons under the oppression of the Conqueror. Ye that oppose independance now, ye know not what ye do: ye are opening a door to eternal tyranny, by keeping vacant the seat of government. There are thousands and tens of thousands, who would think it glorious to expel from the Continent, that barbarous and hellish power, which hath stirred up the Indians and the Negroes to destroy us; the cruelty hath a double guilt, it is dealing brutally by us, and treacherously by them.

To talk of friendship with those in whom our reason forbids us to have faith, and our affections wounded thro' a thousand pores instruct us to detest, is madness and folly. Every day wears out the little remains of kindred between us and them; and can there be any reason to hope, that as the relationship expires, the affection will encrease, or that we shall agree better when we have ten times more and greater concerns to quarrel over than ever?

Ye that tell us of harmony and reconciliation, can ye restore to us the time that is past? Can ye give to prostitution its former innocence? neither can ye reconcile Britain and America. The last cord now is broken, the people of England are presenting addresses against us. There are injuries which nature cannot forgive; she would cease to be nature if she did. As well can the lover forgive the ravisher of his mistress, as the Continent forgive the murders of Britain. The Almighty hath implanted in us these unextinguishable feelings for good and wise purposes. They are the Guardians of his Image in our hearts. They distinguish us from the herd of common animals. The social compact would dissolve, and justice be extirpated from the earth, or have only a casual existence were we callous to the touches of affection. The robber and the murderer would often escape unpunished, did not the injuries which our tempers sustain, provoke us into justice.

O! ye that love mankind! Ye that dare oppose not only the tyranny but the tyrant, stand forth! Every spot of the

old world is overrun with oppression.   Freedom hath been
hunted round the Globe.   Asia and Africa have long expelled her.   Europe regards her like a stranger, and England
hath given her warning to depart.   O! receive the fugitive,
and prepare in time an asylum for mankind.

OF THE PRESENT ABILITY OF AMERICA: WITH SOME
MISCELLANEOUS REFLECTIONS.

I HAVE never met with a man, either in England or
America, who hath not confessed his opinion, that a separation between the countries would take place one time or
other: And there is no instance in which we have shown
less judgment, than in endeavoring to describe, what we call,
the ripeness or fitness of the Continent for independance.

As all men allow the measure, and vary only in their
opinion of the time, let us, in order to remove mistakes,
take a general survey of things, and endeavor if possible to
find out the *very* time.   But I need not go far, the inquiry
ceases at once, for the *time hath found us.*   The general
concurrence, the glorious union of all things, proves the
fact.

'Tis not in numbers but in unity that our great strength lies:
yet our present numbers are sufficient to repel the force of
all the world.   The Continent hath at this time the largest
body of armed and disciplined men of any power under
Heaven: and is just arrived at that pitch of strength, in
which no single colony is able to support itself, and the
whole, when united, is able to do any thing.   Our land force
is more than sufficient, and as to Naval affairs, we cannot be
insensible that Britain would never suffer an American man
of war to be built, while the Continent remained in her
hands.   Wherefore, we should be no forwarder an hundred
years hence in that branch than we are now; but the truth
is, we should be less so, because the timber of the Country
is every day diminishing, and that which will remain at last,
will be far off or difficult to procure.

Were the Continent crowded with inhabitants, her sufferings under the present circumstances would be intolerable.
The more seaport-towns we had, the more should we have
both to defend and to lose. Our present numbers are so
happily proportioned to our wants, that no man need be
idle. The diminution of trade affords an army, and the
necessities of an army create a new trade.

Debts we have none: and whatever we may contract on
this account will serve as a glorious memento of our virtue.
Can we but leave posterity with a settled form of government, an independant constitution of its own, the purchase
at any price will be cheap.   But to expend millions for the
sake of getting a few vile acts repealed, and routing the
present ministry only, is unworthy the charge, and is using
posterity with the utmost cruelty; because it is leaving
them the great work to do, and a debt upon their backs
from which they derive no advantage. Such a thought 's
unworthy a man of honour, and is the true characteristic of
a narrow heart and a pidling politician.

The debt we may contract doth not deserve our regard if
the work be but accomplished. No nation ought to be
without a debt. A national debt is a national bond; and
when it bears no interest, is in no case a grievance. Britain
is oppressed with a debt of upwards of one hundred and
forty millions sterling, for which she pays upwards of four
millions interest. And as a compensation for her debt, she
has a large navy; America is without a debt, and without a
navy; yet for the twentieth part of the English national
debt, could have a navy as large again. The navy of England is not worth at this time more than three millions and
a half sterling.

The first and second editions of this pamphlet were published without the following calculations, which are now
given as a proof that the above estimation of the navy is a
just one. See Entic's " Naval History," Intro., p. 56.

The charge of building a ship of each rate, and furnishing
her with masts, yards, sails, and rigging, together with a

proportion of eight months boatswain's and carpenter's sea-stores, as calculated by Mr. Burchett, Secretary to the navy.

For a ship of 100 guns,	.	.	35,553 *l*.
90	.	.	29,886
80	.	.	23,638
70	.	.	17,785
60	.	.	14,197
50	.	.	10,606
40	.	.	7,558
30	.	.	5,846
20	.	.	3,710

And hence it is easy to sum up the value, or cost, rather, of the whole British navy, which, in the year 1757, when it was at its greatest glory, consisted of the following ships and guns.

Ships.	*Guns.*	*Cost of one.*	*Cost of all.*
6 .	100 .	55,553*l*. .	213,318 *l*.
12 .	90 .	29,886 .	358,632
12 .	80 .	23,638 .	283,656
43 .	70 .	17,785 .	764,755
35 .	60 .	14,197 .	496,895
40 .	50 .	10,605 .	424,240
45 .	40 .	7,558 .	340,110
58 .	20 .	3,710 .	215,180
85 Sloops, bombs, and fireships, one with another, at		2,000 .	170,000

	Cost,	3,266,786*l*.
	Remains for guns,	233,214
	Total,	3,500,000*l*.

No country on the globe is so happily situated, or so internally capable of raising a fleet as America. Tar, timber, iron, and cordage are her natural produce. We need go abroad for nothing. Whereas the Dutch, who make large profits by hiring out their ships of war to the Spaniards and Portugese, are obliged to import most of the materials they use. We ought to view the building a fleet as an article of commerce, it being the natural manufactory of this country.

'Tis the best money we can lay out.   A navy when finished is worth more than it cost :   And is that nice point in national policy, in which commerce and protection are united. Let us build ; if we want them not, we can sell ; and by that means replace our paper currency with ready gold and silver.

In point of manning a fleet, people in general run into great errors ; it is not necessary that one fourth part should be sailors.   The Terrible privateer, captain Death, stood the hottest engagement of any ship last war, yet had not twenty sailors on board, though her complement of men was upwards of two hundred.   A few able and social sailors will soon instruct a sufficient number of active landsmen in the common work of a ship.   Wherefore we never can be more capable of beginning on maritime matters than now, while our timber is standing, our fisheries blocked up, and our sailors and shipwrights out of employ.   Men of war, of seventy and eighty guns, were built forty years ago in New England, and why not the same now?   Ship building is America's greatest pride, and in which she will, in time, excel the whole world.   The great empires of the east are mostly inland, and consequently excluded from the possibility of rivalling her.   Africa is in a state of barbarism ; and no power in Europe, hath either such an extent of coast, or such an internal supply of materials.   Where nature hath given the one, she hath withheld the other ; to America only hath she been liberal to both.   The vast empire of Russia is almost shut out from the sea ; wherefore her boundless forests, her tar, iron, and cordage are only articles of commerce.

In point of safety, ought we to be without a fleet?   We are not the little people now, which we were sixty years ago ; at that time we might have trusted our property in the streets, or fields rather, and slept securely without locks or bolts to our doors and windows.   The case is now altered, and our methods of defence ought to improve with our encrease of property.   A common pirate, twelve months ago, might have come up the Delaware, and laid the city of Philadelphia under contribution for what sum he pleased ;

and the same might have happened to other places. Nay, any daring fellow, in a brig of fourteen or sixteen guns, might have robbed the whole Continent, and carried off half a million of money. These are circumstances which demand our attention, and point out the necessity of naval protection.

Some perhaps will say, that after we have made it up with Britain, she will protect us. Can they be so unwise as to mean, that she will keep a navy in our Harbours for that purpose? Common sense will tell us, that the power which hath endeavoured to subdue us, is of all others, the most improper to defend us. Conquest may be effected under the pretence of friendship; and ourselves, after a long and brave resistance, be at last cheated into slavery. And if her ships are not to be admitted into our harbours, I would ask, how is she to protect us? A navy three or four thousand miles off can be of little use, and on sudden emergencies, none at all. Wherefore if we must hereafter protect ourselves, why not do it for ourselves? Why do it for another?

The English list of ships of war, is long and formidable, but not a tenth part of them are at any one time fit for service, numbers of them are not in being; yet their names are pompously continued in the list, if only a plank be left of the ship: and not a fifth part of such as are fit for service, can be spared on any one station at one time. The East and West Indies, Mediterranean, Africa, and other parts, over which Britain extends her claim, make large demands upon her navy. From a mixture of prejudice and inattention, we have contracted a false notion respecting the navy of England, and have talked as if we should have the whole of it to encounter at once, and, for that reason, supposed that we must have one as large; which not being instantly practicable, has been made use of by a set of disguised Tories to discourage our beginning thereon. Nothing can be further from truth than this; for if America had only a twentieth part of the naval force of Britain, she would be by far an over-match for her; because, as we neither have, nor claim any foreign dominion, our whole force would be employed on our own coast, where we should, in the long run, have two to one the advantage of those who had three or four thousand miles to sail over, before they could attack us, and the same distance to return in order to refit and recruit.   And although Britain, by her fleet, hath a check over our trade to Europe, we have as large a one over her trade to the West Indies, which, by laying in the neighborhood of the Continent, lies entirely at its mercy.

Some method might be fallen on to keep up a naval force in time of peace, if we should not judge it necessary to support a constant navy.   If premiums were to be given to Merchants to build and employ in their service, ships mounted with twenty, thirty, forty, or fifty guns, (the premiums to be in proportion to the loss of bulk to the merchant,) fifty or sixty of those ships, with a few guardships on constant duty, would keep up a sufficient navy, and that without burdening ourselves with the evil so loudly complained of in England, of suffering their fleet in time of peace to lie rotting in the docks.   To unite the sinews of commerce and defence is sound policy; for when our strength and our riches play into each other's hand, we need fear no external enemy.

In almost every article of defence we abound.   Hemp flourishes even to rankness, so that we need not want cordage. Our iron is superior to that of other countries.   Our small arms equal to any in the world.   Cannon we can cast at pleasure.   Saltpetre and gunpowder we are every day producing.   Our knowledge is hourly improving.   Resolution is our inherent character, and courage hath never yet forsaken us.   Wherefore, what is it that we want?   Why is it that we hesitate?   From Britain we can expect nothing but ruin.   If she is once admitted to the government of America again, this Continent will not be worth living in.   Jealousies will be always arising; insurrections will be constantly happening; and who will go forth to quell them?   Who will venture his life to reduce his own countrymen to a foreign obedience? The difference between Pennsylvania and Connecticut, respecting some unlocated lands, shows the insignificance of a British government, and fully proves that nothing but Continental authority can regulate Continental matters.

Another reason why the present time is preferable to all others, is, that the fewer our numbers are, the more land there is yet unoccupied, which, instead of being lavished by the king on his worthless dependants, may be hereafter applied, not only to the discharge of the present debt, but to the constant support of government. No nation under Heaven hath such an advantage as this.

The infant state of the Colonies, as it is called, so far from being against, is an argument in favour of independance. We are sufficiently numerous, and were we more so we might be less united. 'Tis a matter worthy of observation, that the more a country is peopled, the smaller their armies are. In military numbers, the ancients far exceeded the moderns: and the reason is evident, for trade being the consequence of population, men became too much absorbed thereby to attend to any thing else. Commerce diminishes the spirit both of patriotism and military defence. And history sufficiently informs us, that the bravest achievements were always accomplished in the non-age of a nation. With the increase of commerce England hath lost its spirit. The city of London, notwithstanding its numbers, submits to continued insults with the patience of a coward. The more men have to lose, the less willing are they to venture. The rich are in general slaves to fear, and submit to courtly power with the trembling duplicity of a spaniel.

Youth is the seed-time of good habits as well in nations as in individuals. It might be difficult, if not impossible, to form the Continent into one Government half a century hence. The vast variety of interests, occasioned by an increase of trade and population, would create confusion. Colony would be against Colony. Each being able would scorn each other's assistance: and while the proud and foolish gloried in their little distinctions, the wise would lament that the union had not been formed before. Wherefore the present time is the true time for establishing it. The intimacy which is contracted in infancy, and the friendship which is formed in misfortune, are of all others the most lasting and unalterable. Our present union is marked with both these characters: we are young, and we have been distressed ; but our concord hath withstood our troubles, and fixes a memorable Æra for posterity to glory in.

The present time, likewise, is that peculiar time which never happens to a nation but once, viz. the time of forming itself into a government. Most nations have let slip the opportunity, and by that means have been compelled to receive laws from their conquerors, instead of making laws for themselves. First, they had a king, and then a form of government ; whereas the articles or charter of government should be formed first, and men delegated to execute them afterwards : but from the errors of other nations let us learn wisdom, and lay hold of the present opportunity—*to begin government at the right end.*

When William the Conqueror subdued England, he gave them law at the point of the sword ; and, until we consent that the seat of government in America be legally and authoritatively occupied, we shall be in danger of having it filled by some fortunate ruffian, who may treat us in the same manner, and then, where will be our freedom? where our property?

As to religion, I hold it to be the indispensable duty of government to protect all conscientious professors thereof, and I know of no other business which government hath to do therewith. Let a man throw aside that narrowness of soul, that selfishness of principle, which the niggards of all professions are so unwilling to part with, and he will be at once delivered of his fears on that head. Suspicion is the companion of mean souls, and the bane of all good society. For myself, I fully and conscientiously believe, that it is the will of the Almighty that there should be a diversity of religious opinions among us. It affords a larger field for our Christian kindness: were we all of one way of thinking, our religious dispositions would want matter for probation ; and on this liberal principle I look on the various denominations among us, to be like children of the same family, differing only in what is called their Christian names.

In page [97] I threw out a few thoughts on the propriety of a Continental Charter (for I only presume to offer hints, not plans) and in this place, I take the liberty of re-mentioning the subject, by observing, that a charter is to be understood as a bond of solemn obligation, which the whole enters into, to support the right of every separate part, whether of religion, professional freedom, or property. A firm bargain and a right reckoning make long friends.

I have heretofore likewise mentioned the necessity of a large and equal representation; and there is no political matter which more deserves our attention. A small number of electors, or a small number of representatives, are equally dangerous. But if the number of the representatives be not only small, but unequal, the danger is encreased. As an instance of this, I mention the following; when the petition of the associators was before the House of Assembly of Pennsylvania, twenty-eight members only were present; all the Bucks county members, being eight, voted against it, and had seven of the Chester members done the same, this whole province had been governed by two counties only; and this danger it is always exposed to. The unwarrantable stretch likewise, which that house made in their last sitting, to gain an undue authority over the Delegates of that Province, ought to warn the people at large, how they trust power out of their own hands. A set of instructions for their Delegates were put together, which in point of sense and business would have dishonoured a school-boy, and after being approved by a few, a very few, without doors, were carried into the house, and there passed *in behalf of the whole Colony;* whereas, did the whole colony know with what ill will that house had entered on some necessary public measures, they would not hesitate a moment to think them unworthy of such a trust.

Immediate necessity makes many things convenient, which if continued would grow into oppressions. Expedience and right are different things. When the calamities of America required a consultation, there was no method so ready, or at that time so proper, as to appoint persons from the several houses of Assembly for that purpose; and the wisdom with which they have proceeded hath preserved this Continent from ruin. But as it is more than probable that we shall never be without a CONGRESS, every well wisher to good order must own that the mode for choosing members of that body, deserves consideration. And I put it as a question to those who make a study of mankind, whether representation and election is not too great a power for one and the same body of men to possess? When we are planning for posterity, we ought to remember that virtue is not hereditary.

It is from our enemies that we often gain excellent maxims, and are frequently surprised into reason by their mistakes. Mr. Cornwall (one of the Lords of the Treasury) treated the petition of the New York Assembly with contempt, because *that* house, he said, consisted but of twenty-six members, which trifling number, he argued, could not with decency be put for the whole. We thank him for his involuntary honesty.*

TO CONCLUDE, however strange it may appear to some, or however unwilling they may be to think so, matters not, but many strong and striking reasons may be given to show, that nothing can settle our affairs so expeditiously as an open and determined declaration for independance. Some of which are,

First—It is the custom of Nations, when any two are at war, for some other powers, not engaged in the quarrel, to step in as mediators, and bring about the preliminaries of a peace: But while America calls herself the subject of Great Britain, no power, however well disposed she may be, can offer her mediation. Wherefore, in our present state we may quarrel on for ever.

Secondly—It is unreasonable to suppose, that France or

---

* Those who would fully understand of what great consequence a large and equal representation is to a state, should read Burgh's *Political Disquisitions.*—*Author.*

Spain will give us any kind of assistance, if we mean only to make use of that assistance for the purpose of repairing the breach, and strengthening the connection between Britain and America ; because, those powers would be sufferers by the consequences.

Thirdly—While we profess ourselves the subjects of Britain, we must, in the eyes of foreign nations, be considered as Rebels. The precedent is somewhat dangerous to their peace, for men to be in arms under the name of subjects : we, on the spot, can solve the paradox ; but to unite resistance and subjection, requires an idea much too refined for common understanding.

Fourthly—Were a manifesto to be published, and despatched to foreign Courts, setting forth the miseries we have endured, and the peaceful methods which we have ineffectually used for redress; declaring at the same time, that not being able any longer to live happily or safely under the cruel disposition of the British Court, we had been driven to the necessity of breaking off all connections with her; at the same time, assuring all such Courts of our peaceable disposition towards them, and of our desire of entering into trade with them : such a memorial would produce more good effects to this Continent, than if a ship were freighted with petitions to Britain.

Under our present denomination of British subjects, we can neither be received nor heard abroad : the custom of all Courts is against us, and will be so, until by an independance we take rank with other nations.

These proceedings may at first seem strange and difficult, but like all other steps which we have already passed over, will in a little time become familiar and agreeable : and until an independance is declared, the Continent will feel itself like a man who continues putting off some unpleasant business from day to day, yet knows it must be done, hates to set about it, wishes it over, and is continually haunted with the thoughts of its necessity.

APPENDIX TO COMMON SENSE.

SINCE the publication of the first edition of this pamphlet, or rather, on the same day on which it came out, the King's Speech made its appearance in this city [Philadelphia]. Had the spirit of prophecy directed the birth of this production, it could not have brought it forth at a more seasonable juncture, or at a more necessary time. The bloody-mindedness of the one, shows the necessity of pursuing the doctrine of the other. Men read by way of revenge. And the Speech, instead of terrifying, prepared a way for the manly principles of Independance.

Ceremony, and even silence, from whatever motives they may arise, have a hurtful tendency when they give the least degree of countenance to base and wicked performances; wherefore, if this maxim be admitted, it naturally follows, that the King's Speech, as being a piece of finished villany, deserved and still deserves, a general execration, both by the Congress and the people. Yet, as the domestic tranquillity of a nation, depends greatly on the *chastity* of what might properly be called NATIONAL MANNERS, it is often better to pass some things over in silent disdain, than to make use of such new methods of dislike, as might introduce the least innovation on that guardian of our peace and safety. And, perhaps, it is chiefly owing to this prudent delicacy, that the King's Speech hath not before now suffered a public execution. The Speech, if it may be called one, is nothing better than a wilful audacious libel against the truth, the common good, and the existence of mankind; and is a formal and pompous method of offering up human sacrifices to the pride of tyrants. But this general massacre of mankind, is one of the privileges and the certain consequences of Kings; for as nature knows them *not*, they know *not her*, and although they are beings of our *own* creating, they know not *us*, and are become the Gods of their creators.   The speech hath one good quality, which is, that it is not calculated to deceive, neither can we, even if we would, be deceived by it.   Brutality and tyranny appear on the face of it.   It leaves us at no loss: And every line convinces, even in the moment of reading, that he who hunts the woods for prey, the naked and untutored Indian, is less Savage than the King of Britain.

Sir John Dalrymple, the putative father of a whining jesuitical piece, fallaciously called, " *The address of the people of* England *to the inhabitants of* America," hath perhaps from a vain supposition that the people *here* were to be frightened at the pomp and description of a king, given (though very unwisely on his part) the real character of the present one: "But," says this writer, " if you are inclined to pay compliments to an administration, which we do not complain of (meaning the Marquis of Rockingham's at the repeal of the Stamp Act) it is very unfair in you to withhold them from that prince, *by whose* NOD ALONE *they were permitted to do any thing.*"   This is toryism with a witness! Here is idolatry even without a mask: And he who can calmly hear and digest such doctrine, hath forfeited his claim to rationality—an apostate from the order of manhood—and ought to be considered as one who hath not only given up the proper dignity of man, but sunk himself beneath the rank of animals, and contemptibly crawls through the world like a worm.

However, it matters very little now what the king of England either says or does; he hath wickedly broken through every moral and human obligation, trampled nature and conscience beneath his feet, and by a steady and con-stitutional spirit of insolence and cruelty procured for him-self an universal hatred.   It is *now* the interest of America to provide for herself.   She hath already a large and young family, whom it is more her duty to take care of, than to be granting away her property to support a power who is be-come a reproach to the names of men and christians—YE, whose office it is to watch the morals of a nation, of whatsoever sect or denomination ye are of, as well as ye who are more immediately the guardians of the public liberty, if ye wish to preserve your native country uncontaminated by European corruption, ye must in secret wish a separation. But leaving the moral part to private reflection, I shall chiefly confine my further remarks to the following heads:

First, That it is the interest of America to be separated from Britain.

Secondly, Which is the easiest and most practicable plan, RECONCILIATION or INDEPENDENCE? with some occasional remarks.

In support of the first, I could, if I judged it proper, produce the opinion of some of the ablest and most experienced men on this continent: and whose sentiments on that head, are not yet publicly known. It is in reality a self-evident position: for no nation in a state of foreign dependance, limited in its commerce, and cramped and fettered in its legislative powers, can ever arrive at any material eminence. America doth not yet know what opulence is; and although the progress which she hath made stands unparalleled in the history of other nations, it is but childhood compared with what she would be capable of arriving at, had she, as she ought to have, the legislative powers in her own hands. England is at this time proudly coveting what would do her no good were she to accomplish it; and the continent hesitating on a matter which will be her final ruin if neglected. It is the commerce and not the conquest of America by which England is to be benefited, and that would in a great measure continue, were the countries as independant of each other as France and Spain; because in many articles neither can go to a better market. But it is the independance of this country of Britain, or any other, which is now the main and only object worthy of contention, and which, like all other truths discovered by necessity, will appear clear and stronger every day.

First, Because it will come to that one time or other.

Secondly, Because the longer it is delayed, the harder it will be to accomplish.

I have frequently amused myself both in public and private companies, with silently remarking the specious errors of those who speak without reflecting. And among the many which I have heard, the following seems the most general, viz. that had this rupture happened forty or fifty years hence, instead of now, the continent would have been more able to have shaken off the dependance. To which I reply, that our military ability, *at this time*, arises from the experience gained in the last war, and which in forty or fifty years time, would be totally extinct. The continent would not, by that time, have a general, or even a military officer left; and we, or those who may succeed us, would be as ignorant of martial matters as the ancient Indians: and this single position, closely attended to, will unanswerably prove that the present time is preferable to all others. The argument turns thus: At the conclusion of the last war, we had experience, but wanted numbers; and forty or fifty years hence, we shall have numbers, without experience; wherefore, the proper point of time, must be some particular point between the two extremes, in which a sufficiency of the former remains, and a proper increase of the latter is obtained: And that point of time is the present time.

The reader will pardon this digression, as it does not properly come under the head I first set out with, and to which I again return by the following position, viz.:

Should affairs be patched up with Britain, and she to remain the governing and sovereign power of America, (which, as matters are now circumstanced, is giving up the point entirely) we shall deprive ourselves of the very means of sinking the debt we have, or may contract. The value of the back lands, which some of the provinces are clandestinely deprived of, by the unjust extension of the limits of Canada, valued only at five pounds sterling per hundred acres, amount to upwards of twenty-five millions, Pennsylvania currency; and the quit-rents, at one penny sterling per acre, to two millions yearly.

It is by the sale of those lands that the debt may be sunk, without burthen to any, and the quit-rent reserved thereon

will always lessen, and in time will wholly support, the yearly
expense of government. . It matters not how long the debt
is in paying, so that the lands when sold be applied to the
discharge of it, and for the execution of which the Congress
for the time being will be the continental trustees.

I proceed now to the second head, viz.   Which is the
easiest and most practicable plan, Reconciliation or Independence ; with some occasional remarks.

He who takes nature for his guide, is not easily beaten out
of his argument, and on that ground, I answer generally—
That independance *being a* single simple line, *contained within
ourselves ; and reconciliation, a matter exceedingly perplexed
and complicated, and in which a treacherous capricious court is
to interfere, gives the answer without a doubt.*

The present state of America is truly alarming to every
man who is capable of reflection.   Without law, without
government, without any other mode of power than what is
founded on, and granted by, courtesy.   Held together by an
unexampled occurrence of sentiment, which is nevertheless
subject to change, and which every secret enemy is endeavoring to dissolve.   Our present condition is, Legislation without
law ; wisdom without a plan ; a constitution without a name ;
and, what is strangely astonishing, perfect independance contending for dependance.   The instance is without a precedent,
the case never existed before, and who can tell what may be
the event ?   The property of no man is secure in the present
unbraced system of things.   The mind of the multitude is
left at random, and seeing no fixed object before them, they
pursue such as fancy or opinion presents. Nothing is criminal ;
there is no such thing as treason ; wherefore, every one
thinks himself at liberty to act as he pleases.   The Tories
would not have dared to assemble offensively, had they
known that their lives, by that act, were forfeited to the laws
of the state.   A line of distinction should be drawn between
English soldiers taken in battle, and inhabitants of America
taken in arms.   The first are prisoners, but the latter traitors.
The one forfeits his liberty, the other his head.

Notwithstanding our wisdom, there is a visible feebleness in some of our proceedings which gives encouragement to dissentions. The Continental Belt is too loosely buckled: And if something is not done in time, it will be too late to do any thing, and we shall fall into a state, in which neither Reconciliation nor Independance will be practicable. The king and his worthless adherents are got at their old game of dividing the Continent, and there are not wanting among us Printers who will be busy in spreading specious falsehoods. The artful and hypocritical letter which appeared a few months ago in two of the New-York papers, and likewise in two others, is an evidence that there are men who want both judgment and honesty.

It is easy getting into holes and corners, and talking of reconciliation: But do such men seriously consider how difficult the task is, and how dangerous it may prove, should the Continent divide thereon? Do they take within their view all the various orders of men whose situation and circumstances, as well as their own, are to be considered therein? Do they put themselves in the place of the sufferer whose *all* is *already* gone, and of the soldier, who hath quitted *all* for the defence of his country? If their ill-judged moderation be suited to their own private situations *only*, regardless of others, the event will convince them that "they are reckoning without their host."

Put us, say some, on the footing we were in the year 1763: To which I answer, the request is not now in the power of Britain to comply with, neither will she propose it; but if it were, and even should be granted, I ask, as a reasonable question, By what means is such a corrupt and faithless court to be kept to its engagements? Another parliament, nay, even the present, may hereafter repeal the obligation, on the pretence of its being violently obtained, or unwisely granted; and, in that case, Where is our redress? No going to law with nations; cannon are the barristers of crowns; and the sword, not of justice, but of war, decides the suit. To be on the footing of 1763, it is not sufficient, that the laws only be put in the same state, but, that our circumstances likewise be put in the same state; our burnt and destroyed towns repaired or built up, our private losses made good, our public debts (contracted for defence) discharged ; otherwise we shall be millions worse than we were at that enviable period. Such a request, had it been complied with a year ago, would have won the heart and soul of the Continent, but now it is too late. "The Rubicon is passed."

Besides, the taking up arms, merely to enforce the repeal of a pecuniary law, seems as unwarrantable by the divine law, and as repugnant to human feelings, as the taking up arms to enforce obedience thereto. The object, on either side, doth not justify the means ; for the lives of men are too valuable to be cast away on such trifles. It is the violence which is done and threatened to our persons ; the destruction of our property by an armed force ; the invasion of our country by fire and sword, which conscientiously qualifies the use of arms : and the instant in which such mode of defence became necessary, all subjection to Britain ought to have ceased ; and the independance of America should have been considered as dating its era from, and published by, *the first musket that was fired against her.* This line is a line of consistency ; neither drawn by caprice, nor extended by ambition ; but produced by a chain of events, of which the colonies were not the authors.

I shall conclude these remarks, with the following timely and well-intended hints. We ought to reflect, that there are three different ways by which an independancy may hereafter be effected ; and that *one* of those *three*, will, one day or other, be the fate of America, viz. By the legal voice of the people in Congress ; by a military power ; or by a mob : It may not always happen that our soldiers are citizens, and the multitude a body of reasonable men ; virtue, as I have already remarked, is not hereditary, neither is it perpetual. Should an independancy be brought about by the first of those means, we have every opportunity and every encouragement before us, to form the noblest, purest constitution on the face of the earth. We have it in our power to begin the world over again. A situation, similar to the present, hath not happened since the days of Noah until now. The birthday of a new world is at hand, and a race of men, perhaps as numerous as all Europe contains, are to receive their portion of freedom from the events of a few months. The reflection is awful, and in this point of view, how trifling, how ridiculous, do the little paltry cavilings of a few weak or interested men appear, when weighed against the business of a world.

Should we neglect the present favorable and inviting period, and independance be hereafter effected by any other means, we must charge the consequence to ourselves, or to those rather whose narrow and prejudiced souls are habitually opposing the measure, without either inquiring or reflecting. There are reasons to be given in support of independance which men should rather privately think of, than be publicly told of. We ought not now to be debating whether we shall be independant or not, but anxious to accomplish it on a firm, secure, and honorable basis, and uneasy rather that it is not yet began upon. Every day convinces us of its necessity. Even the Tories (if such beings yet remain among us) should, of all men, be the most solicitous to promote it; for as the appointment of committees at first protected them from popular rage, so, a wise and well established form of government will be the only certain means of continuing it securely to them. Wherefore, if they have not virtue enough to be WHIGS, they ought to have prudence enough to wish for independance.

In short, Independance is the only BOND that tye and keep us together. We shall then see our object, and our ears will be legally shut against the schemes of an intriguing, as well as cruel, enemy. We shall then, too, be on a proper footing to treat with Britain; for there is reason to conclude, that the pride of that court will be less hurt by treating with the American states for terms of peace, than with those, whom she denominates "rebellious subjects," for terms of accommodation. It is our delaying in that, encourages her to hope for conquest, and our backwardness tends only to prolong the war. As we have, without any good effect therefrom, withheld our trade to obtain a redress

of our grievances, let us now try the alternative, by inde-
pendantly redressing them ourselves, and then offering to
open the trade. The mercantile and reasonable part of
England, will be still with us; because, peace, with trade, is
preferable to war without it. And if this offer be not accepted, other courts may be applied to.

On these grounds I rest the matter. And as no offer
hath yet been made to refute the doctrine contained in the
former editions of this pamphlet, it is a negative proof,
that either the doctrine cannot be refuted, or, that the party
in favor of it are too numerous to be opposed. WHERE-
FORE, instead of gazing at each other with suspicious or
doubtful curiosity, let each of us hold out to his neighbor
the hearty hand of friendship, and unite in drawing a line,
which, like an act of oblivion, shall bury in forgetfulness
every former dissention. Let the names of Whig and Tory
be extinct; and let none other be heard among us, than
those of *a good citizen ; an open and resolute friend ;* and *a
virtuous supporter of the* RIGHTS *of* MANKIND, *and of the*
FREE AND INDEPENDANT STATES OF AMERICA.

XVI.

EPISTLE TO QUAKERS.

To the Representatives of the Religious Society of the People called Quakers, or to so many of them as were concerned in publishing a late piece, entitled " THE ANCIENT TESTI-MONY *and* PRINCIPLES *of the people called* QUAKERS *renewed, with respect to the* KING *and* GOVERNMENT, *and touching the* COMMOTIONS *now prevailing in these and other parts of* AMERICA, *addressed to the* PEOPLE IN GENERAL." [1]

THE writer of this is one of those few who never dishonors religion either by ridiculing or cavilling at any denomination whatsoever. To God, and not to man, are all men accountable on the score of religion. Wherefore, this epistle is not so properly addressed to you as a religious, but as a political body, dabbling in matters which the professed Quietude of your Principles instruct you not to meddle with.

As you have, without a proper authority for so doing, put yourselves in the place of the whole body of the Quakers, so the writer of this, in order to be in an equal rank with yourselves, is under the necessity of putting himself in the place of all those who approve the very writings and principles against which your testimony is directed: And he hath chosen this singular situation, in order that you might discover in him that presumption of character which you can-

---

[1] The "Testimony" was issued by a general meeting of Pennsylvania and New Jersey Friends held in Philadelphia, January 20, 1776. Paine's "Epistle" was part of the Appendix to the third edition of "Common Sense."—*Editor*.

not see in yourselves. For neither he nor you have any claim or title to *Political Representation.*

When men have departed from the right way, it is no wonder that they stumble and fall. And it is evident from the manner in which ye have managed your testimony, that politics (as a religious body of men) is not your proper Walk; for however well adapted it might appear to you, it is, nevertheless, a jumble of good and bad unwisely put together, and the conclusion drawn therefrom both unnatural and unjust.

The first two pages (and the whole doth make but four) we give you credit for, and expect the same civility from you, because the love and desire of peace is not confined to Quakerism, it is the natural as well as the religious wish of all denominations of men. And on this ground, as men laboring to establish an Independant Constitution of our own, do we exceed all others in our hope, end, and aim. *Our plan is peace for ever.* We are tired of contention with Britain, and can see no real end to it but in a final separation. We act consistently, because for the sake of introducing an endless and uninterrupted peace, do we bear the evils and the burthens of the present day. We are endeavoring, and will steadily continue to endeavor, to separate and dissolve a connection which has already filled our land with blood; and which, while the name of it remains, will be the fatal cause of future mischiefs to both countries.

We fight neither for revenge nor conquest; neither from pride nor passion; we are not insulting the world with our fleets and armies, nor ravaging the globe for plunder. Beneath the shade of our own vines are we attacked; in our own houses, and on our own lands, is the violence committed against us. We view our enemies in the characters of Highwaymen and Housebreakers, and having no defence for ourselves in the civil law, are obliged to punish them by the military one, and apply the sword, in the very case where you have before now applied the halter. Perhaps we feel for the ruined and insulted sufferers in all and every part of the Continent, with a degree of tenderness which hath not yet made its way into some of your bosoms.   But be ye sure that ye mistake not the cause and ground of your Testimony.   Call not coldness of soul, religion ; nor put the Bigot in the place of the Christian.

O ye partial ministers of your own acknowledged principles.   If the bearing arms be sinful, the first going to war must be more so, by all the difference between wilful attack and unavoidable defence.   Wherefore, if ye really preach from conscience, and mean not to make a political hobbyhorse of your religion, convince the world thereof, by proclaiming your doctrine to our enemies, *for they likewise bear* ARMS.   Give us proof of your sincerity, by publishing it at St. James's, to the commanders in chief at Boston, to the admirals and captains who are piratically ravaging our coasts, and to all the murdering miscreants who are acting in authority under HIM whom ye profess to serve.   Had ye the honest soul of Barclay * ye would preach repentance to your king : ye would tell the Royal Wretch his sins, and warn him of eternal ruin.   Ye would not spend your partial invectives against the injured and insulted only, but, like faithful ministers, would cry aloud and *spare none.*   Say not that ye are persecuted, neither endeavor to make us the authors of that reproach which ye are bringing upon yourselves ; for we testify unto all men, that we do not complain against you because ye are *Quakers,* but because ye pretend to *be* and are not Quakers.

Alas ! it seems by the particular tendency of some part of your testimony, and other parts of your conduct, as if all sin

* " Thou hast tasted of prosperity and adversity ; thou knowest what it is to be banished thy native country, to be over-ruled as well as to rule, and sit upon the throne : and being *oppressed* thou hast reason to know how *hateful* the *oppressor* is both to God and man ; If after all these warnings and advertisements, thou dost not turn unto the Lord with all thy heart, but forget him who remembered thee in thy distress, and give up thyself to follow lust and vanity, surely, great will be thy condemnation.—Against which snare, as well as the temptation of those who may or do feed thee, and prompt thee to evil, the most excellent and prevalent remedy will be, to apply thyself to that light of Christ which shineth in thy conscience, and which neither can nor will flatter thee, nor suffer thee to be at ease in thy sins."—*Barclay's Address to Charles II.*

was reduced to, and comprehended in, *the act of bearing arms*, and that by the *people only*. Ye appear to us to have mistaken party for conscience ; because the general tenor of your actions wants uniformity : And it is exceedingly difficult for us to give credit to many of your pretended scruples ; because we see them made by the same men, who, in the very instant that they are exclaiming against the mammon of this world, are nevertheless hunting after it with a step as steady as Time, and an appetite as keen as Death.

The quotation which ye have made from Proverbs, in the third page of your testimony, that "when a man's ways please the Lord, he maketh even his enemies to be at peace with him ;" is very unwisely chosen on your part ; because it amounts to a proof that the king's ways (whom ye are so desirous of supporting) do *not* please the Lord, otherwise his reign would be in peace.

I now proceed to the latter part of your testimony, and that for which all the foregoing seems only an introduction, viz.

"It hath ever been our judgment and principle, since we were called to profess the light of Christ Jesus, manifested in our consciences unto this day, that the setting up and putting down kings and governments, is God's peculiar prerogative ; for causes best known to himself : And that it is not our business to have any hand or contrivance therein ; nor to be busy bodies above our station, much less to plot and contrive the ruin, or overturn of any of them, but to pray for the king, and safety of our nation, and good of all men : That we may live a quiet and peaceable life, in all godliness and honesty ; *under the government which God is pleased to set over us.*"

If these are really your principles why do ye not abide by them ? Why do ye not leave that, which ye call God's work, to be managed by himself? These very principles instruct you to wait with patience and humility, for the event of all public measures, and to receive that event as the divine will towards you. Wherefore, what occasion is there for your *political testimony*, if you fully believe what it contains? And the very publishing it proves that either

ye do not believe what ye profess, or have not virtue
enough to practice what ye believe.

The principles of Quakerism have a direct tendency to
make a man the quiet and inoffensive subject of any, and
every government which is set over him.   And if the setting
up and putting down of kings and governments is God's
peculiar prerogative, he most certainly will not be robbed
thereof by us; wherefore, the principle itself leads you to
approve of every thing which ever happened, or may happen
to kings, as being his work.   Oliver Cromwell thanks you.
Charles, then, died not by the hands of man; and should
the present proud Imitator of him come to the same un-
timely end, the writers and publishers of the testimony are
bound, by the doctrine it contains, to applaud the fact.
Kings are not taken away by miracles, neither are changes
in governments brought about by any other means than
such as are common and human; and such as we now are
using.   Even the dispersing of the Jews, though foretold by
our Saviour, was effected by arms.   Wherefore, as ye refuse
to be the means on one side, ye ought not to be medlers on
the other; but to wait the issue in silence; and, unless you
can produce divine authority to prove that the Almighty,
who hath created and placed this new world at the greatest
distance it could possibly stand, east and west, from every
part of the old, doth, nevertheless, disapprove of its being
independant of the corrupt and abandoned court of Britain;
unless, I say, ye can show this, how can ye, on the ground
of your principles, justify the exciting and stirring up the
people " firmly to unite in the *abhorrence* of all such *writings*,
and *measures*, as evidence a desire and design to break off the
happy connection we have hitherto enjoyed with the kingdom
of Great Britain, and our just and necessary subordination
to the king, and those who are lawfully placed in authority
under him."   What a slap in the face is here !   The men,
who, in the very paragraph before, have quietly and passively resigned up the ordering, altering and disposal of
kings and governments, into the hands of God, are now
recalling their principles, and putting in for a share of the

business. Is it possible, that the conclusion, which is here justly quoted, can any ways follow from the doctrine laid down! The inconsistency is too glaring not to be seen; the absurdity too great not to be laughed at; and such as could only have been made by those whose understandings were darkened by the narrow and crabbed spirit of a despairing political party; for ye are not to be considered as the whole body of the Quakers, but only as a factional and fractional part thereof.

Here ends the examination of your Testimony; (which I call upon no man to abhor, as ye have done, but only to read and judge of fairly;) to which I subjoin the following remark "That the setting up and putting down of kings" must certainly mean, the making him a king who is yet not so, and the making him no king who is already one. And pray what hath this to do in the present case? We neither mean to *set up* nor to *pull down*, neither to *make* nor to *unmake*, but to have nothing to do with them. Wherefore, your testimony, in whatever light it is viewed, serves only to dishonor your judgment, and for many other reasons had better have been let alone than published.

First, Because it tends to the decrease and reproach of all religion whatever, and is of the utmost danger to society, to make it a party in political disputes.

Secondly, Because it exhibits a body of men, numbers of whom disavow the publishing of political testimonies, as being concerned therein and approvers thereof.

Thirdly, Because it hath a tendency to undo that continental harmony and friendship which yourselves, by your late liberal and charitable donations, hath lent a hand to establish; and the preservation of which is of the utmost consequence to us all.

And here, without anger or resentment, I bid you farewell. Sincerely wishing, that as men and christians, ye may always fully and uninterruptedly enjoy every civil and religious right, and be, in your turn, the means of securing it to others; but that the example which ye have unwisely set, of mingling religion with politics, *may be disavowed and reprobated by every inhabitant of* AMERICA.

XVII.

THE FORESTER'S LETTERS.[1]

I.

TO CATO.

To be *nobly wrong* is more manly than to be *meanly right*. Only let the error be disinterested—let it wear *not the mask*, but the *mark* of principle, and 'tis pardonable. It is on this large and liberal ground, that we distinguish between men and their tenets, and generously preserve our friendship for the one, while we combat with every prejudice of the other. But let not Cato take this compliment to himself; he stands excluded from the benefit of the distinction; he deserves it not. And if the sincerity of disdain can add a cubit to the stature of my sentiments, it shall not be wanting.

[1] "The writer of ' Common Sense' and ' The Forester' is the same person," wrote John Adams to his wife. " His name is Paine, a gentleman about two years from England,—a man who, Gen. Lee says, has genius in his eyes." The letters signed " The Forester" are four, and originally appeared in the *Pennsylvania Journal*, the dates of issue being April 3, 10, 24, May 8, 1776. The April letters were replies to " Cato," who was writing a series of letters, in the *Pennsylvania Gazette*, vigorously combating the republican doctrines of Paine's "Common Sense," and its pleas for Independence. " Cato " was the Rev. Dr. William Smith, a Scotch clergyman of the English Church, Provost of the College of Philadelphia, and the most influential preacher in that city until his fall with the royalist cause which he had espoused. The letters of these disputants were widely copied in the country, and the controversy was the most exciting and important immediately preceding the Declaration of Independence. The proposal of such a Declaration was really the issue. It was vehemently opposed by the wealth and aristocracy of Philadelphia, headed by Dr. Smith, and the discussion was almost a battle. This may explain its acrimony, on which neither writer, probably, reflected with satisfaction in after years. The " Cato " letters are not included in the collected Works of Dr. Smith (Philadelphia, 1803), nor have the letters of " The Forester " appeared hitherto in any edition of Paine's Writings. They are, however, of much historical interest. The fourth letter of " The Forester," it will be seen, has no reference to Cato.—*Editor*.

It is indifferent to me who the writer of Cato's letters is, and sufficient for me to know, that they are gorged with absurdity, confusion, contradiction, and the most notorious and wilful falsehoods. Let Cato and his faction be against Independence and welcome ; their consequence will not *now* turn the scale : But let them have regard to justice, and pay some attention to the plain doctrine of reason. Where these are wanting, the sacred cause of truth applauds our anger, and dignifies it with the name of Virtue.

Four letters have already appeared under the specious name of Cato. What pretensions the writer of them can have to the signature, the public will best determine ; while, on my own part, I prophetically content myself with contemplating the similarity of their exits. The first of those letters promised a second, the second a third, the third a fourth ; the fourth hath since made its appearance, and still the writer keeps wide of the question. Why doth he thus loiter in the suburbs of the dispute ? Why hath he not shewn us what the numerous blessings of reconciliation [with Great Britain] are, and *proved them practicable ?* But he cunningly avoids the point. He cannot but discover the rock he is driving on. The fate of the Roman Cato is before his eyes : And that the public may be prepared for his funeral, and for his funeral oration, I will venture to predict the time and the manner of his exit. The moment he explains his terms of reconciliation the typographical Cato dies. If they be calculated to please the [British] Cabinet they will not go down with the Colonies : and if they be suited to the Colonies they will be rejected by the Cabinet : The line of no-variation is yet unfound ; and, like the philosopher's stone, doth not exist. " I am bold," says Cato, " to declare and yet hope to make it evident to every honest man, that the true interest of America lies in *reconciliation* with Great Britain on *constitutional principles*."

This is a curious way of lumping the business indeed ! And Cato may as well attempt to catch lions in a mousetrap as to hope to allure the public with such general and unexplained expressions. It is now a mere bugbear to talk

of *reconciliation* on *constitutional principles* unless the terms
of the first be produced and the sense of the other be defined; and unless he does this he does nothing.

To follow Cato through every absurdity and falsehood in
the compass of a * letter is impossible · neither is it *now*
necessary. *Cassandra* (and I thank him) hath saved me
much trouble; there is a spirit in his remarks which honesty
only can inspire, and a uniformity in the conduct of his
letters which the want of principle can never arrive at.[1]
Mark that, Cato.

One observation which I cannot help making on Cato's
letters, is that they are addressed " *To the People of Pennsylvania* " *only:* In almost any other writer this might have
passed unnoticed, but we know it hath mischief in its meaning. The particular circumstance of a convention is undoubtedly Provincial, but the great business of the day is
Continental. And he who dares to endeavour to withdraw
this province from the glorious union by which all are supported, deserves the reprobation of all men. It is the true
interest of the whole to go hand in hand; and dismal in
every instance would be the fate of that Colony which should
retreat from the protection of the rest.

The first of Cato's letters is insipid in its stile, language
and substance; crowded with personal and private innuen-
dues and directly levelled against " *the Majesty of the People
of Pennsylvania.*" The Committee could only call, propose,
or recommend a Convention;[2] but, like all other public
measures, it still rested with the people at large, whether
they would approve it or not; and Cato's reasoning on the
right or wrong of that choice is contemptible; because, if

---

* *The writer intended at first to have contained his remarks in one letter.—*
Author.

[1] The letter " On sending Commissioners to treat with the Congress," signed
" Cassandra," was particularly dealt with by "Cato" in his second letter.—*Editor.*

[2] This committee was appointed by the Assembly of Pennsylvania in pur-
suance of a recommendation, by the Continental Congress, that the Colonies
should impose on their officers, civil and military, a new patriotic oath. The
course of events led the Committee to summon a Provincial Convention by
which Pennsylvania was entirely reorganized.—*Editor.*

the body of the people had thought, or should still think
that the Assembly (or any of their Delegates in Congress)
by setting under the embarrassment of *oaths*, and entangled
with *government* and *Governors*, are not so perfectly free as
they ought to be, they undoubtedly had and still have both
the *right* and the *power* to place even the whole authority of
the Assembly in any body of men they please ; and whoever
is hardy enough to say to the contrary is an enemy to mankind.   The constitution of Pennsylvania hath been twice
changed through the cunning of former Proprietors; surely,
the people, whose right, power, and property is greater than
that of any single man, may make such alterations in their
mode of government as the change of times and things
require.   Cato is exceedingly fond of impressing us with the
importance of our " *chartered constitution.*"   Alas !   We are
not now, Sir, to be led away by the jingle of a phrase.   Had
we framed our conduct by the contents of the present charters, we had ere now been in a state of helpless misery.
That *very assembly* you mention hath broken it, and been
obliged to break it, in almost every instance of their proceedings.   Hold it up to the Public, and it is transparent
with holes ; pierced with as many deadly wounds as the
body of M'Leod.[1]   Disturb not its remains, Cato, nor dishonour it with another funeral oration.

   There is nothing in Cato's first letter worthy of notice
but the following insinuating falsehood : " Grievous as the
least restraint of the press must always be to a *people* entitled to freedom, it must be the more so, when it is not only
unwarranted by *those* to whom *they* have committed the care
of *their* liberties but cannot be warranted by *them*, consistent
with liberty itself."   The rude and unscholastical confusion
of persons in the above paragraph, though it throws an
obscurity on the meaning, still leaves it discoverable.   Who,
Sir, hath laid any restraint on the liberty of the press ?   I
know of no instance in which the press hath ever been the

---

[1] News had reached Philadelphia of the battle of Moore's Creek Bridge, North
Carolina, in which the " Tory" forces were defeated, and their temporary commander, M'Leod, fell "pierced with twenty balls."—*Editor*.

object of notice in this province, except on account of the tory letter from Kent county, which was first published last spring in the *Pennsylvania Ledger,* and which it was the duty of every good man to detect because the *honesty* of the press is as great an object to society as the *freedom* of it.   If this is the restraint you complain of, we know your true character at once ; and that it is so, appears evident from the expression which immediately follows the above quotation : your words are, " Nevertheless, *we* readily submitted to it while the least colourable pretence could be offered for requiring such a submission."   Who submitted, Cato ? *we* Whigs, or *we* Tories ?   Until you clear up this, Sir, you must content yourself with being ranked among the rankest of the *writing* Tories ; because no other body of men can have any pretence to complain of want of freedom of the press.   It is not your throwing out, now and then, little popular phrases which can protect you from suspicion ; they are only the gildings under which the poison is conveyed, and without which you dared not to renew your attempts on the virtue of the people.

  Cato's second letter, or the greatest part thereof, is taken up with the reverence due from us to the persons and authority of the Commissioners, whom Cato vainly and ridiculously stiles AMBASSADORS *coming to negociate a peace.*   How came Cato not to be let a little better into the secret ?   The act of parliament which describes the powers of these men hath been in this city upwards of a month, and in the hands too of Cato's friends.   No, Sir, they are not the *Ambassadors of peace,* but the distributors of pardons, mischief, and insult. Cato discovers a gross ignorance of the British constitution in supposing that these men *can* be empowered to act as Ambassadors.   To prevent his future errors I will set him right.   The present war differs from every other, in this instance, viz. that it is not carried under the prerogative of the crown as other wars have always been, but under the authority of the whole legislative power united ; and as the barriers which stand in the way of a negociation are not proclamations but acts of parliament, it evidently follows, that were even the King of England here in person, he could not ratify the terms or conditions of a reconciliation; because, in the single character of King he could not stipulate for the repeal of any *acts* of parliament, neither can the Parliament stipulate for him.   There is no body of men more jealous of their privileges than the Commons: Because they sell them.   Mark that, Cato.

I have not the least doubt upon me but that their business (exclusive of granting us pardons) is downright bribery and corruption.   It is the machine by which they effect all their plans.   We ought to view them as enemies of a most dangerous species, and he who means not to be corrupted by them will enter his protest in time.   Are they not the very men who are paid for voting in every measure against us, and ought we not to suspect their designs?   Can we view the barbarians as friends?   Would it be prudent to trust the viper in our very bosoms?   Or to suffer them to ramble at large among us while such doubtful characters as Cato have a being upon the continent?   Yet let their persons be safe from injury and outrage—but trust them not.   Our business with them is short and explicit, viz.:   We are desirous of peace, gentlemen; we are ready to ratify the terms, and will virtuously fulfil the conditions thereof; but we should deserve all and every misery which tyranny can inflict, were we, after suffering such a repetition of savage barbarities, to come under your government again.

Cato, by way of stealing into credit, says, "that the contest we are engaged in is founded on the most noble and virtuous principles which can animate the mind of man.   We are contending (says he) against an arbitrary ministry for the rights of Englishmen."   No, Cato, we are *now* contending against an arbitrary King to get clear of his tyranny.   While the dispute rested in words only, it might be called "contending with the ministry," but since it is broken out into open war, it is high time to have done with such silly and water-gruel definitions.   But it suits not Cato to speak the truth.   It is his interest to dress up the sceptred savage in the mildest colors.   Cato's patent for a large tract of land is yet unsigned.   Alas poor Cato !

Cato proceeds very importantly to tell us, "*that the eyes of all Europe are upon us.*" This stale and hackneyed phrase hath had a regular descent, from many of the King's speeches down to several of the speeches in Parliament; from thence it took a turn among the little wits and bucks of St. James's; till after suffering all the torture of senseless repetition, and being reduced to a state of vagrancy, it was charitably picked up to embellish the second letter of Cato. It is truly of the bug-bear kind, contains no meaning, and the very using it discovers a barrenness of invention. It signifies nothing to tell us "that the eyes of all Europe are upon us," unless he had likewise told us what they are looking at us *for :* which as he hath not done, I will. They are looking at us, Cato, in hopes of seeing a final separation between Britain and the Colonies, that they, the *lookers-on,* may partake of a free and uninterrupted trade with the whole Continent of America. Cato, thou reasonest *wrong.*

For the present, Sir, farewell. I have seen thy soliloquy and despise it. Remember thou hast thrown me the glove, Cato, and either thee or I must tire. I fear not the field of fair debate, but thou hast stepped aside and made it personal. Thou hast tauntingly called on me by name ; and if I cease to hunt thee from every lane and lurking hole of mischief, and bring thee not a trembling culprit before the public bar, then brand me with reproach, by naming me in the list of your confederates.

THE FORESTER.

PHILADELPHIA, March 28, 1776.

II.

TO CATO.

BEFORE I enter on the more immediate purpose of this letter, I think it necessary, once for all, to endeavour to settle as clearly as I can, the following point, viz: How far personality is concerned in any political debate. The general maxim is, that measures and not men are the thing in question, and the maxim is undeniably just when rightly understood. Cato as a refuge for himself, hath quoted the author of *Common Sense* who in his preface says, "That the object for attention is the *doctrine itself* not the *man*," that is, not the *rank* or *condition* of the man. For whether he is with those whose fortune is *already* made, or with those whose fortune is *yet* to make, or among those who seldom think or care whether they make *any*, is a matter wholly out of the question and entirely confined to himself. But the political characters, political dependencies, and political connections of men, being of a public nature, differ exceedingly from the circumstances of private life ; and are in many instances so nearly related to the measures they propose, that to prevent our being deceived by the last, we *must* be acquainted with the first. A total ignorance of men lays us under the danger of mistaking plausibility for principle. Could the wolf bleat like the lamb the flock would soon be enticed into ruin ; wherefore to prevent the mischief, he ought to be *seen* as well as *heard*. There never was nor ever will be, nor ever ought to be, any important political debate carried on, in which a total separation in all cases between men and measures could be admitted with sufficient safety. When hypocrisy shall be banished from the earth, the knowledge of men will be unnecessary, because their measures cannot then be fraudulent ; but until that time come (which never will come) they ought, under proper limitations, to go together. We have already too much secrecy in some things and too little in others. Were men more known, and measures more concealed, we should have fewer hypocrites and more security.

As the chief design of these letters is to detect and expose the falsehoods and fallacious reasonings of Cato, he must not expect (when detected) to be treated like one who had debated fairly ; for I will be bold to say and to prove, that a grosser violation of truth and reason scarcely ever came from the pen of a writer ; and the explanations which he hath endeavoured to impose on the passages which he hath quoted from *Common Sense*, are such as never existed in the mind of the author, nor can they be drawn from the words themselves. Neither must Cato expect to be spared where his carelessness of expression, and visible want of compassion and sentiment, shall give occasion to raise any moral or philosophical reflection thereon. These things being premised, I now proceed to review the latter part of Cato's second letter.

In this place Cato begins his first attack on *Common Sense*, but as he only discovers his ill will, and neither offers any arguments against it, nor makes any quotations from it, I should in this place pass him by, were it not for the following strange assertion: "If little notice," says Cato (*little opposition he means*) "has yet been taken of the publications concerning Independance, it is neither owing to the popularity of the doctrine, the unanswerable nature of the arguments, nor the fear of opposing them, as the vanity of the author would suggest." As Cato has given us the *negative* reasons, he ought to have given us the *real* ones, for as he *positively* tells what it was *not* owing to, he undoubtedly knows what it *was* owing to that *he* delayed *his* answers so long; but instead of telling us that, (which perhaps is not proper to be told) he flies from the argument with the following plump declarations, "Nine tenths of the people of Pennsylvania," says he, "yet abhor the doctrine." But stop, Cato! not quite so fast, friend! If this be true, how came they, so late as the second of March last, to elect for a Burgess of this city, a gentleman of known *Independant Principles*, and one of the very few to whom the author of Common Sense shewed some part thereof while in manuscript.[1]

Cato is just as unfortunate in the following paragraph. "Those," says he, "who made the appeal (that is, published the pamphlet) have but little cause to triumph in its success. Of this they seem sensible : and, like true quacks, are constantly pestering us with additional doses till the stomachs of their patients *begin wholly* to revolt." It is Cato's hard fate to be always detected : for perhaps there never was a pamphlet, since the use of letters were known, about which

---

[1] David Rittenhouse, elected in the place of Franklin, who had left for France.—*Editor*.

so little pains were taken, and of which so great a number went off in so short a time ; I am certain that I am within compass when I say one hundred and twenty thousand. The book was turned upon the world like an orphan to shift for itself; no plan was formed to support it, neither hath the author ever published a syllable on the subject, from that time till after the appearance of Cato's fourth letter ; wherefore what Cato says of additional doses administered by the author is an absolute falsity ; besides which, it comes with an ill grace from one, who frequently publishes two letters in a week, and often puts them both into one paper— Cato here, Cato there, look where you will.

At the distance of a few lines from the above quotations, Cato presents us with a retrospective view of our former state, in which, says he, " we considered our connection with Great Britain as our chief happiness—we flourished, grew rich, and populous to a degree not to be paralleled in history." This assertion is truly of the legerdemain kind, appearing at once both right and wrong. All writers on Cato's side have used the same argument and conceived themselves invincible ; nevertheless, a single expression properly placed dissolves the charm, for the cheat lies in putting the *time* for the *cause*. For the cheat lies in putting the *consequence* for the *cause ;* for had we not *flourished* the *connection* had never *existed* or never been *regarded,* and this is fully proved by the neglect shewn to the first settlers who had every difficulty to struggle with, unnoticed and unassisted by the British Court.

Cato proceeds very industriously to sum up the former declarations of Congress and other public bodies, some of which were made upwards of a year ago, to prove, that the doctrine of Independance hath no sanction from them. To this I shall give Cato one general answer which is, that had he produced a thousand more such authorities they would *now* amount to nothing, they are out of date ; times and things are altered ; the true character of the King was but little known among the body of the poeple of America a year ago ; willing to believe him good, they fondly called him so, but have since found that Cato's Royal Sovereign, is a Royal Savage.

Cato hath introduced the above-mentioned long quotation of authorities against independance, with the following curious preface. " Nor have many weeks," says he, " yet elapsed since the first open proposition for independance was published to the world. By what men of consequence this scheme is supported or whether by any, may possibly be the subject of future enquiry. Certainly it hath no countenance from the Congress, to whose sentiments we look up with reverence. On the contrary, it is *directly repugnant to every* declaration of that respectable body." Now Cato, thou hast nailed thyself with a witness! Directly repugnant to every declaration of that respectable body! Mind that, Cato, and mark what follows. It appears by an extract from the resolves of the Congress, printed in the front of the oration delivered by Dr. Smith, in honor of that brave man General Montgomery, that he, the Doctor, was appointed by that honorable body to compose and deliver the same ; in the *execution* of which, the orator exclaimed loudly against the doctrine of independance ; but when a motion was afterwards made in Congress, (according to former usage) to return the *orator* thanks, and request a copy for the press, the motion was rejected from every part of the house and thrown out without a division.[1]

I now proceed to Cato's third letter, in the opening of which he deserts the subject of independance, and renews

[1] "An Oration in memory of General Montgomery, and of the Officers who fell with him, December 31, 1775, before Quebec ; drawn up (and delivered February 19th, 1776,) at the desire of the Honourable Continental Congress. By William Smith, D.D., Provost of the College and Academy of Philadelphia. Philadelphia, printed : London, reprinted for J. Almon, opposite Burlington-house, Picadilly. MDCCLXXVI." On p. 24 Dr. Smith quotes the petition of Congress " for a ' restoration of the former harmony between Great Britain and these Colonies ' etc." In a footnote Dr. Smith refers to the censures of this passage, and adds that since the petition the situation had changed. It was well known that Dr. Smith was " Cato," and Paine's reference to the resentment of Congress was an especially severe thrust, because " Cato " in his second letter (dated March 11) had repeated his offence, recapitulating all the conciliatory efforts of Congress at an earlier period.—*Editor.*

his attack on the Committee.[1] Cato's manner of writing has as much order in it as the motion of a squirrel. He frequently writes as if he knew not what to write next, just as the other jumps about, only because it cannot stand still. Though I am sometimes angry with him for his unprincipled method of writing and reasoning, I cannot help laughing at other times for his want of ingenuity : One instance of which he gives us in kindly warning us against " *the foul pages of interested writers, and strangers intermedling in our affairs.*" Were I to reply seriously my answer would be this : Thou seemest then ignorant, Cato, of that ancient and numerous order which are related to each other in all and every part of the globe—with whom the kindred is not formed by place or accident, but in principle and sentiment. A freeman, Cato, is a stranger nowhere—a slave, everywhere. But were I disposed to answer merrily, I should tell him, that as his notions of friendship were so very narrow and local, he obliges me to understand, that when he addresses the people with the tender title of " *my dear countrymen* " which frequently occurs in his letters, he particularly means the long list of Macs published in Donald M'Donald's Commission.[2]

In this letter Cato recommends the pamphlet called *Plain Truth*, a performance which hath withered away like a sickly unnoticed weed, and which even its advocates are displeased at, and the author ashamed to own.[3] About the middle of this third letter, Cato gives notice of his being ready to take the field. " I now proceed," says he, " to give my reasons."

---

[1] See note in the preceding letter, p. 129.—*Editor.*

[2] M'Donald was Brigadier-General of the Highlanders who were defeated by the North Carolinians on February 27, 1776, at Moore's Creek Bridge. M'Donald being ill on that day the command devolved on M'Leod, who fell, as mentioned in the preceding letter. Dr. William Smith, a pronounced Scotchman, in alluding to Paine as a "stranger," could hardly have been aware that his identity with " Cato " was known.—*Editor.*

[3] " Plain Truth: addressed to the Inhabitants of America, containing Remarks on a late Pamphlet, intitled Common Sense : etc. Written by CANDIDUS. Will ye turn from Flattery and attend to this Side ? " This pamphlet of 37 pages, published in Philadelphia and London, was the most elaborate of many replies to " Common Sense." It was dull, however, and was out of date almost as soon as it appeared.—*Editor.*

How Cato hath managed the attack we are now to examine;
and the first remark I shall offer on his conduct is, that he
hath most unluckily entered the list on the wrong side, and
discharged his first fire among the tories.

In order to prove this, I shall give the paragraph entire :—
"AGRICULTURE and COMMERCE," says Cato, "have hitherto
been the happy employments, by which these middle colonies
have risen into wealth and importance.   By *them* the face of
the country has been changed from a barren wilderness, into
the hospitable abodes of peace and plenty.   Without *them*
we had either never existed as Americans, or existed only
as savages.   The oaks would still have possessed their
native spots of earth, and never have *appeared in the form of
ships and houses*.   What are now well cultivated fields, or
flourishing cities, would have remained only the solitary
haunts of wild beasts or of men equally wild."   The reader
cannot help perceiving that through this whole paragraph
our connexion with Britain is left entirely out of the question,
and our present greatness attributed to external causes,
agriculture and *commerce*.   This is a strange way, Cato, of
overturning Common Sense, which says, " I challenge the
warmest advocate for reconciliation, to shew a single advantage which this continent can reap by being connected with
Great-Britain ; I repeat," says he, "'the challenge : not a single
advantage is derived.   *Our corn will fetch its price in any
market in Europe ; and our imported goods must be paid for,
buy them where we will.*"   Cato introduces his next paragraph with saying, "that much of our former felicity was
owing to the protection of England *is not to be denied.*"
Yes, Cato, I deny it wholly, and for the following clear and
simple reasons, viz., that our being connected with, and submitting to be protected by her, made, and will still make,
all *her* enemies, *our* enemies, or as *Common Sense* says, " sets
us at variance with nations who would otherwise seek our
friendship, and against whom we have neither anger nor
complaint."

The following passage is so glaringly absurd that I shall
make. but a short comment upon it. " And if hereafter,"

says Cato, "in the fulness of time, it shall be necessary to separate from the land that gave birth to [some of] our ancestors, it will be in a state of perfect manhood, when we can fully wield our *own arms*, and *protect our commerce and coasts by our own fleets*." But how are we to come by *fleets*, Cato, while Britain hath the government of the Continent? Unless we are to suppose, as you have hinted in the former paragraph, that our oaks are to *grow* into ships, and be launched self-built from their "native spots of earth." It is Cato's misfortune as a writer, not to distinguish justly between magic and imagination; while on the other hand there are many passages in his letters so seriously and deliberately false, that nothing but the most hardened effrontery, and a cast of mind bordering upon impiety, would have uttered. He frequently forces me out of the common track of civil language, in order to do him justice; moderation and temper being really unequal to the task of exposing him.

Cato, unless he meant to destroy the ground he stood upon, ought not to have let the following paragraph be seen. "If our present *differences*," says he, "can be accommodated, there is *scarce a probability* that Britain will ever *renew* her late fatal system of policy, or attempt again to employ force against us." How came Cato to admit the *probability* of our being brought *again* into the same bloody and expensive situation? But it is worth remarking, that those who write without principle, cannot help sometimes blundering upon truth. Then there is no *real security*, Cato, in this *reconciliation* of yours on *constitutional principles?* It still amounts to nothing; and after all this expence of life and wealth, we are to rest at last upon hope, hazard, and uncertainty. Why then, by all that is sacred, "*it is time to part.*" But Cato, after admitting the *probability* of our being brought *again* into the same situation, proceeds to tell us how we are to conduct ourselves in the second quarrel; and that is, by the very same methods we have done the present one, viz., to expend millions of treasure, and thousands of lives, in order to patch up a *second union*, that the way may be open for a *third quarrel;* and in this endless and

chequered round of blood and treacherous peace, hath Cato
disposed of the Continent of America.   That I may not be
thought to do Cato injustice, I have quoted the whole passage: "But should Britain be so infatuated," says he, " at
any future period, as to think of subjugating us, either by
the arts of corruption, or oppressive exertions of power, can
we entertain a doubt but we shall AGAIN, with a virtue equal
to the present and with the *weapons of defence in our hands*
(when necessary) convince her that we are willing by a *constitutional connection* with her, to afford and receive reciprocal
benefits; but although subjects of the same King, we will
not consent to be her slaves."—Come hither, ye *little ones*,
whom the poisonous hand of Cato is rearing for destruction,
and remember the page that warns ye of your ruin.

Cato, in many of his expressions, discovers all that calm
command over the passions and feelings which always distinguishes the man who hath expelled them from his heart.
Of this careless kind is the before mentioned phrase, "our
present differences," and the same unpardonable negligence
is conveyed in the following one: "*Although* I consider
her," says he, "as having in her late conduct toward us,
acted the part of a cruel stepdame."   Wonderful sensibility
indeed!   All the havoc and desolation of unnatural war;
the destruction of thousands; the burning and depopulating
of towns and cities; the ruin and separation of friends and
families, are just sufficient to extort from Cato, *this one*
callous confession.   But the cold and creeping soul of Cato
is a stranger to the manly powers of sympathetic sorrow.
He *moves* not, nor *can* he move in so pure an element.   Accustomed to lick the hand that hath made him visible, and to
breathe the gross atmosphere of servile and sordid dependence, his soul would *now* starve on virtue, and suffocate in
the clear region of disinterested friendship.

Surely when Cato sat down to write, he either did not
expect to be called to an account, or was totally regardless
of reputation, otherwise he would not have endeavoured to
persuade the public that the doctrine of Independance was
broached in a kind of seditious manner, at a time "*when*,"

says he, "*some gleams of reconciliation began first to break in upon us.*" Come forth, Cato, and prove the assertion! Where do these gleams of reconciliation spring from? Are they to be found in the King's speech, in the address of either House of Parliament, or in the act which lets loose a whole kennel of pirates upon our property, and commissions another set to insult with pardons the very men whom their own measures had sought to ruin? Either prove the assertion, Cato, or take the reward of it, for it is the part of an incendiary to endeavour with specious falsehoods to mislead the credulity of unwary readers. Cato likewise says, that, while we continue united, and renounce all thoughts of Independance, "we have the *utmost assurance* of obtaining a *full redress* of our *grievances*, and an *ample security* against any *future violation* of our *just rights.*" If Cato means to insinuate that we have *received* such an assurance, let him read the conclusion of the preceeding paragraph again. The same answer will serve for both.

Perhaps when we recollect the long and unabated cruelty of the British court towards us, and remember the many prayers which we have put up both *to* them and *for* them, the following piece of declamation of Cato can hardly be equalled either for absurdity or insanity: "If we now effect independance," says he, "we must be considered as a *faithless people in the sight of all mankind, and could scarcely expect the confidence of any nation upon earth, or look up to Heaven for its approving sentence.*" Art thou mad, Cato, or art thou foolish—or art thou *both*—or art thou *worse* than both? In *this passage* thou hast fairly gone beyond me. I have not language to bring thee back. Thou art safely intrenched indeed! Rest therefore in thy stronghold till *He* who fortified thee in it shall come and fetch thee out.

Cato seems to be possessed of that jesuitical cunning which always endeavours to disgrace what it cannot disprove; and this he sometimes effects, by unfairly introducing *our* terms into *his* arguments, and thereby begets a monster which he sends round the country for a show, and tells the good people that the name of it is *independance*.

Of this character are several passages in his fourth and fifth letters, particularly when he quotes the term "*foreign assistance*," which he ungenerously explains into a surrender of the Continent to France and Spain.   Such an unfair and sophistical reasoner doth not deserve the civility of good manners.   He creates, likewise, the same confusion by frequently using the word *peace* for *union*, and thereby charges us falsely by representing us as being determined to "reject all proposition of *peace*."   Whereas, our wish is *peace* but *not re-union;* and though we would gladly listen to the former, we are determined to resist every proposal for the latter, *come from where it will;* being fully persuaded, that in the present state of affairs *separation of governments is the only and best thing that can be done for both countries.*

The following case is unjustly put.   "There never was a war," says Cato, "so implacable, even among states naturally rivals and enemies, or among savages themselves, as not to have *peace* for its object as well as the end."   But was there ever a war, Cato, which had *union* for its object?   No.   What Cato means by states naturally rivals and enemies, I shall not enquire into, but this I know (for myself at least) that it was not in the power of France or Spain, or all the other powers in Europe, to have given such a wound, or raised us to such a mortal hatred as Britain hath done.   We feel the same kind of undescribed anger at her conduct, as we would at the sight of an animal devouring its young ; and this particular species of anger is not generated in the transitory temper of the man, but in the chaste and undefiled womb of nature.

Cato, towards the conclusion of his third letter, (at which place I shall leave him for the present,) compares the state of Britain and America to the quarrels of lovers, and from thence infers a probability, that our affections will be renewed thereby.   This I cannot help looking on as one of the most unnatural and distorted similes that can be drawn.   Come hither ye that are lovers, or ye that *have been* lovers, and decide the controversy between us !   What comparison is there between the soft murmurs of an heart mourning in secret, and the loud horrors of war—between the silent tears of pensive sorrow, and rivers of wasted blood—between the *sweet* strife of affection, and the *bitter* strife of death—between the curable calamities of pettish lovers, and the sad sight of a thousand slain! " Get thee behind me," Cato, for thou hast not the feelings of a man.

THE FORESTER.

PHILADELPHIA, April 8, 1776.

III.

TO CATO.

CATO'S partizans may call me furious ; I regard it not. There are men, too, who have not virtue enough to be angry and that crime perhaps is Cato's.   He who dares not offend cannot be honest.   Having thus balanced the charge, I proceed to Cato's 4th, 5th, 6th, and 7th letters, all of which, as they contain but little matter, I shall dismiss with as little trouble and less formality.

His fourth letter is introduced with a punning Soliloquy—Cato's title to soliloquies is indisputable ; because no man cares for his company.*   However, he disowns the writing it, and assures his readers that it " was *really* put into his hands."   I always consider this confirming mode of expression as betraying a suspicion of one's self; and in this place it amounts to just as much as if Cato had said, "you know my *failing*, Sirs, but what I tell you now is really true." Well, be it so, Cato ; you shall have all the credit you ask for ; and as to when or where or how you got it, who was the author, or who the giver, I shall not enquire after ; being fully convinced, by the poetical merit of the performance, that tho' the writer of it may be an *Allen*,[1] he 'll never be a Ramsay.†   Thus much for the soliloquy ; and if this gentle

---

* *As this piece may possibly fall into the hands of some who are not acquainted with the word Soliloquy, for their information the sense of it is given, viz. " talking to one's self."—Author.*

[1] Allen was a prominent opponent of Independence in Philadelphia.—*Editor.*

† Allan Ramsay a famous Scotch poet of genuine wit and humour.—*Author.*

chastisement should be the means of preventing Cato or his colleague from mingling their punning nonsense with subjects of such a serious nature as the present one truly is, it will answer *one* of the ends it was intended for.

Cato's fourth, and the greatest part of his fifth letter, are constructed on a false meaning uncivilly imposed on a passage quoted from *Common Sense ;* and for which, the author of that pamphlet hath a right to expect from Cato the usual concessions. I shall quote the passage entire, with Cato's additional meaning, and the inferences which he draws therefrom. He introduces it with saying, " In my remarks on the pamphlet before me I shall first consider those arguments on which, he (the author) appears to lay his chief stress ; and these are collected under four heads in his conclusion, one of which is, ' *It is the custom of nations when any two are at war, for some other powers not engaged in the quarrel, to step in by way of Mediators, and bring about the prelimenaries of a peace ; but while America calls herself the subject of Great-Britain, no power, however well disposed she may be, can offer her mediation.'* " The meaning contained in this passage is so exceedingly plain, and expressed in such easy and familiar terms, that it scarcely admits of being made plainer. No one, I think, could have understood it any other wise, than that while we continue to call ourselves British Subjects, the quarrel between us can only be called a *family quarrel,* in which, it would be just as indelicate for any other nation to advise, or any ways to meddle or make, even with their offers of mediation, as it would be for a third person to interfere in a quarrel between a man and his wife. Whereas were we to make use of that natural right which all other nations have done before us, and erect a government of our own, *independant of all the world,* the quarrel could then be no longer called a *family quarrel,* but a regular war between the two powers of Britain and America, in the same manner as one carried on between England and France ; and in this state of political separation, the neutral powers might kindly render their mediation, (as hath always been the practice) and bring about the preliminaries of a *peace*,—not a *union*, Cato, that is quite another thing. But instead of Cato's taking it in this easy and natural sense, he flies away on a wrong scent, *charges the author with proposing to call in foreign assistance ;* and under this willful falsehood raises up a mighty cry after nothing at all. He begins his wild and unintelligible comment in the following manner : " Is this," says he, (meaning the passage already quoted) "*common sense*, or *common nonsense ?* Surely peace * with Great Britain cannot be the object of this writer, after the horrible character he has given of the people of that country, and telling us, that reconciliation with them would be our ruin. The latter part of the paragraph seems to cast some light upon the former, although it contradicts it, for these mediators are not to interfere for making up the quarrel, but to widen it by supporting us in a declaration, That we are not the subjects of Great Britain. A new sort of business truly for mediators. But this," continues Cato, " leads us directly to the *main enquiry—What foreign power is able to give us this support ?* " What support, Cato ? The passage you have quoted neither says a syllable, nor insinuates a hint about support :—It speaks *only* of neutral powers in the neighbourly character of mediators between those which are at war ; and says it is the custom of European courts to do so. Cato hath already raised Commissioners into Ambassadors ; but how he could transform mediators into men in arms, and mediation into military alliance, is surpassingly strange. Read the part over again, Cato ; if you find I have charged you wrongfully, and will point it out, I will engage that the author of *Common Sense* shall ask your pardon in the public papers, with his name to it : but if the error be yours, the concession on your part follows as a duty.

Though I am fully persuaded that Cato does not believe one half of what himself has written, he nevertheless takes amazing pains to *frighten* his readers into a belief of the whole. Tells them of foreign troops (which he supposes we

---

* It is a strange thing that Cato cannot be taught to distinguish between peace and union.—*Author.*

are going to send for) ravaging up and down the country;
of their "bloody massacres, unrelenting persecutions, which
would *harrow up* (says he) *the very souls of protestants and
freemen.*"   Were they coming, Cato, which no one ever
dreamed of but yourself (for thank God, we want them not,)
it would be impossible for them to exceed, or even to equal,
the cruelties practised by the British army in the East-Indies : The tying men to the mouths of cannon and "*blowing them away*" was never acted by any but an English General, or approved by any but a British Court.*   Read the
proceedings of the Select Committee on Indian Affairs.

From temporal fears Cato proceeds to spiritual ones, and
in a hypocritical panic, asks, "To whose share will Pennsylvania fall—that of his most Catholic, or his most Christian
King ?   I confess," continues he, "that these questions
stagger me."   I don't wonder at it, Cato—I am glad to
hear that some kind of remorse hath overtaken you—that
you begin to *feel* that you are "heavy laden."   You have
had a long run, and the stoutest heart must fail at last.

Cato perceiving that the falsehoods in his fourth letter past
unreproved, ventured boldly on a fifth, in which he continues,
enlarging on the same convenient bugbear.   "In my last,"
says he, "some notice was taken of the dangerous proposition held up by the author of *Common Sense*, for having recourse to foreign assistance."   When will Cato learn to
speak the truth !   The assistance which we hope for from
France is not armies, (we want them not) but arms and
ammunition.   We have already received into this province
only, near two hundred tons of saltpetre and gunpowder,
besides muskets.   Surely we may continue to cultivate a
useful acquaintance, without such malevolent beings as Cato
raising his barbarous slander thereon.   At *this time* it is not
only illiberal, but impolitic, and perhaps dangerous to be
pouring forth such torrents of abuse, as his fourth and fifth
letters contain, against the only power that in articles of
defence hath supplied our hasty wants.

* Lord Clive, the chief of Eastern plunderers, received the thanks of Parliament for " his honourable conduct in the East-Indies.—*Author.*

Cato, after expending near two letters in beating down an idol which himself *only* had set up, proudly congratulates himself on the defeat, and marches off to new exploits, leaving behind him the following proclamation: " Having thus," says Cato, " *dispatched* his (the author of *Common Sense's*) *main argument for independence*, which he founds on the necessity of calling in *foreign assistance*, I proceed to examine some other parts of his work." Not a syllable, Cato, doth any part of the pamphlet in question say of calling in foreign assistance, or even forming military alliances. The dream is wholly your own, and is directly repugnant both to the letter and spirit of every page in the piece. The idea which *Common Sense* constantly holds up, is to have nothing to do with the political affairs of Europe. " As Europe," says the pamphlet, " is our market for trade, we ought to form no political connections with *any part of it. It is the true interest of America to steer clear of all Euro-pean contentions.*" And where it proposes sending a mani-festo to foreign courts (which it is high time to do) it recommends it only for the purpose of announcing to them the *impossibility of our living any longer under the British government, and of "assuring such Courts of our peaceable disposition towards them, and of our desire of entering into trade with them."* Learn to be an honest man, Cato, and then thou wilt not be thus exposed.—I have been the more particular in detecting Cato here, because it is on this *bubble* that his air-built battery against independance is raised—a poor foundation indeed! which even the point of a pin, or a pen, if you please, can demolish with a touch, and bury the formidable Cato beneath the ruins of a vapour.

From this part of his fifth letter to the end of his seventh he entirely deserts the subject of independance, and sets up the proud standard of Kings, in preference to a Republican form of Government. My remarks on this part of the sub-ject will be general and concise.

In this part of the debate Cato shelters himself chiefly in quotations from other authors, without reasoning much on the matter himself; * in answer to which, I present him with a string of maxims and reflexions, drawn from the nature of things, without borrowing from any one. Cato may observe, that I scarcely ever quote; the reason is, I always think. But to return.

Government should always be considered as a matter of convenience, not of right. The scripture institutes no particular form of government, but it enters a protest against the monarchical form; and a negation on *one* thing, where *two only* are offered, and *one* must be chosen, amounts to an affirmative on the *other*. Monarchical government was first set up by the Heathens, and the Almighty permitted it to the Jews as a punishment. " *I gave them a King in mine anger.*" —Hosea xiii. 11. A Republican form of government is pointed out by nature—Kingly governments by an unequality of power. In Republican governments, the leaders of the people, if improper, are removable by vote; Kings only by arms: an unsuccessful vote in the first case, leaves the voter safe; but an unsuccessful attempt in the latter, is death. Strange, that that which is our *right* in the *one*, should be our *ruin* in the *other*. From which reflexion follows this maxim. That that mode of government in which our *right* becomes our ruin, cannot be the *right one*. If all human nature be corrupt, it is needless to strengthen the corruption by establishing a succession of Kings, who, be they ever so base, are still to be obeyed; for the manners of a court will always have an influence over the morals of a people. A Republican government hath more *true grandeur* in it than a Kingly one. On the part of the public it is

---

* *The following is an instance of Cato's method of conducting an argument :* " *If hereditary succession, says* Common Sense, *(meaning succession of monarchial governments) did ensure a race of good and wise men, it would have the seal of divine authority ;*" "thus we find him," says Cato, " with his own hand affixing the seal of heaven to what he before told us the Devil invented and the Almighty entered his protest against." *Cato's 7th letter.—This is a strange argument indeed, Cato, or rather it is no argument at all, for hereditary succession does not ensure a race of good and wise men, consequently has not the seal of divine authority.*"—A*uthor.*

more consistent with freemen to appoint their rulers than to have them born; and on the part of those who preside, it is far nobler to be a ruler by the choice of the people, than a King by the chance of birth. Every honest Delegate is more than a Monarch. Disorders will unavoidably happen in all states, but monarchical governments are the most subject thereto, because the balance hangs uneven. "*Nineteen rebellions and eight civil wars in England since the conquest.*" Whatever commotions are produced in Republican states, are not produced by a Republican spirit, but by those who seek to extinguish it. A Republican state cannot produce its own destruction, it can only suffer it. No nation of people, in their true senses, when seriously reflecting on the rank which God hath given them, and the reasoning faculties he hath blessed them with, would ever, of their own consent, give any *one man* a negative power over the whole: No man since the fall hath ever been equal to the trust, wherefore 'tis insanity in us to entrust them with it; and in this sense, all those who have had it have done us right by abusing us into reason. Nature seems sometimes to laugh at mankind, by giving them so many fools for Kings; at other times, she punishes their folly by giving them tyrants; but England must have offended highly to be curst with both in one. *Rousseau* proposed a plan for establishing a perpetual European peace; which was, for every State in Europe to send Ambassadors to form a General Council, and when any difference happened between any two nations, to refer the matter to arbitration instead of going to arms. This would be forming a kind of European Republic: But the proud and plundering spirit of Kings hath not peace for its object. They look not at the good of mankind. They set not out upon that plan: And if the history of the Creation and the history of Kings be compared together the result will be this—that God hath made a world, and Kings have robbed him of it.

But that which sufficiently establishes the Republican mode of government, in preference to a Kingly one, even when all other arguments are left out, is this simple truth, that all men are Republicans by nature, and Royalists only by fashion. And this is fully proved by that passionate adoration which all men shew to that great and almost only remaining bulwark of natural rights, *trial by juries*, which is founded on a pure Republican basis. Here the power of Kings is shut out. No Royal negative can enter this Court. The Jury, which is here supreme, is a *Republic*, a body of *Judges chosen from among the people.*

The charter which secures this freedom in England, was formed, not in the senate, but in the field; and insisted on by the people, not granted by the crown; the crown in that instance *granted nothing*, but only renounced its former tyrannies, and bound itself over to its future good behaviour. It was the compromise, by which the wearer of it made his peace with the people, and the condition on which he was suffered to reign.

Here ends my reply to all the letters which have at present appeared under the signature of Cato, being at this time seven in number. I have made no particular remarks on his last two, which treat only of the mode of government, but answered them generally. In one place I observe, he accuses the writer of *Common Sense* with inconsistency in having declared, " That no man was a warmer wisher for reconciliation than himself, before the fatal 19th of April, 1775 " [1]; "that is," (says Cato) reconciliation to monarchical government." To which I reply that *war* ought to be no man's *wish*, neither ought any man to perplex a state, already formed, with his private opinions; "the mode of government being a proper consideration for those countries " only "which have their governments yet to form." (*Common Sense*).

On a review of the ground which I have gone over in Cato's letters, (exclusive of what I have omitted) I find the following material charges against him:

First. He hath accused the Committee with crimes generally; stated none, nor proved, nor attempted to prove any.

[1] The " Massacre at Lexington," as it was generally called.—*Editor.*

N. B. The pretence of charging the acts of a body of men on individuals, is too slender to be admitted.*

Secondly. He hath falsely complained to the public of the restraint of the press.

Thirdly. He hath wickedly asserted that "gleams of reconciliation hath lately broken in upon us," thereby grossly deceiving the people.

Fourthly. He hath insinuated, as if he wished the public to believe, that we had *received* "the utmost assurance of having all our grievances redressed, and an ample security against any future violation of our just rights."

Fifthly. He hath spread false alarms of calling in foreign troops.

Sixthly. He hath turned the scripture into a jest.   Ez. 35.

These falsehoods, if uncontradicted, might have passed for truths, and the minds of persons remote from better intelligence might have been greatly embarrassed thereby.   Let our opinions be what they will, truth as to facts should be strictly adhered to.   It was this affecting consideration that drew out the *Forester* (a perfect volunteer) to the painful task of writing three long letters, and occasioned to the public the trouble of reading them.

Having for the present closed my correspondence with Cato, I shall conclude this letter with a well meant affectionate address

To the People.

It is not a time to trifle.   Men, who know they deserve nothing from their country, and whose hope is on the arm that hath fought to enslave ye, may hold out to you, as Cato hath done, the false light of reconciliation.   There is no such

---

* Cato and I differ materially in our opinion of Committees ; I consider them as the only constitutional bodies at present in this province, and that for the following reason ; they were duly elected by the people, and chearfully do the service for which they were elected.   The House of Assembly were likewise elected by the people, but do the business for which they were not elected. Their authority is truly unconstitutional, being self-created.   My charge is as a body, and not as individuals.—*Author*.   The Committee referred to is that mentioned in a note to the Forester's first letter, p. 129.—*Editor*.

thing. 'Tis gone! 'Tis past! The grave hath parted us —and death, in the persons of the slain, hath cut the thread of life between Britain and America.

Conquest, and not reconciliation is the plan of Britain. But admitting even the last hope of the Tories to happen, which is, that our enemies after a long succession of losses, wearied and disabled, should despairingly throw down their arms and propose a re-union; in that case, what is to be done? Are defeated and disappointed tyrants to be considered like mistaken and converted friends? Or would it be right, to receive those for Governors, who, had they been conquerors, would have hung us up for traitors? Certainly not. Reject the offer then, and propose another; which is, *we will make peace with you as with enemies, but we will never re-unite with you as friends.* This effected, and ye secure to yourselves the pleasing prospect of an eternal peace. America, remote from all the wrangling world, may live at ease. Bounded by the ocean, and backed by the wilderness, who hath she to fear, but her GOD?

Be not deceived. It is not a little that is at stake. Reconciliation will not now go down, even if it were offered. 'Tis a dangerous question; for the eyes of all men begin to open. There is now no secret in the matter; there ought to be none. It is a case that concerns every man, and every man ought to lay it to heart. He that *is* here and he that was *born* here are alike concerned. It is needless, too, to split the business into a thousand parts, and perplex it with endless and fruitless investigations, in the manner that a writer signed a *Common Man* hath done. This unparalleled contention of nations is not to be settled like a schoolboy's task of pounds, shillings, pence, and fractions. That writer, though he may mean well, is strangely below the mark: for the first and great question, and that which involves every other in it, and from which every other will flow, is *happiness*. Can this continent be happy under the government of Great Britain or not? Secondly, Can she be happy under a government of our own? To live beneath the authority of those whom we cannot love, is misery, slavery, or what name you please.　In that case, there will never be peace. Security will be a thing unknown, because a treacherous friend in power is the most dangerous of enemies.　The answer to the second question, Can America be happy under a government of her own, is short and simple, viz. As happy as she please; she hath a blank sheet to write upon.　Put it not off too long.*

Painful as the task of speaking truth must sometimes be, yet I cannot avoid giving the following hint, because much, nay almost every thing depends upon it; and that is, *a thorough knowledge of the persons whom we trust.*　It is the duty of the public, at this time, to scrutinize closely into the conduct of their Committee Members, Members of Assembly, and Delegates in Congress; to know what they do, and their motives for so doing.　Without doing this, we shall never know who to confide in; but shall constantly mistake friends for enemies, and enemies for friends, till in the confusion of persons we sacrifice the cause.　I am led to this reflexion by the following circumstance.　That the Gentleman to whom the unwise and arbitrary instructions to the Delegates of this province owe their being, and who hath bestowed all his power to support them, is said to be the same person who, when the ships now on the stocks were wanting timber, *refused to sell it,* and thus by preventing our strength to cry out of our insufficiency.—But his hour of fame is past—he is hastening to his political exit.

THE FORESTER.

IV.

WHOEVER will take the trouble of attending to the progress and changeability of times and things, and the conduct of mankind thereon, will find, that *extraordinary circumstances* do sometimes arise before us, of a species, either so purely natural or so perfectly original, that none but the man of

----

* Forget not the hapless African.—*Author.*

nature can understand them.   When precedents fail to spirit
us, we must return to the first principles of things for information; and *think*, as if we were the *first men* that *thought*.
And this is the true reason that, in the present state of affairs,
the wise are become foolish, and the foolish wise.   I am led
to this reflexion by not being able to account for the conduct of the Quakers on any other: for although they do not
seem to perceive it themselves, yet it is amazing to hear with
what unanswerable ignorance many of that body, wise in
other matters, will discourse on the present one.   Did they
hold places or commissions under the King, were they Governors of provinces, or had they any interest apparently distinct from us, the mystery would cease; but as they have
not, their folly is best attributed to that superabundance of
worldly knowledge which in original matters is too cunning to
be wise.   Back to the first plain path of nature, friends, and
begin anew: for in this business your first footsteps were
wrong.   You have now travelled to the summit of inconsistency, and that with such accelerated rapidity as to acquire
autumnal ripeness by the first of May.   Now your *resting
time* comes on.   You have done your utmost and must abide
the consequences.   Yet who can reflect on such conduct
without feeling concern!   Who can look, unaffected, on a
body of *thoughtful* men, undoing in *one rash hour* the labour
of seventy years: Or what can be said in their excuse, more,
than that they have arrived at their second childhood, the
infancy of threescore and ten.*

   But my chief design, in this letter, is to set forth the inconsistency, partiality, and injustice of the *dependant faction,*[1]

---

   * *The Quakers in 1704 who then made up the whole house of assembly* [in Penn-
sylvania] *zealously guarded their own and the people's rights against the encroach-
ing power of the Proprietor, who nevertheless submitted them by finding means to
abolish the original charter and introduce another, of which they complained in the
following words.   " And then by a subtle contrivance and artifice, ' of thine,'
laid deeper than the capacities of some could fathom, or the circumstances of many
could admit time to consider of, a way was found out to lay the first charter aside
and introduce another."—Query.   Would these men have elected the proprietary
persons which you have done ?—Author.*

   [1] Opponents of American Independence.—*Editor.*

and like an honest man, who courts no favor, to shew to them the dangerous ground they stand upon; in order to do which, I must refer to the *business, event,* and *probable consequences* of the late election.

The business of that day was to do what? Why, to elect four burgesses to assist those already elected, in conducting the military proceedings of this province, against the power of *that crown* by whose authority they pretend to sit: and those gentlemen when elected, are according to the rules of that House (as the rest have done) to take an oath of allegiance to serve the same King against whom this province, with themselves at the head thereof, are at war: and a necessary qualification required of many voters was, that they likewise should swear allegiance to the same King against whose power the same house of assembly had just before obliged them either to fine or take up arms. Did ever national hypocrisy arise to such a pitch as this! Under the pretence of moderation we are running into the most damnable sins. It is now the duty of every man from the pulpit and from the press, in his family and in the street to cry out against it. Good God! Have we no remembrance of duty left to the King of Heaven! No conscientious awe to restrain this sacrifice of sacred things? Is this our chartered privilege? This our boasted constitution, that we can sin and feel it not? The clergy of the English church, of which I profess myself a member, complain of *their* situation, and wish relief; in short, every *thinking man* must feel distress. Yet, to the credit of the people be it spoken, the sin lies not at their door. We can trace the iniquity in this province to the fountain head, and see by what delusions it has imposed on others. The guilt centres in a few, and flows from the same source, that a few years ago avariciously suffered the frontiers of this province to be deluged in blood; and though the vengeance of Heaven hath slept since, it may awake too soon for their repose.

A motion was sometime ago made to elect a convention to take into consideration the state of the province. A more judicious proposal could not be thought of. Our pres-

ent condition is alarming.   We are worse off then other
provinces, and such an enquiry is highly necessary.   The
House of Assembly in its present form is disqualified for
such business, because it is a branch from that power against
whom we are contending.   Besides, they are in intercourse with the King's representative, and the members
which compose the house have, as *members thereof* taken an
oath to discover to the King of England the very business
which, in that inquiry, would unavoidably come before them.
Their minds too are warped and prejudiced by the provincial instructions they have arbitrarily and without right issued forth.   They are again improper because the enquiry
would necessarily *extend to them as a body*, to see how far it
is proper to trust men with such unlimited power as they
have lately assumed.   In times like these, we must trace to
the root and origin of things; It being the only way to become right, when we are got systematically wrong.   The
motion for a Convention alarmed the crown and proprietary
dependants;[1] but, to every man of reflexion, it had a cordial
and restorative quality.   The case is, first, we are got wrong—
Secondly, how shall we get right?   Not by a House of
Assembly ; because *they* cannot sit as *Judges, in a case*, where
their *own existence* under their *present form and authority is
to be judged of.*   However, the objectors found out a way,
as they thought, to supercede the necessity of a Convention,
by promoting a bill for augmenting the number of representatives ; not perceiving at the same time that such an
augmentation would *encrease* the *necessity* of a Convention ;
because, the more any power is augmented, which derives
it's authority from our enemies, the more unsafe and dangerous it becomes to us.   Far be it from the writer of this to
censure the individuals which compose that House ; his aim
being only against the chartered authority under which it
acts.   However, the bill passed into a law, (which shews,
that in Pennsylvania, as well as in England, there is *no constitution*, but only *a temporary form of government.**)   While,

---

[1] Opponents of American Independence.—*Editor.*

* *This distinction will be more fully explained in some future letter.—Author.*

in order to show the inconsistency of the House in its present state, the motion for a convention was postponed, and four conscientious independent gentlemen were proposed as candidates, on the augmentation, who, had they been elected would not have taken the oaths necessary to admit a person as member of that Assembly. And in that case, the house would have had neither one kind of authority or another, while the old part remained sworn to divulge to the King what the new part thought it their duty to declare against him. Thus matters stood on the morning of election.

On our side we had to sustain the loss of those good citizens who are now before the walls of Quebec, and other parts of the continent; while the tories by never stirring out remain at home to take the advantage of elections; and this evil prevails more or less from the Congress down to the Committees. A numerous body of Germans of property, zealots in the cause of freedom, were likewise excluded for non-allegiance. Notwithstanding which, the tory non-conformists, that is those who are advertised as enemies to their country, were admitted to vote on the other side. A strange contradiction indeed! To which were added the testimonizing Quakers, who, after suffering themselves to be duped by the meanest of all passions, religious spleen, endeavour in a vague uncharitable manner to possess the Roman Catholics of the same disease. These parties, with such others as they could influence, were headed by the proprietary dependants to support the British and Proprietary power against the public. They had pompously given out that nine tenths of the people were on their side. A vast majority truly! But it so happened that, notwithstanding the disadvantages we laid under of having many of our votes rejected, others disqualified for non-allegiance, with the great loss sustained by absentees, the manœuvre of shutting up the doors between seven and eight o'clock, and circulating the report of adjourning, and finishing the next morning, by which several were deceived,—it so happened, I say, that on casting up the tickets, the first in numbers on the dependant side, and the first on the independant side, viz. Clymer and Allen, were a tye: 923 each.*

To the description which I have already given of those who are against us, I may add, that they have neither associated nor assisted, or but very few of them ; that they are a collection of different bodies blended by accident, having no natural relation to each other; that they have agreed rather out of spite than right; and that, as they met by chance, they will dissolve away again for the want of a cement.

On our side, our object was *single*, our cause was one; wherefore, we *cannot* separate, neither *will* we separate. We have stood the experiment of the election, for the sake of knowing the men who were against us. Alas, what are they? One half of them ought to be now asking public pardon for their former offences ; and the other half may think themselves well off that they are let alone. When the enemy enters the country, can they defend themselves? Or *will* they defend themselves? And if not, are they so foolish as to think that, in times like these, when it is our duty to search the corrupted wound to the bottom, that we, with ten times their strength and number (if the question were put to the people at large) will submit to be governed by cowards and tories?

He that is wise will reflect, that the safest asylum, especially in times of general convulsion when no settled form of government prevails, is, *the love of the people.* All property is safe under their protection. Even in countries where the lowest and most licentious of them have risen into outrage they have never departed from the path of *natural* honor. Volunteers unto death in defence of the person or fortune of those who had served or defended them, division of property never entered the mind of the populace. It is incompatible with that spirit which impels them into action. An avaricious mob was never heard of ; nay, even a miser pausing in the midst of them, and catching their spirit, would from that instant cease to be covetous.

* *Mr. Samuel Howell, though in their ticket, was never considered by us a proprietary dependant.—Author.*

I shall conclude this letter with remarking, that the English fleet and army have of late gone upon a different plan of operation to what they first set out with ; for instead of going against those Colonies where independence prevails *most*, they go against *those only* where they suppose it prevails *least*. They have quitted Massachusetts-Bay and gone to North-Carolina, supposing they had many friends there. Why are they expected at New-York? But because they imagine the inhabitants are *not* generally independents, (yet that province hath a large share of virtue, notwithstanding the odium which its House of Assembly brought upon it.) From which I argue that the electing the King's Attorney for a Burgess of this city, is a fair invitation for them to come here ; and in that case, will those who have invited them turn out to repulse them ? I suppose not, for in their 923 votes there will not be found more than sixty armed men, perhaps not so many. Wherefore, should such an event happen, which probably will, I here give my *first vote* to levy the expence attending the expedition against them, *on the estates of those who have invited them.*

THE FORESTER.

XVIII.

A DIALOGUE[1]

Between the GHOST of General MONTGOMERY just arrived fom the Elysian Fields; and an American DELEGATE, in a wood near PHILADELPHIA.

Delegate. Welcome to this retreat, my good friend. If I mistake not, I now see the ghost of the brave General Montgomery.

General Montgomery. I am glad to see you. I still love liberty and America, and the contemplation of the future greatness of this Continent now forms a large share of my present happiness. I am here upon an important errand, to warn you against listening to terms of accommodation from the court of Britain.

Del. I shall be happy in receiving instruction from you in the present trying exigency of our public affairs. But suppose the terms you speak of should be just and honorable?

Gen. Mont. How can you expect these, after the King has proclaimed you rebels from the throne, and after both houses of parliament have resolved to support him in carrying on a war against you? No, I see no offers from Great Britain but of PARDON. The very word is an insult upon our cause. To whom is pardon offered?—to virtuous freemen. For what?—for flying to arms in defence of the rights of humanity: And from whom do these offers come?— From a ROYAL CRIMINAL. You have furnished me with a

---

[1] Printed in pamphlet form about the time of the appointment by Congress of a Committee to draft a Declaration of Independence.—*Editor*.

new reason for triumphing in my death, for I had rather have it said that I died by his vengeance, than lived by his mercy.

Del. But you think nothing of the destructive consequences of war. How many cities must be reduced to ashes! how many families must be ruined! and how many widows and orphans must be made, should the present war be continued any longer with Great Britain.

Gen. Mont. I think of nothing but the destructive consequences of slavery. The calamities of war are transitory and confined in their effects. But the calamities of slavery are extensive and lasting in their operation. I love mankind as well as you, and I could never restrain a tear when my love of justice has obliged me to shed the blood of a fellow creature. It is my humanity that makes me urge you against a reconciliation with Great Britain, for if this takes place, nothing can prevent the American Colonies from being the seat of war as often as the King of Great Britain renews his quarrels with any of the Colonies, or with any of the belligerent powers of Europe.

Del. I tremble at the doctrine you have advanced. I see you are for the independence of the Colonies on Great Britain.

Gen. Mont. I am for permanent liberty, peace, and security to the American Colonies.

Del. These can only be maintained by placing the Colonies in the situation they were in the year 1763.

Gen. Mont. And is no satisfaction to be made to the Colonies for the blood and treasure they have expended in resisting the arms of Great Britain? Who can soften the prejudices of the King—the parliament—and the nation, each of whom will be averse to maintain a peace with you in proportion to the advantages you have gained over them? Who shall make restitution to the widows—the mothers— and the children of the men who have been slain by their arms? Can no hand wield the sceptre of government in America except that which has been stained with the blood of your countrymen? For my part if I thought this Continent would ever acknowledge the sovereignty of the Crown of Britain again, I should forever lament the day in which I offered up my life for its salvation.

Del. You should distinguish between the King and his ministers.

Gen. Mont. I live in a world where all political superstition is done away. The King is the author of all the measures carried on against America. The influence of bad ministers is no better apology for these measures, than the influences of bad company is for a murderer, who expiates his crimes under a gallows. You all complain of the corruption of the parliament, and of the venality of the nation, and yet you forget that the Crown is the source of them both. You shun the streams, and yet you are willing to sit down at the very fountain of corruption and venality.

Del. Our distance and charters will protect us from the influence of the crown.

Gen. Mont. Your distance will only render your danger more imminent, and your ruin more irretrievable. Charters are no restraints against the lust of power. The only reason why you have escaped so long is, because the treasure of the nation has been employed for these fifty years in buying up the virtue of Britain and Ireland. Hereafter the reduction of the representatives of the people of America will be the only aim of administration should you continue to be connected with them.

Del. But I foresee many evils from the independence of the Colonies. Our trade will be ruined from the want of a navy to protect it. Each Colony will put in its claim for superiority, and we shall have domestic wars without end.

Gen. Mont. As I now know that Divine Providence intends this country to be the asylum of persecuted virtue from every quarter of the globe, so I think your trade will be the vehicle that will convey it to you. Heaven has furnished you with greater resources for a navy than any nation in the world. Nothing but an ignorance of your strength could have led you to sacrifice your trade for the protection of a foreign navy. A freedom from the restraints of the acts of navigation I foresee will produce such immense additions to the wealth of this country that posterity will wonder that ever you thought your present trade worth its protection. As to the supposed contentions between sister colonies, they have no foundation in truth. But supposing they have, will delaying the independance of the Colonies 50 years prevent them? No—the weakness of the Colonies, which at first produced their union, will always preserve it, 'till it shall be their interest to be separated. Had the Colony of Massachuset's-bay been possessed of the military resources which it would probably have had 50 years hence, would she have held out the signal of distress to her sister colonies, upon the news of the Boston port-bill! No—she would have withstood all the power of Britain alone, and afterwards the neutral colonies might have shared the fate of the colony of Canada. Moreover, had the connection with Great-Britain been continued 50 years longer, the progress of British laws, customs and manners (now totally corrupted) would have been such that the Colonies would have been prepared to welcome slavery. But had it been otherwise, they must have asserted their independance with arms. This is nearly done already. It will be cruel to bequeath another contest to your posterity.

Del. But I dread all innovations in governments. They are very dangerous things.

Gen. Mont. The revolution, which gave a temporary stability to the liberties of Britain, was an innovation in government, and yet no ill consequences have arisen from it. Innovations are dangerous only as they shake the prejudices of a people; but there are now, I believe, but few prejudices to be found in this country, in favor of the old connection with Great-Britain. I except those men only who are under the influence of their passions and offices.

Del. But is it not most natural for us to wish for a connection with a people who speak the same language with us, and possess the same laws, religion, and forms of government with ourselves.

Gen. Mont. The immortal Montesquieu says, that nations

should form alliances with those nations only which are as
unlike to themselves as possible in religion, laws and manners, if they mean to preserve their own constitutions. Your
dependance upon the crown is no advantage, but rather an
injury to the people of Britain, as it increases the power and
influence of the King. The people are benefited only by
your trade, and this they may have after you are independant of the crown. Should you be disposed to forgive the
King and the nation for attempting to enslave you, they
will never forgive you for having baffled them in the
attempt.

Del. But we have many friends in both Houses of
Parliament.

Gen. Mont. You mean the ministry have many enemies
in Parliament who connect the cause of America with their
clamours at the door of administration. Lord Chatham's
conciliatory bill would have ruined you more effectually than
Lord North's motion. The Marquis of Rockingham was
the author of the declaratory bill.[1] Mr. Wilkes has added
infamy to the weakness of your cause, and the Duke of
Grafton and Lord Lyttleton have rendered the minority
junto, if possible, more contemptible than ever.

Del. But if we become independant we shall become a
commonwealth.

Gen. Mont. I maintain that it is your interest to be independant of Great Britain, but I do not recommend any new
form of government to you. I should think it strange that
a people who have virtue enough to defend themselves
against the most powerful nation in the world should want
wisdom to contrive a perfect and free form of government.
You have been kept in subjection to the crown of Britain by
a miracle. Your liberties have hitherto been suspended by a

---

[1] The Act of February, 1766, declaratory of the right of Parliament " to
bind America in all cases whatsoever." In a letter of George III. to Lord
North (February 5, 1778) he remarks that Lord George Germaine " said this
day unto me that the Declaratory Act, though but waste paper, was what galled
them (the Americans) most." (Donne, ii. p. 131.) It was indeed the costliest
bit of waste paper known to history.—*Editor.*

thread. Your connection with Great-Britain is unnatural and unnecessary. All the wheels of a government should move within itself. I would only beg leave to observe to you, that monarchy and aristocracy have in all ages been the vehicles of slavery.

Del. Our governments will want force and authority if we become independant of Great-Britain.

Gen. Mont. I beg leave to contradict that assertion. No royal edicts or acts of assembly have ever been more faithfully or universally obeyed than the resolves of the Congress. I admire the virtue of the colonies, and did not some of them still hang upon the haggard breasts of Great-Britain, I should think the time now come in which they had virtue enough to be happy under any form of government. Remember that it is in a commonwealth only that you can expect to find every man a patriot or a hero. Aristides, Epaminondas, Pericles, Scipio, Camillus, and a thousand other illustrious Grecian and Roman heroes, would never have astonished the world with their names, had they lived under royal governments.

Del. Will not a declaration of independance lessen the number of our friends, and increase the rage of our enemies in Britain?

Gen. Mont. Your friends (as you call them) are too few— too divided—and too interested to help you. And as for your enemies, they have done their worst. They have called upon Russians—Hanoverians—Hessians—Canadians—Savages and Negroes to assist them in burning your towns—desolating your country—and in butchering your wives and children. You have nothing further to fear from them. Go, then, and awaken the Congress to a sense of their importance ; you have no time to lose. France waits for nothing but a declaration of your independance to revenge the injuries they sustained from Britain in the last war. But I forbear to reason any further with you. The decree is finally gone forth. Britain and America are now distinct empires. Your country teems with patriots—heroes—and legislators, who are impatient to burst forth into light and importance. Hereafter your achievements shall no more swell the page of British history. God did not excite the attention of all Europe—of the whole world—nay of angels themselves to the present controversy for nothing. The inhabitants of Heaven long to see the ark finished, in which all the liberty and true religion of the world are to be deposited. The day in which the Colonies declare their independance will be a jubilee to Hampden—Sidney—Russell—Warren—Gardiner—Macpherson—Cheeseman, and all the other heroes who have offered themselves as sacrifices upon the altar of liberty. It was no small mortification to me when I fell upon the Plains of Abraham, to reflect that I did not expire like the brave General Wolfe, in the arms of victory. But I now no longer envy him his glory. I would rather die in *attempting* to obtain permanent freedom for a handful of people, than survive a conquest which would serve only to extend the empire of despotism. A band of heroes now beckon to me. I can only add that America is the theatre where human nature will *soon* receive its greatest military, civil, and literary honours.

XIX.

THE AMERICAN CRISIS.

THOMAS PAINE, in his Will, speaks of this work as *The American Crisis*, remembering perhaps that a number of political pamphlets had appeared in London, 1775–1776, under general title of "The Crisis." By the blunder of an early English publisher of Paine's writings, one essay in the London "Crisis" was attributed to Paine, and the error has continued to cause confusion. This publisher was D. I. Eaton, who printed as the first number of Paine's "Crisis" an essay taken from the London publication. But his prefatory note says: "Since the printing of this book, the publisher is informed that No. 1, or first Crisis in this publication, is not one of the thirteen which Paine wrote, but a letter previous to them." Unfortunately this correction is sufficiently equivocal to leave on some minds the notion that Paine did write the letter in question, albeit not as a number of his "Crisis"; especially as Eaton's editor unwarrantably appended the signature "C. S.," suggesting "Common Sense." There are, however, no such letters in the London essay, which is signed "Casca." It was published August 9, 1775, in the form of a letter to General Gage, in answer to his Proclamation concerning the affair at Lexington. It was certainly not written by Paine. It apologizes for the Americans for having, on April 19, at Lexington, made "an attack upon the King's troops from behind walls and lurking holes." The writer asks : "Have not the Americans been driven to this frenzy? Is it not common for an enemy to take every advantage?" Paine, who was in America when the affair occurred at Lexington, would have promptly denounced Gage's story as a falsehood, but the facts known to every one in America were as yet not before the London writer. The English "Crisis" bears evidence throughout of having been written in London. It derived nothing from Paine, and he derived nothing from it, unless its title, and this is too obvious for its origin to require discussion. I have no doubt, however, that the title was suggested by the English publication, because Paine has followed its scheme in introducing a "Crisis Extraordinary." His work consists of thirteen numbers, and, in addition to these, a "Crisis Extraordinary" and a "Supernumerary Crisis." In some modern collections all of these have been serially numbered, and a brief newspaper article added, making sixteen numbers. But Paine, in his Will, speaks of the number as thirteen, wishing perhaps, in his characteristic way, to adhere to the number of the American Colonies, as he did in the thirteen ribs of his iron bridge. His enumeration is therefore followed in the present volume, and the numbers printed successively, although other writings intervened.

The first "Crisis" was printed in the *Pennsylvania Journal*, December 19, 1776, and opens with the famous sentence, "These are the times that try men's souls"; the last "Crisis" appeared April 19, 1783, (eighth anniversary of the first gun of the war, at Lexington,) and opens with the words, "The times that tried men's souls are over." The great effect produced by Paine's successive publications has been attested by Washington and Franklin, by every leader of the American Revolution, by resolutions of Congress, and by every contemporary historian of the events amid which they were written. The first "Crisis" is of especial historical interest. It was written during the retreat of Washington across the Delaware, and by order of the Commander was read to groups of his dispirited and suffering soldiers. Its opening sentence was adopted as the watchword of the movement on Trenton, a few days after its publication, and is believed to have inspired much of the courage which won that victory, which, though not imposing in extent, was of great moral effect on Washington's little army.

THE CRISIS.

I.

THESE are the times that try men's souls. The summer soldier and the sunshine patriot will, in this crisis, shrink from the service of their country; but he that stands it *now*, deserves the love and thanks of man and woman. Tyranny, like hell, is not easily conquered; yet we have this consolation with us, that the harder the conflict, the more glorious the triumph. What we obtain too cheap, we esteem too lightly: it is dearness only that gives every thing its value. Heaven knows how to put a proper price upon its goods; and it would be strange indeed if so celestial an article as FREEDOM should not be highly rated. Britain, with an army to enforce her tyranny, has declared that she has a right (*not only to* TAX) but "to BIND *us in* ALL CASES WHATSO-EVER," and if being *bound in that manner*, is not slavery, then is there not such a thing as slavery upon earth. Even the expression is impious; for so unlimited a power can belong only to God.

Whether the independence of the continent was declared too soon, or delayed too long, I will not now enter into as an argument; my own simple opinion is, ·that had it been eight months earlier, it would have been much better. We did not make a proper use of last winter, neither could we, while we were in a dependant state. However, the fault, if it were one, was all our own *; we have none to blame but

* The present winter is worth an age, if rightly employed; but, if lost or neglected, the whole continent will partake of the evil; and there is no punishment that man does not deserve, be he who, or what, or where he will, that may be the means of sacrificing a season so precious and useful.—*Author's* note,—a citation from his "Common Sense."

ourselves. But no great deal is lost yet. All that Howe has been doing for this month past, is rather a ravage than a conquest, which the spirit of the Jerseys, a year ago, would have quickly repulsed, and which time and a little resolution will soon recover.

I have as little superstition in me as any man living, but my secret opinion has ever been, and still is, that God Almighty will not give up a people to military destruction, or leave them unsupportedly to perish, who have so earnestly and so repeatedly sought to avoid the calamities of war, by every decent method which wisdom could invent. Neither have I so much of the infidel in me, as to suppose that He has relinquished the government of the world, and given us up to the care of devils; and as I do not, I cannot see on what grounds the king of Britain can look up to heaven for help against us: a common murderer, a highwayman, or a house-breaker, has as good a pretence as he.

'Tis surprising to see how rapidly a panic will sometimes run through a country. All nations and ages have been subject to them: Britain has trembled like an ague at the report of a French fleet of flat bottomed boats; and in the fourteenth [fifteenth] century the whole English army, after ravaging the kingdom of France, was driven back like men petrified with fear; and this brave exploit was performed by a few broken forces collected and headed by a woman, Joan of Arc. Would that heaven might inspire some Jersey maid to spirit up her countrymen, and save her fair fellow sufferers from ravage and ravishment! Yet panics, in some cases, have their uses; they produce as much good as hurt. Their duration is always short; the mind soon grows through them, and acquires a firmer habit than before. But their · peculiar advantage is, that they are the touchstones of sincerity and hypocrisy, and bring things and men to light, which might otherwise have lain forever undiscovered. In fact, they have the same effect on secret traitors, which an imaginary apparition would have upon a private murderer. They sift out the hidden thoughts of man, and hold them up in public to the world. Many a disguised tory has lately shown his head, that shall penitentially solemnize with curses the day on which Howe arrived upon the Delaware.

As I was with the troops at Fort Lee, and marched with them to the edge of Pennsylvania, I am well acquainted with many circumstances, which those who live at a distance know but little or nothing of. Our situation there was exceedingly cramped, the place being a narrow neck of land between the North River and the Hackensack. Our force was inconsiderable, being not one fourth so great as Howe could bring against us. We had no army at hand to have relieved the garrison, had we shut ourselves up and stood on our defence. Our ammunition, light artillery, and the best part of our stores, had been removed, on the apprehension that Howe would endeavor to penetrate the Jerseys, in which case fort Lee could be of no use to us; for it must occur to every thinking man, whether in the army or not, that these kind of field forts are only for temporary purposes, and last in use no longer than the enemy directs his force against the particular object, which such forts are raised to defend. Such was our situation and condition at fort Lee on the morning of the 20th of November, when an officer arrived with information that the enemy with 200 boats had landed about seven miles above : Major General [Nathaniel] Green, who commanded the garrison, immediately ordered them under arms, and sent express to General Washington at the town of Hackensack, distant by the way of the ferry = six miles. Our first object was to secure the bridge over the Hackensack, which laid up the river between the enemy and us, about six miles from us, and three from them. General Washington arrived in about three quarters of an hour, and marched at the head of the troops towards the bridge, which place I expected we should have a brush for; however, they did not choose to dispute it with us, and the greatest part of our troops went over the bridge, the rest over the ferry, except some which passed at a mill on a small creek, between the bridge and the ferry, and made their way through some marshy grounds up to the town of Hackensack, and there passed the river. We brought off as much baggage as the wagons could contain, the rest was lost. The simple object was to bring off the garrison, and march them on till they could be strengthened by the Jersey or Pennsylvania militia, so as to be enabled to make a stand. We staid four days at Newark, collected our out-posts with some of the Jersey militia, and marched out twice to meet the enemy, on being informed that they were advancing, though our numbers were greatly inferior to theirs. Howe, in my little opinion, committed a great error in generalship in not throwing a body of forces off from Staten Island through Amboy, by which means he might have seized all our stores· at Brunswick, and intercepted our march into Pennsylvania ; but if we believe the power of hell to be limited, we must likewise believe that their agents are under some providential controul.

I shall not now attempt to give all the particulars of our retreat to the Delaware ; suffice it for the present to say, that both officers and men, though greatly harassed and fatigued, frequently without rest, covering, or provision, the inevitable consequences of a long retreat, bore it with a manly and martial spirit. All their wishes centred in one, which was, that the country would turn out and help them to drive the enemy back. Voltaire has remarked that king William never appeared to full advantage but in difficulties and in action ; the same remark may be made on General Washington, for the character fits him. There is a natural firmness in some minds which cannot be unlocked by trifles, but which, when unlocked, discovers a cabinet of fortitude ; and I reckon it among those kind of public blessings, which we do not immediately see, that God hath blessed him with uninterrupted health, and given him a mind that can even flourish upon care.

I shall conclude this paper with some miscellaneous remarks on the state of our affairs ; and shall begin with asking the following question, Why is it that the enemy have left the New-England provinces, and made these middle ones the seat of war ? The answer is easy : New-England is not infested with tories, and we are. I have been tender in raising the cry against these men, and used numberless arguments to show them their danger, but it will not do to sacrifice a world either to their folly or their baseness. The period is now arrived, in which either they or we must change our sentiments, or one or both must fall. And what is a tory? Good God! what is he? I should not be afraid to go with a hundred whigs against a thousand tories, were they to attempt to get into arms. Every tory is a coward; for servile, slavish, self-interested fear is the foundation of toryism; and a man under such influence, though he may be cruel, never can be brave.

But, before the line of irrecoverable separation be drawn between us, let us reason the matter together: Your conduct is an invitation to the enemy, yet not one in a thousand of you has heart enough to join him. Howe is as much deceived by you as the American cause is injured by you. He expects you will all take up arms, and flock to his standard, with muskets on your shoulders. Your opinions are of no use to him, unless you support him personally, for 'tis soldiers, and not tories, that he wants.

I once felt all that kind of anger, which a man ought to feel, against the mean principles that are held by the tories: a noted one, who kept a tavern at Amboy, [1] was standing at his door, with as pretty a child in his hand, about eight or nine years old, as I ever saw, and after speaking his mind as freely as he thought was prudent, finished with this unfatherly expression, " *Well! give me peace in my day.*" Not a man lives on the continent but fully believes that a separation must some time or other finally take place, and a generous parent should have said, " *If there must be trouble, let it be in my day, that my child may have peace ;* " and this single reflection, well applied, is sufficient to awaken every man to duty. Not a place upon earth might be so happy as America. Her situation is remote from all the wrangling world, and she has nothing to do but to trade with them. A

---

[1] Early in August, 1776, Paine enlisted in a Pennsylvania division of the Flying Camp, under Gen. Roberdeau, and was first stationed at Amboy, New Jersey.—*Editor.*

man can distinguish himself between temper and principle, and I am as confident, as I am that God governs the world, that America will never be happy till she gets clear of foreign dominion.   Wars, without ceasing, will break out till that period arrives, and the continent must in the end be conqueror ; for though the flame of liberty may sometimes cease to shine, the coal can never expire.

America did not, nor does not want force ; but she wanted a proper application of that force.   Wisdom is not the purchase of a day, and it is no wonder that we should err at the first setting off.   From an excess of tenderness, we were unwilling to raise an army, and trusted our cause to the temporary defence of a well-meaning militia.   A summer's experience has now taught us better ; yet with those troops, while they were collected, we were able to set bounds to the progress of the enemy, and, thank God ! they are again assembling.   I always considered militia as the best troops in the world for a sudden exertion, but they will not do for a long campaign.   Howe, it is probable, will make an attempt on this city ; [1] should he fail on this side the Delaware, he is ruined : if he succeeds, our cause is not ruined.   He stakes all on his side against a part on ours ; admitting he succeeds, the consequence will be, that armies from both ends of the continent will march to assist their suffering friends in the middle states ; for he cannot go everywhere, it is impossible. I consider Howe as the greatest enemy the tories have ; he is bringing a war into their country, which, had it not been for him and partly for themselves, they had been clear of.   Should he now be expelled, I wish with all the devotion of a Christian, that the names of whig and tory may never more be mentioned ; but should the tories give him encouragement to come, or assistance if he come, I as sincerely wish that our next year's arms may expel them from the continent, and the congress appropriate their possessions to the relief of those who have suffered in well-doing.   A single successful battle next year will settle the whole.   America

---

[1] Philadelphia, whither Paine had gone to publish this first " Crisis."— *Editor.*

could carry on a two years war by the confiscation of the property of disaffected persons, and be made happy by their expulsion. Say not that this is revenge, call it rather the soft resentment of a suffering people, who, having no object in view but the *good* of *all*, have staked their *own all* upon a seemingly doubtful event. Yet it is folly to argue against determined hardness; eloquence may strike the ear, and the language of sorrow draw forth the tear of compassion, but nothing can reach the heart that is steeled with prejudice.

Quitting this class of men, I turn with the warm ardor of a friend to those who have nobly stood, and are yet determined to stand the matter out: I call not upon a few, but upon all: not on *this* state or *that* state, but on *every* state: up and help us; lay your shoulders to the wheel; better have too much force than too little, when so great an object is at stake. Let it be told to the future world, that in the depth of winter, when nothing but hope and virtue could survive, that the city and the country, alarmed at one common danger, came forth to meet and to repulse it. Say not that thousands are gone, turn out your tens of thousands; throw not the burden of the day upon Providence, but "*show your faith by your works*," that God may bless you. It matters not where you live, or what rank of life you hold, the evil or the blessing will reach you all. The far and the near, the home counties and the back, the rich and the poor, will suffer or rejoice alike. The heart that feels not now, is dead: the blood of his children will curse his cowardice, who shrinks back at a time when a little might have saved the whole, and made *them* happy. I love the man that can smile in trouble, that can gather strength from distress, and grow brave by reflection. 'Tis the business of little minds to shrink; but he whose heart is firm, and whose conscience approves his conduct, will pursue his principles unto death. My own line of reasoning is to myself as straight and clear as a ray of light. Not all the treasures of the world, so far as I believe, could have induced me to support an offensive war, for I think it murder; but if a thief breaks into my house, burns and destroys my property, and kills or threatens to kill me, or those that are in it, and to "*bind me in all cases whatsoever*"[1] to his absolute will, am I to suffer it? What signifies it to me, whether he who does it is a king or a common man; my countryman or not my countryman; whether it be done by an individual villain, or an army of them? If we reason to the root of things we shall find no difference; neither can any just cause be assigned why we should punish in the one case and pardon in the other. Let them call me rebel, and welcome, I feel no concern from it; but I should suffer the misery of devils, were I to make a whore of my soul by swearing allegiance to one whose character is that of a sottish, stupid, stubborn, worthless, brutish man. I conceive likewise a horrid idea in receiving mercy from a being, who at the last day shall be shrieking to the rocks and mountains to cover him, and fleeing with terror from the orphan, the widow, and the slain of America.

There are cases which cannot be overdone by language, and this is one. There are persons, too, who see not the full extent of the evil which threatens them; they solace themselves with hopes that the enemy, if he succeed, will be merciful. It is the madness of folly, to expect mercy from those who have refused to do justice; and even mercy, where conquest is the object, is only a trick of war; the cunning of the fox is as murderous as the violence of the wolf, and we ought to guard equally against both. Howe's first object is, partly by threats and partly by promises, to terrify or seduce the people to deliver up their arms and receive mercy. The ministry recommended the same plan to Gage, and this is what the tories call making their peace, "*a peace which passeth all understanding*" *indeed!* A peace which would be the immediate forerunner of a worse ruin than any we have yet thought of. Ye men of Pennsylvania, do reason upon these things! Were the back counties to give up their arms, they would fall an easy prey to the Indians, who are all armed: this perhaps is what some tories would not

---

[1] From the Declaratory Act of Parliament, February 24, 1766, concerning British authority over the American Colonies. See *post* p. 199.—*Editor.*

be sorry for.   Were the home counties to deliver up their
arms, they would be exposed to the resentment of the back
counties, who would then have it in their power to chastise
their defection at pleasure.   And were any one state to give
up its arms, *that* state must be garrisoned by all Howe's army
of Britons and Hessians to preserve it from the anger of the
rest.   Mutual fear is the principal link in the chain of mutual
love, and woe be to that state that breaks the compact.
Howe is mercifully inviting you to barbarous destruction,
and men must be either rogues or fools that will not see it.
I dwell not upon the vapours of imagination ; I bring reason
to your ears, and, in language as plain as A, B, C, hold up
truth to your eyes.

I thank God, that I fear not.   I see no real cause for fear.
I know our situation well, and can see the way out of it.
While our army was collected, Howe dared not risk a battle ;
and it is no credit to him that he decamped from the White
Plains, and waited a mean opportunity to ravage the defenceless Jerseys ; but it is great credit to us, that, with a
handful of men, we sustained an orderly retreat for near an
hundred miles, brought off our ammunition, all our field
pieces, the greatest part of our stores, and had four rivers to
pass.   None can say that our retreat was precipitate, for we
were near three weeks in performing it, that the country
might have time to come in. Twice we marched back to
meet the enemy, and remained out till dark.   The sign of
fear was not seen in our camp, and had not some of the cowardly and disaffected inhabitants spread false alarms through
the country, the Jerseys had never been ravaged.   Once
more we are again collected and collecting ; our new army at
both ends of the continent is recruiting fast, and we shall be
able to open the next campaign with sixty thousand men,
well armed and clothed.   This is our situation, and who will
may know it.   By perseverance and fortitude we have the
prospect of a glorious issue ; by cowardice and submission,
the sad choice of a variety of evils—a ravaged country—a
depopulated city—habitations without safety, and slavery
without hope—our homes turned into barracks and bawdy-

houses for Hessians, and a future race to provide for, whose fathers we shall doubt of. Look on this picture and weep over it ! and if there yet remains one thoughtless wretch who believes it not, let him suffer it unlamented.

COMMON SENSE.

December 23, 1776.[1]

THE CRISIS.

II.

TO LORD HOWE.[2]

" What's in the name of *lord,* that I should **fear**
To bring my grievance to the public ear ? "

CHURCHILL.

UNIVERSAL empire is the prerogative of a writer. His concerns are with all mankind, and though he cannot command their obedience, he can assign them their duty. The Republic of Letters is more ancient than monarchy, and of far higher character in the world than the vassal court of Britain ; he that rebels against reason is a real rebel, but he that in defence of reason rebels against tyranny, has a better title to " *Defender of the Faith,*" than George the third.

As a military man your lordship may hold out the sword of war, and call it the " *ultima ratio regum :* " *the last reason of Kings ;* we in return can show you the sword of justice, and call it " the best scourge of tyrants." The first of these two may threaten, or even frighten for a while, and cast a sickly languor over an insulted people, but reason will soon recover the debauch, and restore them again to tranquil for-

---

[1] This was the date of the pamphlet. The essay had appeared on December 19 in the *Pennsylvania Journal.—Editor.*

[2] Richard Viscount Howe had been sent with a view to negotiation with Congress. He had been a friend of Franklin in London, and it was supposed would find favor in America. He issued a Proclamation from H. M. S. " The Eagle," June 20, another from New York Nov. 30, 1776.—*Editor.*

titude. Your lordship, I find, has now commenced author,
and published a Proclamation; I have published a Crisis: as
they stand, they are the antipodes of each other; both cannot rise at once, and one of them must descend; and so quick
is the revolution of things, that your lordship's performance,
I see, has already fallen many degrees from its first place,
and is now just visible on the edge of the political horizon.

It is surprising to what a pitch of infatuation, blind folly
and obstinacy will carry mankind, and your lordship's drowsy
proclamation is a proof that it does not even quit them in
their sleep. Perhaps you thought America too was taking
a nap, and therefore chose, like Satan to Eve, to whisper
the delusion softly, lest you should awaken her. This continent, sir, is too extensive to sleep all at once, and too
watchful, even in its slumbers, not to startle at the unhallowed
foot of an invader. You may issue your proclamations, and
welcome, for we have learned to " reverence ourselves," and
scorn the insulting ruffian that employs you. America, for
your deceased brother's sake, would gladly have shown you
respect, and it is a new aggravation to her feelings, that Howe
should be forgetful, and raise his sword against those, who
at their own charge raised a monument to his brother.[1] But
your master has commanded, and you have not enough of
nature left to refuse. Surely there must be something
strangely degenerating in the love of monarchy, that can so
completely wear a man down to an ingrate, and make him
proud to lick the dust that kings have trod upon. A few
more years, should you survive them, will bestow on you
the title of " an old man: " and in some hour of future reflection you may probably find the fitness of Wolsey's
despairing penitence—" had I served my God as faithfully
as I have served my king, he would not thus have forsaken
me in my old age."

The character you appear to us in, is truly ridiculous.
Your friends, the tories, announced your coming, with high
descriptions of your unlimited powers; but your proclamation has given them the lie, by showing you to be a com-

[1] George Augustus Howe.   See Crisis V., p. 233, note.—*Editor.*

missioner without authority. Had your powers been ever
so great they were nothing to us, further than we pleased;
because we had the same right which other nations had, to
do what we thought was best. " *The* UNITED STATES *of*
AMERICA," will sound as pompously in the world or in history, as " the kingdom of Great Britain ; " the character of
General Washington will fill a page with as much lustre as
that of *Lord Howe:* and the *congress* have as much right to
command the *king and parliament* in London to desist from
legislation, as *they* or *you* have to command the congress.
Only suppose how laughable such an edict would appear
from us, and then, in that merry mood, do but turn the tables
upon yourself, and you will see how your proclamation is
received here. Having thus placed you in a proper position
in which you may have a full view of your folly, and learn to
despise it, I hold up to you, for that purpose, the following
quotation from your own lunarian proclamation.—" And we
(lord Howe and general Howe) do command (and in his
majesty's name forsooth) all such persons as are assembled
together, under the name of general or provincial congresses,
committees, conventions or other associations, by whatever
name or names known and distinguished, to desist and cease
from all such treasonable actings and doings."

You introduce your proclamation by referring to your
declarations of the 14th of July and 19th of September.   In
the last of these you sunk yourself below the character of a
private gentleman.   That I may not seem to accuse you unjustly, I shall state the circumstance : by a verbal invitation
of yours, communicated to congress by General Sullivan,
then a prisoner on his parole, you signified your desire of
conferring with some members of that body as private gentlemen.   It was beneath the dignity of the American congress to pay any regard to a message that at best was but a
genteel affront, and had too much of the ministerial complexion of tampering with private persons ; and which might
probably have been the case, had the gentlemen who were
deputed on the business possessed that kind of easy virtue
which an English courtier is so truly distinguished by. Your

request, however, was complied with, for honest men are
naturally more tender of their civil than their political fame.
The interview ended as every sensible man thought it would;
for your lordship knows, as well as the writer of the Crisis,
that it is impossible for the king of England to promise the
repeal, or even the revisal of any acts of parliament; wherefore, on your part, you had nothing to say, more than to
request, in the room of demanding, the entire surrender of
the continent; and then, if that was complied with, to
promise that the inhabitants should escape with their lives.
This was the upshot of the conference. You informed the
conferees that you were two months in soliciting these
powers. We ask, what powers? for as commissioner you
have none. If you mean the power of pardoning, it is an
oblique proof that your master was determined to sacrifice
all before him; and that you were two months in dissuading
him from his purpose. Another evidence of his savage
obstinacy! From your own account of the matter we may
justly draw these two conclusions: 1st, That you serve a
monster; and 2d, That never was a messenger sent on a
more foolish errand than yourself. This plain language may
perhaps sound uncouthly to an ear vitiated by courtly refinements, but words were made for use, and the fault lies
in deserving them, or the abuse in applying them unfairly.

Soon after your return to New-York, you published a very
illiberal and unmanly handbill against the congress; for it
was certainly stepping out of the line of common civility,
first to screen your national pride by soliciting an interview
with them as private gentlemen, and in the conclusion to
endeavor to deceive the multitude by making a handbill
attack on the whole body of the congress; you got them
together under one name, and abused them under another.
But the king you serve, and the cause you support, afford
you so few instances of acting the gentleman, that out of
pity to your situation the congress pardoned the insult by
taking no notice of it.

You say in that handbill, "that they, the congress, disavowed every purpose for reconciliation not consonant with

their extravagant and inadmissable claim of independence."
Why, God bless me! what have you to do with our independence? We ask no leave of yours to set it up; we ask
no money of yours to support it; we can do better without
your fleets and armies than with them; you may soon have
enough to do to protect yourselves without being burdened
with us. We are very willing to be at peace with you, to
buy of you and sell to you, and, like young beginners in the
world, to work for our living; therefore, why do you put
yourselves out of cash, when we know you cannot spare it,
and we do not desire you to run into debt? I am willing,
sir, that you should see your folly in every point of view I
can place it in, and for that reason descend sometimes to tell
you in jest what I wish you to see in earnest. But to be
more serious with you, why do you say, "their independence?" To set you right, sir, we tell you, that the independancy is ours, not theirs. The congress were authorised
by every state on the continent to publish it to all the
world, and in so doing are not to be considered as the in-
ventors, but only as the heralds that proclaimed it, or the
office from which the sense of the people received a legal
form; and it was as much as any or all their heads were
worth, to have treated with you on the subject of submission
under any name whatever. But we know the men in whom
we have trusted; can England say the same of her parliament?

I come now more particularly to your proclamation of the
30th of November last. Had you gained an entire conquest
over all the armies of America, and then put forth a proclamation, offering (what you call) mercy, your conduct would
have had some specious show of humanity; but to creep by
surprise into a province, and there endeavor to terrify and
seduce the inhabitants from their just allegiance to the rest
by promises, which you neither meant nor were able to fulfil, is both cruel and unmanly: cruel in its effects; because,
unless you can keep all the ground you have marched over,
how are you, in the words of your proclamation, to secure
to your proselytes "the enjoyment of their property?"

What is to become either of your new adopted subjects, or your old friends, the tories, in Burlington, Bordentown, Trenton, Mount Holly, and many other places, where you proudly lorded it for a few days, and then fled with the precipitation of a pursued thief? What, I say, is to become of those wretches? What is to become of those who went over to you from this city and state? What more can you say to them than "shift for yourselves?" Or what more can they hope for than to wander like vagabonds over the face of the earth? You may now tell them to take their leave of America, and all that once was theirs. Recommend them, for consolation, to your master's court; there perhaps they may make a shift to live on the scraps of some dangling parasite, and choose companions among thousands like themselves. A traitor is the foulest fiend on earth.

In a political sense we ought to thank you for thus bequeathing estates to the continent; we shall soon, at this rate, be able to carry on a war without expense, and grow rich by the ill policy of lord Howe, and the generous defection of the tories. Had you set your foot into this city, you would have bestowed estates upon us which we never thought of, by bringing forth traitors we were unwilling to suspect. But these men, you 'll say, "are his majesty's most faithful subjects;" let that honour, then, be all their fortune, and let his majesty take them to himself.

I am now thoroughly disgusted with them; they live in ungrateful ease, and bend their whole minds to mischief. It seems as if God had given them over to a spirit of infidelity, and that they are open to conviction in no other line but that of punishment. It is time to have done with tarring, feathering, carting, and taking securities for their future good behaviour; every sensible man must feel a conscious shame at seeing a poor fellow hawked for a show about the streets, when it is known he is only the tool of some principal villain, biassed into his offence by the force of false reasoning, or bribed thereto, through sad necessity. We dishonor ourselves by attacking such trifling characters while greater ones are suffered to escape; 'tis our duty to find *them* out, and

their proper punishment would be to exile them from the
continent for ever.   The circle of them is not so great as
some imagine ; the influence of a few have tainted many
who are not naturally corrupt.   A continual circulation of
lies among those who are not much in the way of hearing
them contradicted, will in time pass for truth ; and the crime
lies not in the believer but the inventor.   I am not for declaring war with every man that appears not so warm as
myself : difference of constitution, temper, habit of speaking,
and many other things, will go a great way in fixing the
outward character of a man, yet simple honesty may remain
at bottom.   Some men have naturally a military turn, and
can brave hardships and the risk of life with a cheerful face ;
others have not ; no slavery appears to them so great as the
fatigue of arms, and no terror so powerful as that of personal
danger.   What can we say ? We cannot alter nature, neither
ought we to punish the son because the father begot him in
a cowardly mood.   However, I believe most men have more
courage than they know of, and that a little at first is enough
to begin with.   I knew the time when I thought that the
whistling of a cannon ball would have frightened me almost
to death : but I have since tried it, and find that I can stand
it with as little discomposure, and, I believe, with a much
easier conscience than your lordship.   The same dread would
return to me again were I in your situation, for my solemn
belief of your cause is, that it is hellish and damnable, and,
under that conviction, every thinking man's heart *must* fail
him.

From a concern that a good cause should be dishonored
by the least disunion among us, I said in my former paper,
No. I. " That should the enemy now be expelled, I wish,
with all the sincerity of a Christian, that the names of whig
and tory might never more be mentioned ; " but there is a
knot of men among us of such a venomous cast, that they
will not admit even one's good wishes to act in their favor.
Instead of rejoicing that heaven had, as it were, providen-
tially preserved this city from plunder and destruction, by
delivering so great a part of the enemy into our hands with

so little effusion of blood, they stubbornly affected to disbe-
lieve it till within an hour, nay, half an hour, of the prisoners
arriving; and the Quakers put forth a testimony, dated the
20th of December, signed "John Pemberton," declaring
their attachment to the British government.* These men
are continually harping on the great sin of *our* bearing arms,
but the king of Britain may lay waste the world in blood and
famine, and they, poor fallen souls, have nothing to say.

In some future paper I intend to distinguish between the
different kind of persons who have been denominated tories;
for this I am clear in, that all are not so who have been called
so, nor all men whigs who were once thought so; and as I
mean not to conceal the name of any true friend when there
shall be occasion to mention him, neither will I that of an
enemy, who ought to be known, let his rank, station or
religion be what it may. Much pains have been taken by
some to set your lordship's private character in an amiable
light, but as it has chiefly been done by men who know
nothing about you, and who are no ways remarkable for
their attachment to us, we have no just authority for believing it. George the third has imposed upon us by the same
arts, but *time*, at length, has done him justice, and the same
fate may probably attend your lordship. Your avowed purpose here is to kill, conquer, plunder, pardon, and enslave:
and the ravages of your army through the Jerseys have been
marked with as much barbarism as if you had openly professed yourself the prince of ruffians; not even the appearance of humanity has been preserved either on the march or
the retreat of your troops; no general order that I could
ever learn, has ever been issued to prevent or even forbid

---

* I have ever been careful of charging offences upon whole societies of men,
but as the paper referred to is put forth by an unknown set of men, who claim
to themselves the right of representing the whole: and while the whole society
of Quakers admit its validity by a silent acknowledgment, it is impossible that
any distinction can be made by the public: and the more so, because the New
York paper of the 30th of December, printed by permission of our enemies,
says that "the Quakers begin to speak openly of their attachment to the
British constitution." We are certain that we have many friends among them,
and wish to know them.—*Author*.

your troops from robbery, wherever they came, and the only instance of justice, if it can be called such, which has distinguished you for impartiality, is, that you treated and plundered all alike; what could not be carried away has been destroyed, and mahogany furniture has been deliberately laid on fire for fuel, rather than the men should be fatigued with cutting wood.* There was a time when the whigs confided much in your supposed candor, and the tories rested themselves in your favor; the experiments have now been made, and failed; in every town, nay, every cottage, in the Jerseys, where your arms have been, is a testimony against you. How you may rest under this sacrifice of character I know not; but this I know, that you sleep and rise with the daily curses of thousands upon you; perhaps the misery which the tories have suffered by your proffered mercy may give them some claim to their country's pity, and be in the end the best favor you could show them.

In a folio general-order book belonging to Col. Rhal's battalion, taken at Trenton, and now in the possession of the council of safety for this state, the following barbarous order is frequently repeated, "His excellency the *comman-der-in-chief* orders, that all inhabitants who shall be found with arms, not having an officer with them, shall be immediately taken and hung up." [1] How many you may thus have privately sacrificed, we know not, and the account can only be settled in another world. Your treatment of prisoners, in order to distress them to enlist in your infernal service, is not to be equalled by any instance in Europe. Yet this is the humane lord Howe and his brother, whom

---

* As some people may doubt the truth of such wanton destruction, I think it necessary to inform them, that one of the people called Quakers, who lives at Trenton, gave me this information, at the house of Mr. Michael Hutchinson, (one of the same profession,) who lives near Trenton ferry on the Pennsylvania side, Mr. Hutchinson being present.—*Author.*

[1] Col. Johann Gottlieb Rahl, or Rall (as the name is now written), a Hessian, had distinguished himself in compelling the Americans to evacuate Forts Washington and Lee, and in the pursuit of Washington to the Delaware; for such service he had been placed in chief command at Trenton, where he fell.— *Editor.*

the tories and their three-quarter kindred, the Quakers, or some of them at least, have been holding up for patterns of justice and mercy !

A bad cause will ever be supported by bad means and bad men ; and whoever will be at the pains of examining strictly into things, will find that one and the same spirit of oppression and impiety, more or less, governs through your whole party in both countries : not many days ago, I accidentally fell in company with a person of this city noted for espousing your cause, and on my remarking to him, "that it appeared clear to me, by the late providential turn of affairs, that God Almighty was visibly on our side," he replied, "We care nothing for that, you may have Him, and welcome ; if we have but enough of the devil on our side, we shall do." However carelessly this might be spoken, matters not, 'tis still the insensible principle that directs all your conduct and will at last most assuredly deceive and ruin you.

If ever a nation was mad and foolish, blind to its own interest and bent on its own destruction, it is Britain. There are such things as national sins, and though the punishment of individuals may be reserved to *another* world, national punishment can only be inflicted in *this* world. Britain, as a nation, is, in my inmost belief, the greatest and most ungrateful offender against God on the face of the whole earth : blessed with all the commerce she could wish for, and furnished, by a vast extension of dominion, with the means of civilizing both the eastern and western world, she has made no other use of both than proudly to idolize her own " thunder," and rip up the bowels of whole countries for what she could get : Like Alexander, she has made war her sport, and inflicted misery for prodigality's sake. The blood of India is not yet repaid, nor the wretchedness of Africa yet requited. Of late she has enlarged her list of national cruelties by her butcherly destruction of the Caribbs of St. Vincent's, and returning an answer by the sword to the meek prayer for " *Peace, liberty and safety.*" These are serious things, and whatever a foolish tyrant, a debauched court, a trafficking legislature, or a blinded people may think, the national account with heaven must some day or other be settled : all countries have sooner or later been called to their reckoning ; the proudest empires have sunk when the balance was struck ; and Britain, like an individual penitent, must undergo her day of sorrow, and the sooner it happens to her the better : as I wish it over, I wish it to come, but withal wish that it may be as light as possible.

Perhaps your lordship has no taste for serious things ; by your connexions in England I should suppose not ; therefore I shall drop this part of the subject, and take it up in a line in which you will better understand me.

By what means, may I ask, do you expect to conquer America ? If you could not effect it in the summer, when our army was less than yours, nor in the winter, when we had none, how are you to do it ? In point of generalship you have been outwitted, and in point of fortitude outdone ; your advantages turn out to your loss, and show us that it is in our power to ruin you by gifts : like a game of drafts, we can move out of *one* square to let you come in, in order that we may afterwards take two or three for one ; and as we can always keep a double corner for ourselves, we can always prevent a total defeat. You cannot be so insensible as not to see that we have two to one the advantage of you, because we conquer by a drawn game, and you lose by it. Burgoyne might have taught your lordship this knowledge ; he has been long a student in the doctrine of chances.

I have no other idea of conquering countries than by subduing the armies which defend them : have you done this, or can you do it ? If you have not, it would be civil in you to let your proclamations alone for the present ; otherwise, you will ruin more tories by your grace and favor, than you will whigs by your arms.

Were you to obtain possession of this city, you would not know what to do with it more than to plunder it. To hold it in the manner you hold New-York, would be an additional dead weight upon your hands : and if a general conquest is your object, you had better be without the city than with it. When you have defeated all our armies, the cities will fall into your hands of themselves; but to creep into them in the manner you got into Princeton, Trenton, &c. is like robbing an orchard in the night before the fruit be ripe, and running away in the morning. Your experiment in the Jerseys is sufficient to teach you that you have something more to do than barely to get into other people's houses; and your new converts, to whom you promised all manner of protection, and seduced into new guilt by pardoning them from their former virtues, must begin to have a very contemptible opinion both of your power and your policy. Your authority in the Jerseys is now reduced to the small circle which your army occupies, and your proclamation is no where else seen unless it be to be laughed at. The mighty subduers of the continent have retreated into a nutshell, and the proud forgivers of our sins are fled from those they came to pardon; and all this at a time when they were despatching vessel after vessel to England with the great news of every day. In short, you have managed your Jersey expedition so very dexterously, that the dead only are conquerors, because none will dispute the ground with them.

In all the wars which you have formerly been concerned in you had only armies to contend with; in this case you have both an army and a country to combat with. In former wars, the countries followed the fate of their capitals; Canada fell with Quebec, and Minorca with Port Mahon or St. Phillips; by subduing those, the conquerors opened a way into, and became masters of the country: here it is otherwise; if you get possession of a city here, you are obliged to shut yourselves up in it, and can make no other use of it, than to spend your country's money in. This is all the advantage you have drawn from New-York; and you would draw less from Philadelphia, because it requires more force to keep it, and is much further from the sea. A pretty figure you and the tories would cut in this city, with a river full of ice, and a town full of fire; for the immediate consequence of your getting here would be, that you would be cannonaded out again, and the tories be obliged to

make good the damage ; and this sooner or later will be the
fate of New-York.

I wish to see the city saved, not so much from military as
from natural motives. 'Tis the hiding place of women and
children, and lord Howe's proper business is with our armies.
When I put all the circumstances together which ought to be
taken, I laugh at your notion of conquering America. Because you lived in a little country, where an army might run
over the whole in a few days, and where a single company
of soldiers might put a multitude to the rout, you expected
to find it the same here. It is plain that you brought over
with you all the narrow notions you were bred up with, and
imagined that a proclamation in the king's name was to do
great things ; but Englishmen always travel for knowledge,
and your lordship, I hope, will return, if you return at all,
much wiser than you came.

We may be surprised by events we did not expect, and in
that interval of recollection you may gain some temporary
advantage : such was the case a few weeks ago, but we soon
ripen again into reason, collect our strength, and while you
are preparing for a triumph, we come upon you with a defeat. Such it has been, and such it would be were you to
try it a hundred times over. Were you to garrison the
places you might march over, in order to secure their subjection, (for remember you can do it by no other means,)
your army would be like a stream of water running to
nothing. By the time you extended from New-York to
Virginia, you would be reduced to a string of drops not
capable of hanging together ; while we, by retreating from
state to state, like a river turning back upon itself, would
acquire strength in the same proportion as you lost it, and
in the end be capable of overwhelming you. The country,
in the meantime, would suffer, but it is a day of suffering,
and we ought to expect it. What we contend for is worthy
the affliction we may go through. If we get but bread to
eat, and any kind of raiment to put on, we ought not only
to be contented, but thankful. More than *that* we ought
not to look for, and less than *that* heaven has not yet suf-

fered us to want.   He that would sell his birthright for a
little *salt*, is as worthless as he who sold it for pottage without salt ; and he that would part with it for a gay coat, or a
plain coat, ought for ever to be a slave in buff.   What are
salt, sugar and finery, to the inestimable blessings of
" Liberty and Safety ! "   Or what are the inconveniences of
a few months to the tributary bondage of ages ?   The
meanest peasant in America, blessed with these sentiments,
is a happy man compared with a New-York tory ; he can eat
his morsel without repining, and when he has done, can
sweeten it with a repast of wholesome air ; he can take his
child by the hand and bless it, without feeling the conscious
shame of neglecting a parent's duty.

In publishing these remarks I have several objects in
view.

On your part they are to expose the folly of your pretended authority as a commissioner ; the wickedness of your
cause in general ; and the impossibility of your conquering
us at any rate.   On the part of the public, my intention is,
to show them their true and solid interest ; to encourage them
to their own good, to remove the fears and falsities which
bad men have spread, and weak men have encouraged ;
and to excite in all men a love for union, and a cheerfulness
for duty.

I shall submit one more case to you respecting your
conquest of this country, and then proceed to new observations.

Suppose our armies in every part of this continent were
immediately to disperse, every man to his home, or where
else he might be safe, and engage to re-assemble again on a
certain future day ; it is clear that you would then have no
army to contend with, yet you would be as much at a loss
in that case as you are now ; you would be afraid to send
your troops in parties over to the continent, either to disarm
or prevent us from assembling, lest they should not return ;
and while you kept them together, having no arms of ours to
dispute with, you could not call it a conquest ; you might
furnish out a pompous page in the London Gazette or a

New-York paper, but when we returned at the appointed time, you would have the same work to do that you had at first.

It has been the folly of Britain to suppose herself more powerful than she really is, and by that means has arrogated to herself a rank in the world she is not entitled to : for more than this century past she has not been able to carry on a war without foreign assistance. In Marlborough's campaigns, and from that day to this, the number of German troops and officers assisting her have been about equal with her own ; ten thousand Hessians were sent to England last war to protect her from a French invasion ; and she would have cut but a poor figure in her Canadian and West-Indian expeditions, had not America been lavish both of her money and men to help her along. The only instance in which she was engaged singly, that I can recollect, was against the rebellion in Scotland, in the years 1745 and 1746, and in that, out of three battles, she was twice beaten, till by thus reducing their numbers, (as we shall yours) and taking a supply ship that was coming to Scotland with clothes, arms and money, (as we have often done,) she was at last enabled to defeat them. England was never famous by land ; her officers have generally been suspected of cowardice, have more of the air of a dancing-master than a soldier, and by the samples which we have taken prisoners, we give the preference to ourselves. Her strength, of late, has lain in her extravagance ; but as her finances and credit are now low, her sinews in that line begin to fail fast. As a nation she is the poorest in Europe ; for were the whole kingdom, and all that is in it, to be put up for sale like the estate of a bankrupt, it would not fetch as much as she owes ; yet this thoughtless wretch must go to war, and with the avowed design, too, of making us beasts of burden, to support her in riot and debauchery, and to assist her afterwards in distressing those nations who are now our best friends. This ingratitude may suit a tory, or the unchristian peevishness of a fallen Quaker, but none else.

'Tis the unhappy temper of the English to be pleased with any war, right or wrong, be it but successful ; but they

soon grow discontented with ill fortune, and it is an even
chance that they are as clamorous for peace next summer,
as the king and his ministers were for war last winter.   In
this natural view of things, your lordship stands in a very
critical situation : your whole character is now staked upon
your laurels ; if they wither, you wither with them ; if they
flourish, you cannot live long to look at them ; and at any
rate, the black account hereafter is not far off.   What lately
. appeared to us misfortunes, were only blessings in disguise ;
and the seeming advantages on your side have turned out
to our profit.   Even our loss of this city, as far as we can see,
might be a principal gain to us : the more surface you spread
over, the thinner you will be, and the easier wiped away ;
and our consolation under that apparent disaster would be,
that the estates of the tories would become securities for the
repairs.   In short, there is no old ground we can fail upon,
but some new foundation rises again to support us.   " We
have put, sir, our hands to the plough, and cursed be he that
looketh back."

Your king, in his speech to parliament last spring, declared,
" That he had no doubt but the great force they had enabled
him to send to America, would effectually reduce the rebellious colonies."   It has not, neither can it ; but it has done
just enough to lay the foundation of its own next year's ruin.
You are sensible that you left England in a divided, distracted
state of politics, and, by the command you had here, you
became a principal prop in the court party ; their fortunes
rest on yours ; by a single express you can fix their value
with the public, and the degree to which their spirits shall
rise or fall ; they are in your hands as stock, and you have the
secret of the *alley* with you.   Thus situated and connected,
you become the unintentional mechanical instrument of your
own and their overthrow.   The king and his ministers put
conquest out of doubt, and the credit of both depended on
the proof.   To support them in the interim, it was necessary
that you should make the most of every thing, and we can
tell by Hugh Gaine's New-York paper what the complexion
of the London Gazette is.   With such a list of victories the
nation cannot expect you will ask new supplies ; and to

confess your want of them would give the lie to your triumphs, and impeach the king and his ministers of treasonable decep- tion. If you make the necessary demand at home, your party sinks ; if you make it not, you sink yourself ; to ask it now is too late, and to ask it before was too soon, and unless it arrive quickly will be of no use. In short, the part you have to act, cannot be acted ; and I am fully persuaded that all you have to trust to is, to do the best you can with what force you have got, or little more. Though we have greatly exceeded you in point of generalship and bravery of men, yet, as a people, we have not entered into the full soul of enterprise ; for I, who know England and the disposition of the people well, am confident, that it is easier for us to effect a revolution there, than you a conquest here ; a few thousand men landed in England with the declared design of deposing the present king, bringing his ministers to trial, and setting up the Duke of Gloucester in his stead, would assuredly carry their point, while you are grovelling here, ignorant of the matter. As I send all my papers to England, this, like Com- mon Sense, will find its way there ; and though it may put one party on their guard, it will inform the other, and the nation in general, of our design to help them.

Thus far, sir, I have endeavored to give you a picture of present affairs : you may draw from it what conclusions you please. I wish as well to the true prosperity of England as you can, but I consider INDEPENDANCE *as America's natural right and interest*, and never could see any real disservice it would be to Britain. If an English merchant receives an order, and is paid for it, it signifies nothing to him who governs the country. This is my creed of politics. If I have any where expressed myself over-warmly, 'tis from a fixed, immovable hatred I have, and ever had, to cruel men and cruel measures. I have likewise an aversion to monar- chy, as being too debasing to the dignity of man ; but I never troubled others with my notions till very lately, nor ever published a syllable in England in my life.[1] What I

---

[1] This disposes of the notion that Paine was " Junius." He wrote a petition to Parliament for the Excisemen, but it was not published until 1793. His " Wolfe " did not appear in the *Gentleman's Magazine*, as Mr. Burr supposes. —*Editor.*

write is pure nature, and my pen and my soul have ever gone together. My writings I have always given away, reserving only the expense of printing and paper, and sometimes not even that. I never courted either fame or interest, and my manner of life, to those who know it, will justify what I say. My study is to be useful, and if your lordship loves mankind as well as I do, you would, seeing you cannot conquer us, cast about and lend your hand towards accomplishing a peace. Our independance with God's blessing we will maintain against all the world ; but as we wish to avoid evil ourselves, we wish not to inflict it on others. I am never over-inquisitive into the secrets of the cabinet, but I have some notion that, if you neglect the present opportunity, it will not be in our power to make a separate peace with you afterwards ; for whatever treaties or alliances we form, we shall most faithfully abide by ; wherefore you may be deceived if you think you can make it with us at any time. A lasting independent peace is my wish, end and aim ; and to accomplish that, "*I pray God the* Americans *may never be defeated, and I trust while they have good officers, and are well commanded,*" and willing to be commanded, "*that they* NEVER WILL BE."

COMMON SENSE.

PHILADELPHIA, Jan. 13, 1777.

THE CRISIS.[1]

III.

IN the progress of politics, as in the common occurrences of life, we are not only apt to forget the ground we have travelled over, but frequently neglect to gather up experience as we go. We expend, if I may so say, the knowledge of every day on the circumstances that produce it, and

---

[1] This Crisis is dated April 19, 1777, the second anniversary of the collision at Lexington. Two days before (April 17, 1777) Paine had been appointed by Congress Secretary of the Committee of Foreign Affairs, on its constitution. — *Editor.*

journey on in search of new matter and new refinements: but as it is pleasant and sometimes useful to look back, even to the first periods of infancy, and trace the turns and windings through which we have passed, so we may likewise derive many advantages by halting a while in our political career, and taking a review of the wondrous complicated labyrinth of little more than yesterday.

Truly may we say, that never did men grow old in so short a time! We have crowded the business of an age into the compass of a few months, and have been driven through such a rapid succession of things, that for the want of leisure to think, we unavoidably wasted knowledge as we came, and have left nearly as much behind us as we brought with us: but the road is yet rich with the fragments, and, before we finally lose sight of them, will repay us for the trouble of stopping to pick them up.

Were a man to be totally deprived of memory, he would be incapable of forming any just opinion; every thing about him would seem a chaos: he would have even his own history to ask from every one; and by not knowing how the world went in his absence, he would be at a loss to know how it *ought* to go on when he recovered, or rather, returned to it again. In like manner, though in a less degree, a too great inattention to past occurrences retards and bewilders our judgment in everything; while, on the contrary, by comparing what is past with what is present, we frequently hit on the true character of both, and become wise with very little trouble. It is a kind of counter-march, by which we get into the rear of time, and mark the movements and meaning of things as we make our return. There are certain circumstances, which, at the time of their happening, are a kind of riddles, and as every riddle is to be followed by its answer, so those kind of circumstances will be followed by their events, and those events are always the true solution. A considerable space of time may lapse between, and unless we continue our observations from the one to the other, the harmony of them will pass away unnoticed: but the misfortune is, that partly from the pressing necessity of some instant things, and partly from the impatience of our own tempers, we are frequently in such a hurry to make out the meaning of everything as fast as it happens, that we thereby never truly understand it; and not only start new difficulties to ourselves by so doing, but, as it were, embarrass Providence in her good designs.

I have been civil in stating this fault on a large scale, for, as it now stands, it does not appear to be levelled against any particular set of men; but were it to be refined a little further, it might afterwards be applied to the tories with a degree of striking propriety: those men have been remarkable for drawing sudden conclusions from single facts. The least apparent mishap on our side, or the least seeming advantage on the part of the enemy, have determined with them the fate of a whole campaign. By this hasty judgment they have converted a retreat into a defeat; mistook generalship for error; while every little advantage purposely given the enemy, either to weaken their strength by dividing it, embarrass their councils by multiplying their objects, or to secure a greater post by the surrender of a less, has been instantly magnified into a conquest. Thus, by quartering ill policy upon ill principles, they have frequently promoted the cause they designed to injure, and injured that which they intended to promote.

It is probable the campaign may open before this number comes from the press. The enemy have long lain idle, and amused themselves with carrying on the war by proclamations only. While they continue their delay our strength increases, and were they to move to action now, it is a circumstantial proof that they have no reinforcement coming; wherefore, in either case, the comparative advantage will be ours. Like a wounded, disabled whale, they want only time and room to die in; and though in the agony of their exit, it may be unsafe to live within the flapping of their tail, yet every hour shortens their date, and lessens their power of mischief. If any thing happens while this number is in the press, it will afford me a subject for the last pages of it. At present I am tired of waiting; and as neither the enemy, nor the state of politics have yet produced any thing new, I am thereby left in the field of general matter, undirected by any striking or particular object.   This Crisis, therefore, will be made up rather of variety than novelty, and consist more of things useful than things wonderful.

The success of the cause, the union of the people, and the means of supporting and securing both, are points which cannot be too much attended to.   He who doubts of the former is a desponding coward, and he who wilfully disturbs the latter is a traitor.   Their characters are easily fixed, and under these short descriptions I leave them for the present.

One of the greatest degrees of sentimental union which America ever knew, was in denying the right of the British parliament *"to bind the colonies in all cases whatsoever."* [1] The Declaration is, in its form, an almighty one, and is the loftiest stretch of arbitrary power that ever one set of men or one country claimed over another.   Taxation was nothing more than the putting the declared right into practice ; and this failing, recourse was had to arms, as a means to establish both the right *and* the practice, or to answer a worse purpose, which will be mentioned in the course of this number.   And in order to repay themselves the expense of an army, and to profit by their own injustice, the colonies were, by another law, declared to be in a state of actual rebellion, and of consequence all property therein would fall to the conquerors.

The colonies, on their part, *first*, denied the right ; *secondly*, they suspended the use of taxable articles, and petitioned against the practice of taxation : and these failing, they, *thirdly*, defended their property by force, as soon as it was forcibly invaded, and, in answer to the declaration of rebel-

---

[1] "That the King's Majesty, by and with the consent of the Lords spiritual and temporal, and Commons of Great Britain in Parliament assembled, had, hath, and of right ought to have full power and authority to make laws and statutes of sufficient force and validity to bind the colonies and people of America, subjects of the crown of Great Britain, in all cases whatsoever." Paragraph first of the Declaratory Act repealing the Stamp Act, February, 1766. —*Editor*.

lion and non-protection, published their Declaration of Independence and right of self-protection.

These, in a few words, are the different stages of the quarrel; and the parts are so intimately and necessarily connected with each other as to admit of no separation. A person, to use a trite phrase, must be a whig or a tory in a lump. His feelings, as a man, may be wounded; his charity, as a Christian, may be moved; but his political principles must go through all the cases on one side or the other. He cannot be a whig in *this* stage, and a tory in *that*. If he says he is against the united independence of the continent, he is to all intents and purposes against her in all the rest; because *this last* comprehends the whole. And he may just as well say, that Britain was right in declaring us rebels; right in taxing us; and right in declaring her " *right to bind the colonies in all cases whatsoever.*" It signifies nothing what neutral ground, of his own creating, he may skulk upon for shelter, for the quarrel in no stage of it hath afforded any such ground; and either we or Britain are absolutely right or absolutely wrong through the whole.

Britain, like a gamester nearly ruined, hath now put all her losses into one bet, and is playing a desperate game for the total. If she wins it, she wins from me my life; she wins the continent as the forfeited property of rebels; the right of taxing those that are left as reduced subjects; and the power of binding them slaves: and the single die which determines this unparalleled event is, whether we support our independence or she overturn it. This is coming to the point at once. Here is the touchstone to try men by. *He that is not a supporter of the independent states of America in the same degree that his religious and political principles would suffer him to support the government of any other country, of which he called himself a subject, is, in the American sense of the word,* A TORY; *and the instant that he endeavors to bring his toryism into practice, he becomes* A TRAITOR. The first can only be detected by a general test, and the law hath already provided for the latter.

It is unnatural and impolitic to admit men who would

root up our independence to have any share in our legislation, either as electors or representatives; because the support of our independence rests, in a great measure, on the vigor and purity of our public bodies. Would Britain, even in time of peace, much less in war, suffer an election to be carried by men who professed themselves to be not her subjects, or allow such to sit in parliament? Certainly not.

But there are a certain species of tories with whom conscience or principle hath nothing to do, and who are so from avarice only. Some of the first fortunes on the continent, on the part of the whigs, are staked on the issue of our present measures. And shall disaffection only be rewarded with security? Can any thing be a greater inducement to a miserly man, than the hope of making his mammon safe? And though the scheme be fraught with every character of folly, yet, so long as he supposes, that by doing nothing materially criminal against America on one part, and by expressing his private disapprobation against independence, as palliative with the enemy, on the other part, he stands in a safe line between both; while, I say, this ground be suffered to remain, craft, and the spirit of avarice, will point it out, and men will not be wanting to fill up this most contemptible of all characters.

These men, ashamed to own the sordid cause from whence their disaffection springs, add thereby meanness to meanness, by endeavoring to shelter themselves under the mask of hypocrisy; that is, they had rather be thought to be tories from *some kind of principle*, than tories by having *no principle at all*. But till such time as they can show some real reason, natural, political, or conscientious, on which their objections to independence are founded, we are not obliged to give them credit for being tories of the first stamp, but must set them down as tories of the last.

In the second number of the Crisis, I endeavored to show the impossibility of the enemy's making any conquest of America, that nothing was wanting on our part but patience and perseverance, and that, with these virtues, our success, as far as human speculation could discern, seemed as certain as fate. But as there are many among us, who, influenced by others, have regularly gone back from the principles they once held, in proportion as we have gone forward ; and as it is the unfortunate lot of many a good man to live within the neighborhood of disaffected ones ; I shall, therefore, for the sake of confirming the one and recovering the other, endeavor, in the space of a page or two, to go over some of the leading principles in support of independence. It is a much pleasanter task to prevent vice than to punish it, and, however our tempers may be gratified by resentment, or our national expenses eased by forfeited estates, harmony and friendship is, nevertheless, the happiest condition a country can be blest with.

The principal arguments in support of independence may be comprehended under the four following heads.

1st, The natural right of the continent to independence.

2d, Her interest in being independent.

3d, The necessity,—and

4th, The moral advantages arising therefrom.

I. The natural right of the continent to independence, is a point which never yet was called in question. It will not even admit of a debate. To deny such a right, would be a kind of atheism against nature : and the best answer to such an objection would be, " *The fool hath said in his heart there is no God.*"

II. The interest of the continent in being independent is a point as clearly right as the former. America, by her own internal industry, and unknown to all the powers of Europe, was, at the beginning of the dispute, arrived at a pitch of greatness, trade and population, beyond which it was the interest of Britain not to suffer her to pass, lest she should grow too powerful to be kept subordinate. She began to view this country with the same uneasy malicious eye, with which a covetous guardian would view his ward, whose estate he had been enriching himself by for twenty years, and saw him just arriving at manhood.   And America owes no more to Britain for her present maturity, than the ward would to the guardian for being twenty-one years of age. That America hath flourished *at the time* she was under the government of Britain, is true ; but there is every natural reason to believe, that had she been an independent country from the first settlement thereof, uncontrolled by any foreign power, free to make her own laws, regulate and encourage her own commerce, she had by this time been of much greater worth than now.   The case is simply this : the first settlers in the different colonies were left to shift for themselves, unnoticed and unsupported by any European government : but as the tyranny and persecution of the old world daily drove num. bers to the new, and as, by the favor of heaven on their industry and perseverance, they grew into importance, so, in a like degree, they became an object of profit to the greedy eyes of Europe.   It was impossible, in this state of infancy, however thriving and promising, that they could resist the power of any armed invader that should seek to bring them under his authority.   In this situation, Britain thought it worth her while to claim them, and the continent received and acknowledged the claimer.   It was, in reality, of no very great importance who was her master, seeing, that from the force and ambition of the different powers of Europe, she must, till she acquired strength enough to assert her own right, acknowledge some one.   As well, perhaps, Britain as another ; and it might have been as well to have been under the states of Holland as any.   The same hopes of engrossing and profiting by her trade, by not oppressing it too much, would have operated alike with any master, and produced to the colonies the same effects.   The clamour of protection, likewise, was all a farce ; because, in order to make that protection necessary, she must first, by her own quarrels, create us enemies.   Hard terms indeed !

To know whether it be the interest of the continent to be independent, we need only ask this easy, simple question : Is it the interest of a man to be a boy all his life ?   The answer to one will be the answer to both.   America hath been one continued scene of legislative contention from the first king's representative to the last ; and this was unavoidably founded in the natural opposition of interest between the old country and the new. A governor sent from England, or receiving his authority therefrom, ought never to have been considered in any other light than that of a genteel commissioned spy, whose private business was information, and his public business a kind of civilized oppression. In the first of these characters he was to watch the tempers, sentiments and disposition of the people, the growth of trade, and the increase of private fortunes; and, in the latter, to suppress all such acts of the assemblies, however beneficial to the people, which did not directly or indirectly throw some increase of power or profit into the hands of those that sent him.

America, till now, could never be called a *free country*, because her legislation depended on the will of a man three thousand miles distant, whose interest was in opposition to ours, and who, by a single " no," could forbid what law he pleased.

The freedom of trade, likewise, is, to a trading country, an article of such importance, that the principal source of wealth depends upon it; and it is impossible that any country can flourish, as it otherwise might do, whose commerce is engrossed, cramped and fettered by the laws and mandates of another—yet these evils, and more than I can here enumerate, the continent has suffered by being under the government of England. By an independence we clear the whole at once—put an end to the business of unanswered petitions and fruitless remonstrances—exchange Britain for Europe—shake hands with the world—live at peace with the world—and trade to any market where we can buy and sell.

III. The necessity, likewise, of being independent, even before it was declared, became so evident and important, that the continent ran the risk of being ruined every day that she delayed it. There was reason to believe that Britain would endeavor to make an European matter of it, and, rather than lose the whole, would dismember it, like Poland, and dispose of her several claims to the highest bidder. Genoa, failing in her attempts to reduce Corsica, made a sale of it to the French, and such traffics have been com-

mon in the old world. We had at that time no ambassador
in any part of Europe, to counteract her negociations, and
by that means she had the range of every foreign court uncontradicted on our part. We even knew nothing of the
treaty for the Hessians till it was concluded, and the troops
ready to embark. Had we been independent before, we
had probably prevented her obtaining them. We had no
credit abroad, because of our rebellious dependancy. Our
ships could claim no protection in foreign ports, because we
afforded them no justifiable reason for granting it to us.
The calling ourselves subjects, and at the same time fighting against the power which we acknowledged, was a dangerous precedent to all Europe. If the grievances justified
the taking up arms, they justified our separation ; if they
did not justify our separation, neither could they justify our
taking up arms. All Europe was interested in reducing us
as rebels, and all Europe (or the greatest part at least) is interested in supporting us as·independent states. At home
our condition was still worse ; our currency had no foundation, and the fall of it would have ruined whig and tory
alike. We had no other law than a kind of moderated passion ; no other civil power than an honest mob ; and no
other protection than the temporary attachment of one man
to another. Had independence been delayed a few months
longer, this continent would have been plunged into irrecoverable confusion : some violent for it, some against it, till,
in the general cabal, the rich would have been ruined, and
the poor destroyed. It is to independence that every tory
owes the present safety which he lives in ; for by that, and
that only, we emerged from a state of dangerous suspense,
and became a regular people.

The necessity, likewise, of being independent, had there
been no rupture between Britain and America, would, in a
little time, have brought one on. The increasing importance of commerce, the weight and perplexity of legislation,
and the entangled state of European politics, would daily
have shown to the continent the impossibility of continuing
subordinate ; for, after the coolest reflections on the matter,

this must be allowed, that Britain was too jealous of America to govern it justly ; too ignorant of it to govern it well ; and too far distant from it to govern it at all.

IV. But what weigh most with all men of serious reflection are, the *moral advantages* arising from independence : war and desolation have become the trade of the old world ; and America neither could nor can be under the government of Britain without becoming a sharer of her guilt, and a partner in all the dismal commerce of death. The spirit of duelling, extended on a national scale, is a proper character for European wars. They have seldom any other motive than pride, or any other object than fame. The conquerors and the conquered are generally ruined alike, and the chief difference at last is, that the one marches home with his honors, and the other without them. 'Tis the natural temper of the English to fight for a feather, if they suppose that feather to be an affront ; and America, without the right of asking why, must have abetted in every quarrel, and abided by its fate. It is a shocking situation to live in, that one country must be brought into all the wars of another, whether the measure be right or wrong, or whether she will or not ; yet this, in the fullest extent, was, and ever would be, the unavoidable consequence of the connexion. Surely the Quakers forgot their own principles when, in their late Testimony, they called *this connexion*, with these military and miserable appendages hanging to it —" *the happy constitution.*"

Britain, for centuries past, has been nearly fifty years out of every hundred at war with some power or other. It certainly ought to be a conscientious as well as political consideration with America, not to dip her hands in the bloody work of Europe. Our situation affords us a retreat from their cabals, and the present happy union of the states bids fair for extirpating the future use of arms from one quarter of the world ; yet such have been the irreligious politics of the present leaders of the Quakers, that, for the sake of they scarce know what, they would cut off every hope of such a blessing by tying this continent to Britain, like Hector to the chariot wheel of Achilles, to be dragged through all the miseries of endless European wars.

The connexion, viewed from this ground, is distressing to every man who has the feelings of humanity. By having Britain for our master, we became enemies to the greatest part of Europe, and they to us: and the consequence was war inevitable. By being our own masters, independent of any foreign one, we have Europe for our friends, and the prospect of an endless peace among ourselves. Those who were advocates for the British government over these colonies, were obliged to limit both their arguments and their ideas to the period of an European peace only: the moment Britain became plunged in war, every supposed convenience to us vanished, and all we could hope for was not to be ruined. Could this be a desirable condition for a young country to be in?

Had the French pursued their fortune immediately after the defeat of Braddock last war, this city and province had then experienced the woful calamities of being a British subject. A scene of the same kind might happen again; for America, considered as a subject to the crown of Britain, would ever have been the seat of war, and the bone of contention between the two powers.

On the whole, if the future expulsion of arms from one quarter of the world would be a desirable object to a peaceable man; if the freedom of trade to every part of it can engage the attention of a man of business; if the support or fall of millions of currency can affect our interests; if the entire possession of estates, by cutting off the lordly claims of Britain over the soil, deserves the regard of landed property; and if the right of making our own laws, uncontrolled by royal or ministerial spies or mandates, be worthy our care as freemen;—then are all men interested in the support of independence; and may he that supports it not, be driven from the blessing, and live unpitied beneath the servile sufferings of scandalous subjection!

We have been amused with the tales of ancient wonders; we have read, and wept over the histories of other nations:

applauded, censured, or pitied, as their cases affected us. The fortitude and patience of the sufferers—the justness of their cause—the weight of their oppressions and oppressors —the object to be saved or lost—with all the consequences of a defeat or a conquest—have, in the hour of sympathy, bewitched our hearts, and chained it to their fate: but where is the power that ever made war upon petitioners? Or where is the war on which a world was staked till now?

We may not, perhaps, be wise enough to make all the advantages we ought of our independence; but they are, nevertheless, marked and presented to us with every character of *great* and *good*, and worthy the hand of him who sent them. I look through the present trouble to a time of tranquillity, when we shall have it in our power to set an example of peace to all the world. Were the Quakers really impressed and influenced by the quiet principles they profess to hold, they would, however they might disapprove the means, be the first of all men to approve of *independence*, because, by separating ourselves from the cities of Sodom and Gomorrah, it affords an opportunity never given to man before of carrying their favourite principle of peace into general practice, by establishing governments that shall hereafter exist without wars. O! ye fallen, cringing, priest-and-Pemberton-ridden people! What more can we say of ye than that a religious Quaker is a valuable character, and a political Quaker a real Jesuit.

Having thus gone over some of the principal points in support of independence, I must now request the reader to return back with me to the period when it first began to be a public doctrine, and to examine the progress it has made among the various classes of men. The area I mean to begin at, is the breaking out of hostilities, April 19th, 1775. Until this event happened, the continent seemed to view the dispute as a kind of law-suit for a matter of right, litigating between the old country and the new; and she felt the same kind and degree of horror, as if she had seen an oppressive plaintiff, at the head of a band of ruffians, enter the court, while the cause was before it, and put the judge, the jury, the defendant and his counsel, to the sword. Perhaps a more heart-felt convulsion never reached a country with the same degree of power and rapidity before, and never may again. Pity for the sufferers, mixed with indignation at the violence, and heightened with apprehensions of undergoing the same fate, made the affair of Lexington the affair of the continent. Every part of it felt the shock, and all vibrated together. A general promotion of sentiment took place : those who had drank deeply into whiggish principles, that is, the right and necessity not only of opposing, but wholly setting aside the power of the crown as soon as it became practically dangerous (for in theory it was always so), stepped into the first stage of independence ; while another class of whigs, equally sound in principle, but not so sanguine in enterprise, attached themselves the stronger to the cause, and fell close in with the rear of the former ; their partition was a mere point. Numbers of the moderate men, whose chief fault, at that time, arose from entertaining a better opinion of Britain than she deserved, convinced now of their mistake, gave her up, and publicly declared themselves good whigs. While the tories, seeing it was no longer a laughing matter, either sank into silent obscurity, or contented themselves with coming forth and abusing General Gage : not a single advocate appeared to justify the action of that day ; it seemed to appear to every one with the same magnitude, struck every one with the same force, and created in every one the same abhorrence. From this period we may date the growth of independence.

If the many circumstances which happened at this memorable time, be taken in one view, and compared with each other, they will justify a conclusion which seems not to have been attended to, I mean a fixed design in the king and ministry of driving America into arms, in order that they might be furnished with a pretence for seizing the whole continent, as the immediate property of the crown. A noble plunder for hungry courtiers !

It ought to be remembered, that the first petition from

the congress was at this time unanswered on the part of the
British king. That the motion, called lord North's motion,
of the 20th of February, 1775, arrived in America the latter
end of March. This motion was to be laid, by the several
governors then in being, before the assembly of each province; and the first assembly before which it was laid, was
the assembly of Pennsylvania, in May following. This
being a just state of the case, I then ask, why were hostilities commenced between the time of passing the resolve in
the house of commons, of the 20th of February, and the
time of the assemblies meeting to deliberate upon it? Degrading and famous as that motion was, there is nevertheless
reason to believe that the king and his adherents were afraid
the colonies would agree to it, and lest they should, took
effectual care they should not, by provoking them with hostilities in the interim. They had not the least doubt at that
time of conquering America at one blow; and what they
expected to get by a conquest being infinitely greater than
any thing they could hope to get either by taxation or accommodation, they seemed determined to prevent even the
possibility of hearing each other, lest America should disappoint their greedy hopes of the whole, by listening even to
their own terms. On the one hand they refused to hear
the petition of the continent, and on the other hand took
effectual care the continent should not hear them.

That the motion of the 20th February and the orders for
commencing hostilities were both concerted by the same
person or persons, and not the latter by general Gage, as was
falsely imagined at first, is evident from an extract of a letter
of his to the administration, read among other papers in the
house of commons; in which he informs his masters, " *That
though their idea of his disarming certain counties was a right
one, yet it required him to be master of the country, in order
to enable him to execute it.*" This was prior to the commencement of hostilities, and consequently before the motion
of the 20th February could be deliberated on by the several
assemblies.

Perhaps it may be asked, why was the motion passed, if

there was at the same time a plan to aggravate the Americans
not to listen to it ? Lord North assigned one reason himself,
which was *a hope of dividing them.* This was publicly tempting them to reject it ; that if, in case the injury of arms should
fail in provoking them sufficiently, the insult of such a
declaration might fill it up. But by passing the motion and
getting it afterwards rejected in America, it enabled them,
in their wicked idea of politics, among other things, to hold
up the colonies to foreign powers, with every possible mark
of disobedience and rebellion. They had applied to those
powers not to supply the continent with arms, ammunition,
etc., and it was necessary they should incense them against
us, by assigning on their own part some seeming reputable
reason why. By dividing, it had a tendency to weaken the
states, and likewise to perplex the adherents of America in
England. But the principal scheme, and that which has
marked their character in every part of their conduct, was a
design of precipitating the colonies into a state which they
might afterwards deem rebellion, and, under that pretence,
put an end to all future complaints, petitions and remonstrances, by seizing the whole at once. They had ravaged
one part of the globe, till it could glut them no longer ; their
prodigality required new plunder, and through the East
India article *tea* they hoped to transfer their rapine from
that quarter of the world to this. Every designed quarrel
had its pretence ; and the same barbarian avarice accompanied
the *plant* to America, which ruined the country that produced it.

That men never turn rogues without turning fools is a
maxim, sooner or later, universally true. The commencement of hostilities, being in the beginning of April, was, of
all times the worst chosen : the congress were to meet the
tenth of May following, and the distress the continent felt at
this unparalleled outrage gave a stability to that body which
no other circumstance could have done. It suppressed too
all inferior debates, and bound them together by a necessitous affection, without giving them time to differ upon
trifles. The suffering likewise softened the whole body of

the people into a degree of pliability, which laid the principal foundation-stone of union, order, and government; and which, at any other time, might only have fretted and then faded away unnoticed and unimproved : but Providence, who best knows how to time her misfortunes as well as her immediate favors, chose this to be the time, and who dare dispute it?

It did not seem the disposition of the people, at this crisis, to heap petition upon petition, while the former remained unanswered : the measure however was carried in congress, and a second petition was sent; of which I shall only remark that it was submissive even to a dangerous fault, because the prayer of it appealed solely to what it called the prerogative of the crown, while the matter in dispute was confessedly constitutional.   But even this petition, flattering as it was, was still not so harmonious as the chink of cash, and consequently not sufficiently grateful to the tyrant and his ministry.   From every circumstance it is evident, that it was the determination of the British court to have nothing to do with America but to conquer her fully and absolutely. They were certain of success, and the field of battle was the only place of treaty. I am confident there are thousands and tens of thousands in America who wonder *now* that they should ever have thought otherwise ; but the sin of that day was the sin of civility ; yet it operated against our present good in the same manner that a civil opinion of the devil would against our future peace.

Independence was a doctrine scarce and rare, even towards the conclusion of the year 1775 ; all our politics had been founded on the hope of expectation of making the matter up—a hope, which, though general on the side of America, had never entered the head or heart of the British court. Their hope was conquest and confiscation. Good heavens! what volumes of thanks does America owe to Britain ? What infinite obligation to the tool that fills, with paradoxical vacancy, the throne! Nothing but the sharpest essence of villany, compounded with the strongest distillation of folly, could have produced a menstruum that would have effected a separation. The congress in 1774 administered an abortive medicine to independence, by prohibiting the importation of goods, and the succeeding congress rendered the dose still more dangerous by continuing it. Had independence been a settled system with America, (as Britain has advanced,) she ought to have *doubled* her importation, and prohibited in some degree her exportation. And this single circumstance is sufficient to acquit America before any jury of nations, of having a continental plan of independence in view: a charge which, had it been true, would have been honorable, but is so grossly false, that either the amazing ignorance or the wilful dishonesty of the British court is effectually proved by it.

The second petition, like the first, produced no answer; it was scarcely acknowledged to have been received; the British court were too determined in their villainy even to act it artfully, and in their rage for conquest neglected the necessary subtleties for obtaining it. They might have divided, distracted and played a thousand tricks with us, had they been as cunning as they were cruel.

This last indignity gave a new spring to independence. Those who knew the savage obstinacy of the king, and the jobbing, gambling spirit of the court, predicted the fate of the petition, as soon as it was sent from America; for the men being known, their measures were easily foreseen. As politicians we ought not so much to ground our hopes on the reasonableness of the thing we ask, as on the reasonableness of the person of whom we ask it: who would expect discretion from a fool, candor from a tyrant, or justice from a villain?

As every prospect of accommodation seemed now to fail fast, men began to think seriously on the matter; and their reason being thus stripped of the false hope which had long encompassed it, became approachable by fair debate: yet still the bulk of the people hesitated; they startled at the novelty of independence, without once considering that our getting into arms at first was a more extraordinary novelty, and that all other nations had gone through the work of independence before us. They doubted likewise the ability of the continent to support it, without reflecting that it required the same force to obtain an accommodation by arms as an independence. If the one was acquirable, the other was the same ; because, to accomplish either, it was necessary that our strength should be too great for Britain to subdue ; and it was too unreasonable to suppose, that with the power of being masters, we should submit to be servants.*

Their caution at this time was exceedingly misplaced ; for if they were able to defend their property and maintain their rights by arms, they, consequently, were able to defend and support their independence ; and in proportion as these men saw the necessity and correctness of the measure, they honestly and openly declared and adopted it, and the part that they had acted since has done them honor and fully established their characters. Error in opinion has this peculiar advantage with it, that the foremost point of the contrary ground may at any time be reached by the sudden exertion of a thought ; and it frequently happens in sentimental differences, that some striking circumstance, or some forcible reason quickly conceived, will effect in an instant what neither argument nor example could produce in an age.

I find it impossible in the small compass I am limited to,

---

* In this state of political suspense the pamphlet Common Sense made its appearance, and the success it met with does not become me to mention. Dr. Franklin, Mr. Samuel and John Adams, were severally spoken of as the supposed author. I had not, at that time, the pleasure either of personally knowing or being known to the two last gentlemen. The favour of Dr. Franklin's friendship I possessed in England, and my introduction to this part of the world was through his patronage. I happened, when a school-boy, to pick up a pleasing natural history of Virginia, and my inclination from that day of seeing the western side of the Atlantic never left me. In October, 1775, Dr. Franklin proposed giving me such materials as were in his hands, towards completing a history of the present transactions, and seemed desirous of having the first volume out the next spring. I had then formed the outlines of Common Sense, and finished nearly the first part ; and as I supposed the doctor's design in getting out a history, was to open the new year with a new system, I expected to surprise him with a production on that subject, much earlier than he thought of ; and without informing him what I was doing, got it ready for the press as fast as I conveniently could, and sent him the first pamphlet that was printed off.—*Author*.

to trace out the progress which independence has made on the minds of the different classes of men, and the several reasons by which they were moved. With some, it was a passionate abhorrence against the king of England and his ministry, as a set of savages and brutes; and these men, governed by the agony of a wounded mind, were for trusting every thing to hope and heaven, and bidding defiance at once. With others, it was a growing conviction that the scheme of the British court was to create, ferment and drive on a quarrel, for the sake of confiscated plunder: and men of this class ripened into independence in proportion as the evidence increased. While a third class conceived it was the true interest of America, internally and externally, to be her own master, and gave their support to independence, step by step, as they saw her abilities to maintain it enlarge. With many, it was a compound of all these reasons; while those who were too callous to be reached by either, remained, and still remain tories.

The *legal necessity* of being independent, with several collateral reasons, is pointed out in an elegant masterly manner, in a charge to the grand jury for the district of Charleston, by the Hon. William Henry Drayton, chief justice of South Carolina.[1] This performance, and the address of the convention of New York, are pieces, in my humble opinion, of the first rank in America.

The principal causes why independence has not been so universally supported as it ought, are *fear* and *indolence*, and the causes why it has been opposed, are, *avarice, down-right villany*, and *lust of personal power*. There is not such a being in America as a tory from conscience; some secret defect or other is interwoven in the character of all those, be they men or women, who can look with patience on the brutality, luxury and debauchery of the British court, and the violations of their army here. A woman's virtue must sit very lightly on her who can even hint a favorable sentiment in their behalf. It is remarkable that the whole race of prostitutes in New York were tories; and the schemes for support-

[1] April 23, 1776.—*Editor.*

ing the tory cause in this city, for which several are now in jail, and one hanged, were concerted and carried on in common bawdy-houses, assisted by those who kept them.[1]

The connexion between vice and meanness is a fit subject for satire, but when the satire is a fact, it cuts with the irresistible power of a diamond. If a Quaker, in defence of his just rights, his property, and the chastity of his house, takes up a musket, he is expelled the meeting; but the present king of England, who seduced and took into keeping a sister of their society, is reverenced and supported by repeated Testimonies, while the friendly noodle from whom she was taken (and who is now in this city) continues a drudge in the service of his rival, as if proud of being cuckolded by a creature called a king.[2]

Our support and success depend on such a variety of men and circumstances, that every one who does but wish well, is of some use: there are men who have a strange aversion to arms, yet have hearts to risk every shilling in the cause, or in support of those who have better talents for defending it. Nature, in the arrangement of mankind, has fitted some for every service in life: were all soldiers, all would starve and go naked, and were none soldiers, all would be slaves. As *disaffection* to independence is the badge of a tory, so *affection* to it is the mark of a whig; and the different services of the whigs, down from those who nobly contribute every thing, to those who have nothing to render but their wishes, tend all to the same centre, though with different degrees of merit and ability. The larger we make the circle, the more we shall harmonize, and the stronger we shall be. All we

---

[1] In Philadelphia, the only American city with which Paine was then familiar. "Toryism" was of an exceptionally snobbish and self-interested type. It is certain, though not then recognized, that some excellent men made heavy sacrifices for their loyalty to the Crown. Some of these, while sympathizing with the colonies, regarded as sacred official oaths which they had taken to serve the King.—*Editor.*

[2] The Quaker "sister" was of course Hannah Lightfoot, and it would appear that Axford, to whom she was said to have been married, was in Philadelphia.— *Editor.*

want to shut out is disaffection, and, *that excluded*, we must accept from each other such duties as we are best fitted to bestow. A narrow system of politics, like a narrow system of religion, is calculated only to sour the temper, and be at variance with mankind.

All we want to know in America is simply this, who is for independence, and who is not? Those who are for it, will support it, and the remainder will undoubtedly see the reasonableness of paying the charges; while those who oppose or seek to betray it, must expect the more rigid fate of the jail and the gibbet. There is a bastard kind of generosity, which being extended to all men, is as fatal to society, on one hand, as the want of true generosity is on the other. A lax manner of administering justice, falsely termed moderation, has a tendency both to dispirit public virtue, and promote the growth of public evils. Had the late committee of safety taken cognizance of the last Testimony of the Quakers and proceeded against such delinquents as were concerned therein, they had, probably, prevented the treasonable plans which have been concerted since. When one villain is suffered to escape, it encourages another to proceed, either from a hope of escaping likewise, or an apprehension that we dare not punish. It has been a matter of general surprise, that no notice was taken of the incendiary publication of the Quakers, of the 20th of November last: a publication evidently intended to promote sedition and treason, and encourage the enemy, who were then within a day's march of this city, to proceed on and possess it. I here present the reader with a memorial which was laid before the board of safety a few days after the Testimony appeared. Not a member of that board, that I conversed with, but expressed the highest detestation of the perverted principles and conduct of the Quaker junto, and a wish that the board would take the matter up; notwithstanding which, it was suffered to pass away unnoticed, to the encouragement of new acts of treason, the general danger of the cause, and the disgrace of the state.

To the honorable the Council of Safety of the State of Pennsylvania.

At a meeting of a reputable number of the inhabitants of the city of Philadelphia, impressed with a proper sense of the justice of the cause which this continent is engaged in, and animated with a generous fervor for supporting the same, it was resolved, that the following be laid before the board of safety :

" We profess liberality of sentiment to all men ; with this distinction *only*, that those who do not deserve it would become wise and *seek* to deserve it. We hold the pure doctrines of universal liberty of conscience, and conceive it our duty to endeavor to secure that sacred right to others, as well as to defend it for ourselves ; for we undertake not to judge of the religious rectitude of tenets, but leave the whole matter to Him who made us.

" We persecute no man, neither will we abet in the persecution of any man for religion's sake ; our common relation to others being that of fellow-citizens and fellow-subjects of one single community ; and in this line of connexion we hold out the right hand of fellowship to all men. But we should conceive ourselves to be unworthy members of the *free and independent states of America*, were we unconcernedly to see or to suffer any treasonable wound, public or private, directly or indirectly, to be given against the peace and safety of the same. We inquire not into the rank of the offenders, nor into their religious persuasion ; we have no business with either, our part being only to find them out and exhibit them to justice.

" A printed paper, dated the 20th of November, and signed ' *John Pemberton*,' whom we suppose to be an inhabitant of this city, has lately been dispersed abroad, a copy of which accompanies this.[1] Had the framers and publishers of that paper conceived it their duty to exhort the youth and others of their society, to a patient submission under the present trying visitations, and humbly to wait the event of heaven towards them, they had therein shown a Christian temper, and we had been silent ; but the anger and political virulence with which their instructions are given, and

[1] John Pemberton, an eminent Quaker, had been associated with the founding of the Antislavery Society, April 14, 1775, but afterwards led the Quakers into their unpatriotic position, and with more than twenty others was sent to Virginia and confined for some months, at a critical period of the Revolution.— *Editor.*

the abuse with which they stigmatize all ranks of men not thinking like themselves, leave no doubt on our minds from what spirit
their publication proceeded : and it is disgraceful to the pure
cause of truth, that men can dally with words of the most sacred
import, and play them off as mechanically as if religion consisted
only in contrivance. We know of no instance in which the
Quakers have been compelled to bear arms, or to do any thing
which might strain their conscience ; wherefore their advice, ' to
withstand and refuse to submit to the arbitrary instructions and
ordinances of men,' appear to us a false alarm, and could only be
treasonably calculated to gain favor with our enemies, when they
are seemingly on the brink of invading this state, or, what is still
worse, to weaken the hands of our defence, that their entrance
into this city might be made practicable and easy.

" We disclaim all tumult and disorder in the punishment of
offenders ; and wish to be governed, not by temper but by reason,
in the manner of treating them. We are sensible that our cause
has suffered by the two following errors : first, by ill-judged lenity
to traitorous persons in some cases ; and, secondly, by only a
passionate treatment of them in others. For the future we disown both, and wish to be steady in our proceedings, and serious
in our punishments.

" Every state in America has, by the repeated voice of its inhabitants, directed and authorised the continental congress to
publish a formal Declaration of Independence of, and separation
from, the oppressive king and parliament of Great Britain ; and
we look on every man as an enemy, who does not in some line
or other, give his assistance towards supporting the same ; at the
same time we consider the offence to be heightened to a degree
of unpardonable guilt, when such persons, under the show of
religion, endeavor, either by writing, speaking, or otherwise, to
subvert, overturn, or bring reproach upon the independence of
this continent as declared by congress.

" The publishers of the paper signed ' *John Pemberton*,' have
called in a loud manner to their friends and connexions, ' to withstand or refuse ' obedience to whatever ' instructions or ordinances ' may be published, not warranted by (what they call) ' that
happy constitution under which they and others long enjoyed
tranquillity and peace.' If this be not treason, we know not what
may properly be called by that name.

" To us it is a matter of surprise and astonishment, that men with the word '*peace, peace,*' continually on their lips, should be so fond of living under and supporting a government, and at the same time calling it '*happy,*' which is never better pleased than when at war—that hath filled India with carnage and famine, Africa with slavery, and tampered with Indians and negroes to cut the throats of the freemen of America. We conceive it a disgrace to this state, to harbor or wink at such palpable hypocrisy. But as we seek not to hurt the hair of any man's head, when we can make ourselves safe without, we wish such persons to restore peace to themselves and us, by removing themselves to some part of the king of Great Britain's dominions, as by that means they may live unmolested by us and we by them ; for our fixed opinion is, that those who do not deserve a place among us, ought not to have one.

" We conclude with requesting the Council of Safety to take into consideration the paper signed '*John Pemberton,*' and if it shall appear to them to be of a dangerous tendency, or of a treasonable nature, that they would commit the signer, together with such other persons as they can discover were concerned therein, into custody, until such time as some mode of trial shall ascertain the full degree of their guilt and punishment ; in the doing of which, we wish their judges, whoever they may be, to disregard the man, his connexions, interest, riches, poverty, or principles of religion, and to attend to the nature of his offence only."

The most cavilling sectarian cannot accuse the foregoing with containing the least ingredient of persecution. The free spirit on which the American cause is founded, disdains to mix with such an impurity, and leaves it as rubbish fit only for narrow and suspicious minds to grovel in. Suspicion and persecution are weeds of the same dunghill, and flourish together. Had the Quakers minded their religion and their business, they might have lived through this dispute in enviable ease, and none would have molested them. The common phrase with these people is, ' *Our principles are peace.*' To which may be replied, *and your practices are the reverse ;* for never did the conduct of men oppose their own doctrine more notoriously than the present race of the Quakers. They have artfully changed themselves into a

different sort of people to what they used to be, and yet
have the address to persuade each other that they are not
altered; like antiquated virgins, they see not the havoc de-
formity has made upon them, but pleasantly mistaking
wrinkles for dimples, conceive themselves yet lovely and
wonder at the stupid world for not admiring them.

Did no injury arise to the public by this apostacy of the
Quakers from themselves, the public would have nothing to
do with it; but as both the design and consequences are
pointed against a cause in which the whole community are
interested, it is therefore no longer a subject confined to the
cognizance of the meeting only, but comes, as a matter of
criminality, before the authority either of the particular state
in which it is acted, or of the continent against which it
operates. Every attempt, now, to support the authority of
the king and parliament of Great Britain over America, is
treason against *every* state; therefore it is impossible that
any *one* can pardon or screen from punishment an offender
against *all*.

But to proceed: while the infatuated tories of this and
other states were last spring talking of commissioners, accommodation, making the matter up, and the Lord knows
what stuff and nonsense, their *good* king and ministry were
glutting themselves with the revenge of reducing America
to *unconditional submission*, and solacing each other with the
certainty of conquering it in *one campaign*. The following
quotations are from the parliamentary register of the debates
of the house of lords, March 5th, 1776:

"The Americans," says lord Talbot,* "have been obstinate,
undutiful, and ungovernable from the very beginning, from their
first early and infant settlements; and I am every day more and
more convinced that this people never will be brought back to
their duty, and the subordinate relation they stand in to this
country, *till reduced to unconditional, effectual submission; no
concession on our part, no lenity, no endurance,* will have any other
effect but that of increasing their insolence."

* Steward of the king's household.—*Author.*

"The struggle," says lord Townsend,* "is now a struggle for power ; the die is cast, and the *only point* which now remains to be determined is, in what manner the war can be most effectually prosecuted and speedily finished, in order to procure that *unconditional submission*, which has been so ably stated by the noble earl with the white staff" (meaning lord Talbot ;) "and I have no reason to doubt that the measures now pursuing will put an end to the war in the course of a *single campaign.* Should it linger longer, we shall then have reason to expect that some foreign power will interfere, and take advantage of our domestic troubles and civil distractions."

Lord Littleton. "My sentiments are pretty well known. I shall only observe now that lenient measures have had no other effect than to produce insult after insult ; that the more we conceded, the higher America rose in her demands, and the more insolent she has grown. It is for this reason that I am now for the most effective and decisive measures ; and am of opinion that no alternative is left us, but to relinquish America for ever, or finally determine to compel her to acknowledge the legislative authority of this country ; and it is the principle of an *unconditional submission* I would be for maintaining."

Can words be more expressive than these? Surely the tories will believe the tory lords! The truth is, they *do believe them* and know as fully as any whig on the continent knows, that the king and ministry never had the least design of an accommodation with America, but an absolute, unconditional conquest. And the part which the tories were to act, was, by downright lying, to endeavor to put the continent off its guard, and to divide and sow discontent in the minds of such whigs as they might gain an influence over. In short, to keep up a distraction here, that the force sent from England might be able to conquer in "*one campaign.*" They and the ministry were, by a different game, playing into each other's hands. The cry of the tories in England was, "*No reconciliation, no accommodation,*" in order to obtain the greater military force ; while those in America were crying

* Formerly, general Townsend, at Quebec, and late lord-lieutenant of Ireland. —*Author.*

nothing but " *reconciliation and accommodation*," that the force sent might conquer with the less resistance.

But this " *single campaign* " is over, and America not conquered. The whole work is yet to do, and the force much less to do it with. Their condition is both despicable and deplorable: out of cash—out of heart, and out of hope. A country furnished with arms and ammunition as America now is, with three millions of inhabitants, and three thousand miles distant from the nearest enemy that can approach her, is able to look and laugh them in the face.

Howe appears to have two objects in view, either to go up the North river, or come to Philadelphia.

By going up the North river, he secures a retreat for his army through Canada, but the ships must return if they return at all, the same way they went; as our army would be in the rear, the safety of their passage down is a doubtful matter. By such a motion he shuts himself from all supplies from Europe, but through Canada, and exposes his army and navy to the danger of perishing. The idea of his cutting off the communication between the eastern and southern states, by means of the North river, is merely visionary. He cannot do it by his shipping; because no ship can lay long at anchor in any river within reach of the shore; a single gun would drive a first rate from such a station. This was fully proved last October at forts Washington and Lee, where one gun only, on each side of the river, obliged two frigates to cut and be towed off in an hour's time. Neither can he cut it off by his army; because the several posts they must occupy would divide them almost to nothing, and expose them to be picked up by ours like pebbles on a river's bank; but admitting that he could, where is the injury? Because, while his whole force is cantoned out, as sentries over the water, they will be very innocently employed, and the moment they march into the country the communication opens.

The most probable object is Philadelphia, and the reasons are many. Howe's business is to conquer it, and in proportion as he finds himself unable to the task, he will employ his strength to distress women and weak minds, in order to accomplish through *their* fears what he cannot accomplish by his *own* force. His coming or attempting to come to Philadelphia is a circumstance that proves his weakness: for no general that felt himself able to take the field and attack his antagonist would think of bringing his army into a city in the summer time; and this mere shifting the scene from place to place, without effecting any thing, has feebleness and cowardice on the face of it, and holds him up in a contemptible light to all who can reason justly and firmly. By several informations from New York, it appears that their army in general, both officers and men, have given up the expectation of conquering America; their eye now is fixed upon the spoil. They suppose Philadelphia to be rich with stores, and as they think to get more by robbing a town than by attacking an army, their movement towards this city is probable. We are not now contending against an army of soldiers, but against a band of thieves, who had rather plunder than fight, and have no other hope of conquest than by cruelty.

They expect to get a mighty booty, and strike another general panic, by making a sudden movement and getting possession of this city; but unless they can march *out* as well as *in*, or get the entire command of the river, to remove off their plunder, they may probably be stopped with the stolen goods upon them. They have never yet succeeded wherever they have been opposed, but at fort Washington. At Charleston their defeat was effectual. At Ticonderoga they ran away. In every skirmish at Kingsbridge and the White Plains they were obliged to retreat, and the instant that our arms were turned upon them in the Jerseys, they turned likewise, and those that turned not were taken.

The necessity of always fitting our internal police to the circumstances of the times we live in, is something so strikingly obvious, that no sufficient objection can be made against it. The safety of all societies depends upon it; and where this point is not attended to, the consequences will either be a general languor or a tumult. The encouragement and protection of the good subjects of any state, and the suppression and punishment of bad ones, are the principal objects for which all authority is instituted, and the line in which it ought to operate. We have in this city a strange variety of men and characters, and the circumstances of the times require that they should be publicly known ; it is not the number of tories that hurt us, so much as the not finding out who they are ; men must now take one side or the other, and abide by the consequences : the Quakers, trusting to their short-sighted sagacity, have, most unluckily for them, made their declaration in their last Testimony, and we ought *now* to take them at their word. They have involuntarily read themselves out of the continental meeting, and cannot hope to be restored to it again but by payment and penitence. Men whose political principles are founded on avarice, are beyond the reach of reason, and the only cure of toryism of this cast is to tax it. A substantial good drawn from a real evil, is of the same benefit to society, as if drawn from a virtue ; and where men have not public spirit to render themselves serviceable, it ought to be the study of government to draw the best use possible from their vices. When the governing passion of any man, or set of men, is once known, the method of managing them is easy ; for even misers, whom no public virtue can impress, would become generous, could a heavy tax be laid upon covetousness.

The tories have endeavored to insure their property with the enemy, by forfeiting their reputation with us ; from which may be justly inferred, that their governing passion is avarice. Make them as much afraid of losing on one side as on the other, and you stagger their toryism ; make them more so, and you reclaim them ; for their principle is to worship the power which they are most afraid of.

This method of considering men and things together, opens into a large field for speculation, and affords me an opportunity of offering some observations on the state of our currency, so as to make the support of it go hand in hand with the suppression of disaffection and the encouragement of public spirit.

The thing which first presents itself in inspecting the state

of the currency, is, that we have too much of it, and that
there is a necessity of reducing the quantity, in order to increase the value.   Men are daily growing poor by the very
means that they take to get rich; for in the same proportion
that the prices of all goods on hand are raised, the value of
all money laid by is reduced.   A simple case will make this
clear; let a man have 100*l.* in cash, and as many goods on
hand as will to-day sell for 20*l.*; but not content with the
present market price, he raises them to 40*l.* and by so doing
obliges others, in their own defence, to raise cent. per cent.
likewise; in this case it is evident that his hundred pounds
laid by, is reduced fifty pounds in value; whereas, had the
market lowered cent. per cent., his goods would have sold
but for ten, but his hundred pounds would have risen in
value to two hundred; because it would then purchase as
many goods again, or support his family as long again as before.   And, strange as it may seem, he is one hundred and
fifty pounds the poorer for raising his goods, to what he
would have been had he lowered them; because the forty
pounds which his goods sold for, is, by the general raise of
the market cent. per cent., rendered of no more value than
the ten pounds would be had the market fallen in the same
proportion; and, consequently, the whole difference of gain
or loss is on the difference in value of the hundred pounds
laid by, *viz.* from fifty to two hundred. This rage for raising
goods is for several reasons much more the fault of the tories
than the whigs; and yet the tories (to their shame and confusion ought they to be told of it) are by far the most noisy
and discontented.   The greatest part of the whigs, by being
now either in the army or employed in some public service,
are *buyers* only and not *sellers*, and as this evil has its origin
in trade, it cannot be charged on those who are out of it.

But the grievance has now become too general to be
remedied by partial methods, and the only effectual cure is
to reduce the quantity of money: with half the quantity we
should be richer than we are now, because the value of it
would be doubled, and consequently our attachment to it
increased; for it is not the number of dollars that a man

has, but how far they will go, that makes him either rich or poor.

These two points being admitted, *viz.* that the quantity of money is too great, and that the prices of goods can only be effectually reduced by reducing the quantity of the money, the next point to be considered is, the method how to reduce it.

The circumstances of the times, as before observed, require that the public characters of all men should *now* be fully understood, and the only general method of ascertaining it is by an oath or affirmation, renouncing all allegiance to the king of Great Britain, and to support the independence of the United States, as declared by congress. Let, at the same time, a tax of ten, fifteen, or twenty per cent. per annum, to be collected quarterly, be levied on all property. These alternatives, by being perfectly voluntary, will take in all sorts of people. Here is the test; here is the tax. He who takes the former, conscientiously proves his affection to the cause, and binds himself to pay his quota by the best *services* in his power, and is thereby justly exempt from the latter ; and those who choose the latter, pay their quota in money, to be excused from the former, or rather, it is the price paid to us for their supposed, though mistaken, insurance with the enemy.

But this is only a part of the advantage which would arise by knowing the different characters of men. The whigs stake every thing on the issue of their arms, while the tories, by their disaffection, are sapping and undermining their strength ; and, of consequence, the property of the whigs is the more exposed thereby; and whatever injury their estates may sustain by the movements of the enemy, must either be borne by themselves, who have done every thing which has *yet* been done, or by the tories, who have not only done nothing, but have, by their disaffection, invited the enemy on.

In the present crisis we ought to know, square by square and house by house, who are in real allegiance with the United Independent States, and who are not. Let but the line be made clear and distinct, and all men will then know what they are to trust to.   It would not only be good policy but strict justice, to raise fifty or one hundred thousand pounds, or more, if it is necessary, out of the estates and property of the king of England's votaries, resident in Philadelphia, to be distributed, as a reward to those inhabitants of the city and state, who should turn out and repulse the enemy, should they attempt to march this way; and likewise, to bind the property of all such persons to make good the damages which that of the whigs might sustain.   In the undistinguishable mode of conducting a war, we frequently make reprisals at sea, on the vessels of persons in England, who are friends to our cause compared with the resident tories among us.

In every former publication of mine, from Common Sense down to the last Crisis, I have generally gone on the charitable supposition, that the tories were rather a mistaken than a criminal people, and have applied argument after argument, with all the candor and temper which I was capable of, in order to set every part of the case clearly and fairly before them, and if possible to reclaim them from ruin to reason.   I have done my duty by them and have now done with that doctrine, taking it for·granted, that those who yet hold their disaffection are either a set of avaricious miscreants, who would sacrifice the continent to save themselves, or a banditti of hungry traitors, who are hoping for a division of the spoil.   To which may be added, a list of crown or proprietary dependants, who, rather than go without a portion of power, would be content to share it with the devil. Of such men there is no hope;   and their obedience will only be according to the danger set before them, and the power that is exercised over them.

A time will shortly arrive, in which, by ascertaining the characters of persons now, we shall be guarded against their mischiefs then;   for in proportion as the enemy despair of conquest, they will be trying the arts of seduction and the force of fear by all the mischiefs which they can inflict.   But in war we may be certain of these two things, *viz.* that cruelty in an enemy, and motions made with more than usual parade, are always signs of weakness.   He that can conquer, finds his mind too free and pleasant to be brutish ; and he that intends to conquer, never makes too much show of his strength.

We now know the enemy we have to do with.   While drunk with the certainty of victory, they disdained to be civil; and in proportion as disappointment makes them sober, and their apprehensions of an European war alarm them, they will become cringing and artful; honest they cannot be.   But our answer to them, in either condition they may be in, is short and full—"As free and independent states we are willing to make peace with you to-morrow, but we neither can hear nor reply in any other character."

If Britain cannot conquer us, it proves that she is neither able to govern nor protect us, and our particular situation now is such, that any connexion with her would be unwisely exchanging a half-defeated enemy for two powerful ones. Europe, by every appearance, is now on the eve, nay, on the morning twilight of a war, and any alliance with George the third, brings France and Spain upon our backs ; a separation from him attaches them to our side ; therefore, the only road to peace, honour, and commerce, in *Independence.*

Written this fourth year of the UNION,[1] *which God preserve.*

COMMON SENSE.

PHILADELPHIA, April 19, 1777.

THE CRISIS.

IV.

THOSE who expect to reap the blessings of freedom, must, like men, undergo the fatigues of supporting it.   The event of yesterday[2] was one of those kind of alarms which is just sufficient to rouse us to duty, without being of consequence enough to depress our fortitude.   It is not a field of

[1] Paine would seem to date from the formation of the intercolonial committee, in 1773.—*Editor.*

[2] Battle of Brandywine, September 11, 1777.   For the circumstances under which this brief " Crisis " was written, see Paine's letter to Franklin (XXI. of this volume).—*Editor.*

a few acres of ground, but a cause, that we are defending, and whether we defeat the enemy in one battle, or by degrees, the consequences will be the same.

Look back at the events of last winter and the present year, there you will find that the enemy's successes always contributed to reduce them. What they have gained in ground, they paid so dearly for in numbers, that their victories have in the end amounted to defeats. We have always been masters at the last push, and always shall be while we do our duty. Howe has been once on the banks of the Delaware, and from thence driven back with loss and disgrace: and why not be again driven from the Schuylkill? His condition and ours are very different. He has everybody to fight, we have only his *one* army to cope with, and which wastes away at every engagement: we can not only reinforce, but can redouble our numbers; he is cut off from all supplies, and must sooner or later inevitably fall into our hands.

Shall a band of ten or twelve thousand robbers, who are this day fifteen hundred or two thousand men less in strength than they were yesterday, conquer America, or subdue even a single state? The thing cannot be, unless we sit down and suffer them to do it. Another such a brush, notwithstanding we lost the ground, would, by still reducing the enemy, put them in a condition to be afterwards totally defeated.

Could our whole army have come up to the attack at one time, the consequences had probably been otherwise; but our having different parts of the Brandywine creek to guard, and the uncertainty which road to Philadelphia the enemy would attempt to take, naturally afforded them an opportunity of passing with their main body at a place where only a part of ours could be posted; for it must strike every thinking man with conviction, that it requires a much greater force to oppose an enemy in several places, than is sufficient to defeat him in any one place.

Men who are sincere in defending their freedom, will always feel concern at every circumstance which seems to make against them; it is the natural and honest consequence of all affectionate attachments, and the want of it is a vice. But the dejection lasts only for a moment; they soon rise out of it with additional vigor; the glow of hope, courage and fortitude, will, in a little time, supply the place of every inferior passion, and kindle the whole heart into heroism.

There is a mystery in the countenance of some causes, which we have not always present judgment enough to explain. It is distressing to see an enemy advancing into a country, but it is the only place in which we can beat them, and in which we have always beaten them, whenever they made the attempt. The nearer any disease approaches to a crisis, the nearer it is to a cure. Danger and deliverance make their advances together, and it is only the last push, in which one or the other takes the lead.

There are many men who will do their duty when it is not wanted; but a genuine public spirit always appears most when there is most occasion for it. Thank God! our army, though fatigued, is yet entire. The attack made by us yesterday, was under many disadvantages, naturally arising from the uncertainty of knowing which route the enemy would take; and, from that circumstance, the whole of our force could not be brought up together time enough to engage all at once. Our strength is yet reserved; and it is evident that Howe does not think himself a gainer by the affair, otherwise he would this morning have moved down and attacked General Washington.

Gentlemen of the city and country, it is in your power, by a spirited improvement of the present circumstance, to turn it to a real advantage. Howe is now weaker than before, and every shot will contribute to reduce him. You are more immediately interested than any other part of the continent: your all is at stake; it is not so with the general cause; you are devoted by the enemy to plunder and destruction: it is the encouragement which Howe, the chief of plunderers, has promised his army. Thus circumstanced, you may save yourselves by a manly resistance, but you can have no hope in any other conduct. I never yet knew our brave general, or any part of the army, officers or men, out of heart, and I have seen them in circumstances a thousand times more trying than the present. It is only those that are not in action, that feel languor and heaviness, and the best way to rub it off is to turn out, and make sure work of it.

Our army must undoubtedly feel fatigue, and want a reinforcement of rest though not of valour. Our own interest and happiness call upon us to give them every support in our power, and make the burden of the day, on which the safety of this city depends, as light as possible. Remember, gentlemen, that we have forces both to the northward and southward of Philadelphia, and if the enemy be but stopped till those can arrive, this city will be saved, and the enemy finally routed. You have too much at stake to hesitate. You ought not to think an hour upon the matter, but to spring to action at once. Other states have been invaded, have likewise driven off the invaders. Now our time and turn is come, and perhaps the finishing stroke is reserved for us. When we look back on the dangers we have been saved from, and reflect on the success we have been blessed with, it would be sinful either to be idle or to despair.

I close this paper with a short address to general Howe. You, sir, are only lingering out the period that shall bring with it your defeat. You have yet scarce began upon the war, and the further you enter, the faster will your troubles thicken. What you now enjoy is only a respite from ruin; an invitation to destruction; something that will lead on to our deliverance at your expense. We know the cause which we are engaged in, and though a passionate fondness for it may make us grieve at every injury which threatens it, yet, when the moment of concern is over, the determination to duty returns. We are not moved by the gloomy smile of a worthless king, but by the ardent glow of generous patriotism. We fight not to enslave, but to set a country free, and to make room upon the earth for honest men to live in. In such a case we are sure that we are right ; and we leave to you the despairing reflection of being the tool of a miserable tyrant.

COMMON SENSE.

PHILADELPHIA, Sept. 12, 1777.

THE CRISIS.

V.

TO GEN. SIR WILLIAM HOWE.[1]

To argue with a man who has renounced the use and authority of reason, and whose philosophy consists in holding humanity in contempt, is like administering medicine to the dead, or endeavoring to convert an atheist by scripture. Enjoy, sir, your insensibility of feeling and reflecting. It is the prerogative of animals. And no man will envy you these honors, in which a savage only can be your rival and a bear your master.

As the generosity of this country rewarded your brother's services last war, with an elegant monument in Westminster Abbey, it is consistent that she should bestow some mark of distinction upon you.[2] You certainly deserve her notice, and a conspicuous place in the catalogue of extraordinary persons. Yet it would be a pity to pass you from the world in state, and consign you to magnificent oblivion among the tombs, without telling the future beholder why. Judas is as much known as John, yet history ascribes their fame to very different actions.

Sir William hath undoubtedly merited a monument; but of what kind, or with what inscription, where placed or how embellished, is a question that would puzzle all the heralds of St James's in the profoundest mood of historical deliberation. We are at no loss, sir, to ascertain your real character,

---

[1] In October, 1777, Howe being, since September 26, in possession of Philadelphia, Paine was employed by the Pennsylvania Assembly and Council to obtain for it constant intelligence of the movements of Washington's army. (" Life of Paine," i., p. 94.) While writing this, No. V., he saw much of Washington, and the pamphlet was probably to some extent "inspired." It was put into shape at the house of William Henry, Jr., Lancaster, Pa., whose son remembered that he was very long at the work. It was printed at York, Pa., where Congress was in session.—*Editor.*

[2] George Augustus Howe, born 1724, fell at Ticonderoga, July 8, 1758. The General Court of Massachusetts appropriated £250 for the monument in Westminster Abbey.—*Editor.*

but somewhat perplexed how to perpetuate its identity, and preserve it uninjured from the transformations of time or mistake. A statuary may give a false expression to your bust, or decorate it with some equivocal emblems, by which you may happen to steal into reputation and impose upon the hereafter traditionary world. Ill nature or ridicule may conspire, or a variety of accidents combine to lessen, enlarge, or change Sir William's fame; and no doubt but he who has taken so much pains to be singular in his conduct, would choose to be just as singular in his exit, his monument and his epitaph.

The usual honours of the dead, to be sure, are not sufficiently sublime to escort a character like you to the republic of dust and ashes; for however men may differ in their ideas of grandeur or of government here, the grave is nevertheless a perfect republic. Death is not the monarch of the dead, but of the dying. The moment he obtains a conquest he loses a subject, and, like the foolish king you serve, will, in the end, war himself out of all his dominions.

As a proper preliminary towards the arrangement of your funeral honours, we readily admit of your new rank of *knighthood*. The title is perfectly in character, and is your own, more by merit than creation. There are knights of various orders, from the knight of the windmill to the knight of the post. The former is your patron for exploits, and the latter will assist you in settling your accounts. No honorary title could be more happily applied! The ingenuity is sublime! And your royal master hath discovered more genius in fitting you therewith, than in generating the most finished figure for a button, or descanting on the properties of a button mould.

But how, sir, shall we dispose of you? The invention of a statuary is exhausted, and Sir William is yet unprovided with a monument. America is anxious to bestow her funeral favours upon you, and wishes to do it in a manner that shall distinguish you from all the deceased heroes of the last war. The Egyptian method of embalming is not known to the present age, and hieroglyphical pageantry hath outlived the

science of decyphering it. Some other method, therefore,
must be thought of to immortalise the new knight of the
windmill and post. Sir William, thanks to his stars, is not
oppressed with very delicate ideas. He has no ambition of
being wrapped up and handed about in myrrh, aloes and
cassia. Less expensive odours will suffice ; and it fortunately
happens that the simple genius of America hath discovered
the art of preserving bodies, and embellishing them too, with
much greater frugality than the ancients. In balmage, sir,
of humble tar, you will be as secure as Pharaoh, and in a
hieroglyphic of feathers, rival in finery all the mummies of
Egypt.

As you have already made your exit from the moral
world, and by numberless acts both of passionate and deliberate injustice engraved an " *here lyeth* " on your deceased
honour, it must be mere affectation in you to pretend concern at the humours or opinions of mankind respecting you.
What remains of you may expire at any time. The sooner
the better. For he who survives his reputation, lives out of
despite of himself, like a man listening to his own reproach.

Thus entombed and ornamented, I leave you to the inspection of the curious, and return to the history of your
yet surviving actions. The character of Sir William hath
undergone some extraordinary revolutions since his arrival
in America. It is now fixed and known ; and we have
nothing to hope from your candour or to fear from your
capacity. Indolence and inability have too large a share in
your composition, ever to suffer you to be anything more
than the hero of little villainies and unfinished adventures.
That, which to some persons appeared moderation in you at
first, was not produced by any real virtue of your own, but
by a contrast of passions, dividing and holding you in perpetual irresolution. One vice will frequently expel another,
without the least merit in the man ; as powers in contrary
directions reduce each other to rest.

It became you to have supported a dignified solemnity of
character ; to have shown a superior liberality of soul ; to
have won respect by an obstinate perseverance in maintain-

ing order, and to have exhibited on all occasions such an unchangeable graciousness of conduct, that while we beheld in you the resolution of an enemy, we might admire in you the sincerity of a man. You came to America under the high sounding titles of commander and commissioner; not only to suppress what you call rebellion, by arms, but to shame it out of countenance by the excellence of your example. Instead of which, you have been the patron of low and vulgar frauds, the encourager of Indian cruelties; and have imported a cargo of vices blacker than those which you pretend to suppress.

Mankind are not universally agreed in their determination of right and wrong; but there are certain actions which the consent of all nations and individuals hath branded with the unchangeable name of *meanness*. In the list of human vices we find some of such a refined constitution, they cannot be carried into practice without seducing some virtue to their assistance; but *meanness* hath neither alliance nor apology. It is generated in the dust and sweepings of other vices, and is of such a hateful figure that all the rest conspire to disown it. Sir William, the commissioner of George the third, hath at last vouchsafed to give it rank and pedigree. He has placed the fugitive at the council board, and dubbed it companion of the order of knighthood.

The particular act of meanness which I allude to in this description, is forgery. You, sir, have abetted and patronised the forging and uttering counterfeit continental bills. In the same New-York newspapers in which your own proclamation under your master's authority was published, offering, or pretending to offer, pardon and protection to these states, there were repeated advertisements of counterfeit money for sale, and persons who have come officially from you, and under the sanction of your flag, have been taken up in attempting to put them off.

A conduct so basely mean in a public character is without precedent or pretence. Every nation on earth, whether friends or enemies, will unite in despising you. 'Tis an incendiary war upon society, which nothing can excuse or palliate,—an improvement upon beggarly villany—and shows an inbred wretchedness of heart made up between the venomous malignity of a serpent and the spiteful imbecility of an inferior reptile.

The laws of any civilized country would condemn you to the gibbet without regard to your rank or titles, because it is an action foreign to the usage and custom of war; and should you fall into our hands, which pray God you may, it will be a doubtful matter whether we are to consider you as a military prisoner or a prisoner for felony.

Besides, it is exceedingly unwise and impolitic in you, or any other persons in the English service, to promote or even encourage, or wink at the crime of forgery, in any case whatever. Because, as the riches of England, as a nation, are chiefly in paper, and the far greater part of trade among individuals is carried on by the same medium, that is, by notes and drafts on one another, they, therefore, of all people in the world, ought to endeavour to keep forgery out of sight, and, if possible, not to revive the idea of it. It is dangerous to make men familiar with a crime which they may afterwards practise to much greater advantage against those who first taught them. Several officers in the English army have made their exit at the gallows for forgery on their agents; for we all know, who know any thing of England, that there is not a more necessitous body of men, taking them generally, than what the English officers are. They contrive to make a show at the expense of the tailors, and appear clean at the charge of the washer-women.

England, hath at this time, nearly two hundred million pounds sterling of public money in paper, for which she hath no real property: besides a large circulation of bank notes, bank post bills, and promissory notes and drafts of private bankers, merchants and tradesmen. She hath the greatest quantity of paper currency and the least quantity of gold and silver of any nation in Europe; the real specie, which is about sixteen millions sterling, serves only as change in large sums, which are always made in paper, or for payment in small ones. Thus circumstanced, the nation is put to its wit's end, and obliged to be severe almost to criminality, to prevent the practice and growth of forgery. Scarcely a session passes at the Old Bailey, or an execution at Tyburn, but witnesseth this truth, yet you, sir, regardless of the policy which her necessity obliges her to adopt, have made your whole army intimate with the crime. And as all armies at the conclusion of a war, are too apt to carry into practice the vices of the campaign, it will probably happen, that England will hereafter abound in forgeries, to which art the practitioners were first initiated under your authority in America. You, sir, have the honour of adding a new vice to the military catalogue ; and the reason, perhaps, why the invention was reserved for you, is, because no general before was mean enough even to think of it.

That a man whose soul is absorbed in the low traffic of vulgar vice, is incapable of moving in any superior region, is clearly shown in you by the event of every campaign. Your military exploits have been without plan, object or decision. Can it be possible that you or your employers suppose that the possession of Philadelphia will be any ways equal to the expense or expectation of the nation which supports you ? What advantages does England derive from any achievements of yours? To *her* it is perfectly indifferent what place you are in, so long as the business of conquest is unperformed and the charge of maintaining you remains the same.

If the principal events of the three campaigns be attended to, the balance will appear against you at the close of each ; but the last, in point of importance to us, has exceeded the former two. It is pleasant to look back on dangers past, and equally as pleasant to meditate on present ones when the way out begins to appear. That period is now arrived, and the long doubtful winter of war is changing to the sweeter prospects of victory and joy. At the close of the campaign, in 1775, you were obliged to retreat from Boston. In the summer of 1776, you appeared with a numerous fleet and army in the harbor of New-York. By what miracle the continent was preserved in that season of danger is a subject

of admiration! If instead of wasting your time against
Long-Island you had run up the North river, and landed
any where above New-York, the consequence must have
been, that either you would have compelled general Washington to fight you with very unequal numbers, or he must
have suddenly evacuated the city with the loss of nearly all
the stores of his army, or have surrendered for want of
provisions; the situation of the place naturally producing
one or the other of these events.

The preparations made to defend New-York were, nevertheless, wise and military; because your forces were then at
sea, their numbers uncertain; storms, sickness, or a variety
of accidents might have disabled their coming, or so diminished them on their passage, that those which survived
would have been incapable of opening the campaign with
any prospect of success; in which case the defence would
have been sufficient and the place preserved; for cities that
have been raised from nothing with an infinitude of labour
and expense, are not to be thrown away on the bare probability of their being taken. On these grounds the preparations made to maintain New-York were as judicious as the
retreat afterwards. While you, in the interim, let slip
the *very* opportunity which seemed to put conquest in your
power.

Through the whole of that campaign you had nearly
double the forces which general Washington immediately
commanded. The principal plan at that time, on our part,
was to wear away the season with as little loss as possible,
and to raise the army for the next year. Long-Island, New-
York, forts Washington and Lee were not defended after
your superior force was known under any expectation of
their being finally maintained, but as a range of outworks, in
the attacking of which your time might be wasted, your
numbers reduced, and your vanity amused by possessing
them on our retreat. It was intended to have withdrawn
the garrison from fort Washington after it had answered
the former of those purposes, but the fate of that day put a
prize into your hands without much honor to yourselves.

Your progress through the Jerseys was accidental; you had it not even in contemplation, or you would not have sent a principal part of your forces to Rhode-Island beforehand. The utmost hope of America in the year 1776, reached no higher than that she might not then be conquered. She had no expectation of defeating you in that campaign. Even the most cowardly tory allowed, that, could she withstand the shock of *that* summer, her independence would be past a doubt. You had *then* greatly the advantage of her. You were formidable. Your military knowledge was supposed to be complete. Your fleets and forces arrived without an accident. You had neither experience nor reinforcements to wait for. You had nothing to do but to begin, and your chance lay in the first vigorous onset.

America was young and unskilled. She was obliged to trust her defence to time and practice; and hath, by mere dint of perseverance, maintained her cause, and brought the enemy to a condition, in which she is now capable of meeting him on any grounds.

It is remarkable that in the campaign of 1776 you gained no more, notwithstanding your great force, than what was given you by consent of evacuation, except fort Washington; while every advantage obtained by us was by fair and hard fighting. The defeat of Sir Peter Parker was complete.[1] The conquest of the Hessians at Trenton, by the remains of a retreating army, which but a few days before you affected to despise, is an instance of their heroic perseverance very seldom to be met with. And the victory over the British troops at Princeton, by a harassed and wearied party, who had been engaged the day before and marched all night without refreshment, is attended with such a scene of circumstances and superiority of generalship, as will ever give it a place in the first rank in the history of great actions.

When I look back on the gloomy days of last winter, and see America suspended by a thread, I feel a triumph of joy at the recollection of her delivery, and a reverence for the characters which snatched her from destruction. To doubt

[1] At Cape Fear, April, 1776.

now would be a species of infidelity, and to forget the instruments which saved us *then* would be ingratitude.

The close of that campaign left us with the spirit of conquerors. The northern districts were relieved by the retreat of general Carleton over the lakes. The army under your command were hunted back and had their bounds prescribed. The continent began to feel its military importance, and the winter passed pleasantly away in preparations for the next campaign.

However confident you might be on your first arrival, the result of the year 1776 gave you some idea of the difficulty, if not impossibility of conquest. To this reason I ascribe your delay in opening the campaign of 1777. The face of matters, on the close of the former year, gave you no encouragement to pursue a discretionary war as soon as the spring admitted the taking the field; for though conquest, in that case, would have given you a double portion of fame, yet the experiment was too hazardous. The ministry, had you failed, would have shifted the whole blame upon you, charged you with having acted without orders, and condemned at once both your plan and execution.

To avoid the misfortunes, which might have involved you and your money accounts in perplexity and suspicion, you prudently waited the arrival of a plan of operations from England, which was that you should proceed for Philadelphia by way of the Chesapeake, and that Burgoyne, after reducing Ticonderoga, should take his route by Albany, and, if necessary, join you.

The splendid laurels of the last campaign have flourished in the north. In that quarter America has surprised the world, and laid the foundation of this year's glory. The conquest of Ticonderoga, (if it may be called a conquest) has, like all your other victories, led on to ruin. Even the provisions taken in that fortress (which by general Burgoyne's return was sufficient in bread and flour for nearly 5000 men for ten weeks, and in beef and pork for the same number of men for one month) served only to hasten his overthrow, by enabling him to proceed to Saratoga, the place of his destruction. A short review of the operations of the last campaign will show the condition of affairs on both sides.

You have taken Ticonderoga and marched into Philadelphia. These are all the events which the year hath produced on your part. A trifling campaign indeed, compared with the expenses of England and the conquest of the continent. On the other side, a considerable part of your northern force has been routed by the New-York militia under general Herkemer. Fort Stanwix has bravely survived a compound attack of soldiers and savages, and the besiegers have fled. The battle of Bennington has put a thousand prisoners into our hands, with all their arms, stores, artillery and baggage. General Burgoyne, in two engagements, has been defeated; himself, his army, and all that were his and theirs are now ours. Ticonderoga and Independence [forts] are retaken, and not the shadow of an enemy remains in all the northern districts. At this instant we have upwards of eleven thousand prisoners, between sixty and seventy [captured] pieces of brass ordnance, besides small arms, tents, stores, etc.

In order to know the real value of those advantages, we must reverse the scene, and suppose general Gates and the force he commanded, to be at your mercy as prisoners, and general Burgoyne, with his army of soldiers and savages, to be already joined to you in Pennsylvania. So dismal a picture can scarcely be looked at. It has all the tracings and colorings of horror and despair; and excites the most swelling emotions of gratitude by exhibiting the miseries we are so graciously preserved from.

I admire the distribution of laurels around the continent. It is the earnest of future union. South-Carolina has had her day of sufferings and of fame; and the other southern states have exerted themselves in proportion to the force that invaded or insulted them. Towards the close of the campaign, in 1776, these middle states were called upon and did their duty nobly. They were witnesses to the almost expiring flame of human freedom. It was the close struggle of life and death, the line of invisible division ; and on which the unabated fortitude of a Washington prevailed, and saved the spark that has since blazed in the north with unrivalled lustre.

Let me ask, sir, what great exploits have you performed? Through all the variety of changes and opportunities which the war has produced, I know no one action of yours that can be styled masterly. You have moved in and out, backward and forward, round and round, as if valor consisted in a military jig. The history and figure of your movements would be truly ridiculous could they be justly delineated. They resemble the labours of a puppy pursuing his tail ; the end is still at the same distance, and all the turnings round must be done over again.

The first appearance of affairs at Ticonderoga wore such an unpromising aspect, that it was necessary, in July, to detach a part of the forces to the support of that quarter, which were otherwise destined or intended to act against you; and this, perhaps, has been the means of postponing your downfall to another campaign. The destruction of one army at a time is work enough. We know, sir, what we are about, what we have to do, and how to do it.

Your progress from the Chesapeake, was marked by no capital stroke of policy or heroism. Your principal aim was to get general Washington between the Delaware and Schuylkill, and between Philadelphia and your army. In that situation, with a river on each of his flanks, which united about five miles below the city, and your army above him, you could have intercepted his reinforcements and supplies, cut off all his communication with the country, and, if necessary, have despatched assistance to open a passage for general Burgoyne. This scheme was too visible to succeed : for had general Washington suffered you to command the open country above him, I think it a very reasonable conjecture that the conquest of Burgoyne would not have taken place, because you could, in that case, have relieved him. It was therefore necessary, while that important victory was in suspense, to trepan *you* into a situation in which you could only be on the defensive, without the power of affording him assistance. The manœuvre had its effect, and Burgoyne was conquered.[1]

There has been something unmilitary and passive in you from the time of your passing the Schuylkill and getting possession of Philadelphia, to the close of the campaign. You mistook a trap for a conquest, the probability of which had been made known to Europe, and the edge of your triumph taken off by our own information long before.

Having got you into this situation, a scheme for a general attack upon you at Germantown was carried into execution on the 4th of October, and though the success was not equal to the excellence of the plan, yet the attempting it proved the genius of America to be on the rise, and her power approaching to superiority. The obscurity of the morning was your best friend, for a fog is always favourable to a hunted enemy. Some weeks after this you likewise planned an attack on general Washington, while at Whitemarsh. You marched out with infinite parade, but on finding him preparing to attack you next morning, you prudently turned about, and retreated to Philadelphia with all the precipitation of a man conquered in imagination.

Immediately after the battle of Germantown, the probability of Burgoyne's defeat gave a new policy to affairs in Pennsylvania, and it was judged most consistent with the general safety of America, to wait the issue of the northern campaign. Slow and sure is sound work. The news of that victory arrived in our camp on the 18th of October, and no sooner did that shout of joy, and the report of the thirteen cannon reach your ears, than you resolved upon a retreat, and the next day, that is, on the 19th, you withdrew your drooping army into Philadelphia. This movement was evidently dictated by fear; and carried with it a positive confession that you dreaded a second attack. It was hiding

---

[1] This ascription to Washington of a participation in the capture of Burgoyne did him a great and opportune service. The victory at Saratoga had made Gen. Gates such a hero that a scheme was on foot to give him Washington's place as Commander-in-Chief.—*Editor*.

yourself among women and children, and sleeping away the choicest part of the campaign in expensive inactivity. An army in a city can never be a conquering army. The situation admits only of defence. It is mere shelter : and every military power in Europe will conclude you to be eventually defeated.

The time when you made this retreat was the very time you ought to have fought a battle, in order to put yourself in condition of recovering in Pennsylvania what you had lost in Saratoga. And the reason why you did not, must be either prudence or cowardice ; the former supposes your inability, and the latter needs no explanation. I draw no conclusions, sir, but such as are naturally deduced from known and visible facts, and such as will always have a being while the facts which produced them remain unaltered.

After this retreat a new difficulty arose which exhibited the power of Britain in a very contemptible light ; which was the attack and defence of Mud-Island. For several weeks did that little unfinished fortress stand out against all the attempts of admiral and general Howe. It was the fable of Bender realized on the Delaware. Scheme after scheme, and force upon force were tried and defeated. The garrison, with scarce anything to cover them but their bravery, survived in the midst of mud, shot and shells, and were at last obliged to give it up more to the powers of time and gunpowder than to military superiority of the besiegers.[1]

It is my sincere opinion that matters are in much worse condition with you than what is generally known. Your master's speech at the opening of parliament, is like a soliloquy on ill luck. It shows him to be coming a little to his reason, for sense of pain is the first symptom of recovery, in profound stupefaction. His condition is deplorable. He is obliged to submit to all the insults of France and Spain, without daring to know or resent them ; and thankful for the most trivial evasions to the most humble remonstrances. The

---

[1] Paine himself acted an important part in the affair at Mud Island. See my " Life of Thomas Paine," vol. i., pp. 99, 109 ; also Paine's Letter to Franklin, XXI. of this volume.—*Editor.*

time *was* when he could not deign an answer to a petition from America, and the time now *is* when he dare not give an answer to an affront from France. The capture of Burgoyne's army will sink his consequence as much in Europe as in America. In his speech he expresses his suspicions at the warlike preparations of France and Spain, and as he has only the one army which you command to support his character in the world with, it remains very uncertain when, or in what quarter it will be most wanted, or can be best employed; and this will partly account for the great care you take to keep it from action and attacks, for should Burgoyne's fate be yours, which it probably will, England may take her endless farewell not only of all America but of all the West-Indies.

Never did a nation invite destruction upon itself with the eagerness and the ignorance with which Britain has done. Bent upon the ruin of a young and unoffending country, she has drawn the sword that has wounded herself to the heart, and in the agony of her resentment has applied a poison for a cure. Her conduct towards America is a compound of rage and lunacy; she aims at the government of it, yet preserves neither dignity nor character in her methods to obtain it. Were government a mere manufacture or article of commerce, immaterial by whom it should be made or sold, we might as well employ her as another, but when we consider it as the fountain from whence the general manners and morality of a country take their rise, that the persons entrusted with the execution thereof are by their serious example an authority to support these principles, how abominably absurd is the idea of being hereafter governed by a set of men who have been guilty of forgery, perjury, treachery, theft and every species of villainy which the lowest wretches on earth could practise or invent. What greater public curse can befal any country than to be under such authority, and what greater blessing than to be delivered therefrom. The soul of any man of sentiment would rise in brave rebellion against them, and spurn them from the earth.

The malignant and venomous tempered general Vaughan has amused his savage fancy in burning the whole town of Kingston, in York government, and the late governor of that state, Mr. Tryon, in his letter to general Parsons, has endeavoured to justify it and declared his wish to burn the houses of every committeeman in the country.[1]   Such a confession from one who was once intrusted with the powers of civil government, is a reproach to the character.   But it is the wish and the declaration of a man whom anguish and disappointment have driven to despair, and who is daily decaying into the grave with constitutional rottenness.

There is not in the compass of language a sufficiency of words to express the baseness of your king, his ministry and his army.   They have refined upon villany till it wants a name.   To the fiercer vices of former ages they have added the dregs and scummings of the most finished rascality, and are so completely sunk in serpentine deceit, that there is not left among them *one* generous enemy.

From such men and such masters, may the gracious hand of Heaven preserve America!   And though the sufferings she now endures are heavy, and severe, they are like straws in the wind compared to the weight of evils she would feel under the government of your king, and his pensioned parliament.

There is something in meanness which excites a species of resentment that never subsides, and something in cruelty which stirs up the heart to the highest agony of human hatred ; Britain hath filled up both these characters till no addition can be made, and hath not reputation left with us to obtain credit for the slightest promise.   The will of God hath parted us, and the deed is registered for eternity. When she shall be a spot scarcely visible among the nations, America shall flourish the favourite of heaven, and the friend of mankind.

For the domestic happiness of Britain and the peace of the

[1] General Vaughan had been acting with Cornwallis at Cape Fear.   At the beginning of hostilities in North Carolina Tryon was governor there, and on his transfer to New York carried with him a general reputation for cruelty.—*Editor*.

world, I wish she had not a foot of land but what is circumscribed within her own island. Extent of dominion has been her ruin, and instead of civilizing others has brutalized herself. Her late reduction of India, under Clive and his successors, was not so properly a conquest as an extermination of mankind. She is the only power who could practise the prodigal barbarity of tying men to mouths of loaded cannon and blowing them away. It happens that general Burgoyne, who made the report of that horrid transaction, in the house of commons, is now a prisoner with us, and though an enemy, I can appeal to him for the truth of it, being confident that he neither can nor will deny it. Yet Clive received the approbation of the last parliament.

When we take a survey of mankind, we cannot help cursing the wretch, who, to the unavoidable misfortunes of nature, shall wilfully add the calamities of war. One would think there were evils enough in the world without studying to increase them, and that life is sufficiently short without shaking the sand that measures it. The histories of Alexander, and Charles of Sweden, are the histories of human devils; a good man cannot think of their actions without abhorrence, nor of their deaths without rejoicing. To see the bounties of heaven destroyed, the beautiful face of nature laid waste, and the choicest works of creation and art tumbled into ruin, would fetch a curse from the soul of piety itself. But in this country the aggravation is heightened by a new combination of affecting circumstances. America was young, and, compared with other countries, was virtuous. None but a Herod of uncommon malice would have made war upon infancy and innocence : and none but a people of the most finished fortitude, dared under those circumstances, have resisted the tyranny. The natives, or their ancestors, had fled from the former oppressions of England, and with the industry of bees had changed a wilderness into a habitable world. To Britain they were indebted for nothing. The country was the gift of heaven, and God alone is their Lord and Sovereign.

The time, sir, will come when you, in a melancholy hour,

shall reckon up your miseries by your murders in America. Life, with you, begins to wear a clouded aspect. The vision of pleasurable delusion is wearing away, and changing to the barren wild of age and sorrow. The poor reflection of having served your king will yield you no consolation in your parting moments. He will crumble to the same undistinguished ashes with yourself, and have sins enough of his own to answer for. It is not the farcical benedictions of a bishop, nor the cringing hypocrisy of a court of chaplains, nor the formality of an act of parliament, that can change guilt into innocence, or make the punishment one pang the less. You may, perhaps, be unwilling to be serious, but this destruction of the goods of Providence, this havoc of the human race, and this sowing the world with mischief, must be accounted for to him who made and governs it. To us they are only present sufferings, but to him they are deep rebellions.

If there is a sin superior to every other, it is that of wilful and offensive war. Most other sins are circumscribed within narrow limits, that is, the power of *one* man cannot give them a very general extension, and many kinds of sins have only a mental existence from which no infection arises ; but he who is the author of a war, lets loose the whole contagion of hell, and opens a vein that bleeds a nation to death. We leave it to England and Indians to boast of these honors ; we feel no thirst for such savage glory ; a nobler flame, a purer spirit animates America. She has taken up the sword of virtuous defence ; she has bravely put herself between Tyranny and Freedom, between a curse and a blessing, determined to expel the one and protect the other.

It is the object only of war that makes it honourable. And if there was ever a *just* war since the world began, it is this in which America is now engaged. She invaded no land of yours. She hired no mercenaries to burn your towns, nor Indians to massacre their inhabitants. She wanted nothing from you, and was indebted for nothing to you : and thus circumstanced, her defence is honourable and her prosperity is certain.

Yet it is not on the *justice* only, but likewise on the *importance* of this cause that I ground my seeming enthusiastical confidence of our success. The vast extension of America makes her of too much value in the scale of Providence, to be cast like a pearl before swine, at the feet of an European island ; and of much less consequence would it be that Britain were sunk in the sea than that America should miscarry. There has been such a chain of extraordinary events in the discovery of this country at first, in the peopling and and planting it afterwards, in the rearing and nursing it to its present state, and in the protection of it through the present war, that no man can doubt, but Providence hath some nobler end to accomplish than the gratification of the petty elector of Hanover, or the ignorant and insignificant king of Britain.

As the blood, of the martyrs hath been the seed of the Christian church, so the political persecutions of England will and have already enriched America with industry, experience, union, and importance. Before the present era she was a mere chaos of uncemented colonies, individually exposed to the ravages of the Indians and the invasion of any power that Britain should be at war with. She had nothing that she could call her own. Her felicity depended upon accident. The convulsions of Europe might have thrown her from one conqueror to another, till she had been the slave of all, and ruined by every one ; for until she had spirit enough to become her own master, there was no knowing to which master she should belong. That period, thank God, is past, and she is no longer the dependant, disunited colonies of Britain, but the Independent and United States of America, knowing no master but heaven and herself. You, or your king, may call this " delusion," " rebellion," or what name you please. To us it is perfectly indifferent. The issue will determine the character, and time will give it a name as lasting as his own.

You have now, sir, tried the fate of three campaigns, and can fully declare to England, that nothing is to be got on your part, but blows and broken bones, and nothing on hers but waste of trade and credit, and an increase of poverty and taxes. You are now only where you might have been two years ago, without the loss of a single ship, and yet not a step more forward towards the conquest of the continent; because, as I have already hinted, " an army in a city can never be a conquering army." The full amount of your losses, since the beginning of the war, exceeds twenty thousand men, besides millions of treasure, for which you have nothing in exchange. Our expenses, though great, are circulated within ourselves. Yours is a direct sinking of money, and that from both ends at once ; first, in hiring troops out of the nation, and in paying them afterwards, because the money in neither case can return to Britain. We are already in possession of the prize, you only in pursuit of it. To us it is a real treasure, to you it would be only an empty triumph. Our expenses will repay themselves with tenfold interest, while yours entail upon you everlasting poverty.

Take a review, sir, of the ground which you have gone over, and let it teach you policy, if it cannot honesty. You stand but on a very tottering foundation. A change of the ministry in England may probably bring your measures into question, and your head to the block. Clive, with all his successes, had some difficulty in escaping, and yours being all a war of losses, will afford you less pretensions, and your enemies more grounds for impeachment.

Go home, sir, and endeavour to save the remains of your ruined country, by a just representation of the madness of her measures. A few moments, well applied, may yet preserve her from political destruction. I am not one of those who wish to see Europe in a flame, because I am persuaded that such an event will not shorten the war. The rupture, at present, is confined between the two powers of America and England. England finds that she cannot conquer America, and America has no wish to conquer England. You are fighting for what you can never obtain, and we defending what we never mean to part with. A few words, therefore, settle the bargain. Let England mind her own business and we will mind ours. Govern yourselves, and we will govern ourselves. You may then trade where you please unmolested by us, and we will trade where we please unmolested by you ; and such articles as we can purchase of each other better than elsewhere may be mutually done. If it were possible that you could carry on the war for twenty years you must still come to this point at last, or worse, and the sooner you think of it the better it will be for you.

My official situation enables me to know the repeated insults which Britain is obliged to put up with from foreign powers, and the wretched shifts that she is driven to, to gloss them over.[1] Her reduced strength and exhausted coffers in a three years' war with America, hath given a powerful superiority to France and Spain. She is not now a match for them. But if neither councils can prevail on her to think, nor sufferings awaken her to reason, she must e'en go on, till the honour of England becomes a proverb of contempt, and Europe dub her the Land of Fools.

I am, Sir, with every wish for an honourable peace,
Your friend, enemy, and countryman,

COMMON SENSE.

TO THE INHABITANTS OF AMERICA.

WITH all the pleasure with which a man exchanges bad company for good, I take my leave of Sir William and return to you. It is now nearly three years since the tyranny of Britain received its first repulse by the arms of America. A period which has given birth to a new world, and erected a monument to the folly of the old.

I cannot help being sometimes surprised at the complimentary references which I have seen and heard made to ancient histories and transactions. The wisdom, civil governments, and sense of honor of the states of Greece and Rome, are frequently held up as objects of excellence and imita-

---

[1] Paine, elected by Congress, April 17, 1777, Secretary of its Committee of Foreign Affairs, was really the Secretary of Foreign Affairs, and not improperly so styled in many publications.—*Editor*.

tion.   Mankind have lived to very little purpose, if, at this
period of the world, they must go two or three thousand
years back for lessons and examples.   We do great injustice
to ourselves by placing them in such a superior line.   We
have no just authority for it, neither can we tell why it is
that we should suppose ourselves inferior.

Could the mist of antiquity be cleared away, and men
and things be viewed as they really were, it is more than
probable that they would admire us, rather than we them.
America has surmounted a greater variety and combination
of difficulties, than, I believe, ever fell to the share of any
one people, in the same space of time, and has replenished
the world with more useful knowledge and sounder maxims
of civil government than were ever produced in any age
before.   Had it not been for America, there had been no
such thing as freedom left throughout the whole universe.
England hath lost hers in a long chain of right reasoning
from wrong principles, and it is from this country, now, that
she must learn the resolution to redress herself, and the
wisdom how to accomplish it.

The Grecians and Romans were strongly possessed of the
spirit of liberty but *not the principle*, for at the time that
they were determined not to be slaves themselves, they employed their power to enslave the rest of mankind.   But this
distinguished era is blotted by no one misanthropical vice.
In short, if the principle on which the cause is founded, the
universal blessings that are to arise from it, the difficulties
that accompanied it, the wisdom with which it has been
debated, the fortitude by which it has been supported, the
strength of the power which we had to oppose, and the condition in which we undertook it, be all taken in one view,
we may justly style it the most virtuous and illustrious revolution that ever graced the history of mankind.

A good opinion of ourselves is exceedingly necessary in
private life, but absolutely necessary in public life, and of
the utmost importance in supporting national character.   I
have no notion of yielding the palm of the United States
to any Grecians or Romans that were ever born.   We have

equalled the bravest in times of danger, and excelled the wisest in construction of civil governments.

From this agreeable eminence let us take a review of present affairs. The spirit of corruption is so inseparably interwoven with British politics, that their ministry suppose all mankind are governed by the same motives. They have no idea of a people submitting even to temporary inconvenience from an attachment to rights and privileges. Their plans of business are calculated *by* the hour and *for* the hour, and are uniform in nothing but the corruption which gives them birth. They never had, neither have they at this time, any regular plan for the conquest of America by arms. They know not how to go about it, neither have they power to effect it if they did know. The thing is not within the compass of human practicability, for America is too extensive either to be fully conquered or *passively* defended. But she may be *actively* defended by defeating or making prisoners of the army that invades her. And this is the only system of defence that can be effectual in a large country.

There is something in a war carried on by invasion which makes it differ in circumstances from any other mode of war, because he who conducts it cannot tell whether the ground he gains be for him, or against him, when he first obtains it. In the winter of 1776, general Howe marched with an air of victory through the Jerseys, the consequence of which was his defeat ; and general Burgoyne at Saratoga experienced the same fate from the same cause. The Spaniards, about two years ago, were defeated by the Algerines in the same manner, that is, their first triumphs became a trap in which they were totally routed. And whoever will attend to the circumstances and events of a war carried on by invasion, will find, that any invader, in order to be finally conquered must first begin to conquer.

I confess myself one of those who believe the loss of Philadelphia to be attended with more advantages than injuries. The case stood thus: The enemy imagined Philadelphia to be of more importance to us than it really was; for we all know that it had long ceased to be a port: not a cargo of

goods had been brought into it for near a twelvemonth, nor
any fixed manufactories, nor even ship-building, carried on
in it; yet as the enemy believed the conquest of it to be
practicable, and to that belief added the absurd idea that
the soul of all America was centred there, and would be conquered there, it naturally follows that their possession of it,
by not answering the end proposed, must break up the plans
they had so foolishly gone upon, and either oblige them to
form a new one, for which their present strength is not
sufficient, or to give over the attempt.

We never had so small an army to fight against, nor so
fair an opportunity of final success as *now*. The death
wound is already given. The day is ours if we follow it up.
The enemy, by his situation, is within our reach, and by his
reduced strength is within our power. The ministers of
Britain may rage as they please, but our part is to conquer
their armies. Let them wrangle and welcome, but let it not
draw our attention from the *one* thing needful. *Here, in this
spot* is our own business to be accomplished, our felicity
secured. What we have now to do is as clear as light, and
the way to do it is as straight as a line. It needs not to be
commented upon, yet, in order to be perfectly understood I
will put a case that cannot admit of a mistake.

Had the armies under generals Howe and Burgoyne been
united, and taken post at Germantown, and had the northern army under general Gates been joined to that under
general Washington, at Whitemarsh, the consequence would
have been a general action; and if in that action we had
killed and taken the same number of officers and men, that
is, between nine and ten thousand, with the same quantity
of artillery, arms, stores, etc. as have been taken at the
northward, and obliged general Howe with the remains of
his army, that is, with the same number he now commands,
to take shelter in Philadelphia, we should certainly have
thought ourselves the greatest heroes in the world; and
should, as soon as the season permitted, have collected together all the force of the continent and laid siege to the
city, for it requires a much greater force to besiege an enemy

in a town than to defeat him in the field. The case *now* is just the same as if it had been produced by the means I have here supposed. Between nine and ten thousand have been killed and taken, all their stores are in our possession, and general Howe, in consequence of that victory, has thrown himself for shelter into Philadelphia.[1] He, or his trifling friend Galloway, may form what pretences they please, yet no just reason can be given for their going into winter quarters so early as the 19th of October, but their apprehensions of a defeat if they continued out, or their conscious inability of keeping the field with safety. I see no advantage which can arise to America by hunting the enemy from state to state. It is a triumph without a prize, and wholly unworthy the attention of a people determined to conquer. Neither can any state promise itself security while the enemy remains in a condition to transport themselves from one part of the continent to another. Howe, likewise, cannot conquer where we have no army to oppose, therefore any such removals in him are mean and cowardly, and reduces Britain to a common pilferer. If he retreats from Philadelphia, he will be despised ; if he stays, he may be shut up and starved out, and the country, if he advances into it, may become his Saratoga. He has his choice of evils and we of opportunities. If he moves early, it is not only a sign but a proof that he expects no reinforcement, and his delay will prove that he either waits for the arrival of a plan to go upon, or force to execute it, or both ; in *which* case our strength will increase more than his, therefore in *any* case we cannot be wrong if we do but proceed.

The particular condition of Pennsylvania deserves the attention of all the other states. Her military strength must not be estimated by the number of inhabitants. Here are men of all nations, characters, professions and interests.

---

[1] In a private letter to Franklin, in Paris, Paine intimated a probable advantage from the British occupation of Philadelphia. It is said that Franklin, hearing it said that Howe had taken Philadelphia, remarked, " Philadelphia has taken Howe."—*Editor*.

Here are the firmest whigs, surviving, like sparks in the ocean, unquenched and uncooled in the midst of discouragement and disaffection. Here are men losing their all with cheerfulness, and collecting fire and fortitude from the flames of their own estates. Here are others skulking in secret, many making a market of the times, and numbers who are changing to whig or tory with the circumstances of every day.

It is by mere dint of fortitude and perseverance that the whigs of this state have been able to maintain so good a countenance, and do even what they have done. We want help, and the sooner it can arrive the more effectual it will be. The invaded state, be it which it may, will always feel an additional burden upon its back, and be hard set to support its civil power with sufficient authority; aud this difficulty will rise or fall, in proportion as the other states throw in their assistance to the common cause.

The enemy will most probably make many manœuvres at the opening of this campaign, to amuse and draw off the attention of the several states from the *one thing needful.* We may expect to hear of alarms and pretended expeditions to *this* place and *that* place, to the southward, the eastward, and the northward, all intended to prevent our forming into one formidable body. The less the enemy's strength is, the more subtleties of this kind will they make use of. Their existence depends upon it, because the force of America, when collected, is sufficient to swallow their present army up. It is therefore our business to make short work of it, by bending our whole attention to *this one principal point*, for the instant that the main body under general Howe is defeated, all the inferior alarms throughout the continent, like so many shadows, will follow his downfall.

The only way to finish a war with the least possible bloodshed, or perhaps without any, is to collect an army, against the power of which the enemy shall have no chance. By not doing this, we prolong the war, and double both the calamities and expenses of it. What a rich and happy country would America be, were she, by a vigorous exertion, to reduce Howe as she has reduced Burgoyne. Her currency would rise to millions beyond its present value. Every man would be rich, and every man would have it in his power to be happy. And why not do these things? What is there to hinder? America is her own mistress and can do what she pleases.

If we had not at this time a man in the field, we could, nevertheless, raise an army in a few weeks sufficient to overwhelm all the force which general Howe at present commands. Vigor and determination will do any thing and every thing. We began the war with this kind of spirit, why not end it with the same? Here, gentlemen, is the enemy. Here is the army. The interest, the happiness of all America, is centred in this half ruined spot. Come and help us. Here are laurels, come and share them. Here are tories, come and help us to expel them. Here are whigs that will make you welcome, and enemies that dread your coming.

The worst of all policies is that of doing things by halves. Penny-wise and pound-foolish, has been the ruin of thousands. The present spring, if rightly improved, will free us from our troubles, and save us the expense of millions. We have now only one army to cope with. No opportunity can be fairer; no prospect more promising. I shall conclude this paper with a few outlines of a plan, either for filling up the battalions with expedition, or for raising an additional force, for any limited time, on any sudden emergency.

That in which every man is interested, is every man's duty to support. And any burden which falls equally on all men, and from which every man is to receive an equal benefit, is consistent with the most perfect ideas of liberty. I would wish to revive something of that virtuous ambition which first called America into the field. Then every man was eager to do his part, and perhaps the principal reason why we have in any degree fallen therefrom, is because we did not set a right value by it at first, but left it to blaze out of itself, instead of regulating and preserving it by just proportions of rest and service.

Suppose any state whose number of effective inhabitants was 80,000, should be required to furnish 3,200 men towards the defence of the continent on any sudden emergency.

1st, Let the whole number of effective inhabitants be divided into hundreds ; then if each of those hundreds turn out four men, the whole number of 3,200 will be had.

2d, Let the name of each hundred men be entered in a book, and let four dollars be collected from each man, with as much more as any of the gentlemen, whose abilities can afford it, shall please to throw in, which gifts likewise shall be entered against the names of the donors.

3d, Let the sums so collected be offered as a present, over and above the bounty of twenty dollars, to any four who may be inclined to propose themselves as volunteers : if more than four offer, the majority of the subscribers present shall determine which ; if none offer, then four out of the hundred shall be taken by lot, who shall be entitled to the said sums, and shall either go, or provide others that will, in the space of six days.

4th, As it will always happen, that in the space of ground on which an hundred men shall live, there will be always a number of persons who, by age and infirmity, are incapable of doing personal service, and as such persons are generally possessed of the greatest part of property in any country, their portion of service, therefore, will be to furnish each man with a blanket, which will make a regimental coat, jacket, and breeches, or clothes in lieu thereof, and another for a watch cloak, and two pair of shoes ; for however choice people may be of these things matters not in cases of this kind ; those who live always in houses can find many ways to keep themselves warm, but it is a shame and a sin to suffer a soldier in the field to want a blanket while there is one in the country.

Should the clothing not be wanted, the superannuated or infirm persons possessing property, may, in lieu thereof, throw in their money subscriptions towards increasing the bounty ; for though age will naturally exempt a person from personal service, it cannot exempt him from his share of the charge, because the men are raised for the defence of property and liberty jointly.

There never was a scheme against which objections might not be raised. But this alone is not a sufficient reason for rejection. The only line to judge truly upon, is, to draw out and admit all the objections which can fairly be made, and place against them all the contrary qualities, conveniences and advantages, then by striking a balance you come at the true character of any scheme, principle or position.

The most material advantages of the plan here proposed are, ease, expedition, and cheapness; yet the men so raised get a much larger bounty than is any where at present given; because all the expenses, extravagance, and consequent idleness of recruiting are saved or prevented. The country incurs no new debt nor interest thereon; the whole matter being all settled at once and entirely done with. It is a subscription answering all the purposes of a tax, without either the charge or trouble of collecting. The men are ready for the field with the greatest possible expedition, because it becomes the duty of the inhabitants themselves, in every part of the country, to find their proportion of men instead of leaving it to a recruiting sergeant, who, be he ever so industrious, cannot know always where to apply.

I do not propose this as a regular digested plan, neither will the limits of this paper admit of any further remarks upon it. I believe it to be a hint capable of much improvement, and as such submit it to the public.

COMMON SENSE.

LANCASTER, March 21, 1778.

THE CRISIS.

VI.

TO THE EARL OF CARLISLE, GENERAL CLINTON, AND WILLIAM EDEN, ESQ., BRITISH COMMISSIONERS AT NEW YORK.[1]

THERE is a dignity in the warm passions of a whig, which is never to be found in the cold malice of a tory. In the one nature is only heated—in the other she is poisoned. The instant the former has it in his power to punish, he feels a disposition to forgive; but the canine venom of the latter knows no relief but revenge. This general distinction will,

---

[1] Five commissioners were originally appointed to " treat, consult, and agree, upon the Means of quieting the Disorders now subsisting in certain of the Colonies, Plantations and Provinces of North America." The commissioners are thus described by Lord Mahon : " Lord Howe and Sir William were included in the letters patent on the chance of their being still in America when their colleagues should arrive. Of the new commissioners the first was to be Lord Carlisle, with him William Eden and George Johnston. It could not be alleged that the selection of these gentlemen had been made in any narrow spirit of party. George Johnston, who had retained the title of Governor from having filled that post in Florida, was a Member of the House of Commons, and as such a keen opponent of Lord North's. The brother of William Eden had been the last colonial Governor of Maryland. William Eden himself was a man of rising ability on the government side ; in after years, under Mr. Pitt, ambassador in succession to several foreign courts ; and at last a peer with the title of Lord Auckland. Frederick Howard, the fifth Earl of Carlisle, was then only known to the public as a young and not very thrifty man of fashion and pleasure. Against his appointment therefore there were many cavils heard both in and out of Parliament."

The Commissioners reached America just as the British were evacuating Philadelphia. Johnston having made an effort to approach members of Congress privately, and with bribes, that body refused to have anything to do with him, and he had to withdraw from the Commission. General Sir Henry Clinton acted in his place. On June 6, 1778, Congress sent the Commissioners its ultimatum, expressing its willingness to " attend to such terms of peace as may consist with the honour of independent nations, the interest of their constituents, and the sacred regard they mean to pay to treaties." On learning this the King wrote to Lord North (Aug. 12, 1778) : " The present accounts from America seem to put a final stop to all negotiations. Farther concession is a joke." Stevens' invaluable *Facsimiles* shed much light on these events.—*Editor.*

I believe, apply in all cases, and suits as well the meridian of England as America.

As I presume your last proclamation will undergo the strictures of other pens, I shall confine my remarks to only a few parts thereof. All that you have said might have been comprised in half the compass. It is tedious and unmeaning, and only a repetition of your former follies, with here and there an offensive aggravation. Your cargo of pardons will have no market. It is unfashionable to look at them—even speculation is at an end. They have become a perfect drug, and no way calculated for the climate.

In the course of your proclamation you say, " The policy as well as the *benevolence of Great Britain* have thus far checked the extremes of war, when they tended to distress a people still considered as their fellow subjects, and to desolate a country shortly to become again a source of mutual advantage." What you mean by " the *benevolence* of Great Britain " is to me inconceivable. To put a plain question ; do you consider yourselves men or devils ? For until this point is settled, no determinate sense can be put upon the expression. You have already equalled and in many cases excelled, the savages of either Indies; and if you have yet a cruelty in store you must have imported it, unmixed with every human material, from the original warehouse of hell.

To the interposition of Providence, and her blessings on our endeavours, and not to British benevolence are we indebted for the short chain that limits your ravages. Remember you do not, at this time, command a foot of land on the continent of America. Staten-Island, York-Island, a small part of Long-Island, and Rhode-Island, circumscribe your power ; and even those you hold at the expense of the West-Indies. To avoid a defeat, or prevent a desertion of your troops, you have taken up your quarters in holes and corners of inaccessible security ; and in order to conceal what every one can perceive, you now endeavour to impose your weakness upon us for an act of mercy. If you think to succeed by such shadowy devices, you are but infants in the political world; you have the A, B, C, of stratagem yet to learn, and are wholly ignorant of the people you have to contend with. Like men in a state of intoxication, you forget that the rest of the world have eyes, and that the same stupidity which conceals you from yourselves exposes you to their satire and contempt.

The paragraph which I have quoted, stands as an introduction to the following: " But when that country [America] professes the unnatural design, not only of estranging herself from us, but of mortgaging herself and her resources to our enemies, the whole contest is changed : and the question is how far Great Britain may, by every means in her power, destroy or render useless, a connexion contrived for her ruin, and the aggrandizement of France. Under such circumstances, the laws of self-preservation must direct the conduct of Britain, and, if the British colonies are to become an accession to France, will direct her to render that accession of as little avail as possible to her enemy."

I consider you in this declaration, like madmen biting in the hour of death. It contains likewise a fraudulent meanness; for, in order to justify a barbarous conclusion, you have advanced a false position. The treaty we have formed with France is open, noble, and generous. It is true policy, founded on sound philosophy, and neither a surrender or mortgage, as you would scandalously insinuate. I have seen every article, and speak from positive knowledge. In France, we have found an affectionate friend and faithful ally ; in Britain, we have found nothing but tyranny, cruelty, and infidelity.

But the happiness is, that the mischief you threaten, is not in your power to execute; and if it were, the punishment would return upon you in a ten-fold degree. The humanity of America hath hitherto restrained her from acts of retaliation, and the affection she retains for many individuals in England, who have fed, clothed and comforted her prisoners, has, to the present day, warded off her resentment, and operated as a screen to the whole. But even these considerations must cease, when national objects interfere and oppose them. Repeated aggravations will provoke a retort, and policy justify the measure. We mean now to take you seriously up upon your own ground and principle, and as you do, so shall you be done by.

You ought to know, gentlemen, that England and Scotland, are far more exposed to incendiary desolation than America, in her present state, can possibly be. We occupy a country, with but few towns, and whose riches consist in land and annual produce. The two last can suffer but little, and that only within a very limited compass. In Britain it is otherwise. Her wealth lies chiefly in cities and large towns, the depositories of manufactures and fleets of merchantmen. There is not a nobleman's country seat but may be laid in ashes by a single person. Your own may probably contribute to the proof : in short, there is no evil which cannot be returned when you come to incendiary mischief. The ships in the Thames, may certainly be as easily set on fire, as the temporary bridge was a few years ago ; yet of that affair no discovery was ever made ; and the loss you would sustain by such an event, executed at a proper season, is infinitely greater than any you can inflict. The East-India house and the bank, neither are nor can be secure from this sort of destruction, and, as Dr. Price justly observes, a fire at the latter would bankrupt the nation.[1] It has never been the custom of France and England when at war, to make those havocs on each other, because the ease with which they could retaliate rendered it as impolitic as if each had destroyed his own.

But think not, gentlemen, that our distance secures you, or our invention fails us. We can much easier accomplish such a point than any nation in Europe. We talk the same language, dress in the same habit, and appear with the same

[1] The Rev. Dr. Price of London, the eminent defender of America, whose discourses excited the gratitude of Congress. His sermon in 1789 "On the Love of our Country," bearing on events in France, was denounced by Burke. —*Editor*.

manners as yourselves. We can pass from one part of England to another unsuspected ; many of us are as well acquainted with the country as you are, and should you impolitically provoke us, you will most assuredly lament the effects of it. Mischiefs of this kind require no army to execute them. The means are obvious, and the opportunities unguardable. I hold up a warning to your senses, if you have any left, and " to the unhappy people likewise, whose affairs are committed to you." * I call not with the rancor of an enemy, but the earnestness of a friend, on the deluded people of England, lest, between your blunders and theirs, they sink beneath the evils contrived for us.

" He who lives in a glass house," says a Spanish proverb, " should never begin throwing stones." This, gentlemen, is exactly your case, and you must be the most ignorant of mankind, or suppose us so, not to see on which side the balance of accounts will fall. There are many other modes of retaliation, which, for several reasons, I choose not to mention. But be assured of this, that the instant you put your threat into execution, a counter-blow will follow it. If you openly profess yourselves savages, it is high time we should treat you as such, and if nothing but distress can recover you to reason, to punish will become an office of charity.

While your fleet lay last winter in the Delaware, I offered my service to the Pennsylvania navy-board then at Trenton, as one who would make a party with them, or any four or five gentlemen, on an expedition down the river to set fire to it, and though it was not then accepted, nor the thing personally attempted, it is more than probable that your own folly will provoke a much more ruinous act. Say not when mischief is done, that you had not warning, and remember that we do not begin it, but mean to repay it. Thus much for your savage and impolitic threat.

In another part of your proclamation you say, " But if the honours of a military life are become the object of the Americans, let them seek those honors under the banners of

---

* General [Sir H.] Clinton's letter to Congress.—*Author.*

their rightful sovereign, and in fighting the battles of the
united British empire, against our late mutual and natural
enemies." Surely! the union of absurdity with madness
was never marked in more distinguishable lines than these.
Your rightful sovereign, as you call him, may do well enough
for you, who dare not inquire into the humble capacities of
the man; but we, who estimate persons and things by their
real worth, cannot suffer our judgments to be so imposed
upon; and unless it is your wish to see him exposed, it
ought to be your endeavour to keep him out of sight. The
less you have to say about him the better. We have done
with him, and that ought to be answer enough. You have
been often told so. Strange! that the answer must be so
often repeated. You go a-begging with your king as with
a brat, or with some unsaleable commodity you were tired
of ; and though every body tells you no, no, still you keep
hawking him about. But there is one that will have him in
a little time, and as we have no inclination to disappoint
you of a customer, we bid nothing for him.

The impertinent folly of the paragraph that I have just
quoted, deserves no other notice than to be laughed at and
thrown by, but the principle on which it is founded is
detestable. We are invited to submit to a man who has
attempted by every cruelty to destroy us, and to join him in
making war against France, who is already at war against
him for our support.

Can Bedlam, in concert with Lucifer, form a more mad
and devilish request? Were it possible a people could sink
into such apostacy they would deserve to be swept from the
earth like the inhabitants of Sodom and Gomorrah. The
proposition is an universal affront to the rank which man
holds in the creation, and an indignity to him who placed
him there. It supposes him made up without a spark of
honour, and under no obligation to God or man.

What sort of men or Christians must you suppose the
Americans to be, who, after seeing their most humble petitions insultingly rejected; the most grievous laws passed to
distress them in every quarter; an undeclared war let loose

upon them, and Indians and negroes invited to the slaughter; who, after seeing their kinsmen murdered, their fellow citizens starved to death in prisons, and their houses and property destroyed and burned; who, after the most serious appeals to heaven, the most solemn abjuration by oath of all government connected with you, and the most heart-felt pledges and protestations of faith to each other; and who, after soliciting the friendship, and entering into alliances with other nations, should at last break through all these obligations, civil and divine, by complying with your horrid and infernal proposal. Ought we ever after to be considered as a part of the human race? Or ought we not rather to be blotted from the society of mankind, and become a spectacle of misery to the world? But there is something in corruption, which, like a jaundiced eye, transfers the colour of itself to the object it looks upon, and sees every thing stained and impure; for unless you were capable of such conduct yourselves, you would never have supposed such a character in us. The offer fixes your infamy. It exhibits you as a nation without faith; with whom oaths and treaties are considered as trifles, and the breaking them as the breaking of a bubble. Regard to decency, or to rank, might have taught you better; or pride inspired you, though virtue could not. There is not left a step in the degradation of character to which you can now descend; you have put your foot on the ground floor, and the key of the dungeon is turned upon you.

That the invitation may want nothing of being a complete monster, you have thought proper to finish it with an assertion which has no foundation, either in fact or philosophy; and as Mr. Ferguson, your secretary, is a man of letters, and has made civil society his study, and published a treatise on that subject, I address this part to him.[1]

In the close of the paragraph which I last quoted, France is styled the "natural enemy" of England, and by way of

---

[1] Adam Ferguson (b. 1724, d. 1816), Professor of Moral Philosophy in the University of Edinburgh, author of an "Essay on the History of Civil Society" (1767), and "Institutes of Moral Philosophy" (1769).—*Editor*.

lugging us into some strange idea, she is styled " the late mutual and natural enemy" of both countries. I deny that she ever was the natural enemy of either; and that there does not exist in nature such a principle. The expression is an unmeaning barbarism, and wholly unphilosophical, when applied to beings of the same species, let their station in the creation be what it may. We have a perfect idea of a natural enemy when we think of the devil, because the enmity is perpetual, unalterable and unabateable. It admits, neither of peace, truce, or treaty ; consequently the warfare is eternal, and therefore it is natural. But man with man cannot arrange in the same opposition. Their quarrels are accidental and equivocally created. They become friends or enemies as the change of temper, or the cast of interest inclines them. The Creator of man did not constitute them the natural enemy of each other. He has not made any one order of beings so. Even wolves may quarrel, still they herd together. If any two nations are so, then must all nations be so, otherwise it is not nature but custom, and the offence frequently originates with the accuser. England is as truly the natural enemy of France, as France is of England, and perhaps more so. Separated from the rest of Europe, she has contracted an unsocial habit of manners, and imagines in others the jealousy she creates in herself. Never long satisfied with peace, she supposes the discontent universal, and buoyed up with her own importance, conceives herself the only object pointed at. The expression has been often used, and always with a fraudulent design ; for when the idea of a natural enemy is conceived, it prevents all other inquiries, and the real cause of the quarrel is hidden in the universality of the conceit. Men start at the notion of a natural enemy, and ask no other question. The cry obtains credit like the alarm of a mad dog, and is one of those kind of tricks, which, by operating on the common passions, secures their interest through their folly.

But we, sir, are not to be thus imposed upon. We live in a large world, and have extended our ideas beyond the limits and prejudices of an island. We hold out the right

hand of friendship to all the universe, and we conceive that
there is a sociality in the manners of France, which is much
better disposed to peace and negotiation than that of
England, and until the latter becomes more civilized, she
cannot expect to live long at peace with any power. Her
common language is vulgar and offensive, and children suck
in with their milk the rudiments of insult—" The arm of
Britain! The mighty arm of Britain! Britain that shakes
the earth to its centre and its poles! The scourge of France!
The terror of the world! That governs with a nod, and
pours down vengeance like a God."   This language
neither makes a nation great or little; but it shows a sav-
ageness of manners, and has a tendency to keep national
animosity alive.   The entertainments of the stage are calculated to the same end, and almost every public exhibition is
tinctured with insult.   Yet England is always in dread of
France,—terrified at the apprehension of an invasion, suspicious of being outwitted in a treaty, and privately cringing
though she is publicly offending. Let her, therefore, reform
her manners and do justice, and she will find the idea of a
natural enemy to be only a phantom of her own imagination.

Little did I think, at this period of the war, to see a proclamation which could promise you no one useful purpose
whatever, and tend only to expose you.   One would think
that you were just awakened from a four years' dream, and
knew nothing of what had passed in the interval.   Is this a
time to be offering pardons, or renewing the long forgotten
subjects of charters and taxation?   Is it worth your while,
after every force has failed you, to retreat under the shelter
of argument and persuasion?   Or can you think that we, with
nearly half your army prisoners, and in alliance with France,
are to be begged or threatened into submission by a piece of
paper?   But as commissioners at a hundred pounds sterling
a week each, you conceive yourselves bound to do something, and the genius of ill-fortune told you, that you must
write.

For my own part, I have not put pen to paper these
several months.   Convinced of our superiority by the issue

of every campaign, I was inclined to hope, that that which all the rest of the world now see, would become visible to you, and therefore felt unwilling to ruffle your temper by fretting you with repetitions and discoveries. There have been intervals of hesitation in your conduct, from which it seemed a pity to disturb you, and a charity to leave you to yourselves. You have often stopped, as if you intended to think, but your thoughts have ever been too early or too late.

There was a time when Britain disdained to answer, or even hear a petition from America. That time is past and she in her turn is petitioning our acceptance. We now stand on higher ground, and offer her peace ; and the time will come when she, perhaps in vain, will ask it from us. The latter case is as probable as the former ever was. She cannot refuse to acknowledge our independence with greater obstinacy than she before refused to repeal her laws ; and if America alone could bring her to the one, united with France she will reduce her to the other. There is something in obstinacy which differs from every other passion ; whenever it fails it never recovers, but either breaks like iron, or crumbles sulkily away like a fractured arch. Most other passions have their periods of fatigue and rest ; their suffering and their cure ; but obstinacy has no resource, and the first wound is mortal. You have already begun to give it up, and you will, from the natural construction of the vice, find yourselves both obliged and inclined to do so.

If you look back you see nothing but loss and disgrace. If you look forward the same scene continues, and the close is an impenetrable gloom. You may plan and execute little mischiefs, but are they worth the expense they cost you, or will such partial evils have any effect on the general cause ? Your expedition to Egg-Harbour, will be felt at a distance like an attack upon a hen-roost, and expose you in Europe, with a sort of childish phrenzy. Is it worth while to keep an army to protect you in writing proclamations, or to get once a year into winter-quarters ? Possessing yourselves of towns is not conquest, but convenience, and in which you will one day or other be trepanned. Your retreat from

Philadelphia, was only a timely escape, and your next expedition may be less fortunate.

It would puzzle all the politicians in the universe to conceive what you stay for, or why you should have staid so
long.   You are prosecuting a war in which you confess you
have neither object nor hope, and that conquest, could it be
effected, would not repay the charges : in the mean while
the rest of your affairs are running to ruin, and a European
war kindling against you.   In such a situation, there is
neither doubt nor difficulty ; the first rudiments of reason
will determine the choice, for if peace can be procured with
more advantages than even a conquest can be obtained, he
must be an idiot indeed that hesitates.

But you are probably buoyed up by a set of wretched
mortals, who, having deceived themselves, are cringing, with
the duplicity of a spaniel, for a little temporary bread.   Those
men will tell you just what you please.   It is their interest
to amuse, in order to lengthen out their protection.   They
study to keep you amongst them for that very purpose ; and
in proportion as you disregard their advice, and grow callous
to their complaints, they will stretch into improbability, and
season their flattery the higher.   Characters like these are
to be found in every country, and every country will despise
them.

COMMON SENSE.

PHILADELPHIA, Oct. 20, 1778.

THE CRISIS.

VII.

TO THE PEOPLE OF ENGLAND.

THERE are stages in the business of serious life in which
to amuse is cruel, but to deceive is to destroy ; and it is of
little consequence, in the conclusion, whether men deceive
themselves, or submit, by a kind of mutual consent, to the
impositions of each other.   That England has long been
under the influence of delusion or mistake, needs no other
proof than the unexpected and wretched situation that she

is now involved in : and so powerful has been the influence, that no provision was ever made or thought of against the misfortune, because the possibility of its happening was never conceived.

The general and successful resistance of America, the conquest of Burgoyne, and a war in France, were treated in parliament as the dreams of a discontented opposition, or a distempered imagination. They were beheld as objects unworthy of a serious thought, and the bare intimation of them afforded the ministry a triumph of laughter. Short triumph indeed! For everything which has been predicted has happened, and all that was promised has failed. A long series of politics so remarkably distinguished by a succession of misfortunes, without one alleviating turn, must certainly have something in it systematically wrong. It is sufficient to awaken the most credulous into suspicion, and the most obstinate into thought. Either the means in your power are insufficient, or the measures ill planned ; either the execution has been bad, or the thing attempted impracticable ; or, to speak more emphatically, either you are not able or heaven is not willing. For, why is it that you have not conquered us? Who, or what has prevented you? You have had every opportunity that you could desire, and succeeded to your utmost wish in every preparatory means. Your fleets and armies have arrived in America without an accident. No uncommon fortune hath intervened. No foreign nation hath interfered until the time which you had allotted for victory was passed. The opposition, either in or out of parliament, neither disconcerted your measures, retarded or diminished your force. They only foretold your fate. Every ministerial scheme was carried with as high a hand as if the whole nation had been unanimous. Every thing wanted was asked for, and every thing asked for was granted.

A greater force was not within the compass of your abilities to send, and the time you sent it was of all others the most favorable. You were then at rest with the whole world beside. You had the range of every court in Europe uncontradicted by us. You amused us with a tale of commissioners of peace, and under that disguise collected a numerous army and came almost unexpectedly upon us. The force was much greater than we looked for ; and that which we had to oppose it with, was unequal in numbers, badly armed, and poorly disciplined ; beside which, it was embodied only for a short time, and expired within a few months after your arrival. We had governments to form ; measures to concert ; an army to train, and every necessary article to import or to create. Our non-importation scheme had exhausted our stores, and your command by sea intercepted our supplies. We were a people unknown, and unconnected with the political world, and strangers to the disposition of foreign powers. Could you possibly wish for a more favourable conjunction of circumstances ? Yet all these have happened and passed away, and, as it were, left you with a laugh. There are likewise events of such an original nativity as can never happen again, unless a new world should arise from the ocean.

If any thing can be a lesson to presumption, surely the circumstances of this war will have their effect. Had Britain been defeated by any European power, her pride would have drawn consolation from the importance of her conquerors ; but in the present case, she is excelled by those that she affected to despise, and her own opinions retorting upon herself, become an aggravation of her disgrace. Misfortune and experience are lost upon mankind, when they produce neither reflection nor reformation. Evils, like poisons, have their uses, and there are diseases which no other remedy can reach. It has been the crime and folly of England to suppose herself invincible, and that, without acknowledging or perceiving that a full third of her strength was drawn from the country she is now at war with. The arm of Britain has been spoken of as the arm of the Almighty, and she has lived of late as if she thought the whole world created for her diversion. Her politics, instead of civilizing, has tended to brutalize mankind, and under the vain, unmeaning title of " Defender of the Faith," she has made war like an Indian against the religion of humanity.[1] Her cruelties in the East Indies will *never* be forgotten, and it is somewhat remarkable that the produce of that ruined country, transported to America, should there kindle up a war to punish the destroyer. The chain is continued, though with a mysterious kind of uniformity both in the crime and the punishment. The latter runs parallel with the former, and time and fate will give it a perfect illustration.

When information is withheld, ignorance becomes a reasonable excuse; and one would charitably hope that the people of England do not encourage cruelty from choice but from mistake. Their recluse situation, surrounded by the sea, preserves them from the calamities of war, and keeps them in the dark as to the conduct of their own armies. They see not, therefore they feel not. They tell the tale that is told them and believe it, and accustomed to no other news than their own, they receive it, stripped of its horrors and prepared for the palate of the nation, through the channel of the London Gazette. They are made to believe that their generals and armies differ from those of other nations, and have nothing of rudeness or barbarity in them. They suppose them what they wish them to be. They feel a disgrace in thinking otherwise, and naturally encourage the belief from a partiality to themselves. There was a time when I felt the same prejudices, and reasoned from the same errors; but experience, sad and painful experience, has taught me better. What the conduct of former armies was, I know not, but what the conduct of the present is, I well know. It is low, cruel, indolent and profligate; and had the people of America no other cause for separation than what the army has occasioned, that alone is cause sufficient.

The field of politics in England is far more extensive than that of news. Men have a right to reason for themselves, and though they cannot contradict the intelligence in the

---

[1] This is probably the earliest use of the phrase, "the religion of humanity." By "Indian," is meant the aboriginal American, employed by the British officials.—*Editor*.

London Gazette, they may frame upon it what sentiments they please. But the misfortune is, that a general ignorance has prevailed over the whole nation respecting America. The ministry and the minority have both been wrong. The former was always so, the latter only lately so. Politics, to be executively right, must have a unity of means and time, and a defect in either overthrows the whole. The ministry rejected the plans of the minority while they were practicable, and joined in them when they became impracticable. From wrong measures they got into wrong time, and have now completed the circle of absurdity by closing it upon themselves.

I happened to come to America a few months before the breaking out of hostilities. I found the disposition of the people such, that they might have been led by a thread and governed by a reed. Their suspicion was quick and penetrating, but their attachment to Britain was obstinate, and it was at that time a kind of treason to speak against it, They disliked the ministry, but they esteemed the nation. Their idea of grievance operated without resentment, and their single object was reconciliation. Bad as I believed the ministry to be, I never conceived them capable of a measure so rash and wicked as the commencing of hostilities; much less did I imagine the nation would encourage it. I viewed the dispute as a kind of law-suit, in which I supposed the parties would find a way either to decide or settle it. I had no thoughts of independence or of arms. The world could not then have persuaded me that I should be either a soldier or an author. If I had any talents for either, they were buried in me, and might ever have continued so, had not the necessity of the times dragged and driven them into action. I had formed my plan of life, and conceiving myself happy, wished every body else so. But when the country, into which I had just set my foot, was set on fire about my ears, it was time to stir.[1] It was time for every

---

[1] " For my own part, I thought it very hard to have the country set on fire about my ears almost the moment I got into it." (Paine's private letter to Franklin.) Paine arrived in America November 30, 1774.—*Editor*.

man to stir. Those who had been long settled had something to defend ; those who had just come had something
to pursue ; and the call and the concern was equal and universal. For in a country where all men were once adventurers, the difference of a few years in their arrival could
make none in their right.

The breaking out of hostilities opened a new suspicion in
the politics of America, which, though at that time very
rare, has since been proved to be very right. What I allude
to is, " a secret and fixed determination in the British cabinet
to annex America to the crown of England as a conquered
country." If this be taken as the object, then the whole
line of conduct pursued by the ministry, though rash in its
origin and ruinous in its consequences, is nevertheless uniform and consistent in its parts. It applies to every case
and resolves every difficulty. But if taxation, or any thing
else, be taken in its room, there is no proportion between
the object and the charge. Nothing but the whole soil and
property of the country can be placed as a possible equivalent against the millions which the ministry expended. No
taxes raised in America could possibly repay it. A revenue
of two millions sterling a year would not discharge the sum
and interest accumulated thereon, in twenty years.

Reconciliation never appears to have been the wish or the
object of the administration ; they looked on conquest as
certain and infallible, and, under that persuasion, sought to
drive the Americans into what they might style a general
rebellion, and then, crushing them with arms in their hands,
reap the rich harvest of a general confiscation, and silence
them for ever. The dependants at court were too numerous
to be provided for in England. The market for plunder in
the East-Indies was over ; and the profligacy of government
required that a new mine should be opened, and that mine
could be no other than America, conquered and forfeited.
They had no where else to go. Every other channel was
drained ; and extravagance, with the thirst of a drunkard,
was gaping for supplies.

If the ministry deny this to have been their plan, it becomes them to explain what was their plan. For either they have abused us in coveting property they never labored for, or they have abused you in expending an amazing sum upon an incompetent object. Taxation, as I mentioned before, could never be worth the charge of obtaining it by arms; and any kind of formal obedience which America could have made, would have weighed with the lightness of a laugh against such a load of expense. It is therefore most probable that the ministry will at last justify their policy by their dishonesty, and openly declare, that their original design was conquest: and, in this case, it well becomes the people of England to consider how far the nation would have been benefitted by the success.

In a general view, there are few conquests that repay the charge of making them, and mankind are pretty well convinced that it can never be worth their while to go to war for profit's sake. If they are made war upon, their country invaded, or their existence at stake, it is their duty to defend and preserve themselves, but in every other light, and from every other cause, is war inglorious and detestable. But to return to the case in question—

When conquests are made of foreign countries, it is supposed that the *commerce* and *dominion* of the country which made them are extended. But this could neither be the object nor the consequence of the present war. You enjoyed the whole commerce before. It could receive no possible addition by a conquest, but on the contrary, must diminish as the inhabitants were reduced in numbers and wealth. You had the same *dominion* over the country which you used to have, and had no complaint to make against her for breach of any part of the contract between you or her, or contending against any established custom, commercial, political or territorial. The country and commerce were both your own when you *began* to conquer, in the same manner and form as they had been your own an hundred years before. Nations have sometimes been induced to make conquests for the sake of reducing the power of their enemies, or bringing it to a balance with their own. But this could be no part of your plan.   No foreign authority was claimed here, neither was any such authority suspected by you, or acknowledged or imagined by us.   What then, in the name of heaven, could you go to war for?   Or what chance could you possibly have in the event, but either to hold the same country which you held before, and that in a much worse condition, or to lose, with an amazing expense, what you might have retained without a farthing of charges?

War never can be the interest of a trading nation, any more than quarrelling can be profitable to a man in business. But to make war with those who trade with us, is like setting a bull-dog upon a customer at the shop-door.   The least degree of common sense shows the madness of the latter, and it will apply with the same force of conviction to the former.   Piratical nations, having neither commerce or commodities of their own to lose, may make war upon all the world, and lucratively find their account in it; but it is quite otherwise with Britain: for, besides the stoppage of trade in time of war, she exposes more of her own property to be lost, than she has the chance of taking from others. Some ministerial gentlemen in parliament have mentioned the greatness of her trade as an apology for the greatness of her loss.   This is miserable politics indeed!   Because it ought to have been given as a reason for her not engaging in a war at first.   The coast of America commands the West-India trade almost as effectually as the coast of Africa does that of the Straits; and England can no more carry on the former without the consent of America, than she can the latter without a Mediterranean pass.

In whatever light the war with America is considered upon commercial principles, it is evidently the interest of the people of England not to support it; and why it has been supported so long, against the clearest demonstrations of truth and national advantage, is, to me, and must be to all the reasonable world, a matter of astonishment.   Perhaps it may be said that I live in America, and write this from interest.   To this I reply, that my principle is universal. My attachment is to all the world, and not to any particular part, and if what I advance is right, no matter where or who it comes from. We have given the proclamation of your commissioners a currency in our newspapers, and I have no doubt you will give this a place in yours. To oblige and be obliged is fair.

Before I dismiss this part of my address, I shall mention one more circumstance in which I think the people of England have been equally mistaken : and then proceed to other matters.

There is such an idea existing in the world, as that of *national honour*, and this, falsely understood, is oftentimes the cause of war. In a Christian and philosophical sense, mankind seem to have stood still at individual civilization, and to retain as nations all the original rudeness of nature. Peace by treaty is only a cessation of violence for a reformation of sentiment. It is a substitute for a principle that is wanting and ever will be wanting till the idea of *national honour* be rightly understood. As individuals we profess ourselves Christians, but as nations we are heathens, Romans, and what not. I remember the late admiral Saunders declaring in the house of commons, and that in the time of peace, "That the city of Madrid laid in ashes was not a sufficient atonement for the Spaniards taking off the rudder of an English sloop of war." I do not ask whether this is Christianity or morality, I ask whether it is decency ? whether it is proper language for a nation to use? In private life we call it by the plain name of bullying, and the elevation of rank cannot alter its character. It is, I think, exceedingly easy to define what ought to be understood by national honour ; for that which is the best character for an individual is the best character for a nation ; and wherever the latter exceeds or falls beneath the former, there is a departure from the line of true greatness.

I have thrown out this observation with a design of applying it to Great Britain. Her ideas of national honour seem devoid of that benevolence of heart, that universal expansion of philanthropy, and that triumph over the rage of vulgar prejudice, without which man is inferior to himself,

and a companion of common animals. To know who she
shall regard or dislike, she asks what country they are of,
what religion they profess, and what property they enjoy.
Her idea of national honour seems to consist in national
insult, and that to be a great people, is to be neither a Christian, a philosopher, or a gentleman, but to threaten with the
rudeness of a bear, and to devour with the ferocity of a lion.
This perhaps may sound harsh and uncourtly, but it is too
true, and the more is the pity.

I mention this only as her general character. But towards
America she has observed no character at all; and destroyed
by her conduct what she assumed in her title. She set out
with the title of parent, or mother country. The association
of ideas which naturally accompany this expression, are
filled with everything that is fond, tender and forbearing.
They have an energy peculiar to themselves, and, overlook-
ing the accidental attachment of common affections, apply
with infinite softness to the first feelings of the heart. It is
a political term which every mother can feel the force of,
and every child can judge of. It needs no painting of mine
to set it off, for nature only can do it justice.

But has any part of your conduct to America corresponded
with the title you set up? If in your general national character you are unpolished and severe, in this you are inconsistent and unnatural, and you must have exceeding false
notions of national honour to suppose that the world can
admire a want of humanity or that national honour depends
on the violence of resentment, the inflexibility of temper, or
the vengeance of execution.

I would willingly convince you, and that with as much
temper as the times will suffer me to do, that as you opposed
your own interest by quarrelling with us, so likewise your
national honor, rightly conceived and understood, was no
ways called upon to enter into a war with America; had
you studied true greatness of heart, the first and fairest
ornament of mankind, you would have acted directly contrary to all that you have done, and the world would have
ascribed it to a generous cause. Besides which, you had

(though with the assistance of this country) secured a powerful name by the last war. You were known and dreaded
abroad; and it would have been wise in you to have suffered the world to have slept undisturbed under that idea.
It was to you a force existing without expense. It produced to you all the advantages of real power; and you
were stronger through the universality of that charm, than
any future fleets and armies may probably make you. Your
greatness was so secured and interwoven with your silence
that you ought never to have awakened mankind, and had
nothing to do but to be quiet. Had you been true politicians
you would have seen all this, and continued to draw from
the magic of a name, the force and authority of a nation.

Unwise as you were in breaking the charm, you were still
more unwise in the manner of doing it. Samson only told
the secret, but you have performed the operation ; you have
shaven your own head, and wantonly thrown away the locks.
America was the hair from which the charm was drawn that
infatuated the world. You ought to have quarrelled with
no power; but with her upon no account. You had nothing
to fear from any condescension you might make. You might
have humored her, even if there had been no justice in her
claims, without any risk to your reputation; for Europe,
fascinated by your fame, would have ascribed it to your
benevolence, and America, intoxicated by the grant, would
have slumbered in her fetters.

But this method of studying the progress of the passions,
in order to ascertain the probable conduct of mankind, is a
philosophy in politics which those who preside at St. James's
have no conception of. They know no other influence than
corruption and reckon all their probabilities from precedent.
A new case is to them a new world, and while they are seeking for a parallel they get lost. The talents of lord Mans-
field can be estimated at best no higher than those of a
sophist. He understands the subtleties but not the elegance
of nature ; and by continually viewing mankind through the
cold medium of the law, never thinks of penetrating into the
warmer region of the mind. As for lord North, it is his

happiness to have in him more philosophy than sentiment, for he bears flogging like a top, and sleeps the better for it. His punishment becomes his support, for while he suffers the lash for his sins, he keeps himself up by twirling about. In politics, he is a good arithmetician, and in every thing else nothing at all.

There is one circumstance which comes so much within lord North's province as a financier, that I am surprised it should escape him, which is, the different abilities of the two countries in supporting the expense; for, strange as it may seem, England is not a match for America in this particular. By a curious kind of revolution in accounts, the people of England seem to mistake their poverty for their riches; that is, they reckon their national debt as a part of their national wealth. They make the same kind of error which a man would do, who after mortgaging his estate, should add the money borrowed, to the full value of the estate, in order to count up his worth, and in this case he would conceive that he got rich by running into debt. Just thus it is with England. The government owed at the beginning of this war one hundred and thirty-five millions sterling, and though the individuals to whom it was due had a right to reckon their shares as so much private property, yet to the nation collectively it was so much poverty. There is as effectual limits to public debts as to private ones, for when once the money borrowed is so great as to require the whole yearly revenue to discharge the interest thereon, there is an end to further borrowing; in the same manner as when the interest of a man's debts amounts to the yearly income of his estate, there is an end to his credit. This is nearly the case with England, the interest of her present debt being at least equal to one half of her yearly revenue, so that out of ten millions annually collected by taxes, she has but five that she can call her own.[1]

The very reverse of this was the case with America; she

---

[1] This may appear inconsistent with a passage in " Common Sense," on the advantage of a national debt, but it should be observed that the author there made the advantage dependent on such debt not bearing interest.—*Editor.*

began the war without any debt upon her, and in order to carry it on, she neither raised money by taxes, nor borrowed it upon interest, but created it; and her situation at this time continues so much the reverse of yours that taxing would make her rich, whereas it would make you poor. When we shall have sunk the sum which we have created, we shall then be out of debt, be just as rich as when we began, and all the while we are doing it shall feel no difference, because the value will rise as the quantity decreases.

There was not a country in the world so capable of bearing the expense of a war as America; not only because she was not in debt when she began, but because the country is young and capable of infinite improvement, and has an almost boundless tract of new lands in store; whereas England has got to her extent of age and growth, and has not unoccupied land or property in reserve. The one is like a young heir coming to a large improvable estate; the other like an old man whose chances are over, and his estate mortgaged for half its worth.

In the second number of the Crisis, which I find has been republished in England, I endeavored to set forth the impracticability of conquering America. I stated every case, that I conceived could possibly happen, and ventured to predict its consequences. As my conclusions were drawn not artfully, but naturally, they have all proved to be true. I was upon the spot; knew the politics of America, her strength and resources, and by a train of services, the best in my power to render, was honored with the friendship of the congress, the army and the people. I considered the cause a just one. I know and feel it a just one, and under that confidence never made my own profit or loss an object. My endeavor was to have the matter well understood on both sides, and I conceived myself tendering a general service, by setting forth to the one the impossibility of being conquered, and to the other the impossibility of conquering. Most of the arguments made use of by the ministry for supporting the war, are the very arguments that ought to have been used against supporting it; and the plans, by which they thought to conquer, are the very plans in which they were sure to be defeated. They have taken every thing up at the wrong end. Their ignorance is astonishing, and were you in my situation you would see it. They may, perhaps, have your confidence, but I am persuaded that they would make very indifferent members of congress. I know what England is, and what America is, and from the compound of knowledge, am better enabled to judge of the issue than what the king or any of his ministers can be.

In this number I have endeavored to show the ill policy and disadvantages of the war. I believe many of my remarks are new. Those which are not so, I have studied to improve and place in a manner that may be clear and striking. Your failure is, I am persuaded, as certain as fate. America is above your reach. She is at least your equal in the world, and her independence neither rests upon your consent, nor can it be prevented by your arms. In short, you spend your substance in vain, and impoverish yourselves without a hope.

But suppose you had conquered America, what advantages, collectively or individually, as merchants, manufacturers, or conquerors, could you have looked for? This is an object you seemed never to have attended to. Listening for the sound of victory, and led away by the phrenzy of arms, you neglected to reckon either the cost or the consequences. You must all pay towards the expense; the poorest among you must bear his share, and it is both your right and your duty to weigh seriously the matter. Had America been conquered, she might have been parcelled out in grants to the favorites at court, but no share of it would have fallen to you. Your taxes would not have been lessened, because she would have been in no condition to have paid any towards your relief. We are rich by contrivance of our own, which would have ceased as soon as you became masters. Our paper money will be of no use in England, and silver and gold we have none. In the last war you made many conquests, but were any of your taxes lessened thereby? On the contrary, were you not taxed to pay for the charge of making them, and has not the same been the case in every war?

To the parliament I wish to address myself in a more particular manner. They appear to have supposed themselves partners in the chace, and to have hunted with the lion from an expectation of a right in the booty ; but in this it is most probable they would, as legislators, have been disappointed. The case is quite a new one, and many unforeseen difficulties would have arisen thereon. The parliament claimed a legislative right over America, and the war originated from that pretence. But the army is supposed to belong to the crown, and if America had been conquered through their means, the claim of the legislature would have been suffocated in the conquest. Ceded, or conquered, countries are supposed to be out of the authority of parliament. Taxation is exercised over them by prerogative and not by law. It was attempted to be done in the Grenadas a few years ago, and the only reason why it was not done was because the crown had made a prior relinquishment of its claim. Therefore, parliament have been all this while supporting measures for the establishment of their authority, in the issue of which, they would have been triumphed over by the prerogative. This might have opened a new and interesting opposition between the parliament and the crown. The crown would have said that it conquered for itself, and that to conquer for parliament was an unknown case. The parliament might have replied, that America not being a foreign country, but a country in rebellion, could not be said to be conquered, but reduced ; and thus continued their claim by disowning the term. The crown might have rejoined, that however America might be considered at first, she became foreign at last by a declaration of independence, and a treaty with France ; and that her case being, by that treaty, put within the law of nations, was out of the law of parliament, who might have maintained, that as their claim over America had never been surrendered, so neither could it be taken away. The crown might have insisted, that though the claim of parliament could not be taken away, yet, being an inferior, it might be superseded ; and that, whether the claim was withdrawn from the object, or the object taken from the claim, the same separation ensued ; and that America being subdued after a treaty with France, was to all intents and purposes a regal conquest, and of course the sole property of the king. The parliament, as the legal delegates of the people, might have contended against the term "inferior," and rested the case upon the antiquity of power, and this would have brought on a set of very interesting and rational questions.

1st, What is the original fountain of power and honour in any country ?

2d, Whether the prerogative does not belong to the people ?

3d, Whether there is any such thing as the English constitution ?

4th, Of what use is the crown to the people ?

5th, Whether he who invented a crown was not an enemy to mankind ?

6th, Whether it is not a shame for a man to spend a million a year and do no good for it, and whether the money might not be better applied ?

7th, Whether such a man is not better dead than alive ?

8th, Whether a congress, constituted like that of America, is not the most happy and consistent form of government in the world ?—With a number of others of the same import.

In short, the contention about the dividend might have distracted the nation ; for nothing is more common than to agree in the conquest and quarrel for the prize ; therefore it is, perhaps, a happy circumstance, that our successes have prevented the dispute.

If the parliament had been thrown out in their claim, which it is most probable they would, the nation, likewise would have been thrown out in their expectation ; for as the taxes would have been laid on by the crown without the parliament, the revenue arising therefrom, if any could have arisen, would not have gone into the exchequer, but into the privy purse, and so far from lessening the taxes, would not even have been added to them, but served only as pocket money to the crown. The more I reflect on this matter, the more I am satisfied at the blindness and ill policy of my countrymen, whose wisdom seems to operate without discernment, and their strength without an object.

To the great bulwark of the nation, I mean the mercantile and manufacturing part thereof, I likewise present my address. It is your interest to see America an independent, and not a conquered country. If conquered, she is ruined; and if ruined, poor; consequently the trade will be a trifle, and her credit doubtful. If independent, she flourishes, and from her flourishing must your profits arise. It matters nothing to you who governs America, if your manufactures find a consumption there. Some articles will consequently be obtained from other places, and it is right that they should; but the demand for others will increase, by the great influx of inhabitants which a state of independence and peace will occasion, and in the final event you may be enriched. The commerce of America is perfectly free, and ever will be so. She will consign away no part of it to any nation. She has not to her friends, and certainly will not to her enemies; though it is probable that your narrow-minded politicians, thinking to please you thereby, may some time or other unnecessarily make such a proposal. Trade flourishes best when it is free, and it is weak policy to attempt to fetter it. Her treaty with France is on the most liberal and generous principles, and the French, in their conduct towards her, have proved themselves to be philosophers, politicians, and gentlemen.

To the ministry I likewise address myself. You, gentlemen, have studied the ruin of your country, from which it is not within your abilities to rescue her. Your attempts to recover her are as ridiculous as your plans which involved her are detestable. The commissioners, being about to depart, will probably bring you this, and with it my sixth number, addressed to them; and in so doing they carry back more *Common Sense* than they brought, and you likewise will have more than when you sent them.

Having thus addressed you severally, I conclude by addressing you collectively.   It is a long lane that has no turning.   A period of sixteen years of misconduct and misfortune, is certainly long enough for any one nation to suffer under; and upon a supposition that war is not declared between France and you, I beg to place a line of conduct before you that will easily lead you out of all your troubles.   It has been hinted before, and cannot be too much attended to.

Suppose America had remained unknown to Europe till the present year, and that Mr. Banks and Dr. Solander, in another voyage round the world, had made the first discovery of her, in the same condition that she is now in, of arts, arms, numbers, and civilization.   What, I ask, in that case, would have been your conduct towards her?   For *that* will point out what it ought to be now.   The problems and their solutions are equal, and the right line of the one is the parallel of the other.   The question takes in every circumstance that can possibly arise.   It reduces politics to a simple thought, and is moreover a mode of investigation, in which, while you are studying your interest the simplicity of the case will cheat you into good temper.   You have nothing to do but to suppose that you have found America, and she appears found to your hand, and while in the joy of your heart you stand still to admire her, the path of politics rises straight before you.

Were I disposed to paint a contrast, I could easily set off what you have done in the present case, against what you would have done in *that* case, and by justly opposing them, conclude a picture that would make you blush.   But, as, when any of the prouder passions are hurt, it is much better philosophy to let a man slip into a good temper than to attack him in a bad one, for that reason, therefore, I only state the case, and leave you to reflect upon it.

To go a little back into politics, it will be found that the true interest of Britain lay in proposing and promoting the independence of America immediately after the last peace; for the expense which Britain had then incurred by defending America as her own dominions, ought to have shown

her the policy and necessity of changing the *style* of the
country, as the best probable method of preventing future
wars and expense, and the only method by which she could
hold the commerce without the charge of sovereignty.   Besides which, the title which she assumed, of parent country,
led to, and pointed out the propriety, wisdom and advantage
of a separation ; for, as in private life, children grow into
men, and by setting up for themselves, extend and secure
the interest of the whole family, so in the settlement of
colonies large enough to admit of maturity, the same policy
should be pursued, and the same consequences would follow.
Nothing hurts the affections both of parents and children so
much, as living too closely connected, and keeping up the
distinction too long.   Domineering will not do over those,
who, by a progress in life, have become equal in rank to
their parents, that is, when they have families of their own ;
and though they may conceive themselves the subjects of
their advice, will not suppose them the objects of their
government.   I do not, by drawing this parallel, mean to
admit the title of *parent country*, because, if it is due any
where, it is due to Europe collectively, and the first settlers
from England were driven here by persecution.   I mean
only to introduce the term for the sake of policy and to show
from your title the line of your interest.

When you saw the state of strength and opulence, and
that by her own industry, which America arrived at, you
ought to have advised her to set up for herself, and proposed
an alliance of interest with her, and in so doing you would
have drawn, and that at her own expense, more real advantage, and more military supplies and assistance, both of
ships and men, than from any weak and wrangling government that you could exercise over her.   In short, had you
studied only the domestic politics of a family, you would
have learned how to govern the state ; but, instead of this
easy and natural line, you flew out into every thing which
was wild and outrageous, till, by following the passion and
stupidity of the pilot, you wrecked the vessel within sight
of the shore.

Having shown what you ought to have done, I now proceed to show why it was not done. The caterpillar circle of the court had an interest to pursue, distinct from, and opposed to yours; for though by the independence of America and an alliance therewith, the trade would have continued, if not increased, as in many articles neither country can go to a better market, and though by defending and protecting herself, she would have been no expense to you, and consequently your national charges would have decreased, and your taxes might have been proportionably lessened thereby ; yet the striking off so many places from the court calendar was put in opposition to the interest of the nation. The loss of thirteen government ships, with their appendages, here and in England, is a shocking sound in the ear of a hungry courtier. Your present king and ministry will be the ruin of you ; and you had better risk a revolution and call a congress, than be thus led on from madness to despair, and from despair to ruin. America has set you the example, and you may follow it and be free.

I now come to the last part, a war with France. This is what no man in his senses will advise you to, and all good men would wish to prevent. Whether France will declare war against you, is not for me in this place to mention, or to hint, even if I knew it ; but it must be madness in you to do it first. The matter is come now to a full crisis, and peace is easy if willingly set about. Whatever you may think, France has behaved handsomely to you. She would have been unjust to herself to have acted otherwise than she did ; and having accepted our offer of alliance she gave you genteel notice of it. There was nothing in her conduct reserved or indelicate, and while she announced her determination to support her treaty, she left you to give the first offence. America, on her part, has exhibited a character of firmness to the world. Unprepared and unarmed, without form or government, she singly opposed a nation that domineered over half the globe. The greatness of the deed demands respect; and though you may feel resentment, you are compelled both to wonder and admire.

Here I rest my arguments and finish my address. Such as it is, it is a gift, and you are welcome. It was always my design to dedicate a *Crisis* to you, when the time should come that would properly *make it a Crisis;* and when, likewise, I should catch myself in a temper to write it, and suppose you in a condition to read it. *That* time has now arrived, and with it the opportunity for conveyance. For the commissioners—*poor commissioners!* having proclaimed, that "*yet forty days and Nineveh shall be overthrown,*" have waited out the date, and, discontented with their God, are returning to their gourd. And all the harm I wish them is, that it may not *wither* about their ears, and that they may not make their exit in the belly of a whale.[1]

COMMON SENSE.

PHILADELPHIA, Nov. 21, 1778.

P. S.—Though in the tranquillity of my mind I have concluded with a laugh, yet I have something to mention to the *commissioners*, which, to them, is serious and worthy their attention. Their authority is derived from an act of parliament, which likewise describes and *limits* their *official* powers. Their commission, therefore, is only a recital, and personal investiture, of those powers, or a nomination and description of the persons who are to execute them. Had it contained any thing contrary to, or gone beyond the line of, the written law from which it is derived, and by which it is bound, it would, by the English constitution, have been treason in the crown, and the king been subject to an impeachment. He dared not, therefore, put in his commission what you have put in your proclamation, that is, he dared not have authorised you in that commission to burn and

---

[1] George III. writing to Lord North May 12, 1778, recognizes in the rebuff of the Commissioners the end of all negotiation, and begins to abandon the hope of recovering the American Colonies. "All that can now be done is steadily to pursue the plan very wisely adopted in the spring, the providing Nova Scotia, the Floridas, and Canada, with troops." He suggests that New York might be abandoned.—*Editor*.

destroy any thing in America.   You are both in the *act* and
in the *commission* styled *commissioners for restoring peace*,
and the methods for doing it are there pointed out.   Your
last proclamation is signed by you as commissioners *under
that act*.   You make parliament the patron of its contents.
Yet, in the body of it, you insert matters contrary both to
the spirit and letter of the act, and what likewise your king
dared not have put in his commission to you.   The state of
things in England, gentlemen, is too ticklish for you to run
hazards.   You are *accountable to parliament for the execution
of that act according to the letter of it*.   Your heads may pay
for breaking it, for you certainly have broke it by exceeding
it.   And as a friend, who would wish you to escape the paw
of the lion, as well as the belly of the whale, I civilly hint to
you, *to keep within compass*.

Sir Harry Clinton, strictly speaking, is as accountable as
the rest ; for though a general, he is likewise a commissioner,
acting under a superior authority.   His first obedience is due
to the act ; and his plea of being a general, will not and
cannot clear him as a commissioner, for that would suppose
the crown, in its single capacity, to have a power of dispen-
sing with an act of parliament.   Your situation, gentlemen,
is nice and critical, and the more so because England is
unsettled.   Take heed ! Remember the times of Charles the
first !   For Laud and Stafford fell by trusting to a hope like
yours.

Having thus shown you the danger of your proclamation,
I now show you the folly of it.   The means contradict your
design ; you threaten to lay waste, in order to render America a useless acquisition of alliance to France.   I reply, that
the more destruction you commit (if you could do it) the
more valuable to France you make that alliance.   You can
destroy only houses and goods ; and by so doing you increase our demand upon her for materials and merchandize ;
for the wants of one nation, provided it has *freedom* and
credit, naturally produce riches to the other ; and, as you
can neither ruin the land nor prevent the vegetation, you
would increase the exportation of our produce in payment,

which would be to her a new fund of wealth.   In short, had you cast about for a plan on purpose to enrich your enemies, you could not have hit upon a better.

C. S.

THE CRISIS.

VIII.

ADDRESSED TO THE PEOPLE OF ENGLAND.

"TRUSTING (says the king of England in his speech of November last,) in the divine providence, and in the justice of my cause, I am firmly resolved to prosecute the war with vigor, and to make every exertion in order to compel our enemies to equitable terms of peace and accommodation." To this declaration the United States of America, and the confederated powers of Europe will reply, *if Britain will have war, she shall have enough of it.*

Five years have nearly elapsed since the commencement of hostilities, and every campaign, by a gradual decay, has lessened your ability to conquer, without producing a serious thought on your condition or your fate.   Like a prodigal lingering in an habitual consumption, you feel the relics of life, and mistake them for recovery.   New schemes, like new medicines, have administered fresh hopes, and prolonged the disease instead of curing it.   A change of generals, like a change of physicians, served only to keep the flattery alive, and furnish new pretences for new extravagance.

"*Can Britain fail?*"* has been proudly asked at the undertaking of every enterprize ; and that "*whatever she wills is fate,*" † has been given with the solemnity of prophetic confidence ; and though the question has been constantly replied to by disappointment, and the prediction

---

* Whitehead's new-year's ode for 1776.—*Author*.

† Ode at the installation of lord North, for Chancellor of the university of Oxford.—*Author*.

falsified by misfortune, yet still the insult continued, and your catalogue of national evils increased therewith. Eager to persuade the world of her power, she considered destruction as the minister of greatness, and conceived that the glory of a nation like that of an [American] Indian, lay in the number of its scalps and the miseries which it inflicts.

Fire, sword and want, as far as the arms of Britain could extend them, have been spread with wanton cruelty along the coast of America ; and while you, remote from the scene of suffering, had nothing to lose and as little to dread, the information reached you like a tale of antiquity, in which the distance of time defaces the conception, and changes the severest sorrows into conversable amusement.

This makes the second paper, addressed perhaps in vain, to the people of England. That advice should be taken wherever example has failed, or precept be regarded where warning is ridiculed, is like a picture of hope resting on despair : but when time shall stamp with universal currency the facts you have long encountered with a laugh, and the irresistible evidence of accumulated losses, like the handwriting on the wall, shall add terror to distress, you will then, in a conflict of suffering, learn to sympathize with others by feeling for yourselves.

The triumphant appearance of the combined fleets in the channel and at your harbor's mouth, and the expedition of captain Paul Jones, on the western and eastern coasts of England and Scotland, will, by placing you in the condition of an endangered country, read to you a stronger lecture on the calamities of invasion, and bring to your minds a truer picture of promiscuous distress, than the most finished rhetoric can describe or the keenest imagination conceive.

Hitherto you have experienced the expenses, but nothing of the miseries of war. Your disappointments have been accompanied with no immediate suffering, and your losses came to you only by intelligence. Like fire at a distance you heard not even the cry ; you felt not the danger, you saw not the confusion. To you every thing has been foreign but the taxes to support it. You knew not what it was to be alarmed at midnight with an armed enemy in the streets. You were strangers to the distressing scene of a family in flight, and to the thousand restless cares and tender sorrows that incessantly arose. To see women and children wandering in the severity of winter, with the broken remains of a well furnished house, and seeking shelter in every crib and hut, were matters that you had no conception of. You knew not what it was to stand by and see your goods chopped for fuel, and your beds ripped to pieces to make packages for plunder. The misery of others, like a tempestuous night, added to the pleasures of your own security. You even enjoyed the storm, by contemplating the difference of conditions, and that which carried sorrow into the breasts of thousands served but to heighten in you a species of tranquil pride. Yet these are but the fainter sufferings of war, when compared with carnage and slaughter, the miseries of a military hospital, or a town in flames.

The people of America, by anticipating distress, had fortified their minds against every species you could inflict. They had resolved to abandon their homes, to resign them to destruction, and to seek new settlements rather than submit. Thus familiarized to misfortune, before it arrived, they bore their portion with the less regret : the justness of their cause was a continual source of consolation, and the hope of final victory, which never left them, served to lighten the load and sweeten the cup allotted them to drink.

But when their troubles shall become yours, and invasion be transferred upon the invaders, you will have neither their extended wilderness to fly to, their cause to comfort you, nor their hope to rest upon. Distress with them was sharpened by no self-reflection. They had not brought it on themselves. On the contrary, they had by every proceeding endeavored to avoid it, and had descended even below the mark of congressional character, to prevent a war. The national honor or the advantages of independence were matters which, at the commencement of the dispute, they had never studied, and it was only at the last moment that the measure was resolved on. Thus circumstanced, they naturally and conscientiously felt a dependence upon providence. They had a clear pretension to it, and had they failed therein, infidelity had gained a triumph.

But your condition is the reverse of theirs. Every thing you suffer you have sought : nay, had you created mischiefs on purpose to inherit them, you could not have secured your title by a firmer deed. The world awakens with no pity at your complaints. You felt none for others ; you deserve none for yourselves. Nature does not interest herself in cases like yours, but, on the contrary, turns from them with dislike, and abandons them to punishment. You may now present memorials to what court you please, but so far as America is the object, none will listen. The policy of Europe, and the propensity there in every mind to curb insulting ambition, and bring cruelty to judgment, are unitedly against you ; and where nature and interest reinforce with each other, the compact is too intimate to be dissolved.

Make but the case of others your own, and your own theirs, and you will then have a clear idea of the whole. Had France acted towards her colonies as you have done, you would have branded her with every epithet of abhorrence ; and had you, like her, stepped in to succour a struggling people, all Europe must have echoed with your own applauses. But entangled in the passion of dispute you see it not as you ought, and form opinions thereon which suit with no interest but your own. You wonder that America does not rise in union with you to impose on herself a portion of your taxes and reduce herself to unconditional submission. You are amazed that the southern powers of Europe do not assist you in conquering a country which is afterwards to be turned against themselves ; and that the northern ones do not contribute to reinstate you in America who already enjoy the market for naval stores by the separation. You seem surprised that Holland does not pour in her succours to maintain you mistress of the seas, when her own commerce is suffering by your act of navigation ; or that any country should study her own interest while yours is on the carpet.

Such excesses of passionate folly, and unjust as well as unwise resentment, have driven you on, like Pharaoh, to un-pitied miseries, and while the importance of the quarrel shall perpetuate your disgrace, the flag of America will carry it round the world. The natural feelings of every rational being will be against you, and wherever the story shall be told, you will have neither excuse nor consolation left. With an unsparing hand, and an insatiable mind, you have deso-lated the world, to gain dominion and to lose it ; and while, in a phrenzy of avarice and ambition, the east and the west are doomed to tributary bondage, you rapidly earned de-struction as the wages of a nation.

At the thoughts of a war at home, every man amongst you ought to tremble. The prospect is far more dreadful there than in America. Here the party that was against the measures of the continent were in general composed of a kind of neutrals, who added strength to neither army. There does not exist a being so devoid of sense and sentiment as to covet " *unconditional submission*," and therefore no man in America could be with you in principle. Several might from a cowardice of mind, prefer it to the hardships and dangers of opposing it ; but the same disposition that gave them such a choice, unfitted them to act either for or against us. But England is rent into parties, with equal shares of resolution. The principle which produced the war divides the nation. Their animosities are in the highest state of fermentation, and both sides, by a call of the militia, are in arms. No human foresight can discern, no conclusion can be formed, what turn a war might take, if once set on foot by an invasion. She is not now in a fit disposition to make a common cause of her own affairs, and having no conquests to hope for abroad, and nothing but expenses arising at home, her everything is staked upon a defensive combat, and the further she goes the worse she is off.

There are situations that a nation may be in, in which peace or war, abstracted from every other consideration, may be politically right or wrong. When nothing can be lost by a war, but what must be lost without it, war is then the policy of that country ; and such was the situation of America at the commencement of hostilities : but when no security can be gained by a war, but what may be accomplished by a peace, the case becomes reversed, and such now is the situation of England.

That America is beyond the reach of conquest, is a fact which experience has shown and time confirmed, and this admitted, what, I ask, is now the object of contention ? If there be any honor in pursuing self-destruction with inflexible passion—if national suicide be the perfection of national glory, you may, with all the pride of criminal happiness, expire unenvied and unrivalled. But when the tumult of war shall cease, and the tempest of present passions be succeeded by calm reflection, or when those, who, surviving its fury, shall inherit from you a legacy of debts and misfortunes, when the yearly revenue shall scarcely be able to discharge the interest of the one, and no possible remedy be left for the other, ideas far different from the present will arise, and imbitter the remembrance of former follies. A mind disarmed of its rage feels no pleasure in contemplating a frantic quarrel. Sickness of thought, the sure consequence of conduct like yours, leaves no ability for enjoyment, no relish for resentment ; and though, like a man in a fit, you feel not the injury of the struggle, nor distinguish between strength and disease, the weakness will nevertheless be proportioned to the violence, and the sense of pain increase with the recovery.

To what persons or to whose system of politics you owe your present state of wretchedness, is a matter of total indifference to America. They have contributed, however unwillingly, to set her above themselves, and she, in the tranquillity of conquest, resigns the inquiry. The case now is not so properly who began the war, as who continues it. That there are men in all countries to whom a state of war is a mine of wealth, is a fact never to be doubted. Characters like these naturally breed in the putrefaction of distempered times, and after fattening on the disease, they perish with it, or, impregnated with the stench, retreat into obscurity.

But there are several erroneous notions to which you like-wise owe a share of your misfortunes, and which, if continued, will only increase your trouble and your losses. An opinion hangs about the gentlemen of the minority, that America would relish measures under *their* administration, which she would not from the present cabinet. On this rock lord Chatham would have split had he gained the helm, and sev-eral of his survivors are steering the same course. Such dis-tinctions in the infancy of the argument had some degree of foundation, but they now serve no other purpose than to lengthen out a war, in which the limits of a dispute, being fixed by the fate of arms, and guaranteed by treaties, are not to be changed or altered by trivial circumstances.

The ministry, and many of the minority, sacrifice their time in disputing on a question with which they have noth-ing to do, namely, whether America shall be independent or not? Whereas the only question that can come under their determination is, whether they will accede to it or not? They confound a military question with a political one, and undertake to supply by a vote what they lost by a battle. Say she shall not be independent, and it will signify as much as if they voted against a decree of fate, or say that she shall, and she will be no more independent than before. Questions, which, when determined, cannot be executed, serve only to show the folly of dispute and the weakness of disputants.

From a long habit of calling America your own, you sup-pose her governed by the same prejudices and conceits which govern yourselves. Because you have set up a particular denomination of religion to the exclusion of all others, you imagine she must do the same, and because you, with an unsociable narrowness of mind, have cherished enmity against France and Spain, you suppose her alliance must be defective in friendship. Copying her notions of the world from you, she formerly thought as you instructed, but now feeling herself free, and the prejudice removed, she thinks and acts upon a different system. It frequently hap-pens that in proportion as we are taught to dislike persons and countries, not knowing why, we feel an ardor of esteem upon the removal of the mistake : it seems as if something was to be made amends for, and we eagerly give in to every office of friendship, to atone for the injury of the error.

But, perhaps, there is something in the extent of countries, which, among the generality of people, insensibly communicates extension of the mind. The soul of an islander, in its native state, seems bounded by the foggy confines of the water's edge, and all beyond· affords to him matters only for profit or curiosity, not for friendship. His island is to him his world, and fixed to that, his every thing centres in it ; while those who are inhabitants of a continent, by casting their eye over a larger field, take in likewise a larger intellectual circuit, and thus approaching nearer to an acquaintance with the universe, their atmosphere of thought is extended, and their liberality fills a wider space. In short, our minds seem to be measured by countries when we are men, as they are by places when we are children, and until something happens to disentangle us from the prejudice, we serve under it without perceiving it.

In addition to this, it may be remarked, that men who study any universal science, the principles of which are universally known, or admitted, and applied without distinction to the common benefit of all countries, obtain thereby a larger share of philanthropy than those who only study national arts and improvements. Natural philosophy, mathematics and astronomy, carry the mind from the country to the creation, and give it a fitness suited to the extent. It was not Newton's honour, neither could it be his pride, that he was an Englishman, but that he was a philosopher: the heavens had liberated him from the prejudices of an island, and science had expanded his soul as boundless as his studies.

COMMON SENSE.

PHILADELPHIA, March, 1780.

THE CRISIS.

IX.

HAD America pursued her advantages with half the spirit that she resisted her misfortunes, she would, before now, have been a conquering and a peaceful people ; but lulled in the lap of soft tranquillity, she rested on her hopes, and adversity only has convulsed her into action. Whether subtlety or sincerity at the close of the last year induced the enemy to an appearance for peace, is a point not material to know ; it is sufficient that we see the effects it has had on our politics, and that we sternly rise to resent the delusion.

The war, on the part of America, has been a war of natural feelings. Brave in distress ; serene in conquest ; drowsy while at rest ; and in every situation generously disposed to peace ; a dangerous calm, and a most heightened zeal have, as circumstances varied, succeeded each other. Every passion but that of despair has been called to a tour of duty ; and so mistaken has been the enemy, of our abilities and disposition, that when she supposed us conquered, we rose the conquerors. The extensiveness of the United States, and the variety of their resources ; the universality of their cause, the quick operation of their feelings, and the similarity of their sentiments, have, in every trying situation, produced a *something*, which, favored by providence, and pursued with ardor, has accomplished in an instant the business of a campaign. We have never deliberately sought victory, but snatched it ; and bravely undone in an hour the blotted operations of a season.

The reported fate of Charleston, like the misfortunes of 1776, has at last called forth a spirit, and kindled up a flame, which perhaps no other event could have produced. If the enemy has circulated a falsehood, they have unwisely aggravated us into life, and if they have told us the truth, they have unintentionally done us a service. We were returning with folded arms from the fatigues of war, and thinking and sitting leisurely down to enjoy repose. The dependence that has been put upon Charleston threw a drowsiness over America. We looked on the business done—the conflict over—the matter settled—or that all which remained unfinished would follow of itself. In this state of dangerous relaxation, exposed to the poisonous infusions of the enemy, and having no common danger to attract our attention, we were extinguishing, by stages, the ardor we began with, and surrendering by piece-meals the virtue that defended us.

Afflicting as the loss of Charleston may be, yet if it universally rouse us from the slumber of twelve months past, and renew in us the spirit of former days, it will produce an advantage more important than its loss. America ever *is* what she *thinks* herself to be. Governed by sentiment, and acting her own mind, she becomes, as she pleases, the victor or the victim.

It is not the conquest of towns, nor the accidental capture of garrisons, that can reduce a country so extensive as this. The sufferings of one part can never be relieved by the exertions of another, and there is no situation the enemy can be placed in that does not afford to us the same advantages which he seeks himself. By dividing his force, he leaves every post attackable. It is a mode of war that carries with it a confession of weakness, and goes on the principle of distress rather than conquest.

The decline of the enemy is visible, not only in their operations, but in their plans; Charleston originally made but a secondary object in the system of attack, and it is now become their principal one, because they have not been able to succeed elsewhere. It would have carried a cowardly appearance in Europe had they formed their grand expedition, in 1776, against a part of the continent where there was no army, or not a sufficient one to oppose them ; but failing year after year in their impressions here, and to the eastward and northward, they deserted their capital design, and prudently contenting themselves with what they can get, give a flourish of honor to conceal disgrace.

But this piece-meal work is not conquering the continent. It is a discredit in them to attempt it, and in us to suffer

it. It is now full time to put an end to a war of aggravations, which, on one side, has no possible object, and on the
other has every inducement which honor, interest, safety and
happiness can inspire. If we suffer them much longer to
remain among us, we shall become as bad as themselves.
An association of vice will reduce us more than the sword.
A nation hardened in the practice of iniquity knows better
how to profit by it, than a young country newly corrupted.
We are not a match for them in the line of advantageous
guilt, nor they for us on the principles which we bravely set
out with. Our first days were our days of honour. They
have marked the character of America wherever the story of
her wars are told ; and convinced of this, we have nothing
to do but wisely and unitedly to tread the well known track.
The progress of a war is often as ruinous to individuals, as
the issue of it is to a nation ; and it is not only necessary
that our forces be such that we be conquerors in the end, but
that by timely exertions we be secure in the interim. The
present campaign will afford an opportunity which has never
presented itself before, and the preparations for it are equally
necessary, whether Charleston stand or fall. Suppose the
first, it is in that case only a failure of the enemy, not a defeat. All the conquest that a besieged town can hope for,
is, not to be conquered ; and compelling an enemy to raise
the siege, is to the besieged a victory. But there must be a
probability amounting almost to a certainty, that would
justify a garrison marching out to attack a retreat. Therefore should Charleston not be taken, and the enemy abandon the siege, every other part of the continent should
prepare to meet them ; and, on the contrary, should it be
taken, the same preparations are necessary to balance the
loss, and put ourselves in a position to co-operate with our
allies, immediately on their arrival.

We are not now fighting our battles alone, as we were in
1776 ; England, from a malicious disposition to America, has
not only not declared war against France and Spain, but, the
better to prosecute her passions here, has afforded those
powers no military object, and avoids them, to distress us.

She will suffer her West India islands to be overrun by France, and her southern settlements to be taken by Spain, rather than quit the object that gratifies her revenge. This conduct, on the part of Britain, has pointed out the propriety of France sending a naval and land force to co-operate with America on the spot. Their arrival cannot be very distant, nor the ravages of the enemy long. The recruiting the army, and procuring the supplies, are the two things most necessary to be accomplished, and a capture of either of the enemy's divisions will restore to America peace and plenty.

At a crisis, big, like the present, with expectation and events, the whole country is called to unanimity and exertion. Not an ability ought now to sleep, that can produce but a mite to the general good, nor even a whisper to pass that militates against it. The necessity of the case, and the importance of the consequences, admit no delay from a friend, no apology from an enemy. To spare now, would be the height of extravagance, and to consult present ease, would be to sacrifice it perhaps forever.

America, rich in patriotism and produce, can want neither men nor supplies, when a serious necessity calls them forth. The slow operation of taxes, owing to the extensiveness of collection, and their depreciated value before they arrived in the treasury, have, in many instances, thrown a burden upon government, which has been artfully interpreted by the enemy into a general decline throughout the country. Yet this, inconvenient as it may at first appear, is not only remediable, but may be turned to an immediate advantage; for it makes no real difference, whether a certain number of men, or company of militia (and in this country every man is a militia-man), are directed by law to send a recruit at their own expense, or whether a tax is laid on them for that purpose, and the man hired by government afterwards. The first, if there is any difference, is both cheapest and best, because it saves the expense which would attend collecting it as a tax, and brings the man sooner into the field than the modes of recruiting formerly used; and, on this principle, a law has been passed in this state, for recruiting two men from each company of militia, which will add upwards of a thousand to the force of the country.

But the flame which has broke forth in this city since the report from New-York, of the loss of Charleston, not only does honor to the place, but, like the blaze of 1776, will kindle into action the scattered sparks throughout America. The valor of a country may be learned by the bravery of its soldiery, and the general cast of its inhabitants, but confidence of success is best discovered by the active measures pursued by men of property ; and when the spirit of enterprise becomes so universal as to act at once on all ranks of men, a war may then, and not till then, be styled truly popular.

In 1776, the ardor of the enterprising part was considerably checked by the real revolt of some, and the coolness of others. But in the present case, there is a firmness in the substance and property of the country to the public cause. An association has been entered into by the merchants, tradesmen, and principal inhabitants of the city [Philadelphia], to receive and support the new state money at the value of gold and silver; a measure which, while it does them honor, will likewise contribute to their interest, by rendering the operations of the campaign convenient and effectual.

Nor has the spirit of exertion stopped here. A voluntary subscription is likewise begun, to raise a fund of hard money, to be given as bounties, to fill up the full quota of the Pennsylvania line.[1] It has been the remark of the enemy, that every thing in America has been done by the force of government ; but when she sees individuals throwing in their voluntary aid, and facilitating the public measures in concert with the established powers of the country, it will convince her that the cause of America stands not on the will of a few but on the broad foundation of property and popularity.

---

[1] Paine, who was now Clerk of the Pennsylvania Assembly, first proposed the subscription, and headed it with $500.—*Editor*.

Thus aided and thus supported, disaffection will decline, and the withered head of tyranny expire in America. The ravages of the enemy will be short and limited, and like all their former ones, will produce a victory over themselves.

COMMON SENSE.

PHILADELPHIA, June 9, 1780.

☞ At the time of writing this number of the Crisis, the loss of Charleston, though believed by some, was more confidently disbelieved by others. But there ought to be no longer a doubt upon the matter. Charleston is gone, and I believe for the want of a sufficient supply of provisions. The man that does not now feel for the honor of the best and noblest cause that ever a country engaged in, and exert himself accordingly, is no longer worthy of a peaceable residence among a people determined to be free.   C. S.

THE CRISIS EXTRAORDINARY.

ON THE SUBJECT OF TAXATION.

IT is impossible to sit down and think seriously on the affairs of America, but the original principles upon which she resisted, and the glow and ardor which they inspired, will occur like the undefaced remembrance of a lovely scene. To trace over in imagination the purity of the cause, the voluntary sacrifices that were made to support it, and all the various turnings of the war in its defence, is at once both paying and receiving respect. The principles deserve to be remembered, and to remember them rightly is repossessing them. In this indulgence of generous recollection, we become gainers by what we seem to give, and the more we bestow the richer we become.

So extensively right was the ground on which America proceeded, that it not only took in every just and liberal sentiment which could impress the heart, but made it the direct interest of every class and order of men to defend the country. The war, on the part of Britain, was originally a war of covetousness. The sordid and not the splendid passions gave it being. The fertile fields and prosperous infancy of America appeared to her as mines for tributary wealth. She viewed the hive, and disregarding the industry that had enriched it, thirsted for the honey. But in the present stage of her affairs, the violence of temper is added to the rage of avarice; and therefore, that which at the first setting out proceeded from purity of principle and public interest, is now heightened by all the obligations of necessity; for it requires but little knowledge of human nature to discern what would be the consequence, were America again reduced to the subjection of Britain. Uncontrolled power, in the hands of an incensed, imperious, and rapacious conqueror, is an engine of dreadful execution, and woe be to that country over which it can be exercised. The names of whig and tory would then be sunk in the general term of rebel, and the oppression, whatever it might be, would, with very few instances of exception, light equally on all.

Britain did not go to war with America for the sake of dominion, because she was then in possession; neither was it for the extension of trade and commerce, because she had monopolized the whole, and the country had yielded to it; neither was it to extinguish what *she* might call rebellion, because before she began no resistance existed. It could then be from no other motive than avarice, or a design of establishing, in the first instance, the same taxes in America as are paid in England (which, as I shall presently show, are above eleven times heavier than the taxes we now pay for the present year, 1780) or, in the second instance, to confiscate the whole property of America, in case of resistance and conquest of the latter, of which she had then no doubt.

I shall now proceed to show what the taxes in England are, and what the yearly expense of the present war is to her—what the taxes of this country amount to, and what the annual expense of defending it effectually will be to us; and shall endeavor concisely to point out the cause of our difficulties, and the advantages on one side, and the consequences on the other, in case we do, or do not, put ourselves in an effectual state of defence. I mean to be open, candid, and sincere. I see a universal wish to expel the enemy from the country, a murmuring because the war is not carried on with more vigor, and my intention is to show, as shortly as possible, both the reason and the remedy.

The number of souls in England (exclusive of Scotland and Ireland) is seven millions,* and the number of souls in America is three millions.

The amount of taxes in England (exclusive of Scotland and Ireland) was, before the present war commenced, eleven millions six hundred and forty-two thousand six hundred and fifty-three pounds sterling; which, on an average, is no less a sum than one pound thirteen shillings and three-pence sterling per head per annum, men, women, and children; besides county taxes, taxes for the support of the poor, and a tenth of all the produce of the earth for the support of the bishops and clergy.† Nearly five millions of this sum went annually to pay the interest of the national debt, contracted by former wars, and the remaining sum of six millions six hundred and forty-two thousand six hundred pounds was applied to defray the yearly expense of government, the peace establishment of the army and navy, placemen, pensioners, etc.; consequently the whole of the enormous taxes being thus appropriated, she had nothing to spare out of them towards defraying the expenses of the present war or

* This is taking the highest number that the people of England have been, or can be rated at.—*Author*.

† The following is taken from Dr. Price's state of the taxes of England, p. 96, 97, 98.

An account of the money drawn from the public by taxes, annually, being the medium of three years before the year 1776.

Amount of customs in England	2,528,275*l*.
Amount of the excise in England	4,649,892
Land tax at 3*s*.	1,300,000
Land tax at 1*s*. in the pound	450,000
Salt duties	218,739
Duties on stamps, cards, dice, advertisements, bonds, leases, indentures, newspapers, almanacks, etc.	280,788
Duties on houses and windows	385,369

any other.   Yet had she not been in debt at the beginning
of the war, as we were not, and, like us, had only a land and
not a naval war to carry on, her then revenue of eleven millions and a half pounds sterling would have defrayed all her
annual expenses of war and government within each year.

But this not being the case with her, she is obliged to borrow about ten millions pounds sterling, yearly, to prosecute
the war that she is now engaged in, (this year she borrowed
twelve) and lay on new taxes to discharge the interest; allowing that the present war has cost her only fifty millions sterling, the interest thereon, at five per cent., will be two millions
and an half; therefore the amount of her taxes now must be
fourteen millions, which on an average is no less than forty
shillings sterling, per head, men, women and children, throughout the nation.   Now as this expense of fifty millions was
borrowed on the hopes of conquering America, and as it was
avarice which first induced her to commence the war, how
truly wretched and deplorable would the condition of this
country be, were she, by her own remissness, to suffer an
enemy of such a disposition, and so circumstanced, to reduce
her to subjection.

I now proceed to the revenues of America.

I have already stated the number of souls in America to
be three millions, and by a calculation that I have made,
which I have every reason to believe is sufficiently correct,
the whole expense of the war, and the support of the several

Post office, seizures, wine licences, hackney coaches, etc.	250,000
Annual profits from lotteries	150,000
Expense of collecting the excise in England	297,887
Expense of collecting the customs in England	468,703
Interest of loans an the land tax at 4s. expenses of collec-
tion, militia, etc.	250,000
Perquisites, etc. to custom-house officers, &c. supposed	250,000
Expense of collecting the salt duties in England 10 1-2
per cent.	27,000
Bounties on fish exported	18,000
Expense of collecting the duties on stamps, cards, adver-
tisements, etc. at 5 and 1-4 per cent.	18,000

Total 11,642,653*l*

governments, may be defrayed for two million pounds sterling annually; which, on an average, is thirteen shillings and four pence per head, men, women, and children, and the peace establishment at the end of the war will be but three quarters of a million, or five shillings sterling per head. Now, throwing out of the question everything of honor, principle, happiness, freedom, and reputation in the world, and taking it up on the simple ground of interest, I put the following case:

Suppose Britain was to conquer America, and, as a conqueror, was to lay her under no other conditions than to pay the same proportion towards her annual revenue which the people of England pay: our share, in that case, would be six million pounds sterling yearly. Can it then be a question, whether it is best to raise two millions to defend the country, and govern it ourselves, and only three quarters of a million afterwards, or pay six millions to have it conquered, and let the enemy govern it?

Can it be supposed that conquerors would choose to put themselves in a worse condition than what they granted to the conquered? In England, the tax on rum is five shillings and one penny sterling per gallon, which is one silver dollar and fourteen coppers. Now would it not be laughable to imagine, that after the expense they have been at, they would let either whig or tory drink it cheaper than themselves? Coffee, which is so inconsiderable an article of consumption and support here, is there loaded with a duty which makes the price between five and six shillings per pound, and a penalty of fifty pounds sterling on any person detected in roasting it in his own house. There is scarcely a necessary of life that you can eat, drink, wear, or enjoy, that is not there loaded with a tax; even the light from heaven is only permitted to shine into their dwellings by paying eighteen pence sterling per window annually; and the humblest drink of life, small beer, cannot there be purchased without a tax of nearly two coppers per gallon, besides a heavy tax upon the malt, and another on the hops before it is brewed, exclusive of a land-tax on the earth which produces them. In short, the condition of that country, in point of taxation, is so oppressive, the number of her poor so great, and the extravagance and rapaciousness of the court so enormous, that, were they to effect a conquest of America, it is then only that the distresses of America would begin. Neither would it signify anything to a man whether he be whig or tory. The people of England, and the ministry of that country, know us by no such distinctions. What they want is clear, solid revenue, and the modes which they would take to procure it, would operate alike on all. Their manner of reasoning would be short, because they would naturally infer, that if we were able to carry on a war of five or six years against them, we were able to pay the same taxes which they do.

I have already stated that the expense of conducting the present war, and the government of the several states, may be done for two millions sterling, and the establishment in the time of peace, for three quarters of a million.*

As to navy matters, they flourish so well, and are so well attended to by individuals, that I think it consistent on every principle of real use and economy, to turn the navy into hard money (keeping only three or four packets) and apply it to the service of the army. We shall not have a ship the less; the use of them, and the benefit from them, will be greatly increased, and their expense saved. We are now allied with a formidable naval power, from whom we derive the assistance of a navy. And the line in which we can prosecute the war, so as to reduce the common enemy and benefit the alliance most effectually, will be by attending closely to the land service.

I estimate the charge of keeping up and maintaining an army, officering them, and all expenses included, sufficient for the defence of the country, to be equal to the expense of forty thousand men at thirty pounds sterling per head, which is one million two hundred thousand pounds.

* I have made the calculations in sterling, because it is a rate generally known in all the states, and because, likewise, it admits of an easy comparison between our expenses to support the war, and those of the enemy. Four silver dollars and a half is one pound sterling, and three pence over.—*Author*.

I likewise allow four hundred thousand pounds for continental expenses at home and abroad.

And four hundred thousand pounds for the support of the several state governments—the amount will then be:

For the army	1,200,000*l.*
Continental expenses at home and abroad	400,000
Government of the several states	400,000
	Total 2,000,000*l.*

I take the proportion of this state, Pennsylvania, to be an eighth part of the thirteen United States; the quota then for us to raise will be two hundred and fifty thousand pounds sterling; two hundred thousand of which will be our share for the support and pay of the army, and continental expenses at home and abroad, and fifty thousand pounds for the support of the state government.

In order to gain an idea of the proportion in which the raising such a sum will fall, I make the following calculation.

Pennsylvania contains three hundred and seventy-five thousand inhabitants, men, women and children; which is likewise an eighth of the number of inhabitants of the whole United States: therefore, two hundred and fifty thousand pounds sterling to be raised among three hundred and seventy-five thousand persons, is, on an average, thirteen shillings and four pence per head, per annum, or something more than one shilling sterling per month. And our proportion of three quarters of a million for the government of the country, in time of peace, will be ninety-three thousand seven hundred and fifty pounds sterling; fifty thousand of which will be for the government expenses of the state, and forty-three thousand seven hundred and fifty pounds for continental expenses at home and abroad.

The peace establishment then will, on an average, be five shillings sterling per head. Whereas, was England now to stop, and the war cease, her peace establishment would continue the same as it is now, viz. forty shillings per head; therefore was our taxes necessary for carrying on the war, as much per head as hers now is, and the difference to be only whether we should, at the end of the war, pay at the rate of five shillings per head, or forty shillings per head, the case needs no thinking of. But as we can securely defend and keep the country for one third less than what our burden would be if it was conquered, and support the governments afterwards for one eighth of what Britain would levy on us, and could I find a miser whose heart never felt the emotion of a spark of principle, even that man, uninfluenced by every love but the love of money, and capable of no attachment but to his interest, would and must, from the frugality which governs him, contribute to the defence of the country, or he ceases to be a miser and becomes an idiot. But when we take in with it every thing that can ornament mankind; when the line of our interest becomes the line of our happiness; when all that can cheer and animate the heart, when a sense of honor, fame, character, at home and abroad, are interwoven not only with the security but the increase of property, there exists not a man in America, unless he be an hired emissary, who does not see that his good is connected with keeping up a sufficient defence.

I do not imagine that an instance can be produced in the world, of a country putting herself to such an amazing charge to conquer and enslave another, as Britain has done. The sum is too great for her to think of with any tolerable degree of temper; and when we consider the burden she sustains, as well as the disposition she has shown, it would be the height of folly in us to suppose that she would not reimburse herself by the most rapid means, had she America once more within her power. With such an oppression of expense, what would an empty conquest be to her! What relief under such circumstances could she derive from a victory without a prize? It was money, it was revenue she first went to war for, and nothing but *that* would satisfy her. It is not the nature of avarice to be satisfied with any thing else. Every passion that acts upon mankind has a peculiar mode of operation. Many of them are temporary and fluctuating; they admit of cessation and variety. But avarice is a fixed, uniform passion. It neither abates of its vigor nor changes its object; and the reason why it does not, is founded in the nature of things, for wealth has not a rival where avarice is a ruling passion. One beauty may excel another, and extinguish from the mind of man the pictured remembrance of a former one: but wealth is the phœnix of avarice, and therefore it cannot seek a new object, because there is not another in the world.

I now pass on to show the value of the present taxes, and compare them with the annual expense; but this I shall preface with a few explanatory remarks.

There are two distinct things which make the payment of taxes difficult; the one is the large and real value of the sum to be paid, and the other is the scarcity of the thing in which the payment is to be made; and although these appear to be one and the same, they are in several instances not only different, but the difficulty springs from different causes.

Suppose a tax to be laid equal to one half of what a man's yearly income is, such a tax could not be paid, because the property could not be spared; and on the other hand, suppose 'a very trifling tax was laid, to be collected in *pearls,* such a tax likewise could not be paid, because they could not be had. Now any person may see that these are distinct cases, and the latter of them is a representation of our own.

That the difficulty cannot proceed from the former, that is, from the real value or weight of the tax, is evident at the first view to any person who will consider it.

The amount of the quota of taxes for this state for the year, 1780, (and so in proportion for every other state,) is twenty millions of dollars, which at seventy for one,[1] is but sixty-four thousand two hundred and eighty pounds three shillings sterling, and on an average, is no more than three shillings and five pence sterling per head, per annum, per man, woman and child, or threepence two-fifths per head per

[1] The depreciation of Pennsylvania currency.—*Editor.*

month. Now here is a clear, positive fact, that cannot be contradicted, and which proves that the difficulty cannot be in the weight of the tax, for in itself it is a trifle, and far from being adequate to our quota of the expense of the war. The quit-rents of one penny sterling per acre on only one half of the state, come to upwards of fifty thousand pounds, which is almost as much as all the taxes of the present year, and as those quit-rents made no part of the taxes then paid, and are now discontinued, the quantity of money drawn for public service this year, exclusive of the militia fines, which I shall take notice of in the process of this work, is less than what was paid and payable in any year preceding the revolution, and since the last war; what I mean is, that the quit-rents and taxes taken together came to a larger sum then, than the present taxes without the quit-rents do now.

My intention by these arguments and calculations is to place the difficulty to the right cause, and show that it does not proceed from the weight or worth of the tax, but from the scarcity of the medium in which it is paid; and to illustrate this point still further, I shall now show, that if the tax of twenty millions of dollars was of four times the real value it now is, or nearly so, which would be about two hundred and fifty thousand pounds sterling, and would be our full quota, this sum would have been raised with more ease, and have been less felt, than the present sum of only sixty-four thousand two hundred and eighty pounds.

The convenience or inconvenience of paying a tax in money arises from the quantity of money that can be spared out of trade.

When the emissions stopped, the continent was left in possession of two hundred millions of dollars, perhaps as equally dispersed as it was possible for trade to do it. And as no more was to be issued, the rise or fall of prices could neither increase nor diminish the quantity. It therefore remained the same through all the fluctuations of trade and exchange.

Now had the exchange stood at twenty for one, which

was the rate congress calculated upon when they arranged
the quota of the several states, the latter end of last year,
trade would have been carried on for nearly four times less
money than it is now, and consequently the twenty millions
would have been spared with much greater ease, and when
collected would have been of almost four times the value
that they now are.   And on the other hand, was the depreciation to be ninety or one hundred for one, the quantity
required for trade would be more than at sixty or seventy
for one, and though the value of them would be less, the
difficulty of sparing the money out of trade would be
greater.   And on these facts and arguments I rest the
matter, to prove that it is not the want of property, but the
scarcity of the medium by which the proportion of property
for taxation is to be measured out, that makes the embarrassment which we lie under.   There is not money enough,
and, what is equally as true, the people will not let there be
money enough.

While I am on the subject of the currency, I shall offer
one remark which will appear true to everybody, and can
be accounted for by nobody, which is, that the better the
times were, the worse the money grew ; and the worse the
times were, the better the money stood.   It never depreciated by any advantage obtained by the enemy.   The
troubles of 1776, and the loss of Philadelphia in 1777, made
no sensible impression on it, and every one knows that the
surrender of Charleston did not produce the least alteration
in the rate of exchange, which, for long before, and for more
than three months after, stood at sixty for one.   It seems as
if the certainty of its being our own, made us careless of its
value, and that the most distant thoughts of losing it made
us hug it the closer, like something we were loth to part with ;
or that we depreciate it for our pastime, which, when called
to seriousness by the enemy, we leave off to renew again at
our leisure.   In short, our good luck seems to break us, and
our bad makes us whole.

Passing on from this digression, I shall now endeavor
to bring into one view the several parts which I have

already stated, and form thereon some propositions, and conclude.

I have placed before the reader, the average tax per head, paid by the people of England ; which is forty shillings sterling.

And I have shown the rate on an average per head, which will defray all the expenses of the war to us, and support the several governments without running the country into debt, which is thirteen shillings and four pence.

I have shown what the peace establishment may be con-ducted for, viz. an eighth part of what it would be, if under the government of Britain.

And I have likewise shown what the average per head of the present taxes is, namely, three shillings and fivepence sterling, or threepence two-fifths per month ; and that their whole yearly value, in sterling, is only sixty-four thousand two hundred and eighty pounds. Whereas our quota, to keep the payments equal with the expenses, is two hundred and fifty thousand pounds. Consequently, there is a defi-ciency of one hundred and eighty-five thousand seven hun-dred and twenty pounds, and the same proportion of defect, according to the several quotas, happens in every other state. And this defect is the cause why the army has been so indifferently fed, clothed and paid. It is the cause, like-wise, of the nerveless state of the campaign, and the in-security of the country. Now, if a tax equal to thirteen and fourpence per head, will remove all these difficulties, and make people secure in their homes, leave them to follow the business of their stores and farms unmolested, and not only drive out but keep out the enemy from the country ; and if the neglect of raising this sum will let them in, and produce the evils which might be prevented—on which side, I ask, does the wisdom, interest and policy lie ? Or, rather, would it not be an insult to reason, to put the question ? The sum, when proportioned out according to the several abilities of the people, can hurt no one, but an inroad from the enemy ruins hundreds of families.

Look at the destruction done in this city [Philadelphia]. The many houses totally destroyed, and others damaged ;

the waste of fences in the country round it, besides the plunder of furniture, forage, and provisions. I do not suppose that half a million sterling would reinstate the sufferers; and, does this, I ask, bear any proportion to the expense that would make us secure? The damage, on an average, is at least ten pounds sterling per head, which is as much as thirteen shillings and fourpence per head comes to for fifteen years. The same has happened on the frontiers, and in the Jerseys, New-York, and other places where the enemy has been—Carolina and Georgia are likewise suffering the same fate.

That the people generally do not understand the insufficiency of the taxes to carry on the war, is evident, not only from common observation, but from the construction of several petitions which were presented to the Assembly of this state, against the recommendation of Congress of the 18th of March last, for taking up and funding the present currency at forty to one, and issuing new money in its stead. The prayer of the petition was, *that the currency might be appreciated by taxes* (meaning the present taxes) *and that part of the taxes be applied to the support of the army, if the army could not be otherwise supported.* Now it could not have been possible for such a petition to have been presented, had the petitioners known, that so far from *part* of the taxes being sufficient for the support of the army, the *whole* of them falls three-fourths short of the year's expenses.

Before I proceed to propose methods by which a sufficiency of money may be raised, I shall take a short view of the general state of the country.

Notwithstanding the weight of the war, the ravages of the enemy, and the obstructions she has thrown in the way of trade and commerce, so soon does a young country outgrow misfortune, that America has already surmounted many that heavily oppressed her. For the first year or two of the war, we were shut up within our ports, scarce venturing to look towards the ocean. Now our rivers are beautified with large and valuable vessels, our stores filled with merchandize, and the produce of the country has a ready market, and an advantageous price. Gold and silver, that for a while seemed to have retreated again within the bowels of the earth, have once more risen into circulation, and every day adds new strength to trade, commerce and agriculture. In a pamphlet, written by Sir John Dalrymple, and dispersed in America in the year 1775, he asserted that *two twenty-gun ships, nay, says he, tenders of those ships, stationed between Albermarle sound and Chesapeake bay, would shut up the trade of America for* 600 *miles.* How little did Sir John Dalrymple know of the abilities of America!

While under the government of Britain, the trade of this country was loaded with restrictions. It was only a few foreign ports which we were allowed to sail to. Now it is otherwise ; and allowing that the quantity of trade is but half what it was before the war, the case must show the vast advantage of an open trade, because the present quantity under her restrictions could not support itself ; from which I infer, that if half the quantity without the restrictions can bear itself up nearly, if not quite, as well as the whole when subject to them, how prosperous must the condition of America be when the whole shall return open with all the world. By the trade I do not mean the employment of a merchant only, but the whole interest and business of the country taken collectively.

It is not so much my intention, by this publication, to propose particular plans for raising money, as it is to show the necessity and the advantages to be derived from it. My principal design is to form the disposition of the people to the measures which I am fully persuaded it is their interest and duty to adopt, and which need no other force to accomplish them than the force of being felt. But as every hint may be useful, I shall throw out a sketch, and leave others to make such improvements upon it as to them may appear reasonable.

The annual sum wanted is two millions, and the average rate in which it falls, is thirteen shillings and fourpence per head.

Suppose, then, that we raise half the sum and sixty thousand pounds over. The average rate thereof will be seven shillings per head.

In this case we shall have half the supply that we want, and an annual fund of sixty thousand pounds whereon to borrow the other million ; because sixty thousand pounds is the interest of a million at six per cent. ; and if at the end of another year we should be obliged, by the continuance of the war, to borrow another million, the taxes will be increased to seven shillings and sixpence ; and thus for every million borrowed, an additional tax, equal to sixpence per head, must be levied.

The sum to be raised next year will be one million and sixty thousand pounds: one half of which I would propose should be raised by duties on imported goods, and prize goods, and the other half by a tax on landed property and houses, or such other means as each state may devise.

But as the duties on imports and prize goods must be the same in all the states, therefore the rate per cent., or what other form the duty shall be laid, must be ascertained and regulated by congress, and ingrafted in that form into the law of each state ; and the monies arising therefrom carried into the treasury of each state. The duties to be paid in gold or silver.

There are many reasons why a duty on imports is the most convenient duty or tax that can be collected ; one of which is, because the whole is payable in a few places in a country, and it likewise operates with the greatest ease and equality, because as every one pays in proportion to what he consumes, so people in general consume in proportion to what they can afford ; and therefore the tax is regulated by the abilities which every man supposes himself to have, or in other words, every man becomes his own assessor, and pays by a little at a time, when it suits him to buy. Besides, it is a tax which people may pay or let alone by not consuming the articles ; and though the alternative may have no influence on their conduct, the power of choosing is an agreeable thing to the mind. For my own part, it would be a satisfaction to me was there a duty on all sorts of liquors during the war, as in my idea of things it would be an addition to the pleasures of society to know, that when the health of the army goes round, a few drops from every glass becomes theirs.   How often have I heard an emphatical wish, almost accompanied by a tear, *"Oh, that our poor fellows in the field had some of this!"* Why then need we suffer under a fruitless sympathy, when there is a way to enjoy both the wish and the entertainment at once.

But the great national policy of putting a duty upon imports is, that it either keeps the foreign trade in our own hands, or draws something for the defence of the country from every foreigner who participates it with us.

Thus much for the first half of the taxes, and as each state will best devise means to raise the other half, I shall confine my remarks to the resources of this state.

The quota, then, of this state, of one million and sixty thousand pounds, will be one hundred and thirty-three thousand two hundred and fifty pounds, the half of which is sixty-six thousand six hundred and twenty-five pounds ; and supposing one fourth part of Pennsylvania inhabited, then a tax of one bushel of wheat on every twenty acres of land, one with another, would produce the sum, and all the present taxes to cease.   Whereas, the tithes of the bishops and clergy in England, exclusive of the taxes, are upwards of half a bushel of wheat on *every single* acre of land, good and bad, throughout the nation.

In the former part of this paper, I mentioned the militia fines, but reserved speaking to the matter, which I shall now do.   The ground I shall put it upon is, that two millions sterling a year will support a sufficient army, and all the expenses of war and government, without having recourse to the inconvenient method of continually calling men from their employments, which, of all others, is the most expensive and the least substantial.   I consider the revenues created by taxes as the first and principal thing, and fines only as secondary and accidental things.   It was not the intention of the militia law to apply the fines to anything else but the support of the militia, neither do they produce any revenue to the state, yet these fines amount to more than all the taxes: for taking the muster-roll to be sixty thousand men, the fine on forty thousand who may not attend, will be sixty thousand pounds sterling, and those who muster, will give up a portion of time equal to half that sum, and if the eight classes should be called within the year, and one third turn out, the fine on the remaining forty thousand would amount to seventy-two millions of dollars, besides the fifteen shillings on every hundred pounds of property, and the charge of seven and a half per cent. for collecting, in certain instances which, on the whole, would be upwards of two hundred and fifty thousand pounds sterling.

Now if those very fines disable the country from raising a sufficient revenue without producing an equivalent advantage, would it not be for the ease and interest of all parties to increase the revenue, in the manner I have proposed, or any better, if a better can be devised, and cease the operation of the fines? I would still keep the militia as an organized body of men, and should there be a real necessity to call them forth, pay them out of the proper revenues of the state, and increase the taxes a third or fourth per cent. on those who do not attend. My limits will not allow me to go further into this matter, which I shall therefore close with this remark; that fines are, of all modes of revenue, the most unsuited to the minds of a free country. When a man pays a tax, he knows that the public necessity requires it, and therefore feels a pride in discharging his duty; but a fine seems an atonement for neglect of duty, and of consequence is paid with discredit, and frequently levied with severity.

I have now only one subject more to speak of, with which I shall conclude, which is, the resolve of congress of the 18th of March last, for taking up and funding the present currency at forty for one, and issuing new money in its stead.

Every one knows that I am not the flatterer of congress, but in this instance *they are right*; and if that measure is supported, the currency will acquire a value, which, without it, it will not. But this is not all : it will give relief to the finances until such time as they can be properly arranged, and save the country from being immediately double taxed under the present mode. In short, support that measure, and it will support you.

I have now waded through a tedious course of difficult business, and over an untrodden path. The subject, on every point in which it could be viewed, was entangled with perplexities, and enveloped in obscurity, yet such are the resources of America, that she wants nothing but system to secure success.

COMMON SENSE.

PHILADELPHIA, Oct. 6, 1780.

THE CRISIS.

X.

ON THE KING OF ENGLAND'S SPEECH.[1]

OF all the innocent passions which actuate the human mind there is none more universally prevalent than curiosity. It reaches all mankind, and in matters which concern us, or concern us not, it alike provokes in us a desire to know them.

Although the situation of America, superior to every effort to enslave her, and daily rising to importance and opulence, hath placed her above the region of anxiety, it has still left her within the circle of curiosity; and her fancy to see the speech of a man who had proudly threatened to bring her to his feet, was visibly marked with that tranquil confidence which cared nothing about its contents. It was inquired after with a smile, read with a laugh, and dismissed with disdain.

[1] At the opening of Parliament, November 27, 1781. After the surrender of Cornwallis, and the resignation of Lord North, the King, in a letter to North (April 21, 1782), describes himself as " a mind truely tore to pieces."—*Editor*.

But, as justice is due, even to an enemy, it is right to say, that the speech is as well managed as the embarrassed condition of their affairs could well admit of; and though hardly a line of it is true, except the mournful story of Cornwallis, it may serve to amuse the deluded commons and people of England, for whom it was calculated.

"The war," says the speech, " is still unhappily prolonged by that restless ambition which first excited our enemies to commence it, and which still continues to disappoint my earnest wishes and diligent exertions to restore the public tranquillity."

How easy it is to abuse truth and language, when men, by habitual wickedness, have learned to set justice at defiance. That the very man who began the war, who with the most sullen insolence refused to answer, and even to hear the humblest of all petitions, who hath encouraged his officers and his army in the most savage cruelties, and the most scandalous plunderings, who hath stirred up the Indians on one side, and the negroes on the other, and invoked every aid of hell in his behalf, should now, with an affected air of pity, turn the tables from himself, and charge to another the wickedness that 'is his own, can only be equalled by the baseness of the heart that spoke it.

To be nobly wrong is more manly than to be meanly right, is an expression I once used on a former occasion,[1] and it is equally applicable now. We feel something like respect for consistency even in error. We lament the virtue that is debauched into a vice, but the vice that affects a virtue becomes the more detestable: and amongst the various assumptions of character, which hypocrisy has taught, and men have practised, there is none that raises a higher relish of disgust, than to see disappointed inveteracy twisting itself, by the most visible falsehoods, into an appearance of piety which it has no pretensions to.

"But I should not," continues the speech, "answer the trust committed to the sovereign of a *free people*, nor make a suitable

---

[1] Opening sentence of " The Forester's " first letter to " Cato."—*Editor*.

return to my subjects for their constant, zealous, and affectionate attachment to my person, family and government, if I consented to sacrifice, either to my own desire of peace, or to their temporary ease and relief, *those essential rights and permanent interests,* upon the maintenance and preservation of which, the future strength and security of this country must principally depend."

That the man whose ignorance and obstinacy first involved and still continues the nation in the most hopeless and expensive of all wars, should now meanly flatter them with the name of a *free people,* and make a merit of his crime, under the disguise of their essential rights and permanent interests, is something which disgraces even the character of perverseness. Is he afraid they will send him to Hanover, or what does he fear? Why is the sycophant thus added to the hypocrite, and the man who pretends to govern, sunk into the humble and submissive memorialist?

What those essential rights and permanent interests are, on which the future strength and security of England must principally *depend,* are not so much as alluded to. They are words which impress nothing but the ear, and are calculated only for the sound.

But if they have any reference to America, then do they amount to the disgraceful confession, that England, who once assumed to be her protectress, has now become her *dependant.* The British king and ministry are constantly holding up the vast importance which America is of to England, in order to allure the nation to carry on the war: now, whatever ground there is for this idea, it ought to have operated as a reason for not beginning it; and, therefore, they support their present measures to their own disgrace, because the arguments which they now use, are a direct reflection on their former policy.

"The favorable appearance of affairs," continues the speech, "in the East Indies, and the safe arrival of the numerous commercial fleets of my kingdom, must have given you satisfaction."

That things are not *quite* so bad every where as in America may be some cause of consolation, but can be none for triumph. One broken leg is better than two, but still it is not a source of joy: and let the appearance of affairs in the East Indies be ever so favorable, they are nevertheless worse than at first, without a prospect of their ever being better. But the mournful story of Cornwallis was yet to be told, and it was necessary to give it the softest introduction possible.

" But in the course of this year," continues the speech, " my assiduous endeavors to guard the extensive dominions of my crown have not been attended with success equal to the justice and uprightness of my views."—What justice and uprightness there was in beginning a war with America, the world will judge of, and the unequalled barbarity with which it has been conducted, is not to be worn from the memory by the cant of snivelling hypocrisy.

" And it is with *great concern* that I inform you that the events of war have been very unfortunate to my arms in Virginia, having ended in the loss of my forces in that province."—And *our* great concern is that they are not all served in the same manner.

" No endeavors have been wanting on my part," says the speech, " to extinguish that spirit of rebellion which our enemies have found means to foment and maintain in the colonies ; and to restore to my *deluded subjects* in America that happy and prosperous condition which they formerly derived from a due obedience to the laws."

The expression of *deluded subjects* is become so hacknied and contemptible, and the more so when we see them making prisoners of whole armies at a time, that the pride of not being laughed at would induce a man of common sense to leave it off. But the most offensive falsehood in the paragraph is the attributing the prosperity of America to a wrong cause. It was the unremitted industry of the settlers and their descendants, the hard labor and toil of persevering fortitude, that were the true causes of the prosperity of

America.   The former tyranny of England served to people it, and the virtue of the adventurers to improve it.   Ask the man, who, with his axe, hath cleared a way in the wilderness, and now possesses an estate, what made him rich, and he will tell you the labor of his hands, the sweat of his brow, and the blessing of heaven.   Let Britain but leave America to herself and she asks no more.   She has risen into greatness without the knowledge and against the will of England, and has a right to the unmolested enjoyment of her own created wealth.

" I will order," says the speech, " the estimates of the ensuing year to be laid before you.   I rely on your wisdom and public spirit for such supplies as the circumstances of our affairs shall be found to require.   Among the many ill consequences which attend the continuation of the present war, I most sincerely regret the additional burdens which it must unavoidably bring upon my faithful subjects."

It is strange that a nation must run through such a labyrinth of trouble, and expend such a mass of wealth to gain the wisdom which an hour's reflection might have taught. The final superiority of America over every attempt that an island might make to conquer her, was as naturally marked in the constitution of things, as the future ability of a giant over a dwarf is delineated in his features while an infant. How far providence, to accomplish purposes which no human wisdom could foresee, permitted such extraordinary errors, is still a secret in the womb of time, and must remain so till futurity shall give it birth.

" In the prosecution of this great and important contest," says the speech, " in which we are engaged, I retain a firm confidence in the *protection of divine providence*, and a perfect conviction in the justice of my cause, and I have no doubt, but, that by the concurrence and support of my parliament, by the valour of my fleets and armies, and by a vigorous, animated, and united exertion of the faculties and resources of my people, I shall be enabled to restore the blessings of a safe and honorable peace to all my dominions."

The king of England is one of the readiest believers in the world. In the beginning of the contest he passed an act to put America out of the protection of the crown of England, and though providence, for seven years together, hath put him out of *her* protection, still the man has no doubt. Like Pharaoh on the edge of the Red sea, he sees not the plunge he is making, and precipitately drives across the flood that is closing over his head.

I think it is a reasonable supposition, that this part of the speech was composed before the arrival of the news of the capture of Cornwallis: for it certainly has no relation to their condition at the time it was spoken. But, be this as it may, it is nothing to us. Our line is fixed. Our lot is cast; and America, the child of fate, is arriving at maturity. We have nothing to do but by a spirited and quick exertion, to stand prepared for war or peace. Too great to yield, and too noble to insult; superior to misfortune, and generous in success, let us untaintedly preserve the character which we have gained, and show to future ages an example of un-equalled magnanimity. There is something in the cause and consequence of America that has drawn on her the attention of all mankind. The world has seen her brave. Her love of liberty; her ardour in supporting it; the justice of her claims, and the constancy of her fortitude have won her the esteem of Europe, and attached to her interest the first power in that country.

Her situation now is such, that to whatever point, past, present or to come, she casts her eyes, new matter rises to convince her that she is right. In her conduct towards her enemy, no reproachful sentiment lurks in secret. No sense of injustice is left upon the mind. Untainted with ambition, and a stranger to revenge, her progress hath been marked by providence, and she, in every stage of the conflict, has blest her with success.

But let not America wrap herself up in delusive hope and suppose the business done. The least remissness in prepara-tion, the least relaxation in execution, will only serve to prolong the war, and increase expenses. If our enemies can

draw consolation from misfortune, and exert themselves
upon despair, how much more ought we, who are to win a
continent by the conquest, and have already an earnest of
success?

Having, in the preceding part, made my remarks on the
several matters which the speech contains, I shall now make
my remarks on what it does not contain.

There is not a syllable in it respecting alliances. Either
the injustice of Britain is too glaring, or her condition too
desperate, or both, for any neighboring power to come to
her support. In the beginning of the contest, when she had
only America to contend with, she hired assistance from
Hesse, and other smaller states of Germany, and for nearly
three years did America, young, raw, undisciplined and
unprovided, stand against the power of Britain, aided by
twenty thousand foreign troops, and made a complete conquest of one entire army. The remembrance of those things
ought to inspire us with confidence and greatness of mind,
and carry us through every remaining difficulty with content
and cheerfulness. What are the little sufferings of the present day, compared with the hardships that are past? There
was a time, when we had neither house nor home in safety;
when every hour was the hour of alarm and danger; when
the mind, tortured with anxiety, knew no repose, and every
thing, but hope and fortitude, was bidding us farewell.

It is of use to look back upon these things; to call to
mind the times of trouble and the scenes of complicated
anguish that are past and gone. Then every expense was
cheap, compared with the dread of conquest and the misery
of submission. We did not stand debating upon trifles, or
contending about the necessary and unavoidable charges of
defence. Every one bore his lot of suffering, and looked
forward to happier days, and scenes of rest.

Perhaps one of the greatest dangers which any country
can be exposed to, arises from a kind of trifling which sometimes steals upon the mind, when it supposes the danger
past; and this unsafe situation marks at this time the peculiar crisis of America. What would she once have given to

have known that her condition at this day should be what it now is? And yet we do not seem to place a proper value upon it, nor vigorously pursue the necessary measures to secure it. We know that we cannot be defended, nor yet defend ourselves, without trouble and expense. We have no right to expect it; neither ought we to look for it. We are a people, who, in our situation, differ from all the world. We form one common floor of public good, and, whatever is our charge, it is paid for our own interest and upon our own account.

Misfortune and experience have now taught us system and method; and the arrangements for carrying on the war are reduced to rule and order. The quotas of the several states are ascertained, and I intend in a future publication to show what they are, and the necessity as well as the advantages of vigorously providing for them.

In the mean time, I shall conclude this paper with an instance of *British clemency*, from Smollett's History of England, vol. xi., p. 239, printed in London. It will serve to show how dismal the situation of a conquered people is, and that the only security is an effectual defence.

We all know that the Stuart family and the house of Hanover opposed each other for the crown of England. The Stuart family stood first in the line of succession, but the other was the most successful.

In July, 1745, Charles, the son of the exiled king, landed in Scotland, collected a small force, at no time exceeding five or six thousand men, and made some attempts to reestablish his claim. The late duke of Cumberland, uncle to the present king of England, was sent against him, and on the 16th of April following, Charles was totally defeated at Culloden, in Scotland. Success and power are the only situations in which clemency can be shown, and those who are cruel, because they are victorious, can with the same facility act any other degenerate character.

" Immediately after the decisive action at Culloden, the duke of Cumberland took possession of Inverness ; where six and thirty deserters, convicted by a court martial, were ordered to be executed : then he detached several parties to ravage the country. One of these apprehended the lady Mackintosh, who was sent prisoner to Inverness, plundered her house, and drove away her cattle, though her husband was actually in the service of the government. The castle of lord Lovat was destroyed. The French prisoners were sent to Carlisle and Penrith : Kilmarnock, Balmerino, Cromartie, and his son, the lord Macleod, were conveyed by sea to London ; and those of an inferior rank were confined in different prisons. The marquis of Tullibardine, together with a brother of the earl of Dunmore, and Murray, the pretender's secretary, were seized and transported to the tower of London, to which the earl of Traquaire had been committed on suspicion ; and the eldest son of lord Lovat was imprisoned in the castle of Edinburgh. In a word, all the jails in Great Britain, from the capital, northwards, were filled with those unfortunate captives ; and great numbers of them were crowded together in the holds of ships, where they perished in the most deplorable manner, for want of air and exercise. Some rebel chiefs escaped in two French frigates that arrived on the coast of Lochaber about the end of April, and engaged three vessels belonging to his Britannic majesty, which they obliged to retire. Others embarked on board a ship on the coast of Buchan, and were conveyed to Norway, from whence they travelled to Sweden. In the month of May, the duke of Cumberland advanced with the army into the Highlands, as far as fort Augustus, where he encamped ; and sent off detachments on all hands, to hunt down the fugitives, and lay waste the country with fire and sword. The castles of Glengary and Lochiel were plundered and burned ; every house, hut, or habitation, met with the same fate, without distinction ; and all the cattle and provision were carried off ; the men were either shot upon the mountains, like wild beasts, or put to death in cold blood, without form of trial ; the women, after having seen their husbands and fathers murdered, were subjected to brutal violation, and then turned out naked, with their children, to starve on the barren heaths. One whole family was enclosed in a barn, and consumed to ashes. Those ministers of vengeance were so alert in the execution of their office, that in a few days there was neither house, cottage, man, nor beast, to be seen within the compass of fifty miles ; all was ruin, silence, and desolation."

I have here presented the reader with one of the most shocking instances of cruelty ever practised, and I leave it, to rest on his mind, that he may be fully impressed with a sense of the destruction he has escaped, in case Britain had conquered America; and likewise, that he may see and feel the necessity, as well for his own personal safety, as for the honor, the interest, and happiness of the whole community, to omit or delay no one preparation necessary to secure the ground which we so happily stand upon.

TO THE PEOPLE OF AMERICA.

On the expenses, arrangements and disbursements for carrying on the war, and finishing it with honor and advantage.

WHEN any necessity or occasion has pointed out the convenience of addressing the public, I have never made it a consideration whether the subject was popular or unpopular, but whether it was right or wrong; for that which is right will become popular, and that which is wrong, though by mistake it may obtain the cry or fashion of the day, will soon lose the power of delusion, and sink into disesteem.

A remarkable instance of this happened in the case of Silas Deane; and I mention this circumstance with the greater ease, because the poison of his hypocrisy spread over the whole country, and every man, almost without exception, thought me wrong in opposing him. The best friends I then had, except Mr. [Henry] Laurens, stood at a distance, and this tribute, which is due to his constancy, I pay to him with respect, and that the readier, because he is not here to hear it. If it reaches him in his imprisonment, it will afford him an agreeable reflection.

"*As he rose like a rocket, he would fall like a stick,*" is a metaphor which I applied to Mr. Deane, in the first piece which I published respecting him, and he has exactly fulfilled the description. The credit he so unjustly obtained from the public, he lost in almost as short a time.

The delusion perished as it fell, and he soon saw himself stripped of popular support. His more intimate acquaintances began to doubt, and to desert him long before he left America, and at his departure, he saw himself the object of general suspicion. When he arrived in France, he endeavored to effect by treason what he had failed to accomplish by fraud. His plans, schemes and projects, together with his expectation of being sent to Holland to negotiate a loan of money, had all miscarried. He then began traducing and accusing America of every crime, which could injure her reputation. "That she was a ruined country; that she only meant to make a tool of France, to get what money she could out of her, and then to leave her and accommodate with Britain." Of all which and much more, colonel Laurens and myself, when in France, informed Dr. Franklin, who had not before heard of it.[1] And to complete the character of traitor, he has, by letters to his country since, some of which, in his own handwriting, are now in the possession of congress, used every expression and argument in his power, to injure the reputation of France, and to advise America to renounce her alliance, and surrender up her independence.* Thus in France he abuses America, and in his letters to America he abuses France; and is endeavoring to create disunion between two countries, by the same arts of double-dealing by which he caused dissentions among the commissioners in Paris, and distractions in America. But his life has been fraud, and his character has been that of a plodding, plotting, cringing mercenary, capable of any disguise that suited

[1] Paine, as Secretary for Col. John Laurens, visited France early in 1781, and obtained from that country six millions of livres, with clothing and military stores, supplies which resulted in the defeat of Cornwallis.—*Editor.*

* Mr. William Marshall, of this city [Philadelphia], formerly a pilot, who had been taken at sea and carried to England, and got from thence to France, brought over letters from Mr. Deane to America, one of which was directed to "Robert Morris, Esq." Mr. Morris sent it unopened to Congress, and advised Mr. Marshall to deliver the others there, which he did. The letters were of the same purport with those which have been already published under the signature of S. Deane, to which they had frequent reference.—*Author.*

his purpose. His final detection has very happily cleared up those mistakes, and removed that uneasiness, which his unprincipled conduct occasioned. Every one now sees him in the same light; for towards friends or enemies he acted with the same deception and injustice, and his name, like that of *Arnold*, ought now to be forgotten among us.[1] As this is the first time that I have mentioned him since my return from France, it is my intention that it shall be the last. From this digression, which for several reasons I thought necessary to give, I now proceed to the purport of my address.

I consider the war of America against Britain as the country's war, the public's war, or the war of the people in their own behalf, for the security of their natural rights, and the protection of their own property. It is not the war of congress, the war of the assemblies, or the war of government in any line whatever. The country first, by mutual compact, resolved to defend their rights and maintain their independence, *at the hazard of their lives and fortunes;* they elected their representatives, by whom they appointed their members of congress, and said, *act you for us, and we will support you.* This is the true ground and principle of the war on the part of America, and, consequently, there remains nothing to do, but for every one to fulfil his obligation.

It was next to impossible that a new country, engaged in a new undertaking, could set off systematically right at first. She saw not the extent of the struggle that she was involved in, neither could she avoid the beginning. She supposed every step that she took, and every resolution which she formed, would bring her enemy to reason and close the contest. Those failing, she was forced into new measures; and these, like the former, being fitted to her expectations, and

---

[1] Deane was actually in London associating with Benedict Arnold. The extent of his treason was not known until the publication, in 1867, of George the Third's correspondence. The importance of printing the series of The Crisis consecutively has rendered it necessary to postpone Paine's articles concerning Deane (1778–9) to a later page of this volume. (See XXII., XXIII.)— *Editor.*

failing in their turn, left her continually unprovided, and without system. The enemy, likewise, was induced to prosecute the war, from the temporary expedients we adopted for carrying it on. We were continually expecting to see their credit exhausted, and they were looking to see our currency fail; and thus, between their watching us, and we them, the hopes of both have been deceived, and the childishness of the expectation has served to increase the expense.

Yet who, through this wilderness of error, has been to blame? Where is the man who can say the fault, in part, has not been his? They were the natural, unavoidable errors of the day. They were the errors of a whole country, which nothing but experience could detect and time remove. Neither could the circumstances of America admit of system, till either the paper currency was fixed or laid aside. No calculation of a finance could be made on a medium failing without reason, and fluctuating without rule.

But there is one error which might have been prevented and was not; and as it is not my custom to flatter, but to serve mankind, I will speak it freely. It certainly was the duty of every assembly on the continent to have known, at all times, what was the condition of its treasury, and to have ascertained at every period of depreciation, how much the real worth of the taxes fell short of their nominal value. This knowledge, which might have been easily gained, in the time of it, would have enabled them to have kept their constituents well informed, and this is one of the greatest duties of representation. They ought to have studied and calculated the expenses of the war, the quota of each state, and the consequent proportion that would fall on each man's property for his defence; and this must have easily shown to them, that a tax of one hundred pounds could not be paid by a bushel of apples or an hundred of flour, which was often the case two or three years ago. But instead of this, which would have been plain and upright dealing, the little line of temporary popularity, the feather of an hour's duration, was too much pursued; and in this involved condition of things, every state, for the want of a little thinking, or a little information, supposed that it supported the whole expenses of the war, when in fact it fell, by the time the tax was levied and collected, above three-fourths short of its own quota.

Impressed with a sense of the danger to which the country was exposed by this lax method of doing business, and the prevailing errors of the day, I published, last October was a twelvemonth, the *Crisis Extraordinary*, on the revenues of America, and the yearly expense of carrying on the war. My estimation of the latter, together with the civil list of congress, and the civil list of the several states, was two million pounds sterling, which is very nearly nine millions of dollars.

Since that time, congress have gone into a calculation, and have estimated the expenses of the war department and the civil list of congress (exclusive of the civil list of the several governments) at eight millions of dollars; and as the remaining million will be fully sufficient for the civil list of the several states, the two calculations are exceedingly near each other.

The sum of eight millions of dollars they have called upon the states to furnish, and their quotas are as follows, which I shall preface with the resolution itself.

" *By the United States in congress assembled.*

" *October* 30, 1781.

" *Resolved*, That the respective states be called upon to furnish the treasury of the United States with their quotas of eight millions of dollars, for the war department and civil list for the ensuing year, to be paid quarterly, in equal proportions, the first payment to be made on the first day of April next.

" *Resolved*, That a committee, consisting of a member from each state, be appointed to apportion to the several states the quota of the above sum.

"November 2d. The committee appointed to ascertain the proportions of the several states of the monies to be raised for the expenses of the ensuing year, report the following resolutions:

" That the sum of eight millions of dollars, as required to be raised by the resolutions of the 30th of October last, be paid by the states in the following proportion :

New-Hampshire	$ 373,598
Massachusetts	1,307,596
Rhode Island	216,684
Connecticut	747,196
New-York	373,598
New-Jersey	485,679
Pennsylvania	1,120,794
Delaware	112,085
Maryland	933,996
Virginia	1,307,594
North Carolina	622,677
South Carolina	373,598
Georgia	24,905
	$8,000,000

" *Resolved*, That it be recommended to the several states, to lay taxes for raising their quotas of money for the United States, separate from those laid for their own particular use."

On these resolutions I shall offer several remarks.

1st, On the sum itself, and the ability of the country.

2d, On the several quotas, and the nature of a union. And,

3d, On the manner of collection and expenditure.

1st, On the sum itself, and the ability of the country.   As I know my own calculation is as low as possible, and as the sum called for by congress, according to their calculation, agrees very nearly therewith, I am sensible it cannot possibly be lower.   Neither can it be done for that, unless there is ready money to go to market with ; and even in that case, it is only by the utmost management and economy that it can be made to do.

By the accounts which were laid before the British parliament last spring, it appeared that the charge of only subsisting, that is, feeding their army in America, cost annually four million pounds sterling, which is very nearly eighteen millions of dollars.   Now if, for eight millions, we can feed, clothe, arm, provide for, and pay an army sufficient for our defence, the very comparison shows that the money must be well laid out.

It may be of some use, either in debate or conversation, to attend to the progress of the expenses of an army, because it will enable us to see on what part any deficiency will fall.

The first thing is, to feed them and prepare for the sick.

Second, to clothe them.

Third, to arm and furnish them.

Fourth, to provide means for removing them from place to place. And,

Fifth, to pay them.

The first and second are absolutely necessary to them as men. The third and fourth are equally as necessary to them as an army. And the fifth is their just due. Now if the sum which shall be raised should fall short, either by the several acts of the states for raising it, or by the manner of collecting it, the deficiency will fall on the fifth head, the soldiers' pay, which would be defrauding them, and eternally disgracing ourselves. It would be a blot on the councils, the country, and the revolution of America, and a man would hereafter be ashamed to own that he had any hand in it.

But if the deficiency should be still shorter, it would next fall on the fourth head, *the means of removing the army from place to place;* and, in this case, the army must either stand still where it can be of no use, or seize on horses, carts, wagons, or any means of transportation which it can lay hold of; and in this instance the country suffers. In short, every attempt to do a thing for less than it can be done for, is sure to become at last both a loss and a dishonor.

But the country cannot bear it, say some. This has been the most expensive doctrine that ever was held out, and cost America millions of money for nothing. Can the country bear to be overrun, ravaged, and ruined by an enemy? This will immediately follow where defence is wanting, and defence will ever be wanting where sufficient revenues are not provided. But this is only one part of the folly. The second is, that when the danger comes, invited in part by our not preparing against it, we have been obliged, in a number of instances, to expend double the sums to do that which at first might have been done for half the money. But this is not all. A third mischief has been, that grain of all sorts, flour, beef, fodder, horses, carts, wagons, or whatever was absolutely or immediately wanted, have been taken without pay. Now, I ask, why was all this done, but from that extremely weak and expensive doctrine, *that the country could not bear it ?* That is, that she could not bear, in the first instance, that which would have saved her twice as much at last ; or, in proverbial language, that she could not bear to pay a penny to save a pound ; the consequence of which has been, that she has paid a pound for a penny. Why are there so many unpaid certificates in almost every man's hands, but from the parsimony of not providing sufficient revenues? Besides, the doctrine contradicts itself; because, if the whole country cannot bear it, how is it possible that a part should? 'And yet this has been the case: for those things have been had ; and they must be had ; but the misfortune is, that they have been obtained in a very unequal manner, and upon expensive credit, whereas, with ready money, they might have been purchased for half the price, and nobody distressed.

But there is another thought which ought to strike us, which is, how is the army to bear the want of food, clothing and other necessaries ? The man who is at home, can turn himself a thousand ways, and find as many means of ease, convenience or relief: but a soldier's life admits of none of those: their wants cannot be supplied from themselves: for an army, though it is the defence of a state, is at the same time the child of a country, or must be provided for in every thing.

And lastly, The doctrine is false. There are not three millions of people in any part of the universe, who live so well, or have such a fund of ability, as in America. The income of a common laborer, who is industrious, is equal to that of the generality of tradesmen in England. In the mercantile line, I have not heard of one who could be said to be a bankrupt since the war began, and in England they have been without number. In America almost every farmer lives on his own lands, and in England not one in a hundred does. In short, it seems as if the poverty of that country had made them furious, and they were determined to risk all to recover all.

Yet, notwithstanding those advantages on the part of America, true it is, that had it not been for the operation of taxes for our necessary defence, we had sunk into a state of sloth and poverty : for there was more wealth lost by neglecting to till the earth in the years 1776, '77, and '78, than the quota of taxes amounts to. That which is lost by neglect of this kind, is lost for ever : whereas that which is paid, and continues in the country, returns to us again ; and at the same time that it provides us with defence, it operates not only as a spur, but as a premium to our industry.

I shall now proceed to the second head, viz. *on the several quotas, and the nature of a union.*

There was a time when America had no other bond of union, than that of common interest and affection. The whole country flew to the relief of Boston, and, making her cause their own, participated in her cares and administered to her wants. The fate of war, since that day, has carried the calamity in a ten-fold proportion to the southward ; but in the mean time the union has been strengthened by a legal compact of the states, jointly and severally ratified, and that which before was choice, or the duty of affection, is now likewise the duty of legal obligation.

The union of America is the foundation-stone of her independence ; the rock on which it is built ; and is something so sacred in her constitution, that we ought to watch every word we speak, and every thought we think, that we injure it not, even by mistake. When a multitude, extended, or rather scattered, over a continent in the manner we were, mutually agree to form one common centre whereon the whole shall move to accomplish a particular purpose, all parts must act together and alike, or act not at all, and a stoppage in any one is a stoppage of the whole, at least for a time.

Thus the several states have sent representatives to assemble together in congress, and they have empowered that body, which thus becomes their centre, and are no other than themselves in representation, to conduct and manage the war, while their constituents at home attend to the domestic cares of the country, their internal legislation, their farms, professions or employments, for it is only by reducing complicated things to method and orderly connexion that they can be understood with advantage, or pursued with success. Congress, by virtue of this delegation, estimates the expense, and apportions it out to the several parts of the empire according to their several abilities; and here the debate must end, because each state has already had its voice, and the matter has undergone its whole portion of argument, and can no more be altered by any particular state, than a law of any state, after it has passed, can be altered by any individual. For with respect to those things which immediately concern the union, and for which the union was purposely established, and is intended to secure, each state is to the United States what each individual is to the state he lives in. And it is on this grand point, this movement upon one centre, that our existence as a nation, our happiness as a people, and our safety as individuals, depend.

It may happen that some state or other may be somewhat over or under rated, but this cannot be much. The experience which has been had upon the matter, has nearly ascertained their several abilities. But even in this case, it can only admit of an appeal to the United States, but cannot authorise any state to make the alteration itself, any more than our internal government can admit an individual to do so in the case of an act of assembly; for if one state can do it, then may another do the same, and the instant this is done the whole is undone.

Neither is it supposable that any single state can be a judge of all the comparative reasons which may influence the collective body in arranging the quotas of the continent. The circumstances of the several states are frequently varying, occasioned by the accidents of war and commerce, and it will often fall upon some to help others, rather beyond what their exact proportion at another time might be; but even this assistance is as naturally and politically included in the idea of a union as that of any particular assigned proportion ; because we know not whose turn it may be next to want assistance, for which reason that state is the wisest which sets the best example.

Though in matters of bounden duty and reciprocal affection, it is rather a degeneracy from the honesty and ardour of the heart to admit any thing selfish to partake in the government of our conduct, yet in cases where our duty, our affections, and our interest all coincide, it may be of some use to observe their union. The United States will become heir to an extensive quantity of vacant land, and their several titles to shares and quotas thereof, will naturally be adjusted according to their relative quotas, during the war, exclusive of that inability which may unfortunately arise to any state by the enemy's holding possession of a part ; but as this is a cold matter of interest, I pass it by, and proceed to my third head, viz., *on the manner of collection and expenditure.*

It hath been our error, as well as our misfortune, to blend the affairs of each state, especially in money matters, with those of the United States ; whereas it is our case, convenience and interest, to keep them separate. The expenses of the United States for carrying on the war, and the expenses of each state for its own domestic government, are distinct things, and to involve them is a source of perplexity and a cloak for fraud. I love method, because I see and am convinced of its beauty and advantage. It is that which makes all business easy and understood, and without which, everything becomes embarrassed and difficult.

There are certain powers which the people of each state have delegated to their legislative and executive bodies, and there are other powers which the people of every state have delegated to congress, among which is that of conducting the war, and, consequently, of managing the expenses attending it ; for how else can that be managed, which concerns every state, but by a delegation from each ?   When a state has furnished its quota, it has an undoubted right to know how it has been applied, and it is as much the duty of congress to inform the state of the one, as it is the duty of the state to provide the other.

In the resolution of congress already recited, it is recommended to the several states *to lay taxes for raising their quotas of money for the United States, separate from those laid for their own particular use.*

This is a most necessary point to be observed, and the distinction should follow all the way through.   They should be levied, paid and collected, separately, and kept separate in every instance.   Neither have the civil officers of any state, or the government of that state, the least right to touch that money which the people pay for the support of their army and the war, any more than congress has to touch that which each state raises for its own use.

This distinction will naturally be followed by another.   It will occasion every state to examine nicely into the expenses of its civil list, and to regulate, reduce, and bring it into better order than it has hitherto been ; because the money for that purpose must be raised apart, and accounted for to the public separately.   But while the monies of both were blended, the necessary nicety was not observed, and the poor soldier, who ought to have been the first, was the last who was thought of.

Another convenience will be, that the people, by paying the taxes separately, will know what they are for ; and will likewise know that those which are for the defence of the country will cease with the war, or soon after.   For although, as I have before observed, the war is their own, and for the support of their own rights and the protection of their own property, yet they have the same right to know, that they have to pay, and it is the want of not knowing that is often the cause of dissatisfaction.

This regulation of keeping the taxes separate has given rise to a regulation in the office of finance, by which it is directed :

" That the receivers shall, at the end of every month, make out an exact account of the monies received by them respectively, during such month, specifying therein the names of the persons from whom the same shall have been received, the dates and the sums ; which account they shall respectively cause to be published in one of the newspapers of the state ; to the end that every citizen may know how much of the monies collected from him, in taxes, is transmitted to the treasury of the United States for the support of the war ; and also, that it may be known what monies have been at the order of the superintendant of finance. It being proper and necessary, that, in a free country, the people should be as fully informed of the administration of their affairs as the nature of things will admit."

It is an agreeable thing to see a spirit of order and economy taking place, after such a series of errors and difficulties. A government or an administration, who means and acts honestly, has nothing to fear, and consequently has nothing to conceal ; and it would be of use if a monthly or quarterly account was to be published, as well of the expenditures as of the receipts. Eight millions of dollars must be husbanded with an exceeding deal of care to make it do, and, therefore, as the management must be reputable, the publication would be serviceable.

I have heard of petitions which have been presented to the assembly of this state (and probably the same may have happened in other states) praying to have the taxes lowered. Now the only way to keep taxes low is, for the United States to have ready money to go to market with : and though the taxes to be raised for the present year will fall heavy, and there will naturally be some difficulty in paying them, yet the difficulty, in proportion as money spreads about the country, will every day grow less, and in the end we shall save some millions of dollars by it. We see what a bitter, revengeful enemy we have to deal with, and any expense is cheap compared to their merciless paw. We have seen the unfortunate Carolineans hunted like partridges on the mountains, and it is only by providing means for our defence, that we shall be kept from the same condition. When we think or talk about taxes, we ought to recollect that we lie down in peace and sleep in safety ; that we can follow our farms or stores or other occupations, in prosperous tranquillity ; and that these inestimable blessings are pro-cured to us by the taxes that we pay. In this view, our taxes are properly our insurance money ; they are what we pay to be made safe, and, in strict policy, are the best money we can lay out.

It was my intention to offer some remarks on the impost law of five per cent. recommended by congress, and to be established as a fund for the payment of the loan-office cer-tificates, and other debts of the United States ; but I have already extended my piece beyond my intention. And as this fund will make our system of finance complete, and is strictly just, and consequently requires nothing but honesty to do it, there needs but little to be said upon it.

COMMON SENSE.

PHILADELPHIA, March 5, 1782.

THE CRISIS.

XI.

ON THE PRESENT STATE OF NEWS.

SINCE the arrival of two, if not three packets in quick succession, at New York, from England, a variety of un-connected *news* has circulated through the country, and afforded as great a variety of speculation.

That something is the matter in the cabinet and councils of our enemies, on the other side of the water, is certain— that they have run their length of madness, and are under the necessity of changing their measures may easily be seen into ; but to what this change of measures may amount, or how far it may correspond with our interest, happiness and duty, is yet uncertain; and from what we have hitherto experienced, we have too much reason to suspect them in every thing.

I do not address this publication so much to the people of America as to the British ministry, whoever they may be, for if it is their intention to promote any kind of negotiation, it is proper they should know beforehand, that the United States have as much honour as bravery; and that they are no more to be seduced from their alliance than their allegiance; that their line of politics is formed and not dependant, like that of their enemy, on chance and accident.

On our part, in order to know, at any time, what the British government will do, we have only to find out what they ought *not* to do, and this last will be their conduct. Forever changing and forever wrong; too distant from America to improve in circumstances, and too unwise to foresee them; scheming without principle, and executing without probability, their whole line of management has hitherto been blunder and baseness. Every campaign has added to their loss, and every year to their disgrace; till unable to go on, and ashamed to go back, their politics have come to a halt, and all their fine prospects to a halter.

Could our affections forgive, or humanity forget the wounds of an injured country—we might, under the influence of a momentary oblivion, stand still and laugh. But they are engraven where no amusement can conceal them, and of a kind for which there is no recompense. Can ye restore to us the beloved dead? Can ye say to the grave, give up the murdered? Can ye obliterate from our memories those who are no more? Think not then to tamper with our feelings by an insidious contrivance, nor suffocate our humanity by seducing us to dishonour.

In March 1780, I published part of the Crisis, No. VIII., in the newspapers, but did not conclude it in the following papers, and the remainder has lain by me till the present day.

There appeared about that time some disposition in the

British cabinet to cease the further prosecution of the war, and as I had formed my opinion that whenever such a design should take place, it would be accompanied by a dishonourable proposition to America, respecting France, I had suppressed the remainder of that number, not to expose the baseness of any such proposition. But the arrival of the next news from England, declared her determination to go on with the war, and consequently as the political object I had then in view was not become a subject, it was unnecessary in me to bring it forward, which is the reason it was never published.

The matter which I allude to in the unpublished part, I shall now make a quotation of, and apply it as the more enlarged state of things, at this day, shall make convenient or necessary,

It was as follows:

" By the speeches which have appeared from the British parliament, it is easy to perceive to what impolitic and imprudent excesses their passions and prejudices have, in every instance, carried them during the present war. Provoked at the upright and honourable treaty between America and France, they imagined that nothing more was necessary to be done to prevent its final ratification, than to promise, through the agency of their commissioners (Carlisle, Eden, and Johnstone) a repeal of their once offensive acts of parliament. The vanity of the conceit, was as unpardonable as the experiment was impolitic. And so convinced am I of their wrong ideas of America, that I shall not wonder, if, in their last stage of political phrenzy, they propose to her to break her alliance with France, and enter into one with them. Such a proposition, should it ever be made, and it has been already more than once hinted at in parliament, would discover such a disposition to perfidiousness, and such disregard of honour and morals, as would add the finishing vice to national corruption.—I do not mention this to put America on the watch, but to put England on her guard, that she do not, in the looseness of her heart, envelop in disgrace every fragment of reputation."—Thus far the quotation.

By the complexion of some part of the news which has transpired through the New-York papers, it seems probable that this insidious era in the British politics is beginning to make its appearance. I wish it may not; for that which is a disgrace to human nature, throws something of a shade over all the human character, and each individual feels his share of the wound that is given to the whole.

The policy of Britain has ever been to divide America in some way or other. In the beginning of the dispute, she practised every art to prevent or destroy the union of the states, well knowing that could she once get them to stand singly, she could conquer them unconditionally. Failing in this project in America, she renewed it in Europe; and, after the alliance had taken place, she made secret offers to France to induce her to give up America; and what is still more extraordinary, she at the same time made propositions to Dr. Franklin, then in Paris, the very court to which she was secretly applying, to draw off America from France. But this is not all.

On the 14th of September, 1778, the British court, through their secretary, lord Weymouth, made application to the marquis d'Almadovar, the Spanish ambassador at London, to "ask the *mediation*," for these were the words, of the court of Spain, for the purpose of negociating a peace with France, leaving America (as I shall hereafter show) out of the question. Spain readily offered her mediation, and likewise the city of Madrid as the place of conference, but withal, proposed, that the United States of America should be invited to the treaty, and considered as independent during the time the business was negotiating. But this was not the view of England. She wanted to draw France from the war, that she might uninterruptedly pour out all her force and fury upon America; and being disappointed in this plan, as well through the open and generous conduct of Spain, as the determination of France, she refused the mediation which she had solicited.

I shall now give some extracts from the justifying memorial of the Spanish court, in which she has set the conduct

and character of Britain, with respect to America, in a clear
and striking point of light.

The memorial, speaking of the refusal of the British court
to meet in conference with commissioners from the United
States, who were to be considered as independent during
the time of the conference, says,

" It is a thing very extraordinary and even ridiculous, that the
court of London, who treats the colonies as independent, not only
in acting, but of right, during the war, should have a repugnance
to treat them as such only in acting during a truce, or suspension
of hostilities.   The convention of Saratoga ; the reputing general
Burgoyne as a lawful prisoner, in order to suspend his trial ; the
exchange and liberation of other prisoners made from the colonies ;
the having named commissioners to go and supplicate the Americans, at their own doors, request peace of them, and treat with
them and the congress : and, finally, by a thousand other acts of
this sort, authorized by the court of London, which have been,
and are true signs of the acknowledgment of their independence.

" In aggravation of all the foregoing, at the same time the British
cabinet answered the king of Spain in the terms already mentioned, they were insinuating themselves at the court of France by
means of secret emissaries, and making very great offers to her,
to abandon the colonies and make peace with England.   But there
is yet more ; for at this same time the English ministry were
treating, by means of another certain emissary, with Dr. Franklin,
minister plenipotentiary from the colonies, residing at Paris, to
whom they made various proposals to disunite them from France,
and accommodate matters with England.

" From what has been observed, it evidently follows, that the
whole of the British politics was, to disunite the two courts of
Paris and Madrid, by means of the suggestions and offers which
she separately made to them ; and also to separate the colonies
from their treaties and engagements entered into with France, and
induce them to arm against the house of Bourbon, or *more probably to oppress them when they found, from breaking their engagements, that they stood alone and without protection.*

" This, therefore, is the net they laid for the American states ;
that is to say, to tempt them with flattering and very magnificent
promises to come to an accommodation with them, exclusive of

any intervention of Spain or France, that the British ministry might always remain the arbiters of the fate of the colonies.

"But the Catholic king (the king of Spain) faithful on the one part of the engagements which bind him to the Most Christian king (the king of France) his nephew; just and upright on the other, to his own subjects, whom he ought to protect and guard against so many insults; and finally, full of humanity and compassion for the Americans and other individuals who suffer in the present war; he is determined to pursue and prosecute it, and to make all the efforts in his power, until he can obtain a solid and permanent peace, with full and satisfactory securities that it shall be observed."

Thus far the memorial; a translation of which into English, may be seen in full, under the head of State Papers, in the Annual Register, for 1779, p. 367.

The extracts I have here given, serve to show the various endeavors and contrivances of the enemy, to draw France from her connexion with America, and to prevail on her to make a separate peace with England, leaving America totally out of the question, and at the mercy of a merciless, unprincipled enemy. The opinion, likewise, which Spain has formed of the British cabinet's character for meanness and perfidiousness, is so exactly the opinion of America respecting it, that the memorial, in this instance, contains our own statements and language; for people, however remote, who think alike, will unavoidably speak alike.

Thus we see the insidious use which Britain endeavoured to make of the propositions of peace under the mediation of Spain. I shall now proceed to the second proposition under the mediation of the emperor of Germany and the empress of Russia; the general outline of which was, that a congress of the several powers at war should meet at Vienna, in 1781, to settle preliminaries of peace.

I could wish myself at liberty to make use of all the information which I am possessed of on this subject, but as there is a delicacy in the matter, I do not conceive it prudent, at least at present, to make references and quotations in the same manner as I have done with respect to the mediation of Spain, who published the whole proceedings herself ; and therefore, what comes from me, on this part of the business, must rest on my own credit with the public, assuring them, that when the whole proceedings, relative to the proposed congress of Vienna shall appear, they will find my account not only true, but studiously moderate.

We know at the time this mediation was on the carpet, the expectation of the British king and ministry ran high with respect to the conquest of America. The English packet which was taken with the mail on board, and carried into l'Orient, in France, contained letters from lord G. Germaine to Sir Henry Clinton, which expressed in the fullest terms the ministerial idea of a total conquest. Copies of those letters were sent to congress and published in the newspapers of last year. Colonel [John] Laurens brought over the originals, some of which, signed in the handwriting of the then secretary, Germaine, are now in my possession.

Filled with these high ideas, nothing could be more insolent towards America than the language of the British court on the proposed mediation. A peace with France and Spain she anxiously solicited ; but America, as before, was to be left to her mercy, neither would she hear any proposition for admitting an agent from the United States into the congress of Vienna.

On the other hand, France, with an open, noble and manly determination, and the fidelity of a good ally, would hear no proposition for a separate peace, nor even meet in congress at Vienna, without an agent from America : and likewise that the independent character of the United States, represented by the agent, should be fully and unequivocally defined and settled before any conference should be entered on. The reasoning of the court of France on the several propositions of the two imperial courts, which relate to us, is rather in the style of an American than an ally, and she advocated the cause of America as if she had been America herself.—Thus the second mediation, like the first, proved ineffectual.

But since that time, a reverse of fortune has overtaken the British arms, and all their high expectations are dashed to the ground. The noble exertions to the southward under general [Nathaniel] Greene ; the successful operations of the allied arms in the Chesapeake ; the loss of most of their islands in the West-Indies, and Minorca in the Mediterranean ; the persevering spirit of Spain against Gibraltar; the expected capture of Jamaica ; the failure of making a separate peace with Holland, and the expense of an hundred millions sterling, by which all these fine losses were obtained, have read them a loud lesson of disgraceful misfortune, and necessity has called on them to change their ground.

In this situation of confusion and despair, their present councils have no fixed character. It is now the hurricane months of British politics. Every day seems to have a storm of its own, and they are scudding under the bare poles of hope. Beaten, but not humble ; condemned, but not penitent ; they act like men trembling at fate and catching at a straw. From this convulsion, in the entrails of their politics, it is more than probable, that the mountain groaning in labour, will bring forth a mouse, as to its size, and a monster in its make. They will try on America the same insidious arts they tried on France and Spain.

We sometimes experience sensations to which language is not equal. The conception is too bulky to be born alive, and in the torture of thinking, we stand dumb. Our feelings, imprisoned by their magnitude, find no way out—and, in the struggle of expression, every finger tries to be a tongue. The machinery of the body seems too little for the mind, and we look about for helps to show our thoughts by. Such must be the sensation of America, whenever Britain, teeming with corruption, shall propose to her to sacrifice her faith.

But, exclusive of the wickedness, there is a personal offence contained in every such attempt. It is calling us villains : for no man asks the other to act the villain unless he believes him inclined to be one. No man attempts to seduce the truly honest woman. It is the supposed looseness of her mind that starts the thoughts of seduction, and he who offers it calls her a prostitute. Our pride is always hurt by the same propositions which offend our principles; for when we are shocked at the crime, we are wounded by the suspicion of our compliance.

Could I convey a thought that might serve to regulate the public mind, I would not make the interest of the alliance the basis of defending it. All the world are moved by interest, and it affords them nothing to boast of. But I would go a step higher, and defend it on the ground of honour and principle. That our public affairs have flourished under the alliance—that it was wisely made, and has been nobly executed—that by its assistance we are enabled to preserve our country from conquest, and expel those who sought our destruction—that it is our true interest to maintain it unimpaired, and that while we do so no enemy can conquer us, are matters which experience has taught us, and the common good of ourselves, abstracted from principles of faith and honour, would lead us to maintain the connexion.

But over and above the mere letter of the alliance, we have been nobly and generously treated, and have had the same respect and attention paid to us, as if we had been an old established country. To oblige and be obliged is fair work among mankind, and we want an opportunity of showing to the world that we are a people sensible of kindness and worthy of confidence. Character is to us, in our present circumstances, of more importance than interest. We are a young nation, just stepping upon the stage of public life, and the eye of the world is upon us to see how we act. We have an enemy who is watching to destroy our reputation, and who will go any length to gain some evidence against us, that may serve to render our conduct suspected, and our character odious; because, could she accomplish this, wicked as it is, the world would withdraw from us, as from a people not to be trusted, and our task would then become difficult.

There is nothing which sets the character of a nation in a

higher or lower light with others, than the faithfully fulfilling, or perfidiously breaking, of treaties. They are things
not to be tampered with : and should Britain, which seems
very probable, propose to seduce America into such an act of
baseness, it would merit from her some mark of unusual
detestation. It is one of those extraordinary instances in
which we ought not to be contented with the bare negative
of congress, because it is an affront on the multitude as well
as on the government. It goes on the supposition that the
public are not honest men, and that they may be managed
by contrivance, though they cannot be conquered by arms.
But, let the world and Britain know, that we are neither to
be bought nor sold ; that our mind is great and fixed ; our
prospect clear ; and that we will support our character as
firmly as our independence.

But I will go still further; general Conway, who made the
motion, in the British parliament, for discontinuing *offensive*
war in America, is a gentleman of an amiable character.[1]
We have no personal quarrel with him. But he feels not as
we feel ; he is not in our situation, and that alone, without
any other explanation, is enough.

The British parliament suppose they have many friends in
America, and that, when all chance of conquest is over, they
will be able to draw her from her alliance with France.
Now, if I have any conception of the human heart, they will
fail in this more than in any thing that they have yet tried.

This part of the business is not a question of policy only,
but of honour and honesty ; and the proposition will have

---

[1] Henry Seymour Conway, M. P. for St. Edmund's Bury (born 1720), had
been groom of the bedchamber to George II., and to George III. until 1764.
He had moved the repeal of the Stamp Act, while in the Privy Council of
Rockingham. He was afterwards joint Secretary of State with Grafton, resigning in 1772. His fidelity to the Americans made him odious to the king. He
was Governor of Jersey and defended it in 1779. "General Conway," writes
Horace Walpole, "is in the midst of the storm in a nutshell, and I know will
defend himself as if he was in the strongest fortification in Flanders. I believe
the Court would sacrifice the island to sacrifice him." (Letter to Sir H. Mann,
July 7, 1779.) Conway's motion to discontinue the war in America passed Feb.
27, 1782, by 234 to 215.—*Editor*.

in it something so visibly low and base, that their partisans, if they have any, will be ashamed of it. Men are often hurt by a mean action who are not startled at a wicked one, and this will be such a confession of inability, such a declaration of servile thinking, that the scandal of it will ruin all their hopes.

In short, we have nothing to do but to go on with vigour and determination. The enemy is yet in our country. They hold New-York, Charleston, and Savannah, and the very being in those places is an offence, and a part of offensive war, and until they can be driven from them, or captured in them, it would be folly in us to listen to an idle tale. I take it for granted that the British ministry are sinking under the impossibility of carrying on the war. Let them then come to a fair and open peace with France, Spain, Holland and America, in the manner they ought to do ; but until then, we can have nothing to say to them.

COMMON SENSE.

PHILADELPHIA, May 22, 1782.

A SUPERNUMERARY CRISIS.

TO SIR GUY CARLETON.[1]

IT is the nature of compassion to associate with misfortune ; and I address this to you in behalf even of an enemy, a captain in the British service, now on his way to the headquarters of the American army, and unfortunately doomed to death for a crime not his own. A sentence so extraordinary, an execution so repugnant to every human sensation, ought never to be told without the circumstances which produced it : and as the destined victim is yet in existence, and in your hands rests his life or death, I shall briefly state the case, and the melancholy consequence.

Captain Huddy, of the Jersey militia, was attacked in a

---

[1] Sir Guy Carleton—a humane and just man—had succeeded Sir Henry Clinton at New York.—*Editor*.

small fort on Tom's River, by a party of refugees in the British pay and service, was made prisoner, together with his company, carried to New-York and lodged in the provost of that city : about three weeks after which, he was taken out of the provost down to the water-side, put into a boat, and brought again upon the Jersey shore, and there, contrary to the practice of all nations but savages, was hung up on a tree, and left hanging till found by our people who took him down and buried him.

The inhabitants of that part of the country where the murder was committed, sent a deputation to general Washington with a full and certified statement of the fact. Struck, as every human breast must be, with such brutish outrage, and determined both to punish and prevent it for the future, the general represented the case to general Clinton, who then commanded, and demanded that the refugee officer who ordered and attended the execution, and whose name is Lippincut, should be delivered up as a murderer ; and in case of refusal, that the person of some British officer should suffer in his stead. The demand, though not refused, has not been complied with ; and the melancholy lot (not by selection, but by casting lots) has fallen upon captain Asgill, of the guards, who, as I have already mentioned, is on his way from Lancaster to camp, a martyr to the general wickedness of the cause he engaged in, and the ingratitude of those whom he served.

The first reflection which arises on this black business is, what sort of men must Englishmen be, and what sort of order and discipline do they preserve in their army, when in the immediate place of their head-quarters, and under the eye and nose of their commander-in-chief, a prisoner can be taken at pleasure from his confinement, and his death made a matter of sport.

The history of the most savage Indians does not produce instances exactly of this kind. They, at least, have a formality in their punishments. With them it is the horridness of revenge, but with your army it is a still greater crime, the horridness of diversion.

The British generals who have succeeded each other, from the time of general Gage to yourself, have all affected to speak in language that they have no right to. In their proclamations, their addresses, their letters to general Washington, and their supplications to congress (for they deserve no other name) they talk of British honour, British generosity, and British clemency, as if those things were matters of fact; whereas, we whose eyes are open, who speak the same language with yourselves, many of whom were born on the same spot with you, and who can no more be mistaken in your words than in your actions, can declare to all the world, that so far as our knowledge goes, there is not a more detestable character, nor a meaner or more barbarous enemy, than the present British one. With us, you have forfeited all pretensions to reputation, and it is only by holding you like a wild beast, afraid of your keepers, that you can be made manageable. But to return to the point in question.

Though I can think no man innocent who has lent his hand to destroy the country which he did not plant, and to ruin those that he could not enslave, yet, abstracted from all ideas of right and wrong on the original question, captain Asgill, in the present case, is not the guilty man. The villain and the victim are here separated characters. You hold the one and we the other. You disown, or affect to disown and reprobate the conduct of Lippincut, yet you give him a sanctuary; and by so doing you as effectually become the executioner of Asgill, as if you had put the rope on his neck, and dismissed him from the world. Whatever your feelings on this interesting occasion may be are best known to yourself. Within the grave of your own mind lies buried the fate of Asgill. He becomes the corpse of your will, or the survivor of your justice. Deliver up the one, and you save the other; withhold the one, and the other dies by your choice.

On our part the case is exceeding plain; *an officer has been taken from his confinement and murdered, and the murderer is within your lines.* Your army has been guilty of a thousand instances of equal cruelty, but they have been rendered equivocal, and sheltered from personal detection. Here the crime is fixed; and is one of those extraordinary cases which can neither be denied nor palliated, and to which the custom of war does not apply; for it never could be supposed that such a brutal outrage would ever be committed. It is an original in the history of civilized barbarians, and is truly British.

On your part you are accountable to us for the personal safety of the prisoners within your walls. Here can be no mistake; they can neither be spies nor suspected as such; your security is not endangered, nor your operations subjected to miscarriage, by men immured within a dungeon. They differ in every circumstance from men in the field, and leave no pretence for severity of punishment. But if to the dismal condition of captivity with you must be added the constant apprehensions of death; if to be imprisoned is so nearly to be entombed; and if, after all, the murderers are to be protected, and thereby the crime encouraged, wherein do you differ from [American] Indians either in conduct or character?

We can have no idea of your honour, or your justice, in any future transaction, of what nature it may be, while you shelter within your lines an outrageous murderer, and sacrifice in his stead an officer of your own. If you have no regard to us, at least spare the blood which it is your duty to save. Whether the punishment will be greater on him, who, in this case, innocently dies, or on him whom sad necessity forces to retaliate, is, in the nicety of sensation, an undecided question? It rests with you to prevent the sufferings of both. You have nothing to do but to give up the murderer, and the matter ends.

But to protect him, be he who he may, is to patronise his crime, and to trifle it off by frivolous and unmeaning inquiries, is to promote it. There is no declaration you can make, nor promise you can give that will obtain credit. It is the man and not the apology that is demanded.

You see yourself pressed on all sides to spare the life of

your own officer, for die he will if you withhold justice. The murder of captain Huddy is an offence not to be borne with, and there is no security which we can have, that such actions or similar ones shall not be repeated, but by making the punishment fall upon yourselves. To destroy the last security of captivity, and to take the unarmed, the unresisting prisoner to private and sportive execution, is carrying barbarity too high for silence. The evil *must* be put an end to; and the choice of persons rests with you. But if your attachment to the guilty is stronger than to the innocent, you invent a crime that must destroy your character, and if the cause of your king needs to be so supported, for ever cease, sir, to torture our remembrance with the wretched phrases of British honour, British generosity, and British clemency.

From this melancholy circumstance, learn, sir, a lesson of morality. The refugees are men whom your predecessors have instructed in wickedness, the better to fit them to their master's purpose. To make them useful, they have made them vile, and the consequence of their tutored villany is now descending on the heads of their encouragers. They have been trained like hounds to the scent of blood, and cherished in every species of dissolute barbarity. Their ideas of right and wrong are worn away in the constant habitude of repeated infamy, till, like men practised in execution, they feel not the value of another's life.

The task before you, though painful, is not difficult; give up the murderer, and save your officer, as the first outset of a necessary reformation.

COMMON SENSE.[1]

PHILADELPHIA, May 31, 1782.

---

[1] The lot fell on Asgill May 27, 1782, at Lancaster, Pennsylvania; it will be seen by the date of this letter to the commander at New York that it must have been written immediately after the arrival of the news in Philadelphia. With the rest of the world Paine was ignorant of the fact that young Asgill, an officer under Cornwallis, was, by Article 14 of his chief's terms of capitulation, exempted from liability to any such danger as that which now threatened him. On September 7th Paine ventured to write to Washington a plea for Asgill's life, saying, " it will look much better hereafter." The truth of which must be felt by every American who learns, after its long suppression, the ugly fact that it

THE CRISIS.

XII.

TO THE EARL OF SHELBURNE.[1]

MY LORD,—A speech, which has been printed in several of the British and New-York newspapers, as coming from your lordship, in answer to one from the duke of Richmond, of the 10th of July last, contains expressions and opinions so new and singular, and so enveloped in mysterious reasoning, that I address this publication to you, for the purpose of giving them a free and candid examination. The speech that I allude to is in these words:

" His lordship said, it had been mentioned in another place, that he had been guilty of inconsistency. To clear himself of this, he asserted that he still held the same principles in respect to American independence which he at first imbibed. He had been, and yet was of opinion, whenever the parliament of Great Britain acknowledges that point, the sun of England's glory is set forever. Such were the sentiments he possessed on a former day, and such the sentiments he continued to hold at this hour. It was the opinion of lord Chatham, as well as many other able statesmen. Other noble lords, however, think differently, and as the majority of the cabinet support them, he acquiesced in the measure, dissenting from the idea ; and the point is settled for bringing the matter into the full discussion of parliament, where it will be candidly, fairly, and impartially debated. The independence of America would end in the ruin of England ; and that a peace patched up with France, would give that proud enemy the means

was only after a protest from the court of France, whose honor was also involved, that Captain Asgill was released.

It should be added that the guilt of Captain Lippencott was strenuously denied, and that the facts have never been ascertained.—*Editor.*

[1] Afterwards Lord Lansdowne, whose friendship Paine enjoyed when in England some years later. Writing to Jefferson, March 12, 1789, Paine says : ''I believe I am not so much in the good graces of the Marquis of Lansdowne as I used to be—I do not answer his purpose. He was always talking of a sort of reconnection of England and America, and my coldness and reserve on this subject checked communication.''—*Editor.*

of yet trampling on this country. The sun of England's glory he
wished not to see set forever ; he looked for a spark at least to be
left, which might in time light us up to a new day. But if independence was to be granted, if parliament deemed that measure
prudent, he foresaw, in his own mind, that England was undone.
He wished to God that he had been deputed to congress, that he
might plead the cause of that country as well as of this, and that
he might exercise whatever powers he possessed as an orator, to
save both from ruin, in a conviction to congress, that, if their
independence was signed, their liberties were gone forever.

" Peace, his lordship added, was a desirable object, but it must
be an honorable peace, and not an humiliating one, dictated by
France, or insisted on by America. It was very true, that this
kingdom was not in a flourishing state, it was impoverished by
war. But if we were not rich, it was evident that France was
poor. If we were straitened in our finances, the enemy were
exhausted in their resources. This was a great empire ; it
abounded with brave men, who were able and willing to fight in
a common cause ; the language of humiliation should not, therefore, be the language of Great Britain. His lordship said, that he
was not afraid nor ashamed of those expressions going to America.
There were numbers, great numbers there, who were of the same
way of thinking, in respect to that country being dependant on
this, and who, with his lordship, perceived ruin and independence
linked together."

Thus far the speech ; on which I remark—That his lordship is a total stranger to the mind and sentiments of America ; that he has wrapped himself up in fond delusion, that
something less than independence, may, under his administration, be accepted ; and he wishes himself sent to congress,
to prove the most extraordinary of all doctrines, which is,
that *independence*, the sublimest of all human conditions, is
loss of liberty.

In answer to which we may say, that in order to know
what the contrary word *dependance* means, we have only to
look back to those years of severe humiliation, when the
mildest of all petitions could obtain no other notice than the
haughtiest of all insults ; and when the base terms of unconditional submission were demanded, or undistinguishable

destruction threatened. It is nothing to us that the ministry have been changed, for they may be changed again. The guilt of a government is the crime of a whole country; and the nation that can, though but for a moment, think and act as England has done, can never afterwards be believed or trusted. There are cases in which it is as impossible to restore character to life, as it is to recover the dead. It is a phœnix that can expire but once, and from whose ashes there is no resurrection. Some offences are of such a slight composition, that they reach no further than the temper, and are created or cured by a thought. But the sin of England has struck the heart of America, and nature has not left in our power to say we can forgive.

Your lordship wishes for an opportunity to plead before congress *the cause of England and America, and to save*, as you say, *both from ruin.*

That the country, which, for more than seven years has sought our destruction, should now cringe to solicit our protection, is adding the wretchedness of disgrace to the misery of disappointment; and if England has the least spark of supposed honour left, that spark must be darkened by asking, and extinguished by receiving, the smallest favor from America; for the criminal who owes his life to the grace and mercy of the injured, is more executed by living, than he who dies.

But a thousand pleadings, even from your lordship, can have no effect. Honour, interest, and every sensation of the heart, would plead against you. We are a people who think not as you think; and what is equally true, you cannot feel as we feel. The situations of the two countries are exceedingly different. Ours has been the seat of war; yours has seen nothing of it. The most wanton destruction has been committed in our sight; the most insolent barbarity has been acted on our feelings. We can look round and see the remains of burnt and destroyed houses, once the fair fruit of hard industry, and now the striking monuments of British brutality. We walk over the dead whom we loved, in every part of America, and remember by whom they fell.

There is scarcely a village but brings to life some melancholy thought, and reminds us of what we have suffered, and of those we have lost by the inhumanity of Britain. A thousand images arise to us, which, from situation, you cannot see, and are accompanied by as many ideas which you cannot know; and therefore your supposed system of reasoning would apply to nothing, and all your expectations die of themselves.

The question whether England shall accede to the independence of America, and which your lordship says is to undergo a parliamentary discussion, is so very simple, and composed of so few cases, that it scarcely needs a debate.

It is the only way out of an expensive and ruinous war, which has no object, and without which acknowledgment there can be no peace.

But your lordship says, *the sun of Great Britain will set whenever she acknowledges the independence of America.*— Whereas the metaphor would have been strictly just, to have left the sun wholly out of the figure, and have ascribed her not acknowledging it to the influence of the moon.

But the expression, if true, is the greatest confession of disgrace that could be made, and furnishes America with the highest notions of sovereign independent importance. Mr. Wedderburne, about the year 1776, made use of an idea of much the same kind,—*Relinquish America!* says he— *What is it but to desire a giant to shrink spontaneously into a dwarf.*

Alas! are those people who call themselves Englishmen, of so little internal consequence, that when America is gone, or shuts her eyes upon them, their sun is set, they can shine no more, but grope about in obscurity, and contract into insignificant animals? Was America, then, the giant of the empire, and England only her dwarf in waiting! Is the case so strangely altered, that those who once thought we could not live without them, are now brought to declare that they cannot exist without us? Will they tell to the world, and that from their first minister of state, that America is their all in all; that it is by her importance only that they can live, and breathe, and have a being? Will they, who long since threatened to bring us to their feet, bow themselves to ours, and own that without us they are not a nation? Are they become so unqualified to debate on independence, that they have lost all idea of it themselves, and are calling to the rocks and mountains of America to cover their insignificance? Or, if America is lost, is it manly to sob over it like a child for its rattle, and invite the laughter of the world by declarations of disgrace? Surely, a more consistent line of conduct would be to bear it without complaint; and to show that England, without America, can preserve her independence, and a suitable rank with other European powers. You were not contented while you had her, and to weep for her now is childish.

But lord Shelburne thinks something may yet be done. What that something is, or how it is to be accomplished, is a matter in obscurity. By arms there is no hope. The experience of nearly eight years, with the expense of an hundred million pounds sterling, and the loss of two armies, must positively decide that point. Besides, the British have lost their interest in America with the disaffected. Every part of it has been tried. There is no new scene left for delusion: and the thousands who have been ruined by adhering to them, and have now to quit the settlements which they had acquired, and be conveyed like transports to cultivate the deserts of Augustine and Nova-Scotia, has put an end to all further expectations of aid.

If you cast your eyes on the people of England, what have they to console themselves with for the millions expended? Or, what encouragement is there left to continue throwing good money after bad? America can carry on the war for ten years longer, and all the charges of government included, for less than you can defray the charges of war and government for one year. And I, who know both countries, know well, that the people of America can afford to pay their share of the expense much better than the people of England can. Besides, it is their own estates and property, their own rights, liberties and government, that they are defending; and were they not to do it, they would deserve to lose all, and none would pity them. The fault would be their own, and their punishment just.

The British army in America care not how long the war lasts. They enjoy an easy and indolent life. They fatten on the folly of one country and the spoils of another; and, between their plunder and their prey, may go home rich. But the case is very different with the laboring farmer, the working tradesman, and the necessitous poor in England, the sweat of whose brow goes day after day to feed, in prodigality and sloth, the army that is robbing both them and us. Removed from the eye of that country that supports them, and distant from the government that employs them, they cut and carve for themselves, and there is none to call them to account.

But England will be ruined, says lord Shelburne, if America is independent.

Then I say, is England already ruined, for America is already independent: and if lord Shelburne will not allow this, he immediately denies the fact which he infers. Besides, to make England the mere creature of America, is paying too great a compliment to us, and too little to himself.

But the declaration is a rhapsody of inconsistency. For to say, as lord Shelburne has numberless times said, that the war against America is ruinous, and yet to continue the prosecution of that ruinous war for the purpose of avoiding ruin, is a language which cannot be understood. Neither is it possible to see how the independence of America is to accomplish the ruin of England after the war is over, and yet not affect it before. America cannot be more independent of her, nor a greater enemy to her, hereafter than she now is; nor can England derive less advantages from her than at present: why then is ruin to follow in the best state of the case, and not in the worst? And if not in the worst, why is it to follow at all?

That a nation is to be ruined by peace and commerce, and fourteen or fifteen millions a-year less expenses than before, is a new doctrine in politics. We have heard much clamor of national savings and economy ; but surely the true economy would be, to save the whole charge of a silly, foolish, and headstrong war ; because, compared with this, all other retrenchments are baubles and trifles.

But is it possible that lord Shelburne can be serious in supposing that the least advantage can be obtained by arms, or that any advantage can be equal to the expense or the danger of attempting it ? Will not the capture of one army after another satisfy him, must all become prisoners ? Must England ever be the sport of hope, and the victim of delusion ? Sometimes our currency was to fail ; another time our army was to disband ; then whole provinces were to revolt. Such a general said this and that ; another wrote so and so ; lord Chatham was of this opinion ; and lord somebody else of another. To-day 20,000 Russians and 20 Russian ships of the line were to come ; to-morrow the empress was abused without mercy or decency. Then the emperor of Germany was to be bribed with a million of money, and the king of Prussia was to do wonderful things. At one time it was, Lo here ! and then it was, Lo there ! Sometimes this power, and sometimes that power, was to engage in the war, just as if the whole world was mad and foolish like Britain. And thus, from year to year, has every straw been catched at, and every Will-with-a-wisp led them a new dance.

This year a still newer folly is to take place. Lord Shelburne wishes to be sent to congress, and he thinks that something may be done.

Are not the repeated declarations of congress, and which all America supports, that they will not even hear any proposals whatever, until the unconditional and unequivocal independence of America is recognised ; are not, I say, these declarations answer enough ?

But for England to receive any thing from America now, after so many insults, injuries and outrages, acted towards us, would show such a spirit of meanness in her, that we could not but despise her for accepting it. And so far from lord Shelburne's coming here to solicit it, it would be

the greatest disgrace we could do them to offer it.   England
would appear a wretch indeed, at this time of day, to ask or
owe any thing to the bounty of America.   Has not the name
of Englishman blots enough upon it, without inventing
more?   Even Lucifer would scorn to reign in heaven by
permission, and yet an Englishman can creep for only an
entrance into America.   Or, has a land of liberty so many
charms, that to be a door-keeper in it is better than to be an
English minister of state?

But what can this expected something be?   Or, if obtained, what can it amount to, but new disgraces, contentions and quarrels?   The people of America have for years
accustomed themselves to think and speak so freely and con-
temptuously of English authority, and the inveteracy is so
deeply rooted, that a person invested with any authority
from that country, and attempting to exercise it here, would
have the life of a toad under a harrow.   They would look
on him as an interloper, to whom their compassion permitted a residence.   He would be no more than the Mungo
of a farce; and if he disliked that, he must set off.   It would
be a station of degradation, debased by our pity, and despised
by our pride, and would place England in a more contemptible situation than any she has yet been in during the war.
We have too high an opinion of ourselves, even to think of
yielding again the least obedience to outlandish authority;
and for a thousand reasons, England would be the last
country in the world to yield it to.   She has been treacherous, and we know it.   Her character is gone, and we have
seen the funeral.

Surely she loves to fish in troubled waters, and drink the
cup of contention, or she would not now think of mingling
her affairs with those of America.   It would be like a foolish
dotard taking to his arms the bride that despises him, or
who has placed on his head the ensigns of her disgust.   It
is kissing the hand that boxes his ears, and proposing to renew the exchange.   The thought is as servile as the war is
wicked, and shows the last scene of the drama to be as
inconsistent as the first.

As America is gone, the only act of manhood is to *let her go.* Your lordship had no hand in the separation, and you will gain no honor by temporising politics. Besides, there is something so exceedingly whimsical, unsteady, and even insincere in the present conduct of England, that she exhibits herself in the most dishonourable colors.

On the second of August last, general Carleton and admiral Digby wrote to general Washington in these words:

" The resolution of the house of commons, of the 27th of February last, has been placed in your excellency's hands, and intimations given at the same time that further pacific measures were likely to follow. Since which, until the present time, we have had no direct communications with England ; but a mail is now arrived, which brings us very important information. We are acquainted, sir, *by authority*, that negotiations for a general peace have already commenced at Paris, and that Mr. Grenville is invested with full powers to treat with all the parties at war, and is now at Paris in execution of his commission. And we are further, sir, made acquainted, *that his majesty, in order to remove any obstacles to that peace which he so ardently wishes to restore, has commanded his ministers to direct Mr. Grenville, that the independence of the Thirteen United Provinces, should be proposed by him in the first instance, instead of making it a condition of a general treaty.*"

Now, taking your present measures into view, and comparing them with the declaration in this letter, pray what is the word of your king, or his ministers, or the parliament, good for? Must we not look upon you as a confederated body of faithless, treacherous men, whose assurances are fraud, and their language deceit? What opinion can we possibly form of you, but that you are a lost, abandoned, profligate nation, who sport even with your own character, and are to be held by nothing but the bayonet or the halter?

To say, after this, *that the sun of Great Britain will be set whenever she acknowledges the independence of America,* when the not doing it is the unqualified lie of government, can be no other than the language of ridicule, the jargon of inconsistency. There were thousands in America who predicted the delusion, and looked upon it as a trick of treachery, to take us from our guard, and draw off our attention from the only system of finance, by which we can be called, or deserve to be called, a sovereign, independent people. The fraud, on your part, might be worth attempting, but the sacrifice to obtain it is too high.

There are others who credited the assurance, because they thought it impossible that men who had their characters to establish, would begin with a lie. The prosecution of the war by the former ministry was savage and horrid; since which it has been mean, trickish, and delusive. The one went greedily into the passion of revenge, the other into the subtleties of low contrivance; till, between the crimes of both, there is scarcely left a man in America, be he whig or tory, who does not despise or detest the conduct of Britain.

The management of lord Shelburne, whatever may be his views, is a caution to us, and must be to the world, never to regard British assurances. A perfidy so notorious cannot be hid. It stands even in the public papers of New-York, with the names of Carleton and Digby affixed to it. It is a proclamation that the king of England is not to be believed; that the spirit of lying is the governing principle of the ministry. It is holding up the character of the house of commons to public infamy, and warning all men not to credit them. Such are the consequences which lord Shelburne's management has brought upon his country.

After the authorized declarations contained in Carleton and Digby's letter, you ought, from every motive of honor, policy and prudence, to have fulfilled them, whatever might have been the event. It was the least atonement that you could possibly make to America, and the greatest kindness you could do to yourselves; for you will save millions by a general peace, and you will lose as many by continuing the war.

COMMON SENSE.

PHILADELPHIA, Oct. 29, 1782.

P. S. The manuscript copy of this letter is sent your lordship, by the way of our head-quarters, to New-York, inclos-
ing a late pamphlet of mine, addressed to the abbe Raynal,
which will serve to give your lordship some idea of the
principles and sentiments of America.

C. S.

THE CRISIS.

XIII.

THOUGHTS ON THE PEACE, AND THE PROBABLE ADVAN-TAGES THEREOF.

" THE times that tried men's souls,"* are over—and the
greatest and completest revolution the world ever knew,
gloriously and happily accomplished.

But to pass from the extremes of danger to safety—from
the tumult of war to the tranquillity of peace, though sweet
in contemplation, requires a gradual composure of the
senses to receive it.   Even calmness has the power of stun-
ning, when it opens too instantly upon us.   The long and
raging hurricane that should cease in a moment, would leave
us in a state rather of wonder than enjoyment; and some
moments of recollection must pass, before we could be
capable of tasting the felicity of repose.   There are but
few instances, in which the mind is fitted for sudden transitions : it takes in its pleasures by reflection and comparison
and those must have time to act, before the relish for new
scenes is complete.

In the present case—the mighty magnitude of the object
—the various uncertainties of fate it has undergone—the
numerous and complicated dangers we have suffered or
escaped—the eminence we now stand on, and the vast
prospect before us, must all conspire to impress us with
contemplation.

---

* " These are the times that try men's souls,"   The Crisis No. I. published
December, 1776.—*Author.*

To see it in our power to make a world happy—to teach mankind the art of being so—to exhibit, on the theatre of the universe a character hitherto unknown—and to have, as it were, a new creation intrusted to our hands, are honors that command reflection, and can neither be too highly estimated, nor too gratefully received.

In this pause then of recollection—while the storm is ceasing, and the long agitated mind vibrating to a rest, let us look back on the scenes we have passed, and learn from experience what is yet to be done.

Never, I say, had a country so many openings to happiness as this. Her setting out in life, like the rising of a fair morning, was unclouded and promising. Her cause was good. Her principles just and liberal. Her temper serene and firm. Her conduct regulated by the nicest steps, and everything about her wore the mark of honour. It is not every country (perhaps there is not another in the world) that can boast so fair an origin. Even the first settlement of America corresponds with the character of the revolution. Rome, once the proud mistress of the universe, was originally a band of ruffians. Plunder and rapine made her rich, and her oppression of millions made her great. But America need never be ashamed to tell her birth, nor relate the stages by which she rose to empire.

The remembrance, then, of what is past, if it operates rightly, must inspire her with the most laudable of all ambition, that of adding to the fair fame she began with. The world has seen her great in adversity; struggling, without a thought of yielding, beneath accumulated difficulties, bravely, nay proudly, encountering distress, and rising in resolution as the storm increased. All this is justly due to her, for her fortitude has merited the character. Let, then, the world see that she can bear prosperity: and that her honest virtue in time of peace, is equal to the bravest virtue in time of war.

She is now descending to the scenes of quiet and domestic life. Not beneath the cypress shade of disappointment, but to enjoy in her own land, and under her own vine, the sweet of her labours, and the reward of her toil.—In this situation, may she never forget that a fair national reputation is of as much importance as independence. That it possesses a charm that wins upon the world, and makes even enemies civil. That it gives a dignity which is often superior to power, and commands reverence where pomp and splendour fail.

It would be a circumstance ever to be lamented and never to be forgotten, were a single blot, from any cause whatever, suffered to fall on a revolution, which to the end of time must be an honour to the age that accomplished it: and which has contributed more to enlighten the world, and diffuse a spirit of freedom and liberality among mankind, than any human event (if this may be called one) that ever preceded it.

It is not among the least of the calamities of a long continued war, that it unhinges the mind from those nice sensations which at other times appear so amiable. The continual spectacle of wo blunts the finer feelings, and the necessity of bearing with the sight, renders it familiar. In like manner, are many of the moral obligations of society weakened, till the custom of acting by necessity becomes an apology, where it is truly a crime. Yet let but a nation conceive rightly of its character, and it will be chastely just in protecting it. None ever began with a fairer than America and none can be under a greater obligation to preserve it.

The debt which America has contracted, compared with the cause she has gained, and the advantages to flow from it, ought scarcely to be mentioned. She has it in her choice to do, and to live as happily as she pleases. The world is in her hands. She has no foreign power to monopolize her commerce, perplex her legislation, or control her prosperity. The struggle is over, which must one day have happened, and, perhaps, never could have happened at a better time.*
And instead of a domineering master, she has gained an *ally*

---

* That the revolution began at the exact period of time best fitted to the purpose, is sufficiently proved by the event.—But the great hinge on which the whole machine turned, is the *Union of the States:* and this union was naturally produced by the inability of any one state to support itself against any foreign enemy without the assistance of the rest.

whose exemplary greatness, and universal liberality, have
extorted a confession even from her enemies.

With the blessings of peace, independence, and an universal commerce, the states, individually and collectively, will
have leisure and opportunity to regulate and establish
their domestic concerns, and to put it beyond the power of
calumny to throw the least reflection on their honor.   Character is much easier kept than recovered, and that man, if
any such there be, who, from sinister views, or littleness of
soul, lends unseen his hand to injure it, contrives a wound
it will never be in his power to heal.

Had the states severally been less able than they were when the war began,
their united strength would not have been equal to the undertaking, and they
must in all human probability have failed.—And, on the other hand, had they
severally been more able, they might not have seen, or, what is more, might
not have felt, the necessity of uniting : and, either by attempting to stand
alone or in small confederacies, would have been separately conquered.

Now, as we cannot see a time (and many years must pass away before it can
arrive) when the strength of any one state, or several united, can be equal to
the whole of the present United States, and as we have seen the extreme difficulty of collectively prosecuting the war to a successful issue, and preserving
our national importance in the world, therefore, from the experience we have
had, and the knowledge we have gained, we must, unless we make a waste of
wisdom, be strongly impressed with the advantage, as well as the necessity of
strengthening that happy union which had been our salvation, and without
which we should have been a ruined people.

While I was writing this note, I cast my eye on the pamphlet, Common
Sense, from which I shall make an extract, as it exactly applies to the case. It
is as follows :

" I have never met with a man, either in England or America, who hath not
confessed it as his opinion that a separation between the countries would take
place one time or other ; and there is no instance in which we have shown less
judgment, than in endeavoring to describe what we call the ripeness or fitness
of the continent for independence.

" As all men allow the measure, and differ only in their opinion of the time,
let us, in order to remove mistakes, take a general survey of things, and
endeavour, if possible, to find out the *very time*. But we need not to go far, the
inquiry ceases at once, for, *the time has found us*. The general concurrence,
the glorious union of all things prove the fact.

" It is not in numbers, but in a union, that our great strength lies. The continent is just arrived at that pitch of strength, in which no single colony is able
to support itself, and the whole, when united, can accomplish the matter ; and
either more or less than this, might be fatal in its effects."—*Author*.

As we have established an inheritance for posterity, let
that inheritance descend, with every mark of an honourable
conveyance. The little it will cost, compared with the worth
of the states, the greatness of the object, and the value of
the national character, will be a profitable exchange.

But that which must more forcibly strike a thoughtful,
penetrating mind, and which includes and renders easy all
inferior concerns, is the UNION OF THE STATES. On this our
great national character depends. It is this which must give
us importance abroad and security at home. It is through
this only that we are, or can be, nationally known in the
world; it is the flag of the United States which renders our
ships and commerce safe on the seas, or in a foreign port.
Our Mediterranean passes must be obtained under the same
style. All our treaties, whether of alliance, peace, or commerce, are formed under the sovereignty of the United
States, and Europe knows us by no other name or title.

The division of the empire into states is for our own convenience, but abroad this distinction ceases. The affairs of
each state are local. They can go no further than to itself.
And were the whole worth of even the richest of them
expended in revenue, it would not be sufficient to support
sovereignty against a foreign attack. In short, we have no
other national sovereignty than as United States. It would
even be fatal for us if we had—too expensive to be maintained, and impossible to be supported. Individuals, or
individual states, may call themselves what they please; but
the world, and especially the world of enemies, is not to be
held in awe by the whistling of a name. Sovereignty must
have power to protect all the parts that compose and constitute it: and as UNITED STATES we are equal to the importance of the title, but otherwise we are not. Our union, well
and wisely regulated and cemented, is the cheapest way of
being great—the easiest way of being powerful, and the
happiest invention in government which the circumstances
of America can admit of.—Because it collects from each
state, that which, by being inadequate, can be of no use to
it, and forms an aggregate that serves for all.

The states of Holland are an unfortunate instance of the effects of individual sovereignty. Their disjointed condition exposes them to numerous intrigues, losses, calamities, and enemies; and the almost impossibility of bringing their measures to a decision, and that decision into execution, is to them, and would be to us, a source of endless misfortune.

It is with confederated states as with individuals in society; something must be yielded up to make the whole secure. In this view of things we gain by what we give, and draw an annual interest greater than the capital.—I ever feel myself hurt when I hear the union, that great palladium of our liberty and safety, the least irreverently spoken of. It is the most sacred thing in the constitution of America, and that which every man should be most proud and tender of. Our citizenship in the United States is our national character. Our citizenship in any particular state is only our local distinction. By the latter we are known at home, by the former to the world. Our great title is AMERICANS—our inferior one varies with the place.

So far as my endeavours could go, they have all been directed to conciliate the affections, unite the interests, and draw and keep the mind of the country together; and the better to assist in this foundation work of the revolution, I have avoided all places of profit or office, either in the state I live in, or in the United States [1]; kept myself at a distance from all parties and party connexions, and even disregarded all private and inferior concerns: and when we take into view the great work which we have gone through, and feel, as we ought to feel, the just importance of it, we shall then see, that the little wranglings and indecent contentions of personal parley, are as dishonourable to our characters, as they are injurious to our repose.

It was the cause of America that made me an author. The force with which it struck my mind, and the dangerous condition the country appeared to me in, by courting an im-

---

[1] This referred only to the previous two years; before that Paine had been Secretary of the Congressional Committee of Foreign Affairs, and subsequently Clerk of the Pennsylvania Legislature.—*Editor*.

possible and an unnatural reconciliation with those who were determined to reduce her, instead of striking out into the only line that could cement and save her, A DECLARATION OF INDEPENDENCE, made it impossible for me, feeling as I did, to be silent: and if, in the course of more than seven years, I have rendered her any service, I have likewise added something to the reputation of literature, by freely and disinterestedly employing it in the great cause of mankind, and showing that there may be genius without prostitution.

Independence always appeared to me practicable and probable, provided the sentiment of the country could be formed and held to the object: and there is no instance in the world, where a people so extended, and wedded to former habits of thinking, and under such a variety of circumstances, were so instantly and effectually pervaded, by a turn in politics, as in the case of independence; and who supported their opinion, undiminished, through such a succession of good and ill fortune, till they crowned it with success.

But as the scenes of war are closed, and every man preparing for home and happier times, I therefore take my leave of the subject. I have most sincerely followed it from beginning to end, and through all its turns and windings: and whatever country I may hereafter be in, I shall always feel an honest pride at the part I have taken and acted, and a gratitude to nature and providence for putting it in my power to be of some use to mankind.

COMMON SENSE.

PHILADELPHIA, April 19, 1783.[1]

A SUPERNUMERARY CRISIS.

TO THE PEOPLE OF AMERICA.

IN "Rivington's New-York Gazette," of December 6th, is a publication, under the appearance of a letter from London,

------

[1] This was the date of the eighth anniversary of the collision at Lexington, where the first blood was shed in the revolution.—*Editor*.

dated September 30th; and is on a subject which demands the attention of the United States.

The public will remember that a treaty of commerce between the United States and England was set on foot last spring, and that until the said treaty could be completed, a bill was brought into the British parliament by the then chancellor of the exchequer, Mr. Pitt, to admit and legalize (as the case then required) the commerce of the United States into the British ports and dominions. But neither the one nor the other has been completed. The commercial treaty is either broken off, or remains as it began; and the bill in parliament has been thrown aside. And in lieu thereof, a selfish system of English politics has started up, calculated to fetter the commerce of America, by engrossing to England the carrying trade of the American produce to the West India islands.

Among the advocates for this last measure is lord Sheffield, a member of the British parliament, who has published a pamphlet entitled "Observations on the Commerce of the American States." The pamphlet has two objects; the one is to allure the Americans to purchase British manufactures; and the other to spirit up the British parliament to prohibit the citizens of the United States from trading to the West India islands.

Viewed in this light, the pamphlet, though in some parts dexterously written, is an absurdity. It offends, in the very act of endeavoring to ingratiate; and his lordship, as a politician, ought not to have suffered the two objects to have appeared together. The latter alluded to, contains extracts from the pamphlet, with high encomiums on lord Sheffield, for laboriously endeavoring (as the letter styles it) "to show the mighty advantages of retaining the carrying trade."

Since the publication of this pamphlet in England, the commerce of the United States to the West Indies, in American vessels, has been prohibited; and all intercourse, except in British bottoms, the property of and navigated by British subjects, cut off.

That a country has a right to be as foolish as it pleases, has been proved by the practice of England for many years past: in her island situation, sequestered from the world, she forgets that her whispers are heard by other nations; and in her plans of politics and commerce she seems not to know, that other votes are necessary besides her own. America would be equally as foolish as Britain, were she to suffer so great a degradation on her flag, and such a stroke on the freedom of her commerce, to pass without a balance.

We admit the right of any nation to prohibit the commerce of another into its own dominions, where there are no treaties to the contrary; but as this right belongs to one side as well as the other, there is always a way left to bring avarice and insolence to reason.

But the ground of security which lord Sheffield has chosen to erect his policy upon, is of a nature which ought, and I think must, awaken in every American a just and strong sense of national dignity. Lord Sheffield appears to be sensible, that in advising the British nation and parliament to engross to themselves so great a part of the carrying trade of America, he is attempting a measure which cannot succeed, if the politics of the United States be properly directed to counteract the assumption.

But, says he, in his pamphlet, " It will be a long time before the American states can be brought to act as a nation, neither are they to be feared as such by us."

What is this more or less than to tell us, that while we have no national system of commerce, the British will govern our trade by their own laws and proclamations as they please. The quotation discloses a truth too serious to be overlooked, and too mischievous not to be remedied.

Among other circumstances which led them to this discovery none could operate so effectually as the injudicious, uncandid and indecent opposition made by sundry persons in a certain state,[1] to the recommendations of congress last winter, for an import duty of five per cent. It could not but explain to the British a weakness in the national power

Rhode Island.—*Editor*.

of America, and encourage them to attempt restrictions on her trade, which otherwise they would not have dared to hazard. Neither is there any state in the union, whose policy was more misdirected to its interest than the state I allude to, because her principal support is the carrying trade, which Britain, induced by the want of a well-centred power in the United States to protect and secure, is now attempting to take away. It fortunately happened (and to no state in the union more than the state in question) that the terms of peace were agreed on before the opposition appeared, otherwise, there cannot be a doubt, that if the same idea of the diminished authority of America had occurred to them at that time as has occurred to them since, but they would have made the same grasp at the fisheries, as they have done at the carrying trade.

It is surprising that an authority which can be supported with so much ease, and so little expense, and capable of such extensive advantages to the country, should be cavilled at by those whose duty it is to watch over it, and whose existence as a people depends upon it. But this, perhaps, will ever be the case, till some misfortune awakens us into reason, and the instance now before us is but a gentle beginning of what America must expect, unless she guards her union with nicer care and stricter honor. United, she is formidable, and that with the least possible charge a nation can be so; separated, she is a medley of individual nothings, subject to the sport of foreign nations.

It is very probable that the ingenuity of commerce may have found out a method to evade and supersede the intentions of the British, in interdicting the trade with the West India islands. The language of both being the same, and their customs well understood, the vessels of one country may, by deception, pass for those of another. But this would be a practice too debasing for a sovereign people to stoop to, and too profligate not to be discountenanced. An illicit trade, under any shape it can be placed, cannot be carried on without a violation of truth. America is now sovereign and independent, and ought to conduct her affairs in a regular style of character.   She has the same right to say that no British vessel shall enter ports, or that no British manufactures shall be imported, but in American bottoms, the property of, and navigated by American subjects, as Britain has to say the same thing respecting the West Indies.   Or she may lay a duty of ten, fifteen, or twenty shillings per ton (exclusive of other duties) on every British vessel coming from any port of the West Indies, where she is not admitted to trade, the said tonnage to continue as long on her side as the prohibition continues on the other.

But it is only by acting in union, that the usurpations of foreign nations on the freedom of trade can be counteracted, and security extended to the commerce of America.   And when we view a flag, which to the eye is beautiful, and to contemplate its rise and origin inspires a sensation of sublime delight, our national honour must unite with our interest to prevent injury to the one, or insult to the other.

COMMON SENSE.

NEW-YORK, December 9, 1783.

XX.

RETREAT ACROSS THE DELAWARE.[1]

FORT WASHINGTON being obliged to surrender, by a violent attack made by the whole British army, on Saturday the 16th of November, the Generals determined to evacuate Fort Lee, which being principally intended to preserve the communication with Fort Washington, was become in a manner useless. The stores were ordered to be removed and great part of them was immediately sent off. The enemy knowing the divided state of our army, and that the terms of the soldiers inlistments would soon expire, conceived the design of penetrating into the Jersies, and hoped, by pushing their successes, to be completely victorious. Accordingly, on Wednesday morning, the 20th November, it was discovered that a large body of British and Hessian troops had crossed the North river, and landed about six miles above the fort. As our force was inferior to that of the enemy, the fort unfinished, and on a narrow neck of land, the garrison was ordered to march for Hackensack bridge, which, tho' much nearer the enemy than the fort, they quietly suffered our troops to take possession of. The principal loss suffered at Fort Lee was that of the heavy cannon, the greatest part of which was left behind. Our troops continued at Hackensack bridge and town that day and half of the next, when the inclemency of the weather, the want of quarters, and approach of the enemy, obliged

---

[1] From the *Pennsylvania Journal*, Jan. 29, 1777, where it is preceded by a note showing that its late appearance was owing to the paper having for some time suspended publication. It was during this retreat that Paine wrote "Crisis" No. I.—*Editor.*

them to proceed to Aquaconack, and from thence to Newark; a party being left at Aquaconack to observe the motions of the enemy. At Newark our little army was reinforced by Lord Sterling's and Col. Hand's brigades, which had been stationed at Brunswick. Three days after our troops left Hackensack, a body of the enemy crossed the Passaic above Aquaconack, made their approaches slowly towards Newark, and seemed extremely desirous that we should leave the town without their being put to the trouble of fighting for it. The distance from Newark to Aquaconack is nine miles, and they were three days in marching that distance. From Newark our retreat was to Brunswick, and it was hoped the assistance of the Jersey Militia would enable General Washington to make the Banks of the Raritan the bounds of the enemy's progress; but on the 1st of December the army was greatly weakened, by the expiration of the terms of the enlistments of the Maryland and Jersey Flying Camp; and the militia not coming in so soon as was expected, another retreat was the necessary consequence. Our army reached Trenton on the 4th of December, continued there till the 7th, and then, on the approach of the enemy, it was thought proper to pass the Delaware.

This retreat was censured by some as pusillanimous and disgraceful; but, did they know that our army was at one time less than a thousand effective men, and never more than 4000,—that the number of the enemy was at least 8000, exclusive of their artillery and light horse,—that this handful of Americans retreated *slowly* above 80 miles without losing a dozen men—and that suffering themselves to be forced to an action, would have been their entire destruction—did they know this, they would never have censured it at all—they would have called it prudent—posterity will call it glorious—and the names of Washington and Fabius will run parallel to eternity.

The enemy, intoxicated with success, resolved to enjoy the fruits of their conquest. Fearless of an attack from this side the river, they cantoned in parties at a distance from each other, and spread misery and desolation wherever they went. Their rage and lust, their avarice and cruelty, knew no bounds; and murder, ravishment, plunder, and the most brutal treatment of every sex and age, were the first acts that signalized their conquest. And if such were their outrages on the partial subjection of a few villages—good God! what consummate wretchedness is in store for that state over which their power shall be fully established.

While the enemy were in this situation, their security was increased by the captivity of General Lee, who was unfortunately taken in the rear of his army, December 13th, at Baskinridge by a party of light-horse, commanded by Col. Harcourt. The fortune of our arms was now at its lowest ebb—but the tide was beginning to turn—the militia of this city [Philadelphia] had joined General Washington—the junction of the two armies was soon after effected—and the back countries of this state, aroused by the distresses of America, poured out their yeomanry to the assistance of the continental army. General Washington began now to have a respectable force, and resolved not to be idle. On the 26th of December he crossed the Delaware, surprised three regiments of Hessians, and with little or no loss, took near a thousand prisoners.[1]

Soon after this manœuvre, and while the enemy were collecting their scattered troops at Princeton and Brunswick, Gen. Washington crossed the Delaware with all his army. On the 2d of January the enemy began to advance towards Trenton, which they entered in the afternoon, and there being nothing but a small creek between the two armies, a general engagement was expected next day. This it was manifestly our advantage to avoid; and by a master stroke of generalship, Gen. Washington frees himself from his disagreeable situation, and surprises a party of the enemy in Princeton, which obliges their main body to return to Brunswick.

[1] Washington's letter to Congress (December 27, 1776) is here inserted by the editor of the *Pennsylvania Journal.—Editor.*

XXI.

LETTER TO FRANKLIN, IN PARIS.[1]

York Town [Pa.], May 16, 1778.

YOUR favour of October 7th did not come to me till March. I was at Camp when Capt. Folger arrived with the Blank Packet.[2] The private letters were, I believe, all safe. Mr. [President] Laurens forwarded yours to York Town where I afterwards received it.

The last winter has been rather barren of military events, but for your amusement I send you a little history how I have passed away part of the time.

The 11th of September last I was preparing Dispatches for you when the report of cannon at Brandywine interrupted my proceeding. The event of that day you have doubtless been informed of, which, excepting the Enemy keeping the ground, may be deemed a drawn battle. Genl. Washington collected his Army at Chester, and the Enemy's not moving towards him next day must be attributed to the disability they sustained and the burthen of their wounded. On the 16th of the same month the two armies were drawn up in order of battle near White Horse on the Lancaster road, when a most violent and incessant storm of rain prevented an action. Our Army sustained a heavy loss in their Ammunition, the Cartouche Boxes, especially as

---

[1] Copied from the original in the Franklin Papers, by favor of the Philosophical Society, Philadelphia. Congress was in session at York, Pennsylvania, where the house in which Paine kept the papers of the Foreign Affairs Committee of which he was Secretary, still exists. In it, no doubt, this letter to Franklin was written.—*Editor*.

[2] The dispatches sent by the American Commissioners from Paris had been intercepted by the British.—*Editor*.

they were not of the most seasoned leather, being no proof
against the almost incredible fury of the weather, which
obliged Genl. Washington to draw his army up into the
country until those injuries could be repaired, and a new
supply of ammunition procured.   The enemy in the mean
time kept on the west side of Schuylkill.   On Friday the
19th about one in the morning the first alarm of their crossing was given, and the confusion, as you may suppose,
was very great.   It was a beautiful still moonlight morning
and the streets as full of men, women and children as on a
market day.   On the evening before I was fully persuaded
that unless something was done the City [Philadelphia]
would be lost; and under that anxiety I went to Col. Bayard, Speaker of the House of Assembly, and represented, as
I very particularly knew it, the situation we were in, and the
probability of saving the City if proper efforts were made
for that purpose.   I reasoned thus—Genl. Washington was
about 30 Miles up the Schuylkill with an Army properly
collected waiting for Ammunition, besides which a reinforcement of 1500 men were marching from the North River
to join him ; and if only an appearance of defence be made in
the City by throwing up works at the heads of the streets,
it would make the Enemy very suspicious how they threw
themselves between the City and Genl. Washington, and between two Rivers, which must have been the case; for
notwithstanding the knowledge which military gentlemen
are supposed to have, I observe they move exceedingly
cautiously on new ground, are exceedingly suspicious of
Villages and Towns, and more perplexed at seemingly little
things which they cannot clearly understand than at great
ones which they are fully acquainted with.   And I think it
very probable that Genl. Howe would have mistaken our
necessity for a deep laid scheme and not have ventured
himself in the middle of it.   But admitting that he
had, he must either have brought his whole Army down, or a
part of it.   If the whole, Gen. Washington would have followed him, perhaps the same day, in two or three days at
most, and our assistance in the City would have been

material.   If only a part of it, we should have been a match
for them and Gen. Washington superior to those which remained above.   The chief thing was, whether the citizens
would turn out to defend the City.   My proposal to Cols.
Bayard and Bradford was to call them together the next
morning, make them fully acquainted with the situation and
the means and prospect of preserving themselves, and that
the City had better voluntarily assess itself $50,000 for its
defence than suffer an Enemy to come into it.   Cols. Bayard and Bradford were in my opinion, and as Genl. Mifflin
was then in town, I next went to him, acquainted him with
our design, and mentioned likewise that if two or three
thousand men could be mustered up whether we might depend on him to command them, for without some one to
lead, nothing could be done.   He declined that part, not
being then very well, but promised what assistance he could.
A few hours after this the alarm happened.   I went directly
to Genl. Mifflin but he had sett off, and nothing was done.
I cannot help being of opinion that the City might have
been saved, but perhaps it is better otherwise.

I staid in the City till Sunday [September 21,] having sent
my Chest and everything belonging to the Foreign Committee to Trenton in a Shallop.   The Enemy did not cross the
river till the Wednesday following.   Hearing on the Sunday
that Genl. Washington had moved to Sunderford I set off
for that place, but learning on the road that it was a mistake
and that he was six or seven miles above that place, I crossed
over to Southfield, and the next morning to Trenton, to see
after my Chest.   On the Wednesday morning I intended
returning to Philadelphia, but was informed at Bristol of the
Enemy's crossing the Schuylkill.   At this place I met Col.
Kirkbride of Pennsburg Manor, who invited me home with
him.   On Friday the 26th a Party of the Enemy about 1500
took possession of the City, and the same day an account
arrived that Col. Brown had taken 300 of the Enemy at the
old french lines at Ticonderoga, and destroyed all their Water
Craft, being about 200 boats of different kinds.

On the 29th September I sett off for Camp without well

knowing where to find it, every day occasioning some movement.   I kept pretty high up the country, and being unwilling to ask questions, not knowing what company I might be
in, I was there three days before I fell in with it.   The Army
had moved about three miles lower down that morning.   The
next day they made a movement about the same distance,
to the 21 Mile Stone on the Skippach Road,—Headquarters
at John Wince's.   On the 3d October in the morning they
began to fortify the Camp, as a deception ; and about 9 at
night marched for German Town.   The number of Continental Troops was between 8 and 9000, besides Militia, the
rest remaining as Guards for the security of Camp.   Genl.
Greene, whose Quarters I was at, desired me to remain there
till morning.[1]   The Skirmishing with the Pickets began soon
after.   I met no person for several miles riding, which I concluded to be a good sign ; after this I met a man on horse-
back who told me he was going to hasten on a supply of
ammunition, that the Enemy were broken and retreating
fast, which was true.   I saw several country people with
arms in their hands running cross a field towards German
Town, within about five or six miles, at which I met several
of the wounded on waggons, horseback, and on foot.   I
passed Genl. Nash on a litter made of poles, but did not
know him.   I felt unwilling to ask questions lest the information should not be agreeable, and kept on.   About two
miles after this I passed a promiscuous crowd of wounded
and otherwise who were halted at a house to refresh.   Col.
Biddle D. Q. M. G. was among them, who called after me,
that if I went farther on that road I should be taken, for that
the firing which I heard was the Enemy's.   I never could,
and cannot now learn, and I believe no man can inform truly
the cause of that day's miscarriage.

The retreat was as extraordinary.   Nobody hurried themselves.   Every one marched his own pace.   The Enemy kept

---

[1] Paine had been appointed on Gen. Nathaniel Greene's staff at Fort Lee,
1776, and, after his appointment as Secretary of the Foreign Affairs Committee,
his honorary position on the staff remained.   General Greene was much attached
to him.—*Editor*.

a civil distance behind, sending every now and then a shot after us, and receiving the same from us. That part of the Army which I was with collected and formed on the Hill on the side of the road near White Marsh Church; the enemy came within three quarters of a mile and halted. The orders on Retreat were to assemble that night on the back of Perkioming Creek, about 7 miles above the Camp, which had orders to move. The Army had marched the preceding night 14 miles, and having full 20 to march back were exceedingly fatigued. They appeared to me to be only sensible of a disappointment, not a defeat, and to be more displeased at their retreating from German Town, than anxious to get to their rendezvous. I was so lucky that night to get a little house about 4 miles wide of Perkioming, towards which place in the morning I heard a considerable firing, which distressed me exceedingly, knowing that our army was much harassed and not collected. However, I soon relieved myself by going to see. They were discharging their pieces, which, though necessary, prevented several Parties going till next day. I breakfasted next morning at Genl. Washington's Quarters, who was at the same loss with every other to account for the accidents of the day. I remember his expressing his Surprise, by saying, that at the time he supposed every thing secure, and was about giving orders for the Army to proceed down to Philadelphia; that he most unexpectedly saw a Part (I think of the Artillery) hastily retreating. This partial Retreat was, I believe, misunderstood, and soon followed by. others. The fog was frequently very thick, the Troops young and unused to breaking and rallying, and our men rendered suspicious to each other, many of them being in Red. A new Army once disordered is difficult to manage, the attempt dangerous. To this may be added a prudence in not putting matters to too hazardous a tryal the first time. Men must be taught *regular* fighting by practice and degrees, and tho' the expedition failed, it had this good effect—that they seemed to feel themselves more important *after* it than *before*, as it was the first general attack they had ever made.

I have not related the affair at Mr. Chew's house German Town, as I was not there, but have seen it since. It certainly afforded the Enemy time to rally—yet the matter was difficult. To have pressed on and left 500 Men in ye rear, might by a change of circumstances been ruinous. To attack them was a loss of time, as the house is a strong stone building, proof against any 12 pounder. Genl. Washington sent a flag, thinking it would procure their surrender and expedite his march to Philadelphia; it was refused, and circumstances changed almost directly after.

I staid in Camp two days after the Germantown action, and lest any ill impression should get among the Garrisons at Mud Island and Red Bank, and the Vessels and Gallies stationed there, I crossed over to the Jersies at Trenton and went down to those places. I laid the first night on board the Champion Continental Galley, who was stationed off the mouth of the Schuylkill. The Enemy threw up a two Gun Battery on the point of the river's mouth opposite the Pest House. The next morning was a thick fog, and as soon as it cleared away, and we became visible to each other, they opened on the Galley, who returned the fire. The Commodore made a signal to bring the Galley under the Jersey shore, as she was not a match for the Battery, nor the Battery a sufficient Object for the Galley. One shot went thro' the fore sail, which was all. At noon I went with Col. [Christopher] Greene, who commanded at Red Bank [fort,] over to fort Mifflin (Mud Island.) The Enemy opened that day 2 two-gun Batteries, and a Mortar Battery, on the fort. They threw about 30 shells into it that afternoon, without doing any damage; the ground being damp and spongy, not above five or six burst; not a man was killed or wounded. I came away in the evening, laid on board the Galley, and the next day came to Col. Kirkbride's [Bordentown, N. J.]; staid a few days and came again into Camp. An Expedition was on foot the evening I got there in which I went as Aid de Camp to Genl. [Nathaniel] Greene, having a Volunteer Commission for that purpose. The occasion was—a Party of the Enemy, about 1500, lay

over the Schuylkill at Grey's ferry. Genl. McDougall with
his Division was sent to attack them; and Sullivan and
Greene with their Divisions were to favour the enterprise
by a feint on the City, down the Germantown road. They
set off about nine at night, and halted at daybreak, between
German Town and the City, the advanced Party at three
Miles Run. As I knew the ground I went with two light
horse to discover the Enemy's Picket, but the dress of the
light horse being white made them, I thought, too visible,
as it was then twilight; on which I left them with my
horse, and went on foot, till I distinctly saw the Picket at
Mr. Dickerson's place—which is the nearest I have been to
Philadelphia since September, except once at Cooper's ferry,
as I went to the forts. Genl. Sullivan was at Dr. Redman's
house, and McDougall's beginning the attack was to be the
Signal for moving down to the City. But the Enemy either
on the approach of McDougall, or on information of it,
called in their Party, and the Expedition was frustrated.

A Cannonade, by far the most furious I ever heard, began
down the river, soon after daylight, the first Gun of which
we supposed to be the Signal; but was soon undeceived,
there being no small Arms. After waiting two hours beyond
the time, we marched back; the cannon was then less frequent, but on the road between Germantown and White
Marsh we were stuned with a report as loud as a peal from
a hundred Cannon at once; and turning around I saw a
thick smoke rising like a pillar, and spreading from the top
like a tree. This was the blowing up of the Augusta. I did
not hear the explosion of the Berlin.

After this I returned to Col. Kirkbride's, where I staid
about a fortnight, and set off again to Camp. The day after
I got there Genls. Greene, Wayne, and Cadwallader, with a
Party of light horse, were ordered on a reconnoitering Party
towards the forts. We were out four days and nights without meeting with anything material. An East Indiaman,
whom the Enemy had cut down so as to draw but little
water, came up, without guns, while we were on foot on
Carpenter's Island, going to Province Island. Her Guns

were brought up in the evening in a flat, she got in the rear
of the Fort, where few or no Guns could bear upon her, and
the next morning played on it incessantly.   The night following the fort was evacuated.   The obstruction the Enemy
met with from those forts, and the *Chevaux de frise*, was
extraordinary, and had it not been that the Western Channel, deepened by the current, being somewhat obstructed
by the *Chevaux de frise* in the main river, which enabled
them to bring up the light Indiaman Battery, it is a doubt
whether they would have succeeded at last.   By that assistance they reduced the fort, and got sufficient command of
the river to move some of the late sunk *Chevaux de frise*.
Soon after this the fort on Red Bank (which had bravely
repulsed the Enemy a little time before) was evacuated, the
Gallies ordered up to Bristol, and the Captains of such other
armed Vessels as *thought* they could not pass on the Eastward side of Wind Mill Island, very precipitately set them
on fire.   As I judged from this event that the Enemy would
winter in Philadelphia, I. began to think of preparing for
York Town, which however I was willing to delay, hoping
that the ice would afford opportunity for new Manœuvres.
But the season passed very barrenly away.   I staid at Col.
Kirkbride's till the latter end of January.   Commodore
Haslewood, who commanded the remainder of the fleet at
Trenton, acquainted me with a scheme of his for burning
the Enemy's Shipping, which was by sending a charged
boat across the river from Cooper's ferry, by means of a
Rocket fixed in its stern.   Considering the width of the
river, the tide, and the variety of accidents that might
change its direction, I thought the project trifling and insufficient ; and proposed to him, that if he would get a boat
properly charged, and take a Batteau in tow, sufficient to
bring three or four persons off, that I would make one with
him and two other persons that might be relied on to go
down on that business.   One of the Company, Capn. Blewer
of Philadelphia, seconded the proposal, but the Commodore,
and, what I was more surprized at, Col. Bradford, declined
it.   The burning of part of the Delaware fleet, the precipi-

tate retreat of the rest, the little service rendered by them and the great expence they were at, make the only national blot in the proceedings of the last Campaign. I felt a strong anxiety for them to recover their credit, which, among others, was one motive for my proposal. After this I came to Camp, and from thence to York Town, and published the Crisis No. 5, to Genl. Howe. I have begun No. 6, which I intend to address to Lord North.[1]

I was not at Camp when Genl. Howe marched out on the 20th of December towards White Marsh. It was a most contemptible affair, the threatenings and seeming fury he sate out with, and haste and terror the Army retreated with, make it laughable. I have seen several persons from Philadelphia who assure me that their coming back was a mere uproar, and plainly indicated their apprehensions of a pursuit. Genl. Howe, in his Letter to Lord Go. Germain, dated December 13th, represented Genl. Washington's Camp as a strongly fortified place. There was not, Sir, a work thrown up in it till Genl. Howe marched out, and then only here and there a breastwork. It was a temporary Station. Besides which, our men begin to think Works in the field of little use.

Genl. Washington keeps his Station at the Valley forge. I was there when the Army first began to build huts; they appeared to me like a family of Beavers: every one busy; some carrying Logs, others Mud, and the rest fastening them together. The whole was raised in a few days, and is a curious collection of buildings in the true rustic order.

As to Politics, I think we are now safely landed. The apprehension which Britain must be under from her neighbours must effectually prevent her sending reinforcements, could she procure them. She dare not, I think, in the *present* situation of affairs, trust her troops so far from home.

No Commissioners are yet arrived. I think fighting is

[1] It was, however, addressed to the Commissioners sent from England. "Crisis" V. was written at Lancaster, Pa., in the house of the eminent engineer, William Henry, Jr., who has left on record that Paine then explained to him the means by which steam could be applied to navigation. See my "Life of Paine," vol. ii., pp. 280, 408, 462.—*Editor.*

nearly over, for Britain, mad, wicked, and foolish, has done her utmost. The only part for her now to act is frugality, and the only way for her to get out of debt is to lessen her Government expenses. Two Millions a year is a sufficient allowance, and as much as she ought to expend exclusive of the interest of her Debt. The affairs of England are approaching either to ruin or redemption. If the latter she may bless the resistance of America.

For my own part, I thought it very hard to have the Country set on fire about my Ears almost the moment I got into it; and among other pleasures I feel in having uniformly done my duty; I feel that of not having discredited your friendship and patronage.

I live in hopes of seeing and advising with you respecting the History of the American Revolution, as soon as a turn of Affairs make it safe to take a passage for Europe. Please to accept my thanks for the Pamphlets, which Mr. Temple Franklin tells me he has sent. They are not yet come to hand. Mr. and Mrs. Bache [1] are at Mainheim, near Lancaster; I heard they were well a few days ago. I laid two nights at Mr. Duffield's, in the winter. Miss Nancy Clifton was there, who said the Enemy had destroyed or sold a great part of your furniture. Mr. Duffield has since been taken by them and carried into the City, but is now at his own house.[2] I just hear they have burnt Col. Kirkbride's, Mr. Borden's, and some other houses at Borden Town.[3] Governor Johnstone (House of Commons) has written to Mr. Robert Morris informing him of Commissioners coming from England. The letter is printed in the Newspapers

---

[1] Franklin's son-in-law and daughter, to whom he had introduced Paine when he was emigrating to America, in 1774.—*Editor.*

[2] Rev. Dr. George Duffield, pastor of the Third Presbyterian Church, Philadelphia; Associate Chaplain of the first Continental Congress, and afterwards Chaplain in the Army. He was a famous revolutionary preacher, and tradition says a "reward was set on his head." It will be seen, however, from Paine's letter that Dr. Duffield suffered little molestation after falling into the enemy's hands.—*Editor.*

[3] It was in the house of his friend, Col. Kirkbride, at Bordentown, N. J., that Paine made the earliest model of the iron bridge he had invented.—*Editor.*

without signature, and is dated February 5th, by which you will know it.

Please, Sir, to accept this, rough and incorrect as it is, as I have [not] time to copy it fair, which was my design when I began it ; besides which, paper is most exceedingly scarce.[1]

I am, Dear Sir, your obliged and affectionate humble Servt.,

T. PAINE.

The Honble. Benj. Franklin, Esqr.

---

[1] It is a notable thing that the Secretary of the Foreign Affairs Committee, writing in his office to the United States Minister in Paris, mentions this scarcity of paper.—*Editor.*

XXII.

THE AFFAIR OF SILAS DEANE.[1]

TO SILAS DEANE, ESQ'RE.

AFTER reading a few lines of your address to the Public in the Pennsylvania Packet of December 6th, I can truly say, that concern got the better of curiosity, and I felt an unwillingness to go through it. Mr. Deane must very well know that I have no interest in, so likewise am I no stranger to, his negotiations and contracts in France, his difference with his colleagues, the reason of his return to America, and the matters which have occurred since. All these are to me familiar things; and while I can but be surprised at the conduct of Mr. Deane, I lament the unnecessary torture he has imprudently occasioned. That disagreements will arise between individuals, even to the perplexity of a State, is nothing new, but that they should be outrageously brought forward, by one whose station abroad should have taught him a delicacy of manners and even an excess of prudence, is something strange. The mind of a *living* public is quickly alarmed and easily tormented. It not only suffers by the stroke, but is frequently fretted by the cure, and ought therefore to be tenderly dealt with, and *never ought to be* · *trifled with.* It feels first and reasons afterwards. Its jealousy keeps vibrating between the accused and the

[1] From the *Pennsylvania Packet*, December 15, 1778. The recent investigations of MM. Doniol, Delomanie, and others in France, and of Provost Stillé and others in America, concerning Beaumarchais, the subsidies of France to the American Revolution, and the part acted by the American agent in Paris (Deane), render Paine's papers on this subject of much historical interest. They have not appeared in any previous collection of Paine's works.—*Editor*.

accuser, and on a failure of proof always fixes on the latter.
Had Mr. Deane's address produced no uneasiness in the
body he appeals to, it would have been a sign, not of tranquility, but death: and though it is painful to see it unnecessarily tortured, it is pleasant to contemplate the living
cause. Mr. Deane is particularly circumstanced. He has
advantages which seldom happen, and when they do happen,
ought to be used with the nicest care and strictest honor.
He has the opportunity of telling his own tale and there is
none to reply to him. Two of the gentlemen he so freely
censures are three thousand miles off, and the other two he
so freely affronts are Members of Congress; one of them
likewise, Col. R. H. Lee, is absent in Virginia; and however
painful may be their feelings, they must attend the progressive conduct of the house. No Member in Congress can
individually take up the matter without becoming inconsistent, and none of the public understands it sufficiently. With
these advantages Mr. Deane ought to be nicely and strictly
the gentleman, in his language, his assertions, his insinuations and his facts. He presents himself, as his own evidence, upon his honor, and any misrepresentation or disin-
genuous trifling in him will be fatal.

Mr. Deane begins his address with a general display of his
services in France, and strong *insinuations* against the Hon.
Arthur and William Lee, he brings his complaints down to
the time of signing the treaty, and from thence to the fourth
of March, when he received the following Order of Congress
which he inserts at large:

"In Congress, December 8, 1777. Whereas it is of the greatest
importance that Congress should at this critical juncture be well
informed of the state of affairs in Europe. And whereas Congress
have resolved that the Honorable Silas Deane, Esq, be recalled
from the Court of France, and have appointed another Commissioner to supply his place there. Ordered, that the Committee for
foreign correspondence, write to the Honorable Silas Deane, and
direct him to embrace the first opportunity of returning to America,
and upon his arrival to repair with all possible dispatch to Congress."
Mr. Deane then says " and having placed *my papers* and *yours* in

safety, I left Paris the 30th to embark for my native country, on board that fleet which your great and generous ally sent out for your assistance, in *full confidence* that I should not be detained on the *business I was sent for.*" [1]

I am obliged to tell Mr. Deane that this arrangement is somewhat uncandid, for on the reading it, it creates an opinion and likewise carries an appearance that Mr. Deane was only *sent* for, as the necessary and proper person from whom Congress might obtain a history of their affairs, and learn the character of their foreign Agents, Commissioners and Ambassadors, after which Mr. Deane was to return. Is Mr. Deane so little master of address as not to know that censure may be politely conveyed by an apology? For however Mr. Deane may chuse to represent or misrepresent the matter, the truth is that *his* contracts and engagements in France, had so involved and embarrassed Congress, that they found it necessary and resolved to *recall* him, that is *ordered him home,* to give an account of his *own* conduct, and likewise to save him from a train of disagreeable consequences, which must have arisen to him had he continued in France. I would not be supposed to insinuate, that he might be thought *unsafe,* but *unfit.* There is a certain and necessary association of dignity between the person and the employment which perhaps did not appear when Mr. Deane was considered the Ambassador. His address to the public confirms the justness of this remark. The spirit and language of it differ exceedingly from that cool penetrating judgment and refinement of manners and expression which fits, and is absolutely necessary in, the Plenipotentiary. His censures are coarse and vehement, and when he speaks of himself, he begs, nay almost weeps to be believed.—It was the intricacy of Mr. Deane's *own official* affairs, his multiplied contracts in France before the arrival of Dr. Franklin or any of the other Commissioners; his assuming authorities, and entering into engagements, in the time of his Commercial Agency, for which he had neither commission nor instruction, and

---

[1] The italics are Paine's.—*Editor.*

the general unsettled state of his accounts, that were among
the reasons that produced the motion for recalling and super-
seding him.—Why then does Mr. Deane endeavour to lead
the attention of the public to a wrong object, and bury the
real reasons, under a tumult of new and perhaps unnecessary
suspicions?

Mr. Deane in the beginning of his address to the public
says, "What I *write* to you, I would have *said* to your
Representatives, *their ears have been shut against me*, by an
attention to matters, which my respect for them induces me
to believe were of ' *more importance.*' "

In this paragraph Mr. Deane's excuse becomes his accuser, and his justification is his offence; for if the greater
importance of other matters is supposed and given by himself as a reason, why he was not heard, it is likewise a sufficient reason, why he ought not to have complained that
"*their ears were shut*," and a good reason why he ought to
have waited a more convenient time. But besides the inconsistency of this charge, there is something in it that will
suffer by an inquiry, and I am sorry that Mr. Deane's imprudence has obliged me to mention a circumstance which
affects his honour as a gentleman, his reputation as a man.
In order to be clearly understood on this head, I am
obliged to go back with Mr. Deane to the time of his quitting France on account of his being recalled. "I left Paris,"
says Mr. Deane, "on the 30th of March, 1778 to embark for
my native country, having placed ' *my papers and yours in
safety.*' " Would any body have supposed that a gentleman
in the character of a Commercial Agent, and afterwards in
that of a public Minister, would return home after seeing
himself both recalled and superseded, and not bring with
him his papers and vouchers? And why he has done so
must appear to every one exceedingly unaccountable. After Mr. Deane's arrival he had *two audiences* with Congress
in August last, in neither of which did he offer the least
charge against the gentleman he has so loudly upbraided in
his address to the public: neither has he yet accounted for
his expenditure of public money, which, as it might have

been done by a written state of accounts, might for that
reason have been done at any time, and was a part of the
business which required an audience.

There is something curiously intricate and evasive in Mr.
Deane's saying in his address, that he left France "*in full
confidence* that he should not be detained on the *business he
was sent for.*" And the only end it can answer to him is to
furnish out a present excuse for not producing his papers.
Mr. Deane had no right, either from the literal or implied
sense of the resolution itself, to suppose that he should
return to France in his former public character, or that he
was "*sent for*," as he stiles it, on any other personal business
than that which related to himself. Mr. Deane must be
sensible, if he will but candidly reflect, that as an agent
only, he greatly exceeded his line, and embarrassed the
Congress, the continent, the army and himself.

Mr. Deane's address to the public is dated "Nov."—but
without any day of the month; and here a new scene of
ungenteel evasion opens. On the last day of that month,
viz. the 30th, he addressed a letter to Congress signifying
his intentions of returning to France, and pressing to have
his affairs brought to some conclusion, which, I presume, on
account of the absence of his papers could not well be done;
therefore Mr. Deane's address to the public must be written
before the 30th, and consequently before his letter to Congress, which carries an appearance of its being only a feint
in order to make a confused diversion in his favor at the
time his affairs should come under consideration.

What favours this opinion, is that on the next day, that
is December 1st, and partly in consequence of Mr. Deane's
letter to them of the 30th, the Congress entered the following resolution.

"In Congress December 1st, 1778.—*Resolved*, That after to-
morrow Congress will meet two hours at least each evening, beginning at six o'clock, Saturday evening excepted, until the
present state of their foreign affairs be fully considered."

As an enquiry into the state of foreign affairs naturally

and effectually included all and every part of Mr. Deane's, he was thereupon regularly notified by letter to attend ; and on the *fourth* he wrote again to Congress, acquainting them with his having received that notification and expressed his thanks; yet on the day following, viz. the *fifth* he published his extraordinary address in the newspapers, which, on account of its unsupported matter, the fury of its language and temper, and its inconsistency with other parts of his conduct, is incompatible with that character (which on account of the station he had been honoured with, and the sense that should have impressed him in consequence thereof) he ought to have maintained.

On the appearance of Mr. Deane's address of the fifth, the public became jealously uneasy, and well they might. They were unacquainted with the train of circumstances that preceded and attended it, and were naturally led to suppose, that Mr. Deane, on account of the station he had filled, must be too much a gentleman to deceive them. It was Mr. Deane's particular fortune to grow into consequence from accident. Sent to France as a Commercial Agent under the appointment of a Committee, he rose as a matter of convenience to the station of a Commissioner of Congress; and with what dignity he might fill out that character, the public will judge from his conduct since ; and perhaps be led to substitute convenience as an excuse for the appointment.

A delicacy of difficulties likewise arose in Congress on the appearance of the said address ; for setting aside the matter, the irregular manner of it, as a proceeding, was a breach of decency; and as Mr. Deane after being notified to attend an enquiry into foreign affairs, had circumstantially withdrawn from that mode, by appealing to the public, and at the same time said " *their ears were shut against him,*" it was therefore given as a reason by some, that to take any notice of Mr. Deane in the interim would look like suppressing his public information, if he had any to give; and consequently would imply dishonour on the House,—and that as he had transferred his case to the public, before it had been rejected by the Congress, he ought therefore to be left with the

public, till he had done with them and they with him ; and
that whether his information was true or not, it was an insult
on the people, because it was making them the ladder, on
which he insulted their representatives, by an unjust complaint of neglect.   Others who might anticipate the anxiety
of the public, and apprehend discontents would arise from a
supposed inattention, were for adopting measures to prevent
them, and of consequence inclined to a different line of conduct, and this division of sentiment on what might be
supposed the honour of the House, occasioned the then
President, Henry Laurens, Esq., who adhered to the former
opinion, to resign the chair.   The majority on the sentiments
was a single vote.   In this place I take the liberty of remarking, for the benefit of succeeding generations, that the
Honourable President before mentioned, having filled that
station for one year in October last, made his resignation of
the Presidency at the expiration of the year, lest any example
taken from his continuance might have become inconvenient.
I have an additional satisfaction in mentioning this useful
historical anecdote, because it is done wholly unknown to
the gentleman to whom it relates, or to any other gentleman
in or out of Congress.   He was replaced by a unanimous
vote.   But to return to my narration—

In the Pennsylvania Packet of December 8th, Francis
Lightfoot Lee, Esq., brother to the gentleman so rudely
treated in Mr. Deane's publication, and the only one now
present, put in a short address to the public, requesting a
suspension of their judgment till the matter could be fully
investigated by those whose immediate business it became :
meaning Congress.   And Mr. Deane in the paper of the 10th
published another note, in which he informs, " that the Honorable Congress did, on Saturday morning the 5th instant,
assign Monday evening to hear him."   But why does Mr.
Deane conceal the resolution of Congress of December 1st, in
consequence of which he was notified to attend regularly an
enquiry into the state of foreign affairs?   By so doing, he
endeavours to lead the public into a belief that his being
heard on Monday was extorted purely in consequence of his

address of the 5th, and that otherwise he should not have been heard at all. I presume Congress are anxious to hear him, and to have his accounts arranged and settled; and if this should be the case, why did Mr. Deane leave his papers in France, and now complain that his affairs are not concluded? In the same note Mr. Deane likewise says, "that Congress did on that evening, Monday, resolve, that Mr. Deane do report in writing, as soon as may be, his agency of their affairs in Europe, together with any intelligence respecting their foreign affairs which he may judge proper." But why does Mr. Deane omit giving the remaining part of the resolution, which says, "That Mr. Deane be informed, that if he has any thing to communicate to Congress in the interim of *immediate importance*, that he should be heard to-morrow evening." I can see no propriety, in omitting this part, unless Mr. Deane concluded that by publishing it he might put a quick expiration to his credit, by his not being able to give the wondrous information he had threatened in his address. In the conclusion of this note, Mr. Deane like-wise says, " I therefore conceive that I cannot, with propriety, continue my narrative at present. In the mean time I submit it to the good sense of the public, whether I ought to take any notice of a publication signed Francis Lightfoot Lee, opposed to *stubborn and undeniable facts.*"

Thus far I have compared Mr. Deane with himself, and whether he has been candid or uncandid, consistent or inconsistent, I leave to the judgment of those who read it. Mr. Deane cannot have the least right to think that I am moved by any party difference or personal antipathy. He is a gentleman with whom I never had a syllable of dispute, nor with any other person upon his account. Who are his friends, his connections, or his foes, is wholly indifferent to me, and what I have written will be a secret to everybody till it comes from the press. The convulsion which the public were thrown into by his address will, I hope, justify my taking up a matter in which I should otherwise have been perfectly silent; and whatever may be its fate, my intention is a good one; besides which there was no other person who knew the affair sufficiently, or knowing it, could confidently do it, and yet it was necessary to be done.

I shall now take a short review of what Mr. Deane calls "*stubborn and undeniable facts.*" Mr. Deane must be exceedingly unconversant both with terms and ideas, not to distinguish even between a wandering probability and a fact; and between a forced inclination and a proof; for admitting every circumstance of information in Mr. Deane's address to be true, they are still but circumstances, and his deductions from them are hypothetical and inconclusive.

Mr. Deane has involved a gentleman in his unlimited censure, whose fidelity and personal qualities I have been well acquainted with for three years past; and in respect to an absent injured friend, Col. Richard Henry Lee, I will venture to tell Mr. Deane, that in any stile of character in which a gentleman may be spoken of, Mr. Deane would suffer by a comparison. He has one defect which perhaps Mr. Deane is acquainted with, the misfortune of having but one hand.

The charges likewise which he advances against the Honorable Arthur and William Lee, are to me, circumstantial evidences of Mr. Deane's unfitness for a public character; for it is the business of a foreign minister to learn other men's secrets and keep their own. Mr. Deane has given a short history of Mr. Arthur Lee and Dr. Berkenhout in France, and he has brought the last mentioned person again on the stage in America. There is something in this so exceedingly weak, that I am surprised that any one who would be thought a man of sense, should risk his reputation upon such a frivolous tale; for the event of the story, if any can be produced from it, is greatly against himself.

He says that a correspondence took place in France between Dr. Berkenhout and Mr. [Arthur] Lee; that Mr. Lee shewed part of the correspondence to Dr. Franklin and himself; and that in order to give the greater weight to Dr. Berkenhout's remarks he gave them to understand, that Dr. Berkenhout was in the secrets of the British Ministry. What Mr. Deane has related this for, or what he means to infer from it, I cannot understand; for the political inference

ought to be, that if Mr. Lee really thought that Dr. Berkenhout was in the secrets of the British Ministry, he was therefore the very person with whom Mr. Lee ought, as an
Ambassador, to cultivate a correspondence, and introduce
to his colleagues, in order to discover what those secrets
were, that they might be transmitted to America; and if
Mr. Deane acted otherwise, he unwisely mistook his own
character. However, this I can assure Mr. Deane, upon my
own knowledge, that more and better information has come
from Mr. Lee than ever came from himself; and how or
where he got it, is not a subject fit for public enquiry: unless
Mr. Deane means to put a stop to all future informations. I
can likewise tell Mr. Deane, that Mr. Lee was particularly
commissioned by a certain body, and that under every sacred
promise of inviolable secrecy, to make discoveries in England, and transmit them. Surely Mr. Deane must have left
his discretion with his papers, or he would see the imprudence
of his present conduct.

In the course of Mr. Deane's narrative he mentions Dr.
Berkenhout again. " In September last, " says he," I was informed that Dr. Berkenhout, who I have before mentioned,
was in gaol in this city. I confess I was surprised, considering what I have already related, that this man should have
the audacity to appear in the capital of America." But why
did not Mr. Deane confront Dr. Berkenhout while he was
here? Why did he not give information to Congress or to
the Council before whom he was examined, and by whom
he was discharged and sent back for want of evidence against
him? Mr. Deane was the only person that knew anything
of him, and it looks very unfavorable in him that he was
silent when he should have spoke, if he had anything to say,
and now he has gone has a great deal to tell, and that about
nothing. " I immediately, "says Mr. Deane," *sate myself
about* the measures which I conceived necessary *to investigate
his plans and designs.*" This is indeed a trifling excuse, for it
wanted no great deal of *setting about*, the whole secret as
well as the means being with himself, and half an hour's information might have been sufficient. What Mr. Deane
means by " *investigating his plans and designs,*" I cannot

understand, unless he intended to have the Doctor's nativity cast by a conjurer. Yet this trifling round-about story is one of Mr. Deane's "stubborn and undeniable facts." However it is thus far a fact, that Mr. Deane kept it a secret till the man was gone.

He likewise entertains us with a history of what passed at New York between Dr. Berkenhout and Governor Johnstone; but as he must naturally think that his readers must wonder how he came by such knowledge, he prudently supplies the defect by saying " that Providence in whom we put our trust, ' *unfolded it to me*'"—*revealed it, I suppose.* As to what Dr. Berkenhout was, or what he came for, is a matter of very little consequence to us. He appeared to be a man of good moral character, of a studious turn of mind, and genteel behaviour, and whether he had whimsically employed himself, or was employed on a foolish errand by others, is a business not worth our enquiring after; he got nothing here, and to send him back was both necessary and civil. He introduced himself to General Maxwell at Elizabeth-Town, as knowing Mr. Arthur Lee; the General wrote a letter of information to Col. R. H. Lee who presented the same to Congress. But it does not appear that Mr. Deane moved in the matter till a considerable time after the Doctor was sent off, and then Mr. Deane put a series of queries in the newspaper to know why he was let go. I little thought at that time that the queries were Mr. Deane's, as they really appeared to me to be the produce of some little mind.

Mr. Deane likewise tells us that Mr. A. Lee was suspected by some of our best friends because of his acquaintance with Lord Shelburne; and perhaps some Mr. Deane in England might find out that Lord Shelburne ought to be suspected because of his acquaintance with Mr. Lee. Mr. Deane appears to me neither to understand characters nor business, or he would not mention Lord Shelburne on such an occasion whose uniform and determined opposition to the Ministry appears to be known to everybody but Mr. Deane.[1] Mr.

---

[1] Shelburne (afterwards Lord Lansdowne) was the friend of Dr. Priestley. George III. detested Lord Shelburne, whom he described as "the Jesuit of Berkeley-Square." When Paine was in England in 1787-9 Lansdowne was his friend.—*Editor.*

Deane has given us a quotation from a letter [of Arthur
Lee's] which he never saw, and had it likewise from a gentleman in France who had never seen it, but who had heard it
from a correspondent in England to whom it was *not* sent ;
and this traditionary story is another of Mr. Deane's *stubborn
and undeniable facts.*   But even supposing the quotation to
be true, the only inference from it is naturally this, " That
*the sooner England makes peace with America the better it
will be for her.*"   Had the intimation been given before
the treaty with France was signed, it might have been justly
censured, but being given after, it can have but *one* meaning,
and that a *clear* one.   He likewise says, that Charles Fox
" declared pointedly in the House of Commons," that the
treaty between France and America was signed, and as
Charles Fox knows Lord Shelburne, and Lord Shelburne
Mr. Lee, therefore Mr. Deane infers, " as a stubborn and undeniable fact," that Mr. Lee must tell it.   Does Mr. Deane
know that nothing can be long a secret in a Court, especially
where the countries are but twenty miles apart, and that
Charles Fox, from his ingratiating manners, is almost universally known in France ?

Mr. Deane likewise supposes that William Lee, Esquire
continues an Alderman of London, and either himself or
some other gentleman since, under the signature of OBSER-
VATOR, says that " he has *consulted*, on this *point*, the Royal
Kalendar or Annual Register," and finds it true.   To *consult*
a Kalendar to find out a name must be a learned consultation indeed.   An Alderman of London is neither a place at
Court nor a place of profit, and if the city chuses not to expel him, it is a proof they are very good whigs ; and this is
the only proved fact in Mr. Deane's Address.   But there is,
through the whole of it, a barbarous, unmanly and unsupported attack on absent characters, which are, perhaps, far
superior to his own ; an eagerness to create suspicions wherever he can catch an opportunity ; an over-strained desire to
be believed ; and an affected air of giving importance to
trifles.   He accuses Mr. [Arthur] Lee of incivility to the
French nation.   Mr. Lee, if I can judge by his writing, is

too much both of a scholar and a gentleman to deserve such a censure. He might with great justice complain of Mr. Deane's contracts with individuals; for we are fully sensible, that the gentlemen which have come from France since the arrival of Dr. Franklin and Mr. Lee in that country, are of a different rank to the generality of those with whom Mr. Deane contracted when alone. And this observation will, I believe explain that charge no ways to Mr. Deane's honour.

Upon the whole, I cannot help considering this publication as one of the most irrational performances I ever met with. He seems in it to pay no regard to individual safety, nor cares who he may involve in the consequences of his quarrel. He mentions names without restraint, and stops at no discovery of persons. A public man, in Mr. Deane's former character, ought to be as silent as the grave; for who would trust a person with a secret who shewed such a talent for revealing? Under the pretence of doing good he is doing mischief, and in a tumult of his own creating, will expose and distress himself.

Mr. Deane's Address was calculated to catch several sorts of people: The rash, because they are fond of fiery things; the curious, because they are fond of curiosities; the weak, because they easily believe; the good, because they are unsuspicious; the tory, because it comforts his discontent; the high whig, because he is jealous of his rights; the man of national refinement, because it obscurely hints at national dishonor. The clamor, it is true, has been a popular one, and so far as it is the sign of a *living* principle, it is pleasant to see it; but when once understood it will amount to nothing, and with the rapidity that it rose it will descend.

COMMON SENSE.

PHILADELPHIA, Dec. 14, 1788.

P.S.—The writer of this has been waited on by a gentleman, whom he supposes, by his conversation, to be a friend of Mr. Deane's, and whom Mr. Deane, but not any other person, is welcome to know whenever he pleases. The gentleman informed the writer, that some persons, whom he did not mention, had threatened most extraordinary violence against him (the writer of this piece) for taking the matter up; the writer asked, what, whether right or wrong? and likewise informed the gentleman, that he had done it solely with a view of putting the public right in a matter which they did not understand—that the threat served to increase the necessity, and was therefore an excitement to his doing it. The gentleman, after expressing his good opinion of, and personal respect for, the writer, withdrew.

XXIII.

TO THE PUBLIC ON MR. DEANE'S AFFAIR.[1]

HOPING this to be my last on the subject of Mr. Deane's conduct and address, I shall therefore make a few remarks on what has already appeared in the papers, and furnish you with some interesting and explanatory facts ; and whatever I may conceive necessary to say of myself will conclude the piece. As it is my design to make those that can scarcely read understand, I shall therefore avoid every literary ornament, and put it in language as plain as the alphabet.

I desire the public to understand that this is not a personal dispute between Mr. Deane and me, but is a matter of business in which they are more interested than they seemed at first to be apprised of. I rather wonder that no person was curious enough to ask in the papers how affairs stood between Congress and Mr. Deane as to money matters? And likewise, what it was that Mr. Deane has so repeatedly applied to the Congress for without success? Perhaps those two Questions, properly asked, and justly answered, would have unravelled a great part of the mystery, and explained the reason why he threw out, at such a *particular time*, such a strange address. They might likewise have asked, whether there had been any former dispute between Mr. Deane and Arthur or William Lee, and what it was about? Mr. Deane's round-about charges against the Lees, are accompanied with a kind of rancor, that differs exceedingly from public-spirited zeal. For my part, I have but a very slender opinion of those patriots, if they can be called such, who never appear till provoked to it by a personal quarrel, and then blaze

[1] From the *Pennsylvania Packet* of December 31, 1778, and January 2, 5, 7, and 9, 1779.—*Editor*.

away, the hero of their own tale, and in a whirlwind of
their own raising; such men are very seldom what the
populace mean by the word "staunch," and it is only by a
continuance of service that any public can become a judge
of a man's principles.

When I first took up this matter, I expected at least to
be abused, and I have not been disappointed. It was the
last and only refuge they had, and, thank God, I had nothing to dread from it. I might have escaped it if I would,
either by being silent, or by joining in the tumult. A
gentleman, a Member of Congress, an Associate, I believe, of
Mr. Deane's, and one whom I would wish had not a hand in
the piece signed Plain Truth, very politely asked me, a few
days before Common Sense to Mr. Deane came out, whether
on that subject I was *pro* or *con?* I replied, I knew no *pro*
or *con*, nor any other sides than right or wrong.

Mr. Deane had objected to my putting the signature of
Common Sense to my address to him, and the gentleman
who came to my lodgings urged the same objections; their
reasons for so doing may, I think, be easily guessed at.
The signature has, I believe, an extensive reputation, and
which, I trust, will never be forfeited while in my possession.
As I do not chuse to comply with the proposal that was
made to me for changing it, therefore Mr. Plain Truth, as
he calls himself, and his connections, may endeavour to take
off from the credit of the signature, by a torrent of low-
toned abuse without wit, matter or sentiment.

Had Mr. Deane confined himself to his proper line of
conduct, he would never have been interrupted by me, or
exposed himself to suspicious criticism. But departing from
this, he has thrown himself on the ocean of the public, where
nothing but the firmest integrity can preserve him from
becoming a wreck. A smooth and flattering tale may do
for a while, but unless it can be supported with facts, and
maintained by the most incontestible proof, it will fall to
the ground, and leave the inventor in the lurch.

On the first view of things, there is something in Mr.
Deane's conduct which must appear mysterious to every

disinterested man, if he will but give himself time to reflect. Mr. Deane has been arrived in America, and in this city, upwards of five months, and had he been possessed of any secrets which affected, or seemed to affect, the interest of America, or known any kind of treachery, misconduct, or neglect of duty in any of the other Commissioners, or in any other person, he ought, as an honest man, to have disclosed it immediately on his arrival, either to the Committee for Foreign Affairs, of which I have the honor to be Secretary, or to Congress.   Mr. Deane has done neither, notwithstanding he has had two audiences with Congress in August last, and might at any time have laid his written information before them, or before the Committee, through whom all his foreign concerns had passed, and in whose hands, or rather in mine, are lodged all his political correspondence, and those of other Commissioners.

From an unwillingness to expose Mr. Deane and his adherents too much, I contented myself in my first piece with showing their inconsistency rather than their intentions, and gave them room to retract by concealing their discredit.   It is necessary that I should now speak a plainer language.

The public have totally mistaken this matter, and when they come to understand it rightly, they will see it in a very different light to what they at first supposed it.   They seemed to conceive, and great pains have been taken to make them believe, that Mr. Deane had repeatedly applied to Congress to obtain an audience, in order to lay before them some great and important discoveries, and that the Congress had refused to hear such information.   It is, Gentlemen, no such thing.   If Mr. Deane or any one else had told you so, they have imposed upon you.

If you attend to a part of Mr. Deane's Address to you, you will find there, even from his own account, what it was that he wanted an interview with Congress for, viz. *to get some how or other through his own perplext affairs, and obtain an audience of leave and departure that he might embark for France*, and which if he could have obtained, there is every reason to believe, he would have quitted America in silence, and that the public would never have been *favored* with his address, nor I plagued with the trouble of putting it to rights. The part which I allude to is this "*and having placed my papers and yours in safety, I left Paris, in full confidence that I should not be detained in America,*" to which he adds this curious expression, " on the business I was sent for." To be "*detained*" at *home* is a new transposition of ideas, especially in a man who had been absent from it two years and a half, and serves to show that Mr. Deane was become so wonderfully foreignized that he had quite forgotten poor Connecticut.

As I shall have frequent occasions to make use of the name of Congress, I request you to suspend all kind of opinions on any supposed obligations which I am said to lie under to that body, till you hear what I have to say in the conclusion of this address, for if Mr. Deane's accounts stand as clear with them as mine do, he might very easily have brought his papers from France. I have several times repeated, and I again repeat it, that my whole design in taking this matter up, was and is, to prevent the public being imposed upon, and the event must and will convince them of it.

I now proceed to put the affair into such a straight line that you cannot misunderstand it.

Mr. Deane wrote his address to you some time in November, and kept it by him in order to publish or not as it might suit his purpose.* On the 30th day of the same

---

* This is fully proved by the address itself which is dated *November*, but without any day of the month, and the same is likewise acknowledged by his blundering friend Mr. Plain Truth. His words are, " Mr. Deane, it is true, wrote his address " (dated November) " previous to his application to Congress, of the 30th of November." He certainly could not write it after, there being, unfortunately for him, but thirty days in that month ; " but," continues Mr. Plain Truth, " he was determined notwithstanding some *forceable reasons*, which the *vigilant* part of the publick are at no loss to *guess*, not to publish it if he could be assured of an *early* audience with Congress." Mr. Deane was in a confounded hurry, sure that he could not submit to be *detained in America* till the next day, for on that very next day, December 1st, *in consequence of his letter* the Congress, " *Resolved to spend two hours each day, beginning at six in the evening, till the state of their foreign affairs should be fully ascertained.*" This

month he applied by letter to Congress, and what do you
think it was for? To give them any important information?
No. To "tell them what he has wrote to you?" No, it was
to acquaint them *that he had missed agreeable opportunities
of returning to France*; dismal misfortune indeed! And that
the season (of the year) is now becoming as *pressing* as the
business which calls him *back*, and therefore he *earnestly
entreated the attention of Congress*, to what? To his great information? No, to his important discoveries? No, but to
his own *situation and requests.* These are, I believe, his own
words.

Now it only remains to know whether Mr. Deane's official
affairs were in a fit position for him to be permitted to quit
America or not; and I trust, that when I tell you, I have
been secretary for foreign affairs almost two years, you will
allow that I must be some judge of the matter.

You have already heard what Mr. Deane's application to
Congress was for. And as one of the public, under the well
known signature of Common Sense, I humbly conceive, that
the Congress have done that which as a faithful body of

naturally included all and every part of Mr. Deane's affairs, information and
everything else, and it is impossible but he (connected as he is with some late
and present Members of Congress) should know immediately about it.

I should be glad to be informed what those "*forceable reasons*" are at which
the vigilant part of the public "*guess*" and likewise how early Mr. Deane
expected an audience, since the resolution of the *next day* appears to have been
too late. I am suspicious that it was too soon, and that Mr. Deane and his
connections were not prepared for such an *early* examination notwithstanding
he had been here upwards of five months, and if the thing is to be "*guessed*" at
at last, and that by the *vigilant* part of the public, I think I have as great a
right to *guess* as most men, and Mr. Plain Truth, if he pleases, may *guess* what
I mean ; but lest he should mistake I will tell him my guess, it is, that the
whole affair is a juggle to amuse the people with, in order to prevent the state
of foreign affairs being enquired into, and Mr. Deane's accounts, and those he
is connected with in America settled as they ought to be ; and were I to go on
guessing, I should likewise *guess* that this is the reason why his accounts are left
behind, though I know many people inclined to guess that he has them with him
but has forgot them ; for my part I don't chuse at *present* to go so far. If any
one can give a better guess than I have done I shall give mine up, but as the
gentlemen choose to submit it to a guess, I chuse therefore to take them upon
their own terms, and put in for the honor of being right. It was, I think, an
injudicious word for them to use, especially at Christmas time.—*Author.*

Representatives they ought to do, that is, they ordered an enquiry into the state of foreign affairs and accounts which Mr. Deane had been intrusted with, before they could, with justice to you, grant the request he asked ; And this was the more necessary to be done, because Mr. Deane says he has left his papers and accounts behind him : Did ever any steward, when called upon, to surrender up his stewardship make such a weak and frivolous excuse ? Mr. Deane saw himself not only *recalled* but *superceeded* in his office by another person, and he could have no right to think he should *return,* nor any pretence to come away without the necessary credentials.

His friend and associate, and perhaps partner too, Mr. Plain Truth, says, that I have endeavored in my address, to " throw out a suggestion that Mr. Deane is considered by Congress as a defaulter of public money " : The gentlemen seem to wince before they are touched. I have no where said so, but this I will say, that his accounts are not satisfactory : Mr. Plain Truth endeavors to palliate what he cannot contradict, and with a seeming triumph assures the public " that Mr. Deane not long after his arrival laid before Congress a *general* state of the receipts and expenditures of the Monies which passed thro' his hands " ; to which Mr. Plain Truth subjoins the following extraordinary apology : " It is true the account was not accompanied with all the vouchers for the particular expenditures." And why not I ask ? for without those it was no account at all ; it was what the Sailors call a boot account, so much money gone and the Lord knows for what. Mr. Deane had Secretaries and clerks, and ought to have known better than to produce such an account to Congress, especially as his colleague Arthur Lee had declared in an office letter, which is in my possession, that he had no concern in Mr. Deane's contracts.

Neither does the excuse, which his whirligig friend Mr. Plain Truth makes for him, apply to his case ; this random shot gentleman, in order to bring him as easily off as possible, says, " that any person in the least conversant with business, knows the time which is requisite for calling in manufacturers and tradesmen's bills, and prepare accounts and vouchers for a final settlement "; and this he mentions because Mr. Deane received his order of recall the 4th of March, and left Paris the 31st: here is, however, four weeks within a day.   I shall make three remarks upon this curious excuse.

First, it is contradictory.   Mr. Deane could not obtain the total or general expenditure without having the particulars, therefore he must be in the possession of the particulars. He surely did not pass away money without taking receipts, and what was due upon credit, he could only know from the bills delivered in.

Secondly, Mr. Deane's contracts did not lay in the retail way, and therefore were easily collected.

Thirdly, The accounts which it was Mr. Deane's particular duty to settle, were those, which he contracted in the time of being only a commercial Agent in 1776, before the arrival of Dr. Franklin and Arthur Lee, which separate agency of his expired upwards of fifteen months before he left France, —and surely that was time enough,—and in which period of his agency, there happened an unexplained contract of about two hundred thousand pounds sterling.   But more of this when I come to remark on the ridiculous Puffs with which Mr. Plain Truth has set off Mr. Deane's pretended Services in France.

Mr. Deane has not only left the public papers and accounts behind him, but he has given no information to Congress, where or in whose hands they are ; he says in his address to you, that he has left them in a safe place, and this is all which is known of the matter.   Does this look like business ? Has it an open and candid or a mysterious and suspicious appearance ?   Or would it have been right in Congress to have granted Mr. Deane an audience of leave and departure in this embarrassed state of his affairs?   And because they have not, his ready written November address has been thrown out to abuse them and amuse you by directing you to another object; and myself, for endeavoring to unriddle confusion, have been loaded with reproach by his partizans and partners, and represented as a writer, who like an unprincipled lawyer had let himself out for pay. Charges which the propagators of them know to be false, because some, who have encouraged the report, are Members of Congress themselves, and know my situation to be directly the reverse. But this I shall explain in the conclusion ; and I give the gentlemen notice of it, that if they can make out anything against me, or prove that I ever received a single farthing, public or private, for any thing I ever wrote, they may convict me publicly, and if they do not, I hope they will be honest enough to take shame to themselves, for the falsehood they have supported. And I likewise request that they would inform the public what my salary as Secretary for foreign affairs is, otherwise I shall be obliged to do it myself. I shall not spare them and I beg they would not spare me. But to return—

There is something in this concealment of papers that looks like an embezzlement. Mr. Deane came so privately from France, that he even concealed his departure from his colleague Arthur Lee, of which he complains by a letter in my office, and consequently the papers are not in his hands ; and had he left them with Dr. Franklin he would undoubtedly have taken the Doctor's receipt for them, and left nobody to "*guess,*" at what Mr. Deane meant by a *safe place*: A man may leave his own private affairs in the hands of a friend, but the papers of a nation are of another nature, and ought never to be trusted with any person whatever out of the direct line of business. This I conceive to be another reason which justifies Congress in not granting Mr. Deane an audience of leave and departure till they are assured where those papers are. Mr. Deane might have been taken at sea, he might have died or been cast away on his passage back from France, or he might have been settled there, as Madame D'Eon did in England, and quarrelled afterwards as she did with the power that employed him. Many accidents might have happened by which those papers and accounts might have been totally lost, the secrets got into the hands of the enemy, and the possibility of settling the expenditure of public money for ever prevented. No apology can be made for Mr. Deane, as to the danger of the seas, or their being taken by the enemy, in his attempt to bring them over himself, because it ought always to be remembered that he came in a fleet of twelve sail of the line.[1]

I shall now quit this part of the subject to take notice of a paragraph in Mr. Plain Truth.

In my piece to Mr. Deane I said, that his address was dated in November, without any day of the month, that on the last day of that month he applied to Congress, that on the 1st of December the Congress resolved to investigate the state of their foreign affairs, of which Mr. Deane had notice, and that on the fourth he informed them of his receiving that notification and expressed his thanks, yet that on the fifth he published his extraordinary address.

Mr. Plain Truth, in commenting upon this arrangement of facts has helped me to a new discovery. He says, that Mr. Deane's thanks of the fourth of December were only expressed to the President, Henry Laurens Esqr: for personally informing him of the resolution and other attention to his Affairs, and *not*, as I had said, *to Congress for the resolution itself.* I give him credit for this, and believe it to be true ; for my opinion of the matter is, that Mr. Deane's views were to get off without any enquiry, and that the resolution referred to was his great disappointment. By all accounts which have been given both by Mr. Deane's friends and myself, we all agree in this, that Mr. Deane knew of the resolution of Congress before he published his address, and situated as he is he could not help knowing it two or three days before his address came out. Why then did he publish it, since the very thing which he ought to have asked for, viz. an enquiry into his affairs, was ordered to be immediately gone into?

---

[1] There is now little doubt that Deane left his papers in the hands of the British spy George Lupton, whom he employed as a clerk, and who gave his English employers regular information, and the American Dr. Edward Bancroft, who was so royally paid by England. See Donne's "Letters of George III. to Lord North" ; also Stevens' *Facsimiles.* Had the King's correspondence been known in 1842, Deane's family would never have received from Congress the money voted them.—*Editor.*

I wish in this place to step for a moment from the floor of office, and press it on every State, to enquire what mercantile connections any of their *late* or present Delegates have had or now have with Mr. Deane, and that a precedent might not be wanting, it is important that this State, *Pennsylvania should begin.*

The uncommon fury which has been spread to support Mr. Deane cannot be altogether for his sake. Those who were the original propagators of it, are not remarkable for gratitude. If they excel in anything it is in the contrary principle and a selfish attachment to their own interest. It would suit their plan exceedingly well to have Mr. Deane appointed Ambassador to Holland, because so situated, he would make a very convenient partner in trade, or a useful factor.

In order to rest Mr. Deane on the shoulders of the Public, he has been set off. with the most pompous puffs—The Saviour of his Country—the Patriot of America—the True Friend of the Public—the Great Supporter of the cause in Europe,—and a thousand other full-blown bubbles, equally ridiculous and equally untrue. Never were the public more wretchedly imposed upon. An attempt was made to call a town meeting to return him thanks and to march in a body to Congress to demand justice for Mr. Deane. And this brings me to a part in Mr. Plain Truth's address to me, in which he speaks of Mr. Deane's services in France, and defies me to disprove them. If any late or present Member of Congress has been concerned in writing that piece, I think it necessary to tell him, that he either knows very little of the state of foreign affairs, or ought to blush in thus attempting to rob a friendly nation, France, of her honors, to bestow them on a man who so little deserves them.

Mr. Deane was sent to France in the Spring, 1776, as a Commercial Agent, under the authority of the Committee which is now stiled the Committee for foreign affairs. He had no Commission of any kind from Congress; and his instructions were to assume no other character but that of a merchant; yet in this line of action Mr. Plain Truth has the ignorance to dub him a " public Minister " and likewise says,

" that before the first of December, after his arrival he had formed and cultivated the esteem of a valuable political and commercial connection, not only in France but in other parts of Europe, laid the foundation of a public loan, procured thirty thousand stand of arms, thirty thousand suits of cloathes, more than two hundred and fifty pieces of brass cannon, and a great amount of tents and military stores, provided vessels to transport them, and in spite of various and almost inconceivable obstructions great part of these articles were shipped and arrived in America before the operations of the campaign in 1777." To which Mr. Plain Truth adds, " That he has had the means of being acquainted with all these circumstances, avows them to be facts, and *defies* Common Sense or any other person to disprove them."

Poor Mr. Plain Truth, and his avower Mr. Clarkson, have most unfortunately for them challenged the wrong person, and fallen into the right hands when they fell into mine, for without stirring a step from the room I am writing in, or asking a single question of any one, I have it in my power, not only to contradict but disprove it.

It is, I confess, a nice point to touch upon, but the necessity of undeceiving the public with respect to Mr. Deane, and the right they have to know the early friendship of the French Nation towards them at the time of their greatest wants, will justify my doing it. I feel likewise the less difficulty in it, because the whole affair respecting those supplies has been in the hands of the enemy at least twelve months, and consequently the necessity for concealing it is superceded : Besides which, the two nations, viz. France and England, being now come to an open rupture makes the secret unnecessary. It was immediately on the discovery of this affair by the enemy fifteen months ago, that the British Ministry began to change their ground and planned what they call their Conciliatory Bills. They got possession of this secret by stealing the dispatches of October, 1777, which should have come over by Captain Folger, and this likewise explains the Controversy which the British Commissioners carried on with Congress, in attempting to prove that England had planned what they called her conciliatory Bills, before France moved towards a treaty; for even admitting that assertion to be true, the case is, that they planned those Bills in consequence of the knowledge they had stolen.*

The supplies here alluded to, are those which were sent from France in the Amphitrite, Seine and Mercury about two years ago. They had at first the appearance of a present, but whether so, or on credit, the service was nevertheless a great and friendly one, and though only part of them arrived the kindness is the same. A considerable time afterwards the same supplies appeared under the head of a charge amounting to about two hundred thousand pounds sterling, and it is the unexplained contract I alluded to when I spoke of the pompous puffs made use of to support Mr. Deane. On the appearance of this charge the Congress were exceedingly embarrassed as to what line of conduct to pursue. To be insensible of a favor, which has before now

* When Capt. Folger arrived at York-Town [Pa.] he delivered a Packet which contained nothing but blank paper, that had been put under the cover of the dispatches which were taken out. This fraud was acted by the person to whom they were first intrusted to be brought to America, and who afterwards absconded, having given by way of deception the blank packet to Capt. Folger. The Congress were by this means left without any information of European Affairs. It happened that a private letter from Dr. Franklin to myself, in which he wrote to me respecting my undertaking the history of the present revolution, and engaged to furnish me with all his materials towards the completion of that work, escaped the pilfering by not being enclosed in the packet with the dispatches. I received this letter at Lancaster through the favor of the President, Henry Laurens, Esqr., and as it was the only letter which contained any authentic intelligence of the general state of our affairs in France, I transmitted it again to him to be communicated to Congress. This likewise was the only intelligence which was received from France from May, 1777, to May 2d, 1778, when the treaty arrived; wherefore, laying aside the point controverted by the British Commissioners as to which moved first, France or England, it is evident that the resolutions of Congress of April 22d, 1778, for totally rejecting the British Bills, were grounded entirely on the determination of America to support her cause,—a circumstance which gives the highest honour to the resolutions alluded to, and at the same time gives such a character of her fortitude as heightens her value, when considered as an ally, which though it had at that time taken place, was, to her, perfectly unknown.—*Author.*

been practised between nations, would have implied a want of just conceptions; and to have refused it would have been a species of proud rusticity. To have asked the question was both difficult and awkward; to take no notice of it would have been insensibility itself; and to have seemed backward in payment, if they were to be paid for, would have impeached both the justice and the credit of America. In this state of difficulties such enquiries were made as were judged necessary, in order that Congress might know how to proceed. Still nothing satisfactory could be obtained. The answer which Mr. Deane signed so lately as February 16th last past (and who ought to know most of the matter, because the *shipping* the supplies was while he acted alone) is as ambiguous as the rest of his conduct. I will venture to give it, as there is no political secret in it and the matter wants explanation.

" Hear that Mr. B [eaumarchais] has sent over a person to demand a large sum of you on account of arms, ammunition, etc., —think it will be best for you to leave that matter to be settled here (France), as there is a mixture in it of public and private concern which you cannot so well develop."

Why did not Mr. Deane compleat the contract so as it might be developed, or at least state to Congress any difficulties that had arisen? When Mr. Deane had his two audiences with Congress in August last, he objected, or his friends for him, against his answering the questions that might be asked him, and the ground upon which the objection was made, was, because *a man could not legally be compelled to answer questions that might tend to criminate himself.*—Yet this is the same Mr. Deane whose address you saw in the *Pennsylvania Packet* of December 5 signed Silas Deane.

Having thus shewn the loose manner of Mr. Deane's doing business in France, which is rendered the more intricate by his leaving his papers behind, or his not producing them; I come now to enquire into what degree of merit or credit Mr.

Deane is entitled to as to the procuring these supplies, either as a present or a purchase.

Mr. Plain Truth has given him the whole. Mr. Plain Truth therefore knows nothing of the matter, or something worse. If Mr. Deane or any other gentleman will procure an order from Congress to inspect an account in my office, or any of Mr. Deane's friends in Congress will take the trouble of coming themselves, I will give him or them my attendance and show them in a handwriting which Mr. Deane is well acquainted with, that the supplies, he so pompously plumes himself upon, were promised and engaged, and that as a present, before he ever *arrived* in France, and the part that fell to Mr. Deane was only to see it done, and how he has performed that service, the public are now acquainted with. The last paragraph in the account is, " *Upon Mr. Deane's arrival in France the business went into his hands and the aids were at length embarked in the Amphitrite, Mercury and Seine.*"

What will Mr. Deane or his Aid de Camp say to this, or what excuse will they make now? If they have met with any cutting truths from me, they must thank themselves for it. My address to Mr. Deane was not only moderate but civil, and he and his adherents had much better have submitted to it quietly, than provoked more material matter to appear against them. I had at that time all the facts in my hands which I have related since, or shall yet relate in my reply. The only thing I aimed at in the address, was, to give out just as much as might prevent the public from being so grossly imposed upon by them, and yet save Mr. Deane and his adherents from appearing too wretched and despicable. My fault was a misplaced tenderness, which they must now be fully sensible of, and the misfortune to them, is, that I have not yet done.

Had Mr. Plain Truth only informed the Public that Mr. Deane had been industrious in promoting and forwarding the sending the supplies, his assertion would have passed uncontradicted by me, because I must naturally suppose that Mr. Deane would do no otherwise ; but to give him the

whole and sole honour of *procuring* them, and that, without
yielding any part of the honor to the public spirit and
good disposition of those who furnished them, and who
likewise must in every shape have put up with the total loss
of them had America been overpowered by her enemies,
is, in my opinion, placing the reputation and affection of our
allies not only in a disadvantageous, but in an unjust point
of view, and concealing from the public what they ought to
know.

Mr. Plain Truth declares that he knows all the circumstances, why then did he not place them in a proper line,
and give the public a clear information how they arose?
The proposal .for sending over those supplies, appears to
have been originally made by some public spirited gentleman
in France, before ever Mr. Deane arrived there, or was known
or heard of in that Country, and to have been communicated
(personally by Mr. Beaumarchais, the gentleman mentioned
in the letter signed J. L. which letter is given at length by
Mr. Plain Truth) to Mr. Arthur Lee while resident in London about three years ago. From Mr. B's manner of expression, Mr. Lee understood the supplies to be a present,
and has signified it in that light. It is very easy to see that
if America had miscarried, they *must* have been a present,
which probably adds explanation to the matter. But Mr.
Deane is spoken of by Mr. Plain Truth, as having an
importance of his *own*, and procuring those supplies through
that importance; whereas he could only rise and fall with
the country that empowered him to act, and be *in* or *out* of
credit, as to money matters, from the same cause and in the
same proportion; and every body must suppose, that there
were greater and more original wheels at work than he was
capable of setting in motion. Exclusive of the matter being
begun before Mr. Deane's arrival, Mr. Plain Truth has given
him the whole merit of every part of the transaction. America
and France are wholly left out of the question, the former
as to her growing importance and credit, from which all Mr.
Deane's consequence was derived, and the latter, as to her
generosity in furnishing those supplies, at a time, when the

risk of losing them appears to have been as great as our want of them.

I have always understood thus much of the matter, that if we did not succeed no payment would be required, and I think myself fully entitled to believe, and to publish my belief, that whether Mr. Deane had arrived in France or not, or any other gentleman in his stead, those same supplies would have found their way to America. But as the nature of the contract has not been explained by any of Mr. Deane's letters and is left in obscurity by the account he signed the 16th of February last, which I have already quoted, therefore the full explanation must rest upon other authority.

I have been the more explicit on this subject, not so much on Mr. Deane's account, as from a principle of public justice. It shews, in the first instance, that the greatness of the American cause drew, at its first beginning, the attention of Europe, and that the justness of it was such as appeared to merit support; and in the second instance, that those who are now her allies, prefaced that alliance by an early and generous friendship; yet, that we might not attribute too much to human or auxiliary aid, so unfortunate were those supplies, that only one ship out of the three arrived. The Mercury and Seine fell into the hands of the enemy.

Mr. Deane, in his address, speaks of himself as "*sacrificed for the agrandizement of others*" and promises to inform the public of "*what he has done and what he has suffered.*" What Mr. Deane means by being *sacrificed* the Lord knows, and what he has *suffered* is equally as mysterious. It was his good fortune to be situated in an elegant country and at a public charge, while we were driven about from pillar to post. He appears to know but little of the hardships and losses which his countrymen underwent in the period of his fortunate absence. It fell not to his lot to turn out to a Winter's campaign, and sleep without tent or blanket. He returned to America when the danger was over, and has since that time suffered no personal hardship. What then are Mr. Deane's *sufferings* and what the sacrifices he complains of? Has he lost money in the public service? I

believe not. Has he got any? That I cannot tell. I can
assure him that I have not, and he, if he pleases, may make
the same declaration.

Surely the Congress might recall Mr. Deane if they
thought proper, without an insinuated charge of injustice
for so doing. The authority of America must be little indeed when she cannot change a Commissioner without
being insulted by him. And I conceive Mr. Deane as
speaking in the most disrespectful language of the Authority
of America when he says in his address, that in December
1776 he was "honored with one Colleague, and *saddled* with
another." Was Mr. Deane to dictate who should be Commissioner, and who should not? It was time, however, to
saddle him, as he calls it, with somebody, as I shall shew before I conclude.

When we have elected our Representatives, either in Congress or in the Assembly, it is for our own good that we
support them in the execution of that authority they derive
from us. If Congress is to be abused by every one whom
they may appoint or remove, there is an end to all useful
delegation of power, and the public accounts in the hands of
individuals will never be settled. There has, I believe, been
too much of this work practised already, and it is time that
the public should now make those matters a point of consideration. But who will begin the disagreeable talk?

I look on the independence of America to be as firmly
established as that of any country which is at war. Length
of time is no guarantee when arms are to decide the fate of
a nation. Hitherto our whole anxiety has been absorbed in
the means for supporting our independence, and we have
paid but little attention to the expenditure of money; yet
we see it daily depreciating, and how should it be otherwise
when so few public Accounts are settled, and new emissions
continually going on?—I will venture to mention one circumstance which I hope will be sufficient to awaken the
attention of the public to this subject. In October, 1777,
some books of the Commercial Committee, in which, among
other things, were kept the accounts of Mr. Thomas Morris,

appointed a Commercial Agent in France, were by Mr.
Robert Morris's request taken into his possession to be settled, he having obtained from the Council of this State six
months' leave of absence from Congress to settle his affairs.
In February following those books were called for by Congress, but not being compleated were not delivered. In
September, 1778 Mr. Morris returned them to Congress, in,
or nearly in, the same unsettled state he took them, which,
with the death of Mr. Thomas Morris, may probably involve
those accounts in further embarrassment. The amount of
expenditure on those books is considerably above two millions of dollars.*

I now quit this subject to take notice of a paragraph in
Mr. Plain Truth, relative to myself. It never fell to my lot
to have to do with a more illiberal set of men than those of
Mr. Deane's advocates who were concerned in writing that
piece. They have neither wit, manners nor honesty; an instance of which I shall now produce. In speaking of Mr.
Deane's contracts with individuals in France I said in my
address " We are all fully sensible, that the gentlemen who
have come from France since the arrival of Dr. Franklin and
Mr. Lee in that Country are of a different rank from *the generality of those* with whom Mr. Deane contracted when alone."
These are the exact words I used in my address.

---

* There is an article in the constitution of this state, which, were it at this
time introduced as a Continental regulation, might be of infinite service ; I mean
a Council of *Censors* to inspect into the expenditure of public money and call
defaulters to an account. It is, in my opinion, one of the best things in the
Constitution, and that which the people ought never to give up, and whenever
they do they will deserve to be cheated. It has not the most favourable look
that those who are hoping to succeed to the government of this state, by a
change in the Constitution, are so anxious to get that article abolished. Let expenses be ever so great, only let them be fair and necessary, and no good citizen
will grumble.

Perhaps it may be said, Why do not the Congress do those things? To which
I might, by another question reply, Why don't you support them when they
attempt it ? It is not quite so easy a matter to accomplish that point in Congress as perhaps many conceive ; men will always find friends and connections
among the body that appoints them, which will render all such enquiries difficult.—*Author*.

Mr. Plain Truth has misquoted the above paragraph into his piece, and that in a manner, which shews him to be a man of little reading and less principle. The method in which he has quoted it is as follows: " All are fully sensible that the gentlemen who came from France since the arrival of Dr. Franklin and Mr. Lee in that country, are of a different rank from those with whom Mr. Deane contracted when acting separately." Thus by leaving out the words *" the generality of,"* Mr. Plain Truth has altered the sense of my expression, so as to suit a most malicious purpose in his own, which could be no other, than that of embroiling me with the French gentlemen that have remained ; whereas it is evident, that my mode of expression was intended to do justice to such characters as Fleury and Touzard, by making a distinction they are clearly entitled to. Mr. Plain Truth not content with unjustly subjecting me to the misconceptions of those gentlemen, with whom even explanation was difficult on account of the language, but in addition to his injustice, endeavoured to provoke them to it by calling on them, and reminding them that they were the *" Guardians of their own honour."* And I have reason to believe, that either Mr. Plain Truth or some of the party did not even stop here, but went so far as personally to excite them on. Mr. Fleury came to my lodgings and complained that I had done him great injustice, but that he was sure I did not intend it, because he was certain that I knew him better. He confessed to me that he was pointed at and told that I meant him, and he withal desired, that as I knew his services and character, that I would put the matter right in the next paper. I endeavoured to explain to him that the mistake was not mine, and we parted. I do not remember that in the course of my reading I ever met with a more illiberal and malicious mis-quotation, and the more so when all the circumstances are taken with it. Yet this same Mr. Plain Truth, whom no body knows, has the impertinence to give himself out to be a man of *" education "* and to inform the public that " he is not a writer from *inclination* much less by *profession,"* to which he might safely have added, *still less by capacity, and least of all by principle.*

As Mr. Clarkson has undertaken to avow the piece signed Plain Truth, I shall therefore consider him as legally accountable for the apparent malicious intentions of this mis-quotation, and he may get whom he pleases to speak or write a defence of him.

I conceive that the *general* distinction I referred to between those with whom Mr. Deane contracted when alone, and those who have come from France since the arrival of Dr. Franklin and Mr. Lee in that Country, is sufficiently warranted. That gallant and amiable officer and volunteer the Marquis de la Fayette, and some others whom Mr. Plain Truth mentions, did not come from France till after the arrival of the additional Commissioners, and proves my assertion to be true. My remark is confined to the many and unnecessary ones with which Mr. Deane burthened and distracted the army. If he acquired any part of his popularity in France by this means he made the continent pay smartly for it. Many thousand pounds it cost America, and that in money totally sunk, on account of Mr. Deane's injudicious contracts, and what renders it the more unpardonable is, that by the instructions he took with him, he was *restricted* from making them, and consequently by having no authority had an easy answer to give to solicitations. It was Doctor Franklin's answer as soon as he arrived and might have been Mr. Deane's. Gentlemen of science or literature or conversant with the polite or useful arts, will, I presume, always find a welcome reception in America, at least with persons of a liberal cast, and with the bulk of the people.

In speaking of Mr. Deane's contracts with foreign officers, I concealed out of pity to him a circumstance that must have sufficiently shewn the necessity of recalling him, and, either his great want of judgment, or the danger of trusting him with discretionary power. It is no less than that of his throwing out a proposal, in one of his last foreign letters, for contracting with a German prince [1] to command the American

---

[1] Prince Ferdinand of Brunswick, brother-in-law of George III. In Donne's "Correspondence of George III. with Lord North" (ii., p. 116), a letter of the king shows that Prince Ferdinand had actually received such a proposal.—*Editor.*

Army. For my own part I was no ways surprised when I read it, though I presume almost every body else will be so when they hear it, and I think when he got to this length, it was time to *saddle* him.

Mr. Deane was directed by the Committee which employed him to engage four able engineers in France, and beyond this he had neither authority nor commission. But disregarding his instructions (a fault criminal in a negociator) he proceeded through the several degrees of subalterns, to Captains, Majors, Lieutenant Colonels, Colonels, Brigadier Generals and at last to Major Generals; he fixed their rank, regulated their command, and on some, I believe, he bestowed a pension. At this stage, I set him down for a Commander in Chief, and his next letter proved me prophetic. Mr. Plain Truth, in the course of his numerous encomiums on Mr. Deane, says, that—

" The letter of the Count de Vergennes, written by order of his Most Christian Majesty to Congress, speaking of Mr. Deane in the most honorable manner, and the letter from that Minister in his own character, written not in the language of a courtier, but in that of a person who felt what he expressed, would be sufficient to counterbalance, not only the opinions of the writer of the address to Mr. Deane, but even of characters of more influence, who may vainly endeavor to circulate notions of his insignificancy and unfitness for a public minister."

The supreme authority of one country, however different may be its mode, will ever pay a just regard to that of another, more especially when in alliance. But those letters can extend no further than to such parts of Mr. Deane's conduct as came under the immediate notice of the Court as a public Minister, or a political agent; and cannot be supposed to interfere with such other parts as might be disapproved in him here as a Contractor or a Commercial Agent, and can in no place be applied as an extenuation of any imprudence of his either there or since his return; besides which, letters of this kind, are as much intended to compliment the power that employs, as the person employed; and upon the whole,

I fear Mr. Deane has presumed too much upon the polite friendship of that nation, and engrossed to himself, a regard, that was partly intended to express, through him, an affection to the continent.

Mr. Deane should likewise recollect that the early appearance of any gentleman from America, was a circumstance, so agreeable to the nation, he had the honor of appearing at, that he must have managed unwisely indeed to have avoided popularity.   For as the poet says,

> *" Fame then was cheap, and the first comers sped."*

The last line of the couplet is not applicable

> *" Which they have since preserved by being dead."*

From the pathetic manner in which Mr. Deane speaks of his *" sufferings "* and the little concern he seems to have of ours, it may not be improper to inform him, that there is kept in this city a *" Book of Sufferings,"* into which, by the assistance of some of his connections, he may probably get them registered.[1] I have not interest enough myself to afford him any service in this particular, though I am a friend to all religions, and no personal enemy to those who may, in this place, suppose themselves alluded to.

I can likewise explain to Mr. Deane, the reason of one of his sufferings which I know he has complained of.   After the Declaration of Independence was passed, Mr. Deane thought it a great hardship that he was not authorized to announce it in form to the Court of France, and this circumstance has been mentioned as a seeming inattention in Congress.   The reason of it was this, and I mention it from my own knowledge.   Mr. Deane was at that time only a Commercial Agent, without any Commission from Congress, and consequently could not appear at Court with the rank suitable to the for-

---

[1] Some of the Quakers who opposed the Revolution, but whose peace-principles did not prevent their giving assistance to the enemy, so that they had to be dealt with, kept a " Book of Sufferings."   Those interested may find something on the subject, though not much, in a brief " Memoir of John Pemberton," issued by the Quakers.—*Editor.*

mality of such an occasion. A new commission was therefore necessary to be issued by Congress, and that honour was
purposely reserved for Doctor Franklin, whose long services
in the world, and established reputation in Europe, rendered
him the fittest person in America to execute such a great and
original design ; and it was likewise paying a just attention
to the honour of France by sending so able and extraordinary
a character to announce the Declaration.

Mr. Plain Truth, who sticks at nothing to carry Mr. Deane
through everything thick or thin, says :

" It may not be improper to remark that when he (Mr.
Deane) arrived in France, the opinion of people there, and in
the different parts of Europe, not only with respect to the merits,
but the probable issue of the Contest, had by no means acquired
that consistency which they had at the time of Dr. Franklin's
and Mr. Arthur Lee's arrival in that Kingdom."

Mr. Plain Truth is not a bad historian. For it was the
fate of Dr. Franklin and Mr. Lee to arrive in France at the
very worst of times. Their first appearance there was
followed by a long series of ill fortune on our side. Doctor
Franklin went from America in October, 1776, at which time
our affairs were taking a wrong turn. The loss on Long
Island, and the evacuation of New York happened before
he went, and all the succeeding retreats and misfortunes
through the course of that year, till the scale was again
turned by taking the Hessians at Trenton on the 26th day
of December, followed day by day after him. And I have
been informed by a gentleman from France, that the philosophical ease and cheerful fortitude, with which Dr. Franklin
heard of or announced those tidings, contributed greatly
towards lessening the real weight of them on the minds of
the Europeans.

Mr. Deane speaking of himself in his address says, " *While
it* was safe to be silent my lips were closed. Necessity hath
opened them and necessity must excuse this effort to serve,
by informing you." After which he goes on with his address. In this paragraph there is an insinuation thrown out

by Mr. Deane that some treason was on foot, which he had happily discovered, and which his duty to his country compelled him to reveal. The public had a right to be alarmed, and the alarm was carefully kept by those who at first contrived it. Now, if after this, Mr. Deane has nothing to inform them of, he must sink into nothing. When a public man stakes his reputation in this manner, he likewise stakes all his future credit on the performance of his obligation.

I am not writing to defend Mr. Arthur or Mr. William Lee, I leave their conduct to defend itself; and I would with as much freedom make an attack on either of these gentlemen, if there was a public necessity for it, as on Mr. Deane. In my address I mentioned Colonel R. H. Lee with some testimony of honourable respect, because I am personally acquainted with that gentleman's integrity and abilities as a public man, and in the circle of my acquaintance I know but few that have equalled, and none that have exceeded him, particularly in his ardor to bring foreign affairs, and more especially the present happy alliance, to an issue.

I heard it mentioned of this gentleman, that he was among those, whose impatience for victory led them into some kind of discontent at the operations of last Winter. The event has, I think, fully proved those gentlemen wrong, and must convince them of it ; but I can see no reason why a misgrounded opinion, produced by an overheated anxiety for success, should be mixed up with other matters it has no concern with. A man's political abilities may be exceedingly good, though at the same time he may differ, and even be wrong, in his notions of some military particulars.

Mr. Deane says that Mr. Arthur Lee was dragged into a Treaty with the utmost reluctance, a charge which if he cannot support, he must expect to answer for. I am acquainted that Mr. Lee had some objection against the constructions of a particular article [12th], which, I think, shews his judgment, and whenever they can be known will do him honor; but his general opinion of that valuable transaction I shall give in his own words from a letter in my hands.

" France has done us substantial benefits, Great Britain substantial injuries. France offers to guarantee our sovereignty, and universal freedom of commerce. Great Britain *condescends* to *accept* our *submission* and to *monopolize* our commerce. France demands of us to be independent, Great Britain tributary. I do not conceive how there can be a mind so debased, or an understanding so perverted, as to balance between them.

" The journies I have made north and south in the public service, have given me opportunities of knowing the general disposition of Europe on our question. There never was one in which the harmony of opinion was so universal. From the Prince to the peasant there is but one voice, one wish, the liberty of America and the humiliation of Great Britain."

If Mr. Deane was industrious to spread reports to the injury of these gentlemen in Europe, as he has been in America, no wonder that their real characters have been misunderstood. The peculiar talent which Mr. Deane possesses of attacking persons behind their backs, has so near a resemblance to the author of Plain Truth, who after promising his name to the public has declined to give it, and some other proceedings I am not unacquainted with, *particularly an attempt to prevent my publications*, that it looks as if one spirit of private malevolence governed the whole.

Mr. Plain Truth has renewed the story of Dr. Birkenhout, to which I have but one reply to make : why did not Mr. Deane appear against him while he was here ? He was the only person who knew anything of him, and his neglecting to give information, and thereby suffering a suspicious person to escape for want of proof, is a story very much against Mr. Deane ; and his complaining after the man was gone corresponds with the rest of his conduct.

When little circumstances are so easily dwelt upon, it is a sign, not only of the want of great ones, but of weakness and ill will. The crime against Mr. William Lee is, that some years ago he was elected an Alderman of one of the wards in London, and the English Calender has yet printed him with the same title. Is that any fault of his ? Or can he be made accountable for what the people of London may

do? Let us distinguish between whiggishness and waspish-
ness, between patriotism and peevishness, otherwise we shall
become the laughing stock of every sensible and candid
mind. Suppose the Londoners should take it into their
heads to elect the President of Congress or General Washington an Alderman, is that a reason why we should displace
them? But, Mr. Lee, say they, has not resigned. These
men have no judgment, or they would not advance such
positions. Mr. Lee has nothing to resign. He has vacated
his Aldermanship by accepting an appointment under Congress, and can know nothing further of the matter. Were
he to make a formal resignation it would imply his being a
subject of Great Britain; besides which, the character of
being an Ambassador from the States of America, is so superior to that of any Alderman of London, that I conceive Mr.
Deane, or Mr. Plain Truth, or any other person, as doing a
great injustice to the dignity of America by attempting to
put the two in any disputable competition. Let us be
honest lest we be despised, and generous lest we be
laughed at.

Mr. Deane in his address of the 5th of December, says,
"having thus introduced you to your great servants, I now
proceed to make you acquainted with some other person-
ages, which it may be of consequence for you to know. I
am *sorry* to say, that Arthur Lee, Esq., was suspected by
some of the best friends you had abroad, and those in important characters and stations." To which I reply, that I
firmly believe Mr. Deane will *likewise* be sorry he has said
it. Mr. Deane after thus advancing a charge endeavours to
paliate it by saying, "these suspicions, *whether well* or *ill*
founded, were frequently urged to Dr. Franklin and myself."
But Mr. Deane ought to have been certain that they were
well founded, before he made such a publication, for if they
are *not* well founded he must appear with great discredit,
and it is now his duty to accuse Mr. Arthur Lee legally, and
support the accusation with sufficient proofs. Characters
are tender and valuable things; they are more than life to a
man of sensibility, and are not to be made the sport of

interest, or the sacrifice of incendiary malice. Mr. Lee is an absent gentleman, I believe too, an honest one, and my motive for publishing this, is not to gratify any party, or any person, but as an act of social duty which one man owes to another, and which, I hope, will be done to me whenever I shall be accused ungenerously behind my back.

Mr. Lee to my knowledge has far excelled Mr. Deane in the usefulness of his information, respecting the political and military designs of the Court of London. While in London he conveyed intelligence that was dangerous to his personal safety. Many will remember the instance of the rifle man who had been carried prisoner to England alone three years ago, and who afterwards returned from thence to America, and brought with him a letter concealed in a button. That letter was from this gentleman, and the public will, I believe, conclude, that the hazard Mr. Lee exposed himself to, in giving information while so situated, and by such means, deserves their regard and thanks. The detail of the number of the foreign and British troops for the campaign of 1776, came first from him, as did likewise the expedition against South Carolina and Canada, and among other accounts of his, that the English emissaries at Paris had boasted that the British Ministry had sent over half a million of guineas to corrupt the Congress. This money, should they be fools enough to send it, will be very ineffectually attempted or bestowed, for repeated instances have shewn that the moment any man steps aside from the public interest of America, he becomes despised, and if in office, superceeded.

Mr. Deane says, "that Dr. Birkenhout, when he returned to New York, ventured to assure the British Commissioners, that by the alliance with France, America was at liberty to make peace without consulting her ally, unless England declared War." What is it to us what Dr. Birkenhout said, or how came Mr. Deane to know what passed between him and the British Commissioners? But I ask Mr. Deane's pardon, he has told us how. "Providence, (says he) in whom we put our trust, *unfolded* it to me." But Mr. Deane says, that

Col. R. H. Lee, pertinaciously maintained the same doctrine. The treaty of alliance will neither admit of debate nor any equivocal explanation. Had *war not broke out*, or *had not Great Britain, in resentment to that alliance or connection, and of the good correspondence which is the object of the said treaty, broke the peace with France, either by direct hostilities or by hindering her commerce and navigation in a manner contrary to the rights of nations, and the peace subsisting at that time, between the two Crowns,* —in this case, I likewise say, that America, as a *matter of right*, could have made a peace without consulting her ally, though the civil obligations of mutual esteem and friendship would have required such a consultation. But war *has* broke out, though not declared, for the first article in the treaty of alliance is confined to the *breaking out of war*, and *not* to its *declaration*. Hostilities have been commenced; therefore the first case is superseded, and the eighth article of the treaty of alliance has its full intentional force: "*Article 8.*—Neither of the two parties shall conclude either truce or peace without the formal consent of the other first obtained, and they mutually engage not to lay down their arms until the independence of the United States, shall have been formally or tacitly assured, by the treaty or treaties that shall terminate that war."

What Mr. Deane means by this affected appearance of his, both personally and in print, I am quite at a loss to understand. He seems to conduct himself here in a stile, that would more properly become the secretary to a foreign embassy, than that of an American Minister returned from his charge. He appears to be everybody's servant but ours, and for that reason can never be the proper person to execute any commission, or possess our confidence. Among the number of his "*sufferings*" I am told that he returned burthened with forty changes of silk, velvet, and other dresses. Perhaps this was the reason he could not bring his papers.

Mr. Deane says, that William Lee Esq: gives five per cent commission, and receives a share of it, for what was formerly done for two per cent. That matter requires to be cleared up and explained; for it is not the quantity per cent, but the purposes to which it is applied that makes it right or wrong; besides which, the whole matter, like many other of Mr. Deane's charges, may be groundless.

I here take my leave of this gentleman, wishing him more discretion, candour and generosity.

In the beginning of this address I informed the public, that "whatever I should conceive necessary to say of myself, would appear in the conclusion." I chose that mode of arrangement, lest by explaining my own situation first, the public might be induced to pay a greater regard to what I had to say against Mr. Deane, than was necessary they should; whereas it was my wish to give Mr. Deane every advantage, by letting what I had to advance come from me, while I laid under the disadvantage of having the motives of my conduct mistaken by the public. Mr. Deane and his adherents have apparently deserted the field they first took possession of and seemed to triumph in. They made their appeal to you, yet have suffered me to accuse and expose them for almost three weeks past, without a denial or a reply.

I do not blame the public for censuring me while they, though wrongfully, supposed I deserved it. When they see their mistake, I have no doubt, but they will honor me with that regard of theirs which I before enjoyed. And considering how much I have been misrepresented, I hope it will not now appear ostentatious in me, if I set forth what has been my conduct, ever since the first publication of the pamphlet Common Sense down to this day, on which, and on account of my reply to Mr. Deane, and in order to import the liberty of the press, and my right as a freeman, I have been obliged to resign my office of Secretary for foreign affairs, which I held under Congress. But this, in order to be compleat, will be published in the Crisis No 8, of which notice will be given in the papers.

COMMON SENSE.

PHILADELPHIA, January 8, 1779.

XXIV.

MESSRS. DEANE, JAY, AND GÉRARD.[1]

Mr. Dunlap,

In your paper of August 31st was published an extract of a letter from Paris, dated May the 21st, in which the writer, among other things, says:

"It is long since I felt in common with every other well-wisher to the cause of liberty and truth, the obligations I was under to the author of Common Sense, for the able and unanswerable manner in which he has defended those principles. The same public motives I am persuaded induced him to address the public against Mr. Deane and his associates. The countenance and support which Deane has received is a melancholy presage of the future. Vain, assuming, avaricious and unprincipled, he will stick at no crime to cover what he has committed and continue his career.

"The impunity with which Deane has traduced and calumniated Congress to their face, the indulgence and even countenance he has received, the acrimonious and uncandid spirit of a letter containing Mr. Paine's publications which accompanied a resolve sent to Mr. Gerard, are matters of deep concern here to every friend to America."

By way of explaining the particular letter referred to in the above, the following note was added:

[1] From the *Pennsylvania Packet* of September 14, 1779. The French Minister, Gérard, who was interested in the Deane-Beaumarchais claims (though Paine did not know it) complained to Congress of Paine's disclosures. Paine resigned his secretaryship, and the President of Congress, Jay, wrote an effusive and apologetic letter to Gérard. Congress knew that Paine had written only what was true, but after the French Minister's complaint were " obliged," as Hon. Gouverneur Morris said, " to act as if they believed " otherwise.— *Editor.*

"The letter here alluded to can be no other than that signed '*John Jay*,' dated January 13th, and published in Mr. Dunlap's paper of Jan. 16th. It is very extraordinary that Mr. Jay should write such a letter, because it contains the same illiberal reflections which Congress, as a Body, had rejected from their resolve of January 12, as may be seen by any one who will peruse the proceedings of January last. Congress has since declined to give countenance to Mr. Jay's letter; for tho' he had a public authority for writing *a letter* to Mr. Gerard, he had no authority for the reflections he used; besides which, the letter would be perfectly laughable were every circumstance known which happened at that particular time, and would likewise show how exceedingly delicate and cautious a President ought to be when he means to act officially in cases he is not sufficiently acquainted with."

Every person will perceive that the note which explains the letter referred to, is not a part of the letter from Paris, but is added by another person; and Mr. Jay, or any other Gentleman, is welcome to know that the note is in my writing, and that the original letter from Paris is now in my possession. I had sufficient authority for the expressions used in the note. Mr. Jay did not lay his letter to Mr. Gerard before Congress previous to his sending it, and therefore, tho' he had their order, he had not their approbation. They, it is true, ordered it to be published, but there is no vote for approving it, neither have they given it a place in their Journals, nor was it published in any more than one paper in this city (Benjamin Towne's), tho' there were at that time two others. Some time after Mr. Jay's letter appeared in the paper, I addressed another to Congress, complaining of the unjust liberty he had taken, and desired to know whether I was to consider the expressions used in his letter as containing *their* sentiments, at the same time informing them, that if they declined to prove what he had written, I should consider their silence as a disapprobation of it. Congress chose to be silent; and consequently, have left Mr. Jay to father his own expressions.

I took no other notice of Mr. Jay's letter at the time it was published, being fully persuaded that when any man recollected the part I had acted, not only at the first but in the worst of times, he could but look on Mr. Jay's letter to be groundless and ungrateful, and the more so, because if America had had no better friends than himself to bring about independance, I fully believe she would never have succeeded in it, and in all probability been a ruined, conquered and tributary country.

Let any man look at the position America was in at the time I first took up the subject, and published Common Sense, which was but a few months before the declaration of Independence ; an army of thirty thousand men coming out against her, besides those which were already here, and she without either an object or a system ; fighting, she scarcely knew for what, and which, if she could have obtained, would have done her no good. She had not a day to spare in bringing about the only thing which could save her. A REVOLUTION, yet no one measure was taken to promote it, and many were used to prevent it ; and had independance not been declared at the time it was, I cannot see any time in which it could have been declared, as the train of ill-successes which followed the affair of Long Island left no future opportunity.

Had I been disposed to have made money, I undoubtedly had many opportunities for it. The single pamphlet Common Sense, would at that time of day, have produced a tolerable fortune, had I only taken the same profits from the publication which all writers had ever done, because the sale was the most rapid and extensive of any thing that was ever published in this country, or perhaps any other. Instead of which I reduced the price so low, that instead of getting, I yet stand thirty-nine pounds eleven shillings out of pocket on Mr. Bradford's books, exclusive of my time and trouble, and I have acted the same disinterested part by every publication I have made. I could have mentioned those things long ago, had I chosen, but I mention them now to make Mr. Jay feel his ingratitude.

In the Pennsylvania Packet of last Tuesday some person has republished Mr. Jay's letter, and Mr. Gerard's answer of the 13th and 14th January last, and though I was patiently silent upon their first publication, I now think it necessary, since they are republished, to give some circumstances which ought to go with them.

At the time the dispute arose, respecting Mr. Deane's affairs, I had a conference with Mr. Gerard at his own request, and some matters on that subject were freely talked over, which it is here unnecessary to mention. This was on the 2d of January.

On the evening of the same day, or the next, Mr. Gerard, thro' the mediation of another gentleman, made me a very genteel and profitable offer. I felt at once the respect due to his friendship, and the difficulties which my acceptance would subject me to. My whole credit was staked upon going through with Deane's affairs, and could I afterwards have written with the pen of an Angel, on any subject whatever, it would have had no effect, had I failed in that or declined proceeding in it. Mr. Deane's name was not mentioned at the time the offer was made, but from some conversation which passed at the time of the interview, I had sufficient reason to believe that some restraint had been laid on that Subject. Besides which I have a natural inflexible objection to any thing which may be construed into a private pension, because a man after that is no longer truly free.

My answer to the offer was precisely in these words— " Any service I can render to either of the countries in alliance, or to both, I ever have done and shall readily do, and Mr. Gerard's *esteem* will be the only recompense I shall desire." I particularly chose the word *esteem* because it admitted no misunderstanding.

On the fifth of January I published a continuation of my remarks on Mr. Deane's affairs, and I have ever felt the highest respect for a nation which has in every stage of our affairs been our firm and invariable friend. I spoke of France under that general description. It is true I prosecuted the point against Mr. Deane, but what was Mr. Deane to France, or to the Minister of France?

On the appearance of this publication Mr. Gerard presented

a Memorial to Congress respecting some expressions used therein, and on the 6th and 7th I requested of Congress to be admitted to explain any passages which Mr. Gerard had referred to ; but this request not being complied with, I, on the 8th, sent in my resignations of the office of Secretary to the Committee of Foreign Affairs.

In the evening I received an invitation to sup with a gentleman, and Mr. Gerard's offer was, by his own authority, again renewed with considerable additions of advantage. I gave the same answer as before. I was then told that Mr. Gerard was very ill, and desired to see me. I replied, " That as a matter was then depending in Congress upon a representation of Mr. Gerard against some parts of my publications, I thought it indelicate to wait on him till that was determined."

In a few days after I received a second invitation, and likewise a third, to sup at the same place, in both of which the same offer and the same invitation were renewed and the same answers on my part were given : But being repeatedly pressed to make Mr. Gerard a visit, I engaged to do it the next morning at ten o'clock: but as I considered myself standing on a nice and critical ground, and lest my reputation should be afterwards called in question, I judged it best to communicate the whole matter to an honorable friend before I went, which was on the 14th of January, the very day on which Mr. Gerard's answer to Mr. Jay's letter is dated.

While with Mr. Gerard I avoided as much as possible every occasion that might give rise to the subject. Himself once or twice hinted at the publications and added that, " he hoped no more would be said on the subject," which I immediately waived by entering on the loss of the dispatches. I knew my own resolution respecting the offer, had communicated that resolution to a friend, and did not wish to give the least pain to Mr. Gerard, by personally refusing that, which, from him might be friendship, but to me would have been the ruin of my credit. At a convenient opportunity I rose to take my leave, on which Mr. Gerard said " Mr. Paine, I have always had a great respect for you, and should be glad of some opportunity of shewing you more solid marks of my friendship."

I confess I felt myself hurt and exceedingly concerned that the injustice and indiscretion of a party in Congress should drive matters to such an extremity that one side or other must go to the bottom, and in its consequences embarrass those whom they had drawn in to support them. I am conscious that America had not in France a more strenuous friend than Mr. Gerard, and I sincerely wish he had found a way to avoid an affair which has been much trouble to him. As for Deane, I believe him to be a man who cares not who he involves to screen himself. He has forfeited all reputation in this Country, first by promising to give an "*history of matters important for the people to know*" and then not only failing to perform that promise, but neglecting to clear his own suspected reputation, though he is now on the spot and can any day demand an hearing of Congress, and call me before them for the truth of what I have published respecting him.

Two days after my visit to Mr. Gerard, Mr. Jay's letter and the answer to it was published, and I would candidly ask any man how it is possible to reconcile such letters to such offers both done at one and the same time, and whether I had not sufficient authority to say that Mr. Jay's letter would be truly laughable, were all the circumstances known which happened at the time of his writing.

Whoever published those letters in last Tuesday's paper, must be an idiot or worse. I had let them pass over without any other public notice than what was contained in the note of the preceding week, but the republishing them was putting me to defiance, and forcing me either to submit to them afresh, or to give the circumstances which accompanied them. Whoever will look back to last Winter, must see I had my hands full, and that without any person giving the least assistance. It was first given out that I was paid by Congress for vindicating their reputation against Mr. Deane's charges, yet a majority in that House were every day pelting me for what I was doing. Then Mr. Gerard was unfortunately brought in, and Mr. Jay's letter to him and his answer were published to effect some purpose or other. Yet Mr. Gerard was at the same time making the warmest professions of friendship to me, and proposing to take me into his confidence with very liberal offers. In short I had but one way to get thro', which was to keep close to the point and principle I set out upon, and that alone has rendered me successful. By making this my guide I have kept my ground, and I have yet ground to spare, for among other things I have authentic copies of the dispatches that were lost.

I am certain no man set out with a warmer heart or a better disposition to render public service than myself, in everything which laid in my power.[1] My first endeavour was to put the politics of the country right, and to show the advantages as well as the necessity of independance: and until this was done, independance never could have succeeded. America did not at that time understand her own situation; and though the country was then full of writers, no one reached the mark; neither did I abate in my service, when hundreds were afterwards deserting her interest and thousands afraid to speak, for the first number of the Crisis was published in the blackest stage of affairs, six days before the taking the Hessians at Trenton. When this State was distracted by parties on account of her Constitution, I endeavored in the most disinterested manner to bring it to a conclusion; and when Deane's impositions broke out,

---

[1] A heavy reproach does indeed rest upon the Congress and its president for their treatment of the Secretary who saved them from the Beaumarchais-Gérard-Deane imposition, which, had it succeeded, would have crippled the means of the Revolution, and tended to defeat the object of the supplies sent by Louis XVI. Paine was the one man who knew as much about Silas Deane as George III. did, when he wrote to Lord North (March 3, 1781): "I think it perfectly right that Mr. Deane should so far be trusted as to have three thousand pounds for America"; and in the same year (July 19th): "I have received Lord North's boxes containing the intercepted letters of Mr. Deane for America. I have only been able to read two of [them], on which I form the same opinion of too much appearance of being connected with this country, and therefore not likely to have the effect as if they bore another aspect." In August 7th the king suggests what Deane should write (Donne, vol. ii., pp. 380, 381.)—*Editor.*

and threw the whole States into confusion, I readily took up the subject, for no one else understood it, and the country now see that I was right. And if Mr. Jay thinks he derives any credit from his letter to Mr. Gerard, he will find himself deceived, and that the ingratitude of the composition will be his reproach not mine.

COMMON SENSE.

END OF VOLUME I.